CIVIL AIRCRAFT

CIVIL AIRCRAFT

PASSENGER AND UTILITY AIRCRAFT: A CENTURY OF INNOVATION

GENERAL EDITOR: JIM WINCHESTER

amber
BOOKS

This edition first published in 2010 by
Amber Books Ltd
Bradley's Close
74–77 White Lion Street
London N1 9PF
United Kingdom
www.amberbooks.co.uk

ISBN 978-1-907446-38-2

Printed and bound in China

10 9 8 7 6 5 4 3 2 1

Picture Credits

All images courtesy of International Masters Publishers AB except

Airbus: 36 all, 37 top; Alamy: 116 top right & 117 bottom centre (Dan Lamont), 116 bottom right
(Peter Carey); Cody Images: 116 top centre; Corbis: 116 top left & bottom centre (Dan Levine),
117 bottom right (Robert Sorbo); Dreamstime: 116 centre (Roman Snytsar); Qantas: 37 centre;
U.S. Department of Defense: 117 bottom left; Wikimedia Creative Commons Licence: 116 bottom
left (Mark Handel); 117 top & centre (Dave Sizer); Rolando Ugolini: 37, 117 profile artworks; Jim
Winchester: 37 bottom all

This material was originally published as part of the reference set *Aircraft of the World*

Contents

Introduction

In less than ninety years, powered flight went from the Wright Brothers' Flyer, which could stay aloft barely a minute, to the Rutan Brothers' Voyager, which circled the globe without refuelling. Both were private ventures without an immediate commercial or military application when they appeared, but their technology influenced the next generations. The majority of civil aircraft do not stand out from their contemporaries as much as the Flyer or Voyager did, but as this volume shows, they have come in all shapes and sizes, depending on their role.

With a few exceptions, such as Concorde, airliner configurations have largely followed the pattern of the DC-3 of 1935. The Boeing 707 of the 1950s and the Airbus A380 of the 2000s are not an order of magnitude different, at least until you get under the skin where the systems that make them function are worlds apart. Noise issues and rising fuel prices have seen fuel-efficient high-bypass turbofans replace earlier generations of jet engine. The next step will be to further improve efficiency and reduce carbon emissions, both from the engines themselves and the aircraft manufacturing process.

Flying boats and large amphibians were the jumbo jets of their day, allowing swift transcontinental travel for the wealthy few. However, these types are now largely restricted to specialised roles such as fire fighting. Lighter floatplanes continue to be widely used for tourism and supplying islands and remote communities where long runways will never be built.

Rotorcraft all work on the principle of their spinning blades acting like a wing. Over the years different methods to spin those blades have been tried, including tip jets such as the Rotodyne's, or simply the airflow, like the Wallis Autogyros. Most modern helicopters use turboshaft engines and similar airframe configurations, although composite components and digital engine controls have greatly improved efficiency.

Above: the Wright Flyer was the first civil aircraft, but hardly the basis of a passenger transport. Practical airliners would have to wait until after World War I.

Above: The interior of the Airbus A380 could have accommodated the first flight of the Flyer.
The Wright Brothers themselves never built an aircraft with more than two seats.

Private or General Aviation (GA) aircraft have also benefited from advances in materials and avionics. Many aero club and training aircraft now have cockpits that would not look out of place in the latest Airbus.

Business aircraft model their cockpits on fighters and their cabins on private clubs.

The future for civil aviation seems to be one of ever-improving efficiency rather than radical change, but there's always room for a Wright or a Rutan to come along with something that launches the next great leap forwards.

AERO SPACELINES

SUPER GUPPY

● Outsize load-lifter ● Space rocket transporter ● Airbus component carrier

Since 1961, Aero Spacelines has modified ancient piston-powered prop-driven Boeing Stratocruisers to carry outsized rocket boosters and oil derricks. Known as 'Guppies' after the bulbous fish, their most notable features are the huge extensions built into their fuselages. Old it might be, but the Guppy has done a valuable job hauling everything from Saturn V rocket stages to the components of Europe's Airbus.

▲ *For an aircraft that no-one seemed to want when it was conceived, the Guppy family has been a great success. The outsized planes may still be in service for years to come.*

AERO SPACELINES SUPER GUPPY

▼ **Aeromaritime**
Aeromaritime, the freight division of the UTA airline, operated Super Guppy 201s, but these were eventually replaced by modified A300s known as the 'Beluga'.

▲ **Airbus cargo**
The fin of this Airbus A300 started its flying career when a Super Guppy flew it from Hamburg to Toulouse.

◀ **Inside the Guppy**
The cavernous hold of a Guppy is almost unique in being very high. Later Guppies could swallow an entire Airbus A320 wing.

◀ **Filton visit**
Guppies have been frequent visitors to the BAe plant at Filton, England, since the 1980s. Their task was to ship Airbus A320 wings by air to the Toulouse factory.

The world's strangest plane? ▶
The massive swelling of the upper fuselage makes it hard to accept that such a bizarre aircraft could ever get off the ground. But it can fly as well as its Stratocruiser and B-29 ancestors.

FACTS AND FIGURES

➤ The first B-377PG Pregnant Guppy flew on 18 September 1962.

➤ About 15 ground runs and test 'hops' were made before that first flight.

➤ The bigger B-377SG Super Guppy, the first to use turboprop engines, is an ex-military YC-97J and serves with NASA.

➤ The original Guppy could carry three million peanuts.

➤ Other aircraft may be able to carry heavier loads, but the Guppy's forte has always been outsize cargoes.

➤ The A300-600ST 'Beluga' is a 'Guppy' version of the A300 Airbus.

The fattest plane ever

Aero Spacelines in the USA saw the potential of outsized aircraft to haul cargoes which were not unreasonably heavy but had enormous dimensions. In 1961, the company modified its first piston-engined Boeing B-377 Stratocruiser, the military C-97, by stretching the aircraft and creating a 'bubble' structure atop the fuselage.

Eight Guppys were built in six configurations. Four aircraft (including two Guppy 201s converted by UTA) support

Airbus in the multinational manufacture of jetliners by hauling large components from different factories to a central point for final assembly.

A Guppy being loaded is one of the most amazing sights in aviation. The whole cockpit section, complete with nosewheel, is all but detached from the aircraft and swung through 110° to leave unobstructed access to the open fuselage.

These ex-Boeing freighters have proved so practical that

The inventors of the Guppy series succeeded in creating a market of their own with these aircraft. Thirty years on, there are few aircraft capable of handling such outsize loads.

Airbus created a 'Guppy' of its own. The A300-600ST Super Transporter, or 'Beluga', is taking over carrying cargoes for the international aircraft manufacturer.

The cockpit area is much the same as a Stratocruiser, with accommodation for two pilots, a navigator and flight engineer. The cockpit is pressurised, unlike the hold.

The ancestry of the Guppy family is immediately apparent when the wing plan view is seen. It is almost identical to the C-97 Stratocruiser wing.

Despite the huge fuselage doubling the cross-sectional area of the C-97, the Guppy only required six per cent more power to maintain a given airspeed.

Dimensions:	
span	47.63 m (156 ft.)
length	43.84 m (144 ft.)
height	14.78 m (48 ft.)
wing area	182.51 m² (1,964 sq.ft.)

The Super Guppy 201 is the largest member of this unique family. The aircraft have had a busy life, mainly transporting large components for Airbus.

The Super Guppy is powered by Allison 501 turboprops, mounted in the same nacelles as those fitted to the Lockheed P-3 Orion.

The huge area of the fuselage creates very little difference in the stability of the Guppy, and actually improves some aspects of the aircraft's handling.

The Guppy family have extensively modernised tail surfaces compared to the Stratocruisers from which they were derived.

The nose contains a small AVQ-55 weather radar.

AERO SPACELINES

N1038V

The wing centre section of the Super Guppy was extended by about 4 m (12 ft.), to give increased lift and improve propeller clearance.

ACTION DATA

MAXIMUM SPEED

SUPER GUPPY	463 km/h (287 m.p.h.)
An-22 ANTEI	740 km/h (459 m.p.h.)
BELFAST	544 km/h (337 m.p.h.)

Turboprop power meant that the Super Guppy was no slower than its piston-engined predecessors, even though its huge fuselage expansion created more drag. It is still much slower than other large turbo-powered transports of the 1960s, however.

PAYLOAD

SUPER GUPPY 201 24 tonnes (24 tons)	**An-22 ANTEI** 80 tonnes (80 tons)	**BELFAST** 35 tonnes (35 tons)

While the Super Guppy can lift a respectable weight of cargo, it cannot match aircraft designed to lift heavy weights such as the Belfast or the massive Soviet An-22, which for several years was the world's largest aircraft. Neither can match the Super Guppy's abilities with large-volume cargoes, however.

HOLD DIAMETER

SUPER GUPPY 201 7.7 m (25 ft.)	**An-22 ANTEI** 4.5 m (15 ft.)	**BELFAST** 3.5 m (12 ft.)

The Belfast was designed to carry three armoured cars or up to 200 troops. The An-22 was capable of operating out of rough fields while carrying a main battle tank or two huge SA-4 missile launch systems. But neither could have carried the third stage of a Saturn V moon rocket, or the entire wings or fuselage sections of a wide-body airliner, which are the Guppy's stock in trade.

King-size cargo carriers

■ **GLOBEMASTER:** Designed to carry large cargoes for the US Air Force of the 1950s and 1960s, the Douglas C-124 featured a fixed nose with clamshell loading doors.

■ **CANADAIR CL-44:** Based on the Bristol Britannia airliner, the CL-44 had a swinging tail to allow direct access to the cargo hold. But it lacked the Guppy's outsize load ability.

■ **ANTONOV'S GIANTS:** The Ukrainian concern has long specialised in large aircraft, the massive An-124 being its current workhorse. It offers yet another method of hold access.

■ **TWENTY-FIRST CENTURY GUPPY:** Based on the Airbus A300 airframe, the 'Beluga' will ensure that the Guppy concept will be around for many years to come.

AÉROSPATIALE

ALOUETTE II

● High altitude ● Air ambulance ● Excellent handling

Sud-Est, one of the forerunners of Aérospatiale, combined Turboméca's new Artouste turbine with a gearbox adapted from the Sikorsky S-55 to produce power for the Alouette. It flew for the first time in March 1955, and within three months the machine had set a new helicopter altitude record of 8209 m (26,925 ft.). Two years later an Alouette raised the record to 10984 m (36,028 ft.). This altitude performance made the aircraft a natural candidate for mountain rescues.

▲ Spacious and relatively well equipped for rescue work, the Alouette II has found a ready market in both civil and military services as a dependable rescue platform.

AÉROSPATIALE ALOUETTE II

Oral warning ▶
Equipped with a large amplifier, this example is used to issue warnings of avalanches to climbers in the mountains.

◀ Saving lives
A French Air Force Alouette II hoists up another rescued skier. Despite their military role the Alouettes are often tasked with rescuing civilians in distress.

Airborne ambulance ▶
Once retrieved from the mountain, survivors are flown to hospital in special fuselage stretchers.

▲ The search is on
Pilots often look for the survivors themselves, exploiting the excellent visibility from the Alouette's cockpit.

Star performer ▶
Demonstrating the capabilities of the helicopter is this example, lifting a large balloon as part of a publicity stunt. Crews find the helicopter a delight to fly.

FACTS AND FIGURES

➤ The Alouette II first flew on 12 March 1955; French certification on 2 May 1956 cleared the way for production.

➤ Germany has used the helicopter for more than 25 years without any crashes.

➤ Because of the shape of the fuselage the helicopter is known as 'bug-eye.'

➤ Options available for the helicopter include skid landing gear, floats or a wheeled undercarriage.

➤ In the rescue role the Alouette has a 120-kg (264-lb.) capable hoist.

➤ Many civilian examples operating today are ex-military machines.

PROFILE

High mountain rescuer

Even before flight testing had been completed, the Alouette II was showing its abilities as a mountain rescue aircraft. The second prototype Alouette II was in the Alps for performance tests in July 1956 when the test team learned that a climber was dying after having a heart attack in the Vallot Mountain refuge, one of the highest in Europe at 4362 m (14,307 ft.).

The first attempt at a rescue was unsuccessful, but the second worked: within five minutes of landing the helicopter had transported the climber to hospital in Chamonix, thereby saving his life.

At the beginning of 1957 two Alouettes carried out a similar rescue, retrieving six mountain guides, and two pilots of an S-55 rescue helicopter which had crashed, from the same refuge.

Since then the Alouette II and its high-altitude version, the Lama, have carried out many mountain rescues, retrieving stranded climbers from places that would not have been reachable by any other means.

Above: Small and nimble, the Alouette looks very dated compared to modern helicopters.

Right: With the extra-high skids this Alouette derivative is known as the Lama. It combines features from both the Alouette II and III variants.

The Alouette's successor, the Aérospatiale Ecureuil, is now serving with the Nepalese Army. The type has already retrieved climbers from high on Everest.

SA 318C Alouette II

Type: trainer/utility/rescue helicopter

Powerplant: one 395-kW (530-hp.) Turboméca Astazou IIA turboshaft engine

Maximum speed: 205 km/h (127 m.p.h.) at sea level; cruising speed 180 km/h (122 m.p.h.)

Endurance: 5 hr 18 min

Initial climb rate: 396 m/min (1,300 f.p.m.)

Range: 720 km (446 mi.)

Service ceiling: 3300 m (10,824 ft.); hovering ceiling 1550 m (5,080 ft.)

Weights: empty 890 kg (1,958 lb.); maximum take-off, with full rescue equipment 1650 kg (3,630 lb.)

Dimensions: fuselage width 2.22 m (7 ft. 3 in.)
length 9.75 m (32 ft.)
height 2.75 m (9 ft. 1 in.)
main rotor disc area 81.71 m² (879 sq. ft.)

SA 318C ALOUETTE II

The German army has operated the Alouette II for more than 25 years for general duties including scouting and as a VIP transport. Now facing replacement, the helicopters are being sold on the civil market.

Despite reaching the end of its military service, numerous examples of the Alouette II have been purchased by civil operators to be used for liaison duties. Later designs have entered the market but the rescue performance of the Alouette is proving hard to beat.

The Alouette's turboshaft engine gives it excellent performance. Even when loaded with the equipment needed for with the rescue role, the Alouette II has been able to reach exceptional altitudes.

A single twin-bladed rotor is fitted to the Alouette II. Pilots have found that manoeuvring the helicopter is easy.

Despite the dated look of the open tail boom, this network of metal tubes allows the helicopter to be extremely light. This is particularly useful because of the altitudes at which most rescue operations are undertaken in the mountains.

Visibility from the cockpit is excellent because of the extensive glazing.

A range of options is available for the landing gear on the Alouette II. Apart from the traditional skids, floats, wheels and specially adapted extra-wide skids to land on snow are available.

Positioned at the rear of the fuselage boom is a large wire loop, designed to protect the tail rotor from striking the ground during landings.

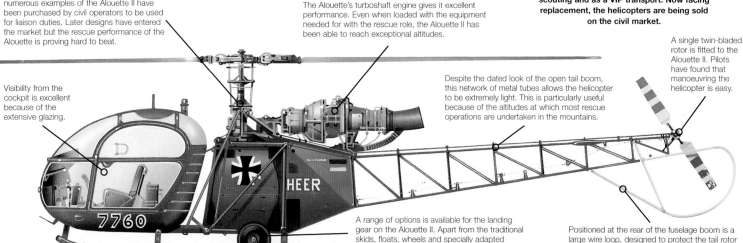

HEER

7760

Help from above

■ **AÉROSPATIALE AS 352 COUGAR:** Derived from the earlier Puma, the Cougar is a far more capable rescue helicopter.

■ **BOEING CH-113 LABRADOR:** Operated by the Canadian Armed Forces, the large Labrador is able to land on water.

■ **WESTLAND SEA KING:** The primary rescue helicopter of the RAF, the Sea King is based at several UK locations.

ACTION DATA

MAXIMUM CRUISING SPEED

Power from a turboshaft engine gives the Alouette II a surprisingly agile performance. Compared to other helicopters of the era Aérospatiale's design was an outstanding performer. Small and low powered, the TH-55A was much slower.

SA 318C ALOUETTE II	180 km/h (112 m.p.h.)
TH-55A	153 km/h (95 m.p.h.)
SKEETER T.Mk 12	171 km/h (106 m.p.h.)

RANGE

Additional auxiliary fuel tanks added to the Alouette allowed the helicopter to have a range beyond that of any of its competitors. The outstanding range of the helicopter has seen it used for patrol duties in both civilian and military guises.

SA 318C ALOUETTE II 720 km (446 mi.)

SKEETER T.Mk 12 422 km (262 mi.)

TH-55A 370 km (229 mi.)

SERVICE CEILING

Although it is used as a mountain rescue helicopter, when compared to the British Skeeter and American TH-55A the basic Alouette had a relatively poor performance at high altitude. Despite this, specially adapted models were developed to allow the Alouettes to fulfil rescue duties.

| SA 318C ALOUETTE II 3300 m (10,824 ft.) | TH-55A 3110 m (10,200 ft.) | SKEETER T.Mk 12 3901 m (12,800 ft.) |

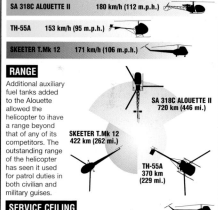

AÉROSPATIALE

ALOUETTE III

● Alpine search and rescue ● Unrivalled high-altitude performance

H igh in the Alps, the Alouette is a guardian angel – risking fierce winds, snow, ice and treacherous terrain to rescue those in trouble on Europe's high mountains. The highly successful Alouette is found in dozens of nations performing hundreds of jobs. None have become better known than its dramatic mercy missions, which it carries out at great risk to the crew to save those in peril.

▲ A roomy cabin
allows the Alouette III to operate as an effective troop transporter. The Alouette has also been used in support of quick-reaction units to intercept terrorist forces.

AÉROSPATIALE ALOUETTE III

▲ High performance
Fitted with a more powerful Astazou XIV engine, the SA 319B has superb high-altitude performance. This example also carries floats for water-based operations.

▲ Taking the load
Where landing is impossible the exceptionally versatile Alouette can still provide vital supplies using an external sling.

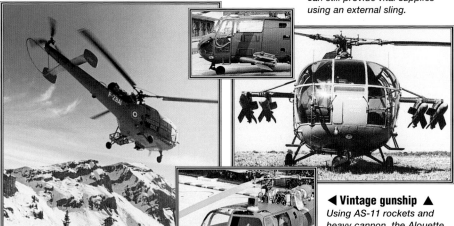

▲ Mountain rescue
An Alouette of the French Sécurité Civil picks up an injured skier from a high mountain top. Alouettes have carried out hundreds of missions like this.

◄ Vintage gunship ▲
Using AS-11 rockets and heavy cannon, the Alouette was a pioneer in the development of helicopter gunships. The Alouette served in the war in Algeria with French forces, and also in the Rhodesian civil war.

FACTS AND FIGURES

➤ In June 1960 an Alouette III proved that it could operate at 4810 m (15,780 ft.) on Mont Blanc, Europe's highest mountain.

➤ The first flight of the Alouette III took place on 28 February 1959.

➤ On 21 June 1972, an SA 315B Lama (Alouette II airframe and III engine) set a height record of 12442 m (40,820 ft.).

➤ Alouettes also serve as light transports, agricultural, liaison, observation and photo-mapping aircraft.

➤ The Alouette III has an external sling for loads up to 750 kg (1,650 lb.) or a rescue hoist which can lift 175 kg (400 lb.).

➤ Indian Alouettes regularly operate in the Himalayas, the world's highest mountains.

PROFILE

Rotors to the rescue, Alpine style

The Aérospatiale SA 319A/C Alouette III, manufactured by the company known today as Eurocopter, has been a spectacular aircraft almost from its first flight in 1959. This fine helicopter exhibits many superb flying qualities, but none is more impressive than the Alouette's high-altitude performance. Part of the credit for the success of Europe's best-known helicopter is due to the Turboméca company, which was the first in the world to develop light turbine aero engines.

On the heels of the earlier Alouette II, 1,305 of which serve around the globe, the Alouette III has reached operators in numbers exceeding 1,500. In every climate, the Alouette is a versatile aircraft and military operators have used the Alouette III for light-attack and anti-submarine duties. However, it has become famous for flying life-saving missions in mountain ranges the world over.

French Alouettes have performed a variety of jobs. As a military light utility transport they have been replaced by the Gazelle and Puma, but the Gendarmerie continues to appreciate its superb high-altitude performance in the mountains.

Alouette III

Type: general-purpose helicopter

Powerplant: one 870-kW (870-shp.) Turboméca Artouste IIIB turboshaft derated to 425 kW/550 shp. (SA-316B); one 649-kW/870-shp. Turboméca Astazou XIV turboshaft derated to 448 kW/600 shp. (SA-319C)

Maximum speed: 210 km/h (137 m.p.h.) at sea level

Hovering ceiling in ground effect: 2880 m (8,400 ft.)

Hovering ceiling out of ground effect: 1520 m (5,000 ft.)

Range: 480 km (375 mi.)

Weights: empty 1143 kg (2,440 lb.); loaded 2200 kg (4,960 lb.)

Dimensions: rotor diameter 11.02 m (36 ft. 2 in.)
length (blades folded) 10.03 m (33 ft.)
height 3.00 m (9 ft. 10 in.)
wing area 95.38 m² (1,027 ft.)

ALOUETTE III

The Netherlands army operates weaponless Alouette IIIs in an observation and light transport role. It is shortly due to replace them with McDonnell Douglas AH-64D Apaches, but the Netherlands air force will retain some for search-and-rescue operations.

The Alouette has a traditional hinged rotor head with three rotor blades. Despite its old design, the Alouette is a nimble machine and is well liked by pilots.

Turboméca's Astazou has proved to be a reliable and powerful engine. The Astazou's light weight and high power output give the Alouette much of its famous performance at altitude.

Tail rotors are a vulnerable area of any helicopter, and even with this large guard below it the pilot is always concerned about the tail. The successors to the Alouette have an enclosed tail rotor in a 'fenestron' fin mounting, for protection and improved performance.

The roomy cabin is a useful feature for search and rescue. Six passengers can be carried, or two stretchers and two seated passengers in the casualty evacuation role.

A-218

The excellent view from the Alouette's cockpit is vital for crews in search-and-rescue work.

Many Alouettes have winches and spotlights fitted for light transport. The maximum 750-kg (1,650-lb.) payload can also be carried externally on a sling.

The six passenger seats in the standard Alouette III's roomy cabin can quickly be removed. The helicopter then becomes a light cargo transport, able to lift payloads of up to 750 kg (1,650 lb.).

The fins on the tailboom give added stability in forward flight, and also help the pilot keep a steady hover when performing delicate rescue manoeuvres in high wind conditions.

ACTION DATA

SERVICE CEILING

The key to the Alouette III's high-altitude performance is the use of the Turboméca Astazou XIV turboshaft. Light but powerful, the engine allows the Alouette to operate at heights most other helicopters cannot reach, making it ideal for mountain rescue. The Gazelle also has a respectable ceiling but rarely operates above 1000 m (3,280 ft.). The less powerful JetRanger struggles above 3000 m (9,850 ft.).

ALOUETTE III
6000 m
(17,700 ft.)

GAZELLE
5000 m
(16,400 ft.)

206 JETRANGER
4100 m
(13,400 ft.)

Alouettes in the mountains

■ **UNDERCARRIAGE:** The ski-equipped undercarriage of an Alouette in a high mountain valley shows that it operates here all year round. The warm summer weather in this picture makes the helicopter's performance lower than usual, as the air density is reduced even more.

■ **SNOW OPERATIONS:** The Alouette's small size, light weight, forgiving flying characteristics and ski undercarriage are essential when operating on snow. Heavy helicopters with normal wheels would probably get stuck in these conditions, as well as finding it hard to fly in the thin alpine air.

■ **RESCUE VETERAN:** Thousands of people owe their lives to the Alouette for saving them in daring winch rescues. This mission needs careful work between all three crew – the pilot, winch operator and the winchman. Long periods in the hover also demand the good performance given by the Alouette.

AÉROSPATIALE

AS 332 SUPER PUMA

● Airborne workhorse ● Increased power ● Civil operations

▲ *Having already developed a highly capable transport helicopter with the Puma, Aérospatiale proposed a model with increased power and cabin volume.*

An established favourite with helicopter companies specialising in the support of offshore oil exploration and production, the Super Puma, along with its Cougar military variant, has also won orders from many other companies and agencies for a wide variety of applications. They range from VIP transport to the support of UN peace-keeping forces in the world's troublespots. The type is readily adaptable for a whole host of other tasks.

▼ **Overseas service**
To increase safety during long over-water flights, the Super Puma can be fitted with emergency flotation bags around the nose. This example operates from Ireland.

◀ **Worthy successor**
The AS 332 was developed from the successful SA 330. This French SA 330 is seen demonstrating fire-fighting equipment.

▲ **Increased volume**
The larger fuselage of the Super Puma is evident in this view of an AS 332C lifting off from a snowy landscape.

▼ **Advanced design**
Aérospatiale was able to utilise the latest advances in aviation technology in the design. One of these was the use of glass-fibre rotors.

◀ **Added strength**
An increase in power along with the larger fuselage has seen the Super Puma employed heavily in the construction industry. Extra nose mirrors are installed to allow the pilot to monitor the load.

FACTS AND FIGURES

➤ The first flight of the AS 332 Super Puma was on 13 September 1978. Service entry occurred in 1981.

➤ Civilian Super Pumas have the capacity to seat 24 passengers.

➤ Luxury variants have been developed to fill the VIP transport role.

➤ In the event of a mishap, the Super Puma is able to land on water because of the fitting of emergency flotation bags.

➤ One variant, the AS 332L, has more than 70 examples in civilian service.

➤ Super Pumas are widely used as transports for oil exploration support.

Aérospatiale's super workhorse

A cabin big enough to accommodate 24 passengers on standard seats is clearly big enough to carry smaller numbers in much greater comfort. Aérospatiale has exploited the possibility in a big way, and claims to have created the market for VIP helicopters by combining the versatility of rotary-wing flight with the all the comforts of a business jet.

The Prestige range of VIP interiors offers luxuriously upholstered seating in a single nine-seat cabin, or separate compartments with four seats forward and another eight aft,

along with such amenities as a bar, individual video screens and telephones.

Super Pumas and Cougars are used to transport no fewer than 25 heads of state, and more than 50 VIP versions are in service. Apart from the 8-m (26-ft.) long cabin, the type's attractions include low noise and vibration levels and large windows along with high performance and long range.

Other roles have included supporting the United Nations peace-keeping force in Mozambique. The Super Puma is well suited to operations in Africa, where it is able to take

off with full tanks even in temperatures of 30°C (86°F).

Above: Taking to the air is the prototype Super Puma; the helicopter is identifiable by its prominent ventral fin.

Right: An increase in the nose volume of the Super Puma has allowed the type to be fitted with a weather radar.

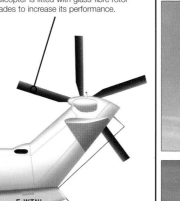

AS 332 SUPER PUMA

Proving to be a highly capable transport helicopter, the Super Puma is fast becoming the first choice for operators who require a dependable and safe helicopter. The exceptional power available coupled with long range will ensure sales success.

AS 332L-1 Super Puma

Type: twin-engined transport/support helicopter

Powerplant: two 1184-kW (1,590-hp.) (continuous rating) Turbomeca Makila 1A1 turboshafts

Cruising speed: 266 km/h (165 m.p.h.)

Initial climb rate: 486 m/min (1,600 f.p.m.) at sea level

Range: 870 km (539 mi.)

Service ceiling: 4600 m (15,100 ft.)

Weights: empty 4460 kg (9,812 lb.); maximum take-off 8600 kg (18,920 ft.)

Accommodation: two pilots plus 24 passengers

Dimensions: rotor diameter 15.60 m (51 ft. 2 in.)
length 16.29 m (53 ft. 5 in.)
height 4.92 m (16 ft. 2 in.)
main rotor disc area 191.10 m² (2,056 sq. ft.)

As a safety precaution the Super Puma can be fitted with emergency flotation bags around the cockpit. These inflate in the event of the helicopter landing on water.

The large cabin area of the Super Puma can accommodate 24 seated passengers or a sizeable cargo load. This particular version operates in the passenger configuration.

Aérospatiale was able to equip the Super Puma with the latest technology. Apart from the improved avionics and radar, the helicopter is fitted with glass-fibre rotor blades to increase its performance.

-LN-OLA

A-S LUFTTRANSPORT

F-WTNI

Positioned either side of the fuselage in streamlined fairings is the large single-wheel high-energy absorption landing gear. The landing gear can be retracted.

The increase in power of the engine required the addition of a large ventral fin. This is a distinguishing feature of the new Super Pumas now on operation.

HELICOPTERS AT WORK

CONSTRUCTION WORKER: Despite its small size, the Aérospatiale SA 315 Lama (pictured left) is a specially developed variant of the SA 318 Alouette II. The helicopter offers a better performance at high altitude and is equipped with raised skids to allow it to operate from any rough terrain.

OIL INDUSTRY: Offering an increase in range and capability, Bell's LongRanger (pictured above) was derived from the extremely successful JetRanger. With its long-range, the helicopter is used to explore potential sites for oil exploration. The helicopter can be equipped with a ski undercarriage, if required, during winter months.

Multi-purpose Pumas

■ **BELGIAN POLICE:** This Puma is one of three examples used by the Belgian Gendarmerie. They are based at Brasschaat in the north of the country and employed for patrol and VIP duties.

OL-GOI

■ **VIP FLIGHTS:** This SA 330C Puma serves with the Gabonese air force. Most are flown by mercenary pilots. The Pumas are used for VIP and support tasks.

TR-KCD

■ **RESCUE ROLE:** With its extended range and improved all-weather radar, Singapore's AS 332Bs operate with No. 125 Squadron at Sembawang. They are used for SAR and VIP flights.

RESCUE 21

AÉROSPATIALE

AS 350 ECUREUIL TV NEWS

● On-the-spot news ● Rapid response ● Economical and reliable

▼ Camera system
When fully equipped, there is little space available inside the Ecureuil.

▲ US TV
Even in America, where Bell and McDonnell Douglas helicopters have traditionally been favoured, the AS 350 has been popular with TV news companies.

◀ UK newscasting
This much-modified, smartly painted Twin Squirrel is operated by ITN.

JetRanger on air ▶
Many other light helicopters are used for TV duties, including the Bell JetRanger.

Chicago ▶ bulletin
This JetRanger is operated by Chicago's WLS-TV. The helicopter also represents a high-profile publicity tool for the TV station.

Helicopters are responsible for some of the most dramatic television news images. The use of these aircraft as TV camera platforms has mushroomed since the late 1970s, when the first microwave transmitters small enough to be carried by a light helicopter appeared. The helicopter usually carries a reporter and a camera operator, and the AS 350 Ecureuil, with its combination of affordability and reliability, has proved popular for the task.

▲ *With its ample cabin space, the Ecureuil makes a perfect camera platform. This was recognised by Aérospatiale, which offered a TV camera installation as standard equipment.*

FACTS AND FIGURES

➤ A Textron Lycoming-engined version of the Ecureuil is marketed in North America as the Astar.

➤ By 1 March 1989 Ecureuils and Astars were flying in 43 countries.

➤ Most of the AS 350's outer skin is made from thermo-formed plastic.

➤ An uprated electrical system on the Ecureuil 2 makes it particularly suited to the TV reporting role.

➤ Apart from its twin engines, the AS 355 Ecureuil 2 is similar to the AS 350.

➤ The Ecureuil is still in production, and is now built by Eurocopter.

PROFILE

Going live with the Ecureuil

Once it became possible to relay live pictures from helicopters, many broadcasters rushed to buy their own machines. Within 18 months there were more than 100 in use across the United States alone. But operating in this way was very expensive, and it became more common to charter an aircraft when it was needed to cover a specific story or event.

The AS 350's main advantages for news-gathering operations are reliability and performance. Good reserves of power, simple flight controls and rapid response mean that the pilot can concentrate on the subject and does not need to be concerned about the machine's limitations.

This is particularly important when the pilot is also the reporter. Keeping clear of other helicopters, respecting minimum height regulations and handling the controls, while selecting the right shot to illustrate the story and describing the scene to viewers, is a full-time job.

In spite of the expense, if a helicopter can get to the scene of a major event as it is happening, or to the aftermath of a natural disaster, there is no substitute for the sense of immediacy it can provide.

Above: Some TV broadcasters use their helicopters as relays for signals transmitted from the ground. This system is especially useful for live broadcasts from built-up areas.

Above: This is ITN's AS 355F-1 in action. A special seat is installed to allow the camera operator to work in safety from the open door.

AS 350B2

Type: general-purpose light helicopter

Powerplant: one 540-kW (724-hp.) Turboméca Arriel 1D1 turboshaft

Maximum cruising speed: 246 km/h (153 m.p.h.) at sea level

Climb rate: 546 m/min (1,790 f.p.m.) at sea level

Range: 690 km (428 mi.) with maximum fuel

Hover ceiling: 3200 m (10,500 ft.) in ground effect

Weights: empty 1132 kg (2,490 lb.); maximum take-off 2250 kg (4,950 lb.)

Accommodation: pilot plus up to five passengers

Dimensions:
main rotor diameter	10.69 m (35 ft)
fuselage length	10.93 m (35 ft. 10 in.)
height	3.14 m (10 ft. 4 in.)
rotor disc area	89.75 m² (966 sq. ft.)

The AS 355 and AS 350 share the same rotor system design. The blades are of glass fibre construction with stainless steel leading-edge sheaths. Glass fibre is also used in the rotor hub.

The Ecureuil 2 can be operated by a single crewmember, which makes the aircraft more economical.

Twin Allison turboshafts give the Twin Squirrel large reserves of power in most flight conditions, allowing the pilot to react to a developing situation.

A broader chord tail rotor is one modification which allows the AS 355F-1 to fly at increased weights.

G-OITN

For night-time or low-light work, this aircraft carries a powerful spotlight which allows filming regardless of conditions.

A remotely-controlled sensor pod, containing a camera system, is mounted on a boom which runs through the forward part of the cabin.

When using heavy camera equipment, the camera operator must remain safely restrained at all times, regardless of flight attitude. There is a large footrest on the side of the cabin and comprehensive harnessing is also fitted.

AS 355F-1 TWIN SQUIRREL

This aircraft contains specialist camera and transmitting equipment. Belonging to Independent Television News Limited, it is appropriately registered G-OITN and has become a common sight across the UK.

ACTION DATA

CABIN HEIGHT

With its spacious cabin, the Ecureuil has plenty of room to accommodate bulky TV camera equipment. The AS 350B also has large sliding cabin doors, which allow good access and give a camera operator an excellent vantage point from which to film or take photographs.

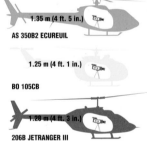

1.35 m (4 ft. 5 in.)
AS 350B2 ECUREUIL

1.25 m (4 ft. 1 in.)
BO 105CB

1.28 m (4 ft. 3 in.)
206B JETRANGER III

MAXIMUM TAKE-OFF

Although the BO 105CB can carry a heavier equipment load than the other types, it is more expensive to operate. The Ecureuil may offer the best compromise between the BO 105CB and the JetRanger.

AS 350B2 ECUREUIL	BO 105CB	206B JETRANGER III
2250 kg (4,950 lb.)	2550 kg (5,610 lb.)	1451 kg (3,192 lb.)

RANGE

Range and endurance are important factors if the aircraft is to remain on station and avoid missing a major event. Again the Ecureuil comes out on top, which makes it popular around the world in this role.

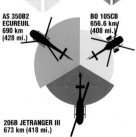

AS 350B2 ECUREUIL 690 km (428 mi.)

BO 105CB 656.6 km (408 mi.)

206B JETRANGER III 673 km (418 mi.)

Multi-purpose Ecureuil

■ **ARMED:** Several air arms use the Ecureuil in its armed form as a light battlefield helicopter. It is compatible with a range of gun pods and guided and unguided missiles.

■ **FIRE-BOMBING:** France's Securité Civile is one operator of the specially equipped fire-bombing Ecureuil. Other aircraft, often with local modifications, are flown in Canada.

■ **RIG SUPPORT:** A few AS 350 Ecureuils are flown on rig support missions in Japan and the US. The twin-engined AS 355, such as this Air Logistics aircraft, is more commonly used for this, however.

17

AÉROSPATIALE (SUD AVIATION)

CARAVELLE

● First French jet airliner ● Rear-mounted turbojet ● 30 years' service

▲ *The Caravelle gave French aviation a huge boost. It proved that France could compete in commercial as well as military aviation, though it relied initially on British design for engines and other components.*

The Caravelle was a pace-setter of the jet age. France's first jet airliner was one of the earliest short- to medium-range turbojet transports, and the first with podded engines fixed to the rear fuselage. This was a successful attempt to ensure improved wing performance and to decrease cabin noise, an idea later copied by many other manufacturers. Hundreds of Caravelles were produced, and served with distinction for three decades.

AÉROSPATIALE (SUD AVIATION) CARAVELLE

▲ Caravelle line
The Toulouse St Martin production line was busy producing these beautiful airliners between 1959 and 1973.

▲ Sterling
The Caravelle 12, as operated by Sterling Airways of Denmark, could carry up to 140 passengers. Sterling was one of 24 operators still using the Caravelle during the 1980s.

◄ Long service
Air Inter used the Caravelle for many years. It had 14 aircraft, which serviced a large French domestic route network.

Luxury liner ►
Some aircraft were fitted out as VIP transports, their luxury interiors having full conference and business facilities which were enhanced by the Caravelle's low noise and smooth ride.

◄ New engines
The Caravelle 7 was a trials version using the General Electric CJ-805 engine. It used the 'short cowl' turbofan in an attempt to increase fuel economy.

FACTS AND FIGURES

➤ The SE 210 Caravelle prototype made its first flight on 27 May 1955.

➤ Design of the front fuselage was based on the de Havilland Comet.

➤ First flown on 3 March 1964, the Super Caravelle was a refinement of the Caravelle III and IV.

➤ Construction of the first two Caravelles was sponsored by the French government.

➤ The 'ultimate' Caravelle variant was the Caravelle 12, the biggest and most powerful model.

➤ The Caravelle 12 took to the air for the first time on 29 October 1970.

PROFILE

Rear-engine pioneer from France

The Caravelle was a product of the early 1950s. Designed by Sud Aviation (now part of Aérospatiale) as a 52-seater, it was to grow considerably after its first flight in 1955. By the time the Caravelle 12 came along in 1970, passenger capacity had increased to 140 and some 35 airlines in two dozen countries were operating the type.

The Caravelle is renowned for being much quieter inside than other first-generation jetliners like the de Havilland Comet and Boeing 707. All versions pampered passengers with a sumptuous interior, plenty of room and excellent vision. Pilots found the Caravelle a very sensible and practical machine. It was also considered a bargain by airline executives nervous about fuel prices.

In the 1980s, approaching old age, Caravelles were gradually withdrawn from most scheduled routes, but with considerable reluctance. Caravelles found other uses. Many succeeded as freighters; some were used as VIP transports, utility craft or electronic intelligence-gatherers for the military.

The Caravelle was a great design success for France. Not only did it have a relatively trouble-free entry into service, but it introduced a totally new engine layout, in rear pods, at a time when American designs used wing-mounted pods and the British persisted with engines mounted in the wingroots.

The Caravelle tailplane was mid-set on the fin to keep it clear of the engine exhaust.

Caravelle 12

Type: short-/medium-range transport

Powerplant: two 64.50-kN (14,470-lb.-thrust) Pratt & Whitney JT8D-9 turbofans

Maximum cruising speed: 825 km/h (512 m.p.h.) at 7620 m (25,000 ft.)

Range: 4040 km (2,860 mi.)

Service ceiling: 10,900 m (35,750 ft.)

Weights: empty 29,500 kg (64,900 lb.); loaded 58,000 kg (127,600 lb.)

Accommodation: 52 to 64 passengers in initial versions; up to 104 passengers on Super Caravelle; up to 140 passengers on Caravelle 12

Dimensions:
span 34.29 m (112 ft. 6 in.)
length 36.23 m (118 ft. 10 in.)
height 9.02 m (29 ft. 7 in.)
wing area 146.70 m² (1,579 sq. ft.)

CARAVELLE III 'ALTAIR'

Alitalia operated one of the largest Caravelle fleets, with 21 aircraft in service by 1965. 'Altair' entered service in 1960 and was eventually sold to an Ecuadorian airline which flew it throughout the 1970s.

A projected Caravelle 10A was designed with a leading-edge root extension and double-slotted flaps, but only one prototype was ever built.

A unique and instant recognition feature of the Caravelle was the graceful swept tail. Early aircraft also had a shallow spine from the fin to the mid-fuselage, housing radio antennas.

Caravelle IIIs were powered by the Rolls-Royce Avon engine, which was powerful but rather thirsty. Fuel economy was much improved with the fitting of Pratt & Whitney JT8D turbofans in the Caravelle 10B.

The forward fuselage of the Caravelle was based upon that of the British de Havilland Comet, the world's first operational jet airliner.

Over the years the fuselage of the Caravelle was 'stretched' many times. The first Caravelles seated only about 50 passengers, but the final version seated about 140 in economy-style layout.

Due to the absence of engine mountings the wing was unusually clean and efficient in design. Two fences were fitted on the outboard of the wing.

ALTAIR

ALITALIA

I-DAXA

CARAVELLE

Only a pilot and co-pilot were usually housed in the flight deck.

The cabin windows had an unusual rounded triangular shape.

Rear-mounted engines meant that the passenger cabin of the Caravelle was quieter than any of the other first-generation jet airliners.

ACTION DATA

MAXIMUM SPEED

The Caravelle was one of the earliest jet liners, so it was marginally slower than some of its contemporaries. But it was the first short-haul jet, and it could travel twice as fast as the piston-engined twins that many airlines were using in the 1950s.

CARAVELLE III 805 km/h (512 m.p.h.)
COMET 4C 861 km/h (534 m.p.h.)
DC-9 900 km/h (558 m.p.h.)

RANGE

As a short-haul jet, a typical Caravelle route had stages ranging from 150 km (100 mi.) to around 1000 km (600 mi.). The later DC-9 was designed for the same market and has a similar layout and range. Although the Comet had a much longer range, it too was largely used on short- and medium-haul routes.

COMET 4C 7000 km (4,300 mi.)
CARAVELLE III 2300 km (1,400 mi.)
DC-9 2000 km (1,250 mi.)

PASSENGER LOAD

Although early Caravelles could carry nearly 100 passengers in a high-density layout, 64 passengers in a two-class configuration was a more usual payload. First-class passengers sat four abreast, with economy seating in rows of five.

CARAVELLE III maximum 99
COMET 4C maximum 118
DC-9 maximum 90

Constant improvement

■ **CARAVELLE III:** Tunis Air operated nine assorted Caravelles between 1961 and 1977. This was a Series III, which mated the original fuselage with more powerful Rolls-Royce Avon engines.

■ **CARAVELLE 11R:** This had a 1.93-m (6-ft. 4-in.) fuselage extension and a large cargo door. This example served in Tahiti for many years, supporting France's nuclear test range in the Pacific.

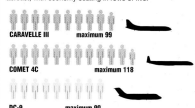

■ **CARAVELLE 12:** The Caravelle 12 was 4.23 m (13 ft. 10 in.) longer than the original. Air Inter operated Caravelles to 23 destinations in France, and this example seated 128 passengers.

AÉROSPATIALE/BAC

CONCORDE

● World's fastest airliner ● Mach 2 performance ● Supreme luxury

MPH
1340

▲ *Although it is a product of 1960s technology, without the benefit of multi-screen cockpits and fly-by-wire controls, Concorde is still the most futuristic airliner to be seen anywhere in the world.*

It is one of the most beautiful aircraft ever built, still capable of turning heads after a quarter of a century. But the Anglo-French Concorde is much more than a work of aeronautic art. A record breaker from the start, it proved to be highly profitable on the prestige air routes between Europe and the USA until shortly before its retirement in October 2003.

◄ Supercruise
Concorde is one of the very few aircraft able to maintain a supersonic cruise without the use of afterburners, which enables it to fly further at Mach 2 than any other aircraft.

Olympus power ▶
Concorde's engines each pour out more than 17 tons of thrust.

▼ Powerpack
To gain additional thrust at critical moments such as take-off and transition to supersonic speed, Concorde's engines are fitted with afterburners.

▲ Streamlining
Even at altitudes above 15,000 m (49,000 ft.), air friction at twice the speed of sound is a significant factor, so Concorde is polished mirror smooth to reduce drag.

AIR FRANCE

▲Elegant travelling
Concorde's aesthetically pleasing shape is matched by a standard of service more luxurious than that of any other scheduled airliner.

FACTS AND FIGURES

➤ Since Concorde entered scheduled service in 1978, British and French aircraft have carried 3,000,000 supersonic passengers.

➤ Concorde's only rival, the Soviet Tu-144, is no longer in service.

➤ During supersonic flight, Concorde's skin heats to 127°C (260°F) at the nose.

➤ Concorde gains 3000 m (9,850 ft.) as fuel is burned off during a flight.

➤ Concorde flies 16 km (10 mi.) while a passenger's champagne glass is filled.

➤ The 14 Concordes have clocked up more supersonic hours than all the fighters used by the world's air forces.

PROFILE

Mach 2 across the Atlantic

Over the past two decades a handful of Concordes have carried more people beyond the speed of sound than all the other supersonic aircraft ever built.

Since its commercial debut in 1976, Concorde has proved deservedly popular. It is the only way a businessman can cross the Atlantic for a meeting and return the same day, while his subsonic competitor faces at the very least two seven-hour flights and serious jet lag. As a result, Concorde flights are nearly always filled with high-paying passengers.

And yet Concorde has been a commercial failure. When it entered service the oil crisis had made the viability of a gas-guzzling supersonic jet questionable, and influential American environmentalists were loud in their protests over the noise its powerful engines generated. As a result, options on 70 aircraft by more than a dozen airlines were cancelled.

Nevertheless, the 14 production aircraft delivered to the national carriers in Britain and France performed splendidly, with higher than average mechanical reliability. They remained the world's only operational supersonic airliners until their retirement in October 2003.

Concorde in flight could never be confused with any other aircraft currently in service. The graceful arrow-like layout, the slender nose and unique curved double delta wing are instant recognition features.

CONCORDE

G-BOAB was the sixth production Concorde, it entered service with British Airways on 21 January 1976.

Concorde

Type: luxury supersonic airliner

Powerplant: four 169.17-kN (227-hp.) Rolls-Royce/SNECMA Olympus 593 Mk 610 turbojets with afterburning

Cruising speed: 2180 km/h (1355 m.p.h.) at 15,000 m (49,000 ft.) (Mach 2.04)

Range: 6250 km (3880 mi.) with maximum payload and reserves

Service ceiling: 18,300 m (60,000 ft.)

Weights: empty 78,700 kg (173,500 lb.); loaded 185,066 kg (408,000 lb.)

Payload: three crew, 100 passengers

Dimensions:
span	25.55 m (83 ft. 10 in.)
length	62.10 m (203 ft. 9 in)
height	11.40 m (37 ft. 5 in.)
wing area	358.22 m² (3,856 sq. ft.)

Concorde's curved double delta wing is a good compromise between supersonic efficiency and low-speed controllability during landing and take-off.

During supersonic flight, the aircraft's equilibrium shifts. To compensate, fuel is pumped during flight from front to rear to ensure that the jet remains stable.

BRITISH AIRWAYS

G-BOAB

AB

Concorde's unique hydraulically-powered nose 'droops' by 12.5° to increase pilot visibility during take-off and landing. At supersonic speeds the nose is raised for streamlining, and a heat-resistant visor protects the cockpit windows.

Concorde's cabin could hold 128 passengers seated at normal airline density, but both operators restrict capacity to 100. This allows the premium-paying passengers even more room than in conventional first-class layout.

Concorde's landing gear is made by Messier Hispano. The wheels, which have to withstand higher landing speeds than normal aircraft, retract inwards towards the fuselage.

Concorde does not have a conventional tailplane. Each wing has three trailing-edge elevons, which combine the pitch control function of elevators and the roll control of ailerons.

Supersonic flight path

1 TAKE-OFF: Concorde uses afterburners for take-off, then cuts them until the aircraft is clear of land. They are engaged again to accelerate through Mach 1.

2 SUPERCRUISE: At Mach 1.7 the afterburners are cut, and the aircraft continues to accelerate to Mach 2 under normal power.

3 CLIMB: As fuel is burned and Concorde becomes lighter, the aircraft drifts upwards from 15,000 to 18,000 m (49,000 to 59,000 ft.).

4 DESCENT: Several hundred kilometres out, Concorde reduces thrust. Speed falls below Mach 1 as the aircraft descends below 11,000 m (36,000 ft.) to normal commercial flight levels and becomes just another airliner.

16000 m
MACH 2
MACH 1.7
MACH 1
10000 m

CONCORDE 3 hours
MACH 2.2
MACH 1

BOEING 747 6 hours

NEW YORK
QUEEN ELIZABETH II 5 Days
1600 km (1,000 mi.)
3200 km (2,000 mi.)
4800 km (3,000 mi.)
LONDON

AGUSTA

A 109 HIRUNDO

● Air taxi ● Military transport ● Anti-tank attack

W idely recognised as one of the most graceful and attractive helicopters ever built, the Agusta A 109 Hirundo has sold well in both civil and military markets. Since 1971 the Hirundo has performed superbly as a light passenger transport, freighter, air ambulance, law-enforcement craft and search-and-rescue ship. In its military guise, the A 109A is employed for anti-tank attack, reconnaissance and electronic warfare.

▲ Agusta 109s are often seen nestling among New York's skyscrapers. Whether ferrying top executives or performing law-enforcement duties the aircraft performs with quiet efficiency.

◀ Maritime missions
Fitted with searchlights, floats and a 360° radar, the A 109 can fulfil a number of maritime roles such as search-and-rescue, coastal patrol and anti-ship duties.

▼ Hot and high
Designed for operations in arid, mountainous regions, the A 109K incorporates more powerful engines, dust filters and improved avionics, giving it the durability to survive in harsh conditions.

▲ Spy launcher
An unusual use of the A 109 is as a launch ship for unmanned reconnaissance drones. These can spy on enemy positions using conventional or infra-red cameras.

Alpine rescue ▶
The A 109 can be fitted with skis and is used in the Alps as an air ambulance, evacuating victims of avalanches or skiing accidents.

▲ Flying ambulance
The A 109's capacious cabin is ideal for casualty rescue. The versatile helicopter can ferry two stretcher cases plus three attendants to hospital.

FACTS AND FIGURES

➤ The first of three civil A 109 prototypes made its initial flight on 4 August 1971.

➤ Deliveries of the first production A 109A began in 1975.

➤ Two of Argentina's four A 109As were captured during the 1982 Falklands War and were used by the British.

➤ In 1981 the civil model was redesignated A 109A Mk II, reflecting changes in transmission and other features.

➤ The A 109C is a 'wide-body' version with more room and increased power.

➤ The Belgian army uses A 109s for scouting and anti-armour duties.

PROFILE

Agusta's best-selling machine

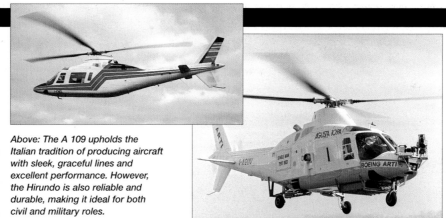

Although Augusta has a solid track record for making helicopters designed by other companies, the A 109 Hirundo (Swallow) was the first mass-produced helicopter actually designed by the Italian company.

The sleek A.109 was originally intended to have a single 551-kW (740-hp.) Turboméca Astazou XII turboshaft, but for additional safety it was redesigned in 1967 around two Allison 250-C14 engines.

Development of the A 109 was protracted, but the result has been satisfying. Large corporations, police departments and military users are pleased with its solid performance. For military and naval use, the Hirundo carries dozens of combinations of electronics gear, weapons and equipment. The hi-tech maritime A 109A ECM (electronic countermeasures) variant has a radar display, direction finder, electromagnetic emission analyser and jamming equipment.

A specialised military utility model, the A 109B, was proposed, but in 1969 this was abandoned in favour of the eight-seat A 109C civil version.

Above: The A 109 upholds the Italian tradition of producing aircraft with sleek, graceful lines and excellent performance. However, the Hirundo is also reliable and durable, making it ideal for both civil and military roles.

Above: A modified A 109 was used as Boeing's Advanced Rotorcraft Technology Integration (ARTI) testbed. The pilot was situated in the passenger cabin and had no external view; he used the cameras on the nose to fly the aircraft.

A 109A Hirundo

Type: light general-purpose helicopter

Powerplant: two Allison 250-C20B turboshaft engines each developing 313 kW (420 hp.) for take-off derated to 258 kW (346 hp.) for continuous twin-engine flight performance

Maximum cruising speed: 266 km/h (165 m.p.h.)

Endurance: 3 hours 18 minutes

Service ceiling: 4968 km (3,080 ft.)

Weights: empty 1415 kg (3,113 lb.); loaded 2450 kg (5,390 lb.)

Armament: (military version) two 7.62-mm machine-guns and two XM157 rocket launchers (seven 70-mm rockets), up to 866 kg (1,905 lb.) of alternate weapons including guns, rockets and missiles

Dimensions: main rotor diameter 11.00 m (36 ft.)
length 10.71 m (35 ft. 2 in.)
height 3.30 m (10 ft. 9 in.)
rotor disc area 95.00 m² (1,022 sq. ft.)

A 109A HIRUNDO

The Argentine army deployed several A 109s to the Falkland Islands in 1982. Some were destroyed in Harrier attacks, but two were captured by the British and are now used by the Special Air Service.

In the newer A 109K the Allison engines are replaced by a pair of Turboméca Arriel turboshafts.

The latest A 109s have composite rotor blades, but earlier versions had conventional aluminium alloy blades with a Nomex core. Blade-folding can be performed manually.

The A 109A has a two-bladed tail rotor. Some military versions have the ventral fin removed and alpine versions have a small tail-ski fitted under the tailboom.

The A 109A Mk II featured a redesigned tailboom structure and a new tail rotor drive shaft.

Military A 109s can be fitted with a Saab Helios sight system and a laser rangefinder on the roof.

The lower rear fuselage contains two bladder-type fuel tanks with a capacity of 560 litres (146 gallons). An auxiliary tank with a capacity of 170 litres (44 gallons) can also be fitted in the fuselage.

ACTION DATA

PASSENGER LOAD

The S-76 was designed more specifically with the civil helicopter market in mind, and therefore has a higher passenger capacity. The A 109 and Bell 222 are smaller all-rounders, with more versatile airframes but lower passenger capacity.

A 109A HIRUNDO 6-7 passengers
MODEL 222 8-9 passengers
S-76 SPIRIT 12 passengers

MAXIMUM CRUISING SPEED

Conventional helicopters have limited speeds due to the laws of aerodynamics. Even so, all these machines are well streamlined, giving them much higher cruising speeds than similar sized helicopters designed 10 or 20 years earlier.

A 109A HIRUNDO 266 km/h (165 m.p.h.)
MODEL 222 265 km/h (164 m.p.h.)
S-76 SPIRIT 269 km/h (167 m.p.h.)

RANGE

The larger S-76 requires more fuel but has greater range than the A 109 or Bell 222. The range of any helicopter varies greatly according to its payload. At maximum all-up weight the amount of fuel carried is often limited, and a large proportion of the force generated by the rotor is used to keep the aircraft flying rather than pushing it forward. Other factors such as ambient air temperature and 'density altitude' also affect range.

A 1094 HIRUNDO 565 km (350 mi.)
S-76 SPIRIT 748 km (464 mi.)
MODEL 222 523 km (324 mi.)

Multi-role middleweights

■ AÉROSPATIALE SA 365 DAUPHIN: This helicopter was designed to replace the Allouette II. The Dauphin II was the main version, featuring twin engines. China bought the production rights to the SA 365 and builds the type as the Z-9 Haitun; a military version armed with anti-tank missiles is also projected.

■ BELL 222: Another capable design, in fierce competition with the S-76 on the civil market, the Bell 222 has had little success in the military field. Its successor, the Bell 230, shows every sign of changing this, with trials on Chilean navy vessels proving very successful and many other nations showing signs of interest.

■ SIKORSKY S-76: The S-76 has been very successful, especially in America. It has also been developed as a military helicopter, but has had far more sales in the civil market. The latest versions have Arriel turboshafts like the A 109K and advanced 'glass' cockpit displays.

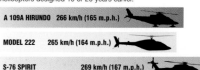

AIRBUS INDUSTRIE

AIRBUS A300

● European collaboration ● Medium-range wide-body airliner

▲ *From the start of its design, the A300 was envisaged as offering wide-body comfort in a twin-aisle arrangement. The large cabin can be readily altered to suit an individual customer's requirements, allowing for maximum density seating for charter operators or a full three-class layout for scheduled airlines.*

The Airbus 300 is the flagship of an international manufacturing enterprise. It was designed as an economical and efficient large jetliner for busy, medium-range routes of up to 2225 km (1,380 mi.) and carrying 250 passengers. When the A300 burst on the scene in 1973, success was far from certain. Today, the A300B model heads a family of airliners that successfully challenges American manufacturers Boeing and McDonnell Douglas.

Modular ▶ construction
Components of the Airbus are built in several countries. These are then brought together and assembled at Toulouse in France.

▼ Global success
The A300 design was the first of the Airbus products and immediately took a large share of the world airliner market.

▲ High-tech wing
Built by British Aerospace, the A300 wing has an advanced supercritical airfoil section for maximum efficiency.

◀ European standard
Many of Europe's airlines, including Olympic, adopted the A300 for their European routes.

Ongoing ▶ development
Airbus Industrie has continued to refine the A300, with greater range and load-carrying ability.

▲ Long-range winglets
The later variants of the A300 feature triangular-shaped surfaces on the wingtips. These reduce drag, increasing range and efficiency.

FACTS AND FIGURES

➤ According to the US-based Air Transport Association, Airbus 300s have flown more than a billion revenue-miles.

➤ The Airbus 300 has its roots in the Anglo-French HBN100 design dating from 1967.

➤ Eleven ex-airline A300s are currently being converted into freighters.

➤ The A300-600ST 'Beluga' is the giant replacement for the Super Guppy used to transport Airbus parts to Toulouse.

➤ The first A300 to fly, an A300B1, took to the air on 28 October 1972.

➤ The A300 is one of the few Western designs flown by Aeroflot of Russia.

PROFILE

Airbus people carrier

Airbus Industrie launched the A300 as the first jetliner in what has become a legendary family of advanced, efficient air transports, successfully challenging America's post-war domination of the world airliner market.

One of the first medium- to long-range passenger craft to be powered by just two engines (in under-wing pods), the A300 was purpose-designed to accommodate any of several engine types. Not readily visible from outside are features of the A300 which have become a

trademark of all Airbus transports – the latest, most advanced technology in cockpit instrumentation and computers which aid the two pilots in every task from taxiing out to navigating.

Airbus has manufactured half a dozen versions of this fine jetliner, including the longer-range A300B4 introduced in 1974 and the A300-600R, which is currently in production. Around the world, nearly 400 A300s are flying in the colours of 53 airlines, with over half operating in Asia and Australasia.

Lufthansa has a large fleet of Airbus aircraft, including the A300-600 (illustrated), A310, A320, A321 and A340.

The A300 can be powered by two families of engines, depending on customer choice. One is the Pratt & Whitney JT9D/PW4000 series: the other is the General Electric CF6 series.

The nose radome covers a small weather-avoidance radar set. There is also room for a second weather radar and a ground proximity warning system.

The A300 introduced a wide range of new construction technologies. The wing skin is milled from one solid piece of metal.

Airbus A300B4

Type: medium-haul twin-engined airliner

Powerplant: two 233.54-kN (52,390-lb.-thrust) General Electric CF6-50CI advanced technology turbofan engines

Maximum cruising speed: 911 km/h (565 m.p.h.) at 7620 m (25,000 ft.)

Service ceiling: with passengers 13,000 m (42,640 ft.); empty 15,000 m (49,200 ft.)

Weights: empty 79,831 kg (175,628 lb.); loaded 165,000 kg (363,000 lb.)

Accommodation: flight deck crew of two; eight to 12 flight attendants; seating layouts for 220 to 336 passengers; maximum capacity 375

Dimensions:
span	44.84 m	(147 ft.)
length	53.62 m	(175 ft. 10 in.)
height	16.53 m	(54 ft. 3 in.)
wing area	260 m²	(279 sq. ft.)

AIRBUS A300B4

In May 1974 Air France introduced the Airbus into service, ushering in a new era of efficient, economic air travel. The A300 was designed to move large numbers of people between major population centres, perfect for the European market where it achieved great sales success. It also made small inroads into the US domestic market.

Fuel is held principally in the wings. The internal structure of the wing has two main spars with the outer skins stretched between them. This forms a very strong box, which is filled with fuel from the wingroot to the tip.

Airbus designed a very efficient wing with a supercritical section for high-speed flight. For take-off and landing, the wing deploys very powerful flaps and leading-edge slats to provide vital extra lift.

The tailplane of the Airbus has conventional elevators on the trailing edge for pitch control, but to accurately trim the aircraft the whole tailplane pivots around a central point. The diamond shape around the tailplane fixture is a sealing plate.

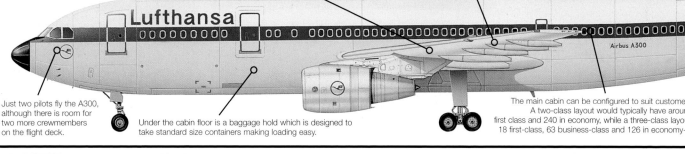

Just two pilots fly the A300, although there is room for two more crewmembers on the flight deck.

Under the cabin floor is a baggage hold which is designed to take standard size containers making loading easy.

The main cabin can be configured to suit customer preferences. A two-class layout would typically have around 20 seats in first class and 240 in economy, while a three-class layout would have 18 first-class, 63 business-class and 126 in economy-class seating.

A true multi-national

One of the unique characteristics of the Airbus project is the fact that parts are manufactured by aircraft companies all over Europe. After completion the individual sections are flown to the Airbus factory at Toulouse for final assembly.

ACTION DATA

PASSENGER LOAD

The modern wide-body airliners have greater capacity than old narrow-body types like the Boeing 727.

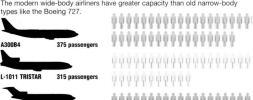

A300B4	375 passengers
L-1011 TRISTAR	315 passengers
MODEL 727	189 passengers

KEY (A300-600)
- ○ Aérospatiale (France)
- ◐ Deutsche Aerospace (Germany)
- ● British Aerospace (UK)
- ◔ Casa (Spain)
- ◑ Fokker (Netherlands)
- ○ General Electric (USA)
- ● Messier (France)

TAIL STRUCTURE: Deutsche Aerospace builds the vertical tail of the A300, with Casa of Spain supplying the tailplane and other small parts. Engines on the A300 series are provided by General Electric of the USA.

FUSELAGE STRUCTURE: Germany supplies the largest part of the Airbus fuselage, with France providing the cockpit section and most of the avionics, as well as the engine pylons and wingroots.

WING STRUCTURE: The Airbus wing is manufactured by British Aerospace. Flaps were made by the now defunct Fokker, but later models have parts from Belgium.

AIRBUS INDUSTRIE

A300-600F

● **Dependable freighter** ● **High-tech design** ● **Economic service**

T he great majority of current commercial cargo aircraft are around 25 years old, leaving many airfreight operators in need of newer and more economical equipment. Using experience gathered through the production of the SATIC Beluga, Airbus has profited from this demand thanks to its modification of surplus or retired A300B4 airliners to freighter configuration, as well as building a new cargo version of the A300. Both types are known by the designation A300-600F.

▲ *British Aerospace at Filton, near Bristol, was responsible for the conversion of the A300 freighter. In the foreground is the first A300 cargo conversion to be delivered, the aircraft being handed over to Channel Express in 1997.*

◀ **Cargo not passengers**
From the outside, the freighter looks similar to the A300-600R airliner, although the entire passenger cabin is removed.

▼ **From airliner to freighter**
As well as the newly built freighter, British Aerospace has provided cargo conversions of standard A300 airliners.

▼ **Great white whale**
The largest variant in the A300 series is the SATIC A300-600ST Beluga, used by Airbus for transporting outsized aircraft components. The Beluga replaced the ageing Super Guppy.

▼ **New freighter at Stansted**
HeavyLift Cargo Airlines, based at Stansted, once operated a fleet of three A300B4 freighters. The airline ceased operating in 2006.

◀ **Filton conversion centre**
The cargo conversion of the A300 took place in England at Filton, near Bristol.

FACTS AND FIGURES

➤ As with the standard A300, the cargo version is available with a range of engines, the GE CF6 being the most popular option.

➤ The maiden flight of a new-build A300 freighter took place on 2 December 1993.

➤ Federal Express became the first customer for the new-build freighter in July 1991.

➤ Newly built A300-600F freighters were built in Toulouse, while cargo conversions of existing A300s took place in Filton.

➤ Airbus also offered a convertible version of the A300, for either passengers or cargo.

➤ Convertible versions are offered, with accommodation for up to 375 passengers.

PROFILE

A new generation of cargo aircraft

The Airbus A300 firmly established Airbus as an important manufacturer of widebody airliners. The aircraft has now been in service for 36 years. As newer models began to enter service, older A300B4s began to be withdrawn from passenger use. Converted to become freighters, these aircraft remain reliable and useful, with many more years of service ahead of them.

In 1996 British Aerospace began to convert surplus or withdrawn A300 airliners to freighter standard at its Filton facility in England. The first two examples were delivered to the freight specialist HeavyLift Cargo Airlines based at Stansted. The conversion work included the installation of a large cargo door in the port side of the fuselage, a cargo-handling system in the main cabin and specialised safety equipment including a smoke-warning system.

Airbus also built a new freighter on the basis of its then-current widebody airliner, the A300-600R. These new-build aircraft are externally identical to the converted machines, but are equipped with a digital cockpit, more powerful

Above: Federal Express is one of the world's biggest cargo airlines, and opted for the A300-600F, primarily for use on its regional routes.

engines, and feature other particular items of equipment that were introduced on the A300-600R airliner. Most A300-600F aircraft are powered by General Electric CF6-80C2A5 turbofans. In 1994, Federal Express became the first recipient and operator of the new-build A300-600F freighter.

By fielding a widebody freighter for the regional route network, Airbus secured a market in which there were practically no other serious rivals. The main cabin is capable of accommodating up to 20 pallets each measuring 2.24 by 3.17 m (7 ft. 4 in. by 10 ft. 5 in.)

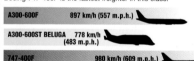

Above: One of the smaller cargo operators, Channel Express entered a new era of cargo services with the introduction of a freighter conversion of the A300B4.

Daimler-Benz Aerospace build the rear fuselage and the tail area, together with the vertical tailfin. Together with the other remaining major components, these are transported from Hamburg by Beluga or Guppy transporter to Toulouse, where final assembly takes place. The aircraft are then returned to Hamburg to receive their cabin interior and other internal fittings.

A300-600F

Type: Medium-range regional freighter

Powerplant: two 274kN (61,626-lb.-thrust) General Electric CF6-80C2A5 turbofan engines

Maximum cruising speed: 897 km/h (557 m.p.h.)

Landing speed: 251 km/h (156 m.p.h.)

Range: 7593 km (4,718 miles)

Service ceiling: 10 000 m (32,000 ft.)

Payload: max. 50 950 kg (112,325 lb.)

Weights: empty 78 335 kg (172,700 lb.); loaded 170 500 kg (375,888 lb.)

Accommodation: flight deck crew of two

Dimensions:		
	span	44.84 m (147 ft.)
	length	53.62 m (175 ft. 10 in.)
	height	16.53 m (54 ft. 3 in.)
	wing area	260 m² (279 sq. ft.)

Compared to earlier variants of the A300, the A300-600F freighter is equipped with a modern-technology cockpit, with digital multi-function displays, automatic navigation and automatic engine and engine systems controls.

A smoke-warning system in the main cabin is one of the special additions to the freighter version of the A300. Other features particular to the cargo version include the freight-loading system on the main cargo deck, which makes the process of loading and unloading much more efficient.

The forward fuselage area including the flight deck, the lower forward fuselage and the engine nacelles were built by Dassault Aérospatiale in France.

Most A300-600Fs are powered by General Electric CF6 turbofan engines, although the PW4158 from Pratt & Whitney was also offered as an option.

Both wings are fitted with two-position slats on the leading edges. The slats are divided into three sections, and are complemented by large, curved flaps that run continuously along the trailing edge. Fitted ahead of the flaps are spoilers, which act as air brakes as well as complementing to the elevator when in descending flight.

A300-600F

This aircraft is one of 10 A300-600F freighters that were received by Korean for service with the carrier's Air Cargo fleet. In addition to these, Korean also operated two older A300F4 aircraft, these being cargo conversions of airliners.

ACTION DATA

SPEED

With its highly efficient and powerful turbofan engines, the A300-600F possesses excellent flight performance, and is faster than the Beluga outsized-cargo transporter. With its four CF6 engines, the Boeing 747-400F is the fastest freighter in this class.

A300-600F	897 km/h (557 m.p.h.)
A300-600ST BELUGA	778 km/h (483 m.p.h.)
747-400F	980 km/h (609 m.p.h.)

RANGE

Modern twin-engines civilian aircraft offer much increased range compared to their predecessors. The A300 freighter has allowed many companies to transport cargo to more different destinations than ever before. As class leader, the 747 can offer an enormous range.

A300-600F 7593 km (4718 miles)

747-400F 13398 km (8325 miles)

A300-600ST BELUGA 1666 km (1035 miles)

CEILING

The ceiling for these aircraft is around 10000 m (32,000 ft.) or more. The jet-engined Beluga is far more capable than the turboprop-powered Guppy that it replaced.

A300-600F	A300-600ST BELUGA	747-400F
10 000 m (32,000 ft.)	10 600 m (34,750 ft.)	13 715 m (45,000 ft.)

European Projects

■ **AIRBUS MRTT:** A number of nations have already introduced the military variant of the A310 to service. Airbus also offers a Multi-Role Tanker Transport. The MRTT, in common with the civil freighter versions, is available as a new-build aircraft or as a conversion.

■ **SATIC A300-600ST BELUGA:** This variant is intended for the transport of oversized items of freight and is based on the extended-range Airbus A300-600R. The Beluga has an entirely new fuselage without cabin pressurisation.

■ **AIRBUS A400M:** Originally known as the Future Large Aircraft, the A400M was designed to replace the C-130 Hercules and Transall with a number of European air arms. It first flew in December 2009.

AIRBUS INDUSTRIE

AIRBUS A310

● Twin turbofan ● Medium/long range ● Advanced technology airliner

B ased on the successful Airbus A300, the smaller, medium-range Airbus A310 was launched in 1978 and was first flown in April 1982. The A310's fuselage is 8.10 m (26 ft. 6 in.) shorter but has the same cross-section, and can accommodate 280 passengers. The type first entered service with Swissair and Lufthansa in April 1983, and the latter currently operates 10 of the longer range A310-300 series.

▲ The Airbus A310
has an advanced two-crew 'glass' EFIS
(electronic flight instrument system)
cockpit. It was one of the first airliners to
dispense with the flight engineer's station.

AIRBUS INDUSTRIE AIRBUS A310

▲ Toulouse assembly
The Airbus international
consortium supplies the major
sections for assembly in France.

▲ New wing
The A310's advanced wing
reduces drag and, therefore,
increases fuel economy. It was
designed by British Aerospace
and is manufactured at the
company's Chester works.

▲ Longer range
This Airbus A310 is one of a pair of long-range
-304s operated by the Czech Republic airline CSA.
The only distinguishing feature externally is the small
winglets, and it has an extra fuel tank in the fin.

▲ Good performance
The A310's powerful engines and high-lift wing give it
a good take-off performance when operating from
small international airports at maximum weight.

Wide body ▶
Like the A300, the A310 was an advance on
previous designs and provided wide-body
capacity for medium-range routes.

FACTS AND FIGURES

➤ Announced in 1978, the A310 was first
flown on 3 April 1982; by this date, 181
had already been ordered by airlines.

➤ First deliveries were made to Swissair
and Lufthansa on 29 March 1983.

➤ Lufthansa introduced the aircraft on
21 April 1983, nine days after Swissair.

➤ The A310 is manufactured in France,
Germany, Spain and the UK; final
assembly is by Aérospatiale at Toulouse.

➤ Three versions of the A310 were planned,
but only the -200 and -300 have been sold.

➤ By January 1997, 254 A310s had been
delivered from total orders for 271.

High-technology European airliner

The success of the twin-engined, medium- to long-range Airbus A300 airliner in the 1970s highlighted the need for the European consortium to develop a smaller, medium-range version. The aircraft was first promoted as the A300B10, and became the A310 in 1978.

The new Airbus retained the wide-body cabin, but was 11 frames shorter than the A300. It had a new BAe-designed wing, a modified undercarriage and a two-crew 'glass' cockpit with the then-current state-of-the-art instrumentation.

The A310 is powered by either General Electric CF6 or Pratt & Whitney PW4152 turbofans. Two versions of the aircraft are offered to airlines: the A310-200 (range 6667 km (4,135 mi.) with General Electric engines) and the -300 (range 7963 km (4,995 mi.) with General Electric engines). The PW4152 engines give slightly greater range.

Airbus delivered the first -300, which had extra fuel capacity, maximum take-off weight increased to 150,000 kg (330,000 lb.) and winglets, to Thai Airways in 1986, after certification on 5 December 1985. The A310 remains in production and Airbus is re-proposing the short-range -100 in an updated, lighter configuration as the A310 Lite.

The Airbus A310-300, powered by Pratt & Whitney JT9D-7R4E turbofans, was first flown at Toulouse, France, on 8 July 1985.

To extend the range of the A310, Airbus developed the -300 with more powerful engines, a fuel tank in the fin and a computerised fuel trimming system.

Currently, two different turbofan engines are offered for the A310-300: the Pratt & Whitney PW4156A (249 kN (56,000-lb. thrust)) or the more powerful General Electric CF6-80C2A8 (262 kN (59,000-lb. thrust)).

Retaining the same basic structure as the A300, the A310's wing is, aerodynamically, completely new. Wingtip fences were introduced on the -300 and fitted retrospectively to earlier aircraft.

A310-300

Type: twin-engined medium- to long-range passenger airliner

Powerplant: two 262-kN (59,000-lb.-thrust) General Electric CF6-80C2A8 or 249-kN (56,000-lb.-thrust) Pratt & Whitney PW4156A turbofans

Maximum speed: 804 km/h (498 m.p.h.) at 9450 m (31,000 ft.)

Range: 8056 km with P&W engines

Service ceiling: 12,192 m (40,000 ft.)

Weights: empty 71,840 kg (158,048 lb.); maximum take-off 150,900 kg (331,980 lb.)

Accommodation: standard seating for 250 passengers; maximum 280

Dimensions: span 43.89 m (144 ft.)
length 46.66 m (153 ft.)
height 15.80 m (51 ft. 10 in.)
wing area 219 m² (2,356 sq. ft.)

A310-204

Hapag-Lloyd Fluggesellschaft has a fleet of four A310-204s and four -304/8s for use on its international scheduled and charter passenger services.

When launched in 1978 the A310 was the first Airbus airliner with a forward-facing two-crew arrangement and an electronic flight instrument system 'glass' cockpit.

Forward fuselage, upper centre fuselage and rear fuselage sections, and their associated doors, are built by Daimler-Benz Aerospace Airbus. Aérospatiale manufactures the majority of the remaining fuselage components, BAe produces the wings and CASA and Fokker construct all other sections.

The A310's wide-body fuselage has eight-abreast seating for economy-class passengers. The rear fuselage is reprofiled to allow seats to be fitted further to the rear.

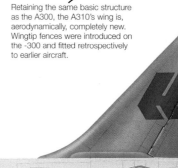

The main passenger access door is situated behind the cockpit on the port side of the fuselage.

The inward-retracting, four-wheel bogie main undercarriage legs on the A310 differ from those on the A300.

More extensive use is made of carbon fibre, such as in the tail control surfaces, to lighten the structure of the A310. The tailcone houses a Garrett GTCP 331-250 auxiliary power unit.

Airbus A310 variants

■ **A310-300:** More -200s have been sold than -300s, but this newer, long-range variant is gaining in popularity.

■ **A310-200F:** Federal Express converted 13 former Lufthansa -200s to freighter configuration with a large cargo loading door

■ **CC-150 POLARIS:** Six A310-300s are flown on passenger and freight transportation duties by the Canadian Armed Forces as the Polaris.

■ **A310 MULTI-ROLE TANKER TRANSPORT:** The MRTT, with a cargo door, extra fuel tanks and refuelling pods, underwent trials in 1995.

ACTION DATA

STANDARD SEATING

Airbus has produced an airliner which offers good payload/range characteristics and which closely matches market requirements. Additional flexibility is offered with a 280-seat, high-density layout.

A310-200 — 250 passengers
767-200 — 224 passengers
Il-96-300 — 235 passengers

TAKE-OFF RUN

When operating from smaller airports, good take-off performance is essential if payload or range is not to be sacrificed. Both the A310 and the Boeing 767-200 are closely matched. The Il-96 has a much longer take-off run.

A310-200 1860 m
767-200 1798 m
Il-96-300 2600 m

RANGE

From this diagram it is evident that the Il-96 theoretically offers greater range than the A310. In practice, however, operators report that excessive fuel consumption limits the Il-96's range. The A310 is therefore the longest ranged of these types, with the added flexibility of being able to fly shorter sectors if required.

A310-200 6667 km (4,135 mi.)
767-200 5963 km (3,628 mi.)
Il-96-300 7500 km (4,650 mi.)

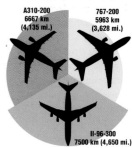

AIRBUS INDUSTRIE

AIRBUS A320

● Revolutionary fly-by-wire airliner ● The aircraft that made Airbus' fortune

Once in a generation, a new aircraft changes aviation for ever. The Airbus A320 is just such a trailblazer. It introduced such far-reaching advances in terms of technology that it stands as the first of a whole new generation of commercial transports – the 'electric' airliners. Designed and built by computers, and flown with the aid of computers, the A320 offers its passengers high-technology safety, reliability and comfort.

▲ *Passenger comfort is everything in a modern airliner. The fly-by-wire controls make the A320 one of the smoothest of modern airliners in even the roughest turbulence.*

AIRBUS INDUSTRIE AIRBUS A320

▲ The glass cockpit
The cockpit of the A320 has TV-style screens in place of the traditional dials. The pilots even have sidesticks, like the F-16 fighter, instead of a central control column.

Advanced aerodynamics ▶
All new A320s have these characteristic wingtip-mounted winglets. Most modern airliners have such additions, designed to reduce drag and so increase range.

▼ Multinational product
Airbus airliners are built by a European consortium, each manufacturing major parts. These are shipped to the central factory at Toulouse, where all the parts are brought together in final assembly.

▲ Family member
The A320 is just one of a whole series of jets with which Airbus Industrie has risen to challenge Boeing and McDonnell Douglas.

◀ Thorough testing
Today's airliners go through rigorous testing before they are allowed into passenger service. Here an A320 simulates a landing on a waterlogged runway.

FACTS AND FIGURES

➤ Airbus Industrie is a true international partnership, bringing together France, Germany, Spain and Great Britain.

➤ The A320 was the first production airliner with a digital flight control system.

➤ Since 1972, Airbus has sold over 4500 airliners to 123 customers worldwide.

➤ The stretched A321 is built in Hamburg, the first Airbus built outside France.

➤ The A320 introduced the new European multinational IAE V2500 turbofan.

➤ Boeing tried to acquire an A320 to park on its 737 assembly line to act as a motivation to its workers.

PROFILE

Europe's fly-by-wire pioneer

The dedicated plane-builders at Europe's Airbus Industrie started from behind, but learned fast to build airliners equal to the champions from Boeing and McDonnell Douglas. With the A320, Airbus have now gone further, introducing a new standard by which other short- and medium-haul airliners are measured.

The Airbus A320 is a technological marvel. Each tiny part of this aircraft is crafted with love, care and the latest in technology. The A320 flight deck uses computers and colour electronic displays in a bigger and better way than any previous airliner, and the pilot controls the aircraft with just a small stick at his side.

Sophistication in the sky is of little benefit unless it boosts business for the airline. The Airbus A320 flies superbly, but it also makes a profit. Advanced aerodynamics and electronic engine systems keep fuel-burn to a minimum, while other onboard systems allow the A320 to self-diagnose any faults as

The A320's high-technology construction and extremely efficient engines make it very economical to run. It has proved successful with small airlines, and more than 930 A320s and their derivatives have been ordered or are on option.

they happen, allowing them to be fixed easily and speedily. Less time in the hangar means more time in the air earning money for the airline.

Until recently, Airbus relied on the Aero Spacelines Super Guppy to transport its airframe components to their final assembly line at Toulouse. These elderly veterans were replaced by the Beluga – a much modified A300 cargolifter.

A320-200

Type: twin-engine short- and medium-haul airliner

Powerplant: two 111.21-kN (20,000-lb.-thrust) IAE V2525 or two 117.98-kN (26,500-lb.-thrust) CFM56 turbofans

Operating speed: 960 km/h (600 m.p.h.)

Range: 5460 km (3,400 mi.) (V2525); 5615 km (3,500 mi.) (CFM56) with optional long-range tanks

Weights: empty 41,500 kg (91,500 lb.); loaded 73,000 kg (161,000 lb.)

Accommodation: two flight deck crew; four cabin attendants; maximum 179 passengers (single class) or 150 passengers (two classes)

Dimensions:
span	33.91 m	(111 ft. 3 in.)
length	37.57 m	(123 ft. 3 in.)
height	11.80 m	(38 ft. 8 in.)
wing area	122.40 m² (1,318 sq. ft.)	

AIRBUS A320

One of Europe's great success stories of recent times, the Airbus company now challenges Boeing as the world's most popular planemaker. High technology is the key to the Airbus success, and the A320 spearheads the campaign.

Only two pilots are needed to fly the A320, with all the necessary information at their fingertips in the high-tech cockpit.

The A320 comes with a choice of engines – either the CFM56 or the IAE V2500. Both types develop about 115 kN (25,000 lb.) of thrust each.

The A320 has a fly-by-wire control system. This has a computer which stops the pilots putting the aircraft into dangerous flight situations.

The A320 is part of the larger Airbus family, but itself forms the lead member of a sub-group. The A319 is a slightly shorter version, while the A321 is about 6 m (20 ft.) longer. All three use the same wing and tail structures.

Large sections of the A320, including the fin and rudder, are manufactured from aramid-fibre-, carbon-fibre- or glass-fibre-reinforced plastic composites. These are stronger and lighter than aluminium.

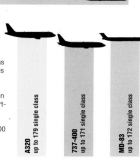

Airlines can tailor the cabin layout to their own requirements. A typical configuration may have a business class section for about 12, and 138 in the economy class section.

BRITISH AIRWAYS
G-BUSC

ACTION DATA

RANGE

The A320 and its competitors are designed for short-haul, frequently-flown high-density air routes. However, the definition of 'short-haul' has changed dramatically in the last 20 years. They still fly the city to city routes for which they were designed, but such airliners can now fly the Atlantic non-stop.

A320	5400 km (3,400 mi.)
737-400	5000 km (3,100 mi.)
MD-83	4851 km (3,000 mi.)

PAYLOAD

The explosive growth in demand for air transport since the 1960s has seen jets at all ends of the market develop greater carrying capacity. In 1970 a typical short-haul airliner might have carried between 80 and 100 passengers; now their capacity has almost doubled.

A320 up to 179 single class
737-400 up to 171 single class
MD-83 up to 172 single class

NOISE LEVELS

Noise pollution is a major environmental hazard, and all new airliners must meet US and European noise abatement regulations. The A320 is one-tenth as noisy as first-generation jet airliners.

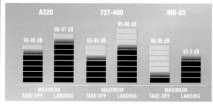

A320	737-400	MD-83
94-95 dB / 96-97 dB	93-95 dB / 95-98 dB	90-95 dB / 93.3 dB
MAXIMUM TAKE-OFF / LANDING	MAXIMUM TAKE-OFF / LANDING	MAXIMUM TAKE-OFF / LANDING

The Airbus family

Airbus Industrie was established in 1970 to handle the production of the Airbus range of airliners. The main companies involved are Aérospatiale (France), Daimler-Benz Aerospace (Germany), British Aerospace (UK) and CASA (Spain). Other European countries such as Belgium, the Netherlands and Italy also have a stake.

A300 (range 7408 km+/4600 mi.+)
First flew 28 October 1972. Two 222.42-kN (50,000-lb.) engines. c.266 seats.

A310 (range 7963 km+/4777 mi.+)
First flew 3 April 1982. Two 222.42-kN (50,000-lb.) engines. c.220 seats.

A320 (range 5300 km+/3290 mi.+)
First flew 22 February 1987. Two 111.21-kN (25,000-lb.) engines. c.150 seats.

A330 (range 8900 km+/5527 mi.+)
First flew 2 November 1992. Two 300.27-kN (67,500-lb.) engines. c.135 seats.

A340 (range 13612 km+/8453 mi.+)
First flew 25 October 1991. Four 138.77-kN (32,000-lb.) engines. c.300 seats.

AIRBUS INDUSTRIE

AIRBUS A321/A319

● International development ● Medium range ● High capacity

Having established the 150-seat A320 as its most successful model in terms of sales, Airbus Industrie decided to go ahead with a stretched A321 version in November 1989. By 1996 another variant, the shortened A319, had also entered service. The three aircraft can be powered by the same engines and can be maintained by the same engineers using the same stock of spare parts – yet they carry passenger loads ranging from 124 to 186 people.

▲ With the competitive nature of the airliner industry, the unveiling of new models is often surrounded by much 'pomp and ceremony'; here, the A321 is rolled out.

▼ **American bird**
Entering the competitive American market, the Airbus family has proved itself to be more than capable of beating the Boeing designs.

▲ **European orders**
Swissair was the third customer for the A321, ordering 19 examples; its aircraft operate across Europe. A follow-up order has been rumoured but, at present, no more examples have entered service.

▼ **First flight**
Traditional coloured tails are a hallmark of the Airbus fleet, particularly on the prototypes.

▲ **Advanced design**
By incorporating the latest design developments, the A321 can perform flight manoeuvres that would otherwise be impossible.

Italian operations ▶
The Italian airline Alitalia chose the A321 because of the exceptional operating economy that the design offers. One of the largest operators, Alitalia has taken options on 107 A321s.

FACTS AND FIGURES

➤ The short-fuselage A319 was announced in May 1992 as the third member of the A320 Airbus 'family'.

➤ British Aerospace designed the wings, and construct them at its Filton site.

➤ Exceptionally wide fuselages are a feature of the A319/A321 designs.

➤ To produce the A321 from the various components takes only 46 days, including a full series of flight tests.

➤ Flight controls of the A319 and A321 utilise 'fly-by-wire' technology.

➤ Both aircraft have received numerous European orders.

PROFILE

Stretched to success

Like the A320, both the shortened A319 and stretched A321 use fly-by-wire flight controls. They also have cockpits which are almost identical, enabling the same pilots to fly any of the three models.

Compared with the A320, the A321 has eight additional fuselage frames forward of the wing and an extra five aft. It entered service with Lufthansa in 1994 and a second version, the A321-200, flew for the first time in December 1996. The -200 has a higher maximum take-off weight of 89,000 kg (195,800 lb.) to accommodate a new centre-section fuel tank, extending its range from 4900 km (3,040 mi.) to 5550 km (3,440 mi.).

The A319 has seven fewer fuselage frames than the standard A320. It entered service with Swissair in April 1996 and, like the other two models in the family, comes with a choice of two engines. Both produce less noise and fewer emissions than those fitted to older airliners.

For passengers, the wide fuselage used by all three variants – with a diameter 19 cm (7 in.) bigger than that of the Boeing 737 and 757 – spells increased comfort, with room for wider seats and aisles and bigger overhead baggage bins.

Above: The prototype of the A321 visited numerous trade exhibitions and flew at air shows to demonstrate its potential.

Above: The A321 is a stretched version of the A320 and seats 185 passengers. This example operates far from European skies, flying with TransAsia Airways which has found the aircraft a major improvement over earlier types.

A319

Type: short- to medium-range airliner

Powerplant: two 97.9-kN (22,025-lb.-thrust) CFM56-5A4 turbofans, or two 104.5-kN (23,510-lb.-thrust) IAE V2524-A5 turbofans

Cruising speed: 903 km/h (560 m.p.h.) at high altitude

Take-off distance: 1829 m (6,000 ft.)

Range: 4907 km (3,040 mi.)

Cruising altitude: 9500 m (31,170 ft.)

Weights: operating empty 40,149 kg (88,328 lb.), maximum take-off 64,000 kg (140,800 lb.)

Accommodation: 124 passengers in two classes

Dimensions: span 33.91 m (111 ft. 3 in.)
length 33.80 m (110 ft. 10 in.)
height 11.80 m (38 ft. 8 in.)
wing area 122.4 m² (1,317 sq. ft.)

A321

Alitalia was the first airline to sign a contract for the A321, and quickly followed this with an order for 20 examples. Operated on the domestic and European networks, the aircraft are proving a success.

The wide-bodied design of the aircraft has only a single central aisle, and can seat 186 passengers in typical first and economy classes. Reports indicate that the less cramped conditions are well appreciated by passengers, particularly on the medium-haul flights.

Design features found to be successful on earlier Airbus aircraft have been incorporated into the A321, so reducing the overall cost of the aircraft.

A fuel dump pipe is located in the extreme rear of the fuselage, allowing the A321 to jettison its fuel load in an emergency while not inhibiting the engines' operation.

An advanced flight deck is fitted with multi-function displays and fly-by-wire controls. Pilot conversion from the A319 to the A321 is easy because of the similarity between the two flight decks. Crews appreciate the handling qualities of the airliner.

There is a choice of engines for the A321: either the CFM 56-5 constructed jointly in the US and England, or the IAE V2500 produced by a consortium of nations including Italy, Japan and Germany. Both powerplants offer the A321 low operating costs.

An advanced wing design, featuring raised wingtips and trailing-edge flaps, affords the Airbus excellent handling. Thanks to this feature and the 'fly-by-wire' inputs, the prototype aircraft performed amazing displays of agility at air shows, creating huge interest in the design.

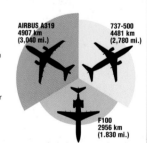

The smaller fleet

■ **BOEING 737-400:** Air UK Leisure was the first airline outside the USA to fly the new super-stretched Boeing. Its five aircraft were used on domestic routes.

■ **FOKKER 100:** Developed in Germany, the Fokker 100 operates as an advanced regional airliner. Variants include dedicated cargo and VIP configurations.

■ **McDONNELL DOUGLAS MD 90:** Powered by twin turbofans, the MD 90 was launched in 1989 with an order for 50 from Delta Air Lines. The design uses the latest advanced technology.

ACTION DATA

MAXIMUM CRUISING SPEED
Operating at a high cruising speed allows airliners to reach their destinations quicker, allowing more flights to be undertaken. The Boeing 757 is the leader in this field.

AIRBUS A319 — 903 km/h (560 m.p.h.)
737-500 — 912 km/h (565 m.p.h.)
F100 — 861 km/h (534 m.p.h.)

RANGE
From experience gained with earlier designs, Airbus's aircraft have grown in both size and capability. These advances have given the Airbus fleet a range advantage over their contemporaries, which has led to an increase in sales in the competition with Boeing's designs.

AIRBUS A319 4907 km (3,040 mi.)
737-500 4481 km (2,780 mi.)
F100 2956 km (1.830 mi.)

CAPACITY
Featuring the widest fuselage in current airliner production, the passenger capacity of the A319 is superior to that of the German design but inferior to that of its American competitor.

AIRBUS A319 124 PASSENGERS
737-500 132 PASSENGERS
F100 107 PASSENGERS

AIRBUS INDUSTRIE

AIRBUS A330

● Twin-engined wide-body airliner ● A340 variant ● 'Glass' cockpit

▲ *Commonality between the four-engined A340 and twin-engined A330 gives an airline operating both aircraft more crewing flexibility and lower training costs.*

Developed in parallel with the four-engined A340, the A330 uses the same fuselage and wings, and has an almost identical cockpit for maximum crewing flexibility. Whereas the A340 was designed for maximum range, the A330 was intended to provide optimum flexibility at the lowest possible operating cost. Thus, a wide range of seating arrangements is possible, and the cargo hold is 60 per cent bigger than that of the Boeing 747.

AIRBUS INDUSTRIE AIRBUS A330

▼ **Mixed fleet**
The 100th aircraft off the A330/340 production line was an A330-322 delivered to Malaysian Airline System in 1995. This aircraft was the 69th example.

▲ **Multi-coloured tailfins**
At the end of 1996, Airbus Industrie had delivered 47 of the 160 A330s ordered.

▼ **Toulouse assembly**
Final A330 assembly is undertaken alongside A340s at Airbus Industrie's main plant.

▲ **Launch carrier**
Air Inter (now Air France Europe) was the airline with which the A330 entered service in 1994. Apart from five Fokker 100s, Airbuses make up the entire fleet.

Asian fleet ▶
Seen landing at Hong Kong's busy Kai Tak airport, this Thai Airways International A330, named Bang Rashan, was one of eight operated by the airline in 1997 alongside A300s and A310s.

FACTS AND FIGURES

➤ In 1996, the annual combined A330/340 production rate was 30 to 35 units, the majority of which were A340s.

➤ F-WWKB, the first A330, flew for the first time on 3 December 1992.

➤ Airbus has been studying enlarged A330 versions, dubbed A330-400.

➤ The A330-200, which entered service in April 1998, is a direct competitor to Boeing's long-range 767-300ER.

➤ Aer Lingus flew the first ETOPS transatlantic A330 service in May 1994.

➤ A 'stretched' A330 may have seats in a forward cargo bay fitted with windows.

PROFILE

A340's twin-engined brother

Flown for the first time in December 1992, the A330 became the first aircraft in history to be certified simultaneously by both the European and US authorities. The original A330-300 entered service with launch customer Air Inter (now Air France Europe) in January 1994, carrying 412 single-class passengers.

Typical seating arrangements for the A330-300 are 295 in three classes or 335 in two. Range is 8982 km (5,140 mi.) with 335

passengers, or up to 10,200 km (6,325 mi.) with a reduced payload, though the aircraft can also operate high-density, short-haul routes with as many as 440 people aboard.

In 1998 the A330-300 was joined by the A330-200, which has a shorter fuselage but has space for 42,000 litres (11,000 gal.) more fuel than the A330-300 – to give it an extended range of 11,700 km (7,250 mi.). It will be able to carry a three-class load of 256.

Above: Hong Kong-based Cathay Pacific Airways operates a modern mixed fleet of at least 50 aircraft, including A330s and A340s and Boeing 747s and 777s.

Economic operation was a principal goal of the A330's design, and it has been achieved so successfully that at least one airline uses its A330s as freighters during the night.

Below: German scheduled, charter and cargo airline LTU was an early operator of the A330-300, from its Düsseldorf base.

A330-300

Type: twin-engined wide-body airliner

Powerplant: (typical) two 300-kN (67,500-lb.-thrust) General Electric CF6-80E1A2 turbofans

Maximum speed: Mach 0.86

Range: (longer-range variant with CF6 engines) 8982 km (5,140 mi.) with 335 passengers and baggage and fuel for 370-km (230-mi.) diversion

Weights: operating empty 120,170 kg (264,374 lb.); maximum take-off 230,000 kg (506,000 lb.)

Accommodation: two flight crew plus cabin crew and (typically) 295 (three-class) or 335 (two-class) passengers; maximum 440 passengers

Dimensions:
span 60.30 m (197 ft. 9 in.)
length 63.65 m (208 ft. 9 in.)
height 16.74 m (54 ft. 11 in.)
wing area 363.10 m² (3,907 sq. ft.)

The almost identical cockpits of the A330 and A340 are also very similar to that of the A320. Six cathode ray tubes (CRTs) display engine and other vital information before the two-person crew. The aircraft is controlled via sidesticks rather than the more conventional yokes favoured by Boeing and uses fly-by-wire technology to operate the control surfaces.

AIRBUS A330-300

In May 1997 Cathay Pacific Airways had a fleet of 11 A330-300s, with options for up to 16 others. Like some other operators, Cathay Pacific also employs a number of A340s.

As with earlier Airbus wide-body types, the construction of the A330 and A340 is divided among the Airbus consortium members. Aérospatiale is responsible for the cockpit, engine pylons and part of the centre fuselage, as well as final assembly at the Toulouse factory. British Aerospace builds the wings, Daimler-Benz Aerospace most of the fuselage, fin and interior, CASA the tailplane and Belairbus the leading-edge slats.

Six cabin crew rest beds or sleeping accommodation for passengers are available as optional equipment for the rear underfloor cargo hold. The passengers' version consists of five mini cabins, each with one or two full-length bunk beds and other equipment.

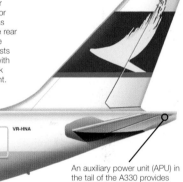

VR-HNA

An auxiliary power unit (APU) in the tail of the A330 provides power for aircraft systems when the main engines are shut down.

To manoeuvre the aircraft on the ground the A330 has nosewheel steering via the rudder pedals. This disengages automatically at speeds above 185 km/h (115 m.p.h.).

Like most modern airliners the A330 is available with a selection of engines. Apart from the latest versions of the G.E. CF6, the A330 is available with Pratt & Whitney PW4000s or Rolls-Royce Trent 700s. All are rated between 300 kN (67,5000 lb.) and 322 kN (72,440 lb.) each.

With a fuel capacity of 97,170 litres (25,670 gal.), the A330 may undertake extended-range twin-engined operations (ETOPS) on transoceanic routes.

A330 hold capacity

SMALLER HOLD THAN THE A340: Though it shares its fuselage with the A340, the A330 has a shorter forward cargo hold. Total capacity is 30 standard LD3 containers compared to 32 in the A340.

ACTION DATA

FUEL CAPACITY

Modern airliners are required to fly vast distances and consequently carry a huge weight in fuel. A larger four-engined aircraft, the A340 carries more fuel than its twin-engined brother, the A330. Boeing's 777-200 is another long-range twin-jet with a capacity of over 100,000 litres (30,000 gal.).

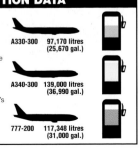

A330-300	97,170 litres (25,670 gal.)
A340-300	139,000 litres (36,990 gal.)
777-200	117,348 litres (31,000 gal.)

A330/A340 commonality

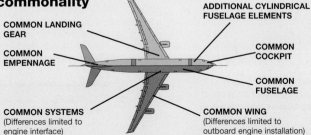

PARALLEL DEVELOPMENT: A major feature of the A330/A340 programme was the 85 per cent commonality of components between the two types, which helped control development costs and had benefits for operators.

COMMON LANDING GEAR

COMMON EMPENNAGE

COMMON SYSTEMS (Differences limited to engine interface)

ADDITIONAL CYLINDRICAL FUSELAGE ELEMENTS

COMMON COCKPIT

COMMON FUSELAGE

COMMON WING (Differences limited to outboard engine installation)

'UNDERFLOOR EARNING POWER': As well as the obvious passenger features, Airbus Industrie has been keen to sell the aircraft's freight-carrying abilities.

AIRBUS

AIRBUS A380

● World's largest airliner ● 520-850 seater ● Double-decker

Initially known as the A3XX, the Airbus A380 was formally launched as a competitor to the 747-400 for high-capacity long-range routes in 2000. Assembled from parts made all over Europe, the A380 is a massive financial and industrial undertaking. The project ran into technical problems and suffered several major delays before and after its first flight in 2005. Slower than expected sales and penalty payments for late deliveries have reduced the profit on aircraft sold, but the A380 is proving popular with airlines and passengers.

▲ To accommodate A380 passengers enlarged check-ins and gate lounges have been built, as have two-level airbridges, although a standard one is shown here.

AIRBUS A380

◄ **Giant wingspan**
At just under 80m (262ft), the A380's wingspan is the longest of any airliner's. Most airports could not handle a larger span without extensive rebuilding.

Wing spar ▶
Most of the A380's wing is built by BAE Systems in Bristol, UK and is transported to Toulouse by barge and road.

◄ **Lufthansa**
The first Lufthansa A380 flew in October 2009. In June 2010 it flew the German football team to the World Cup Finals in South Africa.

Spreading the load ▶
Although the heaviest airliner in service, the A380's 22 wheels help spread the weight so it can use the same runways as the 747.

◄ **Air France**
Air France received its first of 12 planned A380s in October 2009, initially for use on the Paris to New York route.

FACTS AND FIGURES

➤ The list price for an A380 in 2010 was US$327 million. Customers include Virgin, Kingfisher, Qatar Airways, Etihad and British Airways.

➤ In testing, Airbus proved they could evacuate 853 passengers from an A380 in 90 seconds, using only half the exits.

➤ The proposed A380F freighter, ordered by UPS, FedEx and others was cancelled to get passenger 380 deliveries back on track.

➤ The first A380 'Flying Palace' executive aircraft was delivered to Saudi Prince Al-Waleed in 2010 for an estimated US$485 million.

European giant of the skies

After numerous delays, the A380 finally entered service in late 2007 with Singapore Airlines, followed by Emirates, Qantas and Air France in 2008-9. The initial users reported that fuel efficiency was better than forecast and that the aircraft had proved very popular with customers. The enormous interior space of the A380 allows a wide choice of seating configurations and special facilities for premium customers. Emirates offers two shower cubicles for First Class passengers. Virgin Atlantic said they may install a gym, beauty salon or casino on their aircraft. Most airlines have fitted a bar for their First and Business passengers. For the majority in Economy Class, the cabin is similar to that on other wide-body jets, although interior noise is reduced compared to the 747.

Of the initial operators, Emirates is unique in devoting the upper deck to First and Business Class passengers. Air France and Singapore have some Economy seats upstairs alongside Business Class, and Qantas mixes Business and Premium Economy seating on the top deck.

Left: Emirates has ordered 58 A380s, all with Engine Alliance GP7000 turbofans. The Dubai-based airline is by far the biggest customer to date.
Below: Qantas introduced the A380 in September 2008 and flies them from Sydney and Melbourne to Los Angeles, Singapore and London.

Airbus A380

Type: four-engined wide-body double-deck airliner

Powerplant: (typical) Four 355-kN (80,000-lb. thrust) Rolls-Royce Trent 970/B turbofan engines

Maximum speed: 1020 km/h (634 m.p.h.)

Range:) 15,200 km (9,400 mi.)

Weights: operating empty 276,800 kg (610,000 lb.); maximum take-off 569,000 kg (1,250,000 lb.)

Accommodation: two flight crew plus cabin crew and (typically) 525 (three-class) or 644 (two-class) passengers; maximum 853 passengers

Dimensions:
span	79.75 m (261.6 ft.)
length	73 m (240 ft.)
height	24.1 m (79 ft.)
wing area	845m² (9,100 sq. ft.)

AIRBUS A380

Singapore Airlines was the first to put the A380 into service. The inaugural passenger flight was made from Singapore to Sydney on 27 October 2007.

The two-pilot cockpit shares much of its design with other Airbus widebodies. Like all the current Airbus range, it has sidestick controllers.

The First Class section (called 'Suites' by Singapore Airlines) has enclosed compartments for passengers similar to those on a railway sleeping carriage.

Singapore Airlines configures its A380s with a mix of Economy and First Class seats on the lower deck and Business and Economy on the upper deck.

The tail fin is the tallest on any airliner and equal in height to that of the Hughes 'Spruce Goose' flying-boat, tying the record for the world's tallest aircraft.

Singapore Airlines has chosen the Rolls-Royce Trent 900 for its 19 A380s. Other customers to order Trents include Qantas, Virgin Atlantic and Lufthansa.

The A380 VVIP 'Flying Palace'

CONFERENCE ROOM: This conference and dining room allows the A380 VVIP owner and staff to conduct business in flight.

PRIVATE BEDROOM: The upper deck has plenty of room for a full-width private bedroom with all the comforts of home

PRIVATE LOUNGE: A private lounge and breakfast bar is one suggested feature for the A380 VVIP's upper deck.

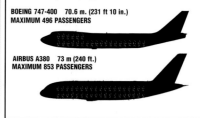

ACTION DATA

LENGTH AND CAPACITY

The A380 is certified to carry up to 853 passengers in all-economy layout. Most airlines configure them for around 525 in three classes. Air Austral has ordered two 840-seat aircraft for services from France to Réunion Island, but in general terms the A380's capacity not massively greater than that of the 747-400. The overall length of the A380 is only 2.4m (8ft) greater than the 747-400.

BOEING 747-400 70.6 m. (231 ft 10 in.)
MAXIMUM 496 PASSENGERS

AIRBUS A380 73 m (240 ft.)
MAXIMUM 853 PASSENGERS

ANTONOV

AN-70

● Commercial transport ● Propfan engines ● Composite structure

▲ *In a time of tightening budgets, Antonov's An-70 will have a tough time achieving sales, despite its advanced design. Political problems have clouded the development of the aircraft.*

Filling a Russian air force requirement for a transport to replace the venerable An-12, the An-70 is the world's first aircraft powered entirely by propfans. Development began in 1975. The new design followed the configuration of the An-12, but incorporated new technologies into the much larger aircraft. The prototype was lost in an accident, but a second was eventually built and flown in 1997. Antonov has high hopes for the aircraft.

◄ **Lightweight design**
Despite the large size of the An-70, 28 per cent of its structure is composed of composite materials, allowing the airframe to be extremely light.

Powered tail ►
The tall tail is fitted with powered upper and lower double-hinged rudders. Trimming devices are fitted to improve the An-70's low-speed handling.

◄ **Conventional design**
High-mounted wings and a large fuselage body are standard design features on current transport aircraft. The An-70 is larger than Europe's FLA.

Ample accommodation ►
Fully pressurised, the circular-section fuselage is able to accommodate the latest Russian main battle tank or seating for 170 troops.

◄ **Advanced propulsion**
The contra-rotating propfans were developed especially for the An-70, and give the large aircraft agile performance.

FACTS AND FIGURES

➤ The first prototype crashed on 10 February 1995 after colliding with its An-72 chase plane.

➤ Antonov has proposed twin-propfan and turbojet-powered An-70 variants.

➤ Antonov's An-70 is much smaller than the American C-17A Globemaster III.

➤ Each propfan has contra-rotating propellers; the front has eight composite blades, the rear just six.

➤ The planned An-70TK will carry either 30 tonnes of cargo or 150 passengers.

➤ Antonov sees other possible An-70 roles as including firefighting and naval patrol.

PROFILE

Russia's revolutionary transport

On 19 August 1997, the second An-70 prototype, registered UR-NTK, was seen in public for the first time at the MAKS '97 air show at Zhukhovskii, near Moscow.

The future of the An-70 programme had been in some doubt after the tragic loss of the first prototype in February 1995, less than three months after its first flight. Funding for the design had passed from the Soviet air force to the new Ukrainian government after dissolution of the USSR. The prototype's crash was a major setback at a time when funding for the Russian aviation industry was scarce.

A STOL (Short Take-Off and Landing) design, with a large, pressurised and air conditioned fuselage, the An-70 has twice the internal capacity of either the An-12 or the Lockheed C-130 and has a maximum payload of 47 tonnes. As well as propfan engines, the aircraft features composite materials in its construction (the entire tail unit, ailerons and flaps), a modern 'glass' cockpit and an avionics fit to Western standards. The first aircraft have three flight crew, but later examples will be able to be flown by two crew.

In a joint Russian/Ukrainian programme, this promising aircraft has recently undergone a wide range of certification tests, and looks set to enter quantity production shortly, with the Russian Air Force likely to be the main recipient.

Left: Antonov's An-70 has exceptional flying characteristics, relying heavily on fly-by-wire controls and large flaps in the wings.

Above: Viewed from head-on, the unique layout of the 14 curved propeller blades fitted to each engine is clearly shown.

An-70

Type: medium-size wide-body transport

Powerplant: four 10290-kW (13,800-hp.) ZMKB Progress D-27 propfans driving SV-27 contra-rotating propellers

Cruising speed: 750 km/h (465 m.p.h.)

Range: 5530 km (3,100 mi.) with max§ payload

Service ceiling: 11000 m (33,000 ft.)

Optimum cruising height: 9000 m (29,500 ft.)

Weights: empty 72800 kg (160,160 lb.); max take-off 133000 kg (292,600 lb.)

Accommodation: 150 passengers and 4 crew

Dimensions:
span	44.06 m (40 ft. 9 in.)
length	40.73 m (133 ft. 7 in.)
height	16.38 m (53 ft. 9 in.)
wing area	200 m² (2,152 sq.ft.)

AN-70

The first aircraft to be powered only by propfans, the An-70 is a remarkable transport aircraft. Despite the abilities of Antonov's design, budget constraints put the entire programme in serious jeopardy. At the time of writing, the An-70's future looks bright, however.

The well-equipped cockpit includes a fly-by-wire control system. Operations can be undertaken with two pilots and one loadmaster.

Approximately 28 per cent of the airframe is of lightweight composite structure, including the complete tail unit, ailerons and flaps. The wings are manufactured at the Chkalov plant at Tashkent in Uzbekistan. Such delegation of construction for the aircraft is an indication of the tough times the aviation industry is facing.

The high-set tail of the An-70, coupled with the high wings, mean that the fuselage is uncluttered with any associated flight controls. Maximum space is available for cargo.

Double-slotted trailing-edge flaps in two sections are located on the wings. They are supplemented by three-section spoilers forward of each outer flap.

The large cargo door is located at the rear of the fuselage. The upper section folds up into the fuselage while the lower sections can be utilised as ramps for loading the aircraft.

354

АНТОНОВ 70

UR-NTK

ACTION DATA

CRUISING SPEED

Its four advanced propfan engines give the An-70 an exceptionally high cruising speed in comparison to the American types. The new C-17 Globemaster III – powered by four turbofans – has a poor cruising performance, only slightly better than that of the C-130J.

An-70T	750km/h (465 m.p.h.)
C-130J	645 km/h (400 m.p.h.)
C-17A GLOBEMASTER III	648 km/h (402 m.p.h.)

MAXIMUM RANGE

The ability to cover huge distances with a large payload is the key requirement for any new transport aircraft. For its class, the An-70 has the greatest range of the current crop of military transport aircraft.

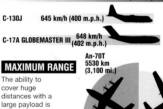

An-70T 5530 km (3,100 mi.)

C-130J 5250 km (3,255 mi.)

C-17A GLOBEMASTER III 5190 km (3,218 mi.)

MAXIMUM PAYLOAD

Built on experience gained with the C-5 Galaxy and C-141 StarLifter, the C-17 Globemaster III offers the largest payload available. Able to accommodate main battle tanks as well as troops, the aircraft is unbeatable in its class.

An-70T	C-130J	C-17A GLOBEMASTER III
47000 kg (66,000 lb.)	18955 kg (41,700 lb.)	78108kg (171,850 lb.)

Russian heavyweights

■ **An-22 'COCK':** Powered by a mass of contra-rotating propellers, the 'Cock' was used extensively in Afghanistan to ferry troops and supplies to the battlefield.

■ **An-124 'CONDOR':** With a configuration similar to that of the American C-5 Galaxy, the 'Condor' is now the primary transport aircraft of the Russian armed forces.

■ **An-225 'COSSACK':** Constructed to support the Russian space shuttle programme (now grounded), the aircraft is used sporadically for cargo flights.

ANTONOV

AN-225 MRIYA 'COSSACK'

● Strategic transport ● World's largest aircraft ● Soviet shuttle carrier

Antonov's An-225 Mriya (Dream), built in the Ukraine, has been given the NATO reporting name of 'Cossack'. It is a stretched derivative of the An-124 'Condor', built for the special purpose of transporting massive 'piggyback' cargoes. This huge machine carries incredible payloads of up to 250 tonnes, and offers the unrivalled ability to move very large items of freight over respectable distances. The An-225 has not so far been used to its full potential.

▲ The An-225 restores the distinction of being the world's largest aircraft to the Antonov design bureau. However, the market for such a super-heavy cargo carrier remains open to doubt.

ANTONOV **AN-225 MRIYA 'COSSACK'**

▼ Large span
Banking gracefully, the An-225 shows off its enormous wing, equipped with almost full-span flaps, similar to those of the earlier An-12.

▲ Buran lifter
The An-225 was used to carry the Buran space shuttle. Britain's cancelled HOTOL space plane was another proposed cargo.

▼ Blast off
The astonishing thrust of the six Lotarev D-18 fan engines gives the An-225 a respectable take-off performance for such a large aircraft.

▼ Wing on wheels
To support its massive weight, the An-225 has seven pairs of main undercarriage wheels arranged in two units and two pairs of nosewheels. The An-225 can 'kneel' by retracting its nosewheels on the ground.

▲ Hinged nose
The nose section of the An-225 hinges upwards to allow outsize cargoes to be easily loaded. Even helicopters and main battle tanks can fit through this doorway.

FACTS AND FIGURES

➤ The An-225 made its first flight carrying the Buran space shuttle orbiter on 13 May 1989 from Baikonur cosmodrome.

➤ On 22 March 1989 the An-225 established 106 payload records.

➤ The Mriya is nearly twice the size of the American Lockheed C-5 Galaxy.

➤ On its record-breaking flights, the huge An-225 took off at an all-up weight of 508200 kg (1,338040 lb.).

➤ Typically, the 'Cossack' carries two pilots, two flight engineers and two navigators.

➤ Like the Su-27, the flight system incorporates fly-by-wire controls.

PROFILE

World's biggest aeroplane

Based on the huge An-124, but with over 50 per cent improvement in payload, the An-225 Mriya is simply the largest aircraft ever built. The An-225 added a stretched fuselage, six engines instead of four and seven pairs of wheels per side instead of five.

This flying juggernaut was developed to replace two Myasischev VM-T Atlants – converted 'Bison' bombers – used to carry outsized loads associated with the Soviet space

programme's Energia rockets. The Mriya's first flight took place on 21 December 1988 and the aircraft flew with the Buran space shuttle on its back five months later.

The break-up of the USSR and the cancellation of the Soviet re-usable orbital project means that the An-225 is now reduced to working on sporadic freight jobs. For most of its life the Mriya has languished in storage and has been cannibalised for parts. Plans to use it as a

launcher for Britain's HOTOL spacecraft have failed to materialise, and a second example remains uncomplete.

Below: Unlike the An-124, which has had considerable success in the heavylift cargo market, the An-225 remains unwanted. The aircraft's sheer size and operating costs make it uneconomical.

The An-225 appeared at a time when Soviet aviation was at its zenith and new designs were stunning Western analysts at every air show.

An-225 Mriya 'Cossack'

Type: very large cargo transport

Powerplant: six ZMKB Progress (Lotarev) D-18T turbofan engines each rated at 229.47 kN (51,355.4-lb.-thrust)

Maximum cruising speed: 850 km/h (527 m.p.h.)

Cruising speed: 700 km/h (434 m.p.h.)

Range: 15400 km (9,548 mi.)

Service ceiling: 11145 m (36,500 ft.)

Weights: empty 350000 kg (770,000 lb.); maximum loaded 600000 kg (1,320,000 lb.)

Accommodation: a crew of up to 12 are involved in carrying the Energia rocket; if used to carry troops it could accommodate over 600

Dimensions: span 88.40 m (290 ft.)
length 84.00 m (276 ft.)
height 18.20 m (60 ft.)
wing area 905.00 m² (9,738 sq.ft.)

AN-225 MRIYA 'COSSACK'

The An-225 first appeared in the West at the Paris Air Show in 1989, making an unprecedented appearance by carrying the Buran space shuttle craft.

The main fuselage has a large cabin above the cargo hold, which can hold 60 to 70 passengers.

Buran was never used operationally, but made an unmanned test flight. Originally, the Russian space shuttle was to be carried by a modified 'Atlant' Mya-4 'Bison'.

The tailplane is canted upwards (known as dihedral) for added stability.

The twin-fin arrangement was a necessity for stable flight when the Buran was carried on the fuselage. A single fin would have caused unacceptable airflow problems.

As well as being the main cargo loading area, the nose contains weather radar and a downward-looking terrain avoidance and ground-mapping radar.

The wing has a leading-edge flap, trailing-edge Fowler flaps and inboard and outboard airbrakes.

The main undercarriage has seven pairs of wheels on each side.

The large Lotarev D-18 turbofan is identical to that used in the smaller An-124 'Condor'. This engine is very powerful, but there have been problems with its reliability in service.

Unlike earlier large Antonovs, for example the An-22, the An-225 has no rear cargo doors and relies on a hinged nose instead.

ACTION DATA

MAXIMUM PAYLOAD

The An-225 is capable of carrying a tonne more than its predecessor, the An-124. The huge Mriya can transport cargo equivalent to the weight of one-and-a-half empty C-5 Galaxies, and also has the ability to carry a load on top of its fuselage.

An-124 'CONDOR' 150000 kg (330,000 lb.)
An-225 MRIYA 'COSSACK' 250000 kg (330,000 lb.)
C-5 GALAXY 118387 kg (260,450 lb.)

TAKE-OFF RUN

The larger the aircraft, the longer it usually takes to get airborne. Even with its massive wing and six engines, the An-225 requires an extensive length of runway.

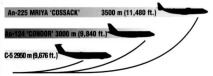

An-225 MRIYA 'COSSACK' 3500 m (11,480 ft.)
An-124 'CONDOR' 3000 m (9,840 ft.)
C-5 2950 m (9,676 ft.)

The world's biggest lifters

■ **ANTONOV An-22 'COCK' (1965):** Once the largest aircraft in the world, the An-22 remains the world's biggest turboprop. Despite its age it remains in demand, as turboprops have comparatively low operating costs. Several payload-to-height records were set by the An-22, some of which still stand.

■ **LOCKHEED C-5 GALAXY (1968):** Still the USAF's largest transport, the C-5 remains in service despite major problems, including structural faults with engine mountings and wing spars. The Galaxy set several records for payload delivery when it entered service, but these were all subsequently broken by the An-124.

■ **ANTONOV An-124 'CONDOR' (1982):** The basis of the An-225 design, the An-124 has been a commercial success. It flies with Aeroflot, Volga Dnepr and several other Russian heavylift carriers. The 'Condor' could even carry a mobile version of the SS-20 intermediate-range ballistic missile system or main battle tanks.

ARMSTRONG WHITWORTH

ARGOSY

● Turboprop transport design ● 30 years of service ● Limited production

▲ While loading and unloading was accomplished with ease, thanks to the nose and rear doors, the Argosy Series 100's relatively small payload forced Hawker Siddeley to redesign the aircraft to carry larger loads. The Series 220 was the result, but it was built in even smaller numbers than the original version.

When it came on the scene in the 1950s, the AW.650 Argosy was an advanced freighter. The company's first customer was Miami freight operator Riddle Airlines, which ordered four aircraft in 1959 for logistic support flights between USAF bases. Other airlines followed suit, including British European Airways, and 56 aircraft were delivered to the RAF. Although it was expensive to operate, the Argosy served for 30 years.

ARMSTRONG WHITWORTH ARGOSY

▼ Ex-RAF Argosy in Africa
Zairean-registered 9Q-COA was originally an RAF Argosy C.Mk 1. After being withdrawn from RAF service in 1971, it was sold and flew in Africa in the late 1970s. It was scrapped in 1981.

▲ One of the last
This Series 222 was delivered to BEA in 1965. After service in Canada and Ireland, in 1973 it was sold to Safe Air in New Zealand and named Merchant Pioneer.

Improved Series 220 ▶
BEA began flying Argosies in 1961, but needed aircraft with a greater payload capacity. Hawker Siddeley (which AW had joined in 1961) redesigned the wing and interior and fitted more powerful Dart engines with larger propellers.

◀ Australasian survivors
IPEC Aviation in Australia flew its aircraft on freight charters into the 1990s. IPEC's last Argosy was retired in 1992.

Twin-boom design ▶
The Argosy's layout was shared by other aircraft, including the twin-engined C-119 and Noratlas.

FACTS AND FIGURES

➤ The first Argosy flew at Bitteswell on 8 January 1959, less than two years after major design work got under way.

➤ BEA received the first of its Argosy Series 100 freighters in 1961.

➤ A BEA Argosy Series 222 was lost in an accident at Milan, Italy, in July 1965.

➤ After the first public appearance of the Argosy at the Paris air show in 1959, two appeared at Farnborough in 1960.

➤ A twin Rolls-Royce Tyne-engined variant, the AW.651, was proposed but not built.

➤ A short-haul version was proposed with a capacity for six cars and 30 passengers.

PROFILE

'Whistling wheelbarrows'

Taking to the sky in 1955, the Argosy was a result of the British Air Ministry's challenge to manufacturers to create a medium-range freighter for military and civilian use. Armstrong Whitworth designed an aircraft with two booms and two turboprop engines. It became the twin-boomed, four-engined Freightliner, and was renamed the Argosy in 1958.

By 1960 British and American officials had given the Argosy permission to undertake commercial operations.

This burly but attractive aircraft was fairly easy to load and unload, held a useful, but limited, amount of cargo and performed well. If it had weaknesses, they were a lack of range and capacity, which, combined with the four turboprop engines (the source of the nickname 'Whistling Wheelbarrow'), made it expensive to operate.

Sixteen civil aircraft, together with 56 C.Mk 1s transports for the RAF, were built between 1959 and 1966.

Below: Series 100 aircraft could be configured for 89 passengers, although Argosies were rarely used in passenger service.

Above: The prototype and 15 of the 16 civil Argosy aircraft built were delivered to BEA and the American operator Riddle Airlines. The Series 200 prototype was scrapped.

Argosy Series 100

Type: four-engined transport aircraft

Powerplant: four 1506-kW (2,020-hp.) Rolls-Royce Dart 526 turboprop engines

Maximum speed: 477 km/h (296 m.p.h.) at 6100 m (20,000 ft.)

Cruising speed: 451 km/h (280 m.p.h.)

Range: 885 km (550 mi.) with maximum payload and fuel

Maximum ferry range: 3660 km (2,270 mi.)

Service ceiling: 6100 m (20,000 ft.)

Weights: empty 20,865 kg (45,903 lb.); maximum take-off 39,916 kg (87,815 lb.)

Accommodation: two pilots, navigator (on some aircraft), two loadmasters, plus up to 12,700 kg (27,940 lb.) of cargo on cabin floor or on six 2.74-m (9-ft.) cargo pallets, or up to 89 passengers

Dimensions:
span 35.05 m (115 ft.)
length 26.44 m (86 ft. 9 in.)
height 8.92 m (29 ft. 3 in.)
wing area 135.45 m² (1,457 sq. ft.)

ARGOSY SERIES 222

First flown in 1965, G-ASXM was one of a number of Argosies built for BEA. It was active until a landing accident in 1990, during its last days with Safe Air in New Zealand.

All the Argosy's fuel tanks were situated in the wings, one outboard of each engine. Total capacity was 15,454 litres (4,080 gal.).

Two small tanks held the water-methanol mixture used to boost engine power on take-off.

A major feature of the Series 220 was its redesigned wing which saved weight and thus contributed to a greater payload capacity.

Like the Bristol 170 Freighter and the Blackburn Beverley transport aircraft, the Argosy's cockpit was positioned above the main hold.

Four of Rolls-Royce's pioneering and highly successful Dart turboprops powered the Argosy. Each drove a four-bladed propeller and provided 2.25 kN (506 lb.) of additional exhaust thrust.

The retractable tricycle undercarriage was hydraulically operated, with the main gears folding into the inner engine nacelle and tail boom. Dunlop Maxaret anti-skid brakes were fitted.

The rear of the Argosy's cargo bay was hinged on the starboard side and swung open for access. Military Argosies had a split 'beaver tail', the bottom half forming a ramp for vehicles. It could be opened in flight.

The tail unit, with its twin fins and rudders, was carried on elliptical-section metal tail booms. These extended rearwards from the inner engine nacelles.

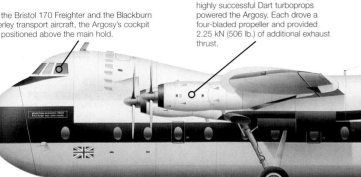

BEA G-ASXM

ACTION DATA

ECONOMIC CRUISING SPEED

Although the Argosy was a fairly fast aircraft compared to piston-engined types, when it appeared in the late 1950s the Armstrong Whitworth aircraft was still slower than the contemporary Hercules.

ARGOSY 220	451 km/h (280 m.p.h.)
CL-44J	612 km/h (379 m.p.h.)
L-100-20 HERCULES	581 km/h (360 m.p.h.)

MAXIMUM PAYLOAD

The CL-44 was able to lift more than 29 tons of cargo, but was not able to carry the outsize loads of the Hercules and Argosy. The L-100 was able to carry 50 per cent more than the Argosy.

ARGOSY SERIES 220 14,095 kg (31,000 lb.)

CL-44J 29,200 kg (64,240 lb.)

L-100-20 HERCULES 21,132 kg (46,490 lb.)

RANGE

Designed to the USAF's exacting specification for a tactical transport, the C-130 Hercules was able to move vehicles and other loads more than 4000 km (2,980 mi.). Lockheed found a ready market for a civil version of the aircraft. The CL-44 was based on the Bristol Britannia airliner and shared its long range.

ARGOSY SERIES 220 885 km (548 mi.)

CL-44J 8460 km (5,245 mi.)

L-100-20 HERCULES 4110 km (2,550 mi.)

Armstrong Whitworth's airliners

■ **ARGOSY:** The 'Argosy' name was first used for this three-engined airliner of the mid-1920s. Seven were built and served with Imperial Airways in Europe and Africa until the mid-1930s.

■ **AW.XV ATALANTA:** Experience with the Argosy led Imperial Airways to standardise with four-engined aircraft. The first example, G-ABPI, flew in 1932. Eight of these 17-seaters were built.

■ **AW.27 ENSIGN:** Built for Imperial Airways, the Ensign of 1938 came in two versions – the 40-seat 'Empire' and the 27-seat 'European'. Many served with the RAF during World War II.

■ **AW.55 APOLLO:** Two Apollos were built to the same specification as the Vickers Viscount, and the first flew in 1949. Intended as a 30-seater, the aircraft suffered engine and other problems.

AVIATION TRADERS

CARVAIR

● Car carrier ● British DC-4 conversion ● Twenty-one delivered

▲ The unique load-carrying capabilities of the Carvair have seen it pressed into service airlifting all manner of different cargoes. Until recent years the plentiful supply of spare parts for the DC-4 made the Carvair a cheap aircraft to operate.

With its unique bulbous nose, the ATL.98 Carvair (a contraction of Car-via-air) filled a niche market in the United Kingdom for a cross-Channel car carrier. The Carvair was an inexpensive solution to the problem as it was not a new aircraft but a conversion of a 20-year-old airliner – the reliable Douglas DC-4. Ultimately, Carvairs served around the world, carrying all manner of outsized loads until their retirement in the 1980s.

AVIATION TRADERS CARVAIR

▲ **British United Air Ferries**
'Chelsea Bridge', the second Carvair conversion, demonstrates the car-loading lift designed by Aviation Traders for use with the aircraft.

▲ **American export**
In the twilight of its career, N55243 was one of several Carvairs based in the United States in the mid-1980s.

▲ **Touching down**
G-AOFW first flew in 1964, one of seven Carvairs delivered to British United Air Ferries.

▲ **Carvair prototype**
The first ATL.98 in hybrid Channel Air Bridge/British United Airways colours. The open fairing for the nosewheel can be seen under the nose.

◀ **Red Cross duty**
This Norwegian-registered Carvair carries the traditional colours of the International Red Cross relief organisation.

FACTS AND FIGURES

➤ In 1966 ATL proposed a Rolls-Royce Dart turboprop-powered DC-7 conversion called the 'Carvair 7', but none was built.

➤ The 'Carvair' name was chosen after a competition was held in Southend.

➤ Carvairs have carried a wide range of cargoes, from radio transmitters to oil.

➤ The managing director of both Channel Air Bridge and ATL was Freddie Laker, later famous for his cut-price airline Skytrain.

➤ Certification of the prototype was delayed after a forklift almost severed its tail.

➤ Two early Carvairs were pure freighters with nine seats behind the flight deck.

PROFILE

From airliner to car carrier

In the late 1950s British airline Channel Air Bridge Limited needed an aircraft to replace their existing Bristol Freighter car ferries. However, with the market for such an aircraft being comparatively small the cost of a new machine was expected to be too high.

Its associated company Aviation Traders came up with an inexpensive option. Second-hand Douglas DC-4s (and ex-military C-54s) could be bought for about $110,000.

With technical help from Douglas, Aviation Traders set about designing the Carvair – a converted DC-4. Nose-loading was essential for a car carrier, therefore the redesigned cockpit was raised 2.08 metres and a hydraulically operated swing nose was fitted. A forward fuselage stretch of 2.64 metres was also carried out. A former World Airways C-54B was chosen to be the first ATL.98 and flew in June 1961. This aircraft entered service between Southend and

Rotterdam the following March and was followed by 20 further conversions, the last in July 1968. Used in at least 10 countries, a handful remained in use in the early 1980s but all have now been grounded, the last being operated in America.

Below: Channel Air Bridge merged with Silver City Airways to form British United Air Ferries, later British Air Ferries (BAF). The lettering on the tailfin of this BAF Carvair advertises the aircraft's 8.5-tonne (8.5-ton) cargo capacity and BAF's telephone number.

Above: 'Big John' was part of British Air Ferries' large fleet. Carvairs retained their DC-4 cabin windows after conversion.

ATL.98 Carvair

Type: four-engined car ferry/freighter

Powerplant: four 1081-kW (1,450-hp.) Pratt & Whitney R-2000-7M2 Twin Wasp radial piston engines

Maximum cruising speed: 296 km/h (212 m.p.h.)

Initial climb rate: 198 m/min (650 f.p.m.)

Range: 3700 km (2,294 mi.) with maximum payload

Service ceiling: 5700 m (18,700 ft.)

Weights: empty 18,999 kg (41,798 lb.); maximum take-off 33,475 kg (73,645 lb.)

Maximum payload: 8500 kg (18,700 lb.)

Dimensions: span 35.81 m (117 ft.)
length 31.27 m (103 ft.)
height 9.09 m (30 ft.)
wing area 135.82 m² (1,461 sq. ft.)

ATL.98 CARVAIR

G-AXAI 'Fat Albert' was the seventeenth of 21 Carvairs converted from Douglas C-54s and DC-4s. Other BAF Carvairs included 'Plain Jane' and 'Porky Pete'.

The new bulbous nose required a raised cockpit to be designed.

Internally, the floor area was increased from the DC-4's 15.19 m² (163 sq. ft.) to over 24 m² (258 sq. ft.) and the maximum useable volume from 104.5 m³ (3,690 cu. ft.)to 123.2 m³ (4,350 cu. ft.).

To offset the increased side area over the DC-4 the taller fin of the DC-7 was fitted.

The initial car-carrying version of the Carvair had a rear cabin for up to 25 passengers as well as room for five cars at the front.

British Air Ferries used several colour schemes on their Carvairs, including this white and blue finish.

A hydraulically operated nose door and lift were installed to ease the loading of cars.

The engines were the same 1081-kW (1,450-hp.) Pratt & Whitney R-2000 Twin Wasps as those fitted to most DC-4s.

To cope with the increased weight of the aircraft the stronger brake system of the DC-6 was fitted.

The passenger cabin at the rear of the Carvair necessitated the fitting of extra windows behind the cargo door. These are not found on a DC-4.

ACTION DATA

MAXIMUM CRUISING SPEED

Designed initially as an airliner, the DC-4 possessed good speed by the standards of the day. The modifications made to create the Carvair slowed the aircraft down. The Bristol Freighter was primarily a cargo plane.

ATL.98 CARVAIR	296 km/h (184 m.p.h.)
DC-4	365 km/h (226 m.p.h.)
FREIGHTER Mk 32	262 km/h (162 m.p.h.)

ACCOMMODATION

The Carvair was intended to replace the Freighter Mk 32 then in service with car-carrying airlines. Its capacity represented an almost 100 per cent improvement over the Freighter with room for half of the DC-4's passengers. Some Carvairs carried freight only.

ATL.98 CARVAIR 5 CARS 25 PASSENGERS	DC-4 44 PASSENGERS	FREIGHTER Mk 32 3 CARS 23 PASSENGERS

RANGE

The Carvair inherited the DC-4's range performance, though the extra weight and regraded aerodynamics of the new nose design reduced this slightly. The Freighter's range, at one third of that of the larger aircraft, was fairly limited. The Carvair allowed operators to fly over considerably longer routes.

ATL.98 CARVAIR 3700 km (2,294 mi.)

DC-4 4025 km (2,496 mi.)

FREIGHTER Mk 32 1320 km (818 mi.)

Airliner freight conversions

CANADAIR CL-44D-4: This variant of the CL-44, itself a derivative of the Bristol Britannia, had a hinged tail to allow straight-in loading of large freight items. First flying in 1960, 27 CL-44D-4s were built.

AEROSPACELINES GUPPY: Derived from the Boeing Stratocruiser, the first Guppy appeared in 1961 to transport outsize parts for the US space programme. More were converted later, including five Super Guppies with Allison turboprops.

SATIC A300-600ST 'BELUGA': Derived from the Airbus A300 series, four Belugas will be built to replace Super Guppies transporting Airbus parts from factories around Europe to Toulouse for final assembly. They are the widest civil jets.

AVIONS DE TRANSPORT RÉGIONAL
ATR 42/ATR 72

● Regional airliner ● Best-selling turboprop ● Freighter

As products of one of the most successful collaborative airliner programmes, the ATR 42 and the later ATR 72 have dominated the twin-turboprop regional airliner market. Built by Aérospatiale of France and Alenia of Italy, the ATR series has been sold worldwide. By the mid-1990s, the aircraft had achieved total sales amounting to over half the world market, with the prospect of more orders to come.

▲ The ATR has many rivals with similar performance, but the marketing effort behind the French/Italian aircraft has been very effective. In particular, sales to the former French colonies and the North American market were high.

◀ Series production
Wing and cabin components are produced at St Nazaire and Nantes, with final assembly taking place in Toulouse.

▼ Multi-function displays
Cockpit technology is very advanced in the ATRs, with multi-function displays and a colour screen for the Honeywell P-800 weather radar.

▲ American Express
PanAm was one of a large number of North American users before the airline went bankrupt.

◀ Air Littoral
Linking 14 French cities and eight other European destinations, Air Littoral is typical of the airlines that appreciate the efficient operation of the ATR.

Cargo-hauling turboprop ▶
With its large fuselage cargo door the ATR 42 Cargo can be swiftly loaded with up to 4000 kg (8,820 lb.) on pallets.

FACTS AND FIGURES

➤ Air Littoral now operates a single ATR 72 and six ATR 42-300s; these serve domestic French and European destinations.

➤ Air Dolomiti operates ATR 42-500s on services like that from Geneva to Trieste.

➤ ATR 42s have been very successful in French-speaking nations of Africa.

➤ The ATR 52 is a military freighter version with a rear-loading ramp, but only one has been ordered – by Gabon.

➤ Aérospatiale manufactures the wing and flight deck and Alenia builds the tail unit.

➤ The ATR 42 Cargo can be reconfigured in just one hour to carry nine containers.

PROFILE

Best-selling turboprop airliner

An example of just how successful collaborative aircraft ventures can be, the ATR series of turboprop airliners has achieved remarkable success in only a few years. Developed by Alenia and Aérospatiale, the Avions de Transport Régional aircraft are named after their seating capacities of 42 and 72, respectively.

The prototype of the ATR 42 first flew in August 1984, and type certification followed in September 1985. The first user of the ATR 42 was Air Littoral, who received the fourth aircraft built.

Since then it has dominated the world market, being purchased almost everywhere outside the former Soviet Union.

The ATR 42-320 has improved-performance PW 121 engines for enhanced hot-and-high power, and the ATR 42-500 is powered by PW 127s. A cargo version, the ATR 42 Cargo, has a cargo door and a reconfigurable cabin.

The stretched ATR 72, powered by PW 124 engines, flew in October 1988. The first recipient was Kar-Air of Finland, and since then more than 170 have been ordered. The problems which

caused the loss of two ATRs have now been solved and the aircraft is currently selling well.

Like joint manufacturers Saab/Fairchild and IPTN/CASA, Alenia and Aérospatiale have produced a highly successful turboprop.

ATR.42-300

Type: short-haul twin-turboprop regional airliner and cargo aircraft

Powerplant: two 1342-kW (1,800-hp.) Pratt & Whitney Canada PW 120 turboprops

Maximum speed: 463 km/h (305 m.p.h.)

Initial climb rate: 640 m/min (2,100 f.p.m.)

Range: 1946 km (1,209 mi.) with 45 passengers

Service ceiling: 3140 m (10,302 ft.)

Weights: empty 10,285 kg (22,674 lb.); loaded 16,700 kg (36,817 lb.)

Passenger capacity: up to 50 at maximum density in four abreast layout

Dimensions:
span	24.57 m	(80 ft. 7 in.)
length	22.67 m	(74 ft. 4 in.)
height	7.58 m	(24 ft. 10 in.)
wing area	54.50 m²	(543 sq. ft.)

The nosecone is constructed of Nomex and Kevlar composite for lightness and strength. Aérospatiale are responsible for the layout of the cabin and flight deck.

Both rudder and elevators are horn balanced to ease control forces in flight.

Lateral control is effected by ailerons and a single spoiler ahead of each outer flap. Two-segment, double-slotted flaps are controlled by Ratier-Fiegeac hydraulic actuators.

The wing is a 'fail safe', two-spar design, with the leading edges being made of a Kevlar/Nomex sandwich.

ATR 42

Many airlines in former French colonial nations have purchased the ATR series. Early customers included Air Mauritius which flies to destinations in Africa.

Two pilots fly the ATR and there is a fold-away seat for an observer. The avionics fit includes a Honeywell DFZ-600 automatic flight control system, a ground proximity warning system, a radio altimeter, two radios, VOR, DME and ILS systems and a digital flight data recorder.

Highly efficient and reliable, the PW 120 turboprops drive four-bladed, constant-speed Hamilton Standard propellers.

AIR MAURITIUS   3B-NAH

ABALEGA

The main baggage and cargo compartment is located between the cockpit and passenger cabin.

The toilet, galley and wardrobe are located at the rear of the cabin. An additional cargo compartment is also located in the rear fuselage.

All the flying controls are mechanically actuated, with electrically actuated trim tabs. The fin and tailplane are mainly constructed of aluminium alloys.

ACTION DATA

PASSENGERS

Standard passenger loads are often less than these maxima. Saab's 2000 is a development of the smaller 340, intended to compete with the larger versions of the ATR 42 and Dash-8.

ATR 42-300   50 passengers

SAAB 2000   58 passengers

DASH-8   56 passengers

MAXIMUM SPEED

The larger Saab 2000 is easily the fastest of this group, because of its more powerful Allison engines. Speed, range and fuel economy are important attributes for this type of aircraft.

ATR 42-300   463 km/h (305 m.p.h.)

SAAB 2000   680 km/h (422 m.p.h.)

DASH-8   527 km/h (327 m.p.h.)

RANGE

The large size of the Saab 2000 gives it extra fuel capacity and therefore greater range. Although the Dash-8 has shorter range, it has superior field performance.

ATR 42-300   1946 km (1,209 mi.)

SAAB 2000   2577 km (1,598 mi.)

DASH-8   1540 km (955 mi.)

Airline customers for the ATR

■ FOSHING: One of the largest Asian ATR customers, Taipei-based Foshing has six ATR 42s and nine ATR 72s in service.

■ HOLLAND AIR: Based at Amsterdam Schipol, Holland Air also operated Boeing 737s and 757s on European regional services.

■ THAI AIR: One of Asia's finest airlines, Thai Air operates two ATR 42s and two ATR 72s, as well as many Boeing jet airliners.

■ TRANSASIA: Based in Taiwan, TransAsia operates three ATR 42s and 12 ATR 72s on regional services from Taipei.

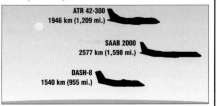

AVRO CANADA

C-102 JETLINER

● Jetliner prototype ● Rolls-Royce engines ● Only one built

Flown for the first time in August 1949, just two weeks after de Havilland's Comet, the C-102 was an audacious attempt by A.V. Roe Canada Limited to build a jet transport with a cruising speed twice that of contemporary piston-engined types. Canadian and American airlines showed interest in the new aircraft, but the outbreak of war in Korea and the Canadian government's demand for CF-100 fighters led to the cancellation of the project.

▲ **Rolls-Royce**
Avon development delays and the British reluctance to release the engine for civil use badly affected a Jetliner programme that was reliant on the new powerplant.

PHOTO FILE

AVRO CANADA C-102 JETLINER

◀ **Conservative lines**
Although a clean design, the C-102 retained the somewhat dated look of a piston-engined aircraft.

▼ **Observation ship**
After cancellation, the Jetliner spent a short time in the US before being returned to Canada for use as an observation aircraft during CF-100 tests. These included gun-pack firing and ejection seat activation.

▲ **Avro Canada products**
The prototype C-102 is seen alongside the CF-100 prototype. The Canadian government cancelled the C-102 in favour of accelerated CF-100 development.

▼ **Trans-Canada Air Lines**
After the powerplant change, TCA was released from its commitment to purchase the C-102. The re-engined aircraft needed to carry more fuel, which reduced payload.

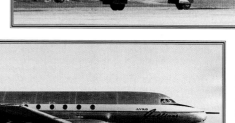

▲ **First flight**
Upon its first flight on 10 August 1949, the C-102 became the first jet transport in North America to take to the air. The Boeing 707 prototype did not fly until 1954.

FACTS AND FIGURES

➤ After testing by the USAF, Avro Canada proposed a trainer variant with four Allison J-33 engines.

➤ Construction of a second C-102 prototype began, but was not completed.

➤ After cancellation, the C-102 was used as an observation platform for CF-100 tests.

➤ Flown for the last time on 23 November 1956, CF-EJD-X was scrapped in December, having flown about 425 hours.

➤ After flying the aircraft in 1952, Howard Hughes considered building the C-102.

➤ The C-102's nose is now in Canada's National Aeronautical Collection.

PROFILE

Canada's first and only jetliner

Only one C-102 was flown, although a second machine was close to completion when the programme was cancelled. The aircraft, registered CF-EJD-X, first flew on 10 August 1949, powered by four Rolls-Royce Derwent 5 turbojet engines.

However, these engines were not the ones originally intended for the new airliner. Avro Canada had hoped to install a pair of Rolls-Royce's new AJ 65 Avon turbojets, but the British government was not prepared to release them for civil use.

Intended to carry 30 to 50 passengers, the C-102 would have covered route stages of around 1750 km (1,085 mi.).

After an early landing accident, the prototype was repaired, demonstrated extensively and later re-engined with more powerful Derwent 8s and 9s (two of each). On one occasion the aircraft flew 587 km (400-plus mi.) from Toronto to New York in 59 minutes with a cargo of mail.

The C-102's launch customer was to be Trans-Canada Air Lines, although US firms were also impressed enough to propose a production order.

The RCAF and USAF also tested the aircraft, but ultimately performance shortcomings, the Korean War and the Canadian government's request that Avro concentrate on the CF-100 fighter led to cancellation in 1951.

Had development continued, the C-102 could have been the world's second jet airliner in service, an honour left to the Soviet Tupolev Tu-104.

The elevators and rudder were in two pieces, the rear portions being manually operated and the front section power-assisted.

Rolls-Royce Derwent turbojets were installed in nacelles designed with the aid of wartime German research.

The Jetliner's twin-spar wing was of conventional stressed-skin construction. Split flaps were fitted.

Had the British government released the Rolls-Royce Avon for civil use, the C-102 would have been fitted with two in single nacelles.

C-102 JETLINER

Although two prototypes were planned, only CF-EJD-X was completed and flown. The tail legend reads 'Designed and built by A.V. Roe Canada Limited, Malton, Ontario'.

Unswept vertical tail surfaces were a feature of many early jet types. Aerodynamic research later showed the benefits of a swept tail.

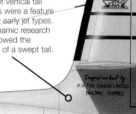

The Jetliner's flightdeck was of conventional layout with fully duplicated controls and seating for two pilots, plus a 'jump' seat between for an observer.

Pressurisation was a feature of the C-102's 3.05-m (10-ft.) diameter fuselage. Seating arrangements for between 30 and 50 passengers were proposed. During demonstration flights passengers were impressed by its low noise levels.

After its second flight the C-102 was unable to lower its main undercarriage and was forced to make a belly landing. It came to rest on its extended nose gear, the ends of its tail pipes and the rear fuselage.

The C-102 was fitted with tricycle undercarriage, with dual mainwheels retracting into the rear of the engine nacelles.

While the prototype was undergoing testing, Avro worked on a production version with a 1.22-m (4-ft.) forward fuselage stretch and a rear fuselage shortened by 0.53 m (nearly 2 ft.). Alternative powerplants were suggested, including Allison J-33s and Pratt & Whitney J-42s (licence-built Rolls-Royce Nenes).

British jet transport prototypes

AVRO 706 ASHTON: Six of these large aircraft were built for the Ministry of Supply for research into jet operations. Four Rolls-Royce Nene turbojets were fitted.

DE HAVILLAND DH.106 COMET: First flown in July 1949, the de Havilland Ghost-powered Comet was to be the world's first jet airliner in service, just under three years later.

VICKERS NENE-VIKING: Rolls-Royce Nene turbojets were installed in a Viking airliner to create the world's first pure-jet transport aircraft. Flown in 1948, it was strictly a test aircraft.

VICKERS VISCOUNT 663: The second Viscount turboprop airliner prototype was rebuilt in 1950 as a flying engine testbed with two Rolls-Royce Tay turbojets.

C-102 Jetliner

Type: medium-range civil transport

Powerplant: four 16.01-kN (3,600-lb.-thrust) Rolls-Royce Derwent 5/17 turbojets

Maximum speed: 804 km/h (498 m.p.h.) at 9145 m (30,000 ft.)

Cruising speed: 692 km/h (429 m.p.h.) at 9145 m (30,000 ft.)

Initial climb rate: 561 m/min (1,840 f.p.m.)

Range: 2012 km (1,250 mi.)

Service ceiling: 11,368 m (37,300 ft.)

Weights: empty 15,050 kg (33,110 lb.); maximum take-off 29,510 kg (64,922 lb.)

Accommodation: (proposed) flight crew of two, plus 30 to 50 passengers in various seating configurations

Dimensions:
span	29.89 m (98 ft.)
length	24.61 m (80 ft. 9 in.)
height	8.06 m (26 ft. 5 in.)
wing area	107.48 m² (1,156 sq. ft.)

ACTION DATA

CRUISING SPEED

The de Havilland Comet flew two weeks before the Jetliner and was the first jet airliner to enter service. Powered by four de Havilland Ghosts, the aircraft had a 96 km/h (60 m.p.h.) speed advantage.

C-102 JETLINER	692km/h (429 m.p.h.)
COMET Mk 1	789 km/h (489 m.p.h.)
Tu-104 'CAMEL'	770 km/h (477 m.p.h.)

PASSENGERS

All three of these jetliners had similar capacity, although with 50 passengers aboard, the C-102 was at its upper limit. The Comet was later 'stretched' to increase seating.

C-102 JETLINER	50 passengers
COMET Mk 1	44 passengers
Tu-104 'CAMEL'	50 passengers

RANGE

In prototype form the C-102 demonstrated a range of just over 2000 km (1,250 mi.). When fitted with four Derwent engines, the Jetliner's fuel capacity was reduced and extra tankage was required to maintain range. Payload capability therefore suffered. Both the Comet and Tu-104 were larger aircraft, the latter having two engines.

C-102 JETLINER 2012 km (1,250 mi.)
COMET Mk 1 2816 km (1,745 mi.)
Tu-104 'CAMEL' 2650 km (1,645 mi.)

AYRES TURBO-THRUSH

LOW-LEVEL SPRAYER

● American turboprop agricultural aircraft ● Developed from a 1950s design

Spraying and dusting crops is hard work and a competitive business. During the summer months pilots routinely work 14-hour days, using every hour of daylight and carrying on into the night if necessary. As the pilots are paid only for the area of land they cover, the Turbo-Thrush was designed to make the most of their time. Based on the earlier piston-engined Thrush, it uses a PT6A turbine to improve performance.

▲ The Turbo-Thrush can trace its origins to the piston-engined Snow S-2 design, which was later built by Rockwell as the Thrush Commander. Piston-engined S-2Rs are still in production.

AYRES TURBO-THRUSH

◀ Spraying or dusting
Different hoppers are fitted at the factory for either dusting, with dry chemicals, or, as shown here, for spraying.

▼ Strong and manoeuvrable
The broad, untapered cantilever wing is designed to be strong and to provide lift for typical spraying manoeuvres.

▲ Piston predecessor
More than 1,600 Thrushes were built by Snow and Rockwell and they remain in production at Ayres Corporation's Georgia factory.

Turbo Sea Thrush ▶
Mounted on amphibious floats, the Turbo Sea Thrush conversion may be operated from land or water as a low-cost water-bomber.

◀ Pratt & Whitney power
Most Turbo-Thrushes are powered by Pratt & Whitney Canada PT6A turbines of varying ratings. The S2R-T34 variant is fitted with the 559-kW PT6A-34AG engine, which is mounted well forwards to maintain the aircraft's centre of gravity position.

FACTS AND FIGURES

➤ The original S-2, designed by Leland Snow, flew in 1958 and was powered by a 336-kW Pratt & Whitney R-985 radial.

➤ A Turbo-Thrush costs about $600,000, depending upon the engine specified.

➤ Ayres markets a military close air support surveillance version called the Vigilante.

➤ By spraying oil into the exhaust system, Turbo-Thrush NEDS can generate smoke to mark marijuana fields for spraying.

➤ Turbo-Thrushes have engine ratings of between 373 kW–1026 kW (500–1075hp).

➤ Piston- and turbine-engined Thrushes operate in about 70 countries.

PROFILE

American agricultural aerobats

Compared with the piston-powered Thrush, the Turbo-Thrush offers shorter take-offs, faster ferry times and an increased load capacity. A fully-reversible propeller makes landing runs shorter and saves taxi time back to the reloading area. Tighter turns between passes and spraying speeds of 150-240 km/h (93–150 mph) add up to less flying time per hectare, or more hectares per hour.

Given the long hours and the need for continuous concentration, pilot comfort is an important consideration. The Turbo-Thrush has better visibility, while the low noise of the PT6A engine and the five-bladed propeller help to reduce pilot fatigue.

In the field, pilots warm up their aircraft's engines before dawn, their hoppers filled with seeds, pesticide or fertiliser, depending on seasonal requirements. Maximum concentration is required over the spraying area. To save time, turns at the end of each pass are flown at just above stalling speed, while pilots keep a constant watch for wires, farm vehicles, embankments and other obstacles.

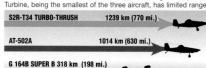

Flown by the International Narcotics Matters Bureau, the NEDS aircraft were operated in Belize on Operation Roundup, spraying commercially-grown marijuana with herbicide.

S2R-T34 Turbo-Thrush

Type: single-/two-seat turboprop agricultural aircraft

Powerplant: one 559-kW (750-hp) Pratt & Whitney Canada PT6A-34AG turboprop

Maximum level speed: 256 km/h (159 mph) with spray equipment

Working speed: 145-241 km/h (90–150 mph)

Climb rate: 530 m/1738 ft. per min. at sea level

Range: 1239 km (770 mi.) at 45 per cent power

Service ceiling: 7620 m (25,000 ft.)

Weights: empty 1633 kg (3,600 lb.); maximum take-off 2721 kg (6,000 lb.)

Dimensions:
span	13.55 m (44 ft. 5 in.)
length	10.06 m (33 ft.)
height	2.80 m (9 ft. 3 in.)
wing area	30.34 m² (326 sq. ft.)

A deflector cable runs from the cockpit to the tail fin to lessen the aircraft's vulnerability to wire strikes.

While earlier members of the Thrush family were built with fabric-covered control surfaces, current models have an all-metal structure and skin.

The stainless steel spray system mounted under the wings is driven by a small propeller between the undercarriage legs. Spray nozzle droplet size is adjustable.

The S2R-T65 variant of the Turbo-Thrush features a 2.82m (9 ft. 3 in.), five-bladed propeller to absorb the extra power of its larger engine. The -T34 model has a three-bladed unit and the Garrett-engined -G10 has a four-bladed propeller.

S2R-T65 TURBO-THRUSH

Also known as the Narcotics Eradication Delivery System (NEDS), this S2R-T65 is one of 19 ordered by the US State Department between 1983 and 1988.

The fibreglass hopper is mounted in front of the cockpit. This one has a capacity of 1514 litres (400 gallons) of chemicals.

Two seats are optional on the Turbo-Thrush and the second seat is often used to carry a ground crew member. In the NEDS aircraft the 'back seater' has a set of controls and can fly the aircraft if necessary. He can also watch for ground fire from the 'blister' windows.

N3090M

Compared to the earlier piston-engined models, the turboprop versions are much longer to accommodate the new engine. The S2R-T65 has a much more powerful engine than standard agricultural models to improve performance and compensate for the weight of armour plate fitted.

The cockpit is sealed to protect the pilot from harmful chemicals and has a steel tube roll cage for protection if the aircraft turns over in a crash. On agricultural aircraft the rear seat may be fitted with dual controls for training.

ACTION DATA

RANGE

Endurance is important for agricultural aircraft; the fewer times they have to stop to refuel, the better. Good range also means that remote air strips can be reached with ease. The Ag-Cat Super B Turbine, being the smallest of the three aircraft, has limited range.

S2R-T34 TURBO-THRUSH	1239 km (770 mi.)
AT-502A	1014 km (630 mi.)
G 164B SUPER B	318 km (198 mi.)

HOPPER VOLUME

Crop-dusters and sprayers are often available with various sizes of hopper for both dry and liquid chemicals. Bigger hoppers usually require the fitting of a larger engine to compensate for the extra weight.

G 164B SUPER B TURBINE	AT-502A	S2R-T34 TURBO-THRUSH
1.51 m³ (53 cu. ft.)	1.89 m² (66.7 cu. ft.)	1.5 m³ (53 cu. ft.)

TAKE-OFF RUN

An agricultural aircraft's take-off run is especially important if it is to be flown from hilly farmland strips. Without a load these aircraft require less than 100 metres (300 ft.) to take off.

TURBO-THRUSH	183 m (600 ft.)
AT-502A	222 m (728 ft.)
G 164B SUPER B TURBINE	274 m (898 ft.)

Agricultural turboprops worldwide

■ **AG-CAT G 164B SUPER B TURBINE:** Powered by the PT6A turbine, the highly agile Ag-Cat biplane was developed from the radial-engined Grumman G-164 of the 1950s.

■ **AIR TRACTOR AT-500:** Designed by Leland Snow after he sold the S-2 to Rockwell International, the Air Tractor is a considerably larger aircraft and uses a PT6A turboprop engine.

■ **EPA NAC 6 FIELDMASTER:** First flown from the Isle of Wight in 1981 by NDN Aircraft (below), only a few of these large, PT6A-engined aircraft were built, the latest by EPA Aircraft.

■ **PAC CRESCO:** Pacific Aerospace in New Zealand continues to build this turboprop development of the Fletcher 'agplane' with Allied Signal (Garrett) or Pratt & Whitney engines.

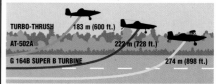

BAC
ONE-ELEVEN

● Short-haul airliner ● Holidaymaker's special ● Licence-built in Romania

BAC ONE-ELEVEN

▲ American service
American Airlines received its first One-Eleven in July 1965. It was successful despite the US Federal Aviation Authority limiting the weight of the aircraft with a two-man crew to only 36288 kg (80,015 lb).

◀ Front end
Most One-Elevens had a two-man crew, even in the United States where three-man flight decks were the norm in the 1960s.

▲ British United
The first production variant was the One-Eleven 200, of which 58 were built. British United Airlines purchased the first 10 aircraft.

High density ▶
The One-Eleven avoided the mistakes of earlier British designs, and had high-density seating.

▲ Dirt runway
The ability to operate from small strips made the One-Eleven a viable operator in Africa, Asia and South America.

◀ Passengers in Peru ▲
Faucett of Peru operated One-Elevens on domestic routes, often from small, unsealed runways at high altitudes.

Designed as a successor to the turboprop-powered Vickers Viscount, the One-Eleven was one of the most efficient British airliner designs. Flying short-haul holiday and inter-city feederliner routes, it sold well in both America and Europe. Despite its design being over 30 years old, the One-Eleven is still a common sight, especially in Europe where the Romanian-built version still thrives.

▲ The One-Eleven was one of the better British airline designs of the 1960s. If legal problems based on noise regulations can be avoided, it will still be a common sight for years to come.

FACTS AND FIGURES

➤ In an ill-fated start, the BAC One-Eleven prototype first flew in August 1963, but crashed three months later.

➤ One-Eleven commercial service began with British United Airlines in April 1965.

➤ The One-Eleven was one of the few British airliners to sell well in the USA.

➤ The 220 One-Elevens sold by 1978 made it Britain's biggest aviation foreign exchange earner of its time.

➤ The Series 500, introduced in 1966, could carry up to 119 passengers.

➤ Rombac of Romania built an upgraded One-Eleven.

PROFILE

Britain's best holiday jet

The One-Eleven began as a design study by Hunting Aircraft, intended as a replacement for the successful Vickers Viscount. The H-107 was to have been a cruciform-tail rear-engined twin, with a capacity of 48 seats and a range of around 1600 km (990 mi.).

In 1960 Hunting was acquired by the British Aircraft Corporation, and the design was expanded to take 65 passengers over 1000 km (600 mi.). In April 1961, production of an initial batch of 20 aircraft was started,

and in May British United Airways became launch customer, ordering 10 Series 200 types. Vital to success was an American purchase, and Braniff International ordered six with six options in October 1961.

The One-Eleven suffered a slight setback when a test aircraft crashed in October 1963 due to a 'deep stall' arising from the T-tail design, but this was cured by control modifications. The One-Eleven then went on to have a trouble-free career, with good sales success. A new

lease of life came in 1977 when the Romanian company Interprederea Avionane took out a licence-build agreement with BAC. The first 'Rombac' One-Eleven was delivered to Tarom Romanian Airlines in 1982, and a hush-kit modification has been proposed to extend the One-Eleven's life still further.

The One-Eleven 500 series was used for inter-city routes by Bavaria Germanair.

The One-Eleven specialised in holiday flights and in servicing commuter routes between cities. American Airlines used it on the busy Boston-New York-Washington 'Jet Express', one of the world's busiest airways.

Fuel tanks with a capacity of 14,024 litres (3,650 gal.) were fitted, one in each wing and one in the centre section.

The wing of the 500 series had an extra 1.52-m (5-ft.) span to improve take-off performance.

One-Eleven Series 500

Type: short-haul twin-jet airliner

Powerplant: two Rolls-Royce 55.82-kN (12,525-lb.-thrust) Spey 512-DW turbofans

Maximum speed: 871 km/h (540 m.p.h.) maximum cruise; 742 km/h (460 m.p.h.) economy cruise

Initial climb rate: 730 m/min (2,400 f.p.m.)

Range: 2380 km (3,870 mi.) with capacity payload; 3458 km (6,015 mi.) with maximum fuel

Service ceiling: 10,600 m (34,800 ft.)

Weights: basic operating weight 24,758 kg (54,468 lb.); maximum take-off weight 47,400 kg (104,498 lb.)

Payload: normal 97 passengers; maximum 119

Dimensions:
span 28.50 m (93 ft. 6 in.)
length 32.61 m (107 ft.)
height 7.47 m (24 ft. 6 in.)
wing area 95.78 m² (1,031 sq. ft.)

ONE-ELEVEN SERIES 414EG

The BAC One-Eleven was one of the most successful European airliners before the Airbus. The 500 series was especially popular, selling well in the face of competition from Boeing and McDonnell Douglas.

A 'stick-pusher' was installed as part of the flight control system. It was intended to warn pilots and prevent a recurrence of the loss of the prototype to a deep stall accident caused by the high T-tail.

BAC considered producing a stretched One-Eleven Series 700, with fuselage lengthened by 3.66 m (12 ft.) compared to the 500 series aircraft.

A small weather radar system is fitted to the One-Eleven.

The One-Eleven was like many of its contemporaries in having five-abreast seating.

Small wing fences are located on the leading edge of the wing to control spanwise airflow.

The Spey 512-14W was capable of producing more thrust, thanks to water injection.

In an attempt to increase the life of the One-Eleven beyond new noise limits, a 'hush kit' was developed for the Spey engine, including a bypass duct lining and six-chute jet mixing exhaust silencer.

A ventral entrance was located in the rear fuselage between the engines, with a hydraulically-powered stairway. Many were sealed shut after a bizarre hijacking incident in America in which the hijacker parachuted out with a large ransom.

ACTION DATA

MAXIMUM SPEED

The new twin-jets were about 200 km/h (125 m.p.h.) faster than turboprops like the Viscount, and twice as fast as the previous decade's piston-engined aircraft. The One-Eleven did not have the speed of its long-haul rivals, but was fast enough over a short haul.

ONE-ELEVEN SERIES 500	871 km/h (540 m.p.h.)
MODEL 737-200	927 km/h (575 m.p.h.)
DC-9 SERIES 30	918 km/h (569 m.p.h.)

RANGE

Typical short-haul routes within Europe and the eastern seaboard of the United States involve flying between cities ranging from 100 km (60 mi.) to 1000 km (600 mi.) apart. The jets designed to operate such flights carry enough fuel to fly several stages without needing replenishment.

DC-9 SERIES 30 3300 km (2,050 mi.)

MODEL 737-200 4075 km (2,525 mi.)

ONE-ELEVEN SERIES 500 3458 km (2,165 mi.)

PASSENGER LOAD

In the late 1950s, when the specification for these jets was first discussed, planners were looking for aircraft with a 50-passenger capacity. However, it quickly became clear that larger planes would be needed. The One-Eleven was never stretched beyond 119 passengers, however, unlike its rivals which entered the 1990s with developed models seating between 150 and 180.

MODEL 737-200 130 passengers

DC-9 SERIES 30 115 passengers

ONE-ELEVEN SERIES 500 119 passengers

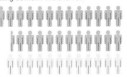

Mass-market air transporters

AÉROSPATIALE CARAVELLE: First flying in the 1950s, the elegant Caravelle was one of the earliest of the short-haul twin-jets, and set the standards by which others have been judged.

MCDONNELL DOUGLAS DC-9: A direct competitor to the One-Eleven, the DC-9 first flew in 1965. Models had a range of passenger capacities, which gave it the commercial edge.

BOEING 737: Although beaten into service by both the One-Eleven and the DC-9, Boeing's spacious twin-jet offered a wider cabin and has become the world's best-selling airliner.

BEDE

BD-10

● Supersonic jet ● Home-built kit ● Composite structure

The Bede BD-10J is a lightweight, single-engine jet aircraft with dual controls and tandem seating. Designed by aviation genius Jim Bede, the BD-10J is meant for the civil market and offers performance characteristics which rival, and in some cases even exceed, those of military fighters. As a privately owned home-build aircraft, the BD-10J astonishingly provides brief supersonic capability at relatively little cost.

▲ Soaring to success; Jim Bede was instrumental in providing the home-built market with high performance aircraft that could be assembled by any individual relatively easily.

PHOTO FILE

BEDE BD-10

◀ Bird of prey
Now called the Peregrine Falcon the BD-10 has been likened to the USAF's F-15 Eagle, both in performance characteristics and the look of the aircraft.

Man with a vision ▶
As president of Bede Aircraft Incorporated, Jim Bede has seen his company produce some of the most innovative aircraft designs ever. His vision is to make flying available to the average person.

▲ Microjet movie star
One of the first sales successes for Jim Bede was the BD-5J. Its high-speed and sparkling performance have seen the jet make numerous guest appearances in a host of films.

▲ Civilian fighter
With the collapse of the Bede Aircraft Corporation, the civil version of the BD-10 is now sold by Peregrine Flight Int.

◀ Model kit aircraft
A display of the components that go up to make the BD-5J; this simple construction is retained on the BD-10.

FACTS AND FIGURES

➤ Design of the BD-10 began in 1983 with the first flight of the aircraft being accomplished on 8 July 1992.

➤ The first kit of the aircraft was delivered in August 1993.

➤ Bede Aircraft Incorporated continues to market the military version of the BD-10.

➤ Peregrine International acquired the design and marketing rights for the civilian sports variant of the BD-10.

➤ One BD-10 was lost in a fatal crash on 30 December 1994.

➤ More than 45 examples of the BD-10 have been ordered within the United States.

PROFILE

Home-built hot rod

The Bede aviation company in St Louis, Missouri held high hopes in the early 1990s for both military and civilian use of the BD-10J, the world's first supersonic, home-built jet aircraft. The fully aerobatic BD-10J has a fighter-style tandem seating arrangement, non-boosted flight controls, and a pressurised cockpit.

Bede launched the BD-10J in 1991, believing it had strong potential for both civil and military use in the developed world and in Third World

countries. The Bede trademark of simplicity was found from one end of the aircraft to the other. It has no hydraulic flight controls and no cables, only manual controls. The flight surfaces are operated by push-rods, rod ends and ball-bearings. The BD-10J is unique in having two control sticks: a side stick and centre stick, mechanically connected, which move in sequence with each other.

Difficulties in development and the loss of the prototype have resulted in the sales of the aircraft being temporarily

suspended. Despite these set-backs huge interest remains in Bede's unique supersonic home-built jet.

Below: Providing a new dimension for the private flying enthusiast, the BD-10 was seen to offer supersonic performance for a fraction of the operating cost of other types.

Above: To reduce the overall weight of the aircraft, the BD-10 uses a composite and aluminium construction. This allows customers to construct their own aircraft in kit form, so reducing the overall purchase cost of the aircraft.

BD-10

Bringing the capabilities of a military jet fighter to the civilian home-built market, the BD-10 is the subject of an enquiry into a crash. Despite this, orders are still forthcoming.

BD-10

Type: home-build supersonic aircraft

Powerplant: one 13.12-kN (2,950-lb.-thrust) General Electric CJ-610 turbojet

Maximum speed: Mach 1.4 at high altitude

Maximum cruising speed: 957 km/h (593 m.p.h.)

Initial climb rate: 9150 m/min (30,000 f.p.m.)

Range: 2499 km (1,550 mi.)

Service ceiling: 13715 m (45,000 ft.)

Weights: maximum take-off 2014 kg (4,430 lb.)

Accommodation: two pilots seated in tandem

Dimensions:
span	6.55 m	(21 ft. 6 in.)
length	8.79 m	(28 ft. 10 in.)
height	2.46 m	(8 ft. 1 in.)
wing area	9.10 m²	(98 sq. ft.)

MILITARY LIGHTWEIGHTS

MICROLIGHT: Currently one of the most advanced microlights flying, the Shadow built by CFM was such a capable machine that military applications were soon envisaged. Equipped with a FLIR pod under its fuselage, the Shadow was to be used as a covert reconnaissance platform. Despite testing, which the Shadow passed with ease, this microlight currently only sees private use.

SAILPLANES: Schweizer has had a long history of constructing highly capable and successful sailplanes for the private market. Various models have also been used by the US military for training since World War II. The latest military application for the sailplanes have seen them being adopted by the US Navy as part of its Test Pilot School fleet.

A simple weather radar is installed within the nose of the BD-10. This provides a limited amount of data for the pilot. Options available on the aircraft are either sophisticated flight instruments or the bare necessities.

A large single piece canopy affords the tandem-seated crew excellent visibility when in flight. The cockpit is pressurised but the pilots are not equipped with ejection seats. Later military training variants were to be fitted with advanced zero-zero ejection seats.

The airframe is composed of 60 per cent metal, 40 per cent composites which include aluminium alloy and aluminium honeycomb structures. These are mounted in a sandwich construction. This has proved to be immensely strong yet incredibly light. Despite this, the fatal crash of the BD-10 was traced to the failure of a wing flap.

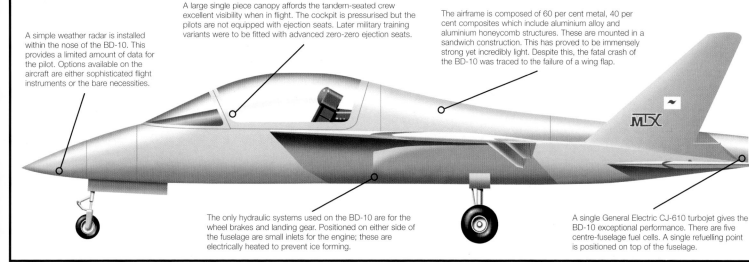

The only hydraulic systems used on the BD-10 are for the wheel brakes and landing gear. Positioned on either side of the fuselage are small inlets for the engine; these are electrically heated to prevent ice forming.

A single General Electric CJ-610 turbojet gives the BD-10 exceptional performance. There are five centre-fuselage fuel cells. A single refuelling point is positioned on top of the fuselage.

Breaking new ground in a Bede

■ **BD-4:** Marketed as a private utility aircraft, the BD-4 was powered by a Lycoming engine, but the design met with little success.

■ **XBD-2:** A revolutionary six-place executive aircraft, the BD-2 featured a single pusher propeller shrouded to increase thrust.

■ **BD-2:** Basically a two-seat Schweizer sailplane, this was the product of an attempt by Jim Bede to fly non-stop around the world.

■ **BD-7:** Developed from the BD-5, an increase in cockpit size allowed passengers to be carried within the small aircraft.

BEECH

17 STAGGERWING

● Pre- and post-war production ● Cabin biplane ● Military users

Beech's Staggerwing is widely regarded as one of the most beautiful aircraft ever built, and is a true classic. The very first Staggerwing biplane was a hand-crafted work of art, completed in 1932 when Walter Beech's Wichita, Kansas, manufacturing company had only eight employees. The last Staggerwing was built in 1949, but this appealing aircraft can still be found flying, today, in the hands of a few loving, proud owners.

▲ *Today the*
Staggerwing is a highly
collectable and valuable classic aircraft. Here,
engineers are seen working on the Pratt & Whitney R-
985-SB Wasp Junior engine fitted to the D17S version.

PHOTO FILE

BEECH 17 STAGGERWING

▼ **RAF transport**
To fill an urgent need for a high-performance light transport aircraft, Britain received 106 Staggerwings. In RAF service they were named Traveller Mk I.

▲ **Staggered wings**
The Staggerwing gets its name from the arrangement of the wings which has the lower wing situated forward of the upper wing.

▼ **Connecting bases**
Used by the USAAF both in the USA and abroad, the UC-43 flew diplomatic and military staff between the many military establishments which existed in the 1940s.

▲ **Wartime delivery**
During World War II, Model 17s were delivered to both the US Navy (GB-1 and GB-2) and US Army Air Force (UC-43). This GB-2 was delivered in 1943.

◄ **US Navy service**
Flying under the US Navy designation GB-2 Traveller, this example was used as a personal transport by US Navy attachés abroad.

FACTS AND FIGURES

➤ Beechcraft records indicate that 785 Model 17 Staggerwings were built between 1932 and 1949.

➤ In 1935 Capt. H.L. Farquhar successfully flew around the world in a Model B17R.

➤ Dwane L. Wallace, future president of Cessna, helped design the Staggerwing.

➤ A Model B17L was impressed into Republican service during the Spanish Civil War and was used as a bomber.

➤ Of around 225 Staggerwings surviving today, over 200 are on the US register.

➤ Each Staggerwing was a custom-built aircraft manufactured by hand.

PROFILE

High-performance personal transport

At the start of the 1930s, Theodore Wells and Walter Beech designed the Model 17 Staggerwing, the first of tens of thousands of Beechcraft aircraft. The Staggerwing was refined over the years but from the beginning it held a unique place in aviation – a majestic aircraft suited for the job of providing elegant transportation to wealthy owners.

The Staggerwing provided quality service in the 1930s to a few corporate and private customers. Some intrepid

aviators, veterans of the 'barnstorming' era of a decade earlier, entered the Staggerwing in racing and endurance events, gaining victory in the Texaco Trophy of 1933 and the Bendix Trophy of 1936 when the successful pilot, Louise Thaden, was voted the outstanding US woman pilot of the year.

The Staggerwing continued to gain fame in races and competitions, but is best remembered as a superb transport carrying passengers in speed and comfort.

It was inevitable that the Staggerwing would be inducted into military service. Many of these aircraft served with a number of armed forces during World War II, and continued to serve both civilian and military customers into the 1950s.

The powerful engine and smooth lines of the Staggerwing helped it establish a number of records. Jacqueline Cochran set new women's speed records over 100 km (62 mi.) and 1000 km (620 mi.).

G17S Staggerwing

Type: four/five-seat cabin biplane

Powerplant: one 336-kW (450-hp.) Pratt & Whitney R-985-AN-4 Wasp Junior radial piston engine

Maximum speed: 341 km/h (211 m.p.h.)

Cruising speed: 298 km/h (185 m.p.h.) at 2895 m (9,500 ft.)

Range: 1610 km (1,000 mi.)

Ceiling: 5805 m (19,000 ft.)

Weights: empty 1270 kg (2,794 lb.); maximum take-off 1928 kg (4,240 lb.)

Accommodation: one pilot and four passengers

Dimensions:		
span	9.75 m (32 ft.)
length	8.15 m (26 ft. 9 in.)
height	2.44 m (8 ft.)
wing area	27.54 m² (296 sq. ft.)

The enclosed cabin could accommodate a pilot and four passengers. The front seats were adjustable, with a bench-type seat in the rear of the cabin. A number of the military versions were supplied with special seats with parachutes forming part of the upholstery.

The equal-span wings have a pronounced back stagger. The upper wing is attached directly to the top of the cabin and is supported by one 'I'-type interplane strut on each side of the fuselage.

Constructed of metal tubing in an oval structure, the fuselage was tapered toward the rear, giving the aircraft its distinctive 'curvaceous' shape. The wings had wooden spars and ribs with ailerons on the top wings and lift flaps on the lower wings.

The cantilever monoplane tail unit had a welded steel framework for the elevators and rudder, and a wooden framework for the tailplane and fin. The entire unit was fabric-covered.

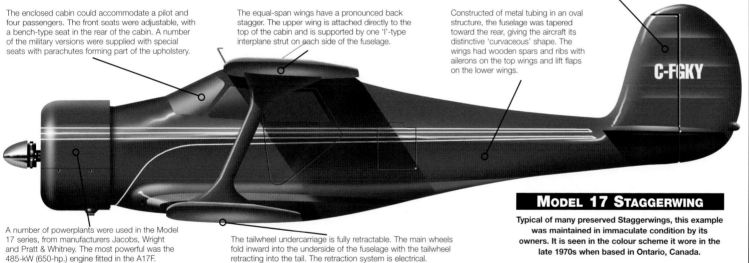

C-FGKY

MODEL 17 STAGGERWING

Typical of many preserved Staggerwings, this example was maintained in immaculate condition by its owners. It is seen in the colour scheme it wore in the late 1970s when based in Ontario, Canada.

A number of powerplants were used in the Model 17 series, from manufacturers Jacobs, Wright and Pratt & Whitney. The most powerful was the 485-kW (650-hp.) engine fitted in the A17F.

The tailwheel undercarriage is fully retractable. The main wheels fold inward into the underside of the fuselage with the tailwheel retracting into the tail. The retraction system is electrical.

ACTION DATA

POWER

The Staggerwing had by far the biggest engine, which is one of the main reasons for its impressive performance. A larger engine means a higher rate of fuel consumption, and as prices have risen economy has become an important factor.

MODEL D17R STAGGERWING	MODEL 195	MODEL 108 VOYAGER
313 kW (420 hp.)	224 kW (300 hp.)	123 kW (165 hp.)

MAXIMUM SPEED

With retractable landing gear and a big engine, combined with its smooth aerodynamics, the Staggerwing outperformed almost all single-engined pre-war lightplanes. The Cessna Model 195 was also quite powerful, with a respectable turn of speed.

MODEL D17R STAGGERWING	339 km/h (210 m.p.h.)
MODEL 195	290 km/h (180 m.p.h.)
MODEL 108	235 km/h (146 m.p.h.)

ACCOMMODATION

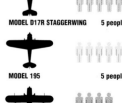

As a light single-engined transport a capacity of five is more than sufficient for the intended tasks. The smaller and less powerful Stinson Model 108 Voyager can carry a pilot plus three passengers. When the Staggerwing carries four passengers, it is not able to carry maximum fuel, so restricting the aircraft's range.

MODEL D17R STAGGERWING — 5 people

MODEL 195 — 5 people

MODEL 108 VOYAGER — 4 people

Cabin lightplanes of the 1930s

■ **TAYLORCRAFT SERIES :** Starting by building the Cub in the 1930s Taylorcraft went on to produce similar designs throughout the 1940s.

■ **CESSNA MODEL A SERIES:** The Type A was Cessna's first production aircraft. This example is a type AW, of which 48 were built.

■ **DE HAVILLAND DH.87B HORNET MOTH:** Introduced in 1935, 165 Hornet Moths were produced before the outbreak of World War II.

■ **PIPER CUB:** Sales of the Cub in 1936 and 1937 represented about one third of the total aircraft sold in the USA.

BEECHCRAFT

65 QUEEN AIR

● Twin-engined business and commuter liner ● 1960s design

Developed from the Twin Bonanza and flown for the first time in August 1958, the Beechcraft Model 65 was the first of a series of twin-engined business aircraft to carry the name Queen Air. Despite its small size, it was equipped like an airliner, with all the systems needed for all-weather operations plus an optional weather radar. It found a ready market, and came to be used widely as an air taxi and short-haul commuter aircraft.

▲ *Beechcraft's top-selling Model 65 Queen Air was the intermediate step between the piston-engined Model 50 Twin Bonanza and the turboprop Model 90 King Air.*

BEECHCRAFT 65 QUEEN AIR

▼ B80 with swept fin
With the Model 65-80 in 1962, Beechcraft introduced a swept tail fin on the Queen Air. Longer-span wings were introduced in 1966 on the Model 65 Queen Air B80, seen here. In all, 242 were built.

▲ Worldwide sales
Queen Airs have sold around the world, including Great Britain. Many were sold to military customers who found the design ideal for communications and training duties.

▼ Queen Airliner
These three Model 70 Queen Airliners are of US operator Commuter Airlines. Certified in 1968, 35 were built, some with cargo pods under the fuselage.

▲ Business liner and airliner
Beechcraft intended the Queen Air for the roles of business and commuter airliner. In high-density configuration, the Model 70 carried nine people.

◀ Turbine popularity
Increasing interest in turboprop-powered commuter liners spelt the end of the piston-engined design in the 1970s. The Model 70 was one of the last models produced.

FACTS AND FIGURES

➤ French companies SFERMA and Sud Aviation designed a Queen Air with two 447-kW Turboméca Astazou turboprops.

➤ Model A65-85 was a planned pressurised version of the Model 65 Queen Air 80.

➤ The Queen Air prototype flew in August 1958, four months after design began.

➤ On 8 February 1960, a Beechcraft test pilot in a Model 65 set a world height record in that class – 10,626 m (34,853 ft.).

➤ The Model 65 Queen Air B80 was the last variant. Production ended in 1977.

➤ Fastest of the Queen Airs was the US Army's U-21A, at 426 km/h (264 m.p.h.).

Beech's regal prop-twins

Walter Beech's company was quick to build on the success of the Model 65. In 1962 the heavier Queen Air 80 introduced a swept tail fin and uprated Lycoming engines, while the Model A65 of the following year had increased fuel capacity. The Queen Air A80 appeared in 1964 with slightly larger wings and a cabin big enough for up to eight passengers, and the B80 introduced further minor changes in 1966. A projected pressurised variant was not built. Beechcraft marketed the Queen Air as both a business aircraft and commuter liner. The Model 70 of 1968 was available as a Queen Airliner with room for nine passenger seats in a high-density configuration.

By 1971, production was switching to a turboprop development, the eight-seat Model 90 King Air. For customers looking for a cheaper alternative to this design, the Model 65-88 was briefly available. It was effectively a piston-engined King Air.

As well as forming the basis for the King Air, the Queen Air was developed as the Swearingen Merlin business aircraft and Metro 19-seat airliner. The US Army used Queen Airs as L-23F/U-8F Seminoles and U-21A Utes.

In addition, Excalibur Aviation has rebuilt more than 160 Model 65s and 70s as Queenaire 800s and 8800s with 298-kW (400-hp.) Lycoming eight-cylinder engines, new engine nacelles and fully-enclosed wheel doors.

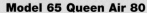

Left: Available from 1968, the Queen Air 70 combined the engines of the Model A65 with the wide-span wings of the Model 80. A Queen Airliner version was also available.

Below: Early production Queen Airs featured a tail assembly inherited from the Model 50 Twin Bonanza, the type it was intended to replace.

Most Queen Airs were powered by versions of Lycoming's O-480 and O-540 flat-six, air-cooled piston engines. However, one of the last variants produced was the Model 65-A90-1 with two Pratt & Whitney PT6A turboprops. This was the only turboprop Queen Air version; the entire production run went to the US Army as the U-21A.

Initially marketed as a seven- to nine-seater, the Queen Air could accommodate up to nine passengers in airliner guise. Beech also intended that the aircraft be used as a freighter if required. To this end, passenger seating and bulkheads were easily removable.

For all-weather operation, de-icing 'boots' could be specified for the leading edges of the wings and tail.

Model A65s introduced the swept tail fin to the Queen Air. In 1968/69 Beech offered the Model A65-8200 Queen Airliner, initially known as the Model 79.

As on a number of other commuter types, the later Queen Air models featured a cargo compartment in the nose. The nose would also house navigation avionics, if fitted.

A two-spar wing of all-metal structure was standard on the Queen Air. Aluminium alloy was used in the semi-monocoque fuselage. This held the main fuel tanks; auxiliary tanks were housed in the wings.

RATS AIR TAXIS

SHOREHAM AIRPORT ☎ (0273) 464011

G-AWKX

MODEL A65 QUEEN AIR

Air taxi firms have been among the biggest users of the Queen Air. This aircraft was eventually reduced to ground instructional airframe status. Between 1967 and 1970, 96 Model A65s were built.

Beechcraft twins

MODEL 60 DUKE: This four- to six-seater, pressurised and turbocharged, first flew in late 1966. Production ended in 1982, with 593 built.

MODEL 76 DUCHESS: Three equipment packages (Weekender, Professional and Holiday) were available on the Duchess, launched in 1978.

MODEL 90/100 KING AIR: Developed directly from the Queen Air, the Model 90 (and 'stretched' Model 100) were turboprop-powered.

MODEL 99 AIRLINER: Beech's largest aircraft type, the 17-seat Airliner, was produced for 20 years, until 1986.

BEECHCRAFT

400

● Business jet ● Multi-engined trainer ● Air ambulance

Beech was chiefly known as a maker of turboprop aircraft until the company acquired the rights to build the Mitsubishi Diamond under licence. The Beech 400 was replaced soon after by the improved Model 400A, which proved more popular with customers than the original model. Despite being known as a civil transport, more Model 400As have in fact been sold as aircrew trainers to the USAF.

▲ When
Beech bought the licence to build the Mitsubishi Diamond, it secured all export rights outside Japan. The aircraft has sold steadily, but has not been as popular as its competitors.

PHOTO FILE

BEECHCRAFT 400 EXECUTIVE TRAVEL

▼ New avionics
One of the few changes made to the original Mitsubishi design was the use of Collins avionics throughout and an electronic flight instrument system.

▲ Computer designed
The Beech 400A wing was computer designed by Mitsubishi, and is certified for unlimited life.

◄ Executive jet
Despite its favourable price tag, the Beech 400A is not cheap, costing about $5 million each in 1995. A Dassault Falcon 50 costs about $16 million.

Production move ►
At first, Beech assembled components built in Japan by Mitsubishi, but in 1989 the whole assembly operation was moved to Wichita in the United States.

◄ Long range
Thrifty Pratt & Whitney JT15 engines give the little Beech 400A a range of more than 3500 km (2,175 mi.), and a high cruise speed.

FACTS AND FIGURES

➤ The Japanese Air Self-Defence Force operates the Beech T-400 as a crew trainer, with direction-finding systems.

➤ Production of the Model 400 totalled 58 aircraft before the 400A was introduced.

➤ The 400A has a radar system for detecting air turbulence.

➤ A Beech 400A was fitted out in air ambulance configuration for the Province of Chubut in Argentina.

➤ Increased ceiling and payload were just two of the improvements of the 400A.

➤ The Beech 400 is known to the USAF as the T-1A Jayhawk.

Beech builds an executive jet

Best known for its turboprop twins, the Beech company branched out into the executive jet market with the purchase of the production rights to the Mitsubishi Diamond in December 1985. The prototype had flown in 1984. Beech acquired all marketing rights outside Japan, and although production was at first carried out using sub-assemblies from Mitsubishi, the company ceased all trading outside Japan in March 1986 and Beech took on production at its base in Wichita, Kansas. The first Beech-assembled aircraft was built in May 1986, and 25 had been delivered by January 1988.

The improved Model 400A was introduced in 1989, and at least 82 aircraft had been delivered by 1995. Designed for civil use, the 400A found success as a military crew systems trainer, winning a USAF competition for a tanker/transport trainer system. Designated T-1A Jayhawk, more than 200 were ordered by the USAF, delivery beginning in 1991. Japan followed suit, ordering a small number of T-400 crew trainers. Civil sales continue, but the Beech aircraft faces ferocious competition from various rivals like the Hawker series, Dassault's Falcon and the evergreen Learjet range.

Below: The world market for corporate jets has been extremely crowded since the late 1980s, with a sharp downturn in world demand and a large number of competing manufacturers. Beech was lucky to secure military orders for its jet at a time of difficulty in the civil market.

Above: Costing $1 million less than a Cessna Citation VII, the 400A represents good value for the corporate client.

Model 400

Type: twin-turbofan executive jet

Powerplant: two Pratt & Whitney JT15D-5 turbofans rated at 13.19 kN (2,968 lb thrust)

Maximum speed: 899 km/h (559 m.p.h.)

Maximum Mach: 0.78

Initial climb rate: 1149 m/min (3,770 f.p.m.)

Range: 2915 km (1811 mi.) with reserves

Service ceiling: 13,230 m (43,400 ft.)

Weights: empty 4819 kg (10,624 lb.); loaded 7303 kg (16,100 lb.)

Accommodation: two crew and eight passengers in standard fit

Dimensions:
span	13.25 m (43 ft. 6 in.)
length	14.75 m (48 ft. 5 in.)
height	4.24 m (13 ft. 11 in.)
wing area	26.09 m² (281 sq. ft.)

MODEL 400A

An increase in business travel saw the demand for small executive jets explode in the late 1980s. Entering an already crowded market, Beech has achieved notable success with its design, offering a reliable and economical aircraft that is proving to be highly adaptable.

Eight passengers are seated in the 400A cabin: four in forward-facing seats and four in adjustable seats that can tilt, rotate and recline. Other seating configurations can be installed to customer requirements, including medical facilities.

The cabin has an independent pressurisation system, with an emergency system available using engine bleed air.

The 400A uses an all-moving tailplane and elevators for pitch control. The tailcone section can accommodate up to 204 kg (450 lb.) of baggage.

Standard avionics include the Collins Pro-Line 4 Electronic Flight Information System, with a three-tube display showing airspeed, altitude, vertical speed, attitude and navigation information.

The wing structure consists of machined upper and lower skins joined to two box spars, forming an integral fuel tank. A refuelling point is fitted on top of each wing. Roll control is effected by small ailerons and full semi-span narrow chord spoilers, which also act as lift dumpers.

The 400A is powered by two Pratt & Whitney JT15D-5 turbofans, fitted with Nordam thrust reversers (unlike the USAF T-1A). The rear-mounting layout reduces cabin noise. The rear fuselage fuel tank is mounted under the floor. The serial number on the tail is a United States registration.

ACTION DATA

MAXIMUM SPEED

Most business jets cruise at a high subsonic speed, usually approaching Mach 0.8. Above this speed there are penalties in airframe design and fuel consumption; it is only the latest business jets like the Gulfstream V and Citation X that can reach Mach 0.9.

BEECH JET 400	899 km/h (599 m.p.h.)
LEARJET 55B	889 km/h (552 m.p.h.)
GULFSTREAM IV	936 km/h (582 m.p.h.)

RANGE

Business jets have a ratio of fuel to empty weight that is broadly proportional. Thus, larger aircraft like the Gulfstream IV have longer range than the smaller Beech 400A. However, a 3000-km (1864-mi.) range and the ability to seat at least eight passengers in comfortable standard is the minimum most manufacturers like to produce.

BEECH JET 400	2915 km (1811 mi.)
LEARJET 55B	4168 km (2590 mi.)
GULFSTREAM IV	7960 km (4946 mi.)

CAPACITY

The exact seating arrangements aboard a business jet depend on the customer's requirements, but Beech offers the 400A in a standard eight-seat layout. More generous club class seating can be fitted to the 400A by moving the forward door.

BEECH JET 400	8
LEARJET 55B	8
GULFSTREAM IV	10

Executive jets

■ **CHALLENGER 601:** Despite being developed as a regional business jet, many 601s have found their way into military service, such as this Canadian air force example.

■ **CITATION VII:** The main rival to the Beech 400 is the similar-looking Cessna Citation, which has been produced in various marks according to the passenger capacity required.

■ **FALCON 10:** Used as a VIP transport for government officials, Dassault's design has seen widespread service across Europe while also being exported to the United States.

■ **GULFSTREAM III:** The type has proved to be highly capable, and the Danish air force has utilised these executive-style jet airliners for SAR duties and fishery patrols.

BEECHCRAFT

1900

● Best-seller ● Commuter airliner ● Corporate transport

Beech re-entered the commuter and corporate airliner market in 1982, with its new 1900 airliner. Few manufacturers have more experience of building twin-engined, prop-driven transports than the company founded by Walter Beech in Wichita, Kansas, that is now part of the Raytheon Corporation. The Beech 1900 continues to be one of the best performers in the 19-seat category and a healthy order book reflects its popularity.

▲ *While examples of the older Model 1900C and C-1 still soldier on, the Model 1900D has become a favourite of feeder airlines, especially in the US.*

BEECHCRAFT 1900

▼ C-1 freighter
With its windows painted out, this Model 1900C-1 is flown as a freighter. A large cargo door on the port side allows cabin access.

▲ First 1900
Having performed much of the early flight testing, the prototype Model 1900 was retired in 1985.

◀ Beech 'down under'
Owned by Manerst Pty, this Model 1900D is flown by the Sydney Morning Post.

▼ Model 1900 upgrade
Having become an early operator of the Model 1900C, Continental Express later upgraded to the more capable Model 1900D.

◀ Airframe modifications
As the Model 1900C evolved into the 1900D, the aircraft acquired a profusion of additional fins, 'tailets' and horizontal surfaces.

FACTS AND FIGURES

➤ Beech flew the prototype for the Model 1900 series from the company's Wichita plant on 3 September 1982.

➤ The 'wet wing' of the Model 1900C-1 increased fuel capacity by 2593 litres (570 gal.).

➤ Mesa Airlines was the first airline to operate the improved 1900D model with a raised, 'stand-up' fuselage.

➤ Having ordered 78 Model 1900Ds by 1992, Mesa ordered a further 40 in 1994.

➤ In 1996 the Beech 1900D was available at US$4.775 million per aircraft.

PROFILE

Commuting around the world

Below: A combination of winglets and a distinctly taller fuselage serves to differentiate the Model 1900D from all previous variants.

Built initially as the Model 1900C Airliner, the Beech 1900 has been produced in several versions, selling well as a commuter-liner, corporate transport and military utility type. After certification by the US Federal Aviation Administration in November 1983, deliveries of the low-wing, twin-engined Model 1900 began in February 1984, with early orders including six for Resort Air of Missouri.

Changing standards within the US certification system led to production of the Model 1900C halting at 72 in 1993, by which time 173 of the improved Model 1900C-1 with additional fuel had also been sold.

In March 1989 Beech had announced its intention to launch the Model 1900D. This improved aircraft featured modified wings and ventral strakes, as well as a taller fuselage which allowed passengers to stand upright in the cabin. The new aircraft gained certification in March 1991 and was in production before the last of the Model 1900Cs had been delivered. The best selling of the Model 1900Ds is the 19-seat commuter

Above: Lifting off from the Beechcraft factory, this Model 1900D clearly shows the winglets of the type. Mesa Air is the largest 1900D operator.

liner, but an executive or corporate version is also available as a replacement for the Model 1900 Exec-Liner, which was derived from the earlier Model 1900C.

Model 1900D

Type: twin-turboprop commuter airliner

Powerplant: two 954-kW (1,280-hp.) Pratt & Whitney Canada PT6A-67D turboprop engines

Maximum cruising speed: 533 km/h (331 m.p.h.) at 4875 m (16,000 ft.) and 6804 kg (15,000 lb.)

Range: 2778 km (1,726 mi.) at 1525 m (5,000 ft.), at long-range cruise power with reserves and 10 passengers

Service ceiling: 10,058 m (33,000 ft.)

Weights: empty 4815 kg (10,615 lb.); maximum take-off 7688 kg (16,949 lb.)

Accommodation: two pilots on flight deck, maximum of 19 passengers and 939 kg (2070 lb.) of baggage

Dimensions:
span	17.67 m (58 ft.)
length	17.63 m (57 ft. 10 in.)
height	4.72 m (15 ft. 6 in.)
wing area	28.80 m² (310 sq. ft.)

MODEL 1900D

USAir Express is one of many feeder lines which have found the capabilities of the Model 1900 well suited to their operations. Many of these airlines are affiliated to large international carriers.

Passenger seating is arranged in two single rows, to either side of a central aisle. Many airlines fly without a cabin attendant and customers may opt for a range of equipment levels, some of which gain extra space and save weight by omitting the toilet.

A small horizontal surface is mounted on both sides of the fuselage just ahead of the wing leading edge. This acts as a vortex generator, energising air at the leading edge to increase wing efficiency at high angles of attack and low air speeds.

Combined fuel capacity of the wing fuel tanks is 2528 litres (556 gal.). Refuelling is accomplished via a filler point in each wing leading edge, inboard of the engine nacelles. The PT6A-67D engines drive four-bladed Hartzell propellers which are fully reversible.

All Model 1900s have featured small fins known as 'tailets' beneath the tailplanes, but the 1900D introduced the ventral strakes, which improve directional stability and allow the aircraft to operate more comfortably in turbulent conditions.

Fixed auxiliary horizontal tail surfaces attached to the rear fuselage of all Model 1900s increase the aircraft's tolerance to centre of gravity changes. This allows greater flexibility of loading and layout.

ACTION DATA

MAXIMUM CRUISING SPEED

Both of the American-built types have higher cruising speeds than the British Aerospace Jetstream 31. The Jetstream has proved very successful, nonetheless, but does not usually fly longer sectors where high speed is more important.

MODEL 1900D	533 km/h (331 m.p.h.)
METRO 23	542 km/h (337 m.p.h.)
JETSTREAM 31	489 km/h (304 m.p.h.)

MAXIMUM PASSENGERS

With a potential load of up to 19 passengers, the Model 1900D and Jetstream allow airlines the option of offering a good number of seats during busy times or flying economically with fewer passengers. The Fairchild Metro 23 rarely flies with 20 seats.

MODEL 1900D — 19
METRO 23 — 20
JETSTREAM 31 — 19

RANGE

With a full load of 19 passengers and fuel reserves, the Jetstream 31 falls far short of the range offered by the Metro 23. With a typical load of ten passengers the Model 1900D achieves 2778 km (1,726 mi.), but with full load range decreases to 1278 km (794 mi.).

MODEL 1900D 2778 km (1,726 mi.)
JETSTREAM 31 1191 km (740 mi.)
METRO 23 2065 km (1,283 mi.)

Raytheon's modern product range

■ **PC-9 Mk II:** Having won the US Joint Primary Aircraft Training System, the Beech/Pilatus PC-9 will be known as the Texan II.

■ **KING AIR 350:** First flown in 1988, the King Air 350 is a worthy successor to the highly successful King Air 300.

■ **BEECHJET 400A:** Based on the Mitsubishi Diamond, the Beechjet has won huge military orders as the T-1A Jayhawk.

■ **HAWKER 1000:** In 1993 Raytheon bought the 125 design from British Aerospace, producing the type under the Hawker name.

BEECHCRAFT

C99

● Feederliner family ● Widespread US service ● Reliable

Combining 1980s technology with Beechcraft's solid experience of the earlier Model 99 and Model B99, the attractive C99 was manufactured at the Selma, Alabama, division and has performed well for about a dozen airlines, allowing small passenger loads to be flown economically. The C99 has now given way to the newer and more commercially successful Beechcraft 1900, but it continues to provide good service on many air routes.

▲ With the Model 99, Beechcraft established a family of sound basic design. A range of improvements and options was offered but the aircraft was never a huge sales success.

BEECHCRAFT C99

▲ Optional cargo door
This demonstrator has the optional forward-hinged cargo door in front of the standard passenger door with its built-in airstair.

▲ Queen Air heritage
In its original form, the Model 99 showed great similarity to the Queen Air.

▲ Extra power for the C99
In addition to extra power, the C99 incorporated a number of other improvements, including modified undercarriage units and more modern avionics.

▲ Excess baggage
A large, streamlined under-fuselage pannier was offered as a customer option. This allowed the carriage of an additional 362 kg (800 lb.) of baggage or other cargo; normal stowage space is in the nose section and behind the rear seats.

▲ Kansas research
Having originally been delivered to Cal-State Air Lines in 1968, this Model 99 is shown flying with the University of Kansas as a research laboratory.

◄ Big Beech
At the time of its introduction, the Model 99 was the largest aircraft produced by the company.

FACTS AND FIGURES

➤ A total of 77 Model C99s was produced between 1982 and 1986, in addition to 163 other Model 99s previously built.

➤ Test-pilot Jim Dolbee took the Model C99 up for its first flight on 20 June 1980.

➤ The C99 is available with an optional, upward-hinged cargo door.

➤ An optional cargo pod that held 272 kg (600 lb.) of freight or baggage was available for the under-fuselage of the C99.

➤ An early Model 99 was returned to the factory and rebuilt as the C99 prototype.

➤ A movable bulkhead enables the C99 to carry a mixture of cargo and passengers.

Early Beechcraft feederliner

Beechcraft used major components from the highly successful Queen Air executive aircraft as the basis for the C99 airliner and its predecessors in the Model 99 family. Wing planform was very similar to that of the Queen Air, but the fuselage was longer and the Model 99 had turboprop rather than piston powerplants.

The purpose was to achieve a practical, affordable charter and feeder airliner that could efficiently carry small numbers of passengers on short flights to small airfields. Unlike the models

that came before it, the C99 had more than enough power, with 533-kW (715-hp.) engines.

Beechcraft ceased building the original Model 99 series in 1975, re-opening the lines to begin manufacture of the C99 in 1980. Deliveries began in 1981 and the aircraft remained in production for five years, before being superseded by the newer and more advanced Beechcraft 1900.

Unfortunately, although the C99 proved capable and reliable in service, it was never a great seller. It did, however, represent

Above: Sunbird Airlines flew a number of C99s, losing one in a crash in August 1985. The C99 has found most favour with US airlines.

Below: Beechcraft converted an early Model 99 into the C99 prototype during 1980. Although the production lines were re-opened, sales still remained elusive.

a great step-up in aircraft size for Beechcraft, and allowed the company to gain valuable feeder-liner production experience.

C99 Airliner

Type: commuter/cargo transport

Powerplant: two 533-kW (715-hp.), flat-rated Pratt & Whitney Canada PT6A-36 turboprops

Maximum speed: 496 km/h (308 m.p.h.) at 2440 m (8,000 ft.)

Cruising speed: 462 km/h (286 m.p.h.) at 2440 m (8,000 ft.)

Range: 1686 km (1,045 mi.) with maximum fuel

Service ceiling: 7620 m (25,000 ft.)

Weights: basic operating empty 3039 kg (6,686 lb.); maximum take-off 5125 kg (11,275 lb.)

Accommodation: two pilots, flight attendant and 14 or 15 passengers, plus provision for up to 782 kg (1,720 lb.) of cargo or baggage, or up to 1990 kg (4,378 lb.) of cargo without passengers. A movable bulkhead allows any combination of passengers and cargo

Dimensions:
span	13.98 m (45 ft. 10 in.)
length	13.58 m (44 ft. 6 in.)
height	4.37 m (14 ft. 4 in.)
wing area	25.98 m² (280 sq. ft.)

MODEL B99 AIRLINER

This early aircraft was originally retained by Beechcraft and used as a demonstrator. It is fitted with the optional double cabin doors which allow large items of cargo to be loaded into the aircraft.

While single crew operation is possible, it is standard practice for the Model 99 to fly with a flight crew of two. Several avionics options were available, including weather radar.

Standard accommodation is for a maximum of 15 passengers. All passenger seats are removable to allow various combinations of commuters and freight.

All B99 Airliners were delivered with a port-side passenger door which incorporated an integral airstair. The port engine was normally shut down as passengers boarded or left the aircraft, with all systems being run from the starboard engine.

Two doors, one on either side of the nose, serve the forward baggage hold. The optional under-fuselage baggage pod increased capacity greatly, but had little effect on speed.

Unlike the Queen Air to which the Model 99 owed much of its basic design, the latter machine had a fully retracting undercarriage. Some pilots found the aircraft difficult to steer on the ground.

Two Pratt & Whitney PT6A-27 turboprops, each of 507 kW (680 hp.), powered the B99, the same engines fitted to the Model 99A Airliner.

Rubber fuel tanks in the wings give a fuel capacity of 1400 litres (370 gal.). The B99 introduced an additional 435 litres (115 gal.) of fuel capacity in the form of engine nacelle tanks.

From its introduction in 1972, the B99 did not sell well. Over four years, only 14 of the standard airliners were built, although some earlier model 99s and 99As were brought up to the B99 standard to benefit from the type's improved hot-and-high performance.

N4299B

Beech turbine twins

■ **KING AIR C90B:** Basically a turboprop derivative of the Queen Air, the King Air was introduced in 1963. The C90B of 1991 introduced four-bladed propellers.

■ **SUPER KING AIR B200:** With a seating capacity in between those of the King Air and the Model 99, the B200 is highly successful. This aircraft was the 1500th built.

■ **MODEL 1900C:** Superseding the C99 in production, the Model 1900 has met with far greater success. The 1900C is the standard airliner, with seating for 19 passengers.

■ **STARSHIP 2000A:** Constructed mainly of composites, the Starship has not achieved the success it deserves. The 2000A is an improved model, based on the initial production version.

ACTION DATA

CRUISING SPEED

Cruising at a height of 2440 metres, the C99 has a marked speed advantage over the EMBRAER EMB-110P2A. It is slower than the Jetstream 31, an aircraft with significant US orders.

C99	462 km/h (286 m.p.h.)
EMB-110P2A	413 km/h (256 m.p.h.)
J31	488 km/h (303 m.p.h.)

PASSENGERS

Although it is slower than the C99, the EMB-110P2A carries more passengers. Larger loads are required for economical operations. However, on rural connections, lower capacity may be desirable.

C99	15 passengers
EMB-110P2A BANDEIRANTE	21 passengers
J31	19 passengers

RANGE

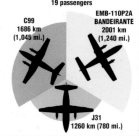

While the J31 has achieved considerable success around the world, it cannot provide the range of the C99 or larger Bandeirante. Each of the aircraft achieves these range figures with a passenger load and reserves. It is significant that both the C99 and J31 are developments of earlier designs.

C99 1686 km (1,045 mi.)

EMB-110P2A BANDEIRANTE 2001 km (1,240 mi.)

J31 1260 km (780 mi.)

BEECHCRAFT

MODEL 18

● Light passenger transport ● Long production run ● Military service

B uilt from the 1930s until the 1960s, the Beechcraft Model 18 was in production longer than any aircraft in the same class. This familiar handyman of the skies is a simple but effective monoplane with two engines, all-metal construction and a cabin for six occupants. The Beechcraft 18 first flew on 15 January 1937 and quickly established itself as a rugged light transport, particularly in Canada where it operated on wheels, floats and skis.

▲ Surprisingly, the Model 18 was not an immediate bestseller. It was the greater capacity and military versions which really launched the machine into worldwide service.

BEECHCRAFT MODEL 18

◀ US Naval service
More than 1500 Model 18s were supplied to the US Navy. Carrying JRB or SNB designations they were equivalent to Army aircraft.

Personnel transport ▶
Known to the US Army as the UC-45, the basic personnel transport and liaison variant was also supplied under Lend-Lease to the UK and Canada.

▼ Kansan
With its gun turret and bomb-bay the AT-11 Kansan was used as a bombing and gunnery trainer.

▼ Model 18D
Powered by Jacobs L-6 engines, the Model 18D was the only successful pre-war variant.

◀ Turbine power
Both Volpar and the Pacific Airmotive Corporation offered lengthened, turboprop-powered conversions based on the Beechcraft 18. Some could carry up to 18 passengers and most had a tricycle undercarriage.

FACTS AND FIGURES

➤ The first Model 18 test pilot, James Peyton, was chosen because of his TWA experience with multi-engine aircraft.

➤ The last of nearly 8,000 Beechcraft 18s were delivered on 26 November 1969.

➤ In the late 1940s, the Model 18 was the world's most popular business aircraft.

➤ A Beechcraft 18 owned by Time magazine flew more than a million kilometres on business assignments.

➤ Turboprop conversions of the Model 18 could carry 15 to 18 passengers.

➤ The first production aircraft was also the first to operate on floats.

PROFILE

Immortal Beechcraft design

Beechcraft created one of aviation's great success stories with its Model 18. Although it looked little different from other aircraft being developed in the 1930s, the Beechcraft 18 captured the hearts and minds of both pilots and operators, and remained in production for a record 32 years.

More recently, the Beechcraft 18 has proven a popular choice for conversion by a number of American companies, with modifications intended to provide improved performance or greater capacity. Many of these updates involved the fitting of turboprop engines and some had major alterations to the airframe and cockpit equipment.

The US Army and the military services of a dozen countries drafted the Model 18 into service during the war years for light transport work, photo-reconnaissance and pilot and navigator training. In US Army service the aircraft was designated the AT-11 Kansan. Often referred to simply as a 'twin Beech', the aircraft was given the name Expeditor by the RAF.

Many pilots who flew this aircraft during the war later piloted it in peacetime. In post-war years, there have been many civil and military versions of this fine aircraft and many hundreds of Beechcraft 18s remain in service around the world.

Left: C-45Fs supplied to Canada became Expeditor IIIs. In the US all C-45 designations changed to UC-45 in January 1945.

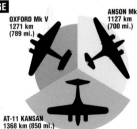

Above: Designed from the outset to operate from optional floats, the Model 18 became very popular in Canada.

Super H18

Type: twin-engine light transport

Powerplant: two 336-kW (450-hp.) Pratt & Whitney R-985-AN-14B radial piston engines

Maximum speed: 375 km/h (233 m.p.h.) at 1370 m (4,495 ft.)

Maximum cruising speed: 354 km/h (220 m.p.h.) at 3050 m (10,000 ft.)

Range: 3060 km (1,900 mi.)

Service ceiling: 6525 m (21,400 ft.)

Weights: empty 2651 kg (5,8854 lb.); maximum take-off 4491 kg (9,900 lb.)

Accommodation: two pilots, plus six to nine passengers

Dimensions: span 15.15 m (49 ft. 8 in.)
length 10.73 m (35 ft. 2 in.)
height 2.84 m (9 ft. 4 in.)
wing area 33.51 m² (361 sq. ft.)

MODEL 18

More than 9000 Model 18s have been built, and several remain in service with third-level airlines worldwide. This Eastern Caribbean Airways aircraft is typical of those still flying with radial engines.

A crew of two is required to fly the Model 18, as the cockpit workload is higher than that of comparable modern designs.

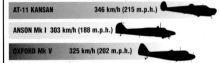

EASTERN CARIBBEAN AIRWAYS

N149L

Twin end-plate fins and rudders were planned for the Model 18 from the outset, even though some have since been converted to a single fin and rudder layout.

Many surviving Model 18s have been continuously modified during their long lives. Non-standard cabin doors, similar to those of the DC-3, have been fitted to this machine.

Pratt & Whitney R-985 Wasp Junior engines have powered almost all production Model 18s, except for a few early aircraft and those converted to turboprop power. The last production aircraft, built in 1969, used the Wasp powerplant.

Beechcraft incorporated an electrically operated retractable undercarriage into the Model 18 design. This advanced feature helped to give the aircraft its high performance and sleek, modern appearance.

The normal seating capacity was for six to seven passengers. A separate compartment to the rear of the cabin accommodates a toilet and baggage compartment. Various cabin configurations have been offered, including a luxury five-seat layout with bar and folding card tables.

Model 18 developments

Many military and civilian models of the Beechcraft Model 18 were built and these are still forming the basis of new conversions.

GUNNERY TRAINER: During World War II 1582 AT-11 Kansans were delivered. Some were armed with twin-gun turrets.

BOMBING TRAINER: A small bomb-bay allowed the AT-11 to carry up to ten 45-kg (100-lb.) bombs. A total of 1582 AT-11s was delivered to the USAF, and some were converted to AT-11A configuration, by the removal of the turret, for navigator training.

FLOATPLANE CONVERSION: One of the most radical and most recent Model 18s is Canada's Vancouver Island Air Seawind. The aircraft first flew in this form in 1994.

COMBAT DATA

MAXIMUM CRUISING SPEED

With its Pratt & Whitney radials, the AT-11 was able to reach 346 km/h even with the drag of its twin-gun dorsal turret. Therefore, the Kansan was able to provide training at speeds close to those of operational aircraft.

AT-11 KANSAN   346 km/h (215 m.p.h.)
ANSON Mk I   303 km/h (188 m.p.h.)
OXFORD Mk V   325 km/h (202 m.p.h.)

MAXIMUM RANGE

Neither of the British aircraft could match the AT-11 for range. The civilian Model 18 had good range for executive and business travel, while the Avro Anson was developed in response to a British short-range airline requirement and the Airspeed Oxford purely as a military trainer.

OXFORD Mk V 1271 km (789 mi.)
ANSON Mk I 1127 km (700 mi.)
AT-11 KANSAN 1368 km (850 mi.)

ARMAMENT

Although the Oxford Mk I could fly as a bombing and gunnery trainer, the majority of those built were multi-engined navigation trainers. The Anson saw active service with RAF Coastal Command.

AT-11 KANSAN   2 x 7.62-mm (.30 cal.) machine-guns 450-kg (990-lb.) bombload

ANSON Mk 1 2 x 7.7-mm (.303 cal.) machine-guns 163-kg (360-lb.) bombload

OXFORD Mk V   none

BEECHCRAFT

STARSHIP 1

● 21st-century executive transport ● Advanced canard design

B eechcraft's Starship 1 cannot show up at any airport in the world without turning heads. This incredibly beautiful aircraft looks as if it comes from another planet, but it has the worldly duty of whisking business executives on important, long-distance trips. The Starship is a bold design, using the latest in lightweight materials to achieve speed and efficiency.

▲ The shape of things to come, or a blind avenue? Beechcraft's Starship is futuristic and a great performer, but it has not sold as well as predicted.

BEECHCRAFT STARSHIP 1

▲ Turning heads
Nothing in the skies looks remotely like the aptly-named Starship 1. The design came from America's futuristic aircraft guru, Burt Rutan.

▲ Tipsails
Lacking a conventional tail, the Starship 1 has rudders on the upturned fins at the end of each wing which enhance flight stability. Beechcraft calls these winglets 'tipsails'.

◀ Creature comforts
For the high-flying executive it's the interior that matters, and the Starship 1 is as plush as any business jet. Leather chairs, drinks bar and washroom facilities are all provided.

▲ Glass cockpit
For the pilots, the Starship 1 cockpit is as modern as the configuration. All data is presented on TV-style screens.

Canard cruiser ▶
Starship 1 has very competitive performance figures thanks to its state-of-the-art aerodynamics and fuel-efficient turboprops.

FACTS AND FIGURES

➤ Beechcraft are now offering their remaining Starships to military customers for use as special missions aircraft.

➤ Beech was known for conservative design until it created the trend-setting Starship 1.

➤ Most Starships are in the USA, but there is one based in Britain and one in Denmark.

➤ The Starship 2000Z model has improved performance and can cross the Atlantic non-stop.

➤ An 85-per-cent-sized prototype Starship was flown by Burt Rutan in August 1983.

➤ The first production Starship 1 was flown by Beechcraft in 1989.

PROFILE

A voyage into tomorrow

In 1983, a bold new aircraft for executive travel was launched when a small prototype of the Beech Starship 1 took to the air. No aircraft like it had been seen before. With its sword-like wing, pusher engines, and canard wings up front, the Starship looks and acts like a rocket ship.

On the inside, the Starship 1 is all space-age technology. Instead of standard metal construction techniques, the Starship 1 uses ultra-light composite and honeycomb materials. These are deceptively strong, but their light weight plays a major part in this futuristic craft's amazing performance.

The first Starship 1 went into service in 1992, giving business users the ultimate power trip with its 21st-century performance. Beech fabricated 53 of these wonderful aircraft, but found the Starship 1 ahead of its time. Seen as too daring and too impertinent by stuffed shirts in the traditional world of business, the Starship 1 is serving valiantly in the hands of a few forward-thinking users, but has now gone out of production.

Putting the engines at the back of the Starship 1 increases their effectiveness, and also makes the cabin very quiet.

The 'pusher' configuration with engines mounted well to the rear means that the passenger compartment is far enough forward to significantly reduce noise in the cabin.

The Starship is powered by two Pratt & Whitney Canada PT6 turboprops. These are mounted close together to reduce yaw in the event that one engine should fail.

Starship 1

Type: eight-passenger fast business aircraft

Powerplant: two 895-kW (1200-hp.) Pratt & Whitney PT6-67A turboprop pusher engines driving McCauley five-bladed propellers

Maximum cruising speed: 621 km/h (386 m.p.h.) at 6700 m (21,982 ft.); economical cruise 546 km/h (339 m.p.h.) at 10,000 m (32,800 ft.)

Range: 2657 km (1,651 mi.) at economy cruise power; 2570 km (1,597 mi.) at maximum cruise

Service ceiling: 10,605 m (34,793 ft.)

Weights: empty 4574 kg (10,084 lb.); max take-off 6577 kg (14,500 lb.)

Accommodation: two crew (but operable by a single pilot) and seven/eight passengers

Dimensions:
span	16.58 m	(54 ft. 5 in.)
length	14.05 m	(46 ft. 1 in.)
height	3.96 m	(13 ft.)
wing area	26.09 m²	(281 sq. ft.)

STARSHIP 1

Designed to be the shape of private commercial aviation for the 21st century, the Beech Starship 1 is a bold step into the forefront of aviation technology.

In keeping with its futuristic design, the Starship has an 'all-glass' cockpit with 12 full colour and two monochrome display screens taking the place of conventional instruments.

The Starship's cabin is 5 m (16 ft. 5 in.) long, 1.68 m (5 ft. 6 in.) wide and 1.61 m (5 ft. 3 in.) high. Luxuriously equipped with reclining seats, it can accommodate eight passengers.

Since the Starship has no conventional tailfin, directional control is provided by fins called 'tipsails' mounted on the wingtips. These are both fitted with rudders.

N8244L

All Starships are equipped with a weather avoidance radar in the nose.

The Starship's foreplanes are of variable geometry, sweeping forward 4° at low speeds and back 30° in high-speed cruise.

The single door at the forward end of the passenger compartment incorporates a built-in air stair.

The wing is composed of a sandwich of Nomex honeycomb, graphite epoxy and glass-reinforced plastic, with main spars of similar material bonded to the upper and lower skins. Aluminium is only used to mount the landing gear and the tipsails.

ACTION DATA

ACCOMMODATION

Two crew and six passengers — **LEARJET 36**

Two crew and eight passengers — **STARSHIP 1**

Two crew and nine passengers — **P.180 AVANTI**

Executive aircraft have varying capacities. Most can be flown by one pilot, but almost invariably have a two-crew cockpit. Passenger capacity varies, but eight to 10 is about average.

RANGE

Most modern executive jets are designed to make long trans-continental flights, allowing busy executives to fly from New York to Chicago or from London to Rome non-stop. Perhaps the Starship's lack of range affected the sales figures, which were disappointing.

P.180 AVANTI 3187 km (1,980 mi.)
LEARJET 36 4600 km (2,858 mi.)
STARSHIP 1 2657 km (1,651 mi.)

MAXIMUM SPEED

LEARJET 36	870 km/h (541 m.p.h.)
STARSHIP 1	621 km/h (386 m.p.h.)
P.180	500 km/h (311 m.p.h.)

The Starship's advanced design enables it to perform as well as a jet but with all the economy of a propeller-driven machine. True jets like the Learjet are faster, but cost much more to run.

The swinging 'moustache'

Part of the highly advanced aerodynamics of the Starship is the canard foreplane, which moves to compensate for aerodynamic changes during different phases of the flight. Made from advanced composite materials, the foreplane is very strong and unlike metal will not corrode.

◄ **CRUISE CONFIGURATION**
In normal cruising flight the Starship has its canard foreplanes swept back at 30°. The sweepback is highly efficient for high-speed flight, and the amount of lift provided by the foreplanes balances that provided by the main wings. When in cruise mode vortex generators increase airflow over the elevators on the foreplane giving more positive control.

◄ **LOW-SPEED CONFIGURATION**
At low speed, the Starship uses flaps on the main wings to increase the amount of lift. These also increase the overall wing area by extending out from the wing. This upsets the delicate balance of the aircraft, so the canard foreplanes swing to 4° of forward sweep to provide extra lift themselves, thereby restoring the balance.

BELL

206 JETRANGER

● Light turboshaft helicopter ● Multi-role civil and military variants

The Bell 206 JetRanger is one of the world's most popular helicopters. Manufactured by Bell in Canada and Agusta in Italy, this civil servant began as a military observation craft but has become a real champion of air commerce. For law enforcement, executive travel, crop spraying and countless other duties, it is one of the best aircraft in its class – a versatile and economical helicopter which is simple to operate and enjoyable to fly.

▲ *The JetRanger is one of the most successful helicopters ever built. Combining simplicity and low operating costs, it has almost completely dominated the small helicopter market.*

BELL 206 JETRANGER

▲ Agile but simple to fly
The JetRanger is agile enough to be used by display teams at air shows. The ease with which it can be flown means that it also makes a good helicopter trainer, both on land and at sea.

▲ Kiowa warrior
Known to the US Army as the OH-58 Kiowa, the latest armed versions of the Model 206 have four-bladed rotors and an anti-glare cockpit, and can carry Hellfire missiles and a mast-mounted sight.

▲ All-rounder
The 206 has performed most light helicopter tasks, but it is often used as an air taxi, typically flying businessmen to and from airports.

▲ Crop sprayer
With a tank and spray bar slung from a cargo hook, the JetRanger can fly crop-spraying missions with notable precision.

Air ambulance ▶
JetRangers have found a ready market as ambulance aircraft, being able to get casualties to hospital in minutes.

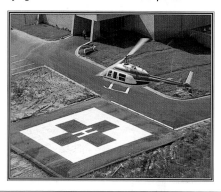

FACTS AND FIGURES

➤ The 1,394 JetRangers and 599 LongRangers on register make up 15 per cent of the US civil helicopter fleet.

➤ Full certification of the Model 206A occurred on 20 October 1966.

➤ The current 206B JetRanger III is built at Bell's facility in Mirabel, Canada.

➤ The normal interior of the JetRanger provides comfortable accommodation for five passengers.

➤ According to Bell figures, the 206 is the world's safest helicopter.

➤ US military trainer versions are the Navy TH-57 and Army TH-67.

PROFILE

Ranging the world with the Bell 206

The Bell 206 series – comprising the JetRanger and its longer, more powerful brother, the 206L LongRanger – virtually created the modern light helicopter market in North America, and have become familiar sights around the world. Bell 206s are seen everywhere, doing everything from ferrying VIPs to swanky race meetings to mounting fire-watching patrols over remote forests.

The 206 originated in Bell's unsuccessful 1964 bid for a US Army light observation helicopter contract. Although the majority of the 7,000 helicopters delivered by Bell have been for military use, well over 2,300 have been sold to civil operators, along with many of the 1,000 aircraft built by Agusta.

Commercial owners like the JetRanger's flexibility and low operating costs. Pilots speak well of its roominess, ease of handling and excellent visibility.

One image which represents what the Bell 206 is all about is that of a US Park Service LongRanger crew rescuing victims from Washington's icy Potomac River in the aftermath of the crash of Air Florida Flight 90 in January 1982.

Left: JetRangers can be used for air ambulance and rescue work. This US Park Police example was first on the scene at the Potomac River air crash of January 1982, which took place in the heart of Washington.

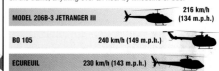

Above: JetRangers are often used by American TV stations to transport reporters to incidents quickly.

Model 206B-3 JetRanger III

Type: light general-purpose helicopter

Powerplant: one 313-kW (420-hp.) Allison 250-C20J turboshaft, flat-rated to 236 kW (316 hp.)

Maximum cruise speed: 216 km/h at 1525 m (134 m.p.h. at 5,000 ft.)

Range: 730 km (450 mi.) with maximum fuel

Service ceiling: 4115 m (13,500 ft.)

Weights: empty 737 kg (1,620 lb.); loaded 1520 kg (3,345 lb.) with external load

Accommodation: one or two pilots, three passengers; provision for medical attendant, litter, and up to 600 kg (1,320 lb.) of ambulance equipment; interior cabin of 2.35 m³ (83 cu. ft.)

Dimensions:
main rotor diameter	10.16 m (33 ft. 4 in.)
length (rotor turning)	11.82 m (38 ft. 9 in.)
height	2.91 m (9 ft. 6 in.)
rotor area	81.10 m² (873 sq. ft.)

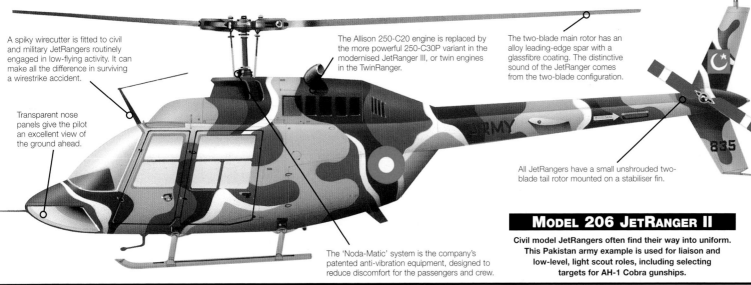

A spiky wirecutter is fitted to civil and military JetRangers routinely engaged in low-flying activity. It can make all the difference in surviving a wirestrike accident.

Transparent nose panels give the pilot an excellent view of the ground ahead.

The Allison 250-C20 engine is replaced by the more powerful 250-C30P variant in the modernised JetRanger III, or twin engines in the TwinRanger.

The two-blade main rotor has an alloy leading-edge spar with a glassfibre coating. The distinctive sound of the JetRanger comes from the two-blade configuration.

All JetRangers have a small unshrouded two-blade tail rotor mounted on a stabiliser fin.

The 'Noda-Matic' system is the company's patented anti-vibration equipment, designed to reduce discomfort for the passengers and crew.

MODEL 206 JetRanger II

Civil model JetRangers often find their way into uniform. This Pakistan army example is used for liaison and low-level, light scout roles, including selecting targets for AH-1 Cobra gunships.

ACTION DATA

MAXIMUM CRUISING SPEED

Light helicopters are not particularly fast by aviation standards, but for short journeys, typically from a city centre heliport to an airport about 50 km (30 miles) distant, they are the fastest means of travel. A journey which takes 10 minutes by JetRanger in those circumstances might take half an hour by train and, depending on the traffic, anything over an hour by limousine or bus.

MODEL 206B-3 JETRANGER III	216 km/h (134 m.p.h.)
BO 105	240 km/h (149 m.p.h.)
ECUREUIL	230 km/h (143 m.p.h.)

RANGE

Helicopters are not the most efficient of aircraft. They tend to use fuel much faster than a conventional aeroplane of similar size, and their range is generally shorter. But although fixed-wing aircraft might be more economical, they cannot put down in a city street to pick up a casualty, or make a rescue from a boat at sea, or land in a forest clearing to check for a possible fire.

BO 105 600 km (370 mi.)
MODEL 206B-3 JETRANGER III 730 km (450 mi.)
ECUREUIL 730 km (450 mi.)

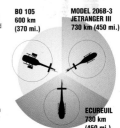

SERVICE CEILING

Since helicopters are most often used for short hops, they rarely need to climb very high. They can reach greatest altitudes in forward flight; in hovering flight their ceiling is much lower. The JetRanger is notable for the fact that its hovering ceiling, using the upwards wash of air known as ground effect, is only 200 m (660 ft.) less than its service ceiling.

ECUREUIL 4800 m (15,750 ft.)
MODEL 206B-3 JETRANGER III 4115 m (13,500 ft.)
BO 105 3050 m (10,100 ft.)

Evolution of the JetRanger

■ **MODEL 206A:** Built as a losing submission for a 1962 US Army observation helicopter contest, the original civil JetRanger flew in 1966 and was an immediate success.

■ **OH-58 KIOWA:** In 1967, the US Army ordered a modified Bell 206 to replace the Hughes OH-6, which won the original competition but proved costly and slow to produce.

■ **LONGRANGER:** Deliveries of the stretched LongRanger began in 1975. Currently built in Canada and Italy, it shares the more powerful engine of the latest JetRanger III.

■ **TWINRANGER:** The latest version of the Model 206 has twin engines. The greater power is expected to give improved payload and range, as well as increased safety.

■ **MODEL 406:** Developed for the US Army as the OH-58D, the Model 406 has a more powerful engine and a four-bladed main rotor, and can carry advanced avionics and missiles.

BELL 206

JETRANGER POLICE

● Airborne crime fighter ● Highway patrol ● Police chase

▲ Criminals no longer have anywhere to hide thanks to the heliborne camera. Here, a JetRanger lifts off to answer a request for assistance from a police patrol on the ground.

Orbiting high over every major American city are the 'eyes in the sky' of the police. The Bell 206 JetRangers, equipped with high-powered cameras, are a vital tool in the fight against crime. Recognising the success of the JetRanger in this role, numerous European police forces have adopted the helicopter for a wide range of duties. They include traffic control, rescue work and searches – all in the service of the public.

BELL 206 JETRANGER POLICE

▼ Beach observer
Keeping a watchful eye on bathing holiday-makers is a JetRanger operated by the New York Police Department. A number of American forces use Bell's JetRanger helicopter.

▲ Eye in the sky
Equipped with a powerful camera, the JetRanger can record activities for the police or TV stations.

◄ European police
Proudly displaying police titles on its fuselage, this Swedish JetRanger starts another patrol.

▼ Highway patrol
The California Highway Patrol is tasked with patrolling the extensive freeways of the state.

◄ Proven design
Operating over city skylines, the Bell JetRanger has proved to be an extremely reliable tool in the fight against crime.

FACTS AND FIGURES

➤ The prototype JetRanger first flew in December 1962. It was originally designed for a military role.

➤ Despite not winning the military contract, many civilian orders were received.

➤ Known as the Model 206, the JetRanger proved an instant sales success.

➤ American law enforcement agencies use the type for observation, traffic control and border patrols.

➤ More than 4,400 examples of the Model 206B were constructed.

➤ JetRangers are also built under licence by Agusta in Italy.

PROFILE

The 'bear in the air'

A police chase ends in a darkened alley; the culprit has escaped the pursuing police officers, and has concealed himself in the nearby woods. A few years ago similar situations often resulted in failure for the police, but now, having surrounded the immediate area, they can ask for airborne assistance.

Within minutes a police helicopter is circling overhead; using a sophisticated infra-red camera, it can detect the suspect through his own body heat. The

pilot directs officers to the location, concluding in an arrest.

Despite failing to win the military contract for which it was designed, the JetRanger has gone on to become one of the most successful civilian helicopters of all time. Gradual upgrades of equipment have allowed police operations to take place at any time of day, in all weathers, leaving criminals little choice but to surrender to the police when they are tracked down.

In a more peaceful guise, airborne patrols are made along

Above: A police helicopter prepares to search for suspects. It is equipped with a powerful searchlight for night-time missions.

America's super-highways as police forces keep an eye on traffic problems.

Despite having been in service for nearly 20 years, the JetRanger will remain the US airborne police officer for years to come.

Below: Orbiting high over a city, the Bell JetRanger allows the police to extend their reach in the fight against crime.

206B Jet Ranger III

Type: general-purpose light utility helicopter

Powerplant: one 313-kW (420-hp.) Allison 250-C20B turboshaft engine

Max speed: 225 km/h (140 m.p.h.) at sea level

Cruising speed: 214 km/h (133 m.p.h.)

Range: 579 km (359 mi.) with maximum load

Hover ceiling: 3870 m (12,700 ft.)

Weights: empty 660 kg (1,452 lb.); maximum take-off 1451 kg (3,192 lb.)

Accommodation: one pilot; three passengers

Dimensions:
span	1.88 m (6 ft. 2 in.)
length	9.50 m (31 ft. 2 in.)
height	2.91 m (9 ft. 6 in.)
main rotor disc area	81.10 m² (873 sq. ft.)

POLICE PATROL

EUROPEAN POLICE: Developed by the European company Aérospatiale, the Ecureuil (pictured below) has been adopted by both military and police organisations. Proving to be a highly capable law enforcement helicopter, it has been successfully used on anti-drug operations throughout Europe.

BRITISH OPERATIONS: Despite the initial cost of acquiring a sophisticated helicopter, the British police have adopted a procedure in which several forces use one machine. An example of this is the MBB 105 (pictured below), which is used by the Devon and Cornwall police force but can also be operated by neighbouring constabularies.

One of the key attributes of the JetRanger for police service was the excellent visibility afforded to the crew.

Most police pilots are ex-patrol officers who have requested training for airborne duty. Missions are often flown with an observer who controls the operation and radios.

A single Allison turboshaft engine powers the JetRanger. Police versions are equipped with an improved engine to allow for the additional weight of equipment associated with their mission.

Many police helicopters have been fitted with the powerful Nitesun searchlight, which can produce a beam of over 1 million candlepower.

POLICE

N203FC

Most police helicopters are fitted with a skid undercarriage. If required, the JetRanger can be modified to carry large floats to undertake operations from water.

206A JetRanger

Having proved to be an extremely capable tool in the fight against crime, the JetRanger is operated across America by a host of police forces. This example flies with the Virginian state police.

Airborne officers

TRAFFIC COP: In the event of car crash, police helicopters are used to monitor the subsequent traffic congestion and send reports to the ground units.

NIGHT PATROL: Criminals no longer have the cover of night to hide their activities, because of the adoption of helicopters with a large searchlight on the nose.

ICE RESCUE: In January 1982 a Boeing 737 crashed into the frozen Potomac River. In a desperate bid to rescue the shocked survivors, a police JetRanger actually submerged its skids in the water.

BELL 206

JETRANGER TAXI

● Top-selling helicopter ● Comfort and refinement ● Thousands sold

One of the world's most popular helicopters, the Bell 206 started life as a loser. Designed to meet a US Army requirement for a utility helicopter in the early 1960s, it was beaten by the Hughes OH-6. When fitted with a bigger, more streamlined fuselage to become the JetRanger, however, the 206 was an immediate success in the civil market. Still in production after 30 years and with more than 4,000 in service, it is one of the mainstays of the air taxi business.

▲ With its comfortable seating, excellent baggage capacity and enviable safety record, the JetRanger continues to be an international sales success.

BELL 206 JETRANGER TAXI

JetRanger II in Canada ▶
Three major variants of the 206B have been produced. These Canadian-registered machines are examples of the JetRanger II.

▼ European air taxi
This JetRanger is painted in one of the smart colour schemes often worn by charter company aircraft. The machine carries a German registration.

▼ Bell in the city
Demonstrating the helicopter's unique ability to operate over cities from the smallest of helipads, this JetRanger flies past London's Big Ben. The helicopter is ideal for transporting personnel to inner-city areas and avoids the problems associated with the road.

▲ Luxury interior
Customers may specify individual requirements. This JetRanger is a luxury version.

Versatile taxi▶
With its skid undercarriage the JetRanger has the versatility to operate from a variety of surfaces. Ground handling can be difficult however, and some aircraft are fitted with auxiliary wheels.

FACTS AND FIGURES

➤ Although it lost to the Hughes OH-6 in the US Army competition, Bell later sold 2,200 JetRangers to the service.

➤ Bell delivered the first Model 206B JetRanger in 1966.

➤ All JetRangers are now built in Canada by Bell Helicopter Textron Canada.

➤ Between 5 August 1982 and 22 July 1983 Dick Smith piloted a JetRanger III around the world, flying 56,742 km (35,180 miles) in 320 hours.

➤ Bell introduced the JetRanger II in 1971 and the JetRanger III in 1977.

➤ Over 7,000 JetRangers have been built.

PROFILE

Bell's flying taxi cab

As an air taxi the JetRanger has many attractions. When it first became available perhaps the most important were its comparatively low levels of noise and vibration. The engine and other mechanical components are fitted on top of the fuselage, keeping the main sources of noise away from the passenger cabin.

The 206 is also safe. One reason for this is that the energy stored in the two heavy rotor blades makes autorotation easy in the event of engine failure. Statistically, JetRangers have suffered fewer accidents than any other single-engined aircraft, either fixed- or rotary-winged.

For the air taxi pilot, no two days are the same. A typical day might include ferrying businessmen to meetings or celebrities to parties, delivering urgent packages or providing the platform for aerial photography. One factor that these tasks have in common is that they all benefit from the unique

versatility of the helicopter, as exemplified by the JetRanger.

Although usually made from airports, flights could be from a hospital roof or the grounds of a country hotel. Wherever it is, the chances are that if a helicopter can land there, then a JetRanger has.

Left: Passenger-friendly features of the JetRanger include wide cabin access doors and steps fitted to the skid undercarriage struts.

Below: As one of the world's most significant helicopter operators, Bristow uses the JetRanger as an air taxi, trainer and utility aircraft.

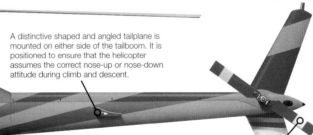

Bell used its tried and tested twin-bladed rotor layout for the JetRanger, keeping rotorhead complexity to a minimum. The main rotor blades are constructed entirely of aluminium.

A 313-kW (420-hp.) Allison 250-C20B powers the JetRanger III. The engine is flat-rated to 236 kW (316 hp.) to maximise engine life.

In normal operations the aircraft is flown by the pilot from the right seat. Dual controls may be fitted as an option, and with a co-pilot in the left-hand seat this reduces passenger capacity to four.

A distinctive shaped and angled tailplane is mounted on either side of the tailboom. It is positioned to ensure that the helicopter assumes the correct nose-up or nose-down attitude during climb and descent.

Up to 113 kg (250 lb.) of baggage may be stowed behind the rear bench seat. This door provides access to the baggage compartment, while passengers enter the main cabin by large doors on either side of the fuselage.

Flight control is by hydraulically-actuated, powered collective and cyclic controls. The tail rotor is controlled by the pilot's foot. Optional equipment includes an autostabiliser, autopilot and instrument flying equipment.

G-BPIE / CABAIR

206B JETRANGER III

This JetRanger is seen in the colours of Cabair, based in the UK. Painted in this colourful blue and white scheme, it flies air taxi services and general charters.

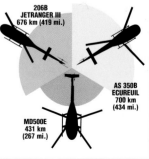
JetRanger civilian operations

■ **OFFSHORE SUPPORT:** Unusually for a single-engined helicopter, some JetRangers are used for rig support flying. The aircraft in the foreground is a 206L LongRanger, a seven-seat development which has a longer cabin.

■ **CROP SPRAYING:** The versatility and load-carrying capabilities of the JetRanger are shown to advantage by its use in the crop-spraying role. Its reliability, economical operating costs and comparative lack of complexity make it ideal for the job.

■ **FIRE-FIGHTING:** Many helicopters have been adapted to the fire-bombing role. While the JetRanger's lifting capacity may be marginal for such duties, it is a useful secondary capability for aircraft serving with police or para-military forces.

BELL

206 JETRANGER RECORD BREAKER

● Solo flights ● Around the world ● Epic journey

Seven men have flown a total of five helicopters in round-the-world record-breaking flights. The first three flights were made in Bell Model 206s – two JetRangers and a 206L LongRanger – and each set a new record. Perhaps the most remarkable was that of Dick Smith, whose 56,740-km (35,257-mile) flight was a solo effort. Ross Perot Jr, who set the first record, had a C-130 for navigation, communications and logistic support, while Ron Bower had GPS navigation to help him beat Perot's record.

▲ Record-breaking pilots stand in front of a Bell JetRanger. This highly successful helicopter has been used for a number of record-breaking flights around the world.

BELL 206 JETRANGER RECORD BREAKER

▼ Colourful example
Having flown around the world in 1994, this Bell 206B-3 is now used by a helicopter training school, to teach the fine art of helicopter flying to new pilots.

▲ Reliable design
Bell has continued to improve the JetRanger, and a number of pilots have achieved fame after accomplishing long-distance flights in the type.

Spirit of Texas ▶
Owned and operated by Ross Perot Jr and Jay Coburn, the Spirit of Texas was used to accomplish the record in 1982, after which it was donated to a museum.

▼ Best seller
The qualities that the JetRanger family showed in their record breaking flights were reflected in the high sales figures the type gained.

▲ Setting off
Crowds cheer and wave as Dick Smith takes off on his record attempt from Fort Worth on 5 August 1982. Ahead lay long solo flights across the world's oceans and deserts that would test both pilot and helicopter to the limit.

FACTS AND FIGURES

➤ Like the Boeing 747, the Bell Model 206B JetRanger is one of the most recognised aircraft in the world.

➤ Ron Bower began his flight on 28 June 1984 from Fort Worth, Texas.

➤ Ross Perot Jr is the youngest son of the Texas oil billionaire.

➤ At the end of a round-the-world flight, a total of at least 37,966 km (23,540 miles) must have been flown.

➤ Pilots maintain that the record can be accomplished in 200 flying hours.

➤ Pilots usually aim to complete the flight in just 28 days.

PROFILE

Around the world in a helicopter

In August 1982, Australian Dick Smith flew solo in a JetRanger III. He was followed by Texans Ross Perot Jr and Jay Coburn in a LongRanger II.

Perot and Coburn completed their flight in 29 days, three hours and eight minutes, to set the first record with an average speed of around 57 km/h (35 m.p.h.). Dick Smith postponed the second half of his journey until the following year, though his total time of 10 months was still a record because his was the first solo flight.

Perot's record stood for 12 years until Ron Bower took up the challenge. Setting off from Bell's factory near Houston, Texas in a brand new 206B-3 JetRanger, he completed the planned 38000-km trip in 24 days, four hours and 36 minutes at an average speed of nearly 65.5 km/h (41 m.p.h.). The total flight time was 229.22 hours, giving an average flying speed of nearly 166 km/h (103 m.p.h.) for the official distance, although Bower actually covered more than 40000 km (24,800 miles).

In 1996 Bower broke his own record in a Model 430, with Bell test pilot John Williams.

In 1997 Mike Smith and Steve Good took the record from Bower flying around the world in their McDD Model 500D in a mere 13 days.

Above: Dick Smith comes in to land in front of cheering and waving crowds, having completed his round-the-world flight on 22 July 1983.

Below: During his record-breaking flight Ross Perot Jr had to obtain his fuel in some extremely isolated and desolate locations.

260B JetRanger

Inspired by the aviators of a bygone era, Dick Smith embarked on long solo flights across the world's oceans and deserts. Equipped with the latest advances in aviation, he still faced many dangers.

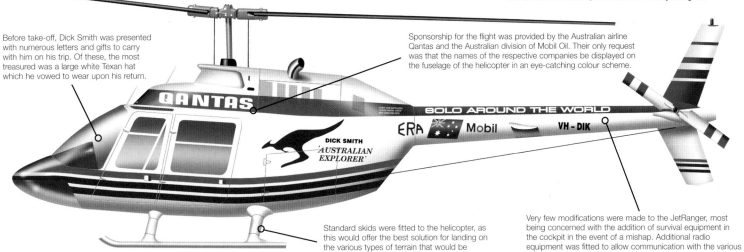

Before take-off, Dick Smith was presented with numerous letters and gifts to carry with him on his trip. Of these, the most treasured was a large white Texan hat which he vowed to wear upon his return.

Sponsorship for the flight was provided by the Australian airline Qantas and the Australian division of Mobil Oil. Their only request was that the names of the respective companies be displayed on the fuselage of the helicopter in an eye-catching colour scheme.

Standard skids were fitted to the helicopter, as this would offer the best solution for landing on the various types of terrain that would be encountered, including ice-floes.

Very few modifications were made to the JetRanger, most being concerned with the addition of survival equipment in the cockpit in the event of a mishap. Additional radio equipment was fitted to allow communication with the various air-traffic control networks that would be encountered.

AVIATION PIONEERS

THE FIRST SOLO FLIGHT from England to Australia was the achievement of Sqn Ldr 'Bert' Hinkler in his Avro 581 Avian light aircraft prototype G-EBOV, as seen below. Flying from Croydon to Darwin, he covered the 17711 km (11,000 miles) via such destinations as Karachi and Singapore. After this flight, the aircraft was placed on display in the Brisbane Museum.

Amy Johnson in her de Havilland 60 named *Jason*, similar to that pictured below, set out for the same destination as 'Bert' Hinkler in an effort to equal his record.

Following this flight was Capt. P. G. Taylor in his Lockheed Altair, called *Lady Southern Cross* (the aircraft pictured below). He was the first to fly between Australia and the United States, in October 1934, leaving from Brisbane and landing in California. He completed the trip on 4 November, after staging through Fiji and Hawaii.

Ron Bower's World Tour

1 TUESDAY MORNING: On 28 June 1994, Ron Bower, Vice-President for Helicopter Marketing at Austin Jet International, took off from Bell's Helicopter plant in Fort Worth, Texas.

2 THE PURPOSE: To set a round-the-world speed record for a solo helicopter pilot. Covering more than 37966 km (24,800 miles) and stopping at 21 capital cities, the helicopter used no specialised ground crews or advance teams in the course of the trip.

3 ON HIS OWN: Bell's Customer Service Facilities located throughout the world provided the only assistance. The trip was completed without any major problems, a testimony to the capabilities of the JetRanger.

Anchorage · Seattle · Fort Worth · Washington · Lisbon · Madrid · London · Berlin · Kazan · Moscow · Bratsk · Yukutsk

BELL

214ST

● Oil rig support ● Military transport ● Gulf War gunship

O riginally intended as a military transport for Iran, the Bell 214ST contract was put in jeopardy with the advent of the Islamic revolution in 1979. Only 100 of these helicopters were built. Although the majority found military customers in utility and support roles, a few ended up in oil rig support. Since then, the 14ST has been replaced by more modern Bell designs and the type is now a rare sight.

▲ Often working
alongside other Bell designs, a handful of Bell 214STs were used by British Caledonian helicopters in the North Sea, transporting oil rig workers.

BELL 214ST

'Huey' heritage ▶
Despite the extensive modifications from the standard Bell 214, the 214ST still has a large twin-blade rotor and twin-blade tail rotor.

▲ Desert colours
Eventually, the 214ST arrived in the Middle East as a gunship, albeit in the hands of Iran's enemy, Iraq.

▲ High capacity
The long stretched cabin of the 214 allowed it to carry 18 passengers on three long bench seats.

▲ Thai navy
Thailand's navy operates five 214STs, and the air force and army operate two each.

Civil colours▶
Painted a distinctive colour, this experimental Bell 214ST carried out testing flights to oil rigs.

FACTS AND FIGURES

➤ Originally, ST stood for Stretched Twin, but was subsequently changed to mean Super Transport.

➤ Oman, Peru und Venezuela all operate three Bell 214STs.

➤ Between 1987 and 1988, Iraq bought 45 Bell 214STs and used them in combat.

➤ The original requirement for Iran was improved hot-and-high performance over the older Bell 214.

➤ The composite rotor blades of the 214ST are wider than the standard Bell 214.

➤ The last of the 100 214STs was produced in 1990; the first was built in 1980.

PROFILE

Biggest of the Bell twins

In the 1970s, the Imperial Iranian armed forces were shopping for new equipment, with a great deal of money. Impressed by the United States Air Cavalry's performance in Vietnam, the air force ordered an upgraded Bell 214.

Bell proposed a substantially improved machine, the 214ST, with increased capacity and power, twin engines and vastly improved hot-and-high performance. The project, worth $575 million to Bell, was suddenly cancelled when the

nation's Islamic revolution occurred in 1979. Bell continued development, and began production in November of that year, hoping for sales to civilian operators as well as other military users.

Luckily for Bell, the 214ST was a success, and despite a modest production run, it was popular with users. Ironically, the largest single user was Iran's mortal enemy in the 1980s, Iraq, which took 45 aircraft in 1987 and recconfigured them as gunships and operated them

alongside Soviet-built Mi-24s.

A few were sold to civil operators, especially for oil rig support where the type's single-engine flight capability was paramount. In 1982 the FAA approved an upgrade capacity to 18 passengers to enhance the appeal of the 214ST to civil users; it has had limited sales.

Left: The North Sea is home to a wide variety of helicopters, including Chinooks, Bell 212s, Pumas and Super Pumas, MBB 105s, Sikorsky S-61s and a few 214STs.

Below: Examples of the 214ST with wheeled undercarriage are extremely rare, but some were sold to China.

214ST

The Fuerza Aérea Venezolana operated three Bell 214STs in the communications role, serving with 42 Escuadrón. Venezuela also operates the Bell 212 and Bell 412 in the VIP transport role.

214ST

Type: medium utility helicopter

Powerplant: two General Electric CT7-2 turboshafts rated at 1212 kW (1,625 hp.) each

Max cruise speed: 259 km/h (161 m.p.h.)

Hover ceiling: 1950 m (6,400 ft.)

Initial climb rate: 543 m/min (1,780 f.p.m.)

Combat radius: 858 km (530 mi.) with standard fuel

Ferry range: 1019 km (630 mi.)

Weight: empty 4284 kg (9,425 lb.); loaded 7938 kg (17,465 lb.)

Dimensions:
Rotor diameter	15.85 m (52 ft.)
Length	18.95 m (62 ft. 2 in.)
Height	4.84 m (15 ft. 10 in.)
Wing area	197.29 m² (2,123 sq. ft.)

Bell used a new rotor suspension system known as Noda-Matic nodal suspension for the rotors. The nodal beam reqires no lubrication. The avanced rotor blades have a glass-fibre spar as well as the more useful glass-fibre coating.

Pilot and co-pilot have full controls. Both crew doors are jettisonable. Avionics can include radar, VLF navigation system, ADF, DME and nav coupling

The main transmission has a one-hour run-dry capability, so the aircraft can still operate safely in the event of loss of lubricant. The twin turboshaft engines are coupled through a combiner gearbox. Single-engine operation is also possible.

FAV 214

FUERZA AEREA VENEZOLANA

Emergency flotation gear can be fitted to the undercarriage. Pop-out life rafts can be installed in the fairing under the rotor mast.

Additional baggage can be stored behind the passenger compartment. The seats can be removed to provide additional cargo space. A special roll-over protection ring is installed in the fuselage structure.

The tail rotor is a conventional design with steel leading edge, honeycomb core and glass-fibre trailing edge. The electronically controlled elevator minimizes trim changes with alternations of power or centre of gravity, and improves stability.

ACTION DATA

TAKE-OFF WEIGHT

The demand for a larger helicopter was not lost on Bell and development of the proven 212 was undertaken. The resulting Bell 214 ST differed little in comparison to the earlier models, but offered a take-off weigt that was significantly greater.

214B	214ST	212
7257 kg (17,465 lb.)	7938 kg (15,965 lb.)	5080 kg (11,176 lb.)

FUEL CAPACITY

Intended to operate over vast stretches of ocean with various petroleum companies, the fuel capacity of the 214ST is of vital importance. Although equal to the 212, the twin-engine design of the 214ST improves safety.

214B	3175 kg (7,685 lb.)
214ST	3493 kg (6,985 lb.)
212	2268 kg (4,990 lb.)

SPEED

Despite the increase in weight due to the larger cabin area and additional engine, the cruising speed is equal to the earlier and lighter Bell 212. Developments in the helicopter series have enabled Bell to meet the increasing demands of the civilian helicopter market.

214B	259 km/h (161 m.p.h.)
214ST	259 km/h (161 m.p.h.)
212	230 km/h (143 m.p.h.)

Bell rotorcraft

■ BELL 206 JETRANGER: The standard by which light civil turbine helicopters are judged, the 216 is still an extremely popular helicopter.

■ BELL 212: Based on the 'Huey', the 212 is a twin-engine design. It has proven popular with civil and military users.

■ BELL 222: Competing against the Agusta 109 and S-76 Spirit, the Bell 222 was itself further developed into the Bell 230.

■ BELL/BOEING V-22: Due to enter service with the US Marine Corps, the V-22 was developed from Bell's XV-15 prototype.

BELL

222 POLICE PATROL

● Police patroller ● Major event surveillance ● Quick-reaction transport

Based at Lippitts Hill in Essex, the Metropolitan Police Air Support Unit found the Bell 222 to be an ideal crime-busting helicopter. Powerful twin engines and stable flight characteristics, as well as good speed, are vital when tracking criminals. The pilots who fly the regular patrols over London's streets are actually employed by Bristow Helicopters and have extensive experience. Whether flying by day or night, the Bell 222 proved to be an invaluable asset in the fight against crime.

▲ The crews of the Metropolitan Police enjoy some of the most varied flying available today. Operating over a large city calls for quick-thinking, good teamwork and accurate flying.

BELL 222 POLICE PATROL

◀ Low level over London
Although London's police helicopters sometimes fly very low, for example during a chase, they normally operate at around 300 metres (1,000 ft.) to avoid noise nuisance and for safety reasons. Accurate navigation and meticulous attention to air traffic control procedures are vital as the local area contains approach lanes for Heathrow airport.

▲ Speed trapper ▶
Using timing marks painted on the motorways, a Bell crew can instantly work out the precise speed of a car and arrange a roadblock.

▲ Round the clock surveillance
The heli-tele system enclosed in the ball on the starboard side provides a close-in view of an incident. The infra-red camera on the port side allows the capability to be maintained at night.

◀ Police pilot
Police helicopter pilots are actually employed by the Bristow company. Usually ex-military, they are trained in firearms and the use of the heli-tele and thermal-imaging systems. Conversion to the Bell 222 was undertaken in the USA.

FACTS AND FIGURES

➤ The first Scotland Yard aerial unit used an airship to observe the crowds at the 1923 Derby.

➤ Just before the war, the Metropolitan Police were using Cierva autogyros.

➤ In the 1970s police helicopters only carried an observer and a radio.

➤ The Air Support Unit started flying the Bell 222 in 1980.

➤ The helicopters carry Nitesun searchlights, stabilised heli-tele TV cameras and infra-red cameras.

➤ The 'Met' always has one helicopter airborne over London in daylight hours.

PROFILE

London police force's eye in the sky

London's famous Metropolitan Police have been using aircraft for observation since 1923. In those days they used an airship, but modern equipment has included the more sophisticated Twin Squirrel and Bell 222 helicopters equipped with advanced sensors and communications systems.

The pilot of the police helicopter works in conjunction with two specialised observers. 'Obs 1' sits beside the pilot and interprets the incoming police messages before guiding him to the location. 'Obs 2', who is positioned behind the pilot in the passenger cabin, locates and follows the target and is responsible for co-ordinating the operation with ground units. Through a large window he observes the scene below using an array of equipment. This includes gyrostabilised binoculars as well as infra-red thermal-imaging and conventional camera systems. During night operations he is also responsible for operating the powerful Nitesun searchlight. This combination of personnel and equipment makes the Bell 222 a highly effective crime-fighting machine.

The Bell 222 is an excellent choice for a police helicopter, having twin-engined clearance for work over crowded cities, and enough capacity to carry dog teams or special firearms officers if needed.

Assignments are numerous and range from searching for missing persons with the infra-red system to covering convoys transporting important criminals to court. Most of this work involves diverting from routine patrols.

Bell helicopters have traditionally been equipped with twin-bladed rotors.

The 222 rotor consists of a stainless-steel 'D' spar, with a honeycomb core behind it, covered in a glass-fibre skin.

Police Bell 222s are powered by a pair of Lycoming LTS101-750C-1 turboshafts.

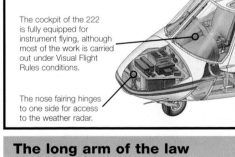

The Bell 222 retains its passenger-carrying capacity, and is sometimes used to ferry special firearms teams to major incidents.

The cockpit of the 222 is fully equipped for instrument flying, although most of the work is carried out under Visual Flight Rules conditions.

The nose fairing hinges to one side for access to the weather radar.

The rear fuselage area contains baggage space and a fuel tank.

A steerable Nitesun searchlight is fitted to the rear fuselage. This can be focused to cover a wide or narrow area.

The tailplane is a fixed unit with a built-in slot, with fixed endplates.

BELL 222A 'G-METC'

The Metropolitan Police Air Support Unit operated a pair of Bell 222s, with the serials G-METB and G-METC, and a leased Eurocopter Ecureuil. The unit is based at Lippitts Hill, near Loughton, on London's eastern edge.

Bell 222A

Type: police patrol helicopter

Powerplant: two 462-kW (620-hp.) Lycoming LTS101-750C-1 turboshafts

Maximum speed: 250 km/h (155 m.p.h.)

Range: 523 km (325 mi.) or 2 hours 30 minutes' endurance at economical cruising speed

Service ceiling: 6100 m (20,000 ft.)

Weights: empty 2204 kg (4,850 lb.); loaded 3560 kg (7,832 lb.)

Accommodation: two pilots, two observers or up to six passengers. Observers are equipped with searchlight, stabilised TV camera, infra-red, thermal imaging and video cameras

Dimensions:
rotor diameter	12.12 m (40 ft.)
fuselage length	10.98 m (36 ft.)
height	3.51 m (12 ft.)
rotor disc area	115.29 m² (1,240 sq. ft.)

ACTION DATA

MAXIMUM SPEED

Although helicopters are not as fast as fixed-wing aircraft, they are still considerably quicker than any land-based transport available in a city. A Bell 222 on patrol over central London can reach an incident anywhere in the the metropolis in minutes.

MODEL 222	250 km/h (155 m.p.h.)
AS 350 ECUREUIL	230 km/h (143 m.p.h.)
BO 105	240 km/h (149 m.p.h.)

ENDURANCE

Excellent though the Bell 222 is for most patrol duties, it is a larger and heavier helicopter than other types in use by police forces around the world. Because of this, it uses more fuel and needs to land for replenishment more often than otherwise less-capable machines.

MODEL 222	AS 350 ECUREUIL	BO 105
2 hours 30 minutes	4 hours	3 hours 30 minutes

CAPACITY

Although the Bell 222's main task is to patrol, it can be pressed into duty as a transport. The helicopters are especially useful for special duty units, such as heavily-armed anti-terrorist teams, who can reach any major incidents with the minimum of delay.

MODEL 222
1 pilot and 7 passengers

AS 350 ECUREUIL
1 pilot and 4 passengers

BO 105
1 pilot and 4 passengers

The long arm of the law

■ **SUSPICIOUS BEHAVIOUR:** Two youths have been seen breaking into cars. A report to the police brings the Bell 222 to the scene, which quickly locates a pair of suspects.

■ **GROUND UNITS CALLED:** As the suspects take a shortcut through an industrial estate, the helicopter directs ground-based police units to cut them off.

■ **POLICE MOVE IN:** The youths are approached and questioned by officers, while the helicopter remains in a surveillance position in case the suspects flee.

■ **AN ARREST IS MADE:** The suspects are found to be carrying goods which may have been stolen. There are now sufficient grounds for holding them, and they are arrested.

BELL
222/230

● Twin-engined light helicopter ● Fifteen years of service ● Exports

Bringing real elegance to the everyday job of carrying people and cargo, the Bell 222 and 230 are considered by many to be the best-looking helicopters on the market. The Bell 222 was launched in 1974, first flew in 1976 as a private venture, and was enthusiastically by helicopter operators around the world. Since it was first delivered in 1980, the 222 has proved popular in roles from executive transport to ambulance.

▲ Bell 222s have been produced for customers worldwide and the later 230 and 430 have continued this success. In 1992 production of the 230 and 430 models was switched to a new factory at Mirabel, Quebec.

▼ Model 430
Bell's 430 is a nine-seat version of the 230 with two 605-kW (810-hp.) Allison engines.

▲ Helikopter Service 222B
This Norwegian-registered 222 flew with Helikopter Service AS of Oslo. The 222B and 222B Executive variants were the original models with a hydraulically retracted wheeled undercarriage.

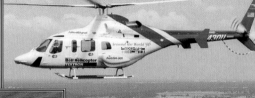

▼ Fenestron trials
This 222 was fitted with a shrouded tail rotor, or fenestron, as used on a number of European designs.

▲ Chilean SAR helicopter
In 1993 this modified 230 was leased to the Chilean navy. Modifications for the search-and-rescue role included a nose-mounted Honeywell radar, Nitesun searchlight, thermal imager and hoist. GPS navigation was also installed, as were extra fuel tanks.

FACTS AND FIGURES

➤ For offshore operations, the 222 can carry a water-activated emergency flotation system and auxiliary fuel tanks.

➤ The first prototype Bell 222 made its maiden flight on 13 August 1976.

➤ A 222 delivered in January 1981 was the 25,000th helicopter built by Bell.

➤ In January 1980 the offshore oil-drilling company Petroleum Helicopters became the first user of the Bell 222.

➤ As of January 1997 Bell 222s were operating in at least 11 countries.

➤ The 430, a stretched version of the 230 with a four-bladed rotor, flew in 1994.

PROFILE

America's first light twin helicopter

The 222 was the first commercial light twin-engined helicopter built in the USA. Its successor, the 230, was manufactured in Canada, which is now the centre for Bell's civil production.

When the 222 first appeared Bell was one of the most experienced helicopter manufacturers in the world, and the new helicopter profited from this experience. The result was a clean, sleek aircraft with retractable landing gear and provision for a number of passenger and cargo configurations.

A single pilot can fly the 222 even under IFR (instrument flight rules) conditions, although on difficult or long-range missions most companies prefer to use two pilots.

So far, the bulk of sales has been to the civil market, but the 222 and 230 have demonstrated great potential for military use. A naval patrol version, with light armament, has been proposed

and a variant for the search-and-rescue role has been employed by the Chilean navy. Civil duties remain the most common, however, and include executive transport and aeromedical and police operations. Succeeded by the 430, Model 230 production ended in 1995, after 38 had been built.

Left: The 230 is distinguished from the 222 by its revised engine air intakes and repositioned exhausts.

Above: The 222B Executive, fitted with retractable wheeled landing gear, has become a favourite with companies as a luxury transport.

230 Utility

Type: light commercial helicopter

Powerplant: two 522-kW (700-hp.) Allison 250-C30G2 or 510-kW (685-hp.) Textron Lycoming LTS 101-750C-1 turboshaft engines

Maximum cruising speed: 254 km/h (157 m.p.h.) at sea level

Range: 702 km (435 mi.)

Service ceiling: 4815 m (15,800 ft.)

Weights: empty 2245 kg (4,940 lb.); maximum take-off 3810 kg (8,380 lb.)

Accommodation: pilot and seven passengers

Dimensions:
main rotor diameter	12.80 m (42 ft.)
fuselage length	12.97 m (42 ft. 6 in.)
height	3.66 m (12 ft.)
rotor disc area	128.71 m² (1,385 sq. ft.)

222UT

The skid-equipped 222UT (Utility Twin) is widely used in the air ambulance role. N77UT carries the livery of the University of Tennessee Research Center and Hospital, Knoxville, Tennessee.

While more modern and updated designs (like the 430) have four-bladed main rotors, the 1970s-designed 222 and 230 are fitted with a two-bladed rotor. This has a stainless steel spar and leading edge with a Nomex body and fibre-glass skin.

Both the 222 and 230 have a two-bladed tail rotor. The 230 and skid-equipped 222s have a curved bar at the rear of the tail boom to protect the tail rotor from ground strikes.

The standard accommodation available in the 222UT is one pilot and six to eight passengers. An optional high-density layout in the 222B allows for up to nine passengers. There is room in both models for 1.05 m³ (37 cu. ft.) of baggage aft of the cabin.

While the 222 was fitted with two AVCO Lycoming (later Textron Lycoming) LTS 101 engines, the 230 is offered with the option of Allison 250-C turboshafts. The latter has been one of the most successful turboshafts and is fitted to many other types, including the Bell 206 JetRanger and Hughes (later McDonnell Douglas) 500.

Those aircraft fitted with wheeled landing gear have hydraulic forward-retracting units. The rear wheels are stowed in sponsons on the outside rear of the cabin. Skid-equipped versions can be fitted with ground handling wheels and retain sponsons, as these contain fuel tanks.

Bell's civil helicopter line-up

■ 206B-3 JETRANGER III: First flown in 1966, the top-selling JetRanger is still in production. NTH is the US Army's trainer version.

■ 206L-4 LONGRANGER: Agusta in Italy continues to produce this 'stretched' seven-seat version of the JetRanger.

■ 407: A development of the 206, the 407 is a single-engined helicopter intended to replace the JetRanger. It first flew in 1994.

■ 412: Announced in 1978, this development of the 212 has a four-bladed main rotor. The 412 is also built in Indonesia and Italy.

ACTION DATA

MAXIMUM SPEED

A top speed of around 270 km/h (167 m.p.h.) is typical of turbine-powered, light commercial helicopters. The popularity of these machines with executive users and air ambulance operators is due to their speed performance and the adaptability of their airframes.

222UT	270 km/h (167 m.p.h.)
BK 117	270 km/h (167 m.p.h.)
S-76 Mk II	278 km/h (172 m.p.h.)

RATE OF CLIMB

The Eurocopter-Kawasaki BK 117 has a superior rate of climb to the similarly sized Bell 222. The S-76 Mk II is a much heavier machine, but has more powerful engines and, consequently, a greater lifting capacity.

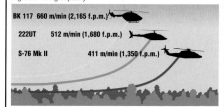

BK 117	660 m/min (2,165 f.p.m.)
222UT	512 m/min (1,680 f.p.m.)
S-76 Mk II	411 m/min (1,350 f.p.m.)

PASSENGER LOAD

The larger S-76 Mk II carries a greater passenger load, although the Bell 222 can be configured for up to nine passengers in a high-density layout. All three types have been used in the air ambulance role, equipped to carry stretchers and medical equipment.

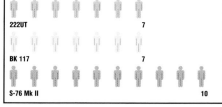

222UT	7
BK 117	7
S-76 Mk II	10

BENSEN

AUTOGYROS

● Do-it-yourself flying ● Evaluated by the USAF ● Low cost

▲ In the 1950s Bensen Aircraft of Raleigh, North Carolina developed the concept of a low-cost, home-built gyrocopter which did not require a pilot's licence to be flown.

Doctor Igor Bensen, former chief of research at Kaman Aircraft, saw the potential for marketing a series of light autogyros and rotary-winged gliders. First flying in the mid-1950s, these strange craft proved very successful, remaining in production for nearly 30 years. Two key factors to their incredible success were a very competitive price and the fact that under US regulations any member of the general public could build and fly one.

BENSEN AUTOGYROS

Gyro-Boat ▶
One of Bensen's most innovative designs was the Gyro-Boat. This craft could only 'fly' while being towed by a normal boat.

◀ Flying Scooter
The 'Sky Skooter' was one of many Benson aircraft. Little is known about this ingenious but apparently unsuccessful design.

Wright tribute ▶
This particular gyrocopter was named Spirit of Kitty Hawk in tribute to the brothers Orville and Wilbur Wright, who made their first ever flight there.

▼ Star Autogyro
Gyrocopters were used for a variety of different roles. This heavily modified example appears to have been used for filming purposes.

▲ VTOL 'shopping trolley'
The strange twin-rotored 'Prop-Copter' resembled something from the supermarket.

FACTS AND FIGURES

➤ When its flight testing was completed Spirit of Kitty Hawk was donated to the Smithsonian Museum in Washington, DC.

➤ The original Bensen Autogyro, first seen in 1959, was known as the B-7M.

➤ Neither machine evaluated by the USAF was adopted by the service.

➤ From his experience at Kaman Aircraft Bensen built a one-off true helicopter which featured twin co-axial rotors.

➤ A single gyrocopter flew non-stop from California to the Catalina Islands.

➤ In 1987 Bensen Aircraft said it was ceasing the production of autogyros.

PROFILE

Flight for the masses

Both unusual and outstanding, the Bensen series of autogyros and gliders represented the first serious attempt to put flying within reach of the average person in the street.

The first craft to be built was the B-8 Gyro-Glider, a simple unpowered device that was towed behind a motorised form of transport such as a car or boat. From this, Bensen developed its series of motorised versions, known as Gyro-copters, of which the most famous was the B-8M. This aircraft proved highly successful, generating half of the total production orders for the company. Among the most interesting variants was a single autogyro acquired by the USAF for parachute experiments.

In 1986, Bensen unveiled its last and possibly best Gyro-copter, known as the Powergyro, at an air show at Lakeland, Florida. Within a year, however, the firm announced that it was ceasing production of all aircraft.

Above: Recreation was a popular advertising theme in 1950s America and signified a new age of optimism. Bensen Aircraft was quick to appreciate the trend.

Right: Hovering in the only true Bensen helicopter, which incorporated co-axial rotors, company founder Igor Bensen demonstrates the relay winch.

Bensen B-8M

Type: single-seat lightweight autogyro

Powerplant: one 54-kW (72-hp.) McCulloch 4318E air-cooled flat-four engine

Maximum speed: 137 km/h (85 m.p.h.)

Endurance: 1.5 hours

Initial climb rate: 610 m/min (2,000 f.p.m.)

Range: 160 km (100 mi.)

Service ceiling: 5030 m (16,500 ft.)

Weights: empty 112 kg (247 lb.); loaded 227 kg (500 lb.)

Take-off run: 15.25 m (50 ft.)

Dimensions:
rotor diameter	6.10 m	(20 ft.)
length	3.45 m	(11 ft. 4 in.)
height	1.90 m	(6 ft. 3 in.)

X-25A

Two Bensen aircraft, a B-8M Gyro-copter and an unpowered B-8 Gyro-glider, were acquired by the USAF in 1968. Known as X-25s, they were used for research into the use of controlled parachutes.

Flight instruments on the B-8M were rudimentary, consisting of a propeller-driven air-speed indicator, altimeter and compass, with an extremely crude artificial horizon mounted above the instrument panel.

Basic flight controls consisted of a large centre-mounted stick with the throttle located to the right of the centre spar. On the original design, the main control column was attached to the rotor head bearing and hung down. Some examples had the stick relocated to a more conventional position and the flight controls reversed for easier handling in the air.

Wooden rotor blades were standard fitments for Bensen B-8Ms, though fabric-covered steel ones could be specified. Quickly detachable blade supports permitted storage in small spaces and enabled the craft to be transported on public roads.

Powering the B-8M was a 1600-cc McCulloch horizontally opposed four-cylinder engine originally designed for unmanned drone targets. This very light engine was powerful for its size and gave the autogyro surprising performance.

For directional stability one vertical and twin horizontal stabilisers were fitted. The latter were fixed, but the vertical surface featured a large rudder to aid control in flight.

THE BENSEN BIRD EXPERIMENTS

Bird strike tests: What happens when a bird flies into the rotor of a B-8M Gyro-copter? The bird comes out second best! Although this picture may appear rather brutal, tests conducted by Bensen Aircraft showed that, on average, three out of four birds would survive such an incident unscathed. Bensen made it clear that no live birds were used during the experiments. The primary objective was to test the strength of the rotor blades.

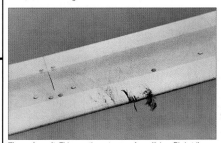

The end result: This was the outcome of a collision. Bird strikes were, and still are, a serious hazard during normal aircraft operations. If large aircraft could suffer severe damage after such a collision, then a small autogyro would fare even worse. Bensen took the matter seriously and the tests were exhaustive. As can be seen from the photo, the damage actually done to the blades was minimal. Happily, such accidents did not occur frequently.

Igor Bensen's amazing B-8

■ FLYING AUTOMOBILE: An interesting feature of the Gyro-Copter was its ability to run on normal automotive fuel. When out on the road, just pull into the nearest filling station for some petrol and groceries!

■ CIVILISED IN TRAFFIC: Despite being designed primarily as an airborne vehicle, the B-8 was surprisingly capable on the road.

■ RUSH HOUR IN THE BENSEN: Negotiating a busy junction, especially in a craft as small as the B-8 Gyro-copter, was no easy task.

■ SUPER BUG: Two main variants of the powered B-8 Gyro-Copter were available, the B-8M and B-8V. The 'V' designation referred to the fitment of a more or less standard 1600cc air-cooled flat-four Volkswagen engine.

BLOHM UND VOSS

HA 139

● Long-range mailplane/freighter ● Three built ● Transatlantic flights

The Ha 139 floatplane was built to a Deutsch Lufthansa specification for a long-range seaplane which was able to take off from, and land on, rough seas. It was also required to carry a 500-kg (1,100-lb.) payload over a distance of 5000 km (3,100 mi.) at 250 km/h (155 m.p.h.). As seaborne bases were envisaged it was realised that the heavy, rugged aircraft would need to be catapult-launched from its depot ship if it was to cross the Atlantic non-stop.

▲ *The three Ha 139s were named* Nordmeer *(North Sea),* Nordwind *(North Wind) and* Nordstern *(North Star) and registered D-AMIE, D-AJEY and D-ASTA, respectively.*

BLOHM UND VOSS **HA 139**

◄ **Fastest flights**
The Ha 139's best transatlantic performances during the 1938 trials were 13 hours 40 minutes east to west by Nordmeer *and 11 hours 53 minutes west to east by* Nordstern.

▲ **Ha 139 V3 at war**
The third Ha 139, Nordstern, *was modified for the Luftwaffe, first as a maritime reconnaissance aircraft and then as a minesweeper when war broke out.*

▲ **Rough sea performance**
The Ha 139's huge floats gave the aircraft the stability required by the DLH specification.

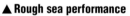

▲ **Third prototype**
Among the changes made to the V3 were lower-mounted engines, greater overall dimensions and increased weights.

◄ **Jumo diesels**
An important factor in the Ha 139's ability to fly the Atlantic was its engines. The two-stroke Jumo diesels had a much lower fuel consumption than equivalent petrol engines.

FACTS AND FIGURES

➤ The 'Ha' in the aircraft's designation stood for Hamburger Flugzeugbau – Blohm und Voss' aircraft design bureau.

➤ During the war the two Ha 139As were modified to Ha 139B standard.

➤ As the war began the Ha 139s' crews were also drafted into the Luftwaffe.

➤ The Ha 139B once left Africa overloaded at 16500 kg after a 90-second take-off run in rough seas.

➤ The BV 142A, a land-based derivative with BMW radial engines, was built for DLH.

➤ A reconnaissance-bomber version was proposed but was not built.

PROFILE

North Wind, Sea and Star

Deutsch Lufthansa's (DLH) specification for a long-range transatlantic mailplane was demanding. Dornier proposed the Do 26 flying-boat based on its proven Wal, while shipbuilders Blohm und Voss offered a floatplane design. Both were powered by economical diesel engines developed by Junkers.

Impressed by the Blohm und Voss design, DLH ordered three prototypes. The first two (V1 and V2, later designated Ha 139A) were delivered in 1937 and trials began immediately between depot ships off the Azores and New York.

Ha 139 V3 (later Ha 139B) was delivered in 1938 and joined the other two for trials. All three entered service on DLH's route between the Gambia and Brazil across the South Atlantic just before World War II began.

During the war the Ha 139s were modified for a maritime reconnaissance role and used as supply aircraft in the Norwegian campaign. All were scrapped in the early 1940s as spare parts became scarce.

Above: Schwabenland was one of two seaplane depot ships fitted with cranes used to hoist the Ha 139 aboard prior to a catapult launch.

HA 139A

Nordwind (North Wind) was the second Ha 139 to be built and was originally known as Ha 139 V2. It was delivered to Deutsch Lufthansa in 1937 and was engaged in trials from mid-August.

Below: In the foreground the Ha 139 V1 is seen suspended from a crane, while the V2 is aboard the Friesenland, from which North Atlantic trials were made in 1937.

Ha 139A

Type: long-distance mailplane

Powerplant: four 451-kW (605-hp.) Junkers Jumo 205C diesel engines

Maximum speed: 315 km/h (195 m.p.h.)

Normal cruising speed: 260 km/h (211 m.p.h.)

Economic cruising speed: 225 km/h (140 m.p.h.)

Climb rate: 6 min to 1000 m (3,100 ft.)

Range: 5300 km (3,285 mi.)

Service ceiling: 3500 m (11,500 ft.)

Weights: empty 10,360 kg (22,792 lb.); loaded for catapult launch 17,500 kg (38,500 lb.)

Dimensions:
span	27.00 m	(88 ft. 7 in.)
length	19.50 m	(63 ft. 11 in.)
height	4.80 m	(15 ft. 9 in.)
wing area	117 m²	(1,259 sq. ft.)

The aircraft's nose featured a mooring compartment and stowage for marine gear. The flight deck seated the two pilots, with positions aft for a flight engineer and radio operator.

The wing's main spar separated the flight deck from the mail and freight compartment. No access between the two was possible in flight. The wing itself was an inverted gull design.

Poor directional stability with the original circular fin and rudder assemblies meant that they were replaced with triangular-shaped fins, the rudders being considerably larger. Other modifications involved the engine cooling system. The float-stub-mounted radiators were prone to corrosion and were removed in favour of a radiator for each engine beneath the wing.

The Ha 139's engines were unusual Junkers Jumo 205C two-stroke diesels with six cylinders and 12 opposed pistons. Initially, radiators were mounted in pairs in the float-stub fairings.

The tubular centre section wing spar was divided into five separate fuel tanks with a total capacity of 6000 litres (1,585 gal.). The wing had a metal-skinned centre section with fabric covering the outer panels.

Modifications for service with the Luftwaffe included a lengthened glazed nose for an observer and a 7.9-mm MG 15 machine-gun. Another machine-gun was fitted in a hatch above the cockpit, with two in mountings either side of the aft fuselage.

LUFTHANS
NORDWIND
NORDWIND D-AJEY

ACTION DATA

MAXIMUM SPEED

Designed to the same specification, the Do 16 and Ha 139 had a similar top speed. Range was the most important factor, however. The Fw 200, as a land-based aircraft with a sleeker fuselage and more powerful engines, was capable of higher speeds. As speeds increased seaplanes fell out of the running.

Ha 139 V1	315 km/h (195 m.p.h.)
Do 26 V6	323 km/h (200 m.p.h.)
Fw 200 V1 CONDOR	374 km/h (232 m.p.h.)

RANGE

In its standard configuration the Fw 200 V1 had a much shorter range than the flying-boats. For the record-breaking flight in 1938 it was fitted with extra tanks and carried a minimal load, other than fuel. This range made it the ideal maritime patrol aircraft.

Ha 139 V1	5300 km (3,285 mi.)
Do 26 V6	7097 km (4,400 mi.)
Fw 200 V1 CONDOR	6558 km (4,065 mi.)

Deutsch Lufthansa mailplanes

■ **DORNIER Do 18:** Designed to replace Lufthansa's Wals on their South Atlantic mail service, the Do 18 flew in 1935 with two Jumo 205 diesels. A number saw war service.

■ **DORNIER Do 26:** Built to the same specification as the Ha 139, the graceful Do 26 flew in 1938. It was employed on South Atlantic routes rather than the northern route, however.

■ **FOCKE-WULF Fw 200 CONDOR:** This modified Fw 200 made a record-breaking pre-war transatlantic crossing in 1938, paving the way for passenger services after the war.

BOEING

247

● Faster than contemporary fighters ● First air-conditioned airliner

▲ Little more
than a month after the first
Boeing 247 was flown on 8 February 1933, it
had been handed over for airline use. By the
end of April, 14 more had been delivered.

America's first low-wing, multi-engined transport, the Boeing 247 was ahead of its time. However, several factors conspired to limit its commercial success, including the rapid rate of change in aeronautical design and aircraft performance in the 1930s. Less than six months after the 247's first flight, the Douglas DC-1 appeared, an aircraft that owed much to the Boeing and paved the way for the famous DC-3.

BOEING 247

▼ 100 million hours
Despite the loss of its mail contracts in 1934, United Air Lines became the first airline in the world to reach a total of 100 million flying hours (mainly on its Boeing 247s) on 17 June 1936.

▲ United Air Lines
United Air Lines (UAL), formed on 1 July 1931, established a fleet of 247s that helped it to reach new highs in passenger and freight revenues.

◀ Miltary service
During World War II the USAAF used 27 Boeing 247Ds for training.

Race success ▶
This United Airlines Boeing 247D achieved third place in the 1934 London to Melbourne air race.

◀ Lufthansa
Two model 247s were supplied to Lufthansa in 1934. They had the new 247D cockpit but kept the old sloping windshield.

FACTS AND FIGURES

➤ In 1934 a militarised version, the 247Y, with two nose-mounted 12.7-mm machine-guns, was delivered to China.

➤ When it first appeared, the 247 was nearly 80 km/h (50 m.p.h.) faster than other airliners.

➤ During World War II the RAF used a 247 for automatic landing system research.

➤ The sole Model 247A was specially modified as an executive transport and research machine for Pratt & Whitney.

➤ In Mexico a number of 247s remained in commercial use in the 1950s.

PROFILE

Boeing's fast airliner twin

When the 247 first entered service in March 1933 it was, above all, fast and comfortable. With United Air Lines it brought coast-to-coast schedules down from 28 hours to 20 hours 30 minutes. The aircraft cruised at 260 km/h (160 m.p.h.), rather than the 180–190 km/h (110–120 m.p.h.) of its Ford, Fokker and Boeing tri-motor predecessors. Its 10-seat cabin featured temperature control and noise insulation.

Almost the entire production run of 75 aircraft was delivered to the various airlines that made up United Air Lines. However, it

was the close commercial tie-ups between UAL and Boeing that hampered attempts to sell more. When one competing airline attempted to purchase 247s and was turned down, it approached Douglas to build the DC-1, the prototype for the larger, faster DC-2.

Another handicap was the aircraft's low all-up weight. Boeing had wanted to build a 7257-kg (15,965-lb.) aircraft, but Boeing Air Transport pilots (one of the UAL companies) insisted that the aircraft would be too heavy for the Hornet engines specified. The design was therefore scaled down to 5443

kg (11,975 lb.), which limited its usefulness.

The last 13 247s were built to a faster 247D standard and most surviving early-build aircraft were eventually rebuilt as such. Some 27 saw wartime service with the USAAF as C-73s.

In 1942 the RAF received this Boeing 247 from Canada. It was used until 1948 in the development of the first automatic landing system.

In planform the tapered wing of the 247 resembled the wing of the later B-17 bomber. The balanced ailerons were constructed from aluminium alloy and a trim tab was fitted to the port aileron only.

Full cowlings were fitted to the engines of the 247D, replacing the cowling rings of earlier models. These, along with improved propellers and new gearing for the Wasp engines, made this variant of the 247 much faster.

Fixed tail surfaces had an aluminium alloy truss structure, with the rudder and elevators fabric-covered. The 247 was the first airliner with trim tabs on the elevators and rudder.

The twin-engined Boeing 247 was the first airliner to use supercharged engines, and the first to be able to climb on one engine with a full passenger load. It was a trendsetter for the next generation of transports.

247D

United Air Line's *City of San Diego* is seen as it looked in 1941. First flown in May 1933, it was converted to 247D configuration with the new windscreen after an accident a month later.

NC13326
U.S.MAIL–A.M.-1-1-1617
AIR EXPRESS

United Air Lines

Retracting into the engine cowling, the 247's main landing gear was very robust. In an emergency the aircraft could land with the interconnected gear in any position from full up to full down.

The all-metal cantilever wing had interchangeable outer wings and wingtips. The wing stub was integral with the fuselage and the engine nacelle supports.

Ten passengers could be carried in the cabin, on five seats either side of a central aisle, with a jump seat for the stewardess at the rear. Baggage was carried in the nose and aft end.

247D

Type: civil transport aircraft

Powerplant: two 410-kW (550-hp.) Pratt & Whitney R-1340S-S1H-1G Wasp radials

Maximum speed: 322 km/h (200 m.p.h.)

Initial climb rate: 350 m/min (217 f.p.m.)

Range: 1199 km (745 mi.)

Service ceiling: 7740 m (25,400 ft.)

Weights: empty 4148 kg (9,125 lb.); maximum take-off 6192 kg (13,625 lb.)

Dimensions:
span	22.56 m (74 ft.)
length	15.72 m (51 ft. 7 in.)
height	3.60 m (11 ft. 10 in.)
wing area	77.68 m² (836 sq. ft.)

ACTION DATA

CRUISING SPEED

Boeing's 247 and Douglas's DC-2 offered a massive increase in speed (around 55 per cent) over previous airliners like the Tri-Motor. Each had powerful engines, an efficient wing and low-drag fuselage. Although speed was one of the most important criteria, each offered improved performance in all flight regimes.

MODEL 247D	304 km/h (188 m.p.h.)
DC-2	306 km/h (190 m.p.h.)
5-AT-D TRI-MOTOR	196 km/h (122 m.p.h.)

PASSENGERS

One area where the Model 247 was woefully inadequate was in passenger accommodation. The restriction was imposed by United Air Lines' insistence on a low all-up weight, a decision which was to have disastrous consequences for later commercial sales.

MODEL 247D	10 passengers
DC-2	14 passengers
5-AT-D TRI-MOTOR	13 passengers

RANGE

The Model 247 offered a huge improvement in range over the Tri-Motor, but was out-ranged itself by its rival, the DC-2, which almost doubled the Tri-Motor's reach. In an era of rapidly expanding air travel, speed and range became the driving factors and any successful design reaped the rewards.

MODEL 247D
1199 km
(745 mi.)

DC-2
1609 km
(1,000 mi.)

5-AT-D TRI-MOTOR
885 km (550 mi.)

1930s airliners

■ **DE HAVILLAND DH.91 ALBATROSS:** The DH.91 was a four-engined, fast and luxurious airliner with distinctive twin fins and rudders.

■ **DOUGLAS DC-2:** Successful rival to the Boeing 247, the DC-2 was developed for TWA and first flown in 1933. It led to the DC-3.

■ **FORD TRI-MOTOR:** In 1926 Ford flew the first prototype of its highly successful Tri-Motor. Some aircraft survived into the 1990s.

■ **JUNKERS Ju 52/3M:** Europe's most successful airliner of the 1930s, the Ju 52/3m also served with the wartime Luftwaffe.

BOEING

307 STRATOLINER

● Long-range airliner ● Military transport ● Only 10 built

F rom some angles, especially from above, the Boeing 307 had a familiar look. The reason for this is that the Stratoliner had a large number of features in common with Boeing's bomber of the same era, the B-17 Flying Fortress. As originally built and flown, this civil airliner was simply a B-17 with a new fuselage and built-in pressurisation system. The Stratoliner was not a commercial success, but some of the 10 aircraft built were used for decades.

▲ In military
service the Stratoliner was
known as the C-75. Modifications to the airliner
included the removal of the pressurisation system
and the installation of a large fuel tank.

BOEING 307 STRATOLINER

▼ Ecuadorian airline
Between 1951 and 1954 this
ex-Pan Am Stratoliner was
operated by Aerovias Ecuatoriana
on routes between Ecuador and
Miami. The aircraft later served
with Quaker City Airways.

▲ Fortress roots
Many of the Stratoliner's features,
including the wings, nacelles,
powerplant and original tail
surfaces, were based on the
B-17C Flying Fortress bomber.

◀ Test flight
A pilot warms up the engines of
the prototype before a test flight
from Boeing Field, Seattle. This
aircraft was later lost during a
test flight for a foreign airline.

▼ Stratoliner at war
In 1942 TWA's five SA-307Bs were requisitioned by the Army Air
Transport Command. In two years of service they flew more than
12 million kilometres (7 million miles) and made 3000 ocean crossings.

▲ Control panel
The cockpit layout of the
Pan Am S-307s was fairly
advanced for the time.
It included duplicate sets
of flight instruments and
a Sperry autopilot.

FACTS AND FIGURES

➤ The first 307 Stratoliner was lost during a test flight before it could be delivered to Pan American.

➤ Pan American's three 307s were named *Comet*, *Flying Cloud* and *Rainbow*.

➤ The advertised price of a brand-new Stratoliner in 1938 was $315,000.

➤ Three French-registered Stratoliners were the only civil aircraft allowed to fly into Hanoi during the Vietnam War.

➤ Howard Hughes' personal 307 was fitted with a luxurious interior costing $250,000.

➤ The only surviving complete 307 is on display at the Pima County Air Museum.

PROFILE

Boeing's pre-war long-range liner

This SB-307B was acquired by Howard Hughes and was converted into an ultra-deluxe aircraft. It was later damaged in a hurricane and was converted into a houseboat.

Engineering work by Boeing aimed at producing a civil transport based on the Flying Fortress bomber resulted in the 307 Stratoliner. The aircraft was built with a circular-section fuselage which was pressurised to provide a cabin altitude of 2440 m (8,000 ft.) when the aircraft was actually flying at 4480 m (14,700 ft.). This enabled the Stratoliner to operate with passengers at about 6000 m (20,000 ft.), an altitude well above most turbulence.

Three Stratoliners were delivered to Pan American World Airways, five to

Transcontinental & Western Airlines (TWA), and one to millionaire industrialist Howard Hughes. In fact, when Hughes' initial attempt to purchase a Stratoliner was thwarted by Boeing's commitment to two airlines, the millionaire bought control of one of the airlines, TWA, and diverted the first of its aircraft for his use. Hughes was a brilliant, eccentric figure but his plans to use the Stratoliner for a round-the-world record flight were cut short by the advent of World War II, and the aircraft ended up being his personal luxury taxi. The other

Boeing 307s enjoyed a brief but successful stint in commercial aviation before being impressed into duties supporting the US armed forces during the war.

After the war, Boeing 307s were used by operators in Ecuador, Honduras, Saudi Arabia and Vietnam.

After the loss of the prototype it was decided to change the B-17C's vertical tail surfaces and install a new rudder and fin. These became a Boeing trademark on later aircraft.

The entirely new fuselage had a completely circular cross-section which gave sufficient room to accommodate cargo and passengers comfortably.

SA-307B Stratoliner

Type: high-altitude long-range transport

Powerplant: four 670-kW (900-hp.) Wright GR-1820 Cyclone radial piston engines

Maximum speed: 396 km/h (245 m.p.h.)

Cruising speed: 354 km/h (222 m.p.h.)

Initial climb rate: 366 m/min (6,527 f.p.m.)

Range: 3846 km (2,390 mi.)

Service ceiling: 7985 m (26,200 ft.)

Weights: empty 13,068 kg (42,000 lb.); maximum take-off 19,050 kg (28,750 lb.)

Accommodation: flight crew of five, plus up to 33 passengers in VIP configuration

Dimensions: span 32.61 m (107 ft. 3 in.)
length 22.66 m (74 ft. 4 in.)
height 6.34 m (20 ft. 9 in.)
wing area 138.05 m² (1,485 sq. ft.)

The flightdeck accommodated captain and co-pilot side-by-side, with a flight engineer and wireless operator situated behind. The navigator sat in a separate cabin behind the flightdeck.

SA-307B STRATOLINER

TWA had the largest fleet of Stratoliners and was the best-known operator. This aircraft received the spurious serial NX1940 for a sales trip. Its true identity was NX19906.

Transcontinental & Western Airlines Stratoliners could carry up to 33 passengers in the pressurised cabin, with a galley situated at the rear. In some configurations, four convertible travel compartments were situated along the starboard side.

Standard Stratoliners were powered by four Wright Cyclone GR-1820-G102 engines of 670 kW (900 hp.). Howard Hughes had his aircraft fitted with more powerful 857-kW (1,150-hp.) Wright R-2600 Twin Cyclones.

The Stratoliner's wing was based on that of the B-17C. Extra leading-edge slots were built into the wingtips and the span was increased by 99 cm (36 in.).

ACTION DATA

PASSENGERS

Of these three pre-war airliners the Stratoliner could carry the most passengers in high-density configuration. However, on longer flights the aircraft would often be fitted with travel compartments, which reduced the capacity but increased passenger comfort.

SA-307B STRATOLINER   33
DH.91 ALBATROSS   22
Fw 200B   26

CRUISING SPEED

With its more streamlined shape the Fw 200 was easily the fastest of this trio. The Fw 200's speed and range were invaluable when it became a maritime patrol aircraft during World War II.

SA-307B STRATOLINER
354 km/h (222 m.p.h.)

DH.91 ALBATROSS
338 km/h (210 m.p.h.)

Fw 200B
390 km/h (242 m.p.h.)

RANGE

The Stratoliner's range allowed it to cover vast distances without the inconvenience of having to land and refuel. Its long range was put to good use when flying trans-oceanic routes with the US armed forces during World War II. The Albatross was let down by its lack of range and just seven were built.

Fw 200B
3219 km
(2,000 mi.)

SA-307B STRATOLINER
3846 km
(2,390 mi.)

DH.91 ALBATROSS
1674 km (1,040 mi.)

From bomber to airliner

■ **AVRO 691 LANCASTRIAN:** This was a high-speed, long-range transport conversion of the famous Lancaster bomber. Operators included the Canadian government and BOAC.

■ **BOEING 377 STRATOCRUISER:** Based on the B-29 Superfortress wartime bomber, the Stratocruiser served with the USAF, major US airlines and the British airline BOAC.

■ **TUPOLEV Tu-104 'CAMEL':** This airliner derivative of the Tu-16 'Badger' bomber could accommodate up to 100 passengers. About 200 were built and the aircraft served until 1981.

■ **TUPOLEV Tu-114 'CLEAT':** Derived from the mighty Tu-95 'Bear', the Tu-114 could carry up to 220 passengers and was the world's largest airliner prior to the Boeing 747.

BOEING

314 CLIPPER

● 1930s transoceanic flying-boat airliner ● Wartime draftee

Pan American Airways introduced the Boeing 314 in 1939. The 'Clipper', as it was known, spanned oceans in the golden age of the flying boat when air travel was a luxury for a privileged few. Following the Martin M-130 and Sikorsky S-42 on Atlantic and Pacific routes, the 314 ushered in new standards in range and speed, as well as passenger comfort. However, World War II brought the era to an end and the flying-boats' days were numbered.

▲ By today's standards flying-boat travel was slow – New York to Marseilles via the Azores and Lisbon took 29½ hours. Compared to a sea crossing, however, it was quick but very expensive.

▲ Double Cyclone power
For minor inflight maintenance the engines could be reached by passageways in the wings.

▲ Three tail configurations
When first built the prototype had a single tailfin, which was later changed to two – one at either end of the tailplane. Production 314s, however, had a triple tail.

Impressed in wartime ▶
Before World War II three 314s had been sold to BOAC. The remaining nine were placed under US Army, then Navy, control.

▼ Hybrid design
The 314's sleek lines belied the fact that its wing was borrowed from the XB-15 bomber, with the hull being a fairly conventional design.

▲ Pan American fleet
Designed to a Pan Am requirement, 12 Clippers were built. NX18601 was the prototype, with the 'NX' prefix indicating an experimental type.

FACTS AND FIGURES

➤ The four passenger cabins of this flying-boat had different floor levels because of the 314's stepped hull.

➤ The first Boeing 314 Clipper made its maiden flight on 7 June 1938.

➤ Clipper flying-boats used the wing and engine nacelles of the XB-15 bomber.

➤ One 314 caught by the outbreak of war in New Zealand escaped by flying west, completing a round-the-world journey.

➤ In 1939 the Clipper was the largest production aircraft in regular airline use.

➤ In 1942 Churchill flew home from the United States via Bermuda in a BOAC 314.

Transoceanic Boeing airliner

Boeing workers were excited in 1936 when their company won a Pan American contract to build six Model 314s. After successful flight tests, the first of these high-wing, triple-tail, four-engined flying-boats, called 'Clippers' by Pan Am, entered transatlantic air mail service on 20 May 1939.

When it began hauling passengers, the Boeing 314 was the world's largest production airliner. Pan Am used its Clippers on the Pacific route to the Far East and New Zealand, across the North Atlantic and on the southerly routes to Brazil and the West Indies.

A second batch of six, known as 314As, were built for Pan Am in the early 1940s, three of these later going to British Overseas Airways Corporation (BOAC) for use in support of the war effort in North Africa. The other nine also saw war service,

requisitioned by the US Army as the C-98. More suited to a naval role, all were turned over to the US Navy as the B-314.

By 1946, when Pan Am made their last Clipper flight, faster landplanes had rendered the majestic 'boats' obsolete.

Above: The large sponsons fitted either side of the hull meant that wing floats were not necessary.

Above: The second batch of six Clippers, known as 314As, incorporated more powerful engines and increased fuel capacity.

314 Clipper

Type: long-range flying-boat transport

Powerplant: four 1118-kW (1,500-hp.) Wright GR-2600 Cyclone 14 radial piston engines

Maximum speed: 311 km/h (193 m.p.h.) at 3050 m (10,000 ft.)

Cruising speed: 295 km/h (183 m.p.h.)

Range: 5633 km (3,495 mi.)

Service ceiling: 4085 m (13,400 ft.)

Weights: empty 22,801 kg (50,162 lb.); maximum take-off 37,421 kg (82,326 lb.)

Accommodation: flight crew and cabin crew of 10, plus up to 74 passengers in four separate cabins (40 passengers in sleeper configuration)

Dimensions:
span	46.33 m	(151 ft. 11 in.)
length	32.31 m	(106 ft.)
height	8.41 m	(27 ft. 7 in.)
wing area	266 m²	(2,866 sq. ft.)

314 CLIPPER

NC18602 'California Clipper' was the second 314 delivered to Pan American Airways. During World War II it served with the Army Transport Command (ATC) and the US Navy.

A crew of six flew the Clipper: pilot, co-pilot, radio operator, flight engineer, navigator and aircraft commander. All were seated in a six-man control cabin.

Wright R-2600 Cyclone 14 engines powered the Clippers; the same engine was fitted to wartime B-25 Mitchell and A-20 Havoc bombers and the PBM Mariner flying-boat.

Painted silver overall, the top surface of the wing carried a broad 'Dayglo' orange band from wingtip to wingtip. This made the aircraft more conspicuous and therefore easier to find in the event of it ditching.

Clippers had enough space for up to 10 crewmembers and 74 passengers, the exact arrangement varying according to the type of flight. As a sleeper, the 314 was limited to 40 passengers.

The cabin area had two decks. The lower deck was divided into compartments: four with seats or bunks, the others including a galley, cocktail bar and promenade deck. The upper level included the flight deck and luggage storage.

Pan Am's Clippers had 'stars and stripes' on the nose and the airline's logo below the cockpit. On the tail was the aircraft's registration and the Boeing trademark.

Transatlantic flying-boats

LATÉCOÈRE 521: The 521 first flew in 1935 before carrying out long-distance flights to South and North America for the Air France Trans-atlantique Company between 1937 and 1939.

SHORT 'G' CLASS: The S.26 'G' class was ordered by Imperial Airways for transatlantic mail services. Three were built and served in World War II before flying with BOAC in the 1940s.

SIKORSKY VS-44 EXCALIBUR: Designed to carry passengers and mail between the USA and Europe, the VS-44 flew cargo and troops to the UK during World War II.

SHORT SOLENT 3: Four of the Hercules-powered Solents were built for Tasman Empire Airways after the end of World War II. They also served with BOAC until 1950.

ACTION DATA

MAXIMUM SPEED

Kawanishi's H6K was another pre-war flying-boat, but was designed as a military aircraft. Its engines were similar in output to those of the Clipper, but powered an airframe which was a fraction of the weight. The post-war Solent used much more powerful engines.

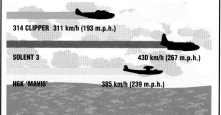

314 CLIPPER 311 km/h (193 m.p.h.)

SOLENT 3 430 km/h (267 m.p.h.)

H6K 'MAVIS' 385 km/h (239 m.p.h.)

BOEING

377 STRATOCRUISER

● Derived from the B-29 ● Luxury airliner ● Cargo lifter

The Boeing 377 set a majestic standard of air travel for the post-war world. Able to handle the New York to London route in just a little over 10 hours, the Stratocruiser pampered its clients. Those who savoured the food, drink and fine service – including sleeping berths for many – remember nostalgically that it was better than anything offered today. Ironically, this legendary servant of the skies owed its origins to the B-29 bomber.

▲ *The combination of a pressurised fuselage and the ability to cruise at high speed above the turbulent lower atmosphere meant that the Boeing 377 offered new standards of comfort.*

BOEING 377 STRATOCRUISER

▼ USAF transport
The USAF's C-97 Stratofreighter was in fact the forerunner to the civil Stratocruiser, and prototype trials of the airliner were conducted using an XC-97, of which three were built.

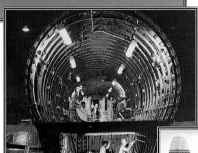

Mass ▶ production
Such was the demand for military Stratofreighters in the 1950s that the aircraft was produced at the rate of one every working day. The 500th was completed in February 1954.

▲ Bomber ancestry
The Stratocruiser's B-29 ancestry was obvious. The Stratofreighter surpassed all previous USAF transports in performance, showing just how advanced the B-29 airframe had been in 1944.

Freight loader ▶
Stratofreighters were still in service long after the passenger versions had all but disappeared from commercial routes.

◀ Crew cabin
The roomy cockpit seated two pilots with full dual controls, a navigator, flight engineer and usually a radio operator.

◀ Cold comfort
Automatic air-conditioning meant that passengers could travel in perfect comfort, even in freezing weather.

FACTS AND FIGURES

➤ When Pan American paid $24.5 million for 20 Stratocruisers, it was the biggest purchase of civil airliners up to that time.

➤ The first aircraft in the series was a military XC-97, which first flew in 1944.

➤ The KC-97 tanker version saw active service with Israel in the 1967 war.

➤ Boeing president Bill Allen decided to build 50 aircraft at the company's risk before airlines invested in the Model 377.

➤ The first Stratocruiser flew from Seattle to Washington DC in 6 hours 4 minutes.

➤ About 15 Stratocruisers were operated by Israel as military freighters.

Sky cruising in comfort

In 1942, Boeing won an Army contract for three XC-97 military transport prototypes based on the B-29 Superfortress but with a pressurised 'double-deck' fuselage optimised for freight and passengers. The C-97 became successful and the KC-97 tanker served the US Air Force and Air National Guard service to the end of the 1970s. But Boeing always saw the design as an airliner superior to the contemporary Lockheed Constellation and

Douglas DC-4, and after the war 55 examples of the civil Stratocruiser entered service with airlines like American, BOAC, Northwest, Pan American and United.

In an age when air travel was only for the rich, the Stratocruiser gave its passengers sheer opulence: well-dressed passengers lounged around the stairway between decks sipping cocktails from the lower deck bar. Later, the Stratocruiser became an unglamorous workhorse – a Red Cross flying ambulance in the 1969/70 Biafra War and a freighter hauling heavy tools for a petroleum

company in Central America. A few examples continued to fly in out-of-the-way parts of the world into the 1990s.

Right: The combination of a large, sleek airframe and features like cocktail bars were very glamorous, but were destined to die out as the age of mass air travel began.

Above: America's urgent demand for a long-range civil transport resulted in the Stratocruiser being built alongside military B-50s at the Seattle plant.

Above: Boeing began 40 years of dominance of the world airline market with the futuristic Stratocruiser.

377 Stratocruiser

Type: long-range commercial transport

Powerplant: four 2610-kW (3,500-hp.) Pratt & Whitney R-4360-TSB-6 Wasp Major 28-cylinder radial piston engines with General Electric superchargers

Maximum speed: 604 km/h (375 m.p.h.)

Cruising speed: 547 km/h (340 m.p.h.)

Range: 6759 km (4,588 mi.)

Weights: empty 38,071 kg (83,756 lb.); loaded 67,133 kg (147,693 lb.)

Accommodation: flight crew of four; typically 50 first-class or up to 117 tourist-class passengers; others with 40 first-class sleeping facilities; some with a mix of 23 first-class plus 40 tourist-class passengers

Dimensions: span 43.05 m (141 ft.)
length 33.63 m (110 ft.)
height 11.68 m (38 ft.)
wing area 164.25 m² (1,767 sq. ft.)

ACTION DATA

SERVICE CEILING
The B-29's wing was optimised for high-altitude flight, and the Stratocruiser inherited its excellent performance at altitude. It could cruise above bad weather, and most of the competition too.

MODEL 377 STRATOCRUISER 9800 m (32,000 ft.)
DC-7 7620 m (25,000 ft.)
B-29 CONSTELLATION 7500 m (24,500 ft.)

PASSENGERS
The unusual 'figure of eight' fuselage gave the Stratocruiser a high capacity. The DC-7 and B-29 Constellation carried almost as many passengers, but the accommodation was less luxurious.

MODEL 377 STRATOCRUISER 117
DC-7 102
B-29 CONSTELLATION 107

RANGE
The broad fuselage meant that the Stratocruiser suffered more aerodynamic drag than the narrow-bodied DC-7 and Constellation, and therefore had slightly less range.

DC-7 7596 km (4,710 mi.)
B-29 CONSTELLATION 7710 km (4,780 mi.)
MODEL 377 STRATOCRUISER 6759 km (4,588 mi.)

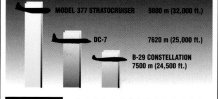
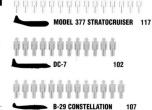
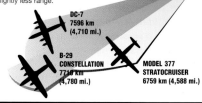

The tall tail was an almost direct copy of the B-50 unit. The rear portion of the fin and rudder could fold sideways to allow hangar storage or maintenance.

A galley with electric ovens and refrigerators was installed in the rear of the aircraft. A water tank was located at the base of the fin.

The tailplane featured thermal anti-icing. Surprisingly for such a large aircraft, the control surfaces were still fabric covered; they were also mass-balanced to ease control.

The principal modification to the Stratofreighter involved fitting large loading doors and an internal ramp. An electrical cargo hoist ran along the entire length of the fuselage.

A stairway linked the upper and lower decks, with the cocktail bar at the foot of the stairs.

Sleeping berths were fitted in the forward upper fuselage, with a ladies' dressing room located ahead of it. Baggage was stored in the hold below. The forward seats in the main cabin could also be converted to berths.

MODEL 377 STRATOCRUISER

This Boeing Stratocruiser entered BOAC service in 1950, and was named RMA Cabot. The aircraft served for eight years, and was then returned to Boeing who sold the machine to Transocean Air Lines.

The main fuselage consisted of an inverted 'figure of eight' section, sometimes referred to as the 'double bubble', designed specifically for the requirements of pressurisation.

Power was provided by the same engines as those fitted to the B-50 Superfortress, namely the massive Pratt & Whitney R-4360 Wasp Major, a 28-cylinder four-row radial.

BOEING
707

● First US jet airliner ● Private venture gamble ● Four decades of production

▲ Built as a private venture by Boeing, the Model 707 airliner revolutionised air transport after PanAm introduced it on scheduled services from New York to Europe on 26 October 1958. Over the next decade major airlines around the world moved into jet power.

The Boeing 707 was the first successful American jet airliner. Moreover, it was a genuine trailblazer, opening a new era of speed and comfort to travellers around the globe. With its four, low-slung jet engines and graceful lines, this aircraft was built for transcontinental service. However, during the decade after it first entered service in 1958, the 707 ended up spanning the world's oceans and became a familiar sight at airports worldwide.

PHOTO FILE

BOEING 707

First of a long line ▶
The very first Boeing 707, appropriately registered N70700, was in fact a Boeing Model 367-80. It was flown for the first time on 15 July 1954 and remained in use as a test aircraft for the next 30 years.

▲ Advanced 320C
This World Airways Model 707-373C is representative of the more advanced 320C versions that did not have the underfin.

▼ American Airlines big order
When American Airlines ordered 30 Boeing 707-123s on 8 November 1955 it enabled the manufacturer to start full-scale production.

▲ Braniff's sprightly 707-220
The US airline Braniff bought the shorter fuselage Model 707-220 that was fitted with the more powerful Pratt & Whitney JT4A engines. These gave it a sprightly take-off performance particularly at hot-and-high airports in South America.

◀ Lufthansa's improved 330B
A fleet of 12 of these bigger, long-range JT3D-3 turbofan-powered 707-330Bs was operated by Lufthansa on intercontinental routes from 1964. This version had new leading- and trailing-edge wing flaps, greater span and modified wingtips.

FACTS AND FIGURES

➤ The first Boeing 707 was actually rolled upside-down on one test flight.

➤ The same prototype flew from Seattle to Baltimore non-stop on 11 March 1957 at an average speed of 985 km/h (611 m.p.h.).

➤ Pan American's first 707-120 flew on 20 December 1957.

➤ Boeing engineers calculated that the 707 used 1710 km (1,060 mi.) of wiring.

➤ Dwight D. Eisenhower was the first US president to have a jet aircraft, a 707-320B.

➤ The purchase of 820 KC-135/Model 717 tankers for the USAF helped to cut the cost of the 707 to the world's airlines.

PROFILE

Boeing's famous family

Boeing entered the commercial jet age in 1954 with the 367-80, its prototype for the incredible 707. Pan American World Airways made history when it purchased jet airliners a year later, investing heavily in the Boeing 707 and contemporary Douglas DC-8.

The 707 became one of the most successful civilian transports ever built, with production exceeding 800 aircraft. A beautiful but practical design, which brought both glamour and common sense to air travel, the 707 was flown by virtually all of the West's major airlines and appeared with several powerplants. A few 707s found military roles as VIP transports, AWACS and communications aircraft.

When the 707 entered service passengers could not believe how smooth flying could be compared to propeller-driven aircraft. Now these wonderful jetliners of the 1960s are referred to as 'narrow body' ships because they gave way, beginning in the 1970s, to 'wide cabin' types like the 747 and DC-10. But every jetliner that ever flew, regardless of its size or shape, owes a debt to the Boeing 707 which came along just when it was needed.

Below: The Boeing 707 became the standard long-distance airliner for almost all of the world's major airlines. It is a testament to the superb initial design that a large number of 707s remain in civilian use 40 years after the type entered service.

Above: BOAC operated the longer range Model 707-320. This had a new, more efficient wing, a longer fuselage to seat 189 passengers and greater fuel capacity. The 707-320 was fitted with powerful Rolls-Royce Conway turbofans.

707-320C

Type: four-engine long-range commercial transport

Powerplant: four 84.52-kN (18,900-lb.-thrust) Pratt & Whitney JT3D-7 turbofan engines

Maximum speed: 1009 km/h (625 m.p.h.)

Cruising speed: 885 km/h (549 m.p.h.)

Service ceiling: 11,890 m (39,000 ft.)

Range: 9262 km (5,742 mi.)

Weights: operating empty 66,406 kg (146,093 lb.); empty weight cargo version 64,002 kg (140,804 lb.); maximum take-off 151,318 kg (332,900 lb.)

Accommodation: two pilots, flight engineer, flight attendants; seating for 147 (14 first-class, 133 coach) to 219 (high density) passengers, plus 48.14 m³ (1,700 cu. ft.) of luggage; plus 2800 kg (6,160 lb.) of cargo

Dimensions:
span	44.42 m (145 ft. 8 in.)
length	46.61 m (152 ft. 10 in.)
height	12.93 m (42 ft. 5 in.)
wing area	283.35 m² (3,049 sq. ft.)

MODEL 720

The Boeing 720 was an intermediate-range development of the 707. It had a shorter fuselage and more efficient wings and engine.

The flight crew comprised a captain and first officer, with room for a navigator seated behind the captain and the flight engineer on the right.

The external outline, dimensions and controls of the Model 720 were almost exactly the same as the older Model 120. This meant that similar flight decks, passenger cabins and facilities could be fitted and were interchangeable.

The main external feature of the Model 720 was a modified wing leading edge giving increased sweepback and decreased thickness. This new wing gave greater fuel efficiency and a higher cruise speed.

Power was provided by four Pratt & Whitney JT3C-7 turbojets mounted in pods beneath the wings.

The 720 had an all-metal tail structure with an electrically and manually operated variable incidence tailplane. A ventral fin was fitted as standard.

IRISH INTERNATIONAL AIRLINES

EI-ALA

The dual nose-wheel undercarriage unit retracts forwards into the fuselage.

Four-wheel main undercarriage bogies retract inwards into wingroot fairings.

ACTION DATA

MAXIMUM CRUISING SPEED

Four-jet airliners could cruise at high subsonic speeds, and a DC-8 was even dived past the sound barrier. Despite claims over speed advantage, all these aircraft were about equal.

MODEL 707-120B	1000 km/h (620 m.p.h.)
DC-8-30	952 km/h (590 m.p.h.)
CV 990	982 km/h (609 m.p.h.)

MAXIMUM PASSENGERS

Of prime importance for these airliners was their ability to carry greater numbers of passengers. The Boeing and DC-8 had a big advantage over Convair.

MODEL 707-120B
189 PASSENGERS

DC-8-30
173 PASSENGERS

CV 990
121 PASSENGERS

RANGE

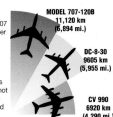

Another advantage of the 707 was its range, especially over the early DC-8s which had less economical engines. These big, four-engined airliners were already flying routes far beyond the capability of smaller airliners like the Comet, and it was not until the advent of the Boeing 747 that airliners had greater range.

MODEL 707-120B
11,120 km (6,894 mi.)

DC-8-30
9605 km (5,955 mi.)

CV 990
6920 km (4,290 mi.)

Early four-jet airliners

■ **DE HAVILLAND DH.106 COMET:** First of the jet airliners, the Comet 1 took to the air in 1949 and initial tests were very positive. However, in 1953 the first of a number of structural failures occurred, causing the Comet to miss out on commercial success.

■ **CONVAIR CV 880:** With a narrow-body five-seat abreast design, the Convair was actually much smaller than the Boeing, and was not a great commercial success, with only 65 built. The CV 990 was a modified version, but just 37 were produced.

■ **DOUGLAS DC-8:** Fiercest rival of the Boeing 707, the DC-8 did not have quite the same success but nevertheless was a capable design. When re-engined with efficient turbofans, it made a final comeback as a cargo aircraft in the late 1980s.

BOEING
727

● **Three-engined** ● **Best-selling airliner** ● **Freight carrier**

Boeing gambled with the 727. One of the first commercial tri-jets, the 727 redeemed the wager and became the world's best-selling jetliner. Put into service in February 1964, the 727 was an instant sensation with flight crews and passengers. Three decades later, after 101 customers purchased 727s from Boeing and dozens more picked them up second-hand, the Boeing 727 has now carried 3.9 billion passengers – more than any other jet.

▲ The 727's great strength was its fine 'hot and high' performance, easily capable of operations out of high-elevation airports like La Paz in Bolivia.

BOEING 727

◀ Into the sunset
Although the 727 is now facing limitations because of new noise regulations, 'hush kits' have been developed to ensure that the aircraft will be around in numbers for many years to come.

▼ Cargo-dropping
Boeing carried out experiments with dropping freight at low speeds, in an attempt to sell a military airlift version.

▲ Tail checks
Routine maintenance on modern commercial jets usually takes place at night, to allow maximum aircraft usage in peak daylight hours.

▲ Interior
The 727 used the Boeing 707's fuselage cross-section, with room for overhead lockers and five- or six-abreast seats.

▲ Going up
Working on the 727 needs a large amount of scaffolding and a 'cherry picker' to reach the high-mounted engines and tail.

▲ Test programme
A test pilot prepares to take the 727 prototype on its next flight. A refuelling hose is plugged into the rear fuselage.

FACTS AND FIGURES

➤ The Boeing 727 first flew at Renton Field near Seattle on 9 February 1963.

➤ In November 1963, a 727 completed a 121,000-km (75,000-mi.) world tour.

➤ Federal Express received the final new-build Boeing 727 (a 727-200F freighter) on 3 September 1984.

➤ The first 727 used by United Air Lines was donated in 1991 to the Museum of Flight in Seattle.

➤ The 727 was the first jetliner with built-in airstairs and single-point refuelling.

➤ The 727 was the first jetliner to operate at the airport in La Paz, Bolivia.

PROFILE

Tri-jet success from Boeing

The jet age began in 1952 with the entry into service of the British Comet and matured in 1958 with the arrival of the Boeing 707, but no jetliner of that era approached the sales record of the versatile, reliable Boeing 727.

Designed specifically for short- and medium-haul operations, the 727's high-lift wing and rear-mounted engines meant that it was the first aircraft capable of bringing regular scheduled jet travel to small city airfields with runways as short as 1550 m (5085 ft.).

Boeing hoped to sell 250 aircraft. The actual number of 727s delivered was nearly eight times that figure – 1,831, in a production run which lasted from 1962 to 1984. The 727 flies today in 17 passenger and freight versions.

There are some military users of the 727, but this classic airliner has made its mark as a hard-working servant of civil air commerce.

The 727 entered service in 1964, and by 1967 it was the most widely used airliner in the world. Air Canada operated the type on domestic and American routes.

Airlines like Texas-based Braniff embraced the 727 as a highly effective, fuel-efficient and reliable workhorse. It could fly several route sectors each day, maximising passenger carriage and increasing profit.

727-200

Type: medium-range passenger or cargo airliner

Powerplant: three Pratt & Whitney 64.50-kN JT8D-9A or 77.38-kN (25,889-lb.-thrust) JT8D-15 turbofans

Maximum cruise speed: 964 km/h (598 m.p.h.)

Range: 4400 km (2,728 mi.)

Service ceiling: 10,000 m (33,000 ft.)

Weights: empty 45,168 kg (99,370 lb.); loaded 86,405 kg (190,090 lb.)

Accommodation: three crew plus flight attendants; maximum 189 single-class passengers; typical load of 14 first class and 131 tourist class

Dimensions:
span	32.92 m	(108 ft.)
length	46.69 m	(153 ft.)
height	10.36 m	(34 ft.)
wing area	157.90 m²	(1,699 sq. ft.)

MODEL 727-200

CS-TBW was the 13th Boeing 727 delivered to Transportes Aereos Portugueses, or TAP. The 727's old engines mean that it does not compare favourably with the latest generation of jets, although it remains a useful performer thanks to its trouble-free reliability.

The rear-mounted three-engine layout was chosen so that the wings were free of engine mountings and could be designed with new features.

With a fuselage width the same as the 707 (and the later 737 and 757), the 727 can seat economy-class passengers six abreast.

The wing fuel tank in the outboard wing contains 31,000 litres (8,000 gal.) of fuel.

The central air intake feeds air to the third engine via a long duct.

The central engine is located on the centreline in the rear of the fuselage.

Most 727s soldier on with the reliable but noisy and uneconomical Pratt & Whitney JT8D turbofan. Rolls-Royce has proposed re-engining Delta Airlines' 727s with its advanced Tay engine.

AIR PORTUGAL

CS-TBW

BOEING 727

The 727 has the three-man cockpit, including a flight engineer, which was standard in the 1960s.

Boeing stretched the 727-100's fuselage by 6 metres to produce the 727-200 series, with maximum passenger capacity increased from 131 to 189.

The 727 wing features ailerons and spoilers for roll control, and Krüger flaps for high efficiency at low speed. The high-lift devices fitted were the most advanced of their day.

Many airlines are fitting 'hush-kit' noise suppression systems to their 727 engines to enable the aircraft to continue operating after 'Stage Three' noise abatement regulations come into force worldwide in the late 1990s.

ACTION DATA

MAXIMUM CRUISE SPEED

The first generation of tri-jets were as fast as their four-jet contemporaries, even though they had 25 per cent less power. They were also far more economical; fitting the engines at the back cuts drag and leaves the wing clear and uncluttered for efficient lift.

MODEL 727-200	964 km/h (598 m.p.h.)
TRIDENT	960 km/h (595 m.p.h.)
Tu-154 'CARELESS'	950 km/h (590 m.p.h.)

RANGE

The tri-jets were not designed for intercontinental flying; they were intended to service routes ranging from 200 km (125 mi.) to 3000 km (1,860 mi.) in length. The ability to use second-line airports and make fast turnarounds was more important than a huge range.

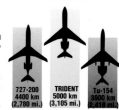

727-200 4400 km (2,780 mi.)
TRIDENT 5000 km (3,105 mi.)
Tu-154 3900 km (2,418 mi.)

The tri-jet rivals

■ **HAWKER SIDDELEY TRIDENT:** An almost exact contemporary of the 727, the Trident was at least as good a flyer, but its smaller capacity and less effective short-field ability meant that it lost out in the sales battles with the Boeing jet.

■ **TUPOLEV Tu-154:** Tupolev engineers copied Boeing's high-lift wing for their tri-jet to enable operations from rough Siberian airfields. Allied to more powerful engines, this gave the 154 the required performance, but economy was never great.

■ **DOUGLAS DC-10:** The explosion in demand for air travel in the 1960s saw the first wide-bodies appear only six years after the 727. Designed to fly similar routes to the 189-seat Boeing jet, the DC-10 could carry up to 380 passengers.

BOEING

737 SERIES 100–500

● Short-haul transport ● Twin-jet ● World's best-selling airliner

B oeing's chunky Model 737 is the world's most popular twin-engined airliner, and has been operated in greater numbers than any commercial aircraft since the classic DC-3. Passengers are seated in a fuselage based on the Boeing 707, wide enough to accommodate six abreast in comfort. The 737's wing provides good lift and handling, and permits this workhorse to use even small-town airfields.

▲ The 737's wide fuselage
has enough room to carry a large number of passengers in a relatively short aircraft, without sacrificing passenger comfort.

BOEING 737 SERIES 100–500

▲ Short-haul workhorse
The Boeing 737 was designed for frequent short-haul flights. Airlines find the latest variants very cost-effective on busy domestic and European routes.

▲ Twin-jet
The wing-mounted engines on the 737 went against the 1960s trend towards rear-mounted jets, but most current jets follow the 737 pattern.

New engines ▼
To fit bigger engines on the low-slung 737 wing, it was necessary to flatten the nacelles.

Spacious cabin ►
Because it uses the 707's hull cross-section the Model 737 comfortably seats six abreast, whereas its 1960s rivals could only seat five.

▲ Mass production
The 737 is the world's most popular airliner. More than 3100 have been built, and orders continue to flood in.

Family of jets ►
The latest variants of the 737 are the stretched 737-400 and the smaller 737-500.

FACTS AND FIGURES

➤ The 737 has passed Boeing's 727 and the competing DC-9/MD-80 to become the world's best-selling airliner.

➤ In all, 3100 Boeing 737s have been delivered; 700 are in the air at any one time.

➤ In 55 million flights, the 737 fleet has carried 4.24 billion passengers.

➤ The Boeing 737-300, -400 and -500 now in production are powered by 97.86-kN (22,000 lb thrust) CFM56-3 engines.

➤ Nineteen Boeing 737s, called CT-43s, are used by the USAF for navigator training.

➤ Indonesia employs the 737 Surveiller for maritime patrol.

Short-haul stalwart

Following the popular 707 and 727, the now-familiar Boeing 737 began enriching air commerce soon after the first aircraft flew on 9 April 1967. From a business standpoint, this twin-engined jet was a stroke of genius. Almost 3000 of these great aircraft are flying, or will fly, with several dozen airlines.

Lufthansa had a strong role in inspiring and backing the 737 and was the first company to offer passenger service, beginning on 10 February 1968. Newer versions with longer fuselage and bigger engines have enabled the Boeing 737 to serve a wider diversity of airfields and operators. Though only two countries (the USA and Indonesia) have found a military duty for this well-known civil servant, others use the 737 as a VIP transport.

To pilots, the Boeing 737 is a super ship to fly, offering excellent handling and performance. The 737 is regarded as the best aircraft in its class, and is likely to be moving passengers in comfort for many years to come.

The 737 was built with the same fuselage cross-section as the Boeing 707 and the 727. Not only did this ease the company's manufacturing requirements, but it also gave the 737 a wider body than its rivals.

The short undercarriage and low-set wings mean that the 737's cabin is not too much of a climb for passengers using airstairs.

Putting the engines on the wings meant that the fuselage could be more lightly built, the weight saved being used to carry as many as 10 extra passengers.

Very few 737s have been delivered for military use. Among the few exceptions are the 737 Surveillers developed by Boeing for the Indonesian air force. They are equipped with a Motorola side-looking radar.

737-400

Type: short-/medium-range transport

Powerplant: two 97.86-kN (22,000 lb thrust) CFM International CFM56-3C turbofan engines

Maximum speed: 935 km/h (581 m.p.h.) at 7165 m (23,500 ft.)

Cruising speed: 900 km/h (559 m.p.h.)

Range: 5000 km (3,107 mi.)

Weights: empty 33,434 kg (73,709 lb.); loaded 62,822 kg (138,499 lb.)

Accommodation: typically, 146 passengers in two classes

Dimensions: span 28.88 m (28 ft. 7 in.)
length 36.45 m (119 ft. 7 in.)
height 11.13 m (36 ft. 6 in.)
wing area 105.40 m² (1,135 sq. ft.)

MODEL 737-200

The first major variant of the Boeing 737, the Model 200 was built in large numbers. More than 1100 examples were delivered between 1967 and 1988.

The 737 was initially powered by two Pratt & Whitney JT8D turbofans. More than 1000 examples of the 737-200 were sold before larger and more fuel-efficient engines became standard.

Passenger capacity aboard the 737-200 varied between 100 and 130, depending on the proportion of economy-class to business-class passengers.

Early 737s included a flight engineer in addition to two pilots, but a two-man flight crew soon became the norm.

Amberair

G-BOSA

A tiny auxiliary power unit at the base of the tail allows the 737 to keep lights and air conditioning running and to start main engines without the need for ground support.

ACTION DATA

MAXIMUM CRUISING SPEED

737-400	900 km/h (559 m.p.h.)	
A320	905 km/h (562 m.p.h.)	
MD-80	885 km/h (550 m.p.h.)	

The 737 has a maximum speed of about 930 km/h (578 m.p.h.), but cruises a little more slowly. To minimise fuel consumption and hence achieve maximum range, the 737 pilot selects an economical cruise speed of about 800 km/h (500 m.p.h.).

AIRCRAFT SALES

The Boeing 737 is easily the most successful post-war airliner in terms of numbers ordered, having overtaken the Boeing 727 in the 1980s. But the short-haul twin-jet market is possibly the busiest and most profitable aircraft manufacturing sector in the world, and demand for such jets is high. By the end of 1993 more than 6150 examples of the 737 and its two main rivals had been delivered or were on order.

BOEING MODEL 737 SERIES 3100

DC-9/MD-80/MD-90 2600

A320 2400

RANGE

Although described as a short-haul airliner, the standard 737-400 could just about make a non-stop transatlantic crossing. However, where it and its competitors are most effective is in the regular, cycle-after-cycle business travel routes, making several flights daily.

5190 km (3,225 mi.)
4600 km (2,858 mi.)
5000 km (3,107 mi.)

MD-80   A320   MODEL 737-400

737s for every occasion

■ **737-100:** The original Boeing 737 first flew on 9 April 1967. Only 30 were sold before production switched to the 737-200.

■ **737-200:** Widely sold to airlines around the world, the Dash-200 was stretched by 2 metres and could seat 12 more passengers.

■ **737-300:** Launched in 1981, the Dash-300 has modern, quiet, fuel-efficient engines, and can carry up to 149 passengers.

■ **737-400:** Success with the Dash-300 led to the even longer Dash-400, which flew in 1988 and can seat up to 170 passengers.

■ **737-500:** The latest variant of the 737 trades capacity for extra range. The Dash-500 first flew in 1989, and has a range of over 5500 km (3,400 mi.).

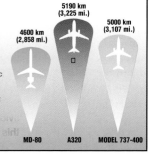

BOEING

747 SERIES 100-200

● World's largest airliner ● Ultra-long-range load carrier

A true giant of the skies, the Boeing 747 revolutionised air travel by carrying more people further, and at lower cost, than any aircraft before it. Called the 'Jumbo Jet' because of its wide-body capacity, the 747 introduced size and economy to the world's airline routes. It is regarded today as the backbone of air transport, and provides efficiency and comfort for business travellers and tourists around the globe.

▲ Few shapes are as distinctive as Boeing's 'Jumbo Jet', the Model 747. Over 1000 of these graceful giants are in service around the globe, and even Concorde could not replace them as the ultimate airline status symbol.

BOEING 747 SERIES 100-200

▼ Plane-maker to the world
The Boeing Airplane Company built its first aircraft in 1919. Since then it has become the largest manufacturer of civil aircraft in history, and 747s will be rolling out for years to come.

◀ Air Force One ▲
Two specially modified 747-200s, called VC-25s, serve as the personal aircraft of the President of the United States. When the President is on board their radio callsign is 'Air Force One'.

▼ Space Shuttle transporter
Every NASA Space Shuttle mission begins with a Boeing 747. NASA operates two Boeing 747s which carry the Space Shuttle from its landing site at Edwards AFB in California across the country to the Shuttle launch site at Cape Canaveral in Florida.

▲ Super freighter
Few aircraft can rival the 747 as a cargo-carrier. Special freight versions, the 747Fs, are fitted with upward-swinging noses and special roller floors so that cargo can easily be rolled in and out. Like ordinary passenger Jumbo Jets the 747 freighter can also carry sizable loads under the floor, in its belly.

FACTS AND FIGURES

➤ With the 747-100's fuel capacity of 178,709 litres (39,310 gal.), a Cessna 150 lightplane can fly 1.8m km (1.1m mi.).

➤ The 747 was chosen for the earthly job of transporting the Space Shuttle orbiter.

➤ 747s carry more passengers each year than the population of Germany.

➤ The interior of a Boeing 747 contains 5000 km (3,100 mi.) of electrical wiring.

➤ The main undercarriage on the 747 has four 'legs' and 16 wheels with disc brakes and individual anti-skid locks.

➤ Special versions of the 747 flying in Japan can carry 566 passengers.

PROFILE

King-size ruler of the airways

The 747 was a huge gamble by Boeing, which risked $1 billion in the belief that the world was ready for a bigger, more efficient airliner able to carry 400 passengers. Made possible by dramatic progress with jet engines, so large that a man can stand in their air intakes, the Boeing 747 suddenly made

airline travel accessible to millions who had never flown before. The 747 first flew in 1969, and it was several years before the number of people snapping up tickets justified such a colossal investment. But Boeing was right in predicting a Jumbo Jet revolution. The 747 has since appeared in several versions, including a long-range model

which easily flies non-stop from London to Tokyo. A handful of 747s have also found freight-carrying and military uses.

Today the 747 is still impressive for its size, and looks awesome when seen close-up. And more than 60 airline companies also appreciate the Boeing 747 for its practical design and economic operating costs.

The demand for Boeing 747s remains strong even today. Airlines are happier with the idea of new 747 versions rather than possible new 600-seat concepts.

Few could have foreseen that Boeing's gamble with the original 747 would pay off with the aircraft becoming the backbone of international travel.

747-200B

Type: high-capacity commercial transport

Powerplant: four 243.55-kN (54,800 lb-thrust) Pratt & Whitney JT9D turbofans

Cruising speed: 940 km/h (584 m.p.h.) at 6096 m (20,000 ft.)

Range: 10,500 km (6,524 mi.) (normal payload)

Cruising ceiling: 13,715 m (45,000 ft.)

Weights: empty 173,272 kg (382,000 lb.); loaded 356,100 kg (785,066 lb.); maximum take-off 377,800 kg (832,906 lb.)

Passenger load: 490 seats maximum; typically 394 seats including 24 first-class, 70 business-class and 290 standard-class passengers

Dimensions:
span	59.64 m (195 ft. 8 in.)
length	70.66 m (231 ft. 10 in.)
height	19.33 m (63 ft. 5 in.)
wing area	510.95 m² (5,500 sq. ft.)

MODEL 747-200F

The Boeing 747 is a true giant of the air. Able to carry nearly 600 passengers or vast amounts of cargo, it lives up to its name – Jumbo Jet.

The upward-swinging nose on the 747F freighter means that even the largest items can be loaded with ease.

The 747 has proved exceptionally popular in Japan, where two airlines, JAL and All Nippon, fly 747s as a commuter airliner with nearly 600 seats on board.

The tip of a 747's fin is more than 19 m (62 ft.) from the ground – taller than a four-storey house.

The fuselage length of the 747 is longer than the distance covered by the Wright Brothers' first flight in 1908.

The 747's main undercarriage needs 16 wheels to spread the load of such a heavy aircraft and avoid damaging runways.

The Saudi Royal family owns several private 747s with sumptuous fittings inside – the ultimate 'bizjet'.

The 747F revolutionised the carriage of freight by air. Several airlines, such as Nippon Cargo Airlines, fly only freighter versions of the Jumbo Jet.

ACTION DATA

MAXIMUM SPEED

The Boeing 747 is the largest airliner ever to have entered large-scale service, but it is also one of the fastest; its four powerful engines drive it to a maximum of almost nine-tenths the speed of sound.

747-200	989 km/h (615 m.p.h.)
DC-10	908 km/h (564 m.p.h.)
DC-8 SERIES 63	960 km/h (597 m.p.h.)

PAYLOAD

The 747 is designed to carry heavy loads of passengers or cargo over great distances. Earlier airliners could not carry as much fuel and could not match the big Boeing's performance.

747-200
394 mixed-class passengers or 100 tons of cargo

DC-10
270 mixed-class passengers or 46 tons of cargo

DC-8 SRS.63
200 mixed-class passengers or 30 tons of cargo

RANGE

Today any modern jet airliner designed for long-haul operations must be able to fly from London to Tokyo non-stop – an unbelievable distance only 20 years ago.

747-200	10,500 km (6,524 mi.)
DC-1	7500 km (4,660 mi.)
DC-8 SRS.63	7250 km (4,505 mi.)

Trans-Atlantic crossing

DEPARTURE: On leaving any American airport bound for Europe, a 747 will climb slowly to about 10,000 m (33,000 ft.). Initially under local control over the United States, after about an hour it will be switched to the air traffic control at Gander in Newfoundland.

OCEANIC CONTROL: Once aircraft are out of VHF radio range (about 300 km (185 mi.) from land) they rely on short-wave radio to talk to Gander Oceanic Control. The controllers there monitor the aircraft's progress, but there is no Atlantic radar coverage.

HIGH POINT: As it burns fuel the 747 gets lighter and climbs higher. Halfway across the Atlantic control is switched to Shanwick, based in Scotland but broadcast from Ireland. First sight of dry land is often the lush green landscape of Ireland.

FINAL APPROACH: At the end of its Atlantic crossing the 747 leaves Oceanic Control and returns to normal air traffic control, relayed across European national air traffic control systems, until it reaches its destination.

BOEING

737 SERIES 600-800

● New generation airliner ● Latest in family ● Three versions

A s the world's best-selling jet airliner, the Model 737 has been the mainstay of Boeing's short-medium haul airliner product range since the 1970s. The success of the new-generation 737s, released in the mid-1980s, proved that the design was as popular as ever and prompted Boeing to design a third generation of Model 737s. Originally called the Model 737X, the three new variants have already received orders from more than 25 airlines.

▲ *Boeing has conducted an extensive promotion and advertising campaign for the new 737s. This demonstrator appeared at the Paris Air Salon in June 1997.*

BOEING 737 SERIES 600-800

◀ **High-tech assembly**
For the manufacture of the aircraft a specially-built integration tool is used. It features electric-driven power cylinders that position the major parts accurately. Laser measurement tools and portable co-ordinate machines ensure alignment and precise fitting.

Reducing costs ▶
To reduce costs the fuselages are manufactured at Wichita, Kansas, and are shipped via rail in one piece to the assembly site at Renton, Washington.

▲ **Largest variant**
The largest of the original series this 737-800 is seen shortly after one of the initial test flights in August 1997. The first delivery was made to Hapag-Lloyd in April 1998.

◀ **Test programme**
Seen in formation with a T-38 Talon chase plane, the first 737-700 to fly undergoes trials. The flight test programme will involve 10 aircraft: four 737-700s, three 737-800s and three 737-600s.

◀ **First of many**
The first of the new series of 737s to be presented to the public was the Series 700. It was unveiled at a lavish ceremony at the company's manufacturing site at Renton, near Seattle, Washington, in December 1996.

FACTS AND FIGURES

➤ All new generation Model 737s are fully digitally defined, as are all the major manufacturing tools.

➤ The largest order so far has been from GE Capital Aviation Services for 80 aircraft.

➤ Boeing launched a fourth and even larger new model, designated 737-900, in 1997.

➤ The new models are powered by the new CFM56-7 engines produced as a joint venture by General Electric and Snecma.

➤ Prices range between US$36-40 million depending on the equipment fit.

➤ The CFM56-7B powerplant was tested on a modified Boeing 747 in January 1996.

PROFILE

Next generation airliner

In the light of the growing success of the European Airbus A320 series Boeing decided, in 1990, to produce a third-generation of its highly successful Boeing 737 airliner. To help tailor the new design to meet customers' requirements, Boeing asked more than 30 airlines to help define the Model 737X.

Results of research culminated in Boeing announcing three new versions. The Series 600 is the smallest of the trio seating 108 passengers in standard layout accommodation. Launch customer is the Scandinavian airline SAS and the first flight was made in January 1998.

The Series 700 was the first of the new generation to fly in December 1996 and carries 128 passengers. Southwest Airlines became the first customer of the new generation, ordering 63 700s before construction of the first aircraft had even begun. Southwest received its first aircraft in October 1997.

The biggest of the family is the Series 800 able to seat 162 in a two-class layout with the first deliveries in April 1998. With 517 of the new generation 737s ordered by 1 January 1997, the aircraft seems to have a very healthy future and with its energy-saving wings and engines it will achieve significant sales well into the 21st century.

Above: The new 737s possess superior range and speed performance compared to the previous variants.

Below: The first airline to receive the 737-700 was Southwest Airlines. They have ordered 63 examples with options on 63 more.

737-800

Type: twin-turbofan short-medium range airliner

Powerplant: two 116.5-kN (26,200-lb.-thrust) CFM International CFM56-7B turbofan engines

Maximum operating speed: Mach 0.82

Range: 5426 km (3,364 mi.) with maximum passenger load

Cruising altitude: 10,730 m (35,200 ft.)

Weights: operating empty 41,554 kg (91,419 lb.); maximum take-off 70,535 kg (155,177 lb.)

Accommodation: Alternative cabin layouts for 162 to 189 passengers; overhead baggage capacity of 9.3 m³ (329 cu. ft.)

Dimensions:
span	34.31 m (112 ft. 6 in.)
length	39.47 m (129 ft. 6 in.)
height	12.55 m (41 ft. 2 in.)
wing area	125 m² (1,345 sq. ft.)

737-800

Olympic Airways of Greece have become the one of the latest customers for the Boeing 737-800. The current deal is for four firm orders and four options. This is expected to grow to a final figure of 25.

The two crew are seated side-by-side. Cockpit instrumentation includes a systems common display screen (CDS) and a six-screen liquid crystal display.

Accommodation can vary between 162 and 189. Typical layouts include 12 four-abreast first class seats plus 150 six-abreast tourist class seats or 189 six-abreast tourist class seats. Lavatories are located forward and aft and an over-wing emergency exit is fitted on both sides of the fuselage. To reduce weight the interior uses advanced crushed core materials.

The tailplane is constructed of aluminium alloy. For strength and reduced weight the elevators and rudder contain graphite/Kevlar, carbon-fibre reinforced plastic (CFRP) and glass-fibre reinforced plastic (GFRP). The tail surfaces are larger than those fitted to second-generation Boeing 737s.

The hydraulically-operated undercarriage is of retractable tricycle type with free-fall emergency extension. The main units have no undercarriage door with the wheels forming the well seal instead. Heavy-duty brakes are fitted as standard.

Two CFM International CFM56-7B turbofan engines power the new generation aircraft. With an improved low-pressure compressor this unit is more efficient than that fitted to second-generation 737s.

Fitted at the rear of the fuselage is the aircraft's auxiliary power unit (APU). The APU provides the air supply and electric power in flight as well as power for engine starting on the ground.

ACTION DATA

CAPACITY

In standard two-class configuration, the Airbus A321 offers the highest passenger capacity which helps reduce the cost per passenger. Boeing's new 737-900 will have similar capacity to this aircraft. Boeing's take-over of McDonnell Douglas in 1997 has placed the MD-90's future in doubt because of its similarity in capacity to Boeing's third-generation 737 series.

737-800	**162 PASSENGERS**
A321	**185 PASSENGERS**
MD-90-30	**153 PASSENGERS**

RANGE

The efficiency of the engines and relatively large fuel capacity for an aircraft of its size ensure that the 737-800 outperforms its competitors in range with a full load of passengers.

737-800 5426 km (3,364 mi.)

MD-90-30 4216 km (2,614 mi.)

A321 4260 km (2,640 mi.)

THRUST

As the lightest of the three types, the MD-90 requires slightly less powerful engines than the 737 or A321. The extra power and size of the A321 allow extra capacity but more power also equates to higher fuel consumption and therefore higher fuel costs.

737-800	233 kW (52,415 lb.-thrust)
A321	266.8 kW (60,020 lb.-thrust)
MD-90-30	222.4 kW (50,030 lb.-thrust)

Other CFM56-powered aircraft

■ **AIRBUS A340:** Four 138.8-kN CFM56-5C2 engines power Airbus' long-range A340. The type entered service with Air France and Lufthansa in March 1993.

■ **BOEING E-3D:** Purchased by the RAF, the E-3D differs from US variants of the E-3 by being powered by the 106.8-kN (24,025-lb.-thrust) CFM56-2A-3.

■ **BOEING E-6 MERCURY:** Based on the venerable Boeing 707, the E-6 is powered by the F108-CF-100 engine which is the military equivalent of the CFM56-2A-2.

■ **DOUGLAS DC-8 SUPER 70:** The CFM56-powered DC-8 established a long distance point-to-point record in March 1983. It flew 13,220 km (8,200 mi.) in 15 hours 46 minutes.

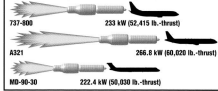

BOEING

747 SERIES 300/400

● Still the world's largest airliner ● Greater range ● More economical

The Boeing 747-300/400 jetliner is the advanced version of the famous 'Jumbo', optimised to carry a large number of passengers at economical cost. While earlier 747s revolutionised air travel with their size, wide bodies and enormous capacity, these 'dash 300' and 'dash 400' versions increase further the number of travellers that can be whisked over intercontinental distances. These are the 'heavy haulers' of air commerce today.

▲ One of the most successful commercial aircraft of all time, the 747 looks set to continue its winning ways thanks to the introduction of the series 300 and much-improved 400.

BOEING 747 SERIES 300/400

▼ World's largest
Just like its predecessors, the high-tech 747-400 has proved a popular choice with many airlines. In the large long-range sector of the market, it remains unrivalled in terms of passenger capacity.

▲ 'Big Top'
Singapore Airlines acquired 14 series 300 aircraft which were christened 'Big Top'. These have since been augmented by 24 747-400 'Mega Tops'.

New freighter ▶
Currently the latest variant to enter service, the 747-400F is a second-generation 747 freighter. It features the strengthened wing and glass cockpit of the passenger 400, but retains the original fuselage profile with the short upper deck.

◀ Belgian Jumbos
Sabena, the Belgian flag carrier, currently operates two 747-300s on long-haul routes. One of its aircraft is seen here on the ramp at Zaventem, near Brussels.

Standardised fleet ▶
Hong Kong's Cathay Pacific, based at Kai Tak airport, has a sizeable number of stretched 'Jumbos'. All 747s in the Cathay fleet are powered by ultra-efficient Rolls-Royce RB211 turbofans.

FACTS AND FIGURES

➤ Initial customers for the 747-300 were UTA of France and Swissair. Their first aircraft were delivered early in 1983.

➤ Today, more than 400 of the stretched upper deck 'Jumbos' have been ordered.

➤ Three different powerplants were simultaneously certified for the 747-400.

➤ A high-density model, designed for the Japanese domestic market, can accommodate up to 509 passengers.

➤ Despite the bulkier upper fuselage, the 747-300 is faster than previous versions.

➤ Unlike in previous versions, the tailplane structure of the 747-400 houses fuel.

PROFILE

Superjet from Seattle

Left: Even lesser known airlines, such as VARIG of Brazil, have acquired 747-300s which are perfectly suited to their requirements.

The Boeing 747-300 of 1982 improved on the world's best-known airliner by adding an upper deck to accommodate up to 91 tourist-class passengers. The first examples of the new 'Stretched Upper Deck' (SUD) variant were delivered to Swissair and UTA, the largest independent airline in France. It has since become a popular aircraft for many carriers on long-haul routes.

Realising the potential of this latest version, Boeing went a step further and unveiled the 747-400 in 1988. This has a fully

digital flight deck for two pilots (eliminating the third flight-crew position), plus wingtip extensions (including upward-pointing, 1.85-m (6-ft.) winglets for greater economy) and increased range. In common with previous variants, three different powerplants manufactured by Pratt & Whitney, General Electric and Rolls-Royce are available as options on the 747-400.

Pilots are delighted with the modern, all-glass cockpit of the 747-400 which has reduced the workload considerably, although

additional complete second crews are often employed by airlines to reduce fatigue. A further version, the 747-400F has since been introduced. This is a dedicated freighter variant and incorporates the cockpit and strengthened wing of the passenger version. It first flew in May 1993 and has subsequently been delivered to 16 operators, the first being Air France.

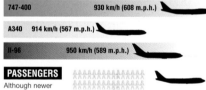

Above: Possibly one of the most famous liveries of recent times is that of Virgin Atlantic airways. In addition to a number of 747s, it also operates the rival Airbus A340.

747-400

Type: high-capacity long haul airliner

Powerplant: four high-bypass-ratio turbofans rated at 258 kN (58,040 lb.-thrust) (engines available Pratt & Whitney PW4056, General Electric CF6-80C2 or Rolls-Royce RB-211 425G)

Maximum speed: 980 km/h (608 m.p.h.)

Range: 13,398 km (8,307 mi.)

Service ceiling: 13,716 m (45,000 ft.)

Weights: empty 182,754 kg (402,059 lb.); loaded 394,625 kg (868,175 lb.)

Take-off run: 3322 m (10,900 ft.)

Accommodation: two (flight deck), 390 passengers in standard configuration

Dimensions:
span	64.44 m	(211 ft. 4 in.)
length	70.66 m	(231 ft. 9 in.)
height	19.41 m	(63 ft. 8 in.)
wing area	511 m²	(5,498 sq. ft.)

747-300

Z5-BAT is one of two series 300s currently flying with Suid Afrikaanse Lugdiens (South African Airways). The airline is based at Johannesburg and uses its 747s on major long-haul routes.

Despite its huge size, the cockpit of the 747 is surprisingly small. On the series 300 the cockpit remains essentially unchanged from earlier variants, with a multitude of conventional dial instruments.

On the upper deck, up to 91 economy-class passengers can be seated. This is more than the entire capacity of the Boeing Model 377 Stratocruiser of 1948. SUD 747s have proved so popular in service that older aircraft are being modified as such. The 747 was designed from the start to permit features introduced on new models to be retrofitted to older aircraft with considerable ease.

Capacity on the main deck remains unaltered from the earlier 747-200B with provision for up to 450 passengers. Some aircraft were delivered as, or have since been modified to 'Combi' variants and designated 747-300BCs. These aircraft can be configured for all-freight, all-passenger or both. A distinguishing feature of this variant is a large cargo door mounted on the port side of the rear fuselage.

Underneath the passenger cabin are two enormous baggage holds, one located fore and the other aft. Many airlines use the excess space for cargo in addition to luggage.

Although the 'Jumbo' was initially powered by Pratt & Whitney high-bypass-ratio JT9D turbofans, other powerplants have since become available. On the series 300, optional engines are the General Electric CF-60 and Rolls-Royce RB-211.

Each wing features two enormous sets of triple-slotted flaps. The amount of lift they generate at slow speeds is immense, considering that a fully laden 747-300 weighs 351,534 kg (773,375 lb.) on take-off. Low speed ailerons and spoilers provide braking.

Mounted in the tail unit is an APU (Auxiliary Power Unit). Whilst the aircraft is on the ground this operates the 747's major systems, such as the electrics, heating and air conditioning.

ACTION DATA

CRUISING SPEED

Modern airliners are powered by highly efficient and powerful turbofans which are also extremely quiet. As the largest airliner in the world, the 747 requires the most powerful engines. Its cruising speed is roughly comparable to that of rival airliners, however.

747-400	930 km/h (608 m.p.h.)
A340	914 km/h (567 m.p.h.)
Il-96	950 km/h (589 m.p.h.)

PASSENGERS

Although newer airliners such as the A340 claim to offer better performance than the 747, the giant aircraft remains untouched in the high-capacity field. The Russian Ilyushin Il-96 is closest, though it has not been a great commercial success.

747-400 421 Passengers

A340 303 Passengers

Il-96 375 Passengers

RANGE

With the 747-400, Boeing has felt no need to offer an improved Special Performance long-range model, thanks to the increased range of the new aircraft. On long, less popular routes, the Airbus A340 has proved successful. It can fly nearly 14,000 km (8,500 mi.) unrefuelled.

747-400 13,390 km (8,3067 mi.)

A340 13,612 km (8,440 mi.)

Il-96 11,482 km (7,120 mi.)

Other 747 variants

■ **747-200B:** Still flying with many carriers around the world, the early 747 variants were pioneers in low-cost air travel for the masses.

■ **747-200F:** Based on the 200 airliner, this version is a freighter with an upward hinging nose. It entered service in the mid-1970s.

■ **747 SP:** An extra-long-range variant, the SP featured a taller tail and short fuselage. Taiwan's China Airlines was a major user of the type.

■ **E-4B COMMAND POST:** These aircraft are equipped to become the wartime emergency base for the US President and his advisors.

BOEING

747SP

● Long-range variant ● Shortened fuselage ● Record breaker

A n almost forgotten member of the Jumbo Jet family, the 747 Special Performance, or SP, is the aircraft that most dramatically altered the 747's appearance. Designed to fly higher, faster and further than any 747 model of its time, the 747SP is easily identified by its compact look caused by its shortened fuselage. As it is lighter and can carry more fuel, the SP can fly non-stop over distances of up to 11,000 km (6,800 mi.).

▲ After exhaustive flight tests, the 747SP was certificated on 4 February 1976. Pan American airlines made the first commercial flight, between New York and Tokyo, two months later.

BOEING 747SP

▼ Long-legged Jumbo
A reduction in passenger capacity and an increase in fuel made the 747SP ideal for lower density, long-range routes.

▲ Launch customer
Pan Am was the first customer for the SP. The airline soon achieved the amazing average daily utilisation rate of 14.1 hours per aircraft.

▼ Major modifications
In addition to its shortened fuselage, the SP also featured a lighter wing structure, a taller fin and rudder, and new trailing-edge flaps.

▲ Far East service
Ideally suited to cover the vast area of Chinese interests, this SP was one of four sold to the Civil Aviation Administration of China.

The Big Orange ▶
One of the most distinctive airlines of the 1970s was Braniff International, which painted its 747 fleet bright orange. After Braniff went into receivership, this aircraft was sold to the government of Oman.

FACTS AND FIGURES

➤ Forty-five Boeing 747SPs were built; 39 with Pratt & Whitney engines and six with Rolls-Royce powerplants.

➤ On its first flight on 4 July 1975, the 747SP reached a speed of Mach 0.92.

➤ Six 747SPs have been operated as luxury VIP transports in the Middle East.

➤ An SAA 747SP broke the non-stop distance record for a civil aircraft, flying 16,560 km (10,270 mi.) from New York to Cape Town.

➤ The height of a Boeing 747SP is equivalent to that of a six-storey building.

➤ A former American Airlines 747SP is now operated by the Kazakhstan government.

Trans-global Jumbo

When the US Federal Aviation Administration certified the Boeing 747SP in February 1976, the world had a jetliner which was able to carry passengers unprecedented distances, at speed and in comfort.

The ability to traverse great distances has always been a challenge to the success of commercial aviation. In the 1950s the propeller-driven Douglas DC-7 could fly from San Francisco to Tokyo with stops only at Honolulu and Wake Island. In the 1960s the jet-powered Boeing 707 still needed to stop in Honolulu. Even the wide-bodied Boeing 747, for all its qualities, was not truly a globe-girdling airliner, until the introduction of the ultra-long-range 747SP.

Although Pan American was the first customer in 1973, the 747SP proved extremely valuable to small national carriers, such as Air Mauritius, which required range but not the capacity of a standard 747.

In April 1976 a Pan Am SP broke the record for the longest non-stop flight by a civil aircraft. This was followed, in 1988, by a special charter flight in which another Pan Am 747SP flew around the world in 46 hours and 26 minutes. Actual flying time on the three-stage flight was 39 hours and 26 minutes.

Many remaining 747SPs are reaching the end of their service lives and are being replaced by the 747-400 and Airbus A340.

Boeing's 'mini-Jumbo' retained the twin-deck forward fuselage of the 747, but three rear-fuselage sections were removed. This gave the SP model its compact shape.

747SP 21

Type: long-range commercial transport

Powerplant: four 208.8-kN (46,970-lb.-thrust) Pratt & Whitney JT9D-7A turbofans or, alternatively, four 222.8-kN (50,120-lb.-thrust) Rolls-Royce RB.211-524B turbofan engines

Cruising speed: 940 km/h at 6096 m

Range: up to 11,397 km (7,070 mi.) with 305 passengers and fuel reserves

Cruising ceiling: 13,715 m (45,000 ft.)

Weights: empty 151,454 kg (333,120 lb.); loaded 317,515 kg (698,530 lb.)

Accommodation: two pilots, flight engineer, up to 12 passenger cabin attendants and (typically) 331 to 370 passengers over distances of up to 10,900 km (6,760 mi.)

Dimensions:
span	59.64 m	(195 ft. 7 in.)
length	56.31 m	(249 ft. 6 in.)
height	19.94 m	(65 ft. 5 in.)
wing area	510.95 m²	(5,498 sq. ft.)

Constructed at Boeing's main production centre in Seattle, the 747SP had a fairly trouble-free seven-month test programme.

MODEL 747SP 21

Named *Clipper Lindbergh* after the pioneering US pilot Charles Lindbergh, this SP was delivered to Pan Am in May 1977. After nine years of service it was transferred to United Air Lines.

A normal crew of three sat on the flightdeck above the main deck. There was also provision for two observer stations. The avionics and equipment were equivalent to that fitted to the standard Boeing 747.

Several versions of different powerplants were available to SP customers. The General Electric CF645A2 or -50E2-F had a power output of 206.8 kN (46,520 lb.-thrust); the Rolls-Royce RB.211-524B had 222.8 kN (50,120 lb.-thrust); and the Pratt & Whitney JT9D-7A had 208.8 kN (46,970 lb.-thrust).

The main consideration of the 747SP design was to reduce weight while maintaining the 747's phenomenal fuel capacity. This was achieved by removing two straight and one tapered section from the fuselage, giving a total reduction in length of 14.60 m (48 ft.).

To give the necessary lateral stability, the tailfin was heightened by 1.52 m (5 ft.). The rudder was also modified into a double-hinged arrangement. To help reduce weight the landing gear had a lighter-weight structure.

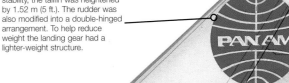

To help counter possible instability in pitch, the tailplane had an increased span of 3.05 m (10 ft.), but maintained a similar form to the conventional 747.

Long-range airliner variants

■ **AIRBUS A300-600R:** First flown in 1987, the 600R featured an extra fuel tank in the tailplane and an increased maximum take-off weight. It had a maximum range of 7840 km (4,870 mi.).

■ **LOCKHEED L1011-500 TRISTAR:** With a shortened fuselage and extra fuel tanks in the centre section, the L1011-500 has a range of 9905 km (6,150 mi.).

■ **McDONNELL DOUGLAS DC-10 SERIES 40:** The Series 40 was fitted with Pratt & Whitney JT9D-59A engines and had a range of 7505 km (4660 mi.).

ACTION DATA

RANGE

Although the TriStar Series 500 and the DC-10 Series 40 were both long-range versions of their standard type, neither could match the globe-spanning range of the SP. It was not until the A340 entered service that an airliner could exceed the SP's performance.

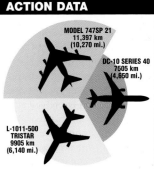

MODEL 747SP 21
11,397 km
(10,270 mi.)

DC-10 SERIES 40
7505 km
(4,650 mi.)

L-1011-500 TRISTAR
9905 km
(6,140 mi.)

BOEING

757

● Short/medium haul ● Twin-engine airliner ● Best-seller

A familiar sight at airports, the Boeing 757 was designed to replace the long-serving 727 tri-jet as the workhorse of the world's airlines. The aircraft incorporated many advanced new features while retaining the traditional Boeing strengths of comfort, economy and reliability. And with that reliability proven, this twin-jet was cleared for trans-ocean operations, previously a preserve of three- or four-engined types. It is now one of the world's most successful airliners.

▲ *The nose of the first 757 takes shape. The 757 and 767 were designed to have a similar profile, but the nose areas are slightly different.*

BOEING 757

Big twin ▶
Boeing's huge four-jet 747 may be the company's most famous product, but since the 757 its airliners have all been efficient twin-engined designs.

▲ Pilot comfort
The 757's cockpit is very comfortable for the crew. It is fitted with a blend of old- and new-style instruments.

◀ Taking shape
The first two Rolls-Royce-powered production 757s, both of which were delivered to Eastern Airlines, undergo final assembly. Two non-production machines had already been built, and were used for 10 months of tests.

▲ Flying to the sun
Iberia is one of many users of 757s, primarily carrying people to sunshine holiday destinations.

▼ Water testing
A vital part of any new airliner's test programme is a water-spray ingestion run. The first 757 was checked to see whether its engines could withstand the water thrown up from the runway.

▲ Rollout day
The rollout of the 757 was a big event for Boeing, as it was the first new airliner the company had built since the 747 in 1969.

FACTS AND FIGURES

➤ Boeing claims that the 757 freighter can hold six million golf balls.

➤ Mexico's Fuerza Aérea Mexicana operates a 757-225 as a VIP presidential aircraft.

➤ The first aircraft, a Boeing 757-200, flew on 18 February 1982.

➤ The 757 fleet has flown almost the equivalent of 5000 round trips between the Earth and the Moon.

➤ Boeing almost built a re-engined and re-designed 727 instead of the 757.

➤ United Airlines is the biggest 757 operator, with 89 in service.

Boeing's ever-popular twin

The Boeing 757 narrow-body airliner is an effective aircraft for commercial carriers all over the world. It was one of the first practical turbofan-powered, short-/medium-range airliners, well known for its passenger-carrying ability but with an equal capability as a freighter.

Originally intended for short-haul duties, the 757ER has been cleared for extended-range ocean flights and now has an intercontinental range.

The fine job being carried out by hundreds of 757s around the globe is due to a number of improvements, including digital instruments in place of some clock-style gauges, advanced flight controls and fuel-efficient engines.

These features put the 757 in the class of new airliners which operate with two flight crew members instead of three. It is also far more economical than preceding jets. For airline companies, these are solid financial incentives, encouraging them to buy the 757.

With hundreds of aircraft on order the 757 promises to be a top-selling airliner, following in the footsteps of Boeing's previous models.

The Pratt & Whitney-powered 757 got off to a firm start when Delta airlines ordered 60 of the aircraft in the mid-1980s.

MODEL 757-2B6

Royal Air Maroc, Morocco's flag-carrier, flies an all-Boeing fleet, including two 757s. They operate throughout Europe and the Middle East as well as to a small number of American destinations.

The tail designs of Singapore Airlines, LTU and Royal Air Maroc, operators of the 757 in three continents.

Most 757s are passenger carriers with a full complement of cabin windows. There is also a pure freighter version which is windowless.

The wing control surfaces consist of flaps, slats and spoilers. The spoilers act as airbrakes and complement the ailerons in flight.

The narrow fuselage profile of the 757 easily distinguished it from the 767. Despite the fuselage having a common cross-section to the 707, 727 and 737, both it and the wing were entirely new designs.

The 757's highly efficient turbofans offered superb fuel efficiency when spiralling fuel costs put a number of operators of older aircraft out of business

The elevators have a lightweight graphite epoxy honeycomb skin construction, built by Vought Aircraft.

Most tourist-class accommodation is in six-abreast configuration. First-class seating is usually four abreast.

The 757's flight deck is made by Boeing's military aircraft division.

Launch customers for the 757 specified Rolls-Royce RB211 engines. Since the mid-1980s, Pratt & Whitney engines have been offered as alternatives.

The landing gear features carbon disc brake technology. The main units have four wheels each.

The lower fuselage has an under-floor cargo volume of over 50 m³ (1,766 cu. ft.).

757-200

Type: twin-engine medium-range transport

Powerplant: two 166.37-kN (37,320-lb.-thrust) Rolls-Royce RB211-535C, or 169.93-kN (38,119-lb.-thrust) Pratt & Whitney PW2037, or 178.38-kN (40,015-lb.-thrust) RB211-535E4, or 185.50-kN (41,613-lb.-thrust) Pratt & Whitney PW2040 high-bypass turbofans

Maximum speed: 981 km/h (608 m.p.h.)

Range: 5150 km (3,193 mi.) with maximum load; 7400 km (4,588 mi.) at maximum economy

Service ceiling: 13,932 m (45,700 ft.)

Weights: empty 57,180 kg (125,796 lb.); loaded 113,400 kg (249,480 lb.)

Accommodation: two pilots, six attendants; typically 194 passengers in mixed-class service; 239 passengers on charter; up to 39,690 kg (87,318 lb.) of cargo and pallets in freighter version

Dimensions:
span	38.05 m (124 ft. 9 in.)
length	47.35 m (155 ft. 9 in.)
height	13.60 m (44 ft. 7 in.)
wing area	181.25 m² (1,950 sq. ft.)

Boeing's narrow-body dynasty

■ **MODEL 707:** The epoch-making Boeing 707 set the future of commercial aviation after the false dawn with Britain's Comet. It introduced the six-abreast cabin now standard on narrow bodies.

■ **MODEL 727:** Boeing's best seller in the 1970s, the 727 was for two decades the dominant short- and medium-haul jet in the world, until dethroned by the 737 and the 757.

■ **MODEL 737:** Originally intended as the 727's short-haul companion, the 737 has fathered its own family of jets in the 100- to 150-seat class, and is the world's best-selling airliner.

ACTION DATA

RANGE

The 757 has greater range than both its Boeing predecessor and the McDonnell Douglas MD-80, a stretched and upgraded version of the old DC-9. Although the 757 is classified as a medium-range airliner, it has been cleared for long-range over-ocean operations.

MODEL 727	MODEL 757	MD-80
4000 km (2,480 mi.)	7400 km (4,588 mi.)	5000 km (3,100 mi.)

BOEING
767

● Third-generation airliner ● Medium-/long-range wide-body

A modern, long-range jetliner, the Boeing Model 767 is a based on design work which was started in the 1970s. One of several twin-engined airliners intended for operation by two flightdeck crew, the 767 entered service in 1982 and has become a familiar sight at airports worldwide. With the same high-tech cockpit as the 757, the 767 offers airlines a profitable aircraft mid-way in size between the narrow-bodied 757 and the 'jumbo' 747 and 777.

▲ The Model 767
was Boeing's first wide-bodied, twin-engined aircraft. The aircraft flies automatically, from the take-off climb until landing, with the help of 140 microprocessors and computers.

PHOTO FILE

BOEING 767

▲ 767-300 cockpit
Six cathode-ray tube displays have replaced many of the traditional dials fitted in earlier airliners. These display both navigation and systems data.

▲ Prototype N767BA in flight
The 767 first flew in September 1981. United Air Lines flew the first passenger services in August 1982.

▼ On the line at Everett
Brand-new 767s await final checks and delivery outside Boeing's Everett Field plant.

▲ The world's favourite airline
In mid-1997 British Airways had 25 Model 767-300ERs, all powered by Rolls-Royce RB211 turbofan engines.

'Star Wars' laboratory ▶
The 767-200 prototype was configured with a 26.2-m (35-ft.) long dorsal cupola to test a long-wavelength infra-red sensor, which was intended to detect ballistic missiles as part of the Strategic Defense Initiative.

FACTS AND FIGURES

➤ The first Model 767 was rolled out on 4 August 1981 and made its maiden flight on 26 September 1981.

➤ A typical Boeing 767, straight out of the factory, has 3,140,000 separate parts.

➤ The production rate in early 1997 was four aircraft a month.

➤ Since 8 September 1982, Model 767s have carried more than 820 million passengers.

➤ Boeing claims that a 767 is 54 per cent more fuel-efficient than a Boeing 727.

➤ By mid-1997, 663 of 764 Boeing 767s ordered had been delivered.

PROFILE

Transoceanic wide-bodied twin

Numerous improvements over previous Boeing jetliners made their first appearance on the Model 767. Its wing is thicker, longer and less swept than those of earlier Boeings, and the shape is said to contribute to its excellent take-off performance and fuel economy. The 767's cabin is more than one metre (three feet) wider than the single-aisle, narrow-bodied Boeing jetliners.

The 767 has been ordered by a dozen of the world's major airlines needing an aircraft with new-generation technology and twin-aisle passenger cabin convenience. Ever since making its first revenue flight with United Air Lines in August 1982, the 767 has established an excellent record for reliability and efficiency. Its extended-range twin-engine operations, or ETOPS, qualification also made the type attractive to airlines flying transoceanic routes.

The 767 has been produced in standard -200 form and as the stretched -300, both of which have an extended-range 'ER' variant. There is also a freighter version. The longer 767-400ER, which will have 303 seats, was announced in 1997 and entered service in 2000.

ZK-NBA Aotearoa was Air New Zealand's first 767-200 and was built in 1985. The airline later operated -200ER and -300ER variants.

An important feature of the 767 family is its ETOPS qualification. This permits the twin-engined aircraft to fly transoceanic routes provided that it remains within two or three hours of an alternative airfield. Such a capability is possible with its modern ultra-reliable engines.

Sub-contractors producing different parts of the 767's structure include Boeing Helicopters (wing leading edges), Northrop Grumman (wing centre section), Canadair (rear fuselage) and Mitsubishi (cargo doors).

The -200ER and -300ER 'extended-range' variants of the basic aircraft have extra fuel tanks, giving a total tankage of 91,379 litres (24,142 gal.). The refuelling point is on the port outer wing.

MODEL 767-2Q8ER

S7-AAS *Aldabra* first flew in July 1989 and was delivered to the International Lease Finance Corporation for lease to Air Seychelles.

One of the innovations of the 767 was its two-person flightdeck, in which the functions of the former flight engineer were performed by the two pilots.

The basic 767-200 accommodates 224 passengers in standard configuration, including 18 in first-class seating. Single-class layouts are possible for between 247 and 290 passengers, although the latter requires eight-abreast seating and extra emergency exits over the wings. The 'stretched' 767-300 can seat between 269 and 350 passengers.

One of three engine types may be specified by the 767 customer. This 767-200ER is powered by General Electric CF6 turbofans. Rolls-Royce RB211s or Pratt & Whitney PW4000s are the other options.

In response to interest from the US company United Parcel Service, Boeing launched a freight version of the -300ER called the -300F. This is distinguished by its lack of passenger windows and a new cargo door on the port side of the forward fuselage.

767-300ER

Type: twin-engined long-range wide-bodied airliner

Powerplant: two 252.4-kN (80,925-lb.-thrust) Pratt & Whitney PW4056 or 266.9-kN (60,042-lb.-thrust) General Electric CF6-80C2B4 or Rolls-Royce RB211-542H turbofans

Cruising speed: Mach 0.80

Range: (with reserves) 11,230 km (6,965 mi.)

Service ceiling: 12,192 m (40,000 ft.)

Weights: empty 81,374 kg (179,023 lb.); maximum take-off 181,437 kg (399,161 lb.)

Accommodation: basic 269 passengers (24 first-class and 245 tourist-class); maximum capacity 350 passengers

Cargo hold volume: 147.0 m³ (5,191 cu. ft.)

Dimensions:
span	47.57 m (156 ft.)
length	54.94 m (180 ft. 3 in.)
height	15.85 m (52 ft.)
wing area	283.30 m² (3,048 sq. ft.)

ACTION DATA

PASSENGERS

The basic 767-200 competes directly with the Airbus A310, the -200 version of which carries a similar number of passengers. The DC-10-30 and -40 also sought sales in the small wide-body market.

MODEL 767-200	224
A310-200	220
DC-10-40	255

CARGO HOLD VOLUME

Underfloor capacity for freight is an important feature of modern airliners as passenger flights often carry small freight items at lucrative rates. The larger DC-10 is the leader in this respect.

MODEL 767-200	111.3 m³ (3,930 cu. ft.)
A310-200	102.1 m³ (3,605 cu. ft.)
DC-10-40	155.4 m³ (5,487 cu. ft.)

MAXIMUM RANGE

The A310 has a better range performance than the 767-200, and this was addressed by Boeing in the extended-range version, the -200ER. DC-10s also had a reputation for long range.

767-200	5963 km (3,700 mi.)
A310-200	6759 km (4,190 mi.)
DC-10-40	6485 km (4,020 mi.)

Model 767 development

■ **TRI-JET 7X7:** Both the 767 and the narrow-bodied 757 can trace their roots back to the 7X7 and 7N7 proposals of the mid-1970s. The 767 was initially a tri-jet design of similar configuration to the DC-10 and TriStar.

■ **NEW DESIGN:** During the design process different tail configurations were proposed, including this T-tail which was similar to that of the 727. The tri-jet was to be produced in co-operation with Italian and Japanese partners.

■ **E-767 AWACS:** Once the twin-jet configuration had been chosen and was in production, Boeing worked on military versions, like the Airborne Warning and Control System 'E-767' for Japan's armed forces.

BOEING
MODEL 777

● Ultra-long-range airliner ● Luxury interior ● Fly-by-wire controls

Developed in partnership with its customer airlines for the first time, the 777 is also Boeing's first fly-by-wire airliner. The entire airframe, all the systems and the cabin were designed with a computer so that every aspect could be examined in three dimensions before being produced. Specially designed laboratories were built to test the aircraft's advanced software, and the finished plane uses more than five-million lines of software code during operation.

▲ The 777 was the first aircraft in service to be designed entirely on computer. Theoretically, a computer could take the place of the pilot; on the 777 some flight functions are computer-controlled.

BOEING MODEL 777

Enormous wingspan ▶
The 777's wings are so large that Boeing offer folding outerwing panels as an option to customers.

▲ Powerplant choice
Boeing 777 customers are offered the choice of three different engines: Pratt & Whitney, General Electric or Rolls-Royce turbofans.

▲ United Airlines
The launch customer of the 777 was United, who placed an order for 34 (plus options on 34) as early as October 1990. The second prototype, flying on 15 July 1994, went on to wear United Airlines livery.

▲ Japanese partnership
Boeing are developing the 777 in co-operation with Mitsubishi, Kawasaki and Fuji, who are involved in producing the airframe.

21st-century cockpit ▶
The 777's crew are treated to an award-winning Boeing-designed flight deck with full fly-by-wire controls and digital Control Display Units (CDUs).

FACTS AND FIGURES

➤ The first export delivery was to British Airways in late-1995; BA has ordered 15 GE90-powered 777-236s.

➤ By mid-1995 Boeing had 164 firm orders for 777-200s, plus 31 for the 777-300.

'A-Market' and 'B-Market' 777-200s are produced; the latter have greater range.

➤ The 'stretched' 777-300 can carry as many passengers as a first-generation 747, but at two-thirds the fuel cost.

Before the 777 entered production it was known as the 7J7 and 767-X.

➤ Twenty per cent of the airframe is built by foreign manufacturers in Japan.

Boeing's big wide-body twin

First flown in 1994, the 777 introduced a whole series of new technologies, which were explored as part of Boeing's 7J7 programme in the 1980s. Many of the traditional black boxes housing electronics and computers have been replaced by an Aircraft Information Management System, or AIMS. Instead of using a separate computer for each function, the designers installed a series of circuit board cards which share the workload.

Cockpit information is presented on liquid-crystal displays instead of cathode-ray tube screens, and the pilots have cursor controls to manipulate these displays. Even the databuses that connect the various sensors and avionic systems are of a new type; there are nine of them, each able to transmit up to two Megabytes of data per second.

To allow airlines maximum flexibility in cabin layout, the galleys and toilets can be moved and the number of seats per row varied between six and 10. Many 777s will also have the latest entertainment systems, including a telephone and personal video screen with a wide range of films

and games for every passenger. Delivering such sophisticated amusement facilities requires more software than is used in the entire flight control system.

A 'stretched' 777-300 is available and there are also plans for a shorter version.

The Pratt & Whitney-powered first prototype, N7771, took to the air on 12 June 1994, flown by Boeing's chief test pilot Captain John Cashman. The flight lasted 3 hours and 48 minutes.

MODEL 777-222A

United Airlines was the first 777 customer, taking delivery of its initial aircraft, the fifth off the production line, on 17 May 1995.

Unlike most earlier large jetliners the 777 has a state-of-the-art, two-person cockpit equipped with multi-function displays rather than traditional instrumentation.

The fuselage diameter of the 777 is between the size of the 767 and 747. Seating arrangements between six- and 10-abreast are possible.

The first of United Airlines' 34 Model 777s can carry 363 passengers in two classes and have a range of over 7700 km (4784 mi.). Maximum take-off weight is 234 tonnes (257 tons).

United's 777-222s have a pair of PW4073 turbofan engines. The 777 prototype also has PW4000-series engines.

An unusual feature of the 777 is its ability (as an option) to fold the outer 6.48 m. (21 ft. 4 in.) of its wings so that it can be accommodated at existing airport terminals.

Composites of carbon and toughened resin are used in the tailplane skin, and the control surfaces and engine nacelles are made from carbon-fibre reinforced plastic.

Aircraft control surfaces are operated by 31 hydraulic actuators, controlled by a 'fly-by-wire' system.

A crew rest module with bunks and seats can be installed under the 777's floor.

The Allied Signal auxiliary power unit (APU) in the extreme rear of the fuselage supplies power for onboard systems when the aircraft is on the ground.

Model 777-200A

Type: twin-engined medium- to very long-range airliner

Powerplant: two 317-kN (71,300-lb thrust) Rolls-Royce RB.211 Trent 870/1, or 327-kN Pratt & Whitney PW4073/A or 331-kN (73,550 lb thrust) General Electric GE90-B2/3 turbofan engines

Maximum speed: Mach 0.87

Range: 7505 km (4663 mi.) with reserves

Service ceiling: 13136 m (43,000 ft.)

Weights: operating empty 135875 kg (299,500 lb.); maximum take-off 242670 kg (534,995 lb.)

Accommodation: two flight deck crew and up to 440 passengers

Dimensions:
span	60.93 m (200 ft.)
length	62.78 m (206 ft.)
height	18.44 m (60 ft. 6 in.)
wing area	427.80 m² (4604 sq. ft.)

Wide-bodied airliners of the 1990s

■ **AIRBUS A330:** The twin-engined A330 shares the structure, wing and cockpit design of the four-engined A340, and deliveries began in 1994. General Electric, Pratt & Whitney or Rolls-Royce engines may be fitted.

■ **AIRBUS A340:** Intended to offer competition in the Boeing 747's share of the airliner market, the A340 can hold a maximum of 440 passengers. Entering service in 1993, the A340 has been dubbed the 'World Ranger'.

■ **ILYUSHIN Il-96:** The Il-96 is a development of the Il-86 with new Kuznetsov NK-86 turbofans. The basic Il-96-300 seats 300 passengers. A prototype Il-96M, with Pratt & Whitney engines, flew in 1995.

■ **McDONNELL DOUGLAS MD-11:** An enlarged and completely updated development of the successful DC-10 tri-jet, the MD-11 had problems meeting its design range guarantees. Service entry took place in 1990.

ACTION DATA

RANGE

While the MD-11 has had problems meeting its advertised range performance figures, it is still a good performer, a feature it inherits from its predecessor, the DC-10.

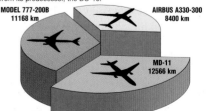

MODEL 777-200B 11168 km

AIRBUS A330-300 8400 km

MD-11 12566 km

BOEING
787 DREAMLINER

● Mid-size widebody ● Composite construction ● Fuel-efficient

The 787 is Boeing's first all-new airliner since the mid 1990s. It uses more composite materials in its construction than any previous large aircraft. New production methods involve widely-separated plants building major components that are brought together and assembled in Washington State. This arrangement proved less efficient than hoped and the first flight and initial deliveries were greatly delayed.

▲ Flightless in Seattle: the 787 had a well-publicised rollout ceremony in July 2007, but was far from complete and was not ready to fly for a further 25 months.

BOEING 787 DREAMLINER

▲ Factory
The 787's cockpit and forward fuselage are completed by Spirit Aerosystems in Wichita, Kansas.

▲ Sonic Cruiser
Many 787 features came from the Sonic Cruiser, a high-speed (but not supersonic) Boeing project that was cancelled in 2002.

First flight ▶
The prototype 787 finally took to the air in December 2009. Three more Rolls-Royce Trent powered test aircraft were flying within two months.

▼ Test programme
The 787 test programme involved six aircraft, the last two with the new General Electric GEnx engine.

▲ Cockpit
The original 7E7 design had a striking wraparound windscreen, but the actual 787's is much more conventional.

FACTS AND FIGURES

➤ List price for the 787 ranges from US $157 million for the 787-8 to $200 million for the 787-9.

➤ Ailerons and flaps are made in Australia, the tailplane in Italy, fairings in Canada and the central wing box in Japan.

➤ As much as 50 per cent of the Dreamliner's structure will be non-metallic composite materials.

➤ The Dreamliner name was chosen after a public competition. 7E7 changed to 787 because 8 is a lucky number in several Asian cultures.

Boeing's fastest-selling airliner

Initially launched as the 7E7 after the shelving of the Sonic Cruiser project, the 787 was designed for efficiency and is expected to use 20 per cent less fuel than other aircraft of its size. It will replace the 767 and A330 but also open up new long-range point-to-point routes where there is not enough demand for large aircraft like the 747 and 777. The Dreamliner was planned in three main versions: the 787-8 with 210-250 seats and up to 8,200 nautical miles (15,200 km) range; the 250-290-seat 787-9 with up to

8,500 nm (15,570 km) range; and the 787-3 (290-330 seats, 3,050 nm/5650 km range) optimised for the high-density Japanese market. ANA of Japan became the launch customer of the 787-8 and Air New Zealand was first to order the 787-9. By early 2010, over 860 787-8s and -9s were on order for over 75 operators and leasing companies, although none were firm orders for the 787-3.

The 787 is offered with a choice of two engines, the Rolls-Royce Trent 1000 and the General Electric GEnX. The Trent

1000 provides 53,000-75,000 lb (240-330 kN) thrust, depending on variant. Both engines use cowlings with distinctive 'chevron' trailing edges, which significantly reduce noise.

Above: The first 787 underwent taxi tests in November and December 2009. At the time of writing the first four 787 test aircraft have flown 898 hours and 30 minutes.

Below: Once the first flight was achieved, an extensive test programme began, eventually involving six 787-8 aircraft. Operations were tested at temperatures from -43°C (-45°F) to +46°C (115°F).

The original 7E7 design had a much longer nose profile and a very different 'shark's fin' vertical tail than appeared on the final design.

The cabin windows are larger than any other current airliner. Instead of sliding shades they use an electronic system to darken the glass.

The wingtips are a refined aerodynamic design, which increases fuel efficiency without using the winglets found on many other aircraft.

787-8

All-Nippon Airlines (ANA) launched the Dreamliner with the first order in April 2004. They took delivery of their first of 55 787-8s in late 2010.

JA801A

Cabin pressure can be maintained at a lower equivalent altitude (6,000 ft/1800 m vs 8,000 ft/2,400 m), which will help reduce passenger fatigue and jetlag.

The fuselage is constructed of composite barrels, which are built in Kansas and delivered by rail to Washington for assembly.

Building the dream

■ The 787 is built in a unique way for a Boeing product. Three highly-modified 747 Large Cargo Freighters, known as Dreamlifters, move components between production sites in Japan, Italy, South Carolina, Kansas and elsewhere. Final assembly is undertaken at Everett in Washington State, but many systems have already been fitted by the time they arrive. The target production rate is 10 aircraft per month.

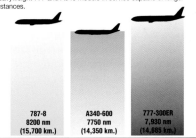

BREGUET

763 PROVENCE

● Twin deck ● Passenger and freight transport ● Long service

After building the twin-engined Breguet 500 airliner during the German occupation, in 1944 Breguet started looking at larger aircraft. To provide a worthwhile passenger and cargo load, the firm decided to develop a twin-deck airliner named the Deux-Ponts, or two decks. The prototype flew in 1949, and 18, called the Sahara, were used as military transports. Air France operated 12 Deux-Ponts under the name Provence.

▲ The 763 Provence airliner and the 765 Sahara military transport were the principal variants which stemmed from the Breguet 761 design. Both types served extensively in Algiers.

BREGUET 763 PROVENCE

▲ Pre-production aircraft
The 761S aircraft had a new central fin and Pratt & Whitney R-2800-B31 engines.

Parachute drop ▶
All three of the 761S were used in the mid-1950s for military trials. Here the rear doors have been removed to drop supplies.

▲ Prototype Breguet 761
Unlike the production models, the prototype was powered by SNECMA-built 1178-kW Gnome-Rhône 14R engines. It also lacked a central fin.

◀ Into Africa
One of the pre-production machines was leased to Air Algerie for a short time early in the 1950s.

◀ Commercial freighter
Air France used its 763s in passenger, combined passenger/freight and all-cargo configurations. The Provence ended its days with the airline as a large-capacity airlifter and served until 1971.

▲ Military lifter
The rear door of the 765 Sahara lowered to form a ramp for loading vehicles.

FACTS AND FIGURES

➤ Air France gave its 12 763s the class name Provence, but they were more popularly known as Deux-Ponts.

➤ Provences were the first post-war French production aircraft to fly with Air France.

➤ Air France was ordered to buy the 763s by the French Minister of Transport.

➤ Military Saharas could hold 146 fully-equipped troops, 85 stretchers with attendants or large military vehicles.

➤ Saharas were powered by R-2800-CB17s with an output of 1417 kW (1,900 hp.).

➤ The last of the Saharas belonging to the Armée de l'Air was retired in 1972.

PROFILE

Twin-deck French design

Below: The sheer size of the 763 dominated airfield parking areas. The Hamilton Standard propellers were 4.22 m (13 ft. 10 in.) in diameter and could provide reverse thrust on landing.

In their original configuration, the Air France Provences had 59 tourist-class seats on the upper deck and 48 second-class seats on the lower. They were used on routes to North Africa and between Paris and London.

The original Deux-Ponts prototype had twin fins and rudders, but a central fin was added on later aircraft. The Provence had a distinctive central rounded fin, and some modifications to the wing camber were required to meet Air France's payload requirements.

The seats on the lower deck, and the rear staircase connecting the two levels, could be stowed to make room for cargo. The rear fuselage sides consisted of doors which opened sideways for loading.

After being replaced by newer airliners, six Provences were sold to the French air force. The other six were modified as freighters, with winches and lifts to the upper deck, under the name Universal. They were used to transport Olympus engines for Concorde from Bristol to

Above: An Air Algerie 761S performs a low-level flypast, showing the tall, double-deck fuselage to advantage.

Toulouse and could also ferry up to 12 cars and their passengers. Maximum payload of the freighter version was increased to 13,150 kg (28,930 lb.), and up to 29 seats could be installed on the upper deck.

763 Provence

Type: twin-deck airliner

Powerplant: four 1566-kW (2,100-hp.) Pratt & Whitney R-2800-CA18 18-cylinder two-row air-cooled radial engines

Maximum cruising speed: 390 km/h (242 m.p.h.) at 3050 m (10,000 ft.)

Range: 2290 km (1,420 mi.) with full load; 4100 km (2,542 mi.) with maximum fuel

Weights: empty 32,241 kg (70,930 lb.); maximum take-off 51,600 kg (23,857 lb.)

Payload: 107 passengers or 10,844 kg (23,857 lb.)

Dimensions:
span	42.99 m (141 ft.)
length	28.94 m (94 ft. 11 in.)
height	9.91 m (32 ft. 6 in.)
wing area	185.40 m² (1,995 sq. ft.)

763 PROVENCE

This Air France aircraft was used exclusively on the airline's North African routes to Algeria and Tunisia.

Before it accepted the Provence, Air France insisted that the cockpit was modified for three-man operation rather than the four crew of the 761S.

Pratt & Whitney engines replaced the French powerplants early on. The R-2800-CA18 radial had its 14 cylinders arranged in two rows and boosted take-off power with water injection.

Passengers sat on two decks: the upper, tourist-class, deck seated 59, while the second-class deck accommodated 48. In the combi role a moveable bulkhead separated the cargo and passengers.

Only the series prototype, the 761, flew without the additional centre fin. This was rounded at its trailing edge to blend into the rear-fuselage contours and was not fitted with any control surfaces.

A high-set position was chosen for the tailplanes, which kept them clear of the considerable propeller wash. Tall fins and rudders, of narrow chord, were mounted inboard of each tailplane tip. A French flag was painted on both sides.

AIR FRANCE

F-BASY

Large clamshell doors allowed easy access to the cabin for loading cargo. An inset door acted as the main passenger entrance, with a staircase to the upper deck.

ACTION DATA

MAXIMUM CRUISE SPEED

A development of the B-29 Superfortress, the Boeing Stratocruiser was a highly advanced and powerful aircraft, which benefited from wartime development in a non-occupied country. The Avro Tudor was faster than the Provence, but was plagued by accidents.

763 PROVENCE	390 km/h (242 m.p.h.)
377 STRATOCRUISER	547 km/h (339 m.p.h.)
G89 TUDOR 2	460 km/h (270 m.p.h.)

PASSENGERS

The Provence could accommodate 107 passengers in comfort, but 135 could be seated in a high-density layout. The Stratocruiser also used a double-deck layout; the lower deck, where the B-29's bomb-bay used to be, was used for baggage and cargo .

763 PROVENCE	107
377 STRATOCRUISER	112
G89 TUDOR 2	80

RANGE

Long range was a key feature of the Stratocruiser, allowing intercontinental flights. Breguet designed the Provence for short- to medium-range services, especially to French colonial states in North Africa for which its 4100-km range was more than adequate.

763 PROVENCE	4100 km (2,542 mi.)
377 STRATOCRUISER	6759 km (4,190 mi.)
G89 TUDOR 2	3750 km (2,330 mi.)

Breguet legacy

273: First flown in 1934, 15 of these reconnaissance bombers were sold to Venezuela and six to China.

470 FULGAR: This sleek, 14-seat airliner was based on the 462 Vultur and built only in prototype form.

482: A post-war design for research into bomber development, only one of these elegant aircraft was built.

941: One prototype and four production examples of this STOL transport were built, but no market was found.

BRISTOL
170 FREIGHTER

● World War II RAF design ● Worldwide service ● Car ferry

Bristol started to design the Type 170 as a military transport in 1944. Then, with the end of World War II in sight, it was changed to a commercial freight and passenger carrier. The original versions were the Mk I Freighter, with nose doors, and the Mk II Wayfarer, which had seats for up to 36 passengers. The first prototype flew in December 1945, and the sole survivor of the 214 that were built was still operating in Canada nearly 50 years later.

▲ *Bristol's Freighter made its name as a car ferry across the English Channel, but Type 170s saw extensive service around the world hauling a multitude of loads.*

BRISTOL 170 FREIGHTER

◀ **Enlarged Freighter Mk 32**
Perhaps the best known version was the Mk 32, which was developed for Silver City Airways for car ferry operations. The fuselage was lengthened by 1.52 m (5 ft.) to accommodate three cars and 23 passengers, and the tail area was increased.

▲ **In its twilight years**
This ex-RNZAF B.170 was briefly flown by the appropriately named Hercules Airways.

◀ **The last airworthy Freighter**
This aircraft was written-off in an accident over Enstone, Oxfordshire, in July 1996.

▲ **Supplying Canada's Eskimos**
Freighters have served around the world, often hauling heavy loads in harsh weather conditions. This Mk 31 spent its short life in Canada with two air freight companies, and crashed in Alberta in 1955.

▲ **Mk 31 modifications**
After two accidents caused by structural failure of the tail fin, a dorsal fin was added. In addition, the Mk 31 had more powerful engines and a higher gross weight. G-AINK was the first production example.

FACTS AND FIGURES

➤ One Silver City Freighter carried 117 refugees on one flight after the break up of India and Pakistan in 1947.

➤ Safe Air of New Zealand flew Freighters for 35 years and, at one time, operated 11.

➤ In all, 214 aircraft, including both civil and military variants, were produced.

➤ Versions of the B.170 with tricycle undercarriage and tail loading ramps were proposed but not built.

➤ Type 170s were built between December 1945 and March 1958.

➤ In 1963 there were 112 still in service; by 1970, 40 civil examples remained.

Jungle freighter turned car ferry

The Type 170 was designed with a fixed undercarriage. Lighter than a retractable type, it was also cheaper, and meant that there was no need for a hydraulic system.

The last 170s were delivered in 1958, but passenger and cargo airlines used them well into the 1980s. Safe Air of New Zealand operated the type for 35 years until 1986. Successive models introduced new wings, more powerful Hercules 734 engines and

bigger fuel tanks (Mk 21), a dorsal fin and an increased gross weight (Mk 31).

Silver City Air Freight Services started a car ferry service between Lympe in England and Le Touquet in France in July 1948. The service continued for many years and in the early 1950s the Mk 32, with its longer fuselage, was developed specifically for car transport. By 1962 Silver City had a total of 24 Freighters in service.

Other Type 170s were built as Mk 31M military transports for the air forces of Australia, Burma, Canada, Iraq, New Zealand and Pakistan. They could carry up to 30 fully equipped troops or 28 stretcher cases plus attendants.

Safe Air (formerly Straits Air Freight Express) in New Zealand was the last major operator of the Freighter. The aircraft were withdrawn from service in 1986.

FREIGHTER MK 31M

Delivered to the Royal New Zealand Air Force (RNZAF) in March 1955, this aircraft was retired in 1978. Sold in 1981, it was used for freight operations in the UK and Canada and, as C-FDFC, was the last airworthy B.170.

The fixed undercarriage was less prone to mechanical failure. As the 170 had a short range and low top speed, the benefits of retractable gear would have been negligible.

Freighter Mk 32

Type: commercial freight and/or passenger transport

Powerplant: two 1476-kW (1,980-hp.) Bristol Hercules 734 radial engines

Maximum speed: 362 km/h (224 m.p.h.)

Initial climb rate: 420 m/min (1,380 f.p.m.) at sea level

Range: 1320 km (820 mi.)

Service ceiling: 7470 m (24,500 ft.)

Weights: empty 13,400 kg (29,480 ft.); maximum take-off 19,960 kg (43,912 lb.)

Payload: three cars plus 23 passengers, or 60 passengers

Dimensions:
span	32.92 m (108 ft.)
length	22.35 m (73 ft. 4 in.)
height	7.62 m (25 ft.)
wing area	138.14 m² (1,486 sq. ft.)

The nose cargo door meant that the cockpit had to be positioned above the forward fuselage. Except for this, the general layout of the 170 was based on that of the RAF's Bombay transport, with which it shared a number of features.

Two of Bristol's own Hercules radial engines powered the Freighter. Those fitted to the earliest versions produced 1249 kW (1,675-hp.), while the Mk 31 was propelled by 1476-kW (1,980-hp.) engines. Renowned for its reliability, Safe Air in New Zealand claimed, in March 1985, to be using an aircraft powered by a Hercules which had accumulated 20,987 hours.

Windows were fitted in the nose doors of a Freighter Mk I employed to survey Persian oilfields in 1947. Later, a number of military Freighters, including those for the RNZAF, were built with nose windows.

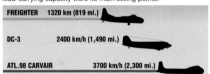

INSTONE

G-BISU

ATLANTIC AIR TRANSPORT

The original RAF specification required that the aircraft was able to carry a 3-tonne (3-ton) Army truck. Loading was made easy by the nose 'clam shell' doors. These were omitted in the Wayfarer all-passenger version.

Most B.170s were built with cabin windows regardless of their intended role. The Wayfarer airliner version could seat up to 32 passengers.

ACTION DATA

RANGE

Range was not a major consideration in the Freighter's design. Because it had to compete for orders with the large numbers of cheap, surplus wartime aircraft like the DC-3 (C-47), its price and load-carrying capacity were its main selling points.

FREIGHTER	1320 km (819 mi.)	
DC-3	2400 km/h (1,490 mi.)	
ATL.98 CARVAIR	3700 km/h (2,300 mi.)	

ACCOMMODATION

The Mk 32 could carry as many as 60 passengers in an all-passenger configuration. As a car ferry it was far more versatile than the DC-3, but its capacity was soon found to be insufficient and led to the development of the Carvair.

FREIGHTER Mk 32	3 cars and 23 passengers
DC-3	24 passengers
ATL.98 CARVAIR	5 cars and 25 passengers

Freighter versatility

■ **SMALL CONSIGNMENTS:** Here a Silver City Air Freight Services Freighter is loaded with ice cream, sometime in the 1960s. The 'clam shell' nose doors, a legacy of the aircraft's military origins, allowed straightforward loading of a variety of cargoes, from the smallest boxes to bulky containers and medium-sized cars.

■ **CUSTOM-BUILT LOADER:** In New Zealand Safe Air, in conjunction with the operators of the country's railway system, operated a 'rail-air' service across Cook Strait. A specially designed, wheeled deck was built for the loading of containers or, in this case, horse boxes. Note the rail tracks under the deck's wheels.

■ **CAR FERRY:** Another of Silver City's Freighters, this time a Mk 32, demonstrates the type's capacity as a car ferry. These Minis were part of a priority consignment en route to France. The Mk 32 was, perhaps, the best known version of the Freighter and ferrying cars across the Channel was its main role. The aircraft was well suited to the task.

BRISTOL

BRITANNIA

● Long-haul airliner ● Early turboprop ● RAF transport

▲ Although the first prototype Britannia flew in 1952, the production aircraft did not enter service until 1957. Only 60 airliners were built, the remaining aircraft being military transports.

With its advanced turboprop engines and long range, the Bristol Type 175 Britannia should have made a great impact in the airliner market of the early 1950s. However, protracted development meant that by the time it entered service in 1957 jet airliners like the Boeing 707 were only a year away. Nevertheless, the Britannia did see valuable service as a passenger- and cargo-carrying aircraft for civil and military operators.

BRISTOL **BRITANNIA**

1950s airliner ▶
Representing the pinnacle of propeller-driven airliners, the Britannia was soon overtaken by the introduction of the first generation of jet airliners.

◀ Luxury accommodation
The original Series 100 aircraft built for BOAC could be configured for either 60 first-class or 93 tourist-class passengers.

▼ Five-man crew
The Britannia carried a flight deck crew of between three and five, including a flight engineer, navigator and two pilots.

Overseas production ▶
Most Britannias were built at Bristol's Filton factory, although a small number were constructed by Short Brothers, Belfast, and by Canadair as the CL-44 with different engines.

▼ Military service
The Britannia was the Royal Air Force Transport Command's first turboprop transport aircraft. Twenty-three were delivered in all.

FACTS AND FIGURES

➤ Israeli airline El Al began a record 9817-km (6,096 mi.) non-stop service between New York and Tel Aviv on 19 December 1957.

➤ The second Britannia built crashed during a test flight in February 1954.

➤ The CL-28 Argus maritime patrol aircraft was another Canadian derivative.

➤ The Britannia's size and relatively quiet engines earned it the nickname 'Whispering Giant'.

➤ Other Britannia airliner users included Cubana and Canadian Pacific.

➤ The Canadair CL-44 was a Britannia derivative with Rolls-Royce Tyne engines.

PROFILE

The 'Whispering Giant'

The Bristol Aircraft Company submitted its Type 175 design in 1947 to meet a British Overseas Airways Corporation requirement for a high-capacity civil transport.

Originally intended to be powered by Bristol Centaurus piston engines, the advanced but troublesome Proteus was substituted early on. At a time when the de Havilland Comet jet airliner appeared risky and untried, the Britannia was expected to sell well. However, teething problems, mainly involving the engines, delayed service entry until early 1957 – the prototype's maiden flight had taken place on 16 August 1952. Potential sales were badly hit when a prototype Britannia force-landed while being evaluated by the chairman of the Dutch airline KLM.

Until the early 1960s the Britannia was progressively developed in different versions with a stretched fuselage, greater range and floor strengthening for freight haulage.

Although produced in relatively small numbers, the type served and operated with great success for airlines all around the world and a few remained in service until the late 1980s, having been converted into cargo freighters.

Early engine problems caused a BOAC Britannia to suffer a complete engine failure in cloud over Uganda in 1956.

BOAC operated both the Series 100 and the stretched, long-range Series 300 versions, numbering 26 in all.

Britannia Series 310

Type: four-engined turboprop airliner

Powerplant: four 3072-kW (4,120-hp.) Rolls-Royce Proteus turboprop engines

Maximum speed: 639 km/h (396 m.p.h.)

Range: 6869 km (4,260 mi.) with maximum payload

Service ceiling: 7315 m (24,000 ft.)

Maximum passengers: 133

Weights: empty 37,438 kg (82,364 lb.); maximum take-off 83,915 kg (184,613 lb.)

Dimensions: span 43.36 m (142 ft. 3 in.)
length 37.87 m (124 ft. 3 in.)
height 11.43 m (37 ft. 6 in.)
wing area 192.77 m² (2,074 sq. ft.)

BRITANNIA C.MK 1

The Britannia 253 entered service with the Royal Air Force as the Britannia C.Mk 1. The second Britannia delivered, XL636, entered service in 1959 with No. 99 Squadron.

The Bristol Proteus turboprop engines were originally designed for the ill-fated Bristol Brabazon II and Saunders-Roe Princess airliners.

The fuselage was a pressurised, aluminium-alloy structure with a maximum diameter of 3.66 m (12 ft.).

When equipped as a troop carrier, the Britannia carried 115 rearward-facing seats.

ROYAL AIR FORCE TRANSPORT COMMAND

636

XL636

While allocated to No. 99 Squadron, XL636 was named 'Argo'.

The 20 Britannia Mk 1s were long-range, all-purpose transports with a strengthened floor and large freight door.

The positioning of the aircraft's engine jet pipes meant that the Messier bogie main landing gear had to retract backwards.

Defence cuts in 1975 spelled the end for the bulk of the RAF Britannia fleet. XL636 was sold and flew briefly as a civilian freighter from 1976.

ACTION DATA

ACCOMMODATION

The Canadair CL-44D was a stretched version of the Britannia and consequently carried more passengers. The Soviet Ilyushin Il-18 had a slightly narrower and shorter fuselage.

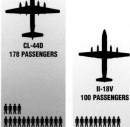

BRITANNIA SERIES 310 133 PASSENGERS

CL-44D 178 PASSENGERS

Il-18V 100 PASSENGERS

Turboprop airliners of the 1950s

■ **CANADAIR CL-44:** This licence-built version of the Britannia was more than 3 m (10 ft.) longer than the largest British-built Britannias. The CL-44D-4 had a hinged aft fuselage section to simplify freight handling.

■ **TUPOLEV Tu-116:** The largest and heaviest commercial airliner before the advent of the Boeing 747, the Tu-116 was a development of the Tu-95 swept-wing turboprop bomber and first flew in 1957.

■ **VICKERS VISCOUNT:** The first civil airliner powered by turboprop engines, the first Viscount flew in 1948 and entered service in 1953. In all, 444 were built for service worldwide, with later versions seating up to 71 passengers.

BRITISH AEROSPACE

JETSTREAM 31/41

● 19-/29-seat commuterliner ● Handley Page design ● In production

▲ Jetstreams
are available in various
configurations: airliner, corporate, executive shuttle
and special role, and can accommodate between
eight and 19 passengers or special equipment.

Developed originally by Handley Page and flown for the first time in August 1967, the Jetstream has been in production for 30 years. It was taken over by Scottish Aviation, which built 26 as navigation trainers for the RAF, and then relaunched as the Jetstream 31 by British Aerospace (BAe) in 1978. In its latest incarnation as the 29-seater Jetstream 41, the design is the sole product of Jetstream Aircraft Limited, a BAe subsidiary.

BRITISH AEROSPACE JETSTREAM 31/41

◀ 31s and Super 31s
Airlines operating under the American Eagle name have taken delivery of several 31s and Super 31s.

▼ In service in the Low Countries
Netherlines, later part of the KLM Cityhopper group, started operating Jetstream 31s in 1985.

▼ Over the Firth of Forth
Loganair's Jetstream 41s have joined the British Regional Airlines fleet, which includes 13 examples of the 29-seat type. G-LOGJ is now G-MAJC.

▲ Birmingham Executive Airways
This company operated Jetstream 31s, with high-quality executive interiors, between the West Midlands and Copenhagen, Milan and Zurich.

◀ Canadian commuterliners
Ontario Express, a Canadian Partner airline, took delivery of the first of 14 Jetstream 31s in 1987. Ontario Express operates services across the province.

FACTS AND FIGURES

➤ The Jetstream started life as the Handley Page H.P.137 with an envisaged capacity of 12 to 20 passengers.

➤ After Handley Page's failure, American backers attempted to restart production.

➤ By June 1996, 101 J41s had been ordered, more than half by North American airlines.

➤ Introduced in 1987, the Jetstream Super 31 has more powerful engines and improved cabin comfort.

➤ Saudi Arabia uses two J31s, fitted with Tornado IDS avionics, to train aircrew.

➤ Field Aircraft finished the interiors of Jetstream 31s.

PROFILE

Handley Page's commuterliner reborn

Flown for the first time in March 1980, the Jetstream 31 was based on the Garrett-engined Mk 3 which the USAF had ordered, but later cancelled, as the C-10A.

In 1987 British Aerospace announced the Jetstream Super 31, which offered a 400-kg (880-lb.) increase in maximum take-off weight (a result of more powerful engines), plus many detail improvements. Both models have found customers as 19-seat regional airliners, although they have also been sold as eight- to 12-seat corporate transports, air ambulance and special missions military aircraft.

Growth in commuter traffic has seen regional aircraft become larger, and in 1989 BAe started the development of the 29-seat Jetstream 41. Again, US-based feeder airlines have been the main customers, but the type is in service worldwide.

The 41 has more powerful TPE331 engines than the 31, enabling it to cruise at 540 km/h (335 m.p.h.) compared to the Super 31's speed of 435 km/h (270 m.p.h.). Payloads have increased steadily since the model's launch, and in 1995 water-methanol injection was introduced to improve performance in 'hot and high' conditions. Since 1996 Jetstreams have been marketed by Aero International (Regional), a consortium of Jetstream, Avro International and ATR.

Below: Delivered in 1993, G-WAWR (now G-MAJD) was the sixth J41 off the production line. Manx Airlines is now part of British Regional Airlines.

Above: Seen prior to delivery, this Jetstream 31 is finished in the livery of Sun-Air of Scandinavia.

Jetstream 41

Type: regional airliner

Powerplant: two 1230-kW (1,650-hp.) Garrett TPE331-14GR/HR turboprops

Maximum speed: 547 km/h (339 m.p.h.) at 6100 m (20,000 ft.)

Initial climb rate: 670 m/min (2,200 f.p.m.)

Range: 1433 km (890 mi.) with 29 passengers and in-flight refuelling reserves

Service ceiling: 7925 m (26,000 ft.)

Weights: empty 6416 kg (14,115 lb.); maximum take-off 10,886 kg (23,949 lb.)

Accommodation: flight crew of two, one attendant plus up to 29 passengers

Dimensions:
span	18.29 m (60 ft.)
length	19.25 m (63 ft. 2 in.)
height	5.74 m (17 ft. 11 in.)
wing area	32.59 m² (351 sq. ft.)

JETSTREAM 31

Flown in June 1985, N409AE was delivered to Metro Express, which operated the aircraft under the American Eagle feederliner banner. After less than two years of service, the aircraft was leased to Chapparal Airlines.

In its original form, the Handley Page design was powered by two Turboméca Astazou turboprops. Scottish Aviation took over the programme after Handley Page went bankrupt, only to be taken over itself by British Aerospace shortly afterwards. At this stage, the Jetstream 31 was developed with more powerful Garrett AiResearch TPE331s.

The main passenger cabin holds up to 19 passengers in a high-density commuter configuration. With an executive interior the aircraft is spacious and fitted with eight to 10 seats. The cabin is pressurised, heated, ventilated and air-conditioned.

Depending upon the regulations of a given country, Jetstream 31s may be fitted with dual controls for operation by one or two pilots.

A commonly fitted extra on Jetstreams in feederliner service is a distinctive underfuselage baggage pod. This allows a maximum number of passengers to be carried.

Aluminium alloy is used in the construction of the semi-monocoque fuselage. In February 1994, the manufacturer increased airframe life from 30,000 to 40,000 hours.

N409AE

American Eagle

ACTION DATA

PASSENGERS

BAe's Jetstream 31 is one of a number of aircraft competing for the lucrative 19-seater market. It has the advantage of being pressurised, unlike the EMB-110 and Do 228, allowing flight at higher altitudes to avoid bad weather.

31	19 passengers
EMB-110P2A BANDEIRANTE	21 passengers
Do 228-200	19 passengers

MAXIMUM CRUISING SPEED

In terms of its maximum cruising speed, the Jetstream 31 has an edge over the EMBRAER EMB-110 and Dornier Do 228. This allows faster journey times and therefore higher aircraft utilisation, which, in turn, give economical operations.

31	489 km/h (303 m.p.h.)
EMB-110P2A	413 km/h (256 m.p.h.)
Do 228-200	428 km/h (265 m.p.h.)

TAKE-OFF RUN

Jetstreams have an appreciably longer take-off run than both the Bandeirante and Do 228. The Dornier's short take-off and landing (STOL) performance is a result of its wing design. Both the Do 228 and EMB-110 have a useful rough-field capability.

Do 228-200	EMB-110P2A BANDEIRANTE	31
411 m (1,350 ft.)	675 m (2,215 ft.)	1569 m (5,150 ft.)

Jetstream 31s worldwide feederliner service

AUSTRALIA: VH-TQK was originally delivered to Queensland Air in September 1986. By 1988 it was serving with Eastern Australia Airlines, operating under the Australian banner.

GERMANY: Contactair was an early Jetstream 31 customer, and received this aircraft in 1983. After a period in Sweden, in 1992 it was leased to Sun-Air in Denmark.

UNITED KINGDOM: The fourth 31 off the production line, G-BKHI operated with Peregrine Air Services for three and a half years. By 1992 it was registered in Denmark.

UNITED STATES: Express Airlines took delivery of this pallet-equipped Jetstream 31 in 1986. It operated in Northwest Airlink colours, and provided feeder services for Northwest Airlines.

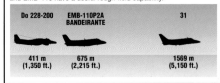

BRITISH AEROSPACE

125

● **Best seller** ● **Civilian and military customers** ● **Luxury interior**

N ow manufactured by Raytheon and known as the Hawker 800, the 125 was built successively by de Havilland, Hawker Siddeley and British Aerospace and was in production for more than 30 years. It became established as the world's best-selling mid-size biz-jet and was one of Europe's most successful civil aircraft programmes. With continuous development, performance has increased and the most recent model can fly across the Atlantic.

▲ *When customers select a 125 or Hawker jet, they receive an aircraft that is equipped to their specification and is backed up by a global servicing network with 30 years of experience.*

BRITISH AEROSPACE **125**

▲ Corporate comfort
Although the exact layout of the cabin is designed to customer requirements, this view represents a typical Hawker 800 interior.

▲ Intercontinental business
British Aerospace launched the BAe 1000 in October 1989 and Raytheon adopted the design as the Hawker 1000. An 84-cm (3-ft.) fuselage extension allows extra fuel to be carried, giving a maximum range of 6204 km (3,850 mi.).

▲ International sales success
BAe 125 and Hawker business jets are in the service of large companies, air forces and individuals worldwide. This is a Yemeni-registered machine.

▼ Australian interest
Carlton and United Breweries use this BAe 125-800 to transport staff across Australia.

▲ British Aerospace biz-jet
British Aerospace first flew the 125-800 in May 1983. This is the company aircraft, which also served as a demonstrator. By January 1995, 273 aircraft had been built and orders continued to be placed. Raytheon bought BAe Corporate Jets, including the 125, for $372 million in August 1993.

FACTS AND FIGURES

➤ Although the 125-800 first flew in 1983 it was not awarded Russian certification until 1993.

➤ Maximum operating altitude was reached on the 125-800's first flight.

➤ On-board entertainments include a CD player and video LCD screen.

➤ Having first flown on 16 June 1990, the BAe 1000 was certified on 26 November 1990 after an 800-hour test programme.

➤ The Hawker 1000 has higher powered engines with thrust reversers.

➤ Maximum passenger capacity of the Hawker 1000 has been increased to 15.

PROFILE

Dominating the luxury market

A primary reason for the 125's popularity is its cabin. The original designers insisted on 1.75 m (5 ft 9 in.) of headroom, which makes long journeys much more comfortable. It is big enough to carry 14 passengers, although eight seats is the norm and three passengers is a typical load.

Another reason the 125 is popular is that the process of continuous development has seen range increase steadily to reach 5318 km (3302 mi.) with maximum payload for the Hawker 800 (formerly the 125-800) and even more for the latest Hawker 1000. For journeys of that length comfort is a necessity, and cabin furnishings usually reflect the highest standards of luxury.

Even before the sale to Raytheon, most 125 interiors were designed by Arkansas Aerospace at Little Rock. Expense is rarely the main consideration in designing the interior, and the experts who furnish the cabin boast that they can literally design the seats to fit the chairman. The finest materials are used to achieve the feel of opulence while minimising weight. Business aircraft have to earn their living, however, and now computers and communications links are likely to be as important as a well stocked drinks cabinet.

Above: Famous excavator manufacturer J.C. Bamford has been a long-standing customer of British Aerospace business jets.

Above: Several earlier aircraft continue in service, a prime example being this BAe 125-700.

125-800

Type: business jet

Powerplant: two 19.13-kN (4,300-lb.-thrust) AlliedSignal TFE731-5R-1H turbofans

Maximum speed: 845 km/h (524 mi.) at 8840 m (29,000 ft.)

Climb rate: 945 m/min (4,000 f.p.m.) at sea level

Range: 5232 km (3,245 mi.) with maximum fuel

Service ceiling: 13,100 m (43,000 ft.)

Weights: empty 7076 kg (15,567 lb.); maximum take-off 12,428 kg (27,342 lb.)

Accommodation: two crew and up to 14 passengers

Dimensions:
span	15.66 m	(51 ft. 4 in.)
length	15.60 m	(51 ft. 2 in.)
height	5.36 m	(17 ft. 7 in.)
wing area	34.75 m²	(374 sq. ft.)

---

125 CC.Mk 3

No. 32 (The Royal) Squadron of the RAF flies six 125 CC.Mk 3 aircraft on Royal and VIP passenger transport duties. The machines are based on the civilian 125-700 airframe.

Individual operators choose their own cabin layout. RAF machines typically fly in an eight-seat configuration for the VIP transport of high-ranking officers.

There are a generous number of large cabin windows, giving passengers a good outside view. In addition, comfort is increased by the provision of individual tables and galley facilities.

AlliedSignal (Garrett) TFE731 turbofans of 16.46 kN (3,700 lb.-thrust) power the CC.Mk 3. To provide fleet commonality and to improve performance, earlier turbojet-powered RAF 125s were re-engined with these turbofans.

Placing the engines at the rear of the cabin minimises internal noise, but requires the tailplanes to be positioned high up on the fin, clear of jet blast.

ZE395

While the CC.Mk 3 can safely be operated by a crew of two, a third crewmember is sometimes carried. The 125 has served the RAF for many years.

A neat fairing covers the wing carry-through structure which runs beneath the cabin floor, allowing maximum internal volume.

A distinctive feature of the Series 700/CC.Mk 3 aircraft is this large ventral fin. Series 800 aircraft dispensed with it, but have an extended fin leading edge.

Other roles of the 125

■ AIR AMBULANCE: Typical of a number of 125s fitted with a hospital interior, this BAe 125-800 is flown by the Swiss air-ambulance service.

■ NAVIGATION TRAINER: Based on the early Hawker Siddeley 125 Series 1A/B, the Dominie T.Mk 1 has been the standard navigation trainer of the RAF since 1966.

■ SEARCH AND RESCUE: Japan's Air Self-Defence Force is currently receiving the U-125A SAR and maritime patrol variant of the Hawker 800.

ACTION DATA

PASSENGERS

In a typical executive layout these aircraft carry similar passenger loads, although all could accommodate more people at the expense of comfort. Typically, passenger loads would be lower than those shown, but the Astra SP lacks the versatility of its competitors.

HAWKER 800 — 8 passengers
LEARJET 60 — 9 passengers
ASTRA SP — 6 passengers

CABIN HEIGHT

To achieve the ultimate in luxury travel, cabin height is an important factor since company executives prefer not to stoop as they move about the aircraft. The Hawker 800 has a distinct advantage.

HAWKER 800 1.75 m (5 ft. 9 in.)
LEARJET 60 1.71 m (5 ft. 7 in.)
ASTRA SP 1.70 m (5 ft. 6 in.)

RANGE

Although the Astra SP has a greater range than the Hawker 800, it cannot match its versatility or pedigree. The Learjet 60 trails in terms of range, but offers greater seating capacity. The similarity of design means that manufacturers must compete fiercely and closely match customer needs to win orders.

HAWKER 800 5232 km (3,245 mi.)
LEARJET 60 5074 km (3,150 mi.)
ASTRA SP 5215 km (3,475 mi.)

BRITISH AEROSPACE/AVRO

146/RJ

● 'WhisperJet' ● STOL performance ● VIP transport

The graceful, efficient British Aerospace 146 (now known by its new name Avro Regional Jet) was designed to provide economical service to small airfields where runway length and noise constraints prohibit most airliners from operating. The Regional Jet lives up to its billing as one of the quietest planes in the sky. It remains popular and successful, although its manufacturer has undergone several corporate changes since 1983.

▲ The 146 had some success in penetrating the American feederliner market during the 1980s. Air Wisconsin was the initial US operator of the type, flying its first passengers in June 1983.

BRITISH AEROSPACE/AVRO **146/RJ**

◄ **Hot and high**
Excellent performance makes the 146 ideal for operations from the high plains of Africa. Good utilisation rates are another major plus.

▼ **All-new cockpit**
The new RJ series features an updated, user-friendly cockpit layout and new flight systems, helping to reduce pilot workload.

◄ **Cabin comfort**
The interior of the 146 is very passenger-friendly. The manufacturer claims that it is the world's most comfortable 100-seat aircraft.

▼ **First off the line**
The first operator of the 146 was Dan-Air who received this aircraft in May 1983.

Environmentally friendly ►
The quiet, efficient and smokeless engines are a far cry from early turbojets.

FACTS AND FIGURES

➤ The 146-200 can accommodate up to 18.3 m³ (24 cu. yd.) of freight.

➤ Textron Inc., manufacturer of the Regional Jet's engines, has built 31,000 turbine engines in 37 years.

➤ Extensive ground tests were equivalent to 168,000 individual 45-minute flights.

➤ The landing gear of the Avro Regional Jet is wider than that of a C-130 Hercules.

➤ The 146 can make 200,000 landings without repairs to its undercarriage.

➤ Standard fuel capacity of the Regional Jet is 11,729 litres (3,100 gal.), and a 12,901-litre (3,400-gal.) option is also offered.

PROFILE

Quiet STOL short-hauler

The Avro Regional Jet whisks passengers aloft at a standard of comfort and convenience that was never before possible in a short-distance transport.

The Regional Jet has survived difficult times since it was first announced on 29 August 1973. It has had three names since then: the Hawker-Siddeley HS 146, followed by British Aerospace 146 and eventually the Avro Regional Jet (RJ). Despite the RJ being very

popular, efforts to sell a military version failed, and commercial sales have not attained their full potential. Passengers like being able to stand in the aisle and pilots enjoy the easy handling qualities of this aircraft.

The first carrier to operate the Regional Jet was Dan-Air, on 27 May 1983, and the BAe 146-200 and 146-300 'stretched' models entered service with Air Wisconsin in 1983 and 1987, respectively.

Because it is quiet and does

not disturb the neighbourhoods around airfields, this is the only jetliner allowed into several city airports, including John Wayne Airport in Orange County, California.

Thanks to its impressive low-noise performance the 146-300QT (Quiet Trader) is widely used on nocturnal courier and freight operations.

The large T-tail provides good longitudinal stability. The manually operated elevators are responsive and the rudder is power assisted.

The key to the 146's quiet performance are the four Textron Lycoming turbofan engines. The aircraft is so quiet in flight that it is nicknamed the 'WhisperJet'.

The highly efficient wings give outstanding field performance and help to reduce fuel consumption. To increase lift for take-off and landing, large Fowler flaps are fitted along 78 per cent of the trailing edge of the wing.

The undercarriage is fairly robust and is suitable for rough-field operations. Anti-skid units are fitted to the braking system.

RJ 100

Type: short-range commercial transport

Powerplant: four 31.14-kN (6,985-hp.) Textron Lycoming LF 507 turbofan engines

Cruising speed: 670 km/h (415 m.p.h.) at 8800 m (29,000 ft.)

Range: 2909 km (1,800 mi.)

Weights: operating empty 22,453 kg (49,397 lb.) (146-100), 23,269 kg (51,192 lb.) (146-200); maximum take-off 38,102 kg (83,824 lb.) (146-100), 42,184 kg (92,805 lb.) (146-200)

Accommodation: two pilots plus 100 passengers in a standard airline layout; maximum of 128 passengers in high-density layout

Dimensions:
span	26.21 m (86 ft.)
length	30.99 m (101 ft. 8 in.)
height	8.59 m (28 ft. 2 in.)
wing area	77.29 m² (832 sq. ft.)

146-200

Continental Express operates the 146-200 on busy business routes in the USA. When production of the 146 ended in 1993 the fleet had flown more than 1.6 million hours.

Almost all the essential flying instruments are duplicated so that either pilot can comfortably fly the 146. From 1990 the RJ series incorporated 'glass cockpit' features.

The 146 has a relatively wide fuselage for an aircraft of its size, allowing six-abreast seating. Stretching the fuselage has produced the varying capacity of the RJ series from the short RJ 70 to the fully stretched RJ 100.

A pair of large petal airbrakes are fitted at the base of the fin. These are spread to increase drag when landing and form the tailcone when closed.

CONTINENTAL EXPRESS

N406XV

ACTION DATA

PASSENGER LOAD

The RJ100 currently competes with Airbus Industrie's twin-engined A319, a shortened version of the A320. These airliners fill the gap left by the retirement of the earlier leader in this class, the Boeing 737-200.

RJ100 128 passengers

A319 130 passengers

737-200 130 passengers

NOISE LEVEL

Noise is becoming a problem for turbo-jet powered airliners of the 1960s and 1970s. Some operators are fitting 'hush kits' to their aircraft to avoid having to replace them altogether.

RJ100	A319	737-200
84-85 db take-off / 97-98 db approach	85-86 db take-off / 96-97 db approach	95-96 db take-off / 101-102 db approach

TAKE-OFF RUN

STOL (Short Take-Off and Landing) ability is a major selling point for the 146/RJ, allowing it to operate from airports with shorter landing strips. They are ideal for small inner-city airports.

737-200 2073 m (6,800 ft.)
A319 1829 m (6,000 ft.)
RJ100 1692 m (5,550 ft.)

Multi-roles for the 146/RJ

QUIET TRADER: With a large side-mounted cargo door, which allows quick loading of bulky freight, the QT is an ideal cargo aircraft especially at night when noise regulations are stringent.

MILITARY ROLE: A 'proof of concept' demonstrator, the 146STA was designed as a military transport. Here a long-wheelbase Land Rover is loaded using a ramp.

MOUNTAIN OPERATIONS: The 146 is ideal for operations in hot or high conditions. Druk Air operates the 146 flying tourists in the Himalaya Mountains of Nepal.

ROYAL APPOINTMENT: No. 32 (The Royal) Squadron operates three 146CC.Mk 2s. Fitted out with high-specification interiors, they are used by the Royal Family for official engagements.

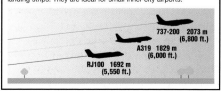

BRITTEN-NORMAN

ISLANDER

● Light utility ● Dirt-strip transport ● Coastal patrol

A brilliant private venture by a pair of British engineers, the Britten-Norman Islander began as a short-haul transport for the African nation of Cameroon and has gone on to become one of the most successful small airliners of all time. The high-wing, twin-engine Islander is testimony to common sense. It is a practical and pragmatic machine which has triumphed in service with 350 operators in 120 countries.

▲ *Reliability and a very adaptable airframe allow the Islander to operate in scorching deserts in Africa and the frozen wastes of Alaska. The aircraft thrives on difficult conditions, and at one time was considered for use in rural China.*

BRITTEN-NORMAN **ISLANDER**

▼ **Police patrol**
Malawi's police received this Islander. The aircraft has sold very widely to military and police forces in Africa and Asia.

◄ **Target tug**
This Islander, towing a bright target drogue, was the 1000th BN-2 to be built at the factory on the Isle of Wight.

▲ **Jungle warrior**
The military Defender is operated by the Belize Defence Force. It is armed with rocket and gun pods, and carries out patrols against drug-runners.

▼ **Survey plane**
Equipped for photographic survey and mapping work, this Islander contains a large camera in the rear cabin.

▲ **Dutch patrol**
The Netherlands police operates two Turbine Islanders fitted with special communications equipment, weather radar and infra-red sensors.

FACTS AND FIGURES

➤ Since 1969, the Islander has been produced in Romania by the manufacturer known today as Romaero.

➤ A three-engine version called the Trislander first flew in 1970.

➤ The Islander made its maiden flight on 13 June 1965.

➤ As late as 1994, Shenzhen Aircraft of China considered building Trislanders.

➤ The Defender 4000 armed version of the Islander made its public debut at the 1994 Farnborough air show.

➤ A turboprop version of the Islander was first tested in 1977.

PROFILE

Flying pick-up for everyone

In 1963, John Britten and Desmond Norman designed an aircraft to operate from crude airfields with low acquisition and operating costs, initially for an air taxi operator flying between Cameroon's cities of Doula and Tiko. The Britten-Norman Islander emerged as a short-haul airliner, mid-way in size between the Piper Apache, which holds

fewer passengers, and the DC-3, which is larger than many users need. By 1967, when Scotland's Loganair became the first airline to put the private-venture Islander into service, it was clear that the Britten-Norman aircraft would be a success with small airlines around the world.

Less obvious were other purposes for which the Islander

was ideal. The aircraft has succeeded with law enforcement, coast guard and drug interdiction agencies. A multi-sensor version carries the APG-66 radar of the F-16 fighter in its enlarged nose. The Defender 4000 is a potent military variant capable of handling Sea Skua missiles and Sting Ray torpedoes, and an AEW version was also projected.

Utility aircraft have a difficult life, often operating in remote areas where maintenance and safety are not a priority. Islanders have a safety record that is second to none.

BN-2B Islander

Type: nine-seat regional transport

Powerplant: two 194-kW (260-hp.) Lycoming O-540-E4C5 piston engines

Maximum speed: 257 km/h (159 m.p.h.)

Range: 2032 km (1,260 mi.)

Service ceiling: 4938 m (16,200 ft.)

Weights: empty 5900 kg (12,890 lb.); maximum take-off 6600 kg (14,520 lb.)

Accommodation: single pilot, nine bench-type passenger seats, provision for 880 kg (1,936 lb.) of personal baggage and cargo

Dimensions:
span	14.93 m	(49 ft.)
length	10.87 m	(35 ft. 7 in.)
height	4.18 m	(13 ft. 8 in.)
wing area	30.19 m²	(325 sq. ft.)

BN-2 ISLANDER

A single Islander was operated by Transkei Airways, flying in the former South African 'homeland'. Transkei Airways acquired the aircraft from a Kenyan operator.

The Islander is powered by simple, reliable Lycoming air-cooled flat six engines. The BN-2T Turbine Islander uses Allison 250 B-17 turboprops, giving increased performance at altitude.

The Islander's span was increased after trials of the prototype to increase the rate of climb.

The Lycoming engine drives a two-bladed constant-speed metal propeller.

The Islander has two seats for a pilot and co-pilot. The nose contains a small baggage compartment.

Fuel is stored in wing tanks, including a wingtip tank.

There is no central aisle in the cabin, so front and rear doors are needed for entry.

ZS-XGF

TRANSKEI AIRWAYS

A specially strengthened undercarriage with low-pressure tyres allows operation from rough strips.

Some Islanders and Defenders have a special rear cabin door that can be opened in flight for use by parachutists.

ACTION DATA

PASSENGER LOAD

The Islander is ideal for short-run flights to and from remote communities, being rugged and dependable yet simple and more economical to operate than the larger Twin Otter or the more complex PC-6. It can also be used to drop parachutists, for which role the bench seats are generally removed.

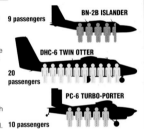

BN-2B ISLANDER — 9 passengers
DHC-6 TWIN OTTER — 20 passengers
PC-6 TURBO-PORTER — 10 passengers

RANGE

Most Islanders have the extended wing which was developed after trials with the prototype, and can carry enough fuel to make fairly long flights. Maximum range is achieved by flying at 59 per cent power at an optimum cruising altitude of 3660 metres.

DHC-6 TWIN OTTER 1700 km (1,050 mi.)
BN-2B ISLANDER 2032 km (1,260 mi.)
PC-6 TURBO-PORTER 1600 km (990 mi.)

TAKE-OFF RUN

The Islander has excellent STOL (short take-off and landing) characteristics. It matches the performance of the Twin Otter, also in worldwide back-country use, but it cannot equal the Turbo-Porter, which has a high-lift wing with double-slotted flaps and single-slotted ailerons.

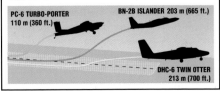

PC-6 TURBO-PORTER 110 m (360 ft.)
BN-2B ISLANDER 203 m (665 ft.)
DHC-6 TWIN OTTER 213 m (700 ft.)

Islanders around the world

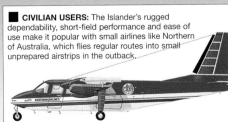

CIVILIAN USERS: The Islander's rugged dependability, short-field performance and ease of use make it popular with small airlines like Northern of Australia, which flies regular routes into small unprepared airstrips in the outback.

MILITARY USERS: The same qualities which make the Islander such a fine bush aircraft make it an ideal light military transport and liaison aircraft. This example of the Mauritanian air force is armed with air-to-surface rockets.

TRISLANDER: The Trislander is a stretched version of the original design with a uniquely positioned third engine. It has been operated by a number of civil and military users, including the Botswana Defence Force.

BRITTEN-NORMAN

TRISLANDER

● Tri-motor feederliner ● Based on Islander design ● More than 70 built

B uilt on the Isle of Wight, the nine-seat Islander has been one of Britain's most successful commercial aircraft. More than 1200 have been sold to operators in more than 120 countries. In 1970, six years after the Islander's first flight, Britten-Norman converted the second prototype to 18-seat configuration by adding a 2.3-m (7-ft. 6-in.) fuselage section and installing a third engine in the tail fin. The result was the Trislander.

▲ The Trislander could carry nearly twice as many passengers as the earlier aircraft. The total number produced, however, was far less than the successful Islander.

BRITTEN-NORMAN TRISLANDER

▼ First Trislander
In prototype form the Trislander's third engine was mounted on a shortened tailfin. This was soon altered with a fin extension above the engine nacelle.

▲ Jamaican feederliner
Like the Islander before it, the Trislander was widely exported and aircraft served on all five continents.

▲ STOL performance
Trislanders had the same short take-off and landing (STOL) capability as the Islander, utilising the lengthened version of the latter's high-lift wing.

▲ Flared wingtips
The Trislander has flared wingtips like the Islander. These were a Britten-Norman trademark.

Launch customer ▶
Aurigny Air Services took delivery of its first Trislander in 1971 and in 1994 had the largest fleet.

FACTS AND FIGURES

➤ First flown on 11 September 1970, the Trislander prototype appeared at the Farnborough air show later that day.

➤ The last factory-built Trislander went to the Botswana defence force in 1984.

➤ In the early-1970s Trislander production was moved to Fairey's Belgian factory.

➤ The Trislander 4 was available with a standby rocket engine in case of engine failure on take-off.

➤ The Trislander 3 was a standard Trislander 2 certified for US operation.

➤ Sixty Trislanders were built for export to Africa, Asia, Australia and South America.

PROFILE

Tri-motor from the Isle of Wight

Loganair used Trislanders to provide a service to the Scottish highlands and islands.

In addition to the stretched fuselage, modified tail and extra engine, the Trislander had a longer wing than the Islander plus new main landing gear with bigger wheels and tyres. Later aircraft also had a baggage compartment in an extended nose assembly.

The Trislander took to the air in September 1970. The first customer was Aurigny Air Services, in the Channel Islands, which remains the biggest operator. Like the original Islander, the three-engined

model has very low operating costs, and additional flights can be scheduled without incurring prohibitive expense. Its seats can be removed quickly so that cargo can be carried when the aircraft does not have a full load of passengers.

In all, 72 Trislanders had been completed by the time production ended in 1984. There have been attempts to return the aircraft to production, but none of these has yet to come to fruition. The rights to the Trislander were sold in 1982

to the International Aviation Corporation of Florida, which planned to build the type as the Tri-Commutair. None was built, however, and the last 10 kits were subsequently sold in Australia. In 1994 Pilatus Britten-Norman (as the company has been known since 1979) had abortive discussions with a Chinese company in an attempt to restart production. Two of these uncompleted airframes were finished and delivered to Aurigny Air Services in 1996.

The Trislander prototype flies alongside a standard Islander, and clearly shows the differences between the two designs.

BN-2A Mk III Trislander 3

Type: tri-motor feederliner

Powerplant: three 194-kW (260-hp.) Lycoming O-540-E4C5 flat-six engines

Maximum speed: 290 km/h (180 m.p.h.) at sea level

Climb rate: 298 m/min (977 f.p.m.) at sea level

Take-off run: 393 m (1,290 ft.)

Maximum range: 1610 km (1,000 mi.)

Service ceiling: 4010 m (13,150 ft.)

Weights: empty 2650 kg (5,830 lb.); maximum take-off 4536 kg (9,979 lb.)

Accommodation: pilot plus up to 17 passengers

Dimensions:
span	16.15 m	(53 ft.)
length	15.01 m	(49 ft. 3 in.)
height	4.32 m	(14 ft. 2 in.)
wing area	31.31 m²	(337 sq. ft.)

BN-2A Mk III Trislander 2

Aurigny Air Services' distinctive yellow-liveried Trislanders continue to provide a service between the Channel Islands and mainland Britain. G-OTSB was later re-registered G-RBSI and was among nine Trislanders operated by the company in 1997.

Originally, a 60-cm (23-in.) fuselage stretch was planned for the Islander (a prototype of which was flown in 1986), but this was abandoned in favour of the 2.3-m (7-ft. 6-in.) extension and extra engine of the Trislander.

The second Islander prototype was rebuilt with a fin-mounted engine to serve as the Trislander prototype. Initially, the tailfin did not extend above the engine nacelle, but later, in an effort to improve handling, the fin area was increased.

An optional feature found on many Trislanders is the extended nose which has 0.62 m³ (22 cu. ft.) of luggage capacity. This is supported by a steerable nosewheel.

Three Lycoming O-540 flat-six cylinder engines, as fitted to most Islanders, power the Trislander. Each is rated at 194 kW (260 hp.) and drives a Hartzell two-bladed propeller. Unlike the Islander, all Trislanders are piston-engined.

To support the extra weight at the rear of the aircraft, new landing gear was fitted with larger wheels and tyres than those of the Islander. The wing is 1.21 m (4 ft.) longer than that of the Islander.

An unusual option on Trislander 4s was a 1.56-kN (350-lb.-thrust) rocket engine which provided 12 seconds of thrust in case of engine failure. This was mounted below the rear engine nacelle.

ACTION DATA

ENGINE POWER

The Trislander's third engine brings its total power output close to that of the Skyservant. The latter can carry a larger load with just two engines, however, making it cheaper to operate. Turboprop engines give the Twin Otter a decided advantage in terms of power output.

BN-2A Mk III TRISLANDER 3 582 kW (780 hp.)	DHC-6 TWIN OTTER SERIES 300 972 kW (1,300 hp.)	Do 28D-2 SKYSERVANT 566 kW (760 hp.)

PASSENGERS

The Trislander provided greater cabin capacity than the Islander, and satisfied the demand for a larger aircraft. However, by the 1980s, turboprop designs, like the DHC-6 Twin Otter, were beginning to dominate the feederliner market.

BN-2A Mk III TRISLANDER 3	17
DHC-6 TWIN OTTER SERIES 300	20
Do 28D-2 SKYSERVANT	13

TAKE-OFF RUN

Although it shared the Islander's wing design, the Trislander did not have the same short field take-off performance. Lighter, twin-engined types are capable of take-off runs of around 200 m (650 ft.), whereas the Trislander has to use just under 400 m (1,300 ft.). Turboprop engines give the DHC-6 a power advantage with little added weight.

DHC-6 TWIN OTTER SERIES 300 213 m (700 ft.)	Do 28D-2 SKYSERVANT 280 m (920 ft.)	BN-2A Mk III TRISLANDER 393 m (1,290 ft.)

Post-war tri-motor transports

■ **DE HAVILLAND AUSTRALIA DHA-3 DROVER:** This utility transport, with eight seats, initially flew in 1948. The first aircraft entered airline service, and others were used by flying doctors.

■ **NORTHROP N.23 PIONEER:** Built as a 40-passenger STOL commercial transport and first flown in 1946, the Pioneer was later developed as the C-125 Raider transport for the USAF.

■ **SPECIALISED AIRCRAFT TRI TURBO-3:** An attempt to breathe new life into the faithful DC-3/C-47, this 1970s conversion involved replacing two radial engines with three PT6 turboprops.

CANADAIR

C-4 ARGONAUT

● Canadian DC-4 ● Merlin engined ● No survivors

During World War II it became obvious that Trans Canada Airlines would need a suitable aircraft for use on both North Atlantic and domestic routes after hostilities ended. The Canadian government selected the Douglas DC-4 and a licence was granted for its manufacture in Canada. This 'north of the border' variant differed from the standard DC-4 in being powered by Rolls-Royce Merlin engines and having a pressurised fuselage.

▲ Compared to previous airliners, the Canadair DC-4M was a considerable improvement. One problem with the aircraft was the exceptionally high level of cabin noise in most variants.

CANADAIR C-4 ARGONAUT

▼ Star performer
Here freight is loaded aboard a North Star, somewhere in Canada. These aircraft proved ideal for high-altitude operations.

▲ First off the line
Serialed CF-TEN-X, the prototype DC-4M first flew in July 1946. It was used on a number of proving flights before being converted into a military C-54GM and delivered to the RCAF in late 1952.

▼ Virtual redesign
Following on from the DC-4M-1 was a pressurised version, the DC-4M-2. Although dimensionally the same, this variant was essentially a new aircraft, featuring many components from the larger DC-6.

▲ Pacific tragedy
Canadian Pacific Airlines operated four North Stars briefly during the early 1950s. This one was lost in a crash in Tokyo.

British Argonauts ▶
Purchased as an interim type, BOAC's C-4s were given the class name Argonaut and primarily employed on services between London, Africa and the Far East. Their service record was so good that the airline operated them for more than 10 years.

FACTS AND FIGURES

➤ Trans Canada Airways began operating DC-4Ms on its transatlantic routes in early 1947, domestic services following.

➤ Royal Canadian Air Force (RCAF) C-54Ms were used extensively in the Korean War.

➤ A Trans Canada machine, CF-TFD, flew into a mountain, killing all on board.

➤ Mrs Howe, wife of the Minister of Reconstruction and Supply, christened the Canadian-built DC-4 the 'North Star'.

➤ By 1975 only a single example of the North Star was still in commercial use.

➤ One RCAF machine was unique in being powered by air-cooled radial engines.

PROFILE

Forgotten cousin of the DC-4

Trans Canada Airways purchased the first of 20 DC-4Ms in October 1947, after having borrowed six unpressurised RCAF aircraft. The British Overseas Airways Corporation (BOAC) ordered 22 aircraft, christened Argonauts, the following November, and all had been delivered by early 1949. Soon after its introduction the type was earning 30 per cent of the airline's revenue.

In service the DC-4M-2s (as the pressurised aircraft were known) were well received.

The Rolls-Royce Merlin engines gave the aircraft much better performance at altitude than standard US-built DC-4s, though the North Stars gained a reputation for excessive cabin noise caused by the engine exhaust systems. This problem was never really solved, so Canadair went ahead with the development of the radial-engined C-5, one of which was built and delivered to the RCAF.

With only 71 airframes built, and a sizeable number lost in flying accidents, a C-4 North Star was a rare sight by the early 1970s. A handful were passed on to small operators, who used them primarily as freighters. In addition, a single example was retained by the RCAF for scientific exploration purposes. This, and the last flying commercial example, another ex-RCAF machine, were finally scrapped in 1976.

Left: RCAF North Stars were all delivered as unpressurised aircraft and featured nose radomes. Most were broken up in the 1960s, but one continued to serve until 1976 on survey duties.

Above: One of the BOAC Argonauts, Atalanta, has a special place in British history; it was the aircraft which carried the newly-crowned Queen Elizabeth II to South Africa in 1952.

C-4 North Star

Type: long-range transport

Powerplant: four 1312-kW (1,760-hp.) Rolls-Royce Merlin 622 liquid-cooled in-line piston engines

Maximum speed: 523 km/h (324 m.p.h.) at 7680 m (25,000 ft.)

Cruising speed: 466 km/h (289 m.p.h.) at 3720 m (12,000 ft.)

Range: 5150 km (3,193 mi.)

Service ceiling: 8990 m (29,500 ft.)

Weights: empty 21,243 kg (46,735 lb.); maximum take-off 37,331 kg (82,128 lb.)

Accommodation: crew of four, plus up to 62 passengers (typically) plus approx. 2600 kg (5,720 lb.) of freight

Dimensions:
span	35.81 m (117 ft. 5 in.)
length	28.54 m (93 ft. 7 in.)
height	8.39 m (27 ft. 6 in.)
wing area	135.63 m² (1,459 sq. ft.)

C-4

Delivered to the British Overseas Airways Corporation in August 1949, this example served with BOAC for 11 years. In February 1960 it was purchased by Aden Airways which operated the aircraft until it was retired in 1963.

When originally delivered to BOAC the C-4 aircraft were configured to carry 40 passengers. This seating plan was very flexible, however, and was altered by Aden Airways to permit carriage of more passengers on high-density routes.

Aden Airways acquired this C-4 from BOAC and it retained a very similar colour scheme to that used by its previous owner. Many fledgling African airlines bought second-hand aircraft from major European airlines.

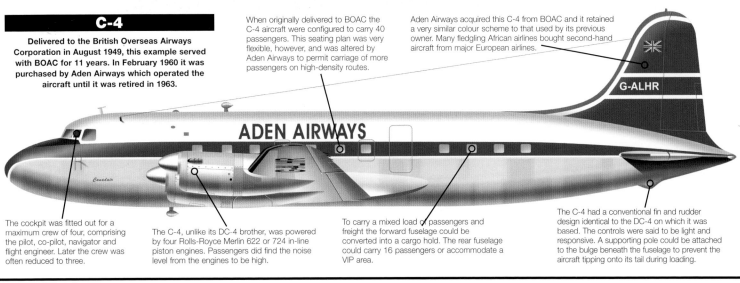

The cockpit was fitted out for a maximum crew of four, comprising the pilot, co-pilot, navigator and flight engineer. Later the crew was often reduced to three.

The C-4, unlike its DC-4 brother, was powered by four Rolls-Royce Merlin 622 or 724 in-line piston engines. Passengers did find the noise level from the engines to be high.

To carry a mixed load of passengers and freight the forward fuselage could be converted into a cargo hold. The rear fuselage could carry 16 passengers or accommodate a VIP area.

The C-4 had a conventional fin and rudder design identical to the DC-4 on which it was based. The controls were said to be light and responsive. A supporting pole could be attached to the bulge beneath the fuselage to prevent the aircraft tipping onto its tail during loading.

ACTION DATA

MAXIMUM SPEED

Fitting Rolls-Royce Merlins to the DC-4 airframe considerably improved performance and the North Star was much faster than its radial-engined American cousin. The Avro Tudor II was also fitted with Merlins but was larger and slightly slower.

C-4	523 km/h (324 m.p.h.)
DC-4-1009	451 km/h (280 m.p.h.)
689 TUDOR II	475 km/h (295 m.p.h.)

SERVICE CEILING

Trans Canada Airlines purchased North Stars with the intention of operating them on North Atlantic routes and at high altitudes. The Merlins were chosen as a powerplant primarily because they offered better performance for this role than the radial engines fitted to the DC-4.

C-4	DC-4-1009	689 TUDOR II
8990 m (29,500 ft.)	6800 m (22,300 ft.)	7790 m (25,550 ft.)

RANGE

In addition to giving the aircraft greater speed and better performance at altitude, the Merlins also increased endurance over that of the American DC-4s. The C-4 was still not as capable in this respect as the Tudor, which was used on long routes to Africa.

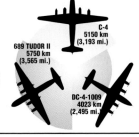

C-4	5150 km (3,193 mi.)
689 TUDOR II	5750 km (3,565 mi.)
DC-4-1009	4023 km (2,495 mi.)

Propeller-driven aircraft from Canadair

■ CANADAIR CL-44: Essentially a copy of the Bristol Britannia, the CL-44 differed in being fitted with more powerful Rolls-Royce Tyne turboprops and featuring a strengthened airframe.

■ CANADAIR CL-28 (CP-107) ARGUS: Also based on the Britannia, this was a dedicated maritime patrol aircraft and featured a completely new unpressurised fuselage.

■ CANADAIR CL-215: Developed in the early 1960s, this amphibian has proved very useful as a water bomber and sizeable numbers have been exported around the world.

CANADAIR

REGIONAL JET

● Extended range ● Pioneering design ● Jet airliner

L aunched in March 1989 as a stretched development of the Challenger 601, Canadair's 50-seat Regional Jet flew for the first time in May 1991 and entered service in November 1992. The idea was to provide an aircraft able to operate on routes that would be uneconomical with bigger jets. It has been highly successful as a regional airliner, and has been used as the basis for the Canadair Special Edition business jet, and the Corporate JetLiner.

▲ In the competitive world of small jet airliners the Canadair Regional Jet offers the client an extremely high level of comfort, not often found in the smaller civil airliners.

PHOTO FILE

CANADAIR REGIONAL JET

◀ **Regional racer**
Owned and operated by the former racing driver Niki Lauda, Lauda Air began operations with the Regional Jet in April 1994. Operating from Austria and using Vienna as a hub, the aircraft flew to Berlin and Manchester.

Advanced airliner ▶
A major milestone was reached on 16 October 1990, when the first Regional Jet reached the closing stages of construction.

▼ **Corporate operations**
Used by the Xerox Corporation for ferrying employees across the United States, the aircraft is able to accommodate 30 passengers.

▼ **High flyer**
Slicing through a city skyline, the Regional Jet takes advantage of all the latest aviation technology for its design. The sleek design and large winglets are a feature of the aircraft.

▲ **Future flights**
Canadair's first Regional Jet wore an extremely smart and complex colour scheme. The aircraft was exhibited at numerous aviation events in a bid to increase sales.

FACTS AND FIGURES

➤ The Regional Jet is the first modern airliner to be designed for the short-to-medium stage length market.

➤ Canadair has produced more than 4000 aircraft in its history.

➤ Flights can be made from Rome to Hamburg non-stop.

➤ With an increase in the demand for small airliners the Regional Jet was designed to replace the Challenger.

➤ The second Regional Jet made its first flight on 2 August 1991.

➤ Several European airlines have adopted the airliner in service.

PROFILE

Flying into the future

Compared with the Canadair Challenger 601, the Regional Jet has a bigger wing for improved lift at low airspeeds, and winglets to reduce drag. The fuselage has been extended by a total of 6.1 m (20 ft.) and there are two additional emergency exits.

As the world's first 50-seat jet airliner, the RJ has opened up a new market for small, high-performance airliners offering the sort of amenities found on traditional airliners, such as galleys for hot meals and ample headroom. It has proved even more economical than expected, burning some 10 per cent less

fuel than originally predicted.

Lufthansa CityLine was the first airline operator, and by September 1997 a total of 16 airlines in 10 countries, mainly in Europe and North America, had ordered 286 examples.

The Corporate JetLiner is intended for use by industrial companies and government agencies as an alternative to airlines. It can be configured to carry from 18 to 35 passengers over ranges of up to 4167 km (2,600 mi.). The Special Edition version is a wide-body business jet with luxurious accommodation for up to 19 passengers and a range of 5778 km (3,528 mi.).

Above: In passing a succession of commercial aviation tests the prototype Regional Jet accomplished the amazing feat of completing five flights within the first week of testing, a civil record that stands to this day.

Right: Used for internal flights, Air Canada's Regional Jets wear a large maple leaf on their tail.

RJ Series 200

Type: long-range regional jet airliner

Powerplant: two 41-kN (9,225-lb.-thrust) General Electric CF34-3A1 single-stage turbofan engines

Cruising speed: 859 km/h (533 m.p.h.); long-range cruise 786 km/h (487 m.p.h.)

Initial climb rate: 463 m/min (1,518 f.p.m.)

Range: 1787 km (1,108 mi.)

Service ceiling: 11,278 m (37,000 ft.)

Weights: empty 13,236 kg (29,119 lb.); maximum take-off 21,523 kg (47,350 lb.)

Accommodation: two pilots, plus flight attendants and up to 50 passengers

Dimensions:
span	21.44 m	(70 ft. 4 in.)
length	26.95 m	(88 ft. 5 in.)
height	6.30 m	(20 ft. 8 in.)
wing area	48.31 m²	(520 sq. ft.)

REGIONAL JET

This example operates with Ansett Aviation Services of Australia. Ansett has chosen to have its aircraft wear a rather muted colour scheme compared to some that are in service.

Though not installed on current aircraft a head-up display has been tested on the Regional Jet. This has proved to be extremely effective during limited visibility landings. As yet no operator has requested this modification.

General Electric worked closely with Canadair to incorporate the changes that were necessary to the engine and engine nacelle. This reduced costs enormously.

Various options are available for the Regional Jet. If required the aircraft can be fitted with a flight management system to reduce the pilots' workload.

During early developmental test flights an instrument boom was attached to the nose of the aircraft to allow data to be recorded and analysed after each flight. This was eventually removed.

A range of seating options is available for the aircraft depending on the operator. For high-density routes the aircraft can accommodate as many as 50 passengers.

A common feature on many modern airliners is the addition of winglets. This provides additional lift, by reducing wing-tip turbulence, and improves the handling of the aircraft.

Power is provided by two General Electric turbofan engines. These were installed on the aircraft after negotiations with GE for an engine that was readily accessible to the market and was easy for airlines to maintain.

Competitive Canadair

■ **CHALLENGER 601:** Developed for domestic civil flights, the Challenger is also operated by the RCAF. The aircraft is currently being replaced in civilian service by the Regional Jet.

■ **DASH-8:** The turbo-prop-powered Dash-8 is seen as a cost-effective alternative to some jet airliners. An all-purpose cargo version has also been produced.

■ **LEARJET 60:** Having established itself as a leader in the civil jet market, the Learjet has been constantly improved. This example is one of the latest variants.

ACTION DATA

MAXIMUM CRUISING SPEED

Canadair has incorporated many of the latest advances in aviation technology in its Regional Jet which has resulted in an impressive service speed. By operating at a high cruise speed the aircraft is able to cover huge distances at relatively little cost to the operator.

REGIONAL JET 200	859 km/h (533 m.p.h.)
F 70	856 km/h (530 m.p.h.)
RJ 85	763 km/h (473 m.p.h.)

RANGE

Having become one of the leaders in the manufacture of small commercial airliners, Canadair sought to improve their aircraft range with the Regional Jet. Though it does not offer the greatest range in its class, the RJ 200 is still very cost effective.

F 70 1981 km (1,228 mi.)

RJ 85 2129 km (1,320 mi.)

REGIONAL JET 200 1787 km (1,108 mi.)

CAPACITY

Designed to operate on domestic routes where the ability to carry a large number of passengers is not essential, the Regional Jet 200 still offers one of the largest passenger loads for its class. Although larger aircraft are able to carry more passengers this has not affected sales of the Regional Jet 200.

REGIONAL JET 200 50 passengers

F 70 79 passengers

RJ 85 85 passengers

CANADAIR

CL-215

● **Multi-purpose amphibian** ● **Aerial firefighter** ● **26-place transport**

The CL-215 is a fighting machine, but not a military one. It is uniquely designed to combat one of mankind's oldest enemies – fire. From the tinder-dry woods of Quebec to the parched and arid scrub of the Mediterranean, forest fires are a regular feature of the hot summer months. And the big Canadian amphibian is the first line of defence in the struggle to protect lives and property.

▲ A Canadair CL-215 of France's Securité Civile dumps five tons of water on a blazing Provençal forest.

CANADAIR **CL-215**

Go-anywhere ▶ firefighter
The CL-215, unlike more conventional aircraft, is not restricted to airfields. It can operate from any sufficiently large body of water – lakes, rivers and the sea.

◀ Turbo power
Many CL-215s have been modified with turbine engines, which are smaller, lighter and more economical than the original piston powerplant.

▲ Fire bomber
The centre of the CL-215's fuselage is devoted to two huge water tanks. Their contents are delivered via large doors in the underside of the hull.

Spray instead ▶ of splatter
Some CL-215s have spray pipes under the wings. These are designed to deliver firefighting water in a fine mist over a wide area of fire, rather than in a single cascading deluge in one spot.

▲ Super scooper
Refilling the CL-215 is a superfast process, thanks to twin scoops under the hull. These enable the machine to replenish from any convenient body of water.

FACTS AND FIGURES

➤ CL-215s are very tough. They have to be to withstand dozens or even hundreds of filling cycles per day.

➤ Using scoops, the amphibian can pick up more than 5 tons of water in 10 seconds.

➤ The CL-215 can empty its tanks over a fire in less than a second.

➤ The CL-215 can fill its tanks in any water more than 1.4 metres deep.

➤ In a four-hour cycle, a water bomber will average about 40 drops.

➤ The record performance was by a Yugoslav plane, which made an incredible 225 drops in 24 hours.

Firefighting over the Timberlands

Once a forest fire takes hold, there is little that firefighters on the ground can do to stop it. But all is not lost. A rising engine roar signals the entrance of the CL-215.

Only 30 metres (100 ft.) above the tree tops, the bright-yellow water-bomber flies directly towards the hottest part of the fire. As it passes overhead, long

doors in its boat-like belly open, and five tons of water cascade down. The aircraft immediately turns away to pick up more.

The CL-215 is an amphibian. It can operate from airfields, where its tanks can be pumped full of fire-retardant chemicals in about two minutes. Or it can head for the nearest open water and in a skimming pass can scoop up an

astonishing 5300 litres (1,400 gal.) of water in just 10 seconds.

As soon as its tanks are full, the plane heads back to the fire. This process is repeated tens or even hundreds of times in a day until the fire is eventually brought under control.

The CL-215 is more than a Canadian water bomber. The Thai navy uses the amphibian for coastal patrol and search and rescue.

CL-215

The Canadian provinces are the largest users of the CL-215, with some 49 aircraft in service.

The CL-215 is powered by a World War II-designed piston engine. Although it is reliable, many aircraft are having lighter, more powerful turbo-props retro-fitted.

A shallow hull means that the CL-215 can use its scoop in just over a metre (three feet) of water, although two metres (six feet) is usually the operational minimum.

The floats positioned at the end of the CL-215's wings mean that the aircraft has great stability when landing on water.

The CL-215 is immensely strongly built. It has to be, since not only does it have to cope with the corrosive effect of thousands of immersions in water, but it regularly flies through the smoke, heat and turbulence created by the fires it is designed to fight.

The CL-215 is an amphibian: its retractable undercarriage means it is equally able to fly from land and water.

Large cargo doors mean that the CL-215 is easily convertible to its secondary function as a 26-man or four-ton capacity light general-purpose transport aircraft.

CF-YXG

35

GOU·ERNEMENT
MINISTERE DES TRA

CL-215

Type: two-seat firefighting amphibian or five-seat patrol aircraft or 26-seat transport

Powerplant: two 1566-kW (2,100-hp.) Pratt & Whitney Double Wasp radial piston engines, or two 1775-kW (2,340-hp.) P&W Canada turboprops

Maximum speed: 290 km/h (174 m.p.h.) at 3000 m (9,800 ft.)

Rate of climb: 305 metres (1,000 ft.) per minute

Operational range: 2000 km (1,240 mi.) with 1600-kg (3,527-lb.) payload

Weights: empty 12,043 kg (26,500 lb.); loaded 19,890 kg (43,850 lb.)

Payload: 6132 litres (1.619 gal.) of water, chemical retardant, oil dispersant or insecticide; with tanks removed 26 passengers or 4 tons of cargo

Dimensions:
span	28.6 m (93 ft. 11 in.)
length	19.82 m (65 ft.)
height (on land)	8.98 m (29 ft. 5 in.)
wing area	100 m² (1,080 sq. ft.)

ACTION DATA

FILLING UP

Touching the surface of the water at about 150 km/h (92 m.p.h.), the pilot immediately applies power to counteract the effect of the scoops, which tend to pitch the nose down. The scoops can pick up more than 5000 litres (1,320 gal.) in about 600 metres (2,000 ft.) and in just 10 seconds.

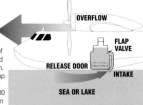

OVERFLOW

FLAP VALVE

RELEASE DOOR

INTAKE

SEA OR LAKE

RELEASE

The CL-215's drop doors are located at the bottom of the boat-shaped hull; early versions have two doors. These can empty the two large tanks in under a second. Later versions have four doors, allowing more flexibility. Whatever the arrangement, the optimum release height is around 30 metres (100 ft.) above the fire.

COVERAGE

A water-bomber pilot has two water delivery options. He can deliver water from both tanks simultaneously, covering a short, wide area of the fire. Or he can empty them in succession, covering a much longer, narrower strip of ground.

12 m (40 ft.)   145 m (465 ft.)

20 m (65 ft.)   85 m (280 ft.)

Water-bombing cycle

3 LOADING: 'Once you are on the water, you wind on the power to keep an indicated airspeed of 85 to 90 knots. The scoops fill the tanks in 10 seconds.'

5 AT THE FIRE: 'We try to bomb from 30 metres (100 ft.) or less. Any higher, especially on really hot days, you lose too much from evaporation. But you don't want to get too low, either – you're flying over a forest, remember. And tough though this plane is, you sure don't want to hit too many trees!'

2 APPROACH: 'You approach like any other water landing. From the cockpit you can't see the surface clearly. We have a couple of retractable probes, about the size of a tea cup, which tell us when we're just a fraction off the right height.'

1 SELECTION: 'Loading up is really straightforward. We can use any piece of water that leaves us enough room to make a touch and go – canals, rivers, lakes, or even the open sea.'

4 CLIMB-OUT: 'Because you're already at flying speed, as soon as the scoops retract you're airborne. Once at safe single-engine climb speed, you're off for the fire as fast as you can.'

CESSNA

401-441

● Air taxi ● Military communications ● Executive transport

A fter dramatic sales success in the 1950s and 1960s with their light, single- and twin-engined private aircraft, in 1962 Cessna made the move into the business aircraft market with the Model 411. This aircraft was an immediate success and it spawned numerous variants, with the latest remaining in production until 1987. The Cessna 400 family is still a common sight around the world today, whether operated as business aircraft or commuter liners.

▲ Not only is the Cessna 400 Series in widespread operation as a passenger carrier, the Cessna 402 Utiliner also has a secondary light freight-carrying ability. This aircraft can have its seats removed and has double doors to facilitate access. Permanent tip tanks are fitted to the wings of the Utiliner to increase the aircraft's endurance.

CESSNA 401-441

Golden Eagle ▶
Pressurised for passenger comfort, the Cessna 421 was developed into the turboprop Model 425 Corsair.

▲ Worldwide service
Cessna 402s were sold to commuter airlines in every continent. This 402B, of Brazilian airline Transportes Aéreos Regionais (TAM), is fitted with turbocharged engines for high-altitude performance.

▲ Avoiding the storms
The Conquest executive version was available with a Bendix colour weather radar to help avoid storms.

◀ Sales success
The basic form of the 411 was kept throughout the series, including the 10-seat Golden Eagle.

Turbo power ▶
Cessna stepped into the turboprop market with the Model 441 Conquest pressurised executive transport, which has accommodation for up to 11 passengers. Some 360 were sold.

FACTS AND FIGURES

➤ Cessna use the 400 Series designation to distinguish medium twin-engined aircraft with a power output of more than 447 kW.

➤ The Cessna 411 gained certification on 17 August 1964.

➤ Cessna 400 Series aircraft are used for communications by more than 20 air arms.

➤ In February 1960, Cessna acquired a 49 per cent stake in French company, Avions Max Holste, which became Reims Aviation.

➤ The basic price for a new Cessna 402C in 1981 was $282,000.

➤ From 1980, Cessna offered a 35-month warranty on all 400 Series aircraft.

PROFILE

Successful twin-engined family

Entering service in 1964, the Cessna 401 introduced the new six-seat 'cabin class' business aircraft to the world. In the following 20 years, this initial design produced a whole family of best-selling twin-engined aircraft, enhancing Cessna's reputation as one of the world's biggest general aviation manufacturers.

The most successful version was the 10-seat Model 402 convertible passenger/freight aircraft also known as the Utiliner or Businessliner. Other versions, such as the pressurised Model 414 Chancellor and 421 Golden Eagle, quickly

followed as sales increased around the world. Showing the versatility of the 400 Series airframe, Cessna decided in the mid-1970s to expand into the twin-turboprop market – previously dominated by the Beech King Air – with the Model 441 Conquest. After early tailplane problems (resulting in a fatal crash), the turboprop Conquest and the smaller Model 425 Corsair became popular with the executive market. In 1975, Cessna launched a stretched version of the Model 402B, called the 404 Titan, which sold well to small commuter airlines. An even larger 14-seat version, called the Caravan II, was

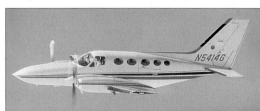

Above: Liability problems in the United States have been resolved and it is hoped that 400 Series production may resume.

Right: To provide a smaller pressurised twin, Cessna developed the six-seat Model 414 Chancellor.

produced by Reims in France. However, by 1986, liability problems had forced Cessna to halt its light/medium piston aircraft production.

Model 441 Conquest

Type: twin-engined pressurised executive transport

Powerplant: two 474-kW (636-hp.) Garrett TPE331-8 turboprop engines

Maximum speed: 547 km/h (340 m.p.h.) at 4875 m (16,000 ft.)

Maximum cruising speed: 542 km/h (337 m.p.h.) at 7315 m (24,000 ft.)

Range: 4096 km (2,545 mi.)

Service ceiling: 11,275 m (37,000 ft.)

Weights: empty 2670 kg (5,886 lb.); maximum take-off 4468 kg (9,850 lb.)

Accommodation: 11 passengers

Dimensions: span 15.04 m (49 ft. 4 in.)
length 11.89 m (39 ft.)
height 4.01 m (13 ft. 2 in.)
wing area 23.56 m² (236 sq. ft.)

MODEL 404 TITAN

Cessna's versatile Titan was available in three versions: the Titan Ambassador passenger carrier, the Titan Courier convertible passenger/freight transport, and the Titan Freighter cargo aircraft.

As well as dual controls, the Titan was usually equipped with factory-installed avionics systems and equipment packages.

Power was provided by two 280-kW (375-hp.) Continental GTSIO-520-M turbocharged engines, giving an increase of more than 30 per cent in kg/km per litre over the Model 402.

The Titan's tail unit differed from the Model 402B in having an extended fin and a tailplane with 12° of dihedral. These measures gave the larger Titan sufficient directional control.

A number of different cabin interiors were offered with the Titan. The Ambassador version was available with an executive interior, whereas the Courier could be fitted with removable seats for up to 10 passengers. The final variant, the Freighter, featured impact-resistant interiors to protect the fuselage from damage by cargo.

The Titan is basically a stretched Model 402B and its nose shares this aircraft's profile. Space in the nose is taken up by a luggage compartment.

The wings and landing gear were similar to those fitted to the Model 441 Conquest, which was developed at the same time.

Cessna 400 Series family

■ **MODEL 402B:** The 10-seat Model 402 was the most numerous variant of the 400 Series, with more than 1000 produced. The prototype first flew in August 1965.

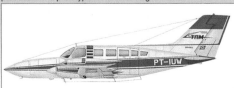

■ **MODEL 404 TITAN:** First flying on 26 February 1975, the Titan was initially delivered at a rate of about 80 per year. In 1981 the basic price for a new Titan was $415,000.

■ **MODEL 441 CONQUEST:** After early structural problems, the Conquest achieved a fair market share of the twin-turboprop executive market. The production run totalled 362 aircraft.

ACTION DATA

CRUISING SPEED

Although the Mojave does not benefit from turboprop power, its sleek lines give it a higher cruising speed than the similarly piston-engined Model 414A. The C90A is turboprop-powered.

MODEL 414A 357 km/h (222 m.p.h.)

KING AIR C90A 448 km/h (278 m.p.h.)

PA-31P-350 MOJAVE 435 km/h (270 m.p.h.)

TAKE-OFF RUN

Again, the added power of turboprop engines gives the King Air a decisive advantage over piston-engined rivals. The Mojave and Model 414 use a similar amount of runway. All the aircraft are able to operate from smaller airfields with short strips.

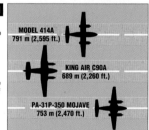

MODEL 414A 791 m (2,595 ft.)

KING AIR C90A 689 m (2,260 ft.)

PA-31P-350 MOJAVE 753 m (2,470 ft.)

RANGE

Early versions of the King Air do not have the range of later models. Both the Mojave and the Model 414 have sufficient range to carry out commuterliner or internal executive flights. The maximum range of the 414A increases to 2459 km (1,528 mi.) if the aircraft is empty, allowing positioning flights over long distances.

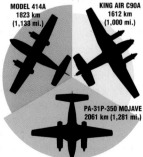

MODEL 414A 1823 km (1,133 mi.)

KING AIR C90A 1612 km (1,000 mi.)

PA-31P-350 MOJAVE 2061 km (1,281 mi.)

CESSNA

MODEL A SERIES

● Air racer ● One-piece cantilever wing ● Commercial aircraft

Clyde V. Cessna's first aircraft was a Blériot-type monoplane built in 1911 and powered by a 45-kW Elbridge engine. By the end of 1927 he had his own company and had constructed the prototype of his first production aircraft, the Model A. It offered high performance, without sacrificing comfort and utility, and served as the basis for the Cessna business for the next 25 years. It was also notable as the first of many light aircraft built by Cessna.

▲ Slender looking and with the performance of a racing aircraft, Cessna's Model A series took the American civil aircraft market by storm, achieving huge sales success.

◀ Firm favourite
A long-time favourite with civilian operators, the Cessna Model AW used a Warner powerplant which overcame some of the problems encountered with the earlier troublesome Anzani engine.

Pioneering design ▶
Cessna was one of the first companies to make practical use of an internally braced wing design, on its Model A.

Surprise performance ▶
The little air-cooled Warner 'Scarab' engine gave the Model A a performance level that was comparable to that of larger aircraft. This allowed the aircraft to compete successfully in numerous air races and exhibitions across America in an effort to increase sales.

◀ Classic design
The design of the Cessna Model A series was so outstanding that it remained relatively unchanged for 25 years, apart from the adoption of different engines.

Engine choice ▶
Cessna sold the aircraft with a range of optional powerplants. This particular aircraft is the Model AC, the suffix 'C' denoting the Comet engine. However, the Warner engine was found to give the best performance.

FACTS AND FIGURES

➤ In 1929 a Model AW became the first civil aircraft to be flown to Siberia, flying more than 16,000 km (9,900 mi.) from the U.S.

➤ Cessna Model As were among the first aircraft used as corporate transports.

➤ Clyde Cessna's aviation activities date back to 1911.

➤ The fuselage was built up of welded chrome-moly steel tubing, lightly faired to shape and fabric covered.

➤ Wheel brakes were available on later models of the aircraft.

➤ Positioned on the rear fuselage was a rubber cord-supported tail-skid.

PROFILE

Wichita's light plane pioneer

Internally braced wings made their debut on a light commercial aircraft in the Cessna Model A. In 1928 a slightly modified Model AA became the first certificated version of the 'Cessna Cantilever Monoplane' series which was to prove so popular with flyers between the wars.

Able to accommodate three or four people, the Model AA was powered by a French 89-kW (120-hp.) Anzani radial engine, as there was no suitable American design in the required power range. A number of variants followed, each powered by a different engine type, as Cessna experimented with alternatives.

The most promising was the Model AW's Warner Scarab; this version was produced during 1929. In all, Model A production totalled 70, including 48 AWs. The Model BW followed, this being a 'sportsman's' version of the Model AW, which was powered by a 164-kW (220-hp.) Wright J5. Thirteen were built.

Chrome-moly steel tube was used in the Model A's fuselage structure, its wings had wooden framing and the entire aircraft was fabric covered. This gave a strong, but lightweight airframe and contributed to its lively performance. In fact, Model As were victorious as racing aircraft during the 1928 US season.

Above: American businesses were quick to adopt the aircraft as executive transports.

Below: Thanks to their excellent construction numerous Model A Series aircraft survive to this day. They are often seen at air shows in the United States.

Model AW

Type: single engine light passenger aircraft

Powerplant: one 82-kW (110-hp.) Warner Scarab seven-cylinder radial engine

Maximum speed: 201 km/h (125 m.p.h.); cruising speed 168 km/h (104 m.p.h.)

Initial climb rate: 188 m/min (617 f.p.m.)

Range: 1013 km (628 mi.)

Service ceiling: 3657 m (12,000 ft.)

Weights: empty 555 kg (1,220 lb.); maximum take-off 1025 kg (2,255 lb.)

Accommodation: one pilot and three passengers

Dimensions:
span	12.19 m	(40 ft.)
length	7.58 m	(24 ft. 10 in.)
height	1.86 m	(6 ft. 2 in.)
wing area	20.80 m²	(224 sq. ft.)

MODEL AW

With performance equal to the racing aircraft of the period, the Cessna Model AW was able to offer the American public a small high-speed passenger aircraft which was purchased readily.

After problems with the early Anzani engine, Cessna installed a Warner Scarab engine on later aircraft, resulting in a marked increase in the performance of the aircraft.

Despite its small dimensions the Model A was capable of carrying three passengers. Two were seated on a bench-type seat in the rear cockpit, with the other seated alongside the pilot.

The fuselage was built up of welded chrome-moly steel tubing faired to shape and then covered with fabric, resulting in a finished fuselage that was light but extremely strong.

A large rudder gave the aircraft excellent handling, which was well appreciated by pilots competing in air races.

NC6448

To meet the requirement of operating from grass runways and unprepared strips, Cessna equipped the Model A with exceptionally large wheels.

The tail section of the undercarriage was a sprung-cord rubber tail-skid. This was lighter than an equivalent tailwheel arrangement which helped to reduced the overall weight of the aircraft.

ACTION DATA

POWER

The lightweight design of the Model A required only a small powerplant to be used on the aircraft. Later models like the AW were fitted with improved engines, ensuring that their performance remained outstanding in comparison to other larger types such as de Havilland's Puss Moth and the Beech Model 10.

MODEL AW
82 kW (110 hp.)

MODEL 10-D
168 kW (225 hp.)

D.H. 80A
PUSS MOTH
97 kW (130 hp.)

MAXIMUM SPEED

Although the Model AW was developed as a passenger aircraft, the high speed of the aircraft saw it competing in numerous air races across America during the twenties, often beating specially constructed designs. Despite this, larger passenger aircraft still just outstripped the Model AW for speed.

MODEL AW   201 km/h (125 m.p.h.)
MODEL 10-D   203 km/h (126 m.p.h.)
D.H. 80A PUSS MOTH 206 km/h (128 m.p.h.)

SERVICE CEILING

Despite its lightweight design, the Model AW was unable to achieve the high altitudes of the larger types such as the Beech Model 10 and de Havilland Puss Moth. For its class, though, the service ceiling of the Model AW was more than adequate.

MODEL AW	MODEL 10-D	D.H. 80A PUSS MOTH
3657 m (12,000 ft.)	3960 m (13,000 ft.)	5334 m (17,500 ft.)

Successful Cessnas

■ **THE COMET:** The first aircraft constructed by Cessna with an enclosed cockpit, the aircraft was displayed at air shows throughout the United States.

■ **DC-6:** Developed in 1928, the DC-6 was produced in two variants. Although it was a capable design, the economic recession in the thirties hindered sales of the aircraft.

■ **MODEL C-34:** Flying for the first time in June 1935, the C-34 displayed all the hallmarks of Cessna's light aircraft. Later models were pressed into limited military service.

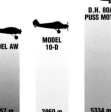

CESSNA

CITATION

● Luxury jet family ● Straight and swept wings ● High performance

On 15 September 1969 the first Cessna Fanjet 500 made its initial flight. Immediately renamed Model 500 Citation, it launched Cessna into the highly competitive business jet market. Competitors doubted the new aircraft, but Cessna persevered and has produced a range of jets which fulfil the needs of business travellers in the USA and around the world. The aircraft have increasingly become a symbol of corporate power.

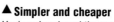

▲ *Business jets have become a useful transport and status symbol for companies and individuals across America. Sports personalities such as Jack Nicklaus are among the Citation customers and serve to give the aircraft an even more glamorous image.*

PHOTO FILE

CESSNA CITATION

▼ Rough business
A Citation 501 prototype demonstrates the aircraft's ability to operate from grass air strips.

▲ Comfort and Citation II
Seating 6 to 10, the 689 Model 550s delivered by January 1995 have luxurious interiors.

Sweeping new Citation ▶
NASA helped Cessna to design the wing for the advanced Model 650 Citation III. Compared to the previous model, the Citation III had only the name in common.

▼ Cessna's 'Nearjet'
Competitors referred to the Citation I as the 'Nearjet' because of its conventional appearance. When production ceased in 1976, 350 had been built.

▲ Simpler and cheaper
Having abandoned the more expensive Citation IV, Cessna developed the lower-cost Citation VI. From the outside this model is identical to the III.

FACTS AND FIGURES

➤ A single-pilot version of the Citation I was certified on 7 January 1977 as the Model 501 Citation I/SP.

➤ During flight tests the Citation III has been taken to Mach 0.90 in a dive.

➤ Golfer Arnold Palmer has also ordered a Model 750 Citation X after his Citation III.

➤ The Citation Excel combines a short version of the Citation X's cabin with Citation V Ultra wings and tail.

➤ Cessna designed the Citation V as a successor to the Citation I and II.

➤ The hi-tech Citation X features a glass cockpit and transatlantic range.

PROFILE

Cessna's winning business jet

Cessna ensured the long-term success of its Citation family by producing a stylish design which offered the utmost in modern jet performance at an affordable price.

Even the original straight-winged models, with their narrow, sleek fuselages and rear-mounted engines, were extremely elegant aircraft. Companies and celebrities were quick to recognise the image-enhancing properties of owning a Citation. Any doubts about

the ability of a manufacturer of light piston-engined aircraft to produce a jet were dispelled by Cessna's experience with the USAF's T-37/A-37 programme.

During 1976 Cessna began work on the Citation III. Intended as a development of the straight-winged I and II, the aircraft emerged as a radically new design with swept wings and a higher cabin ceiling. The increase in height made the aircraft even more desirable, and orders from the US and abroad flooded in. The first

In August 1987 Cessna announced the Citation V. This model brought the straight-winged Citations up to modern standards.

delivery was made to golfer Arnold Palmer in 1983. Subsequent Citations have offered improved performance and comfort, and culminated in the Mach 0.92-capable Citation X.

A gravity refuelling point is located on the upper surface of each wing, with the primary high-pressure point on the starboard rear fuselage.

Most of the airframe is of light-alloy construction. The fuselage is of circular section and of fail-safe structure in pressurised areas.

The wing leading-edge is de-iced by engine bleed air, while the tailplane is de-iced electrically. No provision is made for fin de-icing, although the engine intakes are protected from ice build-up.

The high-mounted T-tail has a variable incidence tailplane and elevators. All tail surfaces are of light alloy.

MODEL 650 CITATION VI

Although it is a smart aircraft with good performance, the Citation VI was launched at a time of general recession. Sales of the $8,200,000 jet have been slow.

A radome at the extreme nose covers a high-resolution Honeywell Primus 300SL colour weather radar. A hold for crew baggage is also incorporated into the nose section.

In order to make the Citation VI more affordable, Cessna limited the avionics options and offered only standard layouts for the cabin. The cabin is heated, pressurised and air-conditioned and is usually configured in a six-seat layout. Passenger seats are fully adjustable and have full harnesses.

The AlliedSignal TFE731 turbofans are pod-mounted high on the rear fuselage and are positioned to provide optimum maintenance convenience with minimum cabin noise. Hydraulically-operated thrust reversers are standard.

Two crew members fly the Citation VI. An electronic flight instrumentation system is optional on this lower-specified model.

Emergency back-up systems are provided for both the nosewheel steering and anti-skid braking system.

This small door on the fuselage side serves the electrically heated 1.56 m³ (55-cu. ft.) passenger baggage compartment. At the forward end of the fuselage the main entrance door incorporates an airstair, while an emergency exit is situated on the starboard side above the wing.

N652CC

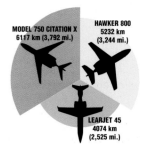
Special mission Citation

■ **FLIGHT CHECKING:** The US Federal Aviation Administration has used this early-model Citation for checking and calibrating airport navigation and approach systems.

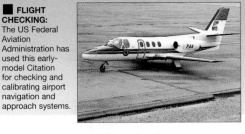

■ **VIP AND PRIORITY TRANSPORT:** A few Citations are used by the military in the VIP and courier roles. This Model 500 belongs to the Venezuelan air force.

■ **RADAR TRAINING:** Fifteen Model 552 Citations replaced T-39 Sabreliners in US Navy service. They operated as T-47As and were used as flying classrooms for student radar operators.

CFM

SHADOW

● Microlight family ● Range of variants ● Affordable flying

When David Cook first fitted a go-kart engine to a hang-glider in 1977, the home-made propeller would not keep him airborne for more than a 150ft (45m) hop. Six years later, when he flew the first Cook Flying Machines Shadow, the authorities had not even considered how to go about certifying such an aircraft. Yet today, microlights are an established route to safe, economical flying, and the Shadow remains a fine machine in its class.

▲ *Cook Flying Machines pioneered microlight production in the 1980s from a small factory in England. Unfortunately, in late 1996, the firm went into receivership.*

CFM SHADOW

◄ **STOL performance**
Microlights are naturally able to use a very short take-off run. The Series B-D has a 90-m (295-ft) run on a metalled surface.

▼ **Variable endurance**
The Shadow has a one-hour, 45-minute endurance, and eight hours with extra fuel tanks.

▼ **At the factory**
CFM's headquarters and chief manufacturing facility was on an industrial estate in Suffolk. Assembly was also undertaken at Old Sarum aerodrome, near Salisbury, Wiltshire.

▼ **Multi-role microlight**
Suggested equipment to be fitted to the Shadow has included spray gear, cameras and thermal imagers.

◄ **Military variant promoted**
This Shadow variant features a British Aerospace infra-red linescan system for military use.

FACTS AND FIGURES

➤ In 1996, CFM's Streak Shadow SA microlight kit cost £10,750, exclusive of engine, propeller and sales tax.

➤ By early 1995, sales of Shadow series microlights had totalled 280.

➤ A multi-function surveillance Shadow variant features a Hasselblad camera fit.

➤ CFM entered a licence-production agreement with a firm in New Mexico.

➤ The last CFM microlight was the SA11 Starstreak, which had a 55-kW (73-hp.) engine.

➤ CFM had plans to establish a licence-production line in South Africa.

Popular pioneering microlight

Nearly 15 years after its first flight, the Shadow has spawned a range of derivatives. There are gliders with an optional 20-kW (27-hp.) motor for self-launching, and a version called the Wizard.

High performance is the preserve of the 48-kW (65-hp.) Streak Shadow and 63-kW (85-hp.) Star Streak. The Streak Shadow has shorter, thinner wings, while the Star Streak's extra power and reduced-chord wings give a top speed of 260 km/h (161 m.p.h.).

But flying a Shadow is mainly about safe, cheap, powered flight. The addition of wing lockers holding 5 kg (10 lb.) of baggage can make the Shadow capable of carrying enough for the pilot and a passenger to spend a weekend away. Carrying only the pilot, the Shadow has also been used for some remarkably long journeys. At least one pilot has crossed the US in such a craft, taking two and a half weeks to cover 6437 kilometres (3,990 mi.), during 69 hours aloft. Another has flown from England to China via Moscow and Siberia in the space of a month, despite thunderstorms, torrential rain and 110-km/h (68-m.p.h.) winds.

Below: In Britain, the first weekend in May sees the Microlight Trade Fair, held at Popham in Hampshire. The fair attracts microlight manufacturers from around Europe.

Above: Shadow Series C-D is the dual-control variant of the company's standard model.

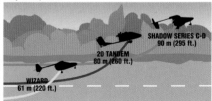

Shadow Series B

Type: two-seat microlight

Powerplant: one 28.3-kW (38-hp.) Rotax 447 two-cylinder engine

Maximum level speed: 153 km/h (95 m.p.h.)

Maximum climb rate: 299 m/min (980 f.p.m.)

Range: 209 km (130 mi.) with reserves

Service ceiling: 6100 m (20,000 ft.)

Weights: empty 150 kg (330 lb.), maximum take-off 348 kg (766 lb.)

Accommodation: pilot and one passenger in tandem seats (dual-control in Series B-D)

Dimensions:
span	10.03 m (32 ft. 11 in.)
length	6.40 m (21 ft.)
height	1.75 m (5 ft. 9 in.)
wing area	15.00 m² (161 sq.ft.)

The Shadow's wings are of aluminium alloy and wood construction, with foam/glass-fibre ribs, plywood covering on the forward section and polyester fabric aft.

Wing design in the Shadow allows no 'defined stall' or spinning. Drooped wingtips increase lift on take-off. Struts are used to strengthen the wing structure.

Microlight design has advanced in leaps and bounds since the early days of the late 1970s. Today's designs feature tricycle undercarriage, enclosed cockpits in a streamlined fuselage, often with two seats, and more powerful engines. The undercarriage is non-retractable, but features brakes. Wheels may be exchanged for floats if required.

Aluminium is used in the Shadow's tailboom. The tailfin and large rudder are positioned below the boom. Finlets are fitted on the ends of the tailplane.

Fuel capacity is 23 litres (50 gallons) in a standard configuration. For long-distance flying, a 43-litre (95-gallon) auxiliary tank is optional.

SHADOW SERIES B-D

The first Shadow flew in 1983 and was in continuous production until CFM went into receivership in 1996. G-MTSG is a dual-control Series B-D, one of a considerable number of Shadows registered in Britain.

The Shadow is one of many microlight designs to employ the Rotax flat-twin cylinder air-cooled engine. The Shadow B-D's engine, rated at 28 kW (38 hp.), drives a 1.3-m (4-ft. 3-in.) diameter three-bladed propeller.

ACTION DATA

MAXIMUM SPEED

Top speeds of around 150-160 km/h (100 m.p.h.) are typical of this type of high-wing, single-engined microlight design. The Ukrainian Aeroprakt 20 is the slowest of the three designs, because of its inferior power-to-weight ratio.

SHADOW SERIES C-D	164 km/h (102 m.p.h.)
20 TANDEM	150 km/h (93 m.p.h.)
WIZARD	161 km/h (100 m.p.h.)

TAKE-OFF RUN

Wing design, weight and engine power largely determine the take-off run of a microlight aircraft. The figures quoted are for an aircraft using a metalled airstrip. Performance from a grass surface is likely to be poorer.

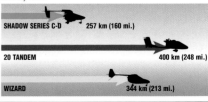

SHADOW SERIES C-D 90 m (295 ft.)
20 TANDEM 80 m (260 ft.)
WIZARD 61 m (220 ft.)

RANGE

While basic range is variable according to the capacity of fuel tanks fitted, most types are able to have optional extra tanks installed. The Shadow has an endurance of up to eight hours with auxiliary tanks.

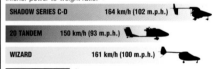

SHADOW SERIES C-D	257 km (160 mi.)
20 TANDEM	400 km (248 mi.)
WIZARD	344 km (213 mi.)

Diverse microlight designs

AEROSTRUCTURE PIPISTRELLE: Designed in France in mid-1981, this 'tail-dragging' craft had an open cockpit and vee-tail.

TIRITH FIREFLY: Two ducted propellers drove the Firefly, a design sharing its configuration with the Shadow.

TISSERAND HYDROPLUM: This unusual French amphibious design first flew in 1983 and was displayed at the 1985 Paris Air Show.

ULTRAFLIGHT LAZAIR: Canadian company, Ultraflight, offered several versions of the Lazair twin-engined design.

CHRISTEN

EAGLE

● Competition aerobatics ● Amateur construction ● 1970s design

After Frank Christensen had tried, unsuccessfully, to buy the famous Pitts Special designs, he decided to design and market a very similar aircraft, named the Christen Eagle. Available only in kit form, the original single-seat Eagle I was replaced by the Eagle II, which sold widely to amateur constructors around the world. In 1981 Christensen finally acquired the Pitts business and marketed his new acquisition alongside his well established Eagle design.

▲ With a large bubble canopy, the cockpit acts like a greenhouse in hot, sunny weather. Pilots tend to keep the canopy open, providing air to the cockpit until take-off is imminent.

CHRISTEN EAGLE

◄ **Eagle finish**
Eagle IIs are almost exclusively finished with an eagle design extending down the fuselage side.

▼ **Bubble canopy**
A large canopy covers both occupants, giving the pilot a 360° field of vision.

▼ **Thrilling the crowds**
After helping form the 'Eagle Aerobatic Flight Team' in 1979, Gene Soucy still regularly performs at air shows in the USA.

▼ **Training or touring**
Built with equipment and comfort levels suitable for advanced aerobatic training or cross-country touring, the Eagle II appeals to a range of customers.

◄ **Powerful engine**
To give the Eagle II superior performance over the Pitts, a 149-kW (200-hp.) Lycoming engine was fitted, bestowing an excellent rate of climb.

FACTS AND FIGURES

➤ Construction of the prototype Eagle II began in 1975 and it flew for the first time in February 1977.

➤ The Eagle II has a maximum rate of roll of over 200° per second.

➤ The special-purpose Eagle I was not available for amateur constructors.

➤ The prototype Eagle I was built under tight security and made its debut in the 1978 US National Championships.

➤ Designed for aerobatics, the Eagle II is certified to +9/-6g.

➤ The specially adapted fuel system allows unlimited inverted flight.

High-performance homebuild

Looking remarkably similar to the famous Pitts Special, the high-performance, aerobatic Eagle II gained a reputation in the late 1970s as a world-beating competition aerobat, despite being available only in kit form.

From its base in Wyoming, Christen marketed the Eagle II in 25 separate kits. Each kit makes a part of the aircraft and is supported by a very detailed construction manual. Christen

claims that no construction experience is required and only common hand tools are needed. A typical homebuilder takes 1,400 to 1,600 hours to complete an Eagle II.

Construction of the prototype Eagle II began in 1975 and manufacture started in 1977. By this time the single-seat Eagle I was flying, and in 1978 aerobatic champion Gene Soucy flew the aircraft in the US National Championships,

gaining a creditable third place.

To demonstrate the superior capabilities of the Eagle over the competing Pitts design, Christensen provided aircraft for the famous 'Red Devils' aerobatic team. The name was changed to the 'Eagles Aerobatic Flight Team' and they were soon performing at more than 60 air shows a season.

By 1986 at least 600 kits had been sold, with 250 completed and in flying condition.

Visibility from the cockpit is generally good, but the top wing blocks out a section of the pilot's forward view. On the ground, the pilot has a restricted view over the aircraft's nose.

Eagle II

Type: two-seat homebuilt aerobatic biplane

Powerplant: one 149-kW (200-hp.) Avco Lycoming AEIO-360-A1D piston engine

Maximum speed: 296 km/h (184 m.p.h.)

Initial climb rate: 645 m/min (2,115 f.p.m.)

Range: 611 km (380 mi.) with max payload

Service ceiling: 5180 m (17,000 ft.)

Weights: empty 465 kg (1,023 lb.); max take-off 725 kg (1,595 lb.)

Dimensions:
span	6.07 m	(19 ft. 11 in.)
length	5.64 m	(18 ft. 6 in.)
height	1.98 m	(6 ft. 6 in.)
wing area	11.61 m²	(125 sq. ft.)

The Eagle II is powered by an Avco Lycoming AEIO-360-A1D piston engine driving a Hartzell constant-speed propeller. The fuel tank is situated in the fuselage and has a capacity of 98.4 litres (26 gallons), with a fuel system which allows unlimited inverted flight.

Two seats are arranged in tandem beneath the one-piece side-hinged bubble canopy. Equipment levels are fairly low, with only essential instruments and a radio fitted. A baggage hold in the turtledeck has a capacity of 13.6 kg (30 lb.).

Pilots Gene Soucy, Tom Poberenzy and Charlie Hillard established 'Team Eagle' and still demonstrate the aircraft's aerobatic qualities.

For simplicity, the landing gear is a fixed tail-wheel arrangement. The large spats fitted to the main wheels improve aerodynamic flow and reduce drag, giving an increase in performance.

The braced biplane wings are supported by steel tube interplane struts. Constructed from wooden spars and ribs, the lower wing has slight dihedral and ailerons are fitted to both the upper and lower wings to increase the rate of roll.

EAGLE II

Purchased as a kit from the Christen company, this Eagle II was constructed by an amateur in the UK. The number '33' was worn on the tail during participation in the Digital Schneider Trophy air race.

ACTION DATA

MAXIMUM SPEED

Fitted with a more powerful engine, and not handicapped by the drag induced by biplane wings, the Yak-50 is the fastest of these types. Although the Eagle II and Pitts S-2A are very similar, the Eagle's more powerful engine gives it an edge in performance.

EAGLE II	296 km/h (184 m.p.h.)
YAK-50	320 km/h (198 m.p.h.)
S-2A	253 km/h (157 m.p.h.)

CLIMB RATE

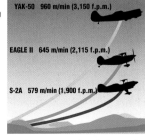

The Yak's powerful engine gives it excellent climb performance, which is vital for competition aerobatics. The Pitts and Christen designs have a slower rate of climb, but they compensate by having a tremendous rate of roll.

YAK-50 960 m/min (3,150 f.p.m.)

EAGLE II 645 m/min (2,115 f.p.m.)

S-2A 579 m/min (1,900 f.p.m.)

Competition aerobatic biplanes

■ **CASA 1.131 JUNGMANN:** Bücker-built Jungmanns competed in the World Aerobatic Championships in the 1960s.

■ **DE HAVILLAND DH.82 TIGER MOTH:** A number of Tiger Moths were flown in both British and World Championships in the 1950s.

■ **PITTS S-1 SPECIAL:** The Pitts Special dominated the US Championships in the late-1960s and 1970s, setting new standards.

■ **STAMPE SV.4A:** Superior to the British Tiger Moth, the Stampe dominated the European aerobatic scene in the 1950s.

CIERVA

AUTOGYROS

● Rotary-winged aircraft ● Spanish inventor ● British manufacture

Juan de la Cierva was born in September 1895. He designed and built a glider when he was 15, and his first three-engined aeroplane in 1918. His true aim was to design an aircraft that would be able to maintain lift, and land safely after an engine failure. Practical helicopters were impossible with the engines and materials then available, so he turned to the concept of an aircraft using an unpowered rotor for lift and a conventional propeller for propulsion.

▲ *Cierva's autogyros were among the first practical rotorcraft. However, it was not until the mid-1930s that vertical take-off in an autogyro was possible. By the end of World War II, the helicopter had demonstrated unbeatable versatility.*

CIERVA AUTOGYROS

Vertically rising C.40 ▶
The C.40 of 1938 was able to make a direct vertical take-off. This was accomplished by spinning the main rotor at a high speed with the blades at zero incidence, then selecting positive pitch to create lift.

◀ First successes
With subsidies from the Spanish government, Cierva built the C.6 series, using Avro 504K fuselages. Such was its success that Cierva established a company in the UK.

Commercial successes ▶
The most commercially successful early design was the C.19, the first purpose-built autogyro. Twenty-nine were built.

Air Ministry craft ▶
British Air Ministry interest in Cierva's designs began in the 1920s with the C.6. Avro was among several British companies eventually licensed to build autogyros. The RAF evaluated several prototypes, including C.6s, a C.8L and C.19s. In 1934/35, 12 C.30As were delivered.

Cierva's first autogyro ▶
Using the fuselage of a French Deperdussin monoplane, Cierva built the C.1, an aircraft that refused to fly!

FACTS AND FIGURES

➤ Twelve C.30As (designated Rota Mk I) were delivered to the RAF in the 1930s, followed by 13 civil examples after 1939.

➤ Among preserved Autogyros is a Rota Mk I (C.30A) at the RAF Museum, London.

➤ British-built C.19s were sold in countries like New Zealand, Japan and Australia.

➤ During World War II, a Jeep was fitted with a rotor and towed behind an aircraft, using the autogyro principle.

➤ Juan de la Cierva became the first autogyro passenger in a C.6D on 30 July 1927.

➤ In the late 1920s, Cierva learned to fly his own autogyros.

Spanish rotary-wing pioneer

Cierva patented the autogyro (or autogiro) design for his aircraft. Their key feature – a vital contribution to helicopter development – was the articulated rotor hub. Its drag and flapping hinges allowed the individual rotor blades to rise and fall and 'evened out' the lift. The first workable craft, the C.4,

flew 4 km (3 miles) in January 1923. By September 1928, Cierva's C.8L Mk II design, powered by a 149-kW (200-hp.) Lynx engine and based on an Avro 504 fuselage, made a 40-km (25-mile) flight across the English Channel and on to Paris.

Cierva died in an airliner crash at Croydon in December 1936, by which time his ideas had been accepted. He had

formed his own company in England, and his designs were produced in the UK, US, France and Germany. The C.40 had a newly developed tilting rotor, allowing it to take off vertically.

Below: Early autogyro flights were plagued by accidents. The first three designs failed to become airborne; it was the C.4 that finally flew in 1923.

Above: de Havilland's distinctive lines were evident in the C.24, designed and built by the company in 1931.

Cierva C.30A

Type: utility autogyro

Powerplant: one 104-kW (140-hp.) Armstrong Siddeley Genet Major IA radial engine

Maximum speed: 177 km/h (110 m.p.h.)

Cruising speed: 153 km/h (95 m.p.h.)

Range: 459 km (285 mi.)

Service ceiling: 5800 m (19,000 ft.)

Weights: empty 553 kg (1,217 lb.); max take-off 816 kg (1,795 lb.)

Accommodation: pilot and observer

Dimensions: main rotor diameter 11.28 m (37 ft.)
length 6.01 m (19 ft. 9 in.)
height 3.38 m (11 ft. 1 in.)
rotor area 99.89 m² (1,075 sq.ft.)

ROTA MK IA

One of three Cierva C.30s impressed into RAF service in World War II, this aircraft was previously G-ACWH. No. 529 Squadron employed a number of Rotas for radar calibration duties during 1943-44.

To start the main rotor spinning before take-off, the C.19 and later designs introduced a drive transmission system from the main engine. This was controlled by a rotor clutch and brake operated from the cockpit.

The C.30 was a two-seater, the pilot occupying the rear cockpit. The pilot was able to unlock and tilt (laterally, as well as fore and aft) the main rotor using the control column attached to the rotor head.

A seven-cylinder Armstrong Siddeley Genet Major IA radial rated at 104 kW (139 hp.) was installed in the C.30A. To the RAF, the engine was known as the Civet I.

For yaw stability, the C.30's vertical surfaces were of a sizeable area. A large fixed fin had a small trimmer at the extreme rear. A small ventral fin was also fitted. The horizontal fins had upturned ends for extra stability.

Although the initial Cierva designs used existing aircraft fuselages, the C.19 and subsequent models were purpose-built. Sixty-six were licence-built by A.V. Roe and Co. Ltd, all at Manchester. In France, Lioré-et-Olivier built 25 designated LeO C301, while Focke-Wulf built 40 examples.

The C.30's fuselage structure was of Duralumin tubing with a fabric skin covering. The later C.40 used wooden skinning over a metal internal frame.

Among the new features of the C.30A were folding rotor blades to allow easier hangarage, and a reverse aerofoil section on the port tailplane to counteract rotor torque.

ACTION DATA

MAXIMUM SPEED

Rota Mk Is (C.30As) had a top speed comparable to the fixed-wing Fieseler Storch. Although RAF Rotas were attached to the School of Army Co-operation, they were soon assigned a coastal radar calibration role. The Storch was a widely-used German STOL liaison aircraft.

C.30A	177 km/h (110 m.p.h.)
FI 282 V21 KOLIBRI	150 km/h (93 m.p.h.)
Fi 156C-1 STORCH	175 km/h (109 m.p.h.)

POWER

With an engine of little more power, the FI 282 search-and-rescue and spotting helicopter was able to accomplish vertical flight using two intermeshed rotors. The Storch STOL aircraft had a larger engine but none of the versatility of the rotary-winged types, relying on an airstrip from which to operate.

C.30A	FI 282 V21 KOLIBRI	Fi 156C-1 STORCH
104 kW (140 hp.)	119 kW (160 hp.)	179 kW (240 hp.)

RANGE

Cierva C.30As had a good range performance, comparable to that of the Storch. Lack of range was a shortcoming of early helicopter designs. The Kolibri was a small two-seater with little internal fuel capacity, whereas the Cierva used a larger fuselage, similar to a fixed-wing aircraft, with more tankage.

C.30A 459 km (285 mi.)
FI 282 V21 KOLIBRI 170 km (105 mi.)
Fi 156C-1 STORCH 467 km (290 mi.)

Getting airborne in an autogyro

CIERVA'S AUTOGYRO: The term 'autogyro' was coined by Juan de la Cierva to describe his aircraft, in which the freewheeling main rotor provided lift for vertical flight.

FORWARD MOTION: With the rotor locked, the engine was started and pulled the aircraft forward. On early designs the rotor was unlocked and air flow made the rotor rotate.

TILTING ROTOR: The C.30 used a driveshaft from the engine to initiate rotor rotation. Once the rotor had reached the required number of revolutions per minute, it was tilted backwards.

LIFT FROM THE ROTOR: Combined with the aircraft's forward motion, the spinning rotor disc provided lift, much like a helicopter.

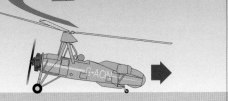

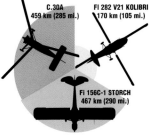

CONVAIR

880/990

● Long-range airliner ● Rival of the Boeing 707 ● Freighter

onvair's 880 and 990 were less successful than first-generation jetliners produced by Boeing (707) and Douglas (DC-8), but during their moment of glory they made an impact. Aerodynamically the aircraft was quite impressive, and an 880 was even dived through the sound barrier. Unfortunately, it was also troublesome and costly to operate. Despite their grace and beauty, these aircraft eventually brought ruin to the manufacturer.

▲ Raquel Tejada christened the 990 over its distinctive wing bulges with champagne. Despite its high speed, the Convair was not as commercially viable as its rivals and had little success.

CONVAIR 880/990

▲ Asia Pacific
Garuda of Indonesia operated the 990 on Pacific routes. The 990 was modified with Krueger flaps and new engine nozzle fairings.

NASA Convair ▶
NASA operated three Convair 990s, including this one named Galileo II based at Dryden Air Force Base. Among the aircraft's many tasks was testing the undercarriage for the Space Shuttle.

▲ Interior
Convair made much of the 880's interior, but it was the five-abreast seating that airlines did not find attractive.

◀ Spantax takes off
Charter airline Spantax was a major customer. It operated 14 Convair 990s, with a maximum of 12 in service at any one time.

▲ Japanese 880
Japan Air Lines took delivery of seven 880s, two of which were destroyed in service.

FACTS AND FIGURES

➤ Convair cancelled plans to finish the 880 airliner in gold metal and to nickname it the Golden Arrow.

➤ The Convair 880 first flew on 27 January 1959; the 990 on 24 January 1961.

➤ Total production of these jetliners was 65 Convair 880s and 37 Convair 990s.

➤ When Convair first built the 880 it offered the aircraft at only $4.7 million, compared to $130 million for today's Boeing 777.

➤ Initial customers for the 990 included American, Swissair and Garuda airlines.

➤ A single Convair 880, known as the UC-880, was flown by the US Navy.

PROFILE

Convair's last gamble

It should have been a great success, offering high performance and stylish interior fittings, but the Convair 880 eventually bankrupted its manufacturer. The 880 came on to the market just before the Boeing 707 and Douglas DC-8, but it was flawed by having five-abreast seating unlike the six-abreast arrangement of its rivals. The reduced passenger capacity meant potential customers did not favour the 880 despite its slightly higher speed. The aircraft's numerical designation, 880, was in fact its maximum speed in feet per second.

Sadly, the Convair jetliners were followed by a great deal of financial difficulty, with aircraft being sold in unprofitable deals. While the 880 developed normally, the 990 was impaired by aerodynamic shortcomings that took time and investment to fix. The distinct bulges on the wings, known as 'Küchemann's Carrots' reduced transonic drag. One Convair 880 was even dived through the sound barrier.

Research improved the entire fleet, but in the end money was the ruin of the 880 and 990, and the financial aftermath shortened Convair's life. By 1981 only Spantax was operating the 990 commercially, the remnants of just 37 built. In 1987, one aircraft was taken out of storage and delivered to South Africa, and one is also used by NASA for testing new equipment.

Above: Peru was one of the last customers for new-build 990s, together with Garuda of Indonesia. The 990 had a brief life with its original operators, and often went on to serve with charter lines.

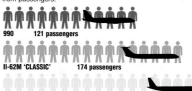

Above: It was lack of orders from domestic users which brought about the end of the 880. Deals with airlines it did attract were often badly negotiated, like the one with American Airlines that involved buying back DC-7s at twice their value.

990

Type: medium-range transport

Powerplant: four 68.57-kN (15,425-lb.-thrust) General Electric CJ805-23B turbofan engines

Maximum speed: 990 km/h (615 m.p.h.) at 6095 m (20,000 ft.)

Cruising speed: 895 km/h (555 m.p.h.) at 10,670 m (35,000 ft.)

Range: 8770 km (5,440 mi.)

Service ceiling: 12,495 m (41,000 ft.)

Weights: empty 54,839 kg (120,645 lb.); maximum take-off 114,759 kg (252,469 lb.)

Accommodation: two pilots, flight engineer, flight attendants and 121 passengers, 12 in first-class seating and 108 in economy seating, plus up to 8000 kg (17,600 lb.) of cargo

Dimensions:
span 36.58 m (120 ft.)
length 42.43 m (139 ft.)
height 12.04 m (39 ft 6 in.)
wing area 209.03 m² (2,249 sq. ft.)

990

Despite offering higher performance and better capacity than its predecessor, the 990 was no more successful. Scandinavian Airways System is one of a very few airlines to have operated Convair's last production airliner.

The cockpit accommodated a pilot and co-pilot side by side and a navigator and flight engineer behind.

Power for the early 880s was supplied by four J79 turbojets, the same engine that powered the McDonnell Douglas Phantom. The 990 used the modified General Electric CJ-805 turbofan.

The 990 had increased capacity over the 880, being about 3 m (10 ft.) longer and accommodating 96–121 passengers in five-abreast seating.

At the rear of the fuselage there was a plug-type door and toilets behind the passenger cabin. A Hamilton Standard air-conditioning system was fitted in the cabin.

Scandinavian Airways System ordered two 990s and also leased two aircraft purchased by Swissair.

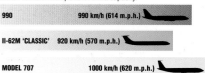

Passengers entered through a door on the port side. The four-abreast first class section was immediately behind.

The four engines were fitted with thrust reversers and noise suppressors. Four of the so-called 'Küchemann's Carrots' mounted in the trailing edge were filled with fuel.

The highly swept wing was an all-metal, twin-spar structure mounted at 7° dihedral. The wing had an additional auxiliary spar at the root. The leading edge was double-skinned, with the space between used as a duct for thermal de-icing.

ACTION DATA

PASSENGERS
Lack of passenger capacity was the downfall of the 990. The jet used almost as much fuel as other airliners but earned less money from passengers.

990 — 121 passengers
Il-62M 'CLASSIC' — 174 passengers
MODEL 707 — 189 passengers

MAXIMUM SPEED
Thanks to its sleek lines and powerful engines, the 990 was as fast as any other large airliner, although most airlines would gladly have traded some of the speed for extra capacity.

990 — 990 km/h (614 m.p.h.)
Il-62M 'CLASSIC' — 920 km/h (570 m.p.h.)
MODEL 707 — 1000 km/h (620 m.p.h.)

RANGE
Another fault of the 990 was its lack of range. This was not a great problem for those sold to the American market, but it limited international sales.

990 — 8770 km (5,440 mi.)
Il-62M 'CLASSIC' — 7800 km (4,836 mi.)
MODEL 707 — 11,120 km (6,894 mi.)

Convair 880 and 990 operators

CATHAY PACIFIC: Flying routes from Hong Kong, Cathay Pacific were among the last non-charter operators of the Convair jets.

DELTA: Flying international and domestic services, Delta also operated the rival Boeing 707 and DC-8 in large numbers.

NORTHEASTERN: One of the American customers that made more use of the 880 than most, Northeastern used it on domestic routes.

TRANSWORLD AIRLINES: TWA first flew 880s in 1961, but three years later it supplemented them with Boeing 707s and 727s.

CONVAIR

CV 240-CV 440

● **Best-selling airliners** ● **Turboprop conversions** ● **Long-serving freighters**

▲ The secret of the 240's success was its ability to be constantly upgraded, at a time when rapid advances in technology could make an aircraft obsolete in only a few years.

American Airlines' search for a DC-3 replacement in 1945 was the spur to the development of the long-serving series of twin-engined airliners from Convair. Originating with the Convair 240, it was to evolve into the 440, one of the top-performing piston airliners of all time. They were a real success in the new age of post-war air commerce, particularly when converted to turboprop power.

PHOTO FILE

CONVAIR **CV 240-CV 440**

◄ Immaculate
This beautifully cared-for Convair 440 was operated by Prinair. The Allison-powered version was later known as the 580, and was the most powerful variant.

Napier turboprop ▶
Convair tested the 340 series with the latest-technology Napier Eland turboprops. The modified aircraft were known as 'Eland Convairs' and were designated Convair 540.

USAF models ▶
The USAF used the CV 240 (as the C-131) for cargo, medevac and electronics testing. It was also used for navigation training, designated T-29.

▲ Lufthansa
The Convair 340 was the first type ordered by the new Lufthansa after the war. The aircraft began operations in 1955, and Convair 440s appeared in 1957.

No more flying ▶
Although Convair twins still serve in South America, their numbers are dwindling and many are being cannibalised for spares.

FACTS AND FIGURES

➤ The 'Convairliner' first flew in July 1946, six months ahead of the Martin 2-0-2.

➤ The Convair 340 introduced in 1951 had a fuselage 'stretch' of 1.37 m (4 ft. 6 in.) and typically hauled 44 passengers.

➤ The final new model, the piston Convair 440, was the heaviest and most powerful.

➤ Military versions of the Convair included the US Air Force T-29 trainer and C-131 transport.

➤ At least 200 Convair twins were converted to turboprop propulsion.

➤ More than 500 Convairliners were built between 1947 and 1958.

PROFILE

Convair's long-lasting twins

Consolidated Vultee, or Convair, was a key player in the post-war race with Boeing, Douglas and Martin to build short- and medium-haul airliners for the blossoming aircraft market. No one achieved the impossible dream of replacing the DC-3, but the 'Convairliner' series came close. The Convair 240 first flew a year after the war and was of great interest to potential users. When it entered service with American Airlines in 1948, it was immediately hailed as one of the finest aircraft in its class.

The piston-engined 240 was improved over time with more powerful engines and greater strength. It was succeeded by the 340 and 440, and the turboprop 540, 580, 600 and 640. Convairliners served with airlines large and small in 33 countries, and their economy and reliability meant that they remained in use well into the jet age.

For many years Convair twins were put to use hauling skiers and package tourists into remote mountain townships, while others were used as VIP transports. John F. Kennedy used a Convair to travel around the USA on his successful 1960 Presidential campaign.

Dozens of Convairs can still be seen in service today, many having been converted to serve as freighters.

Below: Still going strong. This Aerochacos 240 receives the careful attention of a marshal with a fire extinguisher while starting engines. Many 240s remain in service, especially as freight carriers.

Above: One of the earliest customers for Convair twins was KLM, who used them from 1948 to 1964.

CV 440
Type: medium-range transport

Powerplant: two 1864-kW (2,500-hp.) Pratt & Whitney R-2800-CB16 or -CB17 piston engines

Maximum cruising speed: 493 km/h (306 m.p.h.) at 3960 m (13,000 ft.)

Range: 2100 km (1,300 mi.) with max. payload

Service ceiling: 7590 m (25,000 ft.)

Weights: empty 15,111 kg (33,244 lb.); loaded 22,226 kg (48,897 lb.)

Accommodation: two pilots, flight engineer, two stewardesses; 52 passengers

Dimensions: span 27.97 m (91 ft. 9 in.)
length 22.76 m (74 ft. 8 in.)
height 8.20 m (26 ft. 11 in.)
wing area 75.90 m² (817 sq. ft.)

CV 240

Braniff International Airlines used both the Convair 240, acquired when it merged with Mid-Continent Airlines, and Convair 340s, which it purchased directly.

The cockpit accommodated two pilots. Some airlines also flew with a radio operator.

The original Twin Wasp radial piston engines fitted to the 240 model were almost identical to the engines that powered the Hellcat fighters of the wartime US Navy.

Even though pressurisation and higher cruising altitudes enhanced the ride for the passengers, cabin noise was an ever-present problem with the early Convair twins, as it was with all piston-powered airliners. The problem was greatly reduced in the turboprop versions.

Freight versions of the Convair twins featured a large cargo door on the rear of the fuselage.

The distinctive tall tail design remained almost unchanged throughout the production run of the Convair twins.

Weather-mapping radar was optional in the Convair 340 and standard in the 440.

Curtiss and Hamilton Standard propellers were fitted to the Convair 240.

Engine cowling changes were frequent in the Convair twins. The original 240s had an efficient design that maximised cooling with low drag.

The wing of the 240 was enlarged for the 340 version, to give better high-altitude performance.

ACTION DATA

MAXIMUM SPEED

The Convair's powerful Wasp engines and clean lines gave it a far superior speed to earlier aircraft. However, the days of the piston engine were numbered, as turboprop-powered airliners like the Viscount were already in service.

CV 240 — 430 km/h (267 m.p.h.)
DC-3 — 350 km/h (217 m.p.h.)
VISCOUNT — 560 km/h (347 m.p.h.)

PASSENGER LOAD

When the DC-3 was designed, civil air travel was still in its infancy. Both the Convair and the Viscount were designed from the outset with much greater capacity, reflecting the growing size of post-war passenger air travel.

CV 240 — 40 PASSENGERS
DC-3 — 21 PASSENGERS
VISCOUNT — 47 PASSENGERS

RANGE

Bigger overall size and a large fuel load gave the Convair a good range with a typical passenger load. This was much reduced when flying at maximum all-up weight.

CV 240 3200 km (1,985 mi.)
DC-3 2575 km (1,600 mi.)
VISCOUNT 2775 km (1,720 mi.)

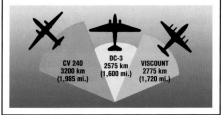

Successors to the DC-3

MARTIN 4-0-4: Built for the same market as the Convair, and similar in appearance and performance, the Martin did not sell as well.

VICKERS VIKING: Britain's Viking was contemporary with the Convair, but its tubby, tail-dragging design was the product of an earlier generation.

ILYUSHIN Il-14: Built in huge numbers, the Il-14 was smaller than the Convair. It can still be found flying in many former Communist states.

FOKKER F27: The turboprop revolutionised airliner design. Flying a decade after the Convair, the F27 was faster and more economical.

HAWKER SIDDELEY HS.748: Dating from the early 1960s, the turboprop HS.748 has been sold to more than 70 operators worldwide.

155

CURTISS

CONDOR II

● 1930s biplane airliner ● Overseas service ● Antarctic pioneer

At first sight the T-32 Condor II appeared to be an anachronism – a new biplane transport at a time, in the early-1930s, when the all-metal monoplane was the way of the future. Curtiss-Wright, however, had seen a niche in the market for a 'stop-gap' aircraft that offered performance improvements over contemporary designs, pending the arrival of the truly advanced Boeing 247 and Douglas DC-2, then under development.

▲ *Condor IIs*
were destined to have a very short history in US airline service. However, overseas airlines and Antarctic explorers soon put the aircraft to work elsewhere.

CURTISS CONDOR II

▼ **On floats in Colombia**
Seen here on floats prior to delivery, this BT-32 operated as a transport from rivers in Colombia and flew Atlantic anti-submarine patrols during World War II.

▲ **Design advances**
Although cheap to produce, the Condor II introduced new features, including zip-fastened panels for easy maintenance. The batteries could also be changed in less than a minute.

▼ **Military sales**
There were just four T-32s in US military service. Overseas sales, however, were made in Colombia (below) and Argentina.

▲ **Chinese bomber**
This, the first military Condor II, flew in 1934 and was immediately demonstrated to the Chinese. After repairs following a landing accident it became the personal transport of Chiang Kai-shek (the head of Chinese central government).

Airline service in America ▶
The Condor II's use as an airliner in the US was shortlived as more advanced types like the Douglas

FACTS AND FIGURES

➤ In all, only 45 Condor IIs were built, including a prototype, 28 airliners, 15 military aircraft and one survey machine.

➤ Swissair's sole AT-32 was the first airliner in Europe to carry a stewardess.

➤ The three Condor IIs used in the Antarctic were fitted with floats or skis.

➤ In the late 1930s a Canadian railroad company used a Condor based in Alaska to reach isolated Yukon communities.

➤ The last operational Condor II was used by the Peruvian air force until 1956.

➤ Four ex-Eastern Air Transport T-32s served as cargo aircraft in England in 1937/38.

PROFILE

Last of the US biplane airliners

Two Condor IIs were purchased by the US Navy in 1934 for transport duties. Both were lost in the Antarctic.

Curtiss-Wright's St Louis factory had been closed for two years by the great depression and the company needed an aircraft with which to resume production. It had to be developed cheaply and quickly.

The result was the XT-32 (Experimental Transport to carry a payload of 7055 kg (3,200 lb.)), the first of which flew on 30 January 1933. The name Condor II was adopted to cash in on

the solid reputation of the earlier Model 18 Condor, which it resembled in basic layout.

Among the T-32's innovative features was an electrically-retracted undercarriage, flexible engine mounts (to reduce vibration) and even hot and cold running water in the toilet.

Eastern Air Transport and American Airways placed orders. By the end of 1935, however, the Condor II was

being replaced with DC-2s. Ultimately, Condor IIs saw a great deal more service overseas. Bomber (BT-32) and transport (CT-32) versions were sold in South America and US civil and Navy examples made pioneering survey flights over the Antarctic.

AT-32-B CONDOR II

American Airways bought Condor IIs to replace the smaller Ford Trimotor. However, the Trimotor was to outlive the Condor IIs, the last of which was retired by AA in 1937. NC12394 was destroyed in a hangar fire in July 1937.

The T-32's simple design and Curtiss-Wright's efficient management allowed the company to offer the aircraft to US airlines at a comparatively cheap price, quoted as 'less than $60,000'.

The AT-32-A was a convertible dayplane/sleeper aircraft with capacity for 12 passengers. The AT-32-C carried 15 passengers in a dayplane-only configuration; other models had engines of varying horsepower ratings. American Airlines was the biggest customer for the A-model with 10 examples.

The engines were mounted on rubber bushes to reduce vibration. To ease maintenance Condor IIs had no less than 125 access panels, closed with zip fasteners.

Passenger comfort was an important selling point for the T-32. The cabin was soundproofed and each seat was provided with individual hot and cold air outlets. Cabin furnishings were composed of a combination of fabric and leather.

Two Wright SGR-1820 Cyclone geared radial engines powered early T-32s. The improved AT-32 used a supercharged variant driving a variable-pitch propeller.

The electrically-retracted undercarriage was the first to be used on a twin-engined airliner and was among a number of innovations that set the Condor apart from other airliners of the period. The airframe, however, retained a metal structure and fabric skin.

NC12394
AMERICAN AIRLINES
155

AT-32-A Condor II

Type: twin-engined biplane airliner

Powerplant: two 529-kW (710-hp.) Wright SGR-1820-F3 Cyclone radial engines

Maximum speed: 306 km/h (190 m.p.h.) at 2438 m (8,000 ft.)

Cruising speed: 245 km/h (152 m.p.h.) at 2438 m (8,000 ft.)

Climb rate: 366 m/min (1,200 f.p.m.)

Range: 1152 km (715 mi.) at 2438 m (8,000 ft.)

Service ceiling: 7010 m (23,000 ft.)

Weights: empty 5550 kg (12,210 lb.); loaded 7938 kg (17,464 lb.)

Accommodation: 12 passengers

Dimensions:
span		24.99 m (82 ft.)
length		14.81 m (48 ft. 7 in.)
height		4.98 m (16 ft. 4 in.)
wing area		112.2 m² (1,207 sq. ft.)

ACTION DATA

CRUISING SPEED

Despite being a twin-engined biplane, the AT-32 had almost a 50-km/h advantage over the three-engined Trimotor monoplane. The DC-2 showed an even better turn of speed, setting new standards in airliner performance.

AT-32-A CONDOR II	245 km/h (152 m.p.h.)
TRIMOTOR	198 km/h (123 m.p.h.)
DC-2	306 km/h (190 m.p.h.)

RANGE

The Condor II's range was also an improvement over that of the Trimotor, despite being considerably heavier. This was largely due to its twin engines, which used less fuel than the Ford's three powerplants. Once again, the DC-2 set new standards.

AT-32-A CONDOR II 1152 km (715 mi.)
DC-2 1609 km (1,000 mi.)
MODEL 5-AT-B TRIMOTOR 708 km (440 mi.)

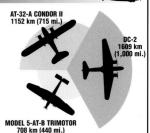

ACCOMMODATION

Early model Condor IIs carried fewer passengers than the Trimotor, but could be flown in a sleeper/dayplane configuration. Later AT-32 variants could carry 15 passengers, more than the first DC-2s.

AT-32-A CONDOR II	12
MODEL 5-AT-B TRIMOTOR	15
DOUGLAS DC-2	14

From the Americas to Antarctica

ANTARCTIC PIONEER: The first Condor II on the southern continent accompanied Admiral Byrd's second expedition.

ARMY TRANSPORT: There were just two USAAC Condor IIs. Designated YC-30 and fitted out as VIP transports, they were retired in 1938.

SWISSAIR'S SOLE EXAMPLE: A few T-32s saw service in Europe. Swissair's was the last civil Condor II built, but it crashed after four months.

BT-32 BOMBER IN CHINA: The turret- and bomb rack-equipped BT-32 appeared in February 1934. This, the first, went to China.

CURTISS

JN-4 'JENNY'

● Two-seat World War I trainer ● Barnstorming aircraft

CURTISS **JN-4 'JENNY'**

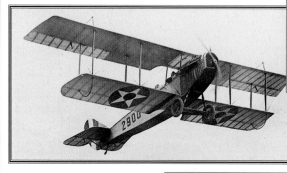

▲ JN-3 collision
The JN-4 was developed from the interim JN-3, 91 of which were sold to Britain and two were purchased by the US Army.

▲ Wartime Army JN-4D
Between November 1917 and January 1919 over 2,800 JN-4Ds were built. To speed up delivery, six manufacturers built the D model.

Barnstorming in the 1920s ▶
Unhampered by regulations governing their use, post-war pilots used JN-4s for stunt flying.

▼ Half-scale Jenny
In 1961, F. A. Murray of Rockford, Illinois, built this half-scale replica of a JN-4D-2, and called it the JN-2D-1 'Jennette'. Power was supplied by a converted Ford Model 'A' 37-kW (50-hp.) car engine.

▲ In the Navy
Most of the US Navy's JN-4s were H models powered by112-kW (150-hp.) engines. Thirty were purchased for advanced pilot training in 1918 and were followed by 90 JN-4HG gunnery trainers.

The JN-4 'Jenny' had a double career. It was America's universal aircraft of the 1920s, having been developed as a military trainer early in the Great War and then becoming the machine of post-war flying instructors and barnstormers. An open field, a nice day and a few heads cranked upwards in curiosity were all that were needed for the JN-4 to bring the thrill of aviation to ordinary people. Many of them learned about aircraft by watching the 'Jenny' perform.

▲ From 1919 to the late-1920s thousands of 'Jennys' were flown in what was known as the 'barnstorming era', introducing many Americans to aircraft for the first time. Surplus JN-4s were bought from the US Army for as little as $50 each.

FACTS AND FIGURES

➤ The contract to build 1,400 JN-4Ds for the US Army was worth $4,417,337 for the Curtiss Corporation.

➤ Approximately 7,280 JN-4s were built, including 4,800 for the US Army.

➤ Of American and Canadian pilots in the World War I, 95 per cent trained on JN-4s.

➤ The 'Jenny' first appeared in July 1916 when an initial batch of planes was sold to Britain and the US Army.

➤ After more than a decade, the last US Army JN-4s were retired in 1927.

➤ As well as pilot training, JN-4s were used for observation and bomber training.

From training to 'barnstorming'

A development of the 1915 JN-3 that flew combat reconnaissance with General Pershing during the US Army's expedition against Pancho Villa on the Mexican border, the Curtiss JN-4 'Jenny' was conceived to replace the antiquated pusher-type, open-to-the-wind trainers that had served the military until that time.

The military JN-4, a two-seater made of fabric, wood and wire, became the standard US Army trainer during World War I and for about seven years after. In the air, the 'Jenny' seemed to have no vices. Even for the beginner it was an easy machine to fly.

After the war, 'Jennys' had a lively time in the civil world. Many pilots-turned-barnstormers purchased JN-4s from the government for very little and set out to earn their fortunes flying for fun, giving joy rides and displays. Stuntmen like Ormer Locklear were called the 'Flying Fools' for their wild antics in the air – indeed, crashes were not infrequent.

The JN-4 gained immortality as a trainer aircraft and as a machine that brought aviation to the people.

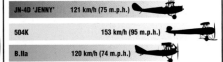

Below: Wearing Army JN-4H markings, this 'Jenny' was preserved in the US. As with the de Havilland Moth family, the numbers built ensured that examples still survive.

Above: This preserved 'Jenny' clearly shows the unequal-span wings. It carries the markings applied to US Army aircraft at the end of World War I.

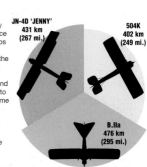

JN-4D 'Jenny'

Type: two-seat military trainer

Powerplant: one 67-kW (90-hp.) Curtiss OX-5 inline piston engine

Maximum speed: 121 km/h (75 m.p.h.)

Cruising speed: 97 km/h (60 m.p.h.)

Service ceiling: 1980 m (6,500 ft.)

Weights: empty 630 kg (1,386 lb.); maximum take-off 871 kg (1,916 lb.)

Accommodation: two pilots in tandem open cockpits

Dimensions:
span	13.30 m	(43 ft. 8 in.)
length	8.33 m	(27 ft. 4 in.)
height	3.01 m	(9 ft. 10 in.)
wing area	32.70 m²	(352 sq. ft.)

The Curtiss OX-5 inline piston engine drove a two-bladed wooden propeller on the JN-4Can. Later variants had a Wright-built Hispano-Suiza engine.

Privately owned, Canadian-built JN-4s remained in use into the 1930s. A few were built as late as 1927, using reconditioned parts. Some had a third cockpit and were known as the Ericson Special Three.

The JN-4 had a larger tailfin and tailplane than earlier members of the JN family.

JN-4CAN

The School of Aerial Fighting in Canada was equipped with the JN-4Can (for 'Canadian'). This was built by the Canadian Aeroplane Corporation of Toronto and known as the 'Canuck'.

CITY OF TORONTO C368

Behind the wheel covers were the spokes and wheel-rim, to which a rubber tyre was fitted. The undercarriage was of the cross-axle type.

Underwing skids near the wingtip prevented the wing from touching the ground during a rough landing.

The two-seat trainer aircraft was arranged to have an instructor in the rear seat and the pupil in the front. In civil aircraft the latter position was used for joy riders.

Control wires on aircraft of this era were often exposed, taking the shortest route between cockpit and the control surface.

The airframe structure was almost entirely wooden with a doped fabric covering.

ACTION DATA

MAXIMUM SPEED

The Avro 504 used a more powerful engine than the early JN-4s, giving the aircraft improved performance; it was also more aerodynamically streamlined. The Albatros B.IIa was primarily an observation aircraft that was used for a secondary training role.

JN-4D 'JENNY'	121 km/h (75 m.p.h.)
504K	153 km/h (95 m.p.h.)
B.IIa	120 km/h (74 m.p.h.)

RANGE

Designed originally as a reconnaissance aircraft, the Albatros had a marginally better range than the 'Jenny' and 504K. Range figures for these machines tend to be converted into endurance – the time the aircraft can spend in the air, on a training flight for example. An endurance of three to four hours is typical for all three types.

JN-4D 'JENNY' 431 km (267 mi.)

504K 402 km (249 mi.)

B.IIa 476 km (295 mi.)

ENGINE POWER

The 504's rotary engine was the most powerful of those fitted to these three types; later versions of the JN-4 had bigger powerplants. The extra power of the 504 is reflected in its shorter range due to higher fuel consumption. All three aircraft had two-bladed propellers.

JN-4D 'JENNY'	67 kW (90 hp.)
504K	82 kW (110 hp.)
B.IIa	75 kW (100 hp.)

Two-seaters of the inter-war years

■ **AVRO 504:** Famous as a trainer from World War I until the mid-1920s, the 504 started life as a bomber and reconnaissance aircraft.

■ **DE HAVILLAND DH.60 MOTH:** The first of the famous Moth family that ended with the Tiger Moth, DH.60s appeared in the early 1920s.

■ **HANDLEY PAGE GUGNUNC:** Designed for a US competition to find an aircraft that was 'safe' to fly, only one Gugnunc was built.

■ **HANRIOT H.433:** A dual-role observation and training aircraft of the late 1920s, the H.433 shared the JN-4's unequal-span wing layout.

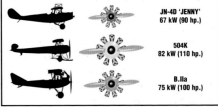

CURTISS
R3C

● Navy floatplane racers ● Schneider Trophy winners ● Seven built

▲ Air races were seen by the
US armed services as valuable proving grounds for
new engines and equipment. To obtain funding, the
aircraft were given spurious designations – the CR-1
was known as the CF-1 fighter.

Sleek Curtiss biplane racers will forever be linked with the prestigious 1920s Schneider Trophy races and with America's best-known military racing pilot, James H. Doolittle. Beginning with the CR-1 and CR-2, Curtiss produced seven aircraft, mainly for the US Navy. As well as taking part in the Schneider Trophy races, these aircraft also participated successfully in the Pulitzer Trophy races, helping to establish Curtiss as a builder of fighter aircraft.

CURTISS R3C

The magnificent Schneider Trophy ▶
Presented by Jacques Schneider, this coveted prize for a dozen races between 1913 and 1931 is now on display at London's Science Museum.

▲ Pulitzer-winning R2C-1
After the Army won the 1922 Pulitzer Trophy Race in its Curtiss R-6 racers, the Navy ordered two R2C-1s, which won the 1923 races.

▲ Army R3C-1 on wheels
Of the three R3C-1s, two were built for the Navy and one for the Army. All were landplanes.

▲ Second place at Cowes
A6080 was the second CR-3 (originally a CR-1) and was placed second in the 1923 Schneider Trophy Race, in the hands of Navy Lieutenant Paul Irvin.

Curtiss 12-cylinder powerplants ▶
While the CR and R2C used the D-12 engine, the R3C introduced the V-1400 of 421 kW (565 hp).

FACTS AND FIGURES

➤ The predecessor of the R3C, Curtiss's R2C, was a world-class racer but was plagued by a series of accidents.

➤ With a bigger engine, the sole R3C-3 reached 410.37 km/h (255 m.p.h.).

➤ US Army R3C-2 A6979 is preserved at the National Air and Space Museum.

➤ After the 1923 Pulitzer race, R2C-1 A6691 was sold to the Army for $1.00 and redesignated R-8. It crashed in 1924.

➤ Each successive racer type used a new aerofoil section wing to improve speed.

➤ A6878, as an R3C-4, crashed before the 1926 Schneider Trophy race.

PROFILE

World-beating racers from Long Island

Curtiss was chosen as the builder of two aircraft for the US Navy in 1921. These aircraft, the CR-1 and CR-2, were to be raced for the Pulitzer Trophy which had been won by the Army in 1920. The Navy withdrew shortly before the race, leaving Curtiss to enter the CR-2 and win the event.

In 1922, victory eluded both machines, but in 1923, after the aircraft were rebuilt to CR-3 floatplane standard, they were entered in the prestigious Schneider Trophy event, taking first and second places.

Meanwhile, for racing in the US, Curtiss had produced an improved design, the R2C. Again a landplane in its original form, the R2C had wing surface radiators to reduce drag. After winning the Pulitzer event in 1923, one aircraft was fitted with floats for the cancelled 1924 Schneider Trophy races. Next came the R3C, with a new V-1400 engine, three of which were built, two for the Navy and one for the Army. Once again, the Pulitzer

and Schneider Trophies were the targets, the Army R3C-1 winning the Pulitzer Trophy and, rebuilt as a float-equipped R3C-2, taking the Schneider Trophy as well, with James Doolittle at the controls.

Army pilot, Lieutenant James H. Doolittle, stands on the float of the R3C-2 in which he won the 1925 Schneider Trophy at a speed of 374.289 km/h (232.572 m.p.h.).

In order to provide cooling for the engine, without bulky, drag-inducing radiators, the CR-2 and subsequent designs employed wing surface radiators.

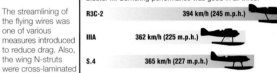

At the heart of the CR-3 was a 336-kW (450-hp.) Curtiss D-12 5DL 12-cylinder, Vee-configuration engine driving a Reed fixed-pitch, two-bladed forged aluminium propeller. This replaced the original wooden airscrew and allowed higher engine speeds.

The two CR-3s were originally built as a CR-1 and CR-2, each with wheeled undercarriage. Floats were fitted for the 1923 Schneider Trophy races.

The CR-3's pilot was snugly enclosed in a cramped cockpit, surrounded by a 'horsecollar' coaming to reduce drag.

Curtiss's established laminated wood veneer construction technique was used for these naval racers. It provided a strong yet relatively lightweight airframe.

After the 1924 Schneider Trophy races were cancelled, A6081 went on to set a closed-circuit seaplane speed record of 302.681 km/h (188.077 m.p.h.). It was fitted with a later version of the D-12 engine and redesignated CR-4.

The streamlining of the flying wires was one of various measures introduced to reduce drag. Also, the wing N-struts were cross-laminated to produce a more aerodynamic form, and the original Lamblin radiators fitted to the CR-1 and CR-2 were replaced with wing surface radiators.

CR-3

Bearing the race number '4', CR-3 A6081 was flown by David Rittenhouse during the 1923 Schneider Race at Cowes. In 1924, it set 100-km (60-mi.), 200-km (120-mi.) and 500-km (300-mi.) closed-circuit world speed records.

CR-3

Type: single-seat racing seaplane

Powerplant: one 336-kW (450-hp.) Curtiss D-12 5DL Vee-configuration liquid-cooled piston engine

Maximum speed: 312 km/h (194 m.p.h.) at sea level

Initial climb rate: 6 mins to 1524 m (5,000 ft.)

Range: 840 km (522 mi.)

Service ceiling: 5852 m (19,200 ft.)

Weights: empty 961 kg (2,119 lb.); gross 1246 kg (2,747 lb.)

Dimensions:
span	6.93 m	(22 ft. 9 in.)
length	7.63 m	(25 ft.)
height	3.27 m	(10 ft. 9 in.)
wing area	15.61 m²	(168 sq. ft.)

ACTION DATA

MAXIMUM SPEED

Unfortunately, the Supermarine S.4 did not get a chance to demonstrate its top speed, as it crashed before the 1925 race. The Curtiss R3C-2 was some 30 km/h faster than the S.4 and Gloster III. Cornering performance was good in all three.

R3C-2	394 km/h (245 m.p.h.)
IIIA	362 km/h (225 m.p.h.)
S.4	365 km/h (227 m.p.h.)

MAXIMUM TAKE-OFF WEIGHT

The S.4 was the heaviest of the three designs, by some 200 kg (440 lb.), but had a less powerful engine than the Gloster III. However, as a more streamlined monoplane design, the S.4 suffered far less from drag and was capable of higher speeds.

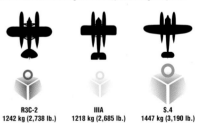

R3C-2	IIIA	S.4
1242 kg (2,738 lb.)	1218 kg (2,685 lb.)	1447 kg (3,190 lb.)

POWER

The Schneider Trophy Races were an ideal testing ground for new technology, like engines, destined for fighter aircraft. This was reflected in the sponsorship of teams by military services such as the US Army and Navy. Most engines were liquid-cooled, in-line types, like the Curtiss D-12 and Napier Lion, which minimised frontal area and therefore reduced drag.

R3C-2	IIIA	S.4
421 kW (565 hp.)	522 kW (700 hp.)	507 kW (680 hp.)

The 1925 Schneider Trophy Race

REPEAT PERFORMANCE: The 1924 Schneider Trophy meeting, planned for Baltimore, Maryland in the US, had been cancelled after the French and Italian teams pulled out, Supermarine produced no design and Gloster's aircraft crashed. Foreign attendance was assured for 1925. The Curtiss CR-3s had won the 1923 event; with the improved R3C, the US Army/Navy team was poised for further glory. As the race date neared, Supermarine's S.4 suffered a crash, leaving Gloster and Macchi to challenge the Americans. On the day (26 October), the R3C's superior speed was telling. The British Gloster III took second place, the Macchi M.33 third.

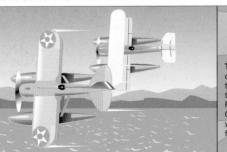

THE VENUE: The site of the 1925 race was the sheltered mouth of the Susquehanna River, near Baltimore. Good water conditions were an important feature.

Start & Finish

CHESAPEAKE BAY

THE COURSE: From a start/finish line at Bay Shore, the aircraft turned at a pylon and lighthouse on the triangular course.

CURTISS

R-6

● US Army racer and record breaker ● Inspired by Navy CR floatplane

▲ Air racing became steadily more popular during the inter-war years, especially in the United States where a number of contests were held each year. Success at home was followed by success abroad as landplane designs were adapted for seaplane racing.

During the 1920s Curtiss was America's leading builder of racing aircraft. Its first successful machine was the CR, built for the US Navy so they could compete for the annual Pulitzer Trophy. The US Army had won this race in 1920, inter-service rivalry spurring the Navy to compete again the following year. Entered by Curtiss, the Navy-owned CR won the 1921 event. Thus, with pride at stake, the Army asked Curtiss to build the R-6.

PHOTO FILE

CURTISS R-6

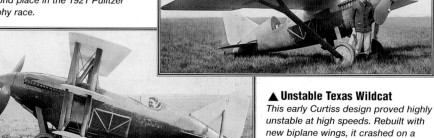

▼ Second-placed Curtiss Cox
Cox triplane Cactus Kitten took second place in the 1921 Pulitzer Trophy race.

▲ Unstable Texas Wildcat
This early Curtiss design proved highly unstable at high speeds. Rebuilt with new biplane wings, it crashed on a cross-country flight.

R-6 descendent ▶
After successes with the CR and R-6 aircraft, Curtiss continued to develop the basic design. It built three R3C-1s, powered by a 421-kW (565-hp.) V-1400 engine, two for the US Navy and one for the Army.

▼ Pulitzer success in 1925
Army flyers were again successful in 1925, racing the latest Curtiss racer, the R3C-1, to victory.

▲ Lieutenant Maitland and his R-6
Lester Maitland flew the R-6 for the first time on 27 September 1922. He took it to second place in the following month's Pulitzer race.

FACTS AND FIGURES

➤ The Pulitzer Trophy for air racing was presented annually by American newspaper owners the Pulitzer brothers.

➤ Two R-6 racers cost the Army $71,000, plus $5,000 for spare parts.

➤ R-6 A.S. 68564 was lost in a fatal crash during the 1924 Pulitzer Trophy race.

➤ Brigadier General 'Billy' Mitchell allegedly 'pulled rank' in order to make the October 1922 record-breaking flight.

➤ During speed trials in April 1923, A.S. 68563 was damaged in two accidents.

➤ Both R-6s were later fitted with large-bore D-12A engines rated at 373 kW (500 hp.).

Army racer and record breaker

S ervice interest in air races arose largely because they were recognised as a valuable proving ground for new designs.

Curtiss cut their racing 'teeth' on two racers built for a Texan oil millionaire, S. E. J. Cox – Texas Wildcat and Cactus Kitten – the latter finishing second behind the CR in the 1921 Pulitzer race.

Determined to beat the Navy in 1922, the Army ordered two racers from Curtiss. The R-6 was a development of the CR series

but introduced a new Curtiss D-12 engine rated at 343 kW.

So it was that on 14 October Lieutenant Russell Maughan took the second of the two machines (A.S. 68564) to victory at a speed of 331.19 km/h (205.79 m.p.h.) – an unofficial world speed record. Lieutenant Lester Maitland in the other aircraft, A.S. 68563, gained second place.

Having achieved their goal and shattered the world speed mark, the Army then set about gaining official recognition. Just four days later Brigadier General William Mitchell took the race winning aircraft to 358.923 km/h (223.024 m.p.h.) before official observers.

The following February a French flyer pushed the world mark to 375 km/h (233 m.p.h.). Not to be outdone, Maughan managed 380.751 km/h (236.588 m.p.h.) on 19 March – a record that lasted seven months.

Inside the Curtiss factory, three of the company's racing designs are seen in various states of repair. In the foreground is an R-6, to its right the US Navy's CR-2, and behind is the Cox Racer Cactus Kitten.

The R-6 was essentially an all-wood aircraft comprising a stressed-skin, all-wood monocoque weighing 57.6 kg (127 lb.) with a two-ply veneer skin covered with doped linen. The wings were also wooden with plywood skinning and fabric-covered ailerons.

After the success of their geared-drive C-12 and direct-drive CD-12 engines, Curtiss developed the all-new D-12 liquid-cooled, vee-configuration 12-cylinder powerplant. The engine's full potential was not realised until 1923 when metal propellers were employed for racing.

A breakthrough in airframe drag reduction introduced on the R-6 was the use of wing-mounted radiators on both surfaces of the upper wings; these replaced the French Lamblin units attached to the undercarriage legs of earlier designs. Surface radiators subsequently became standard on racing aircraft.

R-6 Army racers carried the Air Service bald eagle insignia. The ribbon carried in the eagle's beak read 'US Army Air Service'. The aircraft's fuselage was black overall with gold wings.

R-6

A.S. 68563 was the first of the two R-6s built to contest the 1922 Pulitzer Trophy race, for which it carried the race number '44'. It finished second in the hands of Lieutenant Lester Maitland. In the 1923 event it finished fifth and then second in 1924. The following year it was written off during static testing.

R-6
Type: single-seat biplane racer

Powerplant: one 343-kW (460-hp.) Curtiss D-12 v-configuration liquid-cooled piston engine

Maximum speed: 380 km/h (237 m.p.h.)

Landing speed: 121 km/h (75 m.p.h.)

Range: 455 km (283 m.p.h.) at full throttle

Weights: empty 659 kg (1,453 lb.); gross 884.5 kg (1,950 lb.)

Dimensions: span 5.79 m (18 ft. 10 in.)
length 5.76 m (18 ft. 11 in.)
height 2.41 m (7 ft. 11 in.)
wing area 12.82 m² (138 sq. ft.)

ACTION DATA

POWER
Crucial to a racing aircraft's success was its engine. Curtiss was heavily involved in engine as well as airframe development and introduced various engines for racing, culminating in the D-12, which powered the R-6 and the Navy's CR-3. The Curtiss Cox racer *Texas Wildcat* was fitted with the earlier geared-drive C-12 engine. Gearing was required to reduce engine revolutions because of the strength limitations of wooden propellers used at the time.

| R-6 343 kW (460 hp.) | TEXAS WILDCAT 318 kW (426 hp.) | CR-3 336 kW (450 hp.) |

MAXIMUM SPEED
The maximum speeds achievable by racing aircraft between the wars leapt ahead at an astonishing rate. Though the R-6 was the fastest aircraft in the world during 1922–23 it was outclassed within 12 months by the Navy's R2C which, at the end of 1923, had set a new world record of over 428 km/h (266 m.p.h.). Not until 1932 did the United States again hold a world record, when the Granville Brothers' Gee Bee R-1 achieved almost 474 km/h (295 m.p.h.).

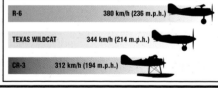

R-6 380 km/h (236 m.p.h.)
TEXAS WILDCAT 344 km/h (214 m.p.h.)
CR-3 312 km/h (194 m.p.h.)

Curtiss racing landplanes

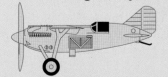
CURTISS COX *TEXAS WILDCAT*: Built as a monoplane for the 1920 Gordon Bennett race in France, the *Wildcat* proved unstable and was rebuilt as a biplane, only to crash.

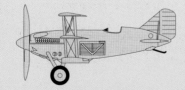
CURTISS COX *CACTUS KITTEN*: The second of the Cox racers was shipped to France but was not assembled. A triplane, it came second in the 1921 Pulitzer race.

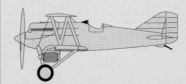
CR-1/CR-2: The US Navy's CRs employed a wheeled undercarriage for the Pulitzer races. Both were fitted with floats for the Schneider Trophy racing and seaplane record breaking.

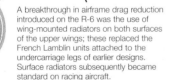
R-6: The R-6's resemblance to the CR racers was readily apparent. A major change was the use of evaporative engine cooling for the new Curtiss D-12 powerplant.

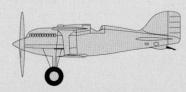
R2C-1/R-8: The 1923 Pulitzer race was won by the Navy in their improved R2C-1 aircraft. One of the two built was then sold to the Army as the R-8, crashing in 1924.

DASA/Eurospace/NASA

SÄNGER/HERMES/X-30

● New age spacecraft ● Trans-continental interest ● Futuristic

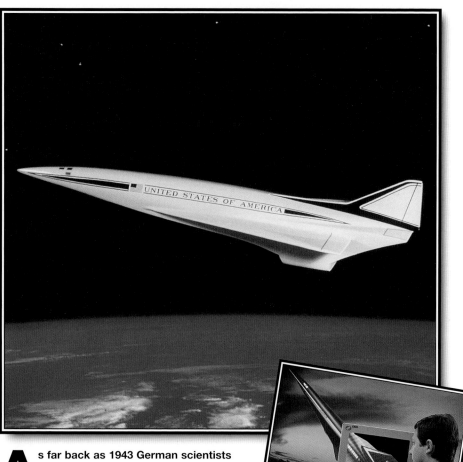

◄ Definitive X-30
After several different design proposals, this rendering of the National Aerospace Plane was selected for further development. Two machines were to be built.

Scale Model ►
A mock-up of the now defunct Hermes illustrates the cargo bay with its characteristic double shielded doors and long loading arm.

French Space Shuttle? ►
One of the more conventional looking trans-atmospheric vehicles, the Hermes was similar in concept to the Rockwell International 'Space Shuttle' and would have reached orbit riding on a larger booster, in this case the Ariane 5 rocket.

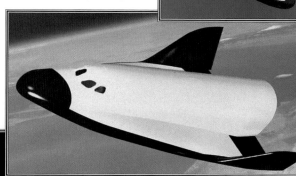

◄ True spaceship
The X-30 was to be capable of reaching orbit on its own power, taking-off from a conventional airfield. Ramjets were the intended propulsion system.

German X-30 ►
Another ambitious European nation is Germany which has developed its own transonic re-useable space vehicle, known locally as the Sänger.

As far back as 1943 German scientists investigated the possibility of a rocket-launched intercontinental bomber, able to skip across the upper atmosphere to reach its target. Further research was conducted in the US and elsewhere in the 1950s and 60s leading to such aircraft as the X-20 Dyno-Soar, used in the Space Shuttle project. By the late 1980s the US X-30, the European Hermes and the Sänger were all being developed.

▲ Several countries, notably France, Germany and the USA have studied the concept of Trans-Atmospheric Vehicles (TVAs), designed to operate on the fringes of space.

FACTS AND FIGURES

➤ Studies related to the X-30 programme have been around since the 1940s but, until 1981, were shrouded in secrecy.

➤ Both Aérospatiale and Dassault were major contractors for Hermes.

➤ Both the German and the French concepts employ a two-stage setup.

➤ Had development continued, it is estimated that more than $10 billion would have been required for the X-30.

➤ Development of such projects remains in doubt because of defence cuts.

➤ At present, the Sänger spacecraft is rumoured still to be under development.

PROFILE

Beyond the frontiers

The most exotic of the late 1980s space-plane projects was the NASA X-30, also known as the National Aerospace Plane (NASP) and the Orient Express. It was to use ramjet/scramjet propulsion and other new technologies enabling it to reach Mach 25, but would have needed an outlay of at least $10 billion to develop.

Hermes was designed to be launched into low earth orbit by an Ariane 5 booster. It was intended to support the

European elements of the International Space Station, but was cancelled in 1993. Some of the technology may be used in a proposed crew rescue vehicle for the space station.

Sänger is a much more ambitious project. It involves a probably unmanned turbo-ramjet-powered first stage that would carry the second stage – a reusable manned vehicle or disposable cargo carrier – to a height of 30000 m (98,000 ft) and a speed of Mach 6. Then the second stage would use its

rocket in order to reach orbit.

By 1997 NASA had switched its attention to the Lockheed Martin X-33 VentureStar reusable launch vehicle. The European Space Agency has continued to study concepts for future space launchers, with the Sänger being one of those projects that may still be under consideration.

Left: The Sänger would be a two-stage reusable aero-space plane configured to carry both cargo and passengers.

Above: France's Hermes was unique among the designs in having a conventional cockpit layout and fuselage, not dissimilar to that of the current Rockwell Space Shuttle.

SÄNGER

Deutsche Aerospace has so far made considerable progress with the Sänger Trans Atmospheric Vehicle and a 1:8 scale mock-up was unveiled to the public. The future of this project remains uncertain.

The tail surfaces resemble those of current high tech combat aircraft, such as the F/A-18, with large canted fins and conventional style rudders.

Mounted on top of the stage one craft is the smaller, rocket-powered manned cargo carrier, which is similar in concept to the Space Shuttle. It has been designed as a manned craft, and would return to earth once the mission was complete.

Extensive research into such craft has resulted in a clean, integrated delta wing configuration being the most popular, in order to achieve greatest aerodynamic efficiency. Not surprisingly, the Sänger resembles something out of a science fiction film.

Some illustrations depict the stage one booster as an unmanned device, though a scale mock-up was fitted with some sort of cockpit windows perhaps indicating otherwise.

For such a machine to be capable of reaching orbit, powerful ramjet/scramjet motors would be required. Developing such a powerplant would be hideously expensive and it would be difficult to produce using current technology.

As it is designed to return to earth once the second stage has separated, the booster features a retractable undercarriage very similar to that of a normal airliner. On the mock-up, this comprised twin nosewheels on a single oleo and twin main legs, each fitted with twelve wheels and tyres to help distribute the incredible weight of this machine.

Besides its role as a Low Earth Orbit (LEO) vehicle, the Sänger was conceived as a conventional airliner, albeit one which could fly at much greater speeds and over even greater distances than commercial jets. Because the performance envelope will be so large, with huge differences between landing and and orbit speeds, very advanced materials and construction techniques will be needed.

Hermes

Payload: up to 4.5 tonnes

Crew: 2 to 6

Weights: launch 29000 kg (63,800 lb.), re-entry 15000 kg (33,000 lb.)

Dimensions: span 9 m (29 ft. 6 in.)
length 13 m (43 ft.)

Sänger

Powerplant: six 400-kN (90,000-lb.-thrust) turbo-ramjets, one 1280-kN (287,950-lb.-thrust) liquid-fuelled ATCRE rocket

Weights: empty 188000 kg (413,600 lb.), max take-off 366000 kg (805,200 lb.)

Dimensions: span 41.04 m (134 ft. 8 in.)
length 84.05 m (275 ft. 8 in.)

X-30

Powerplant: one 1372.9-kN (308,850-lb.-thrust) scramjet

Weights: empty 60000 kg (132,000 lb.), max take-off 140000 kg (308,000 lb.)

Dimensions: span 36 m (118 ft. 1 in.)
length 80 m (262 ft. 5 in.)

ACTION DATA

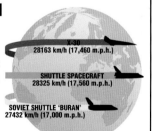

ORBITAL SPEED

Only the Rockwell International Space Shuttle is in use at present. This incredible machine has an orbital speed of 28325 km/h (17,560 m.p.h.). Had the X-30 been built, it would have flown at more or less the same velocity, but directly from the airfield without the aid of a booster.

X-30 28163 km/h (17,460 m.p.h.)
SHUTTLE SPACECRAFT 28325 km/h (17,560 m.p.h.)
SOVIET SHUTTLE 'BURAN' 27432 km/h (17,000 m.p.h.)

LANDING SPEED

To design a craft which can fly at 25000 km/h (17,000 m.p.h.) in orbit and yet still land at around 300 km/h (220 m.p.h.) is difficult. A disadvantage with the shuttle craft is that it cannot land under its own power and only one landing attempt can be made. The X-30 would have been able to make several attempts if required.

X-30 346 km/h (215 m.p.h.)
SHUTTLE SPACECRAFT 363 km/h (225 m.p.h.)
SOVIET SHUTTLE 'BURAN' 340 km/h (211 m.p.h.)

Ambitious ideas

■ **BRITISH AEROSPACE HOTOL:** Conceived in the heady days of the 1980s this was one attempt to rival US dominance in the space race.

■ **DASSAULT STAR-H:** Incorporating the Hermes, this French project was to have been an element of the International Space Station.

■ **LOCKHEED TAV:** An early study for the US Air Force was this combined spacecraft/conventional air transport design.

■ **NASA SHUTTLE BOOSTER:** The differences between concept and reality are evident in this 1970 impression of the booster.

DASSAULT

FALCON

- Long-range business transport ● Dassault's executive jet family

DASSAULT FALCON

◄ Family formation
The secret of the Falcon's success has been in having an aircraft for every customer's requirements. Shown here are (front to rear) the Falcon 100, 200, 50 and 900.

▲ Bizjet office
Like most business jets, the Falcon has a pleasant, spacious cockpit. The latest versions have multi-function displays and state-of-the-art navigation systems.

▼ Company flagship
The largest of the Falcon family is the 900. Its vast range and high capacity make it the king of corporate jets.

▲ Falcon factory
The Falcon 50 is assembled at the Dassault factory at Bordeaux-Mérignac. After 30 years the Falcon is still in production, with the 2000 variant.

Corporate limousine ▶
A Falcon 200 is the stylish way for an executive to arrive in town. Many Falcons have luxurious cabin interiors with every facility, as well as high performance and very long range.

Designed in the late 1950s, the Falcon opened up new horizons in business transportation. This is an exciting executive jet intended for easy adaptation to other duties. Combining luxury with long range and superb flying characteristics, the Falcon has evolved into a family of aircraft. In varying sizes and configurations, these are among the world's best executive transports. Falcons are also used for coastal patrol and other duties.

▲ Most Falcons are in civilian use, but the French Aéronavale uses the aircraft for radar training and transport and to act as an intercept target.

FACTS AND FIGURES

➤ Nearly 1000 examples of the Falcon family are now flying around the world.

➤ The first prototype in the Falcon family made its initial flight on 4 May 1963.

➤ Nine engine types have been offered to customers or considered for use with different versions of the Falcon.

➤ The US Coast Guard's 41 HU-25 Guardians include nine HU-25C Night Stalkers, which use AN/APG-66 radar to detect smugglers.

➤ Falcon jets have flown over 1400 million km (930 million mi.), equal to 10 trips to Mars.

➤ The latest Falcon 2000 (Falcon X) has twin CFE738 engines.

PROFILE

France's flying limousine

Dassault, together with Sud-Aviation, developed the beautiful, twin-jet Falcon 20 (originally known in France as the Mystère 20) as the first in a successful line of attractive, sensible aircraft for business transport and other uses in 1963. This great flying-machine acquired intercontinental range as new Falcons took to the air, including the Falcon 50 and Falcon 900 tri-jets and the powerful twin-jet Falcon 2000, each larger and further-reaching.

Together, this family of aircraft has revolutionised executive travel and brought distant cities in the world closer together.

It was inevitable that this quality jet would be used for VIP transport by dignitaries ranging from the French president to the King of Morocco. The Falcon 20 freighter has proven a reliable hauler in the hands of users like Federal Express. Members of the Falcon family are also doing a fine job in maritime patrol for operators which include the US

Coast Guard and the Japanese Air Self-Defence Force. The Royal Navy uses the Falcon 20 for simulating attacks on shipping and for electronic warfare training.

The Falcon 50 is a rarity among bizjets in having three engines, though the larger Russian-designed Yak-42 also has three.

The advanced technology wing sweeps back at 29° inboard and 24.5° outboard. The structural boxes within the wing also serve as fuel tanks.

The sharply waisted rear fuselage and engine pods were computer-designed for maximum smoothness of airflow.

Falcon 50

Type: long-range executive jet

Powerplant: three 16.46-kN (3,700 lb-thrust) Garrett TFE731-3-1C turbofans

Maximum cruising speed: 870 km/h (541 m.p.h.)

Range: 6500 km (4,039 mi.) at Mach 0.75 with eight passengers

Weights: empty 9000 kg (19,842 lb.); loaded 17,600 kg (38,801 lb.)

Accommodation: two pilots and eight to 10 passengers; up to 14 passengers in a maximum-density layout

Dimensions:
span	18.86 m	(61 ft. 11 in.)
length	18.52 m	(60 ft. 9 in.)
height	6.97 m	(22 ft. 10 in.)
wing area	46.83 m²	(504 sq. ft.)

FALCON 900

The Falcon 900 has vast intercontinental range carrying a highly impressive load of 19 passengers. This capability, along with its relatively low operating costs, has helped to establish good sales figures in the all-important corporate jet market.

The capacious wide-body fuselage of the Falcon 900 gives the cabin almost twice the volume of the Falcon 50. It also has a greater fuel capacity than the twin-jet Falcons, giving much greater range.

The interior of the Falcon can incorporate a wide range of layouts. Typically the cabin is divided into three sections containing swivel 'sleeping' chairs, a dining area, fold-away beds and a conference table.

Falcons are powered by Garrett TFE731 turbofans. These efficient and reliable engines are also used in Learjets, Cessna Citations and BAe 125s.

Falcons have a crew of two pilots, and usually a cabin attendant. Military Falcons often have navigation students or electronic warfare operators as well.

N327K

The Falcon 50/900 wing is a more modern design than that of the 20/200. It is optimised to provide maximum comfort and economy at Mach 0.82 cruise.

Falcons have a 2.55-m³ (90-cu. ft.) baggage compartment at the rear of the fuselage. It is located within the pressurised section of the fuselage, so that delicate or pressure-sensitive items can be carried in safety.

ACTION DATA

RANGE

Modern multinational companies do business all over the world. The corporate jets they use reflect that trend, those at the top of the scale having intercontinental range. The Falcon is one of the best performers on the market, with capabilities beaten only by the very sophisticated and very expensive American-built Gulfstream IV.

BAe 125-800: 5500 km (3,418 mi.)
FALCON 50: 6500 km (4,039 mi.)
GULFSTREAM IV: 7820 km (4,859 mi.)

MAXIMUM CRUISING SPEED

BAe 125-800	845 km/h (525 m.p.h.)
GULFSTREAM IV	936 km/h (582 m.p.h.)
FALCON 50	870 km/h (541 m.p.h.)

The first generation of business jets were often slower than commercial jets. Modern executive jets have grown in speed, range and capability, and an aircraft like the Falcon has airliner-like performance but with considerably greater comfort for the passengers.

PAYLOAD

The Falcon 50 is a little smaller than other high-end corporate jets. To provide more competition for the likes of Gulfstream and British Aerospace, Dassault introduced the Falcon 900 in the mid-1980s. This has a wide range of seating options to a maximum of 19 passengers, doubling the capacity of the Falcon 50.

GULFSTREAM IV
3 crew
19 passengers

BAe 125-800
2 crew
14 passengers

FALCON 50
2 crew
8/10 passengers

Dassault's bizjet family

FALCON 10/100: First flown in 1970, the 100 was originally called the Minifalcon, as it was essentially a scaled-down Falcon 20.

FALCON 20/200: This features General Electric CF700 turbofans. Later Falcon 20s had enlarged fuel capacity and engine power.

FALCON 50: The first Falcon with three engines, the 50 was a larger aircraft with much greater range than earlier twin-jets.

FALCON 900: The top-of-the-range Falcon 900 is designed to carry up to 19 passengers over intercontinental ranges.

DASSAULT-BREGUET

MERCURE

● Short-range airliner ● One operator ● Financial disaster

DASSAULT-BREGUET MERCURE

◄ First to fly
The first Mercure prototype was registered F-WTCC. 'TCC' stood for Transport Court-Courier (short-range transport).

▼ Production centre
Final assembly of the Mercure took place at the Dassault factory in Istres, southeast France.

▼ Unveiling the Mercure
The first Mercure was rolled out at Bordeaux-Mérignac airport on 4 April 1971, just 23 months after work began.

Sole customer ►
Air Inter was the only airline to operate the Mercure. The airline received an annual subsidy of £850,000 during the 1980s to offset the high cost of spares.

Destined to fail ►
Unable to compete with the American Boeing 737 and Douglas DC-9 in terms of range or operating economy, the Mercure never received the orders anticipated as airlines opted for the US-built aircraft.

Despite its similarity to the successful Boeing 737 the Mercure never gained the success of its US counterpart. When Dassault developed the Mercure at the start of the 1970s it seemed ideal for short-haul air routes, but it was rushed into production prematurely, when orders for only 10 had been received. With inferior fuel capacity, the Mercure could not compete with the 737 and the aircraft gained no further orders.

▲ When the Dassault company placed the Mercure into production they were anticipating sales of 300 examples by 1980. The total sale of only 10 aircraft led to a large loss.

FACTS AND FIGURES

➤ An annual subsidy from the French government helped to underwrite operating costs for the Mercure fleet.

➤ The prototype Dassault Mercure first took to the air on 28 May 1971.

➤ Air Inter placed its initial order for 10 Mercures on 29 January 1972.

➤ The first Mercure equipped for airline operations was delivered to Air Inter on 16 May 1974.

➤ The prototype was at first equipped with less powerful JT8D-11 turbofan engines.

➤ For the Mercure to break even it needed to achieve sales of 125 to 150 aircraft.

PROFILE

France's failed twin-jet

Dassault produced the Mercure airliner following the success of the manufacturer's Mystère/Falcon business jets. The Mercure was similar to (but had shorter range than) the Boeing 737, which brilliantly took advantage of the need for a short- to medium-haul passenger craft. However, Dassault made a major financial mistake by giving the 'go ahead' to the Mercure after only 10 had been ordered by Air Inter.

This low-wing, twin-jet aircraft was very pleasing in its general configuration and was equipped to provide travellers with speed and comfort. Pilots found the Mercure to be friendly and relatively easy to master.

With hindsight, however, it is easy to see that the Mercure was a miscalculation: faced with strong competition, especially from the Boeing 737 and the Douglas DC-9, Dassault's designers erred badly in providing so small a fuel capacity that the Mercure could not complete most services without time-consuming refuelling. Even though much of the design and development of this plane was subsidised by the French government, the Mercure never proved economical for Air Inter, the domestic carrier which ordered all 10 machines.

Orders for the improved Mercure 200 never materialised and the project was abandoned at a huge loss.

The Mercure has now been retired from service, although several examples have been saved for museums.

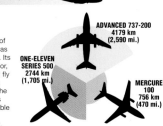

Above: The Air Inter Mercures appeared in a number of colour schemes. This scheme was the last, applied in the mid-1980s.

Left: The second prototype, F-WTMD, was fitted with the production JT8D-15 engine.

MERCURE 100

In the mid-1980s Air Inter operated Mercure 100s on short-haul routes, mainly within France. This aircraft served with Air Inter throughout its service life before being retired in the early 1990s.

Mercure 100

Type: twin-engined short-range transport

Powerplant: two 68.95-kN (15,510-lb.-thrust) Pratt & Whitney JT8D-15 turbofan engines

Maximum speed: 941 km/h (583 m.p.h.) at 6096 m (20,000 ft.)

Maximum cruising speed: 925 km/h (574 m.p.h.) at 6096 m (20,000 ft.)

Range: 756 km (470 mi.)

Service ceiling: est. 12,000 m (39,300 ft.)

Weights: empty operating 31,800 kg (69,960 lb.); maximum take-off 56,500 kg (124,300 lb.)

Accommodation: two pilots, flight engineer, two cabin crew, passenger load of (typically) 120 to 150, maximum 162, plus up to 4400 kg (9,680 lb.) of baggage

Dimensions:
span	30.56 m	(100 ft. 3 in.)
length	34.84 m	(114 ft. 3 in.)
height	11.37 m	(37 ft. 4 in.)
wing area	116 m²	(1,248 sq. ft.)

The crew of two were seated side-by-side in the cockpit with two extra optional seats. The basic Mercure 100 was designed for all-weather (Cat III) operation and a Garrett AiResearch auxiliary power unit provided emergency electrical power and power for engine starting.

The typical mixed-class layout for the interior of the cabin comprised 12 four-abreast seats at 96.5-cm (38-in.) pitch and 120 six-abreast seats at 81.5-cm (32-in.) pitch. Galleys were included at the front and rear and the cabin windows were polarised to reduce glare.

Of cantilever low-wing monoplane form, the Mercure's wings were of two-spar fail-safe structure. Two triple-slotted flaps and a single aileron were fitted on the trailing edge of each wing. Spoilers were fitted to the upper surface to reduce lift when necessary.

For lateral control the rudder was divided into two independent parts, negating the need for trim tabs. The tailplane was of variable incidence type, to be used for emergency pitch control in the event of elevator failure.

AIR INTER
Mercure
F-BTTJ

The retractable tricycle-type undercarriage had twin wheels with shock absorbers on each unit. The nosewheel was steerable through 70° left or right.

Fitted in underwing pods were two Pratt & Whitney JT8D-15 turbofan engines with thrust reversers and Dassault-developed noise absorbers.

The Mercure contained three baggage holds beneath the cabin floor. One was situated forward of the wings and two aft. The two cargo service doors were fitted to the starboard side of the fuselage.

ACTION DATA

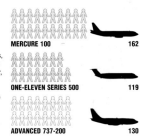

PASSENGERS

Although the Mercure 100 was capable of carrying more passengers than contemporary twin-jets, it could not operate as economically. However, if the Model 737 had not been such an exceptional airliner, the Mercure, with its good capacity, would have been more successful.

MERCURE 100	162
ONE-ELEVEN SERIES 500	119
ADVANCED 737-200	130

SPEED

One area where the Mercure excelled was cruising speed, reducing travel time for passengers. Unfortunately, the Mercure was only suitable for short-range routes, making the extra speed irrelevant.

MERCURE 100	925 km/h (574 m.p.h.)
ONE-ELEVEN	871 km/h (540 m.p.h.)
737-200	856 km/h (530 m.p.h.)

RANGE

The major disadvantage of the Mercure was its poor range. Its main competitor, the 737, could fly more than five times as far. The BAC 1-11 was also only suitable for routes of modest length.

ADVANCED 737-200 4179 km (2,590 mi.)
ONE-ELEVEN SERIES 500 2744 km (1,705 mi.)
MERCURE 100 756 km (470 mi.)

French airliner projects

■ **AÉROSPATIALE SE 210 CARAVELLE:** As the first French turbojet-powered airliner, the Caravelle had a then-unique engine layout of twin engines attached to the rear fuselage. A small number are still in service more than 40 years after the first flight.

STERLING OY-SAS

■ **AÉROSPATIALE/BAC CONCORDE:** The world's only supersonic jet airliner in regular service was an Anglo-French product which became the flagship of Air France and British Airways. It remained in service for over a quarter of a century.

AIR FRANCE

■ **AIRBUS INDUSTRIE A300:** The first in the line of successful Airbus products, the A300 first flew in 1972. It sold well and there is a successful freighter version. The European Airbus concern is based at Toulouse, France.

EGYPTAIR

DE HAVILLAND
DH.18/34

● Commercial airliner ● European flights ● Wooden construction

Airco's first commercial aircraft designed as such from the outset, the DH.18 achieved considerable savings for its operators compared to the ex-military types commonly in use after World War I. Only six were built, but they gave reliable service, mainly on routes between London and the Continent. The DH.18's successor, the DH.34, addressed the main weaknesses of the DH.18 by carrying a greater payload at a higher speed.

▲ For the privileged
passengers who could afford the fare, the DH.18 and DH.34 allowed weekend trips to Paris without the need for a long sea crossing.

DE HAVILLAND DH.18/34

Luggage space ▶
Passengers were accommodated in the forward section of the fuselage, with their luggage stored under the pilot's seat. The traditional triangular shaped hatch was used throughout the series.

▲ Airport operations
This DH.34 is fitted with larger mainwheels, which allowed it to operate from less well-equipped airports.

▲ Landing run
An unusually tall undercarriage was installed on the DH.34, which enabled it to make short landing runs. Traditional bungee shock absorbers were replaced with a rubber cord system and offered better performance during rough landings.

▲ Wider horizons
Passengers board an Instone Airline's DH.18 for a flight to the Continent during the 1920s.

Continental service ▶
The first scheduled flights were between Croydon and Paris and took less than 2 hours 40 minutes.

FACTS AND FIGURES

➤ The first de Havilland aircraft to be built at its Stag Lane, Middlesex, factory were the two DH.18Bs.

➤ DH.18s boasted an operating cost of just two shillings and sixpence per ton-mile.

➤ G-EARO, the first DH.18A, flew 144840 km during its airline career.

➤ After its retirement, G-EARO was used for fuel consumption tests by the Royal Aircraft Establishment at Farnborough.

➤ One DH.34 was exported to Russia for service with the airline Dobrolet.

➤ DH.34 G-EAWW was deliberately ditched during flotation tests by the Air Ministry.

PROFILE

Airliners for an expanding industry

Powered by a 336-kW Napier Lion engine, the DH.18 had a standard de Havilland rear fuselage of fabric-covered, wire-braced wooden construction. However, the plywood-covered cabin was revolutionary, with a watertight door in case of a forced landing, and seating for eight people. With seats removed there was room for 7.25 m³ (265 cu. ft.) of cargo, weighing 998 kg (2,195 lb.). The pilot sat in an open cockpit behind the cabin.

The first aircraft flew from Airco's Hendon factory in 1920 and after testing entered service with Aircraft Transport & Travel Ltd flying between Croydon and Paris.

Five DH.18As and Bs (the latter with a higher all-up weight and inertia engine starting) followed, and were operated by Daimler Hire and the Instone Airline. Most were withdrawn from airline use by 1923.

The DH.34 (built by Geoffrey de Havilland's new company, bearing his name) differed from the DH.18 in having a larger fuselage (from the DH.29

10-seater monoplane) and the cockpit was positioned behind the engine. The prototype flew on 22 March 1922 and entered service on the cross-Channel route in April. Eleven were built, 10 of which eventually served with Imperial Airways until 1926. Two were converted to DH.34B standard in 1924/5 by increasing their wing area to reduce their stalling speed.

Left: The large dimensions of the DH.18 allowed a replacement engine to be installed from inside the fuselage

Above: Awaiting its next flight from Croydon Aerodrome, this DH.34 was capable of reaching Paris, Brussels and Cologne on the first regular commercial flights. These aircraft pioneered passenger flights to Europe.

DH.34

Type: early commercial biplane

Powerplant: one 336-kW (450-hp.) Napier Lion in-line piston engine

Maximum speed: 206 km/h (128 m.p.h.)

Maximum cruising speed: 169 km/h (105 m.p.h.)

Landing speed: 112 km/h (70 m.p.h.)

Range: 587 km (364 mi.)

Service ceiling: 4876 m (16,000 ft.)

Weights: empty 2075 kg (4,565 lb.); maximum take-off 3266 kg (7,185 lb.)

Accommodation: 10 passengers and one pilot

Dimensions:
span	15.65 m (51 ft. 4 in.)
length	11.89 m (39 ft.)
height	3.66 m (12 ft.)
wing area	54.81 m² (590 sq. ft.)

DH.34

Building on experience gained from the DH.18, de Havilland's DH.34 offered benefits to both travellers and airlines, and began a new era in passenger travel.

Constructed from wood, the two mainplanes were fitted with ailerons operated by an effective differential gear mechanism.

Passengers were seated underneath the pilot away from the noise of the engine. The cabin was accessed via a small triangular door on the starboard side.

The rear fuselage followed de Havilland's established method of construction and consisted of wire bracing around a strengthened wooden box structure.

Hinged platforms were fitted around either side of the nose to allow the engine to be serviced.

The pilot was seated in an open cockpit above the fuselage. To keep him warm during long overseas flights, hot air was drawn from a muff which surrounded the exhaust pipe.

Rubber cord shock absorbers were installed on each undercarriage leg to allow the aircraft to operate from rough airfields.

With most major airports still in their infancy, flights were often made from grass runways so a tailwheel was rarely installed. Most DH.34s were fitted with a skid.

G-EBBQ DAIMLER HIRE L. LONDON

ACTION DATA

MAXIMUM SPEED

Many early airliners were ex-military types with low full-load speeds. With the introduction of pure civil designs there was an overall improvement in performance. The DH.34 was faster despite being single engined.

DH.34	206 km/h (128 m.p.h.)
H.P.42	160 km/h (99 m.p.h.)
DH.9C	185 km/h (115 m.p.h.)

RANGE

For the expanding market of air travel an aircraft's range was particularly important. As larger designs capable of carrying greater loads and with longer ranges entered service, the less sophisticated types such as the DH.34 and DH.9C were replaced.

DH.34 587 km (364 mi.)
H.P.42 800 km (496 mi.)
DH.9C 804 km (498 mi.)

PASSENGERS

Although still restricted to the rich, a new era of air travel saw larger aircraft carrying increased passenger loads. Compared to the converted DH.9C, the DH.34 offered a respectable lifting capability, but it was a lot smaller than the later H.P.42.

DH.34 10
H.P.42 38
DH.9C 2

Imperial Airways: the early years

A.W. ARGOSY: Banking over London, an Argosy returns from Paris on one of the first scheduled flights between the two capital cities.

SUPERMARINE SEA EAGLE: One of the first flying-boats used by Imperial Airways, the Sea Eagle flew to the Channel Islands.

DE HAVILLAND DH.66: The three engines improved safety margins and increased the lifting capacity of the DH.66.

HANDLEY PAGE W.10: Awaiting passengers at Croydon in the 1920s, the W.10 offered a much improved capability to Imperial Airways.

DE HAVILLAND
DH.51

● Rare biplane ● Pleasure flights ● Oldest airworthy de Havilland

▲ In the early 1920s, the de Havilland Company unveiled its DH.51. A real effort was made to produce an aircraft for the masses powered by a war surplus engine. Only three were built.

This touring biplane could be described as the aircraft that launched de Havilland's highly successful Moth family, the most successful member of which was the DH.82 Tiger Moth. Using proven, conventional construction methods, de Havilland aimed to produce a cheap, practical, two- or three-seat aircraft and although only three were built, they helped prove the concept of 'affordable flying for the masses' in the 1920s.

DE HAVILLAND **DH.51**

▼ **de Havilland trademark**
Many de Havilland aircraft from the inter-war period displayed the distinctive tail profile and wing-mounted fuel tank. This example is operated by the Shuttleworth Trust alongside Miss Kenya, the sole surviving DH.51.

▲ **Grounded**
Initially powered by a surplus RAF 1A engine, the DH.51 was denied a certificate of airworthiness because of its single ignition system.

Fathering success ▶
The design of the DH.51 was unmistakably de Havilland and, although the aircraft was not a great commercial success, it led to the famous Moth series of classic British biplanes of the late 1920s.

▼ **Flying antique**
Since 1965, G-EBIR Miss Kenya, has been part of the Shuttleworth Collection in Bedfordshire, where it is still flown regularly.

▲ **New engine, greater cost**
Ending the prospect of a low-cost DH.51 was the adoption of a war surplus Renault engine with redesigned cylinder heads and valve gear.

FACTS AND FIGURES

➤ The third DH.51, G-EBIR Miss Kenya, was flown after restoration in 1973; it currently flies with the Shuttleworth Trust.

➤ Registered G-KAA, Miss Kenya was the first aircraft registered in Kenya.

➤ War surplus RAF 1A engines reputedly cost 14s 6d (72.5 pence) each.

➤ The first DH.51 was rebuilt in 1924 as a DH.51A with short-span wings and automatic camber-changing flaps.

➤ After being sold in Australia, the first DH.51 was fitted with floats, as a DH.51B.

➤ G-EBIR was restored by apprentices from Rolls-Royce and Hawker Siddeley.

PROFILE

Forerunner of the Moths

A two-bay biplane with all the hallmarks of a de Havilland design, the DH.51 had a plywood-covered fuselage and was powered by a war surplus, 67-kW (90-hp.) Royal Aircraft Factory (RAF) 1A, air-cooled, eight-cylinder engine, which drove a large, four-bladed, wooden propeller.

This latter feature allowed the DH.51 to climb easily from small fields, an ability that de Havilland felt a small

touring aircraft should be able to demonstrate.

With a cruising speed of 140 km/h (84 m.p.h.), the prototype flew for the first time in July 1924, but immediately struck certification problems. The Air Ministry refused to grant the design a Certificate of Airworthiness without changes to the RAF engine. Unwilling to bear the cost, de Havilland instead re-engined the aircraft with an Airdisco engine (itself a Renault wartime design, reworked by the Aircraft Disposal Company to produce 89 kW

Above: Second of the three DH.51s was G-EBIM, which participated in the 1925 King's Cup air race, but did not finish.

(120 hp.). However, this change pushed up the cost of the type; only two more were built.

The first of these took part, along with the prototype, in the 1925 King's Cup Race; both failed to finish. Also in 1925, the third machine flew to Kenya where it remained airworthy until 1937. Stored during World War II, the aircraft was shipped to the UK in 1965 and subsequently restored to flying condition.

In late 1924, the DH.51 prototype was retrofitted with new short-span single bay wings. These featured automatic camber altering flaps and proved so successful, that they were retained. Atop the upper wing was the fuel tank, a characteristic of de Havilland designs of the mid- to late 1920s.

Above: Today, the sole airworthy DH.51 remains the oldest de Havilland aircraft still capable of flight. It looks set to continue flying for many years to come.

The tail unit was a typical de Havilland design and covered in fabric. To keep things as simple as possible, the rudder did not incorporate a trim tab, but made use of a spring actuated elevator.

Intended primarily for pleasure flights, the DH.51 was designed as a three seater, with the pilot sitting at the rear for a clear and unobstructed view.

MISS KENYA

G-EBIR

Originally powering the DH.51 was a 67-kW (90-hp.) RAF 1A eight-cylinder engine. The Air Ministry's dislike of its single ignition prompted the installation of a more powerful Airdisco engine.

Low unit cost was the order of the day and the DH.51 made extensive use of abundant materials, including balsa wood.

DH.51
Type: three-seat touring biplane

Powerplant: one 89-kW (120-hp.) Airdisco V8 in-line piston engine

Maximum speed: 174 km/h (108 m.p.h.)

Stalling speed: 69 km/h (43 m.p.h.)

Initial climb rate: 292 m/min (960 f.p.m.)

Range: 579 km (360 mi.)

Service ceiling: 4572 m (15,000 ft.)

Weights: empty 609 kg (1,340 lb.); loaded 1016 kg (2,235 lb.)

Accommodation: one pilot, sitting to the rear, and two passengers

Dimensions:
span	11.28 m	(37 ft.)
length	8.08 m	(26 ft. 6 in.)
height	2.97 m	(9 ft. 9 in.)
wing area	40.32 m²	(434 sq. ft.)

DH.51
This was the last of the three DH.51s built and also had the most interesting career. It was shipped out to Kenya in late 1925 and was the first aircraft to be registered in the African state. It still flies today.

ACTION DATA

MAXIMUM SPEED
Once fitted with the Airdisco engine, the DH.51 became a great performer and had the edge on many other contemporary biplanes in terms of speed. It was faster than both the Avro Avian and the Russian Polikarpov Po-2 in level flight.

DH.51	174 km/h (108 m.p.h.)
AVIAN Mk IIIA	164 km/h (102 m.p.h.)
PO-2/U-2	156 km/h (97 m.p.h.)

RANGE
Tailored as it was for long distance flying, it was no surprise that the Avro Avian had a greater range than the other aircraft. The DH.51 had a slightly greater endurance than the Po-2, though the latter was adaptable for military use.

DH.51 579 km (360 mi.) — AVIAN Mk IIIA 643 km (399 mi.) — PO-2/U-2 400 km (248 mi.)

SERVICE CEILING
Compared to the DH.51 and the Po-2, the Avian also had the edge in service ceiling, able to climb to around 5000 m. Compared to the two British designs, the Polikarpov had a poor ceiling, though it was most often flown on low level sorties.

D.H.51 4572 m (15,000 ft.) — AVIAN Mk IIIA 5486 m (18,000 ft.) — PO-2/U-2 4000 m (13,100 ft.)

de Havilland biplanes of the mid-1920s

DH.37: This aircraft has the significance of being the first private aircraft built by de Havilland. Only two were built.

DH 42: Developed in response to an Air Ministry requirement for a fighter/reconnaissance aircraft, it did not enter service.

DH.50: Much larger than the DH.51 these four-seat airliners were used on long-range survey flights to Australia.

DE HAVILLAND

DH.60G GIPSY MOTH 'JASON'

● **Record-breaking craft** ● **Amy Johnson's epic flight** ● **Preserved today**

May 1930 was at the height of the era of trail-blazing long-distance flights, but this one was different. Twenty-six-year-old Amy Johnson was planning to fly from England to Australia. Amy had less than one year of solo experience, but as she set off single-handed in her fragile de Havilland Gipsy Moth biplane 'Jason', she faced one of the longest and most adventurous flights ever attempted.

▲ *Amy Johnson took part in a triumphant procession through London on 8 August 1930, with enormous crowds turning out to see her. Pioneer aviators, especially female ones, were extremely popular.*

▲ **Engine checks**
Amy Johnson had to complete all her own maintenance and repairs during her epic flights. Luckily, the small Gipsy engine was a simple one to fix. Johnson was also a talented navigator, plotting her position by means of 'dead reckoning' and a simple compass.

▲ **Return from the Cape**
Amy Johnson snatched from her husband Jim Mollison the record for flying to the South African Cape in 1932.

▼**A warm welcome**
On landing at Darwin, Australia, Amy was greeted by the Australian Government's chief medical officer, who found her fit but tired.

◀ **Moth skeleton**
The fuselage frame of a Moth was simple, but very strong. The central section of the upper wing contained a fuel tank. The engine installation consisted of a bolted steel tube framework.

Ready to go ▶
Amy Johnson waves goodbye just before setting off. She survived fuel shortages, ferocious headwinds, primitive landing strips and a monsoon, She died in a mysterious accident over England in 1941.

FACTS AND FIGURES

➤ Amy Johnson's target was to beat the 15-day record set by Bert Hinkler in 1928.

➤ Her six-day flight to Karachi knocked two days off the previous best time from England to India.

➤ Maintaining her aircraft by night, she averaged only three hours of sleep.

➤ Returning to Britain by Imperial Airways, Amy found herself a national heroine.

➤ Up to one million people lined the streets as her motorcade made its way from Croydon to central London.

➤ King George V made Amy a Commander of the Order of the British Empire (CBE).

Solo to the far side of the world

Amy Johnson set off from Croydon aerodrome on the morning of 5 May 1930. The first day, leaking petrol fumes almost suffocated the intrepid aviatrix. In cloud over Turkey, she almost hit a mountain, and later a sandstorm forced her to land in the desert outside Baghdad. Covering the engine, she stood guard, revolver in hand, in case she was attacked

by wild dogs. She reached Karachi on 10 May.

Continuing via Jhansi – where she was forced down by a petrol shortage – Allahabad and Calcutta, she crossed the Bay of Bengal to Burma, where 'Jason' was damaged, putting paid to any chance of the record. It took two days for locals to help her repair the wheels and propellers, but she pressed on – only to disappear over the Timor Sea.

Amy had been forced down on East Timor, but resourceful as ever she managed to persuade a priest and local tribesmen to clear a runway. The last stage of the flight saw her making the 800-km (500-mi.) overwater passage to Port Darwin, which she reached on 24 May after 19 days.

Amy Johnson's valiant little Moth can still be seen today, preserved with other famous aircraft in the aviation hall at London's Science Museum.

DH.60G Gipsy Moth

Type: one-/two-seat light aircraft

Powerplant: one 75-kW (60 hp.) de Havilland Gipsy I four-cylinder piston engine

Maximum speed: 160 km/h (100 km/h)

Cruising speed: 135 km/h (84 m.p.h.)

Range: 520 km (323 mi.) (Amy Johnson's aircraft had extra tanks for a range of about 1100 km (680 mi.))

Service ceiling: 4500 m (14,764 ft.)

Weights: empty 417 kg (919 lb.); loaded 750 kg (1,653 lb.)

Dimensions:
span	9.14 m (30 ft.)
length	7.29 m (23 ft. 11 in.)
height	2.68 m (8 ft. 10 in.)
wing area	22.57 m² (243 sq. ft.)

The de Havilland company was unusual in building its own engines. The Gipsy series were built because of a shortage of the Cirrus engines previously used in Moths. The Gipsy was extremely reliable – some RAF Chipmunks used 40-year-old Gipsy Majors until 1995.

To extend the range of the standard Gipsy Moth, 'Jason' was fitted with extra fuel tanks. This fuel had to be manually pumped to the top wing tank. Fumes from this tank caused problems for Amy Johnson on several occasions.

The tail profile of the Moth was retained throughout the family, and is still seen in the sky on the many remaining Tiger Moths. The rudder had no trim, requiring constant attention from the pilot to make accurately balanced turns.

The Moth used a fixed-pitch twin-bladed wooden propeller. Only when the Chipmunk arrived in the 1950s did de Havilland trainers use metal propellers.

The wing was built entirely of wood, with a doped fabric covering. This was very strong and light. The control forces on Moths were exceptionally light, and they were very responsive to the controls.

The fuselage structure consisted of a wooden frame with fabric covering. When flying in remote areas this was susceptible to damage, so the DH.60G introduced a metal-tube frame in 1928.

DH.60G GIPSY MOTH 'JASON'

This was the aircraft used by Amy Johnson on her 19-day pioneering flight from England to Australia. The Gipsy Moth was an improved and re-engined version of the original DH.60 of 1925, and began its career by winning the 1928 King's Cup Air Race and setting a new altitude record of 6090 metres.

AMY JOHNSON

AN ADVENTUROUS LIFE

Born in the English provincial city of Hull, Amy Johnson moved to London in her early 20s. There, she was introduced to flying by a friend and took a job as a typist to help pay for flying lessons. A year after going solo for the first time, she set off on her epoch-making flight to Australia. Hailed as a heroine, she was feted in Australia and on her return to England. Amy, known as 'Johnnie' to her friends, carried on flying and in 1931 made a record breaking flight to Tokyo in another de Havilland Moth. A year later she married fellow aviator Jim Mollison and celebrated by taking 10 hours off his record time to South Africa. In 1936, with her marriage breaking up, she set another record time for the flight to Cape Town, pioneering the route down the West African coast in the process. She then retired from public life. As an experienced pilot and a first-class navigator, she volunteered to join the Air Transport Auxiliary at the outbreak of war in 1939 and ferried combat aircraft from the factories to RAF bases around Britain. In January 1941, at the age of 37, she was flying an Airspeed Oxford, like the one below, which ran out of fuel in thick cloud over the Thames Estuary. Amy's body was never found, but she is thought to have baled out of her stricken aircraft and then died of exposure in the freezing winter waters.

Blazing the Australian trail

■ ROSS AND KEITH SMITH: Flying a Vickers Vimy, the Smith brothers reached Australia in December 1919, after a 27-day flight from London.

■ ALAN COBHAM: Long-range specialist Cobham flew a Giant Moth from London to Melbourne and back between June and October 1926.

■ BERT HINKLER: The Australian officer made the first lightplane solo flight to Australia in 1928. He was killed on a second attempt in 1933.

■ MacROBERTSON RACE: Won by Scott and Campbell-Black, whose de Havilland Comet took under three days to reach Melbourne.

■ NON-STOP: A Qantas Boeing 747 made the first non-stop flight from England to Australia, taking 20 hours on its 1989 delivery flight.

DE HAVILLAND

DH.66 HERCULES

● 1920s mailplane ● Middle East service ● Three engines

▲ From 1921
the RAF used DH.9As for the
Cairo to Baghdad mail service. When Imperial
Airways took it over, they received £87,000
($130,000) per annum for a fortnightly service.

Establishing air mail services to India, and ultimately Australia, was a major goal for Britain in the 1920s. The existing British airlines were amalgamated to form Imperial Airways in 1924, and in 1927 Imperial took over the RAF's route from Cairo to Karachi. A new aircraft was required, and the DH.66 Hercules was selected for the task. The first of five Hercules flew to Egypt in December 1926, ready to start the service the following month.

◀ **Cockpit open to elements**
The first DH.66s had open cockpits. The four machines built for Australia introduced an enclosed cockpit, which was later fitted to earlier machines.

▼ **More than 10 years' service**
Although G-EBMY was withdrawn in 1935, the last South African aircraft served until 1943.

▲ **Joy-rides**
At an air pageant held in Perth in October 1932, a Hercules of West Australian Airways was used for joy-rides at a price of five shillings.

◀ **Imperial's first**
G-EBMW was the first DH.66 to enter service, in January 1927, and was later named City of Cairo by King Faud of Egypt.

G-EBMX arrives in India ▶
Soon after the first Hercules had left for Egypt, the second aircraft arrived in Delhi on 8 January 1927. Two days later the wife of the Viceroy officially named this DH.66 the City of Delhi. Imperial Airways received a subsidy to run a mail service between Cairo and Karachi.

FACTS AND FIGURES

➤ Three engines were specified to minimise the risk of power loss on take-off and during forced landings.

➤ The name 'Hercules' was chosen in a magazine competition run in 1926.

➤ An Australian aircraft in New Guinea was destroyed by Japanese forces in 1942.

➤ South African DH.66s flew courier services throughout Africa during the early days of World War II.

➤ In all, 11 DH.66s were built at de Havilland's Stag Lane, Middlesex, plant.

➤ All 11 Hercules were named after cities in Australia, India and the Middle East.

Imperial's Middle Eastern mailplane

Designed specifically for the Cairo to Karachi route, which Imperial Airways took over from the RAF, the DH.66 entered service in January 1927.

The service from Cairo reached only as far as Basra, in Iraq, until April 1929, when it was extended to Karachi. Later that year it was extended to Delhi. Air mail services had reached Cape Town by January 1932, with DH.66s being used for the journey south of Nairobi.

West Australian Airways

ordered four DH.66s, modified to carry 14 passengers, for use on the Perth to Adelaide route from June 1929. Two of these aircraft were later sold to Imperial Airways, which by this time already had seven aircraft. These two DH.66s were used to establish an air service in New Guinea.

By 1935 four of the Imperial DH.66s had been lost, one of them during a trial mail service to Australia in April 1931. Two more were scrapped, and the remaining three went to the South

African air force. In mid-1935 one of these aircraft was used to drop arsenical dust on locust swarms – a far cry from the glory days at Imperial Airways.

Below: West Australian Airways used four DH.66s for its Perth to Adelaide passenger and mail service, which had an express train connection to Melbourne. G-AUJO City of Perth (later VH-UJO) was its first aircraft.

Above: The DH.66 prototype crashed in 1931 while flying between Karachi and Darwin, on an England to Australia mail service.

DH.66 Hercules

Type: medium-range airliner

Powerplant: three 313-kW (420-hp.) Bristol Jupiter VI nine-cylinder air-cooled radial engines

Maximum speed: 206 km/h (128 m.p.h.)

Cruising speed: 177 km/h (110 m.p.h.)

Initial climb rate: 233 m/min (764 f.p.m.)

Service ceiling: 3962 m (13,000 ft.)

Weights: empty 4110 kg (3,040 lb.); maximum take-off 7103 kg (15,630 lb.)

Accommodation: (Imperial Airways aircraft) three crew, seven passengers and up to 13.2 m³ (466 cu. ft.) of mail

Dimensions: span 24.23 m (79 ft. 6 in.)
length 16.92 m (55 ft. 6 in.)
height 5.56 m (18 ft. 3 in.)
wing area 143.7 m² (1,547 sq. ft.)

DH.66 HERCULES

G-AAJH City of Basra was the penultimate Imperial Airways DH.66 and was delivered in late 1929. It was sold to the South African Air Force for £775 ($1,662) in 1934 and was finally scrapped in 1943.

Mainplane construction followed standard practice at the time with two wooden box main spars and spruce ribs. After initial flights revealed deficiencies in lateral control, ailerons were fitted to all four wings.

In light of experience in hotter climates, Imperial Airways' standard colour scheme was changed from dark blue to a less heat-absorbent all-over silver dope finish.

G-AAJH

All 11 Hercules were fitted with three of the reliable Bristol Jupiter nine-cylinder air-cooled radials. These were also used on other Imperial Airways aircraft, like the Handley Page HP.42E.

Two pilots flew the Hercules, and the cabin could hold a wireless operator, seven passengers and up to 13.2 m³ (466 cu. ft.) of mail. Australian DH.66s had sufficient seating for 14 passengers and more mail.

The fuselage was of tubular steel construction with two large plywood boxes suspended inside to form the cabin and luggage compartment. A wooden structure had been abandoned because of the risk of deterioration in tropical conditions.

The DH.66 had a large biplane tail with three fins. Below this, a skid supported the rear fuselage. The aircraft built for West Australian Airways had a tailwheel, but this did not survive rough handling and was removed in service.

ACTION DATA

ENGINE POWER

The Vickers Vanguard was a 20-seat biplane derived from the Vimy bomber and had a slight power advantage over the DH.66. The Argosy, which was also used by Imperial Airways, was built to fill a need for a Middle East transport aircraft, but served in Europe.

| DH.66 HERCULES 939 kW (1,260 hp.) | VANGUARD 969 kW (1,300 hp.) | ARGOSY II 917 kW (1,230 hp.) |

CRUISING SPEED

Slower than the Vanguard in cruising configuration, the DH.66 had a similar performance to the Argosy, which was also a tri-motored aircraft. All three types were slow even by the standards of the 1930s.

DH.66 HERCULES	177 km/h (110 m.p.h.)
VANGUARD	180 km/h (112 m.p.h.)
ARGOSY II	177 km/h (110 m.p.h.)

PASSENGERS

A contemporary of the DH.66, the Argosy had an impressive passenger cabin capacity. This guaranteed a long service life as the mainstay of Imperial Airways' European fleet until the HP.42 was introduced in 1931. The earlier Vanguard was a one-off design.

DH.66 HERCULES 7 passengers

VANGUARD 20 passengers

ARGOSY II 20 passengers

In Imperial Airways service

AVRO TEN: Avro's Type 618 was, in fact, a licence-built Fokker F.VIIb-3m. The aircraft was so successful that Imperial bought a number of these eight-seater transports.

HANDLEY PAGE HP.42: A larger airliner, with specific versions for Imperial's European (HP.42W) and eastern Empire (HP.42E) air routes, this four-engined biplane first flew in 1930.

HANDLEY PAGE W.8B: Modelled on wartime bombers and powered by two Rolls-Royce Eagle engines, three W.8Bs served on Imperial Airways' London to Paris route from 1924.

DE HAVILLAND
DH.80A PUSS MOTH

● Late 1920s cabin monoplane ● Long-range flights by Jim Mollison

Having designed a cabin monoplane in traditional wood and plywood (the DH.80), de Havilland knew that to gain overseas sales a metal fuselage structure would be necessary. Thus, the DH.80A was flown in 1930. Although marred by early crashes, the Puss Moth's career was notable for worldwide sales and a series of ground-breaking, long-distance flights, some of the most notable being flown by well known aviator, Jim Mollison.

▲ As private
flying flourished after 1918 and pilots ventured further afield, aircraft with enclosed cabins became popular. In this respect, the DH.80A was a trend-setter.

PHOTO FILE

DE HAVILLAND DH.80A PUSS MOTH

▼ **First in Ceylon**
Flown by Neville Vincent, G-AAXJ (the sixth production aircraft) became the first aircraft to visit Ceylon (now Sri Lanka) when it arrived there in early 1931. Note the long exhaust pipe under the aircraft's fuselage.

▲ **Puss Moth on floats**
G-AAVB, the third production Puss Moth, was temporarily fitted with Short floats. It flew the 1674 km (1,040 mi.) from London to the Stockholm Aero Show in 12 hours on 4 September 1930.

Commemorative flight ►
In 1984, this aircraft was flown from Mildenhall, England to Melbourne, Australia to mark the 50th anniversary of the MacRobertson Air Race, in which a DH.80A took part.

▼ **Preserved in Canada**
Built in 1931 for the US Naval Air Attaché in London, this aircraft found its way to Canada, where it now resides as a museum exhibit.

▲ **Folding wings**
The Puss Moth's folding wings were built in two halves and shoulder-mounted to cut down centre-section drag. Shock-absorbing legs on the main undercarriage were attached to the front wingroot fittings.

FACTS AND FIGURES

➤ A Puss Moth in the 1934 MacRobertson Air Race from England to Australia finished third on handicap.

➤ In all, 260 DH.80As were built in England; another 30 were assembled in Canada.

➤ The first trans-Canada return flight was made by a DH.80A.

➤ Amy Mollison (née Johnson) broke her husband's England to South Africa record in a time of 4 days 6 hours 54 mins.

➤ Airworthy DH.80s exist today in the UK and New Zealand.

➤ Several DH.80As were impressed by the RAF in 1939 for communications duties.

Mollison's long-distance Moth

Left: De Havilland designed the DH.80A with a view to improving cabin comfort on long-distance flights.

With private flying flourishing during the 1920s, pilots demanded more cabin comfort as they began to fly longer distances. De Havilland answered the call with the DH.80, a high-wing, wooden monoplane resembling a scaled-down DH.75 Hawk Moth. The Gipsy II engine was modified to run inverted (as the Gipsy III), which improved the pilot's forward view, and the cabin seated two passengers behind the pilot. Only one DH.80 was built. Subsequent production aircraft, known as DH.80A Puss Moths, used a welded steel fuselage structure.

Almost half of the total production run went overseas, initial deliveries going as far afield as Argentina, Japan and New Zealand. Early structural problems (that had resulted in several fatal crashes) were remedied and a second production line was established in Canada. Among notable DH.80A flights were those by Jim Mollison in G-ABXY The Hearts Content (fitted with a 727-litre (160-gal.) fuel tank, giving a 5800-km (3,600-mi.) (range) in 1932. After flying from Britain to South Africa (in G-ABKG), he made the first solo east–west crossing of the North Atlantic. In 1933, Mollison flew G-ABXY to South America from England, completing the first solo east–west South Atlantic crossing.

Above: Jim Mollison crosses the Irish coast near Portmarnock Strand on 18 August 1932, bound for the US. Thirty-one hours and 20 minutes later, he arrived in New Brunswick, having made the first solo east-west Atlantic crossing.

DH.80A Puss Moth

Type: three-seat cabin monoplane

Powerplant: one 89.5-kW (120-hp.) de Havilland Gipsy III air-cooled in-line piston engine

Maximum speed: 206 km/h (128 m.p.h.)

Cruising speed: 174 km/h (108 m.p.h.)

Initial climb rate: 186 m/min (610 f.p.m.)

Range: 482 km (300 mi.)

Service ceiling: 5334 m

Weights: empty 574 kg (1,265 lb.); maximum take-off 930 kg (2,050 lb.)

Dimensions:
span	11.20 m	(36 ft. 9 in.)
length	7.85 m	(25 ft. 9 in.)
height	2.52 m	(8 ft. 3 in.)
wing area	20.62 m²	(222 sq. ft.)

A key to the Puss Moth's design was modifying the de Havilland Gipsy II engine to operate inverted, so that its cylinder heads were no longer in the pilot's line of view. This improved the pilot's visibility and allowed a shortened undercarriage design.

A series of fatal crashes in the early 1930s were traced to wing failure during high-speed flight in turbulent weather conditions. A mass-balanced rudder and ailerons helped to cure the problem.

Using what was essentially a scaled-down version of the Hawk Moth's fuselage, the DH.80 Moth Three was of traditional wooden construction with a plywood covering. Experience with the DH.60M biplane convinced de Havilland that metal construction was essential for overseas sales success. The metal design was designated DH.80A and named Puss Moth.

G-ABXY

The Hearts Content

De Havilland's air-cooled, four-cylinder, 89.5-kW (120-hp.) Gipsy III was fitted to production Puss Moths. For a flight from England to South Africa, Amy Mollison had G-ACAB fitted with a 97-kW (130-hp.) Gipsy Major.

For the long-distance flights made by Jim Mollison, G-ABXY was modified with a large 727-litre (160-gal.) fuel tank in the cabin, allowing a 5794-km (3,600-mi.) range. To make room for the tank, the pilot's seat was moved back and the controls suitably modified. The standard cabin doors were removed and a smaller door fitted below the trailing edge of the wing.

DH.80A Puss Moth

G-ABXY *The Hearts Content* was Jim Mollison's specially built, long-range DH.80A in which he made a number of landmark transoceanic and transcontinental flights between 1932 and 1933.

Mollison's Puss Moth flights

ENGLAND TO SOUTH AFRICA: On 24 March 1932 Jim Mollison left Lympne, Kent in G-ABKG, en route to South Africa via the Sahara and the west coast of Africa. Cape Town was reached four days, 17 hours and 19 minutes later.

SOLO ACROSS THE ATLANTIC: Taking off on 18 August 1932 in G-ABXY, Mollison made the first solo east-west crossing of the Atlantic Ocean, from Portmarnock, Ireland to Pennfield, New Brunswick, Canada in 31 hours and 20 minutes.

FIRST ENGLAND TO SOUTH AMERICA FLIGHT: Arriving in Port Natal, Brazil on 9 February 1933 – three days, 10 hours and eight minutes after leaving Lympne – Mollison became the first man to fly from England to South America, the first to make a solo east–west crossing of the South Atlantic and the first to cross the North and South Atlantic Oceans. Long-distance Puss Moth G-ABXY was, once again, the record-setting aircraft.

ACTION DATA

CRUISING SPEED

Successive de Havilland designs boasted increased speeds as engine power increased. The basic Moth biplane design was developed in a number of directions during the 1920s and 1930s. To provide a cabin version of the Tiger Moth, the Fox Moth was produced.

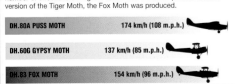

DH.80A PUSS MOTH	174 km/h (108 m.p.h.)
DH.60G GYPSY MOTH	137 km/h (85 m.p.h.)
DH.83 FOX MOTH	154 km/h (96 m.p.h.)

RANGE

In standard configuration, the Puss Moth had a modest range performance, in part because of the extra weight of an additional passenger. For long-distance flights, extra fuel tankage was required. The Fox Moth combined passenger accommodation with extra fuel tankage in order to maintain range.

DH.80A PUSS MOTH 482 km (300 mi.)

DH.60G GYPSY MOTH 515 km (320 mi.)

DH.83 FOX MOTH 579 km (360 mi.)

PASSENGERS

As the Puss Moth was, in effect, a scaled-down version of the Hawk Moth, so the Fox Moth was a small version of the Giant Moth, with capacity for four passengers in an enclosed cabin and the pilot in an open cockpit aft. The design was largely made up of standard de Havilland parts, including DH.82 Tiger Moth wings and the DH.80A's nose section.

DH.80A PUSS MOTH	DH.60G GYPSY MOTH	DH.83 FOX MOTH
2 PASSENGERS	1 PASSENGER	4 PASSENGERS

DE HAVILLAND

DH.89 DRAGON RAPIDE

● Pocket airliner ● Vintage design ● Fabric and fretwork

Designed in the 1930s, the de Havilland DH.89 Dragon Rapide was one of many reasonably successful light commercial transports of the era. But the outbreak of war was to see production soar to keep pace with demand for communications and navigation trainers. After the war, hundreds of ex-service aircraft came onto the market, and the faithful old biplane was to become an important part of the post-war boom in commercial aviation, flying in a multitude of roles from scheduled airliner to fun flier.

▲ The Rapide was a versatile machine capable of many tasks. RAF versions flew as ambulances with two stretchers in a modified fuselage, and others fought local tribesmen in Iraq.

DE HAVILLAND DH.89 DRAGON RAPIDE

▲ Best of British
The Dragon Rapide served with British Airways after the airline bought up many small regional airlines.

Ancient cockpit ▶
Although the Rapide and its relatives served into the 1960s, the spartan cockpit was an ever-present reminder of the biplane's true age.

Gipsy power ▲
The little Gipsy Major was a four cylinder inline air-cooled engine, delivering about 97 kW (130 hp.). The later Gipsy Six delivered 149 kW (200 hp.), and with the extra power allied to a certain amount of streamlining late-model DH.89As could reach a speed of 253 km/h (157 m.p.h.).

▼ Navigator trainer
Military navigation and communication trainers were known as Dominies. These were almost the same as civil models, except for the loop aerial and green paint.

▲ In the Navy
The Royal Navy used Dominies for training duties, and they could still be found as station flight communications aircraft into the 1960s, when they were replaced by Devons.

FACTS AND FIGURES

➤ The prototype DH.84 flew for the first time on 24 November 1932.

➤ The Rapide was proposed as a coastal patrol aircraft, and saw combat as a light bomber in the Spanish Civil War.

➤ Float- and ski-equipped Rapides could be found in Canada, Chile and New Zealand.

➤ The very first Rapide was sold to Switzerland, where for 30 years it flew skiers from Zürich to St Moritz.

➤ During World War II more than 180 DH.89s were produced each year.

➤ The Royal Navy used DH.89s into the 1960s, mainly for cadet training.

The fretwork airliner

The DH.89A was a twin-engined development of the high-performance DH.84 Dragon. First flying in April 1934, its reliability and economy proved popular with small airlines. Officially called the Dragon Rapide but known to most of its users simply as the Rapide, it was soon in world-wide use with operators from the tropics to the high Arctic, and by the outbreak of war

more than 200 had been built.

World War II increased demand for the aircraft, and 521 were completed as de Havilland Dominie navigation trainers. After the war, several hundred surplus machines were supplied to overseas air forces and, stripped of military equipment, to civil buyers.

After the war Rapides could be found working for major government and commercial

organisations, small charter airlines and air taxi companies. They shipped freight in the South American interior, flew businessmen to important meetings around Europe, took tourists on pleasure trips over the Florida Everglades, and maintained island-hopping commercial services in areas as diverse as Scotland's outer isles and the volcanic chains of French Polynesia.

The reason the Rapide remained in service for so long is that many examples were bought at bargain prices after the war, and they proved very economical in operation.

DH.89A Dragon Rapide

Type: six-/eight-seat commercial transport

Powerplant: two 149-kW (200-hp.) de Havilland Gipsy Queen inline piston engines

Cruising speed: 217 km/h (132 m.p.h.)

Range: 950 km (578 mi.)

Service ceiling: 5950 m (19,500 ft.)

Weights: empty 1485 kg (3,267 lb.); loaded 2500 kg (5,500 lb.)

Accommodation: one or two crew, six to eight passengers

Dimensions:
span	14.63 m (48 ft.)
length	10.52 m (34 ft. 6 in.)
height	3.12 m (10 ft. 3 in.)
wing area	31.2 m² (336 sq. ft.)

DH.89A DRAGON RAPIDE

The de Havilland Rapide served with British European Airways after the war, with 45 examples in service from 1947. They served on British domestic routes, notably around the Scottish Highlands and Islands.

Cockpits were generally of single-pilot configuration, with a very basic standard of instruments and controls.

Rapides were driven by two-blade fixed-pitch wooden propellers. The rear of each engine nacelle contained a 273-litre (72-gal.) fuel tank.

The main structure of the Dragon Rapide was a spruce and birch framework with light alloy and fabric skin.

The cabin held up to eight passengers, seated in pairs.

The curved tail of the Rapide was a classic de Havilland feature, which also appeared on the Tiger Moth.

BRITISH EUROPEAN AIRWAYS

G-AFEZ

ROYAL MAIL

The Rapides used Gipsy Six and Gipsy Major engines. The Gipsy Major engine was also used in the post-war de Havilland Chipmunk trainer.

In an attempt to reduce drag, the undercarriage was faired into the engine cowling.

The rudder was covered entirely in fabric.

de Havilland airliners of the 1930s

■ **DH.84 DRAGON:** First flown in 1932, the Dragon was a simple wood-and-fabric biplane identifiable from later aircraft by its exposed wheels.

■ **DH.86 EXPRESS AIR LINER:** Basically an enlarged four-engined Dragon, the D.H.86 entered service from Singapore to Brisbane in 1934.

■ **DH.90 DRAGONFLY:** A smaller version of the Rapide, the four-passenger Dragonfly flew in 1936. It had a wooden monocoque fuselage.

■ **DH.91 ALBATROSS:** Designed as a luxurious high-speed inter-continental transport, the graceful Albatross took to the air in 1937.

■ **DH.95 FLAMINGO:** The company's first all-metal design, the 18-seater D.H.95 was completed just before the start of World War II.

ACTION DATA

MAXIMUM SPEED

The Rapide was in many ways an anachronism, since all-metal monoplane airliners like the Boeing 247 had been flying in America since 1930. But the Rapide was simple to fly, easy to maintain and had excellent short-field capability.

DH.89A DRAGON RAPIDE	217 km/h (132 m.p.h.)
MODEL 247	304 km/h (188 m.p.h.)
LOCKHEED 10	325 km/h (201 m.p.h.)

RANGE

Unlike its bigger DH.86 cousin, the Rapide was designed for short-haul operations. Its range could not match more advanced designs, but it was enough for domestic flights in Britain and around the world, and it was very economical to run.

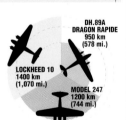

DH.89A DRAGON RAPIDE 950 km (578 mi.)

LOCKHEED 10 1400 km (1,070 mi.)

MODEL 247 1200 km (744 mi.)

PAYLOAD

Early air travel was expensive, and few could afford it. As a result, small airliners of the 1930s could only carry as many passengers as business aircraft of today.

DH.89A DRAGON RAPIDE 8 passengers

MODEL 247 10 passengers

LOCKHEED 10 10 passengers

DE HAVILLAND
DH.104 DOVE

● Light transport ● Executive versions ● Military communications

DE HAVILLAND DH.104 DOVE

◀ Devon down under
With the RAF and the Royal Navy, New Zealand also operated the Devon military variant.

▼ Riley conversion
Sky Tours Hawaii operated five modernised Doves featuring a swept tail and Lycoming engines.

▼ Float equipped
The sole Dove to be fitted with floats was converted by de Havilland Canada and is seen flying over Toronto in 1947. It was quickly realised that the Dove was more suited to land operations.

Indian ▶ service
Three Devon C.Mk 1s, from an initial batch of four, are seen in formation prior to delivery to the Indian air force.

◀ Company transport
Painted in British Aerospace colours, this Dove 8 served as a company transport from Brough in Yorkshire until the late 1980s.

Designed immediately after the end of World War II, the DH.104 Dove was an excellent transport aircraft which was produced to carry passengers over short distances. It was meant to fill the short-haul transport role that had been performed by the elegant pre-war DH.89 Dragon Rapide biplane. The Dove was a pleasing and practical airliner and a general-purpose aerial servant. It was also developed for military communications duties as the Devon.

▲ *As well as having a long and successful career as a short-haul airliner, the Dove was also used extensively by large commercial companies such as Imperial Oil Limited.*

FACTS AND FIGURES

➤ The Dove was the first British transport to use reversible-pitch propellers for assisted braking.

➤ Versions of the Dove were used for pest control and as air ambulances.

➤ More than 500 Doves were manufactured before production ended in 1968.

➤ Apache Airlines of Arizona used much-modified Doves for passenger flights over the Grand Canyon.

➤ About 100 aircraft were built for military use as the Devon.

➤ More than 30 Doves have been preserved in museums around the world.

PROFILE

First of the executive transports

The Dove was an attractive, low-wing, twin-engined aircraft with tricycle gear, which was developed to take advantage of the prosperous market for short-haul airliners that was expected at the end of World War II.

From 1945, the Dove proved that it was one aircraft that had been designed correctly from the start. Production Doves had a dorsal fin (not found on the prototype) and a domed roof to provide more headroom for the pilots, but the first Dove was very

much like the last. Owners, pilots and passengers always had high confidence in this very satisfying aircraft.

Several engines were used on the Dove. It was a flexible and versatile machine, and performed well in most climates. The pilot was not provided with any luxury in terms of leg room or moving space, but he held a commanding view from his perch located about one metre behind and above the nosewheel. Pilots admired the Dove's responsiveness and gentle

Above: The Dove prototype, G-AGPJ, took to the air on 25 September 1945, coinciding with de Havilland's 25th anniversary.

Below: Development of the Dove involved only a minor tail redesign thanks to the excellence of the initial design.

handling qualities.

Although the Dove has now retired from the commercial airline scene, a small number of these fine aircraft still perform charter work and business flying.

DH.104 Dove 7

Type: twin-engined light transport

Powerplant: two 246-kW (330-hp.) de Havilland Gipsy Moth Queen 70 or 298-kW (400-hp.) Gipsy Queen 70 Mk 3 in-line piston engines

Maximum speed: 378 km/h (234 m.p.h.)

Cruising speed: 261 km/h (178 m.p.h.)

Range: 1891 km (1,175 mi.)

Service ceiling: 6615 m (21,700 ft.)

Weights: empty 2985 kg (6,567 lb.); maximum take-off 4060 kg (8,932 lb.)

Accommodation: two pilots, flight attendant, eight to 11 passengers or up to 9300 kg (20,503 lb.) of freight or cargo

Dimensions:
span	17.37 m (57 ft.)
length	11.99 m (39 ft 4 in.)
height	4.06 m (13 ft. 4 in.)
wing area	31.12 m² (335 sq. ft.)

DH.104 DOVE 1

In 1947 Belgian airline SABENA ordered six Dove 1s. Three were used for regional operations in the Belgian Congo, and three for services between Brussels and Deauville.

The de Havilland Gipsy Queen engines were developed throughout the Dove's 14-year production life. The Gipsy Queen 70-3 fitted to this model could produce 246 kW (330 hp.).

The domed roof above the cockpit gave the aircrew sufficient headroom for comfortable operation. Many of the early Doves had a full glass cabin roof to increase the field of vision.

Developed to replace the Dragon Rapide, the Dove was a low-wing monoplane of semi-monocoque, entirely metal construction except for the fabric-covered elevators and rudder.

The only significant design change during development was a remodelling of the dorsal fin into the now familiar curve. This change gave improved control when flying on one engine.

The Dove was initially offered to airlines with accommodation for eight passengers, or 11 with reduced baggage space and no toilet. The successful executive Dove 2 had luxury seating for six.

SABENA
OO-AWD

One company which offered modernised Doves was the Riley Aeronautics Corporation, which fitted Lycoming engines and totally redesigned the tail, fitting an angular swept fin.

Post-war de Havilland airliners

■ **DH.106 COMET:** The world's first jet-engined airliner took to the air in July 1949. Early versions were plagued by a number of crashes.

■ **DH.114 HERON:** The Heron was basically a scaled-up Dove with four engines. Able to carry up to 17 passengers, it first flew in May 1950.

■ **DH.121 TRIDENT:** Designed as a short-haul jet transport, the Trident was eventually produced by the Hawker Siddeley company.

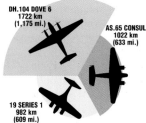

■ **DH.125:** Another design started before the absorption into Hawker Siddeley, the 125 replaced the Dove in the executive market.

ACTION DATA

CRUISING SPEED

Of the three designs, only the Dove was a new aircraft. The Avro 19 was a civilian variant of the wartime Anson, and the Consul was developed from the Oxford. The more modern Dove had a higher cruising speed than its two rivals.

DH.104 DOVE 6	288 km/h (178 m.p.h.)
19 SERIES 1	280 km/h (174 m.p.h.)
AS.65 CONSUL	233 km/h (144 m.p.h.)

PASSENGERS

All three aircraft were intended for the feederliner market and therefore had a fairly low passenger capacity. The Consul was the weakest of the three, being able to carry only six passengers.

DH.104 DOVE 6	8
19 SERIES 1	9
AS.65 CONSUL	6

RANGE

Intended for the executive market as well as being a feederliner aircraft, the Dove had by far the best range performance, giving it greater flexibility. The Avro 19 and Consul could only operate on short-haul routes and were not suitable for executive use.

DH.104 DOVE 6 1722 km (1,175 mi.)

AS.65 CONSUL 1022 km (633 mi.)

19 SERIES 1 982 km (609 mi.)

DE HAVILLAND
DH.106 COMET

● World's first jet airliner ● Long service history ● Military transport

Triumph and tragedy stalked the de Havilland Comet. The world's first jet airliner was so advanced that it had no rival after inaugurating civil jet services in 1952. But when Comets mysteriously started plunging from the sky, detective work on the wreckage revealed a structural fault. Comets were grounded, and headlines called the plane a tragic failure. Although the improved Comet 4 was the first transatlantic jet airliner and flew successfully for many years, the plane was never to live down its early problems.

▲ World War II
night-fighter ace John Cunningham flew the prototype Comet in 1949, revolutionising passenger air transport and ushering in the jet age.

PHOTO FILE
DE HAVILLAND DH.106 COMET

▼ Veteran workhorse
The last UK operator was Dan-Air who used the Comet 4B for charter flights to Mediterranean holiday destinations. After its initial design and safety problems the Comet gave its customers great service for 30 years.

▲ Sleek design
Fitting four engines in the wingroots reduced drag, and gave the Comet pleasing lines. But engineers did not much like this layout, as it gave poor access during maintenance.

▲ Flying the world
A reception committee greets the first Comet to arrive in New Zealand. The aircraft slashed flight times dramatically, establishing jet routes all over the world.

▲ Comet becomes Nimrod
The Nimrod maritime aircraft was derived from the Comet 4 airframe. Entering service in October 1969, Nimrods will be patrolling Britain's coasts for some time.

Airborne radar testbed ▶
The Comet airframe was used as a testbed for an airborne early-warning radar aircraft. The aircraft did not prove successful in this role.

FACTS AND FIGURES

➤ The first production Comet made its maiden flight on 9 January 1951.

➤ The first commercial flights by the Comet were freight-only trips between Britain and South Africa.

➤ Britain and Canada were the only users of military transport Comets.

➤ The Comet 2 used Rolls-Royce Avon engines, as used in the Lightning fighter.

➤ Two Comet 4C airframes were converted as prototypes for the Nimrod maritime patrol aircraft.

➤ The sole Comet 3 introduced the long fuselage used on production Comet 4s.

PROFILE

The world's first jet airliner

When the Comet began commercial jet service in May 1952, it was the flagship of Britain's aviation industry. Apart from its grace and elegance, the Comet was an engineering marvel, almost unmatched in its aerodynamics, structure and propulsion.

The Comet 1 and 2 were the envy of the world until tragedy struck and they began falling from the sky. The inflight destruction of a Comet near Calcutta on 2 May 1953, the first anniversary of BOAC's commercial service, captured attention everywhere.

Two more disasters followed. Eventually, investigators found fatigue cracks on wreckage recovered from the Mediterranean, the evidence of a structural fault. Planes were grounded and production halted. The Comet seemed doomed. But de Havilland made 'fixes' and regained public confidence with the Comet 4 in the 1960s.

Unfortunately, by this time, the de Havilland jet was flying in a world dominated by bigger and faster airliners from Boeing and Douglas, and although it proved reliable and effective, the Comet never achieved the

success that had seemed certain in the heady days of a decade before. Nevertheless, the Comet 4 continued giving excellent service until the end of the 1970s, a remarkable achievement for an aircraft designed in the 1940s.

The extended-range Comet 4C introduced jet operations to a number of airlines in South America and the Middle East. Sudan Airways operated the type until the mid-1970s.

The short-span Comet 4B was designed for short-haul operations, and could carry 100 passengers. It was initially purchased by British European Airways and Olympic Airways of Greece.

DH.106 Comet 4B

Type: medium-range passenger transport

Powerplant: four 46.71-kN (10,500-lb.-thrust) Rolls-Royce Mk 542 Avon turbojets; later Mk 525B

Maximum cruising speed: 856 km/h (532 m.p.h.) at sea level

Range: 3700 km (2,300 mi.) with maximum load, later increased to 5400 km (3,360 mi.)

Service ceiling: 12,500 m (41,000 ft.)

Weights: empty 33,483 kg (73,800 lb.); loaded 70,762 kg (156,000 lb.), later increased to 73,483 kg (162,000 lb.)

Accommodation: two pilots, one or two flight engineers, stewardesses, and 101 to 119 passengers in one or two classes

Dimensions: span 32.87 m (107 ft. 9 in.)
length 35.97 m (118 ft.)
height 8.69 m (28 ft. 6 in.)
wing area 191.28 m² (2,060 sq. ft.)

DH.106 COMET 4C

The Comet 4C was the most successful of the series, and featured a long fuselage and new wing. Middle East Airways was one of many customers from the region to purchase this aircraft.

The Comet was one of the first pressurised commercial aircraft, and once the catastrophic metal fatigue problem was solved it offered passengers a very comfortable flight.

The Comet 4 series was nearly 8 m (26 ft.) longer than the Comet 1. Originally designed to house a maximum of 101 passengers, as a charter airliner in its later life it had a capacity of 119.

The wing was very efficient and gave the Comet a lower stall speed than many contemporary propeller-driven aircraft. Most of it was taken up by a huge sealed fuel tank.

The fuselage was pressurised to give a 2000-m (6,500 ft) cabin pressure when flying at 12,000 m (40,000 ft). Four-abreast one- or two-class seating was the norm.

The Comet originated long before swept-wing data became general knowledge, and the tail was of conventional straight design.

MIDDLE EAST AIRLINES M·E·A   OD-ADT

The flight deck accommodated two pilots, a flight engineer and a navigator.

The Comet's engines were buried in the wingroots. More efficient aerodynamically than 'podded' engines as on the Boeing 707, they were less easy to maintain and upgrade.

The external fuel tank mounted on the lower leading edge of the wing was the main identification feature of the Comet 4C.

Half a century of service

■ **COMET 2:** Serving as a military transport until the late-1960s, the Comet 2 was redesigned following the tragic accidents involving the original civil aircraft. It had thicker skin, and the square-cut windows which had generated the metal fatigue causing the crashes were replaced by oval cut-outs.

■ **COMET 4:** The first jet into regular transatlantic service, the Comet 4 proved itself a safe and reliable airliner. The most successful of the Comets, it was manufactured in three versions and could seat up to 119 passengers. The 67 aircraft built served with airlines all over the world.

■ **NIMROD:** Based on the Comet airframe, the heavily modified Nimrod maritime patrol aircraft has equipped the RAF since the 1970s. One of the most effective anti-submarine patrollers in the world, the Nimrod is still in front-line use. The Comet family has completed more than half a century of service.

ACTION DATA

SERVICE CEILING

The big advantage of the jet over piston-engined airliners is its ability to fly far above the weather. It also creates far less vibration in the airframe than propellers. Passengers on early Comet flights could not believe the smoothness of the ride, compared to the bumping and bouncing of even the best prop-driven machines. It also made good business sense: jet fuel economy improves at high altitude, giving early jet airliners such as the Comet and Boeing 707 transatlantic range.

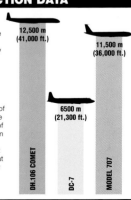

DH.106 COMET	DC-7	MODEL 707
12,500 m (41,000 ft.)	6500 m (21,300 ft.)	11,500 m (36,000 ft.)

DE HAVILLAND

DH.114 HERON

● Based on the Dove ● VIP variants ● Re-engined versions

Responding to the growth in demand for short- and medium-range airliners in post-war Europe, de Havilland designed a larger, four-engined version of the Dove. Named Heron, it was built in smaller numbers than its predecessor but went on to serve with distinction with both civil and military operators. In the 1970s a number of Herons were fitted with Lycoming turboprops and many of these remained in service until the late 1980s.

▲ *The well laid-out cockpit accommodated two pilots with dual controls side-by-side. Passengers were seated two abreast. The cabin had a central aisle and a toilet at the rear.*

DE HAVILLAND DH.114 HERON

◄ In the outback
Butler Air Transport operated the Heron Mk I on mail and air-bus services in New South Wales.

▼ Heron commuterliner
Heron Mk Is of the Belgian airline SABENA established one of the first commuterline routes in Europe.

▼ By Royal Command
Delivered to the Queen's Flight in 1955, XH375 was flown extensively by HRH Prince Philip.

▼ Turbine power
In May 1969 Saunders Aircraft Corp. of Canada flew its first Heron fitted with two PT-6A turboprop engines. Renamed ST-27, 13 aircraft were converted, including this ex-Queen's Flight example which was delivered to Skywest Canada in 1972.

◄ Riley conversions
Named Riley Turbo Skyliners, these Herons were fitted with turbocharged Lycoming engines, which gave improved payload and performance.

FACTS AND FIGURES

➤ The Heron prototype, registered G-ALZL, was first flown by G.H. Pike at Hatfield on 10 May 1950.

➤ With retractable landing gear the Mk 2 was 32 km/h (20 m.p.h.) faster.

➤ A Heron Mk 2B was the personal aircraft of Prince Talal al Saud of Saudi Arabia.

➤ A custom-built version, the Mk 2E, with 12 seats (including four VIP seats) and a galley was flown by Ferranti Ltd.

➤ VIP Herons were used by King Feisal of Iraq and King Hussein of Jordan.

➤ Total Heron production reached 148, of which 52 were fixed-undercarriage Mk Is.

PROFILE

Big brother of the Dove

Two fixed undercarriage Mk IBs were operated by the Scottish division of BEA. Often operating from beach airstrips, they flew ambulance and scheduled services between Scottish islands.

Designed in 1949 under the direction of W.A. Tamblin, the Heron was intended to be a simple and rugged machine, economical enough for short- and medium-range services in areas without properly prepared airfields. Based largely on the Dove, the Heron had four Gipsy Queen engines, which gave the aircraft exceptional short-field performance. After 180 hours of development flying, the only major alteration was the fitting of a sharply dihedral tailplane.

After tropical trials had been completed at Khartoum and Nairobi, production was established at Hatfield. The first example was flown 21000 km to be delivered to New Zealand National Airways.

After only seven aircraft had been built, production was moved to Chester and the improved Mk 2, with retractable landing gear, was introduced. By the mid-1960s the type had seen service in more than 30 countries and many examples had been fitted with luxury interiors for VIP and executive transport duties.

Herons were also operated as air ambulances by British European Airways and as mailplanes in Australia, as well as serving with the RAF's Queen's Flight and the Royal Navy.

DH.114 Heron Mk 2B

Type: four-engined short- to medium-range airliner or executive aircraft

Powerplant: four 186.4-kW (250-hp.) de Havilland Gipsy Queen 30 Mk 2 piston engines

Cruising speed: 266 km/h (165 m.p.h.)

Initial climb rate: 323 m/min (1,060 f.p.m.)

Range: 1296 km (805 mi.)

Service ceiling: 5639 m (18,500 ft.)

Weights: empty 3622 kg (7,698 lb.); maximum take-off 5897 kg (12,975 lb.)

Accommodation: two pilots and 14 passengers (17 passengers if fitted without toilet)

Dimensions:
span	21.79 m	(71 ft. 6 in.)
length	14.78 m	(48 ft. 6 in.)
height	4.75 m	(15 ft. 7 in.)
wing area	46.36 m²	(499 sq. ft.)

The prototype Heron was fitted with a straight tailplane, but testing revealed that one with dihedral provided greater stability and this was therefore adopted on subsequent marks.

The wing was basically a scaled-up version of that fitted to the Dove. It was set at a lower dihedral than the tailplane.

TURBO SKYLINER

When Riley re-engined a number of Herons the resulting Turbo Skyliner gave the aircraft a new lease of life. This example was operated by Sunflower Airlines of Fiji on tourist flights.

Very similar to the Dove, the Heron's cockpit was well-equipped for the 1950s but did not feature modern equipment such as weather radar.

With two-abreast seating, most airliner Herons were configured to carry 14 passengers. A central aisle allowed access for a flight attendant.

The tail unit was similar to that of the Dove. The rounded form of the fin and rudder was typical of de Havilland designs.

Re-engined Turbo Skyliners replaced the original Gipsy Queen units with turbo-charged Lycoming IO-540 piston engines.

The original Mk I Herons had fixed landing gear, but this was replaced by a retractable unit from the Mk 2 onwards. The Riley conversions had the retractable gear.

The upwardly-swept rear fuselage prevented the tail hitting the ground during rotation. A baggage hold and a toilet was situated in the rear fuselage.

ACTION DATA

CRUISING SPEED

Designed 15 years after the ubiquitous DC-3, the Heron had an edge in speed, although in short-range operations the difference was negligible. The smaller, more streamlined Beech Model 18 was faster, making it an ideal executive aircraft.

DH.114 HERON Mk 2D	295 km/h (183 m.p.h.)
DC-3C	274 km/h (170 m.p.h.)
MODEL H18	339 km/h (210 m.p.h.)

PASSENGERS

The DC-3 was a much larger design and was intended to carry more passengers over longer distances than the Heron. The Heron could carry 17 passengers but 14 was a normal load. The smaller Model 18 carried fewer passengers, making it less economic.

DH.114 HERON Mk 2D	17
DC-3C	32
MODEL H18	10

RANGE

All three types could operate short- or medium-range services. Good range was significant for sales in Africa and North America, where towns and cities are separated by long distances. Range was also very important in the executive role to reduce travelling time for businessmen.

DH.114 HERON Mk 2D 1473 km (805 mi.)

DC-3C 1650 km (1,025 mi.)

MODEL H18 1200 km (745 mi.)

De Havilland short-haul propliners

■ **DH.84 DRAGON:** First flown in 1932, the Dragon was the result of a Hillman Airways requirement for a six-seat passenger aircraft.

■ **DH.89 DRAGON RAPIDE:** A direct development of the Dragon, more than 700 DH.89s were built for civil and military customers.

■ **DH.95 FLAMINGO:** Able to carry up to 18 passengers, only one DH.95 entered civilian service before World War II halted production.

■ **DH.104 DOVE:** The Dove was Great Britain's first post-war airliner to enter service, and could carry up to 11 passengers.

DE HAVILLAND CANADA

DHC-2 BEAVER

● Rugged dependability ● Short take-off and landing

Flying in the frozen north presents a real challenge. It takes a very special aircraft to slip into narrow fjords on floats, or to take off from a glacier using skis. Whether you are a cargo hauler delivering people and supplies to remote communities or a policeman enforcing the law over thousands of square kilometres of trackless wilderness, you need an aircraft like the remarkable Canadian de Havilland Beaver to do the job.

▲ *The Beaver is a classic wild-country floatplane. It has an immensely tough high-wing airframe with a capacious cabin, and is powered by a rugged and dependable radial engine.*

DE HAVILLAND CANADA DHC-2 BEAVER

Fishing trip ▶
The annual salmon season brings thousands of well-heeled anglers to the rivers and lakes of Canada. Very often, the only way to the best waters is by Beaver.

▼ On the water
New rules apply when you fly from water. Apart from the obvious like avoiding floating debris on take-off, pilots have to learn tricks such as using the propeller thrust and water rudder to prevent the aircraft 'weather cocking' into wind.

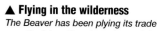

▲ Flying in the wilderness
The Beaver has been plying its trade over the lakes, forests and mountains of Canada's northern wilderness and other countries for nearly 50 years.

◀ Forest fire
The basic concept of the Beaver as a high-wing, STOL-capable transport has been expanded to produce the larger DHC-3 Otter. Both designs have been adapted as fire-bombers, using specially modified floats to scoop up water from lakes.

▲ Amphibian
Deploying wheels within its floats, the versatile Beaver can land on runways. Landing on lakes is actually easier than using a normal runway.

FACTS AND FIGURES

➤ The prototype Beaver made its first flight on 16 August 1947.

➤ Its five-hour endurance makes the slow-flying Beaver ideal for wilderness search-and-rescue missions.

➤ Sixty enlarged, 10-passenger turboprop-powered Beaver IIIs were produced.

➤ The Beaver inspired a larger cousin, the 14-passenger DHC-3 Otter, also widely used for bush flying in the Arctic.

➤ Civil and military DHC-2s have been operated by 65 countries.

➤ More than 1700 Beavers were produced between 1947 and 1965.

PROFILE

Flying in grizzly bear country

The Royal Canadian Mounted Police set an example for all when they carry out bush flying missions with the sturdy DHC-2 Beaver. Designed in 1946-47, the Beaver was tailor-made for adventurous flying under harsh conditions.

With its ability to use wheels, skis, floats or amphibious pontoons, the Beaver can go just about everywhere. Bush pilots use the DHC-2 to haul provisions to remote locations, both in summer and in winter, when temperatures in northern Canada can be as low as minus 40°C (-40°F).

At the height of its career, the Beaver could be found hard at work in every continent, including Antarctica. Superb short take-off ability means that it can operate in remote locations that other aircraft would find impossible.

It is that quality which even now, half a century after its first flight, makes the DHC-2 Beaver a highly effective bush transport.

DHC-2 Beaver

Still in service all over the world, the DHC-2 Beaver remains the classic bush float aircraft, its name being almost synonymous with the role.

The Beaver has an extremely austere cockpit, but it has everything required for its role, including a good view down to the water from the large side windows.

Almost all floatplanes are high-winged, since this gives the pilot the best view of the water. It also keeps the wing free of any high waves during take-off and landing.

The Beaver's long, straight wing configuration gives it a good short take-off capability. This design feature was retained for its larger brother, the DHC-3 Otter.

In plan view, the huge area of the twin floats is immediately apparent. While essential for water operations, they cause a lot of drag in flight. This is why floatplanes are never as fast or as economical as planes with conventional landing gear.

The prominent wires leading to the tail are aerials; good radio communications are essential to bush pilots. Beavers frequently carry long-range HF sets as well as air-band radios.

CF-MPE

Most Beavers are powered by the tried-and-tested Pratt & Whitney Wasp Junior engine, but other engines have been fitted. The turboprop Garrett TPE 331 gives a useful increase in performance.

Designed to house a pilot and seven passengers, the cabin can alternatively hold up to 680 kg (1,500 lb.) of cargo.

The Beaver's fuselage is of all-metal monocoque construction. The door is wider than usual, specifically to allow standard American 45-gallon (205 litres) oil drums to be rolled directly into the cabin, and hatches in the rear cabin bulkhead allow long cargo such as drilling rods to be carried.

Compartmentalised to maintain buoyancy even when holed, the floats are built to withstand the severe pounding they get on take-off and landing. They have small retractable rudders, and are fitted with bilge pumps to flush out the water that inevitably finds its way through joints and seams.

DHC-2 Beaver

Type: light utility transport

Powerplant: one 936-kW (1.255-hp.) Pratt & Whitney R-985 Wasp Junior radial piston engine

Maximum speed: 262 km/h (163 m.p.h.) at 1524 m (5000 ft.)

Range: 1180 km (733 mi.)

Service ceiling: 5485 m (18,000 ft.)

Weights: empty 1923 kg (4,240 lb.); loaded 2313 kg (5,100 lb.)

Accommodation: pilot and up to seven passengers, or 680 kg (1,500 lb.) of freight on strengthened cabin floor

Dimensions:
span	14.63 m (48 ft.)
length	9.22 m (30 ft. 3 in.)
height	2.74 m (9 ft.)
wing area	23.22 m² (250 sq. ft.)

The Royal New Zealand Air Force, one of more than 20 air arms to use the type, used ski-fitted Beavers to patrol the snow-covered peaks and fjords of the country's South Island.

ACTION DATA

PAYLOAD

Light aircraft are a key to communications in wilderness areas, and the most successful aircraft are those that can be modified to carry cargo as well as passengers. The popular aircraft of the Cessna 180 series are, like the Beaver, landplanes which can be fitted with floats. The Buccaneer is by contrast a flying-boat, whose hull provides the buoyancy in water.

DHC-2 BEAVER
7 passengers or 680 kg (1,500 lb.) of cargo

CESSNA 185
5 passengers or 360 kg (794 lb.) of cargo

LA-4 BUCCANEER
5 passengers plus baggage

Water manoeuvres

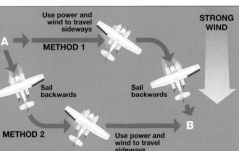

PLOUGH TURN:
Floatplanes, like sailboats, will turn into the wind if left to themselves. To turn across the wind, you need to use a lot of engine power. This pulls the nose high, digging the rudders deep into the water. A small turn to the right allows the rudders to have more effect.

SAILING FLOATPLANES:
In strong wind, you can use two methods to manoeuvre from A to B:

1 Use engine power to taxi across the wind, then trim and cut power and sail backwards.

2 Drift backwards and then use power in combination with the wind to travel sideways.

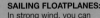

Use power and wind to travel sideways

METHOD 1

STRONG WIND

Sail backwards

Sail backwards

METHOD 2

Use power and wind to travel sideways

DE HAVILLAND CANADA
DHC-6 TWIN OTTER

● Short take-off ● Regional airliner ● Utility floatplane

Admired for its versatility and flexibility, the DHC-6 Twin Otter is a great commuter airliner and utility transport. It was developed in the mid-1960s to provide passenger services to remote airstrips, like those in the hinterlands of Canada where short take-off and landing capability is a 'must'. The Twin Otter also excels at air ambulance and maritime surveillance duties, and is used as a military light transport.

▲ *The smallest of de Havilland of Canada's fleet of short take-off aircraft, the Twin Otter has set the standard by which light utility aircraft are judged.*

DE HAVILLAND CANADA **DHC-6 TWIN OTTER**

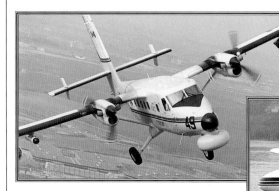

▼ **Float liner**
In British Columbia's lake district, the DHC-6 offers the only way to reach remote areas. All floatplane versions have the early-series style short nose.

▲ **Surveillance Otter**
Demonstrated at the Paris Air Show, this Twin Otter was fitted with a chin-mounted radar for surveillance and search-and-rescue missions.

◄ **Water bomber**
Firefighting is another important role of the DHC-6. Water is carried in the floats.

Brymon Airways ►
One of the many small operators using Twin Otters was Brymon Airways, based in the UK.

Ice skater ►
The British Antarctic Survey uses a ski-equipped Twin Otter for resupply missions in the frozen South Pole.

FACTS AND FIGURES

➤ Engine power of the Twin Otter was increased by changing from PT6A-6 to PT6A-20 to PT6A-27 powerplants.

➤ The US Air Force Academy uses three Twin Otters for parachute training.

➤ When production ended in 1988 more than 830 Twin Otters had been built.

➤ Twin Otters with large 'Vistaliner' windows are used for aerial tours of the Grand Canyon.

➤ The prototype, with PT6A-6 engines, made its initial flight on 20 May 1965.

➤ Twin Otters at Sondrestrom, Greenland, routinely fly in temperatures of -10°C (14°F).

PROFILE

Canada's pocket turboprop

A Twin Otter can handle just about any job. It is the champion of small airlines eager to provide comfort and economy while carrying passengers into remote locations. As a landplane the Twin Otter operates successfully from semi-paved runways as short as 200 m (700 ft.). In its pontoon-equipped seaplane version the DHC-6 is a lifeline for the remote areas of Canada where lakes are more numerous than airfields. Twin Otters also fly routinely on skis in Greenland and on the polar ice cap.

This aircraft was improved constantly during manufacture. As three major versions rolled out of the factory, speed, take-off and landing characteristics, and load-carrying capacity were upgraded. Later series 200 and 300 Twin Otters are distinguished by a longer nose.

Intended for service with commuter airlines, Twin Otters have also seen widespread use with air forces and government agencies. In 1982, DHC offered the DHC-6-300M COIN counter-insurgency aircraft, with a cabin-mounted machine-gun and armour, and the -300MR maritime patrol version, with a search radar under the nose.

Left: Twin Otters are seen all over the world, but especially in hilly countries, such as Chile, Nepal and Switzerland, where short take-off performance is essential.

Above: DHC-6s are vital to many small Third World countries, often making up the majority of some airline fleets.

DHC-6-300 Twin Otter

Type: utility STOL (short take-off and landing) transport

Powerplant: two 486-kW (650-hp.) Pratt & Whitney Canada PT6A-27 turboprop engines

Maximum speed: 338 km/h (210 m.p.h.) at 3050 m (10,000 ft.)

Range: 1297 km (804 mi.)

Service ceiling: 8140 m (26,700 ft.)

Weights: operating empty 3363 kg (7,400 lb.); maximum take-off 5670 kg (12,474 lb.)

Accommodation: two pilots, 13 to 18 passengers (early aircraft), 20 passengers (later aircraft)

Dimensions:
span	19.81 m (65 ft.)
seaplane length	15.09 m (49 ft. 5 in.)
landplane length	15.77 m (51 ft. 9 in.)
height	6.05 m (19 ft. 10 in.)
wing area	39.02 m² (420 sq. ft.)

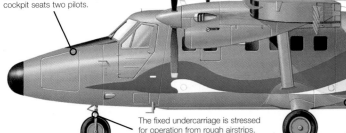

DHC-6-300 TWIN OTTER

Produced between 1964 and 1988, the Twin Otter sold widely to regional airlines around the world, as well as to Canadian operators like norOntair.

This Twin Otter is one of the longer nosed aircraft. The cockpit seats two pilots.

The Twin Otter's short take-off performance is aided by full-span, double-slotted trailing-edge flaps. The outer sections operate differentially as ailerons.

Reliability is a great feature of the Twin Otter, thanks to its PT6 turboprops.

The Twin Otter design used basically the same fuselage section as de Havilland's Otter.

The military versions with nose radar often have extra vertical tailfins outboard to provide greater stability.

The fixed undercarriage is stressed for operation from rough airstrips. Skis or floats are optional.

A special ventral baggage pod can be fitted to the Twin Otter for carrying up to 272 kg (600 lb.) of baggage or freight.

CF-TVP / *norOntair*

ACTION DATA

TAKE-OFF RUN

The Twin Otter has good take-off performance. The An-28 is almost as capable and often flies from desolate airstrips deep in the Russian taiga, like the Twin Otter in Canada's interior.

DHC-6-300 TWIN OTTER	213 m (700 ft.)
An-28 'CASH'	260 m (850 ft.)
Do 28	347 m (1,138 ft.)

RANGE

Twin Otters generally fly short-range missions from one city to another, typically around 800 km. The range figure given for the Twin Otter is with a 1134-kg payload. The Twin Otter offers a useful range and payload capability for a small aircraft.

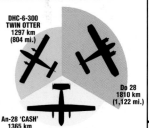

DHC-6-300 TWIN OTTER	1297 km (804 mi.)
An-28 'CASH'	1365 km (846 mi.)
Do 28	1810 km (1,122 mi.)

PAYLOAD

Larger than the Do 28, the Twin Otter can lift greater loads. However, the small An 28 can also carry two tons. The Twin Otter and the Antonov both carry 17 passengers.

DHC-6-300 TWIN OTTER	1941 kg (4,270 lb.)
An-28 'CASH'	2000 kg (4,400 lb.)
Do 28	700 kg (1,540 lb.)

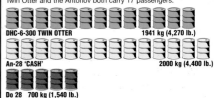

Twin Otters at work

■ COASTAL PATROL: This series 300M has a radar nose and twin rocket pods under the port wing for offensive maritime patrol work.

■ SKI OTTER: This Canadian-registered Twin Otter takes off from a frozen lake on a passenger flight using skis. In summer the same aircraft can take off from lakes with the simple addition of a float undercarriage.

■ SPRAY MISSION: With a large ventral hopper fitted, the Twin Otter can carry out missions like crop spraying or locust spraying.

■ FIRE BOMBER: Another vital mission for Canadian Twin Otters is fire-bombing. Using nearby lakes for a refill of its float tanks, the Twin Otter can respond to a fire in minutes and make many flights a day.

DE HAVILLAND CANADA

DHC-7 DASH 7

● Four engines ● STOL performance ● Low noise output

Possessing an impressive STOL (Short Take Off and Land) capability, the Dash 7 offers the medium level airline operator an economical aircraft that is large enough to carry up to 50 passengers in four-engine safety. Turboprops not only use less fuel than jets, they can also be considerably quieter and the Dash 7 has been particularly welcomed by managers of urban airports where low aircraft noise levels are of paramount importance.

▲ The first British airline operator of the Dash 7 was Brymon Airways. Like many smaller airlines they found the aircraft highly efficient on short haul commuter routes to regional airports.

▲ **In control**
The cockpit layout is fairly conventional. The dual controls allow either pilot to fly the aircraft, with the major instruments also duplicated.

▲ **Four-prop power**
The four Pratt & Whitney turboprops that power the Dash 7 give the aircraft unrivaled STOL performance for airliners in the 50-seat class.

◀ **Island-hopping**
Danish airline Grønlandsfly operated their Dash 7 on flights connecting provincial airports and to islands such as the Faroes.

▼ **Regional airliner**
Dash 7s have been a common sight at regional hub airports all over the United States. Quick turnaround times and a useful passenger load are major assets.

▲ **Best seller**
In the mid 1980s the Dash 7 was probably the world's most popular STOL airliner. This example flew with Norwegian airline Widerøe.

FACTS AND FIGURES

➤ The DHC-7 was announced in October 1968 as the first QSTOL (Quiet Short Take Off and Land) airliner.

➤ The total production run of Dash 7s was 1110.

➤ Customers for the Dash 7 totalled 35, located in 22 different countries.

➤ The Canadian Armed Forces ordered two military Dash 7s designated CC-132.

➤ The Dash 7 is one of the few airliners currently allowed to operate into London City Airport.

➤ The U.S. Army use 'Grizzly Hunter' Dash 7s for drug interdiction duties.

Dashing STOL performer

The first of two prototype Dash 7s made its maiden flight on 27 March 1975, and in basic Series 100 configuration the aircraft's launch customer was Rocky Mountain Airways, which inaugurated services on 3 February 1978. Further development produced the Series 150 and the similar 151 Freighter of 1986 with an increased maximum take-off weight of 21,275 kg (46,900 lb.) compared to the standard 19,913 kg (43,900 lb.). The extra weight was partially taken up by a greater fuel capacity.

The Dash 7's outstanding STOL capability and low engine noise levels made it popular with regional airlines serving some of the more demanding airports in the world, and those like London City Airport, which were obliged to impose strict aircraft noise levels as a condition of the operating license. Among the world's airlines that fly the Dash 7 are Brymon Airways, Hawaiian Airlines, Greenlandair and Air Niugin.

The Dash 7 production lines closed some two years after the takeover of de Havilland Canada by the US giant Boeing in 1986, the decision being taken to concentrate on a twin-engine successor, the Dash 8. The last Dash 7 was delivered to Tyrolean Airways of Austria in 1988.

Amazing short take-off and landing performance allows the Dash 7 to operate from small airfields where other airliners of this size cannot. A long wing fitted with large flaps combined with four powerful engines are the key to its performance.

The tail unit is of cantilever all-metal construction in a T-tail form. The horn balance elevators are cable operated and are fitted with a de-icing boot.

The slightly dihedral wings have double-slotted flaps extending over approximately 80 percent of the trailing edge.

Dash 7

Type: STOL regional airliner

Powerplant: four 835-kW (1,120-hp.) Pratt & Whitney Canada PT6A-50 turboprops.

Maximum cruising speed: 426 km/h (265 m.p.h.)

Service ceiling: 7315 m (24,000 ft.)

Initial climb rate: 372 m/min (1,220 f.p.m.)

Accommodation: 50 passengers (standard).

Range: 1270 km (790 mi.)

Weights: empty 12,534 kg (27,633 lb.); max take-off 21,274 kg (46,902 lb.)

Dimensions:
span	28.35 m (93 ft.)
length	24.54 m (80 ft. 6 in.)
height	7.98 m (26 ft. 2 in.)
wing area	82.31 m² (886 sq. ft.)

DASH 7 SERIES 100

England's Brymon Airways initially ordered three Dash 7s, of which G-BRYA was the first delivered. They primarily served connecting Heathrow to Plymouth, Newquay and the Channel Islands.

The flight crew of two have dual controls fitted as standard. Other pilot aids include an RCA Primus 40 weather radar and a Sperry SPZ-700 autopilot.

Dash 7s are powered by four Pratt & Whitney Canada PT6A-50 tuboprops rated at 835 kW (1,120 hp.). Each engine drives a Hamiliton Standard constant-speed fully-feathering reversible-pitch four-blade propeller of slow-turning type to reduce noise level.

The cabin can hold up to 50 passengers seated in pairs on each side of the central aisle. Emergency exits are provided on each side at the front of the cabin and on the starboard side at the rear.

The landing gear is of Menasco retractable type, with twin wheels on all units. The wheels are fitted with an anti-skid braking system.

The baggage compartment at the rear of the aircraft can carry up to 1000 kg (2,200 lb.) of luggage or cargo.

Under the rear fuselage is a small retractable tailskid. This prevents the rear fuselage touching the runway on takeoff or landing.

BRYMON

G-BRYA

ACTION DATA

SPEED

The high-lift wing which gives the Dash 7 its tremendous STOL performance causes more drag than the wings of its competitors. This drag makes the Dash 7 about 30 m.p.h. slower at maximum cruising speed.

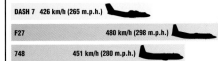

DASH 7	426 km/h (265 m.p.h.)
F27	480 km/h (298 m.p.h.)
748	451 km/h (280 m.p.h.)

TAKE-OFF RUN

The Dash 7's STOL performance is emphasized by comparing its take-off run to that of its competitors. It can become airborne in less than half the distance of the 748 and just over one-third of the distance of the F27.

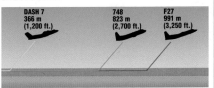

DASH 7	748	F27
366 m (1,200 ft.)	823 m (2,700 ft.)	991 m (3,250 ft.)

ACCOMMODATION

All three types carry a similar passenger load. However, only the Dash 7 can offer passenger services from smaller regional or city airports. Despite having four engines to its competitors' two, the Dash 7 has similar fuel economy with a full passenger load.

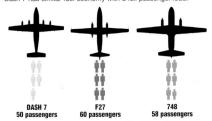

DASH 7	F27	748
50 passengers	60 passengers	58 passengers

Operating from a STOLport

The Dash 7's ability to operate from short runways at small regional or inner city airports with very low noise output is almost unique in the 50-seat class airliners.

STEEP APPROACH: To operate into a city STOLport the Dash 7 adopts a very steep approach path to clear obstacles such as large buildings.

TAKE-OFF: City STOLports have a limited length of runway for operations. The Dash 7 can get airborne with a short take-off run even with a full load.

DEPARTURE: Not only does the Dash 7 have to climb steeply to avoid tall buildings within a city, but it also has to do so within strict noise regulations. The Dash 7 achieves this by using powerful but very quiet engines.

DE HAVILLAND CANADA

DHC-8 DASH 8

● Short-range transport ● Stretched variants ● USAF applications

Since the first Dash 8 made its maiden flight in June 1983, the type has become a regional airline workhorse. The original 37-seat fuselage has been stretched to accommodate 50 passengers in the Series 300, and the Dash 8-400 will have capacity for 70 seats. In the meantime, ownership of de Havilland Canada has passed from the Canadian government via Boeing to its current owner, Bombardier Aerospace.

▲ Launched in 1980, the Dash 8 had attracted 519 orders by early 1997, with a total of 447 delivered. Each costs approximately US $10 million. The type appears to have a rosy future.

DE HAVILLAND CANADA **DHC-8 DASH 8**

◀ **Indigenous powerplant**
All Dash 8s are powered by Pratt & Whitney Canada turboprops. Reversible-pitch propellers are standard.

▼ **Stretched version**
Featuring a 6.83-m fuselage stretch, the Dash 8 Series 400 first flew in early 1998. It has been developed with Mitsubishi of Japan.

▼ **Regional airliner routes**
British Airways Express, based at Gatwick Airport, flies the Dash 8 alongside other regional rivals, the ATR 42, ATR 72 and the RJ 100. In the summer additional routes are flown to Bremen and Luxembourg.

▼ **American sales**
A subsidiary of one of the largest airlines, United, United Express operates 10 Dash 8s, flying feeder services from over 60 US cities.

◀ **Dash family**
Canada's City Express airline not only operates the Dash 8 Series 100, but also its four-engined predecessor, the Dash 7. Here both types overfly the city of Toronto.

FACTS AND FIGURES

➤ With its increased speed and payload the Series 200 is operated by, among others, National Jet Systems for maritime patrol.

➤ Introduced in 1990, the Series 100A features increased passenger headroom.

➤ Canada's military Dash 8s are known as the CC-142, and the CT-142 trainer.

➤ A single Dash 8 Series 100 is used by the Norwegian Civil Aviation Administration for navaid calibration.

➤ The original prototype Dash 8, registered C-GDNK, first flew on 20 June 1983.

➤ The Dash 8 received its FAA certification for civil operations in September 1984.

Canada's capable commuter

Although they may be small in comparison with the big jets operated by the major airlines, modern turboprops lack little in sophistication. The Dash 8-400 will have 3602-kW (4,830-hp.) PW150 engines and an integrated avionics suite featuring large liquid-crystal display screens. Earlier versions of the twin-turboprop were equipped more conventionally. They have found customers around the world, operating as feeders for major airlines, often flying from smaller airports on short-haul, low-density routes whose traffic would not support operations by bigger types, and as corporate

transports fitted with fewer, but larger, seats.

The original Series 100 was available with either 1603-kW (2,150-hp.) PW121 engines as the higher-performance Model 103, or with 1491-kW (2,380-hp.) PW120As as the Model 102. Considerably larger, the Series 300 seats a maximum of 56 passengers and is powered by 1775-kW (3,000-hp.) PW123s. Otherwise, the 300's main change is a fuselage stretch of 3.43 m

(11 ft. 3 in.). Along with the regional airliners, there have been special-purpose military versions of the Dash 8. Canada uses the CC-142 transport and CT-142 navigation trainer, while the US Air Force has two E-9s equipped with a comprehensive avionics suite for range support operations.

The sales potential of the Dash 8 range has been increased by the stretched 300 and new 400 Series aircraft.

DASH 8 SERIES 100

C-GGTO was the fifth Dash 8 to be built and was delivered to City Express in September 1985. Subsequently withdrawn from service and stored at Toronto, it is owned by Canopus.

In typical configuration, the Dash 8 Series 100 carries a payload of 37 passengers in four-abreast seating, plus buffet, toilet and luggage section.

Each of the twin wheel main undercarriage units retracts into an engine nacelle. The nose wheels are steerable, and have Goodrich brakes.

A crew of two flies the Dash 8, with accommodation also provided on the flight deck for a cabin attendant. Avionics include a Primus 800 colour weather radar. The fuselage is fully pressurised and air-conditioned, and the Dash 8Q version features reduced cabin noise.

The Pratt & Whitney Canada PW120A turboprop mounted in each nacelle powers a Hamilton Standard four-bladed constant-speed propeller. A pressure refuelling point is mounted above each engine.

As well as emergency exits on each side of the aircraft, the port fuselage side contains a large airstair door for passenger access, and an inward-opening cargo door aft.

C-GGTO

The structure of the DHC Dash 8 is primarily of conventional adhesive bonded aluminium, but trailing edges and wheel doors are made of strong yet light Kevlar/Nomex composites.

Dash 8 Series 300A

Type: twin-turboprop regional transport

Powerplant: two 1775-kW (2,380-hp.) Pratt & Whitney Canada PW123A turboprops

Maximum cruising speed: 532 km/h (330 m.p.h.)

Take-off field length: 1085 m (3,360 ft.)

Maximum climb rate: 549 m/min (1,800 f.p.m.) at sea level

Range: 1527 km (950 mi.) with 50 passengers

Service ceiling: 7620 m (25,000 ft.)

Weights: operating empty 11,666 kg (25,665 lb.), maximum take-off 18,642 kg (41,012 lb.)

Accommodation: maximum 56 passengers

Dimensions:
span	27.43 m	(90 ft.)
length	25.68 m	(84 ft 3 in.)
height	7.49 m	(24 ft. 7 in.)
wing area	56.21 m²	(605 sq. ft.)

ACTION DATA

MAXIMUM PASSENGERS

Standard seating for up to 50 passengers is offered by the Dash 8 Series 300, but accommodation for 56 is possible in a high-density configuration. The ATR 42-300 is a main competitor.

DASH 8-300 56 passengers
DASH 7-100 54 passengers
ATR 42-300 50 passengers

TAKE-OFF FIELD LENGTH

De Havilland Canada aimed the Dash 7 at specialist operators, with Short Take-Off and Landing (STOL) requirements as a priority. This capability was less important for the Dash 8, which was built to offer a take-off field length of about 1000 m (3,300 ft.), and has similar take-off performance to the ATR 42-300.

DASH 8-300 1085 m (3,360 ft.)
DASH 7-100 689 m (2,260 ft.)
ATR 42-300 1090 m (3,575 ft.)

RANGE

With a maximum passenger load, the Dash 8 Series 300 is able to fly a 1527-km (955-mi.) sector on standard fuel. The ATR 42-300 offers better range, but only with a smaller passenger load, while the more specialised Dash 7 Series 100 offers least range but has a far superior short-field performance.

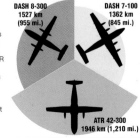

DASH 8-300 1527 km (955 mi.)
DASH 7-100 1362 km (845 mi.)
ATR 42-300 1946 km (1,210 mi.)

Dash 8 civil operators

■ **TALAIR (PAPUA NEW GUINEA):** Four Dash 8s are currently flown in New Guinea; all carry native P2 codes. The Talair aircraft shown here, the 102nd built, was delivered in 1986.

■ **BRYMON EUROPEAN (UK):** Based in Plymouth, Brymon's mid-1997 fleet included seven Series 300 Dash 8s, and two Dash 7s, flying from throughout the UK to Paris and Jersey.

■ **EASTERN METRO EXPRESS (US):** This, the seventh Dash 8 to be delivered, flew with Westinghouse's Metro Airlines before being transferred to Allegheny Commuter Airlines in early 1993.

DEPERDUSSIN

MONOCOQUE RACER

● Advanced construction ● Schneider Trophy winner ● Early monoplane

▲ The company started by a former silk merchant made winning aeroplanes. Most of the famous names in French aviation, like Garros and Blériot, were eventually associated with the firm.

Deperdussin's SPAD company went on to produce some of the best fighters of World War I, but during the last months of peace racing planes carrying the name of Armand Deperdussin were the fastest in the world. With the help of designer Louis Bechereau and pilot Maurice Prévost, his machines dominated the air races and set nine world speed records.

DEPERDUSSIN MONOCOQUE RACER

Powerful start ▶
Like most fast aircraft, the Monocoque owed much of its success to its powerful engine. The Gnome was a 14-cylinder two-row rotary and was quite superior to almost any other engine.

◀ Streamlined
Compared to most of the ungainly aircraft of the era, the Monocoque flew like a bullet.

Ready to race ▶
With an assistant holding the fuselage as the pilot revved the engine, the Deperdussin made a rapid start when racing.

▲ Snapped tail
Not everything went smoothly at Monaco, with the Monocoque's slender, rear fuselage being damaged during taxiing. But after being repaired it went on to beat the rival Nieuport and Morane-Saulnier aircraft.

▼ Still going
This Deperdussin was flown by Wing Commander Kent at the Royal Aeronautical Society's party in 1949.

▲ Pylon turn
When racing, the pilots flew tightly around large marker pylons at the turning points.

FACTS AND FIGURES

➤ A Deperdussin, flown by Eugene Gilbert, won the Henry Deutsch de la Meurthe race around Paris in 1913.

➤ Armand Deperdussin was imprisoned for embezzlement in 1913.

➤ The land-based racers of 1913 often had clipped wings for reduced drag.

➤ Maurice Prévost almost failed to complete the course at Monaco when he initially forgot to fly across the finishing line.

➤ After Deperdussin's arrest, Louis Blériot renamed the company SPAD.

➤ One of the 1913 racers featured unusual reverse tapering on the trailing edge.

PROFILE

Schneider winner

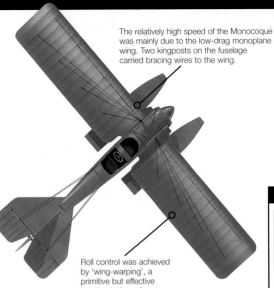

One of the key factors of the Deperdussin aircraft's extraordinary performance was the powerplant. The rotary engine, with its cylinders rotating around a central shaft for cooling, was difficult to control but light and powerful. Another factor was the method of construction. Instead of building the fuselage around an internal frame, Deperdussin's designer saved weight and increased strength by using monocoque – literally, single

eggshell – construction. Three 1.5-mm layers of tulipwood were glued, one on top of the other, around a cigar-shaped mould to produce a fuselage whose skin needed no internal bracing.

The aircraft took first and second places in the 1912 James Gordon-Bennett Cup Race at Chicago. The following year Prévost won the Schneider Trophy Air Race at Monaco, for which the aircraft was equipped with floats.

At Reims in September 1913

Monoplanes were a radical design in 1913 and many designers would not consider building them. The success of the Fokker Eindeker showed just how good the concept was.

Prévost did even better. With the racer fitted with smaller wings, he completed the 200-km (124-mile) race in just under an hour, as well as pushing the world speed record over a 1 km distance above 200 km/h (125 m.p.h.) for the first time.

The relatively high speed of the Monocoque was mainly due to the low-drag monoplane wing. Two kingposts on the fuselage carried bracing wires to the wing.

Roll control was achieved by 'wing-warping', a primitive but effective solution before ailerons were invented.

The cockpit seated two, but when racing only a single pilot flew the aircraft. The lack of a windscreen meant that the cockpit was very draughty.

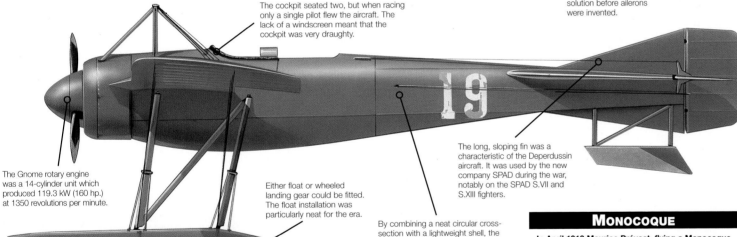

The Gnome rotary engine was a 14-cylinder unit which produced 119.3 kW (160 hp.) at 1350 revolutions per minute.

Either float or wheeled landing gear could be fitted. The float installation was particularly neat for the era.

By combining a neat circular cross-section with a lightweight shell, the Monocoque's designer reduced weight and drag. The lack of internal bracing made it easier to fit control cables and fuel lines.

The long, sloping fin was a characteristic of the Deperdussin aircraft. It was used by the new company SPAD during the war, notably on the SPAD S.VII and S.XIII fighters.

Monocoque

Type: rotary engine monoplane racing aircraft with monocoque fuselage

Powerplant: one 119-kW (160-hp.) Gnome 14-cylinder twin-row rotary engine

Maximum speed: 203.85 km/h (126 m.p.h.)

Weights: maximum take-off 450 kg (990 lb.)

Dimensions:
span	6.55 m (21 ft.)
length	6.10 m (20 ft.)
height	2.30 m (8 ft.)
wing area	9.66 m² (104 sq. ft.)

MONOCOQUE

In April 1913 Maurice Prévost, flying a Monocoque floatplane, won the Schneider Trophy Air Race in Monaco, ensuring that France would host the next Schneider race.

HISTORY OF DEPERDUSSIN

1912 Deperdussin TT observation and patrol monoplane.

Armand Deperdussin was a wealthy French silk merchant who founded the Société Pour les Appareils Deperdussin, or SPAD, in 1910, at Bethernay, near Reims. After Deperdussin was imprisoned in 1913, two talented employees, André Herbemont and Louis Becherau, carried on where he had left off. They designed a number of successful high-speed lightweight monocoque Gnome-powered monoplanes. On 9 September 1912 a Monocoque flown by Jules Véderines won the fourth James Gordon-Bennett Aviation Cup Race at Chicago, Illinois, and further successes followed.

The record-breaking Deperdussin Monocoque Gordon-Bennett Racer.

On 16 April 1913 Maurice Prévost won the first ever Schneider Trophy Air Race at Monaco. He won the Reims Gordon-Bennett race on 29 September, setting a new absolute speed record of 203.85 km/h (126 m.p.h.). A successful year was completed when Eugène Gilbert won the Henry Deutsch de la Meurthe Air Race around Paris on 27 October. In just a few months Herbemont and Becherau had built the world's fastest aircraft and given prestige to the Deperdussin name. By 1914 the company had been taken over by premier aviation pioneer Louis Blériot and named Société Pour L'Aviation Dérives (also SPAD).

A SPAD S.VII C.1 of 'Lafayette' Escadrille, French army, during World War I.

First-generation floatplanes and flying-boats

■ **CURTISS A-SERIES 'HYDROPLANES':** Exhibited to the US Navy by Curtiss himself, the A-1 and A-2 paved the way for a series of successful production aircraft. They flew in 1911, and undertook aircraft-carrier deck trials.

■ **OERTZ W6:** Oertz's W6 Flugschoner of 1917 was an innovative design for the German navy. Powered by two 179-kW (240-hp) Maybach engines, the aircraft had twin sets of biplane wings mounted onto a boat's wooden hull.

■ **SHORT TYPE 74:** One of Short's Admiralty Class floatplanes, this aircraft entered RNAS service in 1914 when Type 74s took part in the historic Christmas Day raid on Cuxhaven, flying from the carriers *Arthusa*, *Engadine* and *Riviera*.

■ **SOPWITH BAT BOAT:** Britain's first flying-boat, the Bat Boat served with the No. 118 Naval Wing from 1913, performing Scapa Flow patrol duties until late 1914. It had an Austro-Daimler, or Green, 75-kW (100-hp.) engine.

DORNIER

KOMET/DELPHIN/MERKUR

● All-metal airliners ● Flying-boats and landplanes ● In service until 1934

▲ *Unusual for their all-metal construction, the Delphin, Komet and Merkur airliners gave good performance and were well equipped for their era. Services were flown by Lufthansa across Germany and Europe.*

Although it might fairly be considered one of the ugliest aircraft ever built, the Do Cs II Delphin (Dolphin), or L 1, led to a long line of German airliners which served faithfully from water and land between 1920 and 1934. Serving mainly in Germany, the Delphin/Komet/Merkur series also sold in modest numbers to operators around the world. A float-equipped Merkur (Mercury) was used on a daring flight from Zürich to Cape Town in 1926–27.

DORNIER KOMET/DELPHIN/MERKUR

First of the Komets ▶
Seated in an open cockpit mounted at the wing leading edge and directly behind the engine, the pilot of the Komet I had a very uncomfortable workplace. The four passengers were accommodated in more comfort.

▼ **Dolphin gets airborne**
Less angular than previous models, the Delphin III seated the pilot at the front of the cabin.

▲ **Foreign evaluation**
During the late 1920s a single Delphin III was evaluated by Britain's Air Ministry. No more examples were acquired.

◀ **South American floatplane**
Syndicato Condor used this float-equipped Merkur on airline services in Brazil. A similar aircraft, CH 171, flew with two passengers from Zürich to Cape Town in 100 hours of flying during 1926–27.

Route extensions ▶
From 2 May 1927, the Moscow-Königsberg route flown by Deruluft was extended to Berlin. The airline was a German-Russian organisation and employed up to nine Merkurs on the service.

FACTS AND FIGURES

➤ Early Komets were powered by 138-kW (185-hp.) BMW IIIa engines, but they exceeded Allied-imposed ceiling limits.

➤ Two designations were applied to the Delphin III: Do L 3 and Do L Bas.

➤ One example of the Komet was flown with the cockpit behind the wing.

➤ Delphin III customers could specify either round or square windows for the rear part of the cabin.

➤ All Lufthansa Komet Is were converted to Komet IIs with 186-kW (250-hp.) engines.

➤ Komet IIIs in Japan were given several Merkur features.

PROFILE

All-metal Dolphin, Comet and Mercury

Even by the standards of 1920, the Delphin was an odd-looking aircraft which paid no attention to the concept of streamlining. Constructed from duralumin and steel, the aircraft seated four or five passengers in the cabin, with the pilot sitting in an exposed position immediately behind the high-mounted engine.

A lengthened version known as the Do L 1a appeared in 1922, with an engine cowling which extended back over the cockpit to form a roof. Further lengthening produced the six- or seven-seat Do L 2 Delphin II,

which placed the pilot in the forward section of the passenger cabin. Like all of the early Delphins, the Do L 2 did not sell well. Dornier's Swiss factory produced a 13-seat Delphin III during 1927 which sold in some numbers.

Both the Komet I and II were basically landplane variants of the L 1 Delphin. The first Do CIII Komet flew in 1921 and both types served faithfully until the last was retired in 1930. Following the trend of Delphin development, Dornier produced the Komet III as a derivation of

the Delphin III. A more powerful engine and minor airframe modifications produced the well-used Merkur, examples of which were built new and by conversion.

Below: This Do L 1a Delphin wears Japanese markings. Several countries were keen to gain experience of the Delphin's all-metal construction, which employed a combination of steel and light alloys.

Above: Two aircraft were used by Ad Astra Aero, the second registered as CH 171. Both were later passed to Swissair, CH 171 gaining floats.

Aerodynamic balancing surfaces were applied to the ailerons and elevators of the Merkur. They were also a feature of the Delphin and Komet.

Komet and Merkur pilots enjoyed few comforts and must have suffered particularly on flights into the Soviet Union. The wing of the Komet III and Merkur did at least provide some protection, the cockpits of earlier Komets being mounted above the wing.

MERKUR I

Lufthansa appears to have operated at least 36 Merkurs, seven of which were converted from Komet IIIs. The last was withdrawn in 1934.

D-1102

LUFT HANSA

BMW VI engines of 335 kW (450 hp.) powered the Merkur and some modified Komet IIIs. The radiator was strut-mounted beneath the engine cowling.

Up to eight passengers could be accommodated in the Merkur, with large cabin windows providing an excellent view of the ground.

Like the Komet and earlier Delphin, the Merkur featured all-metal construction. This was an advanced feature for the period and provoked a great deal of evaluative testing by other manufacturers.

There were few obvious differences between the Komet III and Merkur. The latter, however, had no external bracing of the tailplane. It did have a more powerful engine, and featured a cut-out in the trailing edge of the wing centre-section.

Inter-war civilian Dorniers

■ **LIBELLE:** In answer to an anticipated enthusiasm for seaplanes in post-World War I Germany, Dornier produced the Libelle (Dragonfly) training flying-boat.

■ **Do J WAL:** Built in large numbers and in a confusing array of variants, the Wal was one of the most successful inter-war flying-boats. Early aircraft were completed in Italy.

■ **Do X:** Only three examples of this remarkable flying-boat were built, one for Germany and two for Italy. In 1929 a record 169 people were carried on a single flight.

■ **Do 11:** Few examples of the Do 11 commercial freighter were built. Although a few appeared on the German civil register, it is likely that they saw only limited use.

DORNIER

Do 228

● Twin-engined commuter ● Advanced wing ● Military versions

DORNIER Do 228

◀ Analogue panel
The Do 228 contains relatively old-fashioned instrumentation, rather than a modern 'glass cockpit'.

▲ Maritime reconnaissance
The Royal Thai Navy has three Do 228s equipped to carry out maritime reconnaissance. The radome under the fuselage contains a Bendix 1500 radar scanner. Indian coast guard aircraft also carry radar, plus additional equipment.

▲ Family likeness
The Do 228 uses the same fuselage cross-section as the earlier Dornier 128 – a turboprop version of the Do 28D Skyservant of the 1960s.

▼ Military users
Although the German armed forces make little use of the Do 228, India has become the largest military customer with examples flying with the air force, navy and coast guard.

▲ Advanced wing
Known as the Tragflügel Neuer Technologie, or TNT, the advanced technology wing fitted to the Do 228 was trialled on a modified Do 28 in June 1979. A similar wing is also used on the new Do 328.

With its advanced wing design, which contributes to an excellent range and load capability, the Dornier Do 228 has become a top seller around the world. In production since the mid-1980s, it has been the economical choice of small airlines and air forces in both hemispheres. Because of its versatility the Do 228 has been adapted to perform a variety of roles from transport to pollution surveillance.

▲ The Do 228 has sold well,
especially in smaller aviation markets like the Kingdom of Bhutan. Its rugged yet advanced design has made it a prime candidate for overseas construction and a number have been assembled in India.

FACTS AND FIGURES

➤ Work on the Do 228's wing was partly financed by the German Federal Ministry of Research and Technology.

➤ The air ambulance version can carry six stretchers with nine patients sitting.

➤ By early 1996 227 Do 228s had been delivered to 80 customers.

➤ Over a million kilometres of flying time in the Do 228 helped with the design of the new Do 328 airliner.

➤ Used Do 228 airliners are now being converted into cargo aircraft.

➤ The Royal Omani police air wing operates two Do 228-100s.

PROFILE

Dornier's turboprop twin

Left: A number of special versions of the Do 228 are available, including maritime patrol and pollution surveillance models.

With its drooping nose and bulging main undercarriage fairing, the Do 228 was developed by Dornier (now part of Deutsche Aerospace AG) and was the first post-war aircraft from this famous company to reflect advanced engineering skills.

In fact, the Do 228 was an amalgamation of the basic fuselage design of earlier post-war Dorniers and a new advanced composite wing. From the outset two airframe sizes were offered: the 15-seater Do 228-100, which first flew on 28 March 1981, and the larger -200 series, which took to the air just six weeks later.

By 1986 orders from 40 customers had been received, many from small airlines in Third World states. The Dornier has also been produced under licence by India's Hindustan Aeronautics, while China's Harbin company considered plans to manufacture the aircraft. Sales in the United States and other developed nations have been limited, however, partly due to the aircraft's lack of cabin pressurisation.

An American analysis of the Do 228 concluded that no other airliner can carry the same passenger load over the same distances. Production of the improved Do 228-212 is winding down, although manufacture of the Do 228-201 continues in India.

Below: Being a high-wing design, the Do 228 has an undercarriage which retracts into the fuselage.

Do 228-200

Type: twin-engine commuter airliner

Powerplant: two 533-kW (715-hp.) Allied Signal (Garrett AiResearch) TPE331-5-252D turboprop engines

Maximum speed: 440 km/h (273 m.p.h.)

Range: 2704 km (1,676 mi.)

Service ceiling: 8535 m (28,000 ft.)

Weights: empty 3547 kg (7,800 lb.); maximum take-off 5700 kg (12,640 lb.)

Accommodation: two pilots, flight attendant and up to 19 passengers, or up to six stretchers (air ambulance role) or 2200 kg (4,480 lb.) of freight

Dimensions:
span	16.97 m	(55 ft. 8 in.)
length	16.56 m	(54 ft. 4 in.)
height	4.86 m	(15 ft. 11 in.)
wing area	32 m²	(344 sq. ft.)

Do 228-200

F-OGOF is a Do 228-200 working in the colours of Air Guadeloupe. The majority of Dorniers have been equipped as commuter aircraft.

The leading-edge, wingtips, Fowler single-slotted trailing-edge flaps and ailerons are all of composite construction.

The widely used Allied Signal (formerly Garrett) TPE331 turboprop powers the Do 228.

A Hartzell four-blade, constant-speed, fully feathering, reversible-pitch metal propeller is fitted to each engine.

A flight deck crew of two occupy the cockpit, and the cabin is able to accommodate up to 19 passengers.

AIR GUADELOUPE

F-OGOF

The main undercarriage retracts into a large fairing beneath the fuselage, which saves internal space. Landing lights are incorporated ahead of the undercarriage doors.

The main passenger entry and exit point is the large double door at the rear of the aircraft. This also functions as a cargo door on freight versions.

The fuselage of the Do 228-200 is 1.52 m (5 ft.) longer than the earlier Do 228-100. It is able to carry four more passengers and additional baggage.

ACTION DATA

MAXIMUM CRUISING SPEED

The Do 228 was designed some time after the L-410 and DHC-6 and benefits from better aerodynamics and more powerful engines. It therefore has a higher top speed.

Do 228-200	428 km/h (273 m.p.h.)
DHC-6-300	338 km/h (210 m.p.h.)
L-410UVP-E	380 km/h (339 m.p.h.)

RANGE

The Dornier's fuel efficiency and therefore range have benefited from the design of its wing. The DHC-6's wing is optimised for short take-off and landing (STOL) performance rather than range.

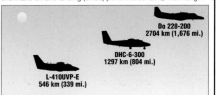

Do 228-200 2704 km (1,676 mi.)

DHC-6-300 1297 km (804 mi.)

L-410UVP-E 546 km (339 mi.)

SERVICE CEILING

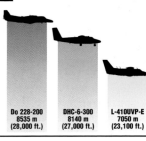

The Dornier has a slightly higher service ceiling than is typical of modern commuter aircraft of its type and size. This is largely a result of the good lifting properties of the wing and the efficiency of the Allied Signal engines at high altitude.

Do 228-200 8535 m (28,000 ft.)	DHC-6-300 8140 m (27,000 ft.)	L-410UVP-E 7050 m (23,100 ft.)

Twin-engined light commuters

■ **DE HAVILLAND CANADA DHC-6 TWIN OTTER:** Building on their single-engined STOL aircraft experience, de Havilland of Canada came up with the DHC-6 which first flew in 1965. Over 800 were built before production ceased in 1988.

■ **LET L-410:** Still in production in the Czech Republic, the L-410 19-seater dates from 1969 and has seen wide use in the former Eastern Bloc, in particular the former Soviet Union. A larger L-610 is under development for the Western market.

■ **BRITISH AEROSPACE JETSTREAM:** A Handley Page design until the company went bankrupt, the Jetstream became a Scottish Aviation product in the 1970s. Early versions used Astazou engines; more recent models have Garrett powerplants.

DORNIER

DO J WAL

● Flying-boat ● Transatlantic aircraft ● Deutsche Luft-Hansa mailplane

▲ With its tandem engines, open cockpit and broad wing, the Wal was an instantly recognisable design. Despite being clumsy and heavy, it set several range, payload and distance records in the 1930s and was exported to several countries, including Argentina.

Dornier's Wal was a superb flying-boat that was probably the most important aircraft designed by Dornier in the 1920s. This big craft established a flying-boat configuration of classic lines that was to endure, in refined form, for many years. With its broad, metal, two-step hull the Wal was also one of the most advanced flying-boats in the world in its era, operating on long-distance flights as far afield as South America and Africa.

DORNIER DO J WAL

▲ **Arctic Wal**
In the hands of intrepid pilots like Wolfgang von Gronau and Roald Amundsen, Wals ranged across the world's vast oceans. von Gronau's 1932 record flight to New York took him over the North Atlantic and the Arctic Circle.

Taifun take-off ▶
Like ships or modern airliners, Wals were given individual names. This Deutsche Luft-Hansa Wal, 'Taifun', is ready for deck launch.

▲ **Wal on the stocks**
Although most Wals were built in Italy, 56 examples were produced by Dornier at its factory in Friedrichsafen.

▼ **Ship launch**
Wals were even carried and launched from civil liners. This Deutsche Luft-Hansa aircraft was launched from the Schlebenland.

▲ **Lion heart**
This aircraft is a Wal 40, powered by British Napier Lion engines. Power for the series ranged from 223.6-kW (300-hp.) to 559-kW (750-hp.) engines.

FACTS AND FIGURES

➤ On 18 August 1930, Wolfgang von Gronau flew a Wal from List to New York in 44 hours 25 minutes.

➤ The Italian-built prototype Wal made its first flight on 6 November 1922.

➤ About 300 Wals were manufactured before production stopped in the 1930s.

➤ One aircraft downed on the ice in the Arctic was rebuilt under difficult conditions and reflown.

➤ Wal services from Stuttgart to Buenos Aires began on 3 February 1934.

➤ The Wal was used in the Spanish Civil War by the Nationalist forces.

Dornier's whale takes to the sea

Built in Italy to get around restrictions placed on Germany after World War I, the Dornier Do J Wal flying-boat soon proved a commercial success and was used on European and international civil routes. Some were built in Japan, Netherlands, Spain and Switzerland before German production began at Friedrichshafen in 1933.

The Wal's star status as a heavy lifter was demonstrated in February 1925 when it set

20 world-class records with payloads of 250 to 2000 kg (550 to 4,400 lb.). That year, explorer Roald Amundsen took two Wals to the North Pole. Wals also featured in a round-the-world flight during 1932, and a record-breaking flight from Germany to New York. In 1934, Do Js began a mail service from Germany to South America.

By the mid-1930s, the Wal was supplemented by the Do R SuperWal, with greater wing span and a longer fuselage. In addition to production by

Dornier, Super Wals were built in several countries. They gave valuable service to a number of airlines, including Deutsche Luft-Hansa, predecessor of today's Lufthansa. In this capacity they were launched from specially fitted-out ships, which served as refuelling bases.

The Wal was succeeded by the Do R2 SuperWal with four engines and which could accommodate more passengers.

Above: This Wal 1 was produced in Italy, with a BMW licence-built Rolls-Royce Eagle engine. The Wal was manufactured by SCMP and its successor CMASA, a Fiat subsidiary.

Left: The 10-ton Wal of 1933 was used by Deutsche Luft-Hansa. Flying from the depot ships Westfalen and Schlebenland, they made 328 crossings of the South Atlantic on regular long-distance mail flights.

Do R2 SuperWal

Type: four-engined commercial flying-boat

Powerplant: four 391-kW (525-hp.) Siemens built Bristol Jupiter radial piston engines (Do R4); four 268-kW (360-hp.) Rolls-Royce Eagle IX engines (Spanish Navy Wals)

Maximum speed: 210 km/h (130 m.p.h.)

Cruising speed: 161 km/h (100 m.p.h.)

Range: 1000 km (620 mi.) with maximum payload

Weights: empty 9850 kg (21,670 lb.); maximum take-off 14,000 kg (30,800 lb.)

Accommodation: two pilots, nine to 19 passengers

Dimensions:
span	28.60 m	(93 ft. 10 in.)
length	24.60 m	(80 ft. 8 in.)
height	6.00 m	(19 ft. 8 in.)
wing area	137 m²	(1,474 sq. ft.)

Do R2 SuperWal

Dornier built 16 of the four-engined SuperWals, this one (D-1337 'Pottwal') being the only one powered by Napier Lion engines. The others had Siemens-built Bristol Jupiter air-cooled radial engines.

One of the imperfections of the Wal design was the very broad wingtip which caused high induced drag. This inhibited its impressive range.

The aerofoil-shaped float sponsons gave the Wal extra stability on water.

Flying the first Wals in cold weather required a lot of determination. The later models at least had an enclosed cockpit.

The tandem engine configuration was most unusual. Although it offered lower drag than separate engines, the rear propeller often felt the strain of the airstream from the forward engine. Various engines were fitted to Wals, including Hispano Suiza 42, Rolls-Royce Eagle, Liberty 42, Napier Lion, BMW VI, Jupiter IV, Lorraine Dietrich, Isotta Fraschini and Fiat R.22.

LUFT HANSA POTTWAL

D-1337

Deutsche Luft-Hansa Wals always had the aircraft's name painted on the front of the hull.

Dornier had a reputation for building very seaworthy flying-boat hulls and the Wals were no exception, as pilot Wolfgang von Gronau proved when landing on rough seas in Greenland.

The cabin was very luxurious and had boat-style portholes.

The long rear fuselage and triangular tail shape was a distinct Dornier trademark. This was retained on the later Do 18 flying-boat used in World War II.

ACTION DATA

MAXIMUM SPEED

Speed was not an outstanding feature of bulky and underpowered flying-boats. Wals at least had more powerful engines to offset this, as did the Beriev MP-1.

Do R2 SUPERWAL 210 km/h (130 m.p.h.)

SEA EAGLE 149 km/h (92 m.p.h.)

MP-1 214 km/h (133 m.p.h.)

PASSENGER CAPACITY

Little could compare with the mighty Wals; even the earlier versions could carry up to nine passengers compared to six in the Sea Eagle and MP-1.

Do R2 SUPERWAL 19 PASSENGERS

SEA EAGLE 6 PASSENGERS

MP-1 6 PASSENGERS

RANGE

The Superwals had very impressive range. The Beriev MP-1 was a similar configuration aircraft, with a powerful engine. The Sea Eagle was a much smaller aircraft and had shorter range.

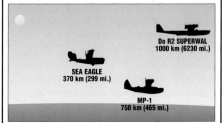

Do R2 SUPERWAL 1000 km (6230 mi.)

SEA EAGLE 370 km (299 mi.)

MP-1 750 km (465 mi.)

Transatlantic record flight

In July 1932 a Wal piloted by von Gronau broke the Transatlantic record. He subsequently made the first round-the-world flight in a flying-boat, taking 111 days.

1 LIST-SYLT: Wolfgang von Gronau set out from List-Sylt on 22 July 1932. He made his first stop in the Faroe Islands, refuelled and set off for Iceland.

2 FROZEN NORTH: He stopped again in Iceland's Seydis Fjord, after flying across the North Sea. The next stop was Ivitgut Fjord in Greenland.

3 NEW YORK: Finally sighting the coast of Newfoundland, von Gronau landed in Labrador and after refuelling he set off for New York, landing just over 44 hours after leaving Germany.

DORNIER

Do X

● Pioneering flying-boat ● Largest aircraft of its time

Today, it is the haunt of holidaying sailors and windsurfers. But in 1929 Lake Constance was the home of the world's largest aeroplane. Created by the legendary designer Dr Claudius Dornier as a trans-Atlantic passenger carrier, the huge 12-engined Dornier Do X was a marginal performer which was never to be a commercial proposition. But it pushed back the boundaries of aviation.

▲ *The appropriately-named Richard Wagner, Dornier's chief test pilot, was behind the huge control wheel of the titanic flying-boat for its first flight.*

PHOTO FILE

DORNIER Do X

The main attraction ▶
The Do X drew great crowds wherever and whenever it appeared.

▲ Innovation
Claudius Dornier was one of aviation's great pioneers. He had many successful flying-boats in the early 1920s, refining the design features that would eventually appear on the Do X.

▲ Luxury accommodation
Flying in the 1920s and 1930s was only for the rich, and the sumptuous interior of the Do X reflects the luxury which they would have expected.

▲ Power
Twelve radial engines made the Do X the most powerful aircraft of its day.

At home on water ▶
The Do X was a boat that could fly, rather than an aeroplane that could float.

FACTS AND FIGURES

➤ The Do X's record passenger load stood at a crew of 10, 150 invited passengers, and nine stowaways.

➤ In its initial form, the Do X took a snail-like 20 minutes to reach a height of 600 metres (2,000 ft.).

➤ The wings were thick enough to allow an engineer access to the engines.

➤ On one attempted flight, the Do X ran for 13 km (8 miles) without being able to lift off.

➤ Even with more powerful engines, the Do X cruised at a leisurely 175 km/h (110 m.p.h.).

➤ The Do X was in the air for a total of 211 hours on its maiden transatlantic voyage – spread over a period of 19 months!

Transatlantic Titan

The only revolutionary thing about the massive Dornier Do X was its size. But this alone represented a huge leap into the unknown.

At 56 tons all-up weight, it was by far the largest aircraft in the world. But in spite of having more power than any aircraft of its time, the Do X was never more than a marginal performer. The huge flying-boat was painfully slow, and took an age to reach its meagre operating height of less than 1250 metres (3,300 ft.).

But the Do X represented Germany's reappearance on the world aviation stage, only a decade after its industry had been dismantled at the end of World War I. And that rebirth was celebrated by an epoch-making maiden voyage, from Europe to Africa, across the Atlantic to South America, and on to New York and back.

The Do X lifts majestically from the surface of Lake Constance on the morning of 12 July 1929.

The huge machine was eventually handed over to Lufthansa, but the airliner was not commercially viable, and never took any fare-paying passengers. It was to end its days in a Berlin museum and was destroyed in an air raid in 1945.

The Do X's successful, if delayed, flight to New York gave a great boost to the German aircraft industry, which was recovering from the crippling blow of World War I.

Do X

Type: experimental passenger flying-boat

Powerplant: 12 450-kW (660-hp.) Curtiss Conqueror nine-cylinder radial engines

Maximum speed: 210 km/h (130 m.p.h.); cruising speed 175 km/h (110 m.p.h.)

Time to height: 14 minutes to 1000 m (3,280 ft.)

Maximum range: 2200 km (1,370 mi.)

Service ceiling: 1250 m (4,100 ft.)

Weights: empty 32,675 kg (72,040 lb.); loaded 56,000 kg (123,406 lb.)

Payload: 15,325 kg (33,790 lb.), comprising 14 crew, 66 passengers; record flight from Lake Constance, 10 crew, 150 passengers and nine stowaways – a total of 169 people

Dimensions:
span	48.00 m	(157 ft. 5 in.)
length	40.05 m	(131 ft. 2 in.)
height	10.10 m	(33 ft. 1 in.)
wing area	250 m²	(2,690 sq. ft.)

DO X 'MONSTER OF THE SEA'

Dornier's huge flying-boat was an attempt to revolutionise air transport. Unfortunately ambition out-stripped available technology, and it was not a success.

The pilot of the Do X sat at the front of the upper deck, behind a large steering-wheel. Smaller wheels controlled trim in flight and the rudder in the water.

The Do X had 12 engines in six nacelles above the wing. The wing was thick enough for a crawlspace, which led to ladders up to each nacelle, allowing engineers free access to the engines, even in flight.

The upper deck was occupied by the flight engineer, navigators, maintenance technicians and radio operators.

The Do X was originally powered by 12 British-designed Bristol Jupiter radial engines, but for the Atlantic crossing they were replaced by 12 slightly more powerful Curtiss Conquerors.

D-1929

The hull and wing of the Do X was of all-metal construction, but the heavy weight and lack of power meant that it could never reach its designed operating altitude.

Large tail surfaces gave the Do X fair stability. For added control, an extra horizontal tailplane was attached to the fuselage.

The Do X was fitted with a rudder at the rear of the keel to enable the aircraft to be steered while on the water.

Passengers were carried in two cabins fore and aft of the wing leading edge. The bar and smoking room were in the bow, and the galley was at the rear. Baggage was stowed aft of the galley.

With the Do X across the Atlantic

■ **DEPARTURE:** The trip was made in easy stages, with calls at seaplane bases at Amsterdam (left) and Calshott in the south of England. Wherever the Do X went, it drew sightseeing crowds.

■ **WEST AFRICA:** In spite of its huge fuel load the Do X had limited range, so the Atlantic crossing had to be made at its narrowest point. On 3 June 1931 the Do X set off from Portuguese Guinea.

■ **FLYING DOWN TO RIO:** Seventeen days later, the Do X reached Rio de Janeiro. The widest part of the crossing, from the Cape Verde Islands to Fernando Noronha, took 13 hours.

■ **WELCOME TO NEW YORK:** Over the next eight weeks, the Do X worked its way up South and North America via the Caribbean. The huge plane caused a sensation on reaching New York.

■ **HOME AGAIN:** After wintering in America, the Do X crossed the North Atlantic via Newfoundland and the Azores. On 24 May 1932 it landed on Berlin's Müggelsee to a tumultuous welcome.

DOUGLAS
DC-3

● Twin-prop airliner ● Most important transport in history

The DC-3 changed the world. No other aircraft has done as much. First flown in the 1930s, this classic Douglas airliner has operated in every country across the face of the globe. It has succeeded at just about every job it has been given, from crop-spraying via executive transport to cargo-hauling. But the DC-3 achieved immortality because it created commercial passenger travel as we know it today.

▲ The DC-3 was a dramatic improvement over passenger aircraft that had gone before. It is a stunning testament to the excellence of the design that hundreds are still in operational service after 60 years.

DOUGLAS DC-3

Commercial pioneer ▶
A Swissair DC-3 heads out over the English Channel on its way to Zurich. The DC-3 was standard equipment with most European airlines in the early post-war years.

▼ Comfortable travel
The DC-3 revolutionised air travel in the USA, offering its pre-war passengers speedy flights and unrivalled comfort.

▲ Still working after all these years
More than 300 civil DC-3s still fly in the 21st century, doing everything from hauling cargo around South America to giving pleasure trips and making air show appearances as examples of flying history.

Military survivor ▶
Variants of the DC-3 continue to serve in large numbers with more than 30 air forces. This is a South African Defence Force Dakota.

▼ Mercy mission
DC-3s have been used all over the world for flying aid missions, including United Nations work. The DC-3 is suited to such work because of its low operational costs.

▲ Heyday of the DC-3
Howard Hughes was the second customer for the DC-3, ordering a dozen examples for Trans-continental and Western (which became TWA).

FACTS AND FIGURES

➤ The 17 December 1935 maiden flight of the DC-3 was the 32nd anniversary of the Wright Brothers' first powered flight.

➤ 10,636 DC-3s were manufactured in the USA, 4878 being built in 1944 alone.

➤ The Super DC-3, first flown on 23 June 1949, offered many improvements but was not purchased by airlines.

➤ Air Atlantique, based in Coventry in the UK, use a fleet of DC-3's as pollution control aircraft.

➤ In continuous service for more than 60 years, the DC-3 is the most important civil aircraft in history.

➤ At least 300 civil DC-3s remain in service in more than 30 countries.

Workhorse for the world

The DC-3 first entered service with American Airlines in 1936, and before World War II conscripted the great Douglas transport for military duty a dozen airlines seized the chance to provide travellers with its unprecedented comfort and convenience. Five distinct series were built for civil customers before the war. Since then, over 100 airlines have flown DC-3s, often using ex-military aircraft from the 10,000 built during World War II.

Originally, the DC-3 was a sleeper transport with 14 double seats which became upper and lower berths. Over time, the interior has carried people and things in every combination imaginable. Sixty years after its first flight, the DC-3 is still flying and working around the world.

Military DC-3s acquired many new names, including Dakota, C-47 and R4D. General Dwight Eisenhower called the C-47 one

Many hundreds of commercial DC-3s are still plying their trade all around the world.

of the four most important weapons of World War II.

The military DC-3 has tackled just about every job, from electronic spying to Antarctic exploration. It has even fought: decades after first donning camouflage, the AC-47 gunship was one of the most potent warplanes used in Vietnam.

The DC-3 was flown by two pilots, with one or two cabin crew to take care of the paying passengers.

The immensely strong cantilever wing was skinned with aluminium. The sweepback of the outer leading edge made the DC-3 easy to recognise.

The DC-3's smooth lines gave it an economic edge. It cost about the same to fly a given route as a Ford Trimotor, but carried three times the payload and did it in half the time.

DC-3 SLEEPER TRANSPORT

American Airlines were the launch customers for the DC-3. They wanted an aircraft which could outclass the Boeing 247s and DC-2s used by their rivals, and the new airliner provided everything they wanted.

American Airlines, today one of the world's largest carriers, was founded in 1934 as a successor to American Airways. The company has a long history of sponsoring major aircraft designs.

The cabin of the DC-3 was originally designed to house 14 passengers in sleeping berths. This was soon changed to an all-seater arrangement, however, with 21 passengers being carried in seven rows of three seats.

The retractable main undercarriage was driven by a hydraulic pump, and took 15 seconds to raise or lower.

The DC-3 could be powered either by nine-cylinder Wright Cyclone or 14-cylinder Twin Wasp radial engines. Each could deliver about 750 kW (975 hp.).

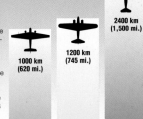

From biplanes to monoplanes: the early American airliners

CURTISS CONDOR: This large biplane was pretty much the state-of-the-art in airliner design in the 1920s, and it was used extensively on mail and passenger routes in the USA well into the 1930s. It could not compete in speed or comfort with the new monoplanes, however.

FORD TRIMOTOR: As revolutionary in its way as the DC-3, the Trimotor was the impetus behind the first great expansion in airline travel. Although uncomfortable and noisy for modern tastes, by the standards of the time it offered its passengers a lot.

BOEING MODEL 247: Flying in 1933, the Model 247 was the first twin-engined, all-metal, low-wing monoplane airliner with retractable landing gear to enter service.

DOUGLAS

DC-4 SKYMASTER

● Four-engined airliner ● Many surplus C-54s converted

A generation of skilled pilots, who had learned their trade in wartime, took the DC-4 on its global expeditions, allowing aviation to truly touch the entire world for the first time. The Douglas DC-4 had the ability to span oceans and allowed intercontinental travel. Although the development of this four-engined airliner was placed in limbo by World War II, in the immediate post-war years the DC-4 was a trailblazer.

▲ *During World War II the C-54 gained an impressive reputation as a transoceanic aircraft. USAAF machines made 79,642 such flights with only three ditchings, one of which was a deliberate test crash.*

DOUGLAS DC-4 SKYMASTER

▲ **Reliable workhorse**
Many USAAF and RAF pilots who had flown C-54s during World War II became airline pilots after the war.

▲ **Dutch Skymaster**
Dutch airlines KLM and KNILM took delivery of both converted C-54s and new-build DC-4-1009s. These were used on routes to the Dutch East Indies after a proving flight in November 1945.

▲ **North Atlantic service**
Air France began its North Atlantic service with new and war-surplus DC-4s.

▲ **Down-under freighter**
The DC-4 was used worldwide during the post-war years. This Australian example was flown by Ansett, and Australian National Airways operated DC-4s on Pacific routes from 1946.

▲ **Pan Am pioneer**
Pan American used the DC-4 to pioneer trans-pacific routes and also for cargo services.

◄ **Preserved in Holland**
This South African-registered aircraft is operated by the Dutch Dakota Association.

FACTS AND FIGURES

➤ Some US airlines painted square black frames around their DC-4s' round windows to make them look like DC-6s.

➤ The DC-4 could fly from New York to Los Angeles in 14 hours 30 minutes.

➤ American, Eastern and United Airlines ordered the first commercial DC-4s.

➤ US airline Braniff used JATO (jet-assisted take-off) for high-altitude DC-4 take-offs from La Paz, Bolivia.

➤ The DC-4 prototype was actually a C-54 and first flew on 14 February 1942.

➤ Canadair built one DC-4 with R-2800 radial engines as the C-5.

PROFILE

Skymaster service

DC-4s and converted C-54s soldiered on with some of the world's smaller airlines for a number of decades.

Designed as a civil airliner but first taking to the air as the C-54 wearing military colours, the DC-4 initially flew in 1942. The dream of new standards in US domestic air travel had to be put aside while the war was in progress, but when military needs receded after 1945 Douglas built 79 civil DC-4s.

These, along with large numbers of ex-military versions, gave valuable service in the United States on long-range passenger and cargo flights and went on to pioneer many transoceanic routes. DC-4s served as the backbone of many airlines until more advanced, pressurised types became available.

Several versions of the DC-4 were built, including those produced in Canada by Canadair as the C-4, powered by Rolls-Royce engines. Both civil and military models are remembered for their contribution to the 1948 Berlin Airlift.

Operators found the DC-4 extremely reliable, which was important on long flights, especially over transoceanic routes when fatigue, bad weather and communications made flying difficult. Although not a match for the DC-6s and Constellations which replaced the DC-4, the type was to see extensive service with smaller airlines for many years.

C-4 'ARGONAUT'

Astraea was one of 22 C-4s delivered to the British Overseas Airways Corporation in 1949. As BOAC's 'Argonaut' class they were used on Far Eastern, Middle Eastern and South American routes until 1960.

As a cost-cutting measure BOAC specified as much British equipment as possible to be fitted to its C-4s. This produced a saving of $200,000 per aircraft.

The main wing had a constant taper to the leading and trailing edges and a cross-section typical of Douglas aircraft with three spars.

Although Douglas sold 79 new DC-4s after World War II, most of the machines that entered service were converted ex-USAAF aircraft. These often retained the port-side cargo door that was not fitted to aircraft built before and after the war.

The original cabin layout of the DC-4 allowed for 40 passengers, or 28 sleeping births for overnight services. After World War II some converted C-54s could carry as many as 86 passengers in a high-density seating arrangement. Canadair C-4s were distinguished by their square windows, which indicated that the cabin was pressurised, unlike most DC-4s.

All three DC-4 undercarriage units retracted forwards; the nose gear into the forward fuselage, the main gear into the engine nacelle.

Four Rolls-Royce Merlin 626s replaced the Pratt & Whitney R-2000s installed in DC-4s. Merlins were fitted with superchargers and had better high-altitude performance. They were also cheaper, as they could be purchased duty-free unlike the American engines.

When loading the aircraft without the engines running, a pole could be fitted between the special tail bracket and the ground to prevent the aircraft from overbalancing.

DC-4-1009

Type: long-range transport

Powerplant: four 1081-kW (1,450-hp.) Pratt & Whitney R-2000-2SD13G Twin Wasp radial piston engines

Maximum speed: 451 km/h (280 m.p.h.) at 4265 m (14,000 ft.)

Cruising speed: 365 km/h (226 m.p.h.) at 3050 m (10,000 ft.)

Range: 4023 km (2,500 mi.)

Service ceiling: 6800 m (22,300 ft.)

Weights: empty 19640 kg; maximum take-off 33,112 kg (72,846 lb.)

Accommodation: crew of five, plus up to 44 passengers, baggage and freight for day use, or 22 passengers, baggage and freight as a sleeper transport

Dimensions:
span	35.81 m (117 ft. 6 in.)
length	28.60 m (93 ft. 10 in.)
height	8.38 m (29 ft. 2 in.)
wing area	135.63 m² (1,459 sq. ft.)

ACTION DATA

CRUISING SPEED

Here, the cruisng speeds of the DC-4 and its predecessor and successor are compared. Intended for domestic use, the DC-4 delivered major improvements in coast-to-coast travel times.

DC-4-1009	365 km/h (226 m.p.h.)
DC-3C	274 km/h (170 m.p.h.)
DC-6A	507 km/h (314 m.p.h.)

PASSENGER LOAD

The larger capacity of the DC-4 and DC-6 allowed greater economies for operators, who in turn were able pass this on to the passenger in the form of cheaper fares. This increased the popularity of air travel.

DC-4-1009	44
DC-3C	32
DC-6A	52

RANGE

One of the greatest improvements of four-engined types was their range performance. Although originally designed for domestic use, the DC-4 pioneered transoceanic routes. Its use was short-lived, however, as new pressurised types like the DC-6 began to enter service.

DC-3C 1650 km (1,025 mi.)
DC-6A 4710 km (2,920 mi.)
DC-4-1009 4023 km (2,500 mi.)

War surplus aircraft for the airlines

■ **AVRO YORK:** The York was designed to an RAF specification for a long-range transport. A number were sold to airlines after the war.

■ **CURTISS C-46 COMMANDO:** The CW-20 was another pre-war design that was pressed into military service and was used mainly as a freighter.

■ **DOUGLAS C-47 SKYTRAIN:** Like the DC-4, the war-surplus military versions of the DC-3 were converted into airliners in large numbers.

■ **LOCKHEED C-69 CONSTELLATION:** Ordered by TWA and flown from 1943, the first 20 'Connies' were impressed into USAAF service.

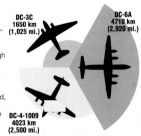

DOUGLAS
DC-6

● Long-range airliner ● Freighter ● Military transport

A beautiful and functional airliner of the post-World War II years, the Douglas DC-6 was a fine aircraft that advanced the contribution made to aerial commerce by the successful Douglas family of transports. When it entered service in 1947, the DC-6 combined a high standard of comfort with long range. Primarily a passenger carrier, the DC-6 also performed well as a civil freighter and, in small numbers, as a military transport.

▲ Based on the successful wartime Douglas DC-4, which had made more than 80,000 transatlantic crossings, the pressurised DC-6 offered greater range and increased passenger comfort.

DOUGLAS DC-6

◄ **Atlantic Clipper**
Pan American used the improved DC-6 on transatlantic routes throughout the 1950s, until propeller-driven airliners were replaced by vastly more efficient jets like the Boeing 707.

▲ **Long service**
Even when it was overtaken by turboprops and jets, the DC-6 continued to be an economic proposition for cargo charters well into the 1990s. Although expensive to run, they were very cheap to buy.

▲ **Airline stalwart**
The DC-6B was the main passenger variant, with 288 being completed and delivered to airlines all over the world. Some were used on scheduled services into the 1970s.

Tourist special ▶
Pan American ordered 45 88-seat DC-6Bs for use on the airline's tourist-class services. Previous airliners had catered almost exclusively to the luxury trade, and 54 passengers was a more normal first-class load.

FACTS AND FIGURES

➤ The DC-6 made its maiden flight in Santa Monica, California, on 15 February 1946.

➤ The first DC-6s were delivered to American Airlines and United Air Lines on 20 November 1946.

➤ Two DC-6Bs were modified with a swinging tail to ease cargo loading.

➤ The US Air Transport Association estimates that first-line DC-6s carried over 100 million passengers.

➤ Total production of DC-6s, including military variants, numbered 704 aircraft.

➤ The final DC-6 was delivered to Yugoslavia on 17 November 1958.

PROFILE

Piston power across the oceans

In the 1950s, when air travel was still an experience available to only a small, well-heeled segment of the population, the Douglas DC-6 offered style and elegance. Seating space was generous, and travellers were pampered with gourmet meals and fine wines.

The DC-6, with its clean lines and straightforward shape, was a development of the earlier DC-4. It offered improved performance and the lowest operating costs of any airliner in its class, making it the most sought-after long-range commercial transport of its time.

It was the first Douglas transport to have cabin pressurisation. Later versions, the DC-6A, DC-6B and DC-6C, introduced improvements in the R-2800 piston engines, passenger accommodation and cargo capacity.

The introduction of jet-powered airliners such as the Boeing 707 in the late-1950s rapidly relegated the DC-6 to second-level routes, but the aircraft remained popular because of its low purchase price, operating costs and reputation for reliability.

US Air Force C-118 and US Navy R6D transports were successful military versions of this fine aircraft, serving troops throughout the world.

Half a century on, the DC-6 is still going strong. In recent years it has worked for cargo airlines like Instone (below) and Air Atlantique (above), which still uses the type from its base in Coventry.

DC-6B

Type: long-range transport

Powerplant: four 1864-kW (2,500-hp.) Pratt & Whitney R-2800-CB17 Double Wasp radial piston engines

Maximum speed: 645 km/h (400 m.p.h.)

Cruising speed: 507 km/h (314 m.p.h.)

Range with maximum payload: 4836 km (3,000 mi.)

Range with maximum fuel: 7596 km (4,700 mi.)

Service ceiling: 7620 m (25,000 ft.)

Weights: empty 25,110 kg (55,357 lb.); maximum take-off 48,534 kg (106,775 lb.)

Accommodation: two pilots, flight engineer and stewardesses; 48 to 52 passengers in standard seating; up to 88 passengers in high-density configuration

Dimensions:
span	35.81 m (117 ft. 6 in.)
length	32.18 m (105 ft. 6 in.)
height	8.74 m (28 ft. 8 in.)
wing area	135.91 m² (1,462 sq. ft.)

DC-6B

KLM operated the DC-6 throughout the 1950s, using the type on the company's extensive route network to Africa and South America.

Early piston-engined airliners like the DC-6 usually had a five-man flight crew on long-haul flights, including two pilots, two flight engineers and a navigator.

Developed from the DC-4, the DC-6 had a new pressurised fuselage of larger dimensions. It was able to carry more passengers in greater comfort than its predecessor.

Passenger capacity of the DC-6B varied considerably. As a luxury transport it could carry 54 people, but this increased to 88 passengers in tourist configuration, or 92 for short-haul high-density routes.

The square cabin windows were a feature of the DC-6 and the succeeding DC-7, replacing the round windows of the DC-4 from which they were developed. They offered a larger glazed area and gave passengers a better view.

After their passenger-carrying days were over, two DC-6Bs were converted to freighters, with swinging tails to allow for the loading of bulky cargo.

PH-DFK

THE FLYING DUTCHMAN

KLM

JAN HUYGHEN VAN LINSCHOTEN

The DC-6 had no radar, although the stretched DC-7 was one of the first commercial aircraft to be fitted with weather radar as standard.

Power was provided by four Pratt & Whitney Double Wasp radial piston engines, initially delivering 1790 kW (2,400 hp.) of power, but later upgraded to 1864 kW (2,500 hp.) with water injection.

The DC-6 used the same 35.81-m (117-ft. 6-in.) span wings as the DC-4, the only difference being a more rugged undercarriage to cope with heavier take-off weights.

The DC-6B was designed as a passenger carrier, and lacked the large upward-hinging cargo doors fitted to most freighter variants.

ACTION DATA

PASSENGER LOAD

The explosive growth in commercial aviation is reflected in the increase in passenger loads of Douglas airliners. Capacity more than doubled in the 15 years between the DC-3 and DC-6, and a decade later the DC-8 was carrying over seven times as many people.

DC-3 — 24 passengers

DC-6 — 58 passengers

DC-8 — 173 passengers

Variations on the DC-6

■ **MILITARY TRANSPORT:** Designed to a military specification, the DC-6 was ordered by the US Air Force as the C-118A. It could carry 74 fully-equipped troops or more than 12 tons of cargo.

■ **GOOD SAMARITAN:** The C-118 could hold 60 stretchers and was often used as a flying ambulance. It was the main USAF aeromedical evacuation aircraft in the early Vietnam years.

■ **FIRE BOMBER:** Several DC-6s have been modified as fire-fighters, with a ventral pannier tank which is normally loaded with fire retardant chemicals.

■ **FREIGHT MASTER:** Starting out as a freighter design, the DC-6 has returned to the role in the twilight of its career. It is used to carry a wide variety of cargo – even light aircraft.

DOUGLAS

DC-7

● Piston-engined airliner ● Improved DC-6 ● Trans-oceanic flights

▲ *In a scene*
from a bygone era of luxury
travel, passengers drive out to the
tarmac to be greeted by the crew of
their DC-7 before boarding for a flight
to South Africa.

L ast of the Douglas propeller-driven airliners, the DC-7 was developed for head-to-head competition with the Lockheed Super Constellation. The DC-7 became a classic in its own right, spanning the world's oceans in an age when air commerce was slower than today, but provided luxurious service. The ultimate version, the DC-7C 'Seven Seas', was slightly enlarged and had very long range, allowing it to cover marathon distances.

DOUGLAS DC-7

◀ **Douglas airliners**
Lined up with other Douglas products, the DC-7 brought major improvements to operators.

▼ **British operations**
Passengers disembark from a BOAC-operated DC-7 after returning to one of London's airports.

▲ **All American operations**
DC-7s were supplied to American airline operators in the process of establishing themselves in what was a growing market. Pan American operated the type as the 'Super 7'; orders also came from overseas.

▲ **Graceful lines**
Displaying the beauty that only piston airliners possessed, a DC-7 sets out on a long flight.

◀ **Second hand**
After serving as airliners many aircraft were sold to be used as cargo carriers in the Third World.

FACTS AND FIGURES

➤ The initial DC-7 was a direct development of the DC-6B with the fuselage lengthened for extra seats.

➤ Total production of DC-7s amounted to 337 of all variants.

➤ A non-stop route between London and New York began on 13 June 1955.

➤ In the late 1990s fewer than 10 DC-7's remained in service, as cargo aircraft in South America and Africa.

➤ Some aircraft had an under-fuselage tank fitted and were used for fire-fighting.

➤ The DC-7 was eventually replaced by the jet-powered Douglas DC-8.

PROFILE

Transatlantic pioneer

Entering service in 1953, the Douglas DC-7 was the jewel in the crown of a dynasty of Douglas passenger aircraft. It was created to compete with Lockheed's Super Constellation, but as it turned out, the two aircraft represented the pinnacle of the development of piston-engined airliners.

American Airlines was the first purchaser of the DC-7, a direct development of the successful DC-6B. Its Wright Turbo-Compound engines added exhaust 'push' to the thrust provided by propellers. Many

users bought DC-7s with greater fuel capacity, among them Pan American which inaugurated a non-stop London-New York service on 13 June 1955. Even then, more fuel capacity was needed. To improve the reach of this airliner, Douglas created the DC-7C 'Seven Seas' version with longer 'legs'.

Although the DC-7 series was popular, its operating costs were comparatively high, largely because of its complicated engines. DC-7s were soon replaced by the first turboprop- and turbojet-powered machines.

Above: With its cargo doors open, a DC-7 is loaded with supplies for a flight to South America. Many small airlines operated the aircraft in the transport role.

Right: Resplendent in a blue and white airliner finish, an early production DC-7B climbs high into the sky for a transatlantic flight.

DC-7C

Type: passenger transport

Powerplant: four 2535-kW (3,400-hp.) Wright R-3350-18EA-1 Turbo-Compound radial piston engines

Maximum speed: 653 km/h (405 m.p.h.) at 6615 m (21,700 ft.)

Accommodation: 189 passengers plus crew

Initial climb rate: 536 m/min (21,700 ft.)

Range: 7410 km (4,600 mi.) with maximum payload; 9075 km (5,626 mi.) with maximum fuel

Service ceiling: 6615 m (21,700 ft.)

Weights: empty 33,005 kg (72,611 lb.); maximum take-off 64,864 kg (142,700 lb.)

Dimensions:
span	38.86 m (127 ft. 5 in.)
length	34.21 m (112 ft. 3 in.)
height	9.70 m (31 ft. 10 in.)
wing area	152.08 m² (1,636 sq.ft.)

DC-7C

The flight deck of the aircraft remained similar throughout the DC-7 series and allowed pilots to convert from earlier Douglas aircraft with ease.

With a stretched fuselage, the passenger cabin of the DC-7 was spacious compared to that of the DC-6. This was an advantage on long transatlantic flights. Passenger comfort was an important feature.

Delivered to Pan American World Airways in 1956 this DC-7 was known as the *Clipper Blue Jacket*. After sterling service it was sold to an operator in Bermuda, where the aircraft was written-off in an accident.

To allow the aircraft to operate at higher weights, various structural modifications were made to the DC-7. One of these was an increase in the height of the tail.

Many airline operators name their aircraft to increase publicity for their expanding fleets. Pan American World Airways was a leader in this field, painting names on the noses of all its aircraft.

The four Wright engines proved to be unreliable on early versions on the aircraft, but after modifications requested by operators a satisfactory level of performance was achieved. Compared to later jet engines, maintenance turned out to be costly, however.

After being retired as commercial airliners many DC-7s found themselves serving as cargo aircraft on shorter domestic routes in South America. This often necessitated the installation of two large cargo doors on the left side of the fuselage.

ACTION DATA

MAXIMUM SPEED

Steady advances in piston engine design saw a gradual increase in the speeds of post-war airliners. The DC-7 offered a vast improvement compared to the wartime DC-3, but both were eventually superseded by the new jet powered DC-8.

DC-7C	653 km/h (405 m.p.h.)
DC-3C	274 km/h (170 m.p.h.)
DC-8-50	932 km/h (578 m.p.h.)

MAXIMUM RANGE

An increase in range offered airliner operators a wider choice of destinations. The DC-7 brought with it the ability routinely to fly non-stop across the Atlantic and over many Pacific routes. Gradual development of the aircraft saw the fuel load increased allowing further destinations to be reached. The DC-3 was not able to compete.

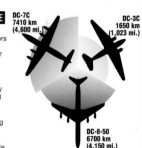

DC-7C 7410 km (4,600 mi.)
DC-3C 1650 km (1,023 mi.)
DC-8-50 6700 km (4,150 mi.)

PASSENGERS

As the power of the engines increased, so airliners became larger, allowing an increase in passenger loads. The small size of the DC-3 is obvious when compared to the later Douglas products such as the DC-7.

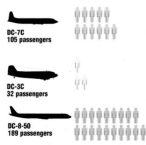

DC-7C 105 passengers
DC-3C 32 passengers
DC-8-50 189 passengers

Douglas airliner family

DC-3: After achieving legendary status during World War II, the civilian DC-3 variant continues to serve with various airlines.

DC-4: Developed from the DC-3 to offer improved range and a larger load capability the DC-4 operated with many non-US airlines.

DC-6: Having served its time as an airliner this example now operates as a 'fire-bomber', fighting forest fires in France.

DC-8: The first Douglas jet airliner brought an end to its propeller-driven airliners. Reduced operating costs were a vital feature.

DOUGLAS
DC-8

● Four-jet airliner ● Long-serving cargo carrier ● Rival of the 707

▲ Technically just as good as its rivals, the DC-8 had a mixed history. Airline economics meant that it was often worth more second-hand in the late 1960s than when it was first built.

Airlines converted from propellers to jets with two aircraft, the Douglas DC-8 and the Boeing Model 707. Douglas leaped into the jet transport field with great success, even though it had no indirect subsidy from the US military, which Boeing received for its jet tankers. It seemed as though the DC-8 had lost the edge to the Boeing 707, but with modifications it has had a longer career, especially as a freighter.

DOUGLAS DC-8

▲ Swissair into the jet age
Having used Douglas turboprops, Swissair chose the DC-8 to go into the jet age, with the first aircraft entering service in 1960. The airline also ordered the rival Convair 880, which was less cost effective.

▲ Ground school
Learning to fly a DC-8 with United Airlines meant starting on the ground. With 30 aircraft refitted, United was the biggest customer for the re-engined DC-8 Super 71.

▼ San Francisco
American operators acquired many second-hand DC-8s in the 1960s. This group is at San Francisco airport in 1967.

▲ Ageing flight deck
The technology of flight decks in the 1950s was a long way from modern aircraft, with simple dials and switches and no screens.

▲ Freight hauler
Cargolux was one of many airlines that bought up DC-8s for freight operations. These aircraft, which were not re-engined, were replaced by Boeing 747s in the late 1980s.

Big and noisy ▶
Built with Rolls-Royce Conway or Pratt & Whitney JT4 engines, DC-8s were thirsty and noisy, but many have been fitted with the quiet and efficient CFM-56.

FACTS AND FIGURES

➤ The DC-8 prototype first flew on 30 May 1958 at Edwards air base in California.

➤ The DC-8 entered service in September 1959, but at first lacked range.

➤ In August 1961 a DC-8 became the first jetliner to fly faster than sound by diving steeply from 15,877 m (52,000 ft.).

➤ The DC-8 Super 61 flew in March 1966, the first of many stretched models.

➤ The stretched DC-8 had the longest range of any jetliner when United used it on Baltimore – Honolulu flights.

➤ A single DC-8 is operated by the US Navy as an electronic research aircraft.

Douglas flies into the jet age

Douglas' long experience with passenger travel was epitomised by the great DC-8 family of successful jetliners, from the elegant prototype of 1958 to the 'stretched' Super 60/70 series, many of which still fly today with secondary users.

The DC-8 was a more conservative design than the rival Boeing 707, with a less swept wing and no leading-edge lift devices and, unusually for the time, no wing fences or vortex generators. It was slightly cheaper, and the later-series aircraft introduced in the mid-1960s had very long range.

With the oil crisis of 1973, the DC-8 gained new popularity because it was the biggest narrow-body aircraft available. Though production ended in 1972, second-hand aircraft with low airframe hours were trading at high prices.

New noise regulations drafted in the 1970s threatened to put many DC-8s out of business before their time, so many were re-engined in the early 1980s with CFM-56 engines. Once again the DC-8 made a come-back, with 'scrap value' examples suddenly in demand as freighters. Many still fly today, some with modernised cockpits and engine 'hush kits'.

The DC-8 was never as successful as the rival Boeing 707, but it has gained a niche of its own, especially with new engines. The development of wide bodies meant that it was obsolete by the 1970s.

DC-8 Super 63

Type: long-range transport

Powerplant: four 84.52-kN (19,000-lb.-thrust) Pratt & Whitney JT3D-7 turbofans

Maximum cruising speed: 966 km/h (599 m.p.h.) at 9145 m (30,000 ft.)

Range: with max. payload 7242 km (4,490 mi.)

Service ceiling: about 12,690 m (42,000 ft.)

Weights: empty 69,739 kg (153,426 lb.); loaded 158,760 kg (502,698 lb.)

Accommodation: as a freighter, maximum payload over short distances up to 52,000 kg (114,400 lb.); as an airliner, up to 259 passengers depending on configuration

Dimensions:
span	45.24 m (148 ft. 5 in.)
length	57.12 m (187 ft. 4 in.)
height	12.93 m (42 ft. 5 in.)
wing area	271.92 m² (2,926 sq.ft.)

Many early DC-8s had a navigator as well as a pilot, co-pilot and flight engineer. United Parcels Service has upgraded its DC-8s with advanced EFIS cockpits.

DC-8 SERIES 30

KLM Royal Dutch Airlines began using the DC-8 in 1960, and subsequently used Series 30, 53 and Super 63 variants on services to New York, Sydney and Tokyo. They were replaced by Airbus A310s in 1983.

Five small spoilers were mounted ahead of the flap sections. These automatically activated when the nosewheel hit the ground, to destroy any remaining wing lift on landing.

The DC-8 had an unusual aileron arrangement. The aileron consisted of two parts, the outer being used only at low speeds. Tabs were mounted on the inner sections.

The tail was a three-spar unit with a full-span one-piece rudder. It housed the aerials for the HF and VHF radios and the VOR navigation system.

KLM ROYAL DUTCH AIRLINES

PH-DCD

Small cheek inlets admitted air for the air-conditioning system. A weather radar dish was housed in the nose behind a black dielectric radome.

Large baggage holds were provided forward and aft of the wing, with a combined capacity of 36 m³ (1,272 cu. ft.). The doors were on the starboard side.

The DC-8 was most commonly powered by Pratt & Whitney engines. The JT3D had distinct half cowls that ejected bypass air from the compressor.

The wing was virtually one enormous fuel tank between the spars, containing 87,360 litres (23,000 gal.) of fuel.

The fuselage was of double circular section, with the upper lobe being of greater diameter than the lower lobe, giving the characteristic 'pinched' look to the airframe.

ACTION DATA

PASSENGER CAPACITY

Airliners designed in the late 1950s were intended to have a passenger capacity of around 120. The unprecedented rise in demand for air transport saw larger, longer versions quickly put into production, with much more densely packed seating. None of the big four-jets were stretched as far as the DC-8, however, which could carry more passengers than any other airliner until the arrival of the wide-body jets in the 1970s.

707-320B	189 passengers
DC-8 SUPER 63	259 passengers
SUPER VC10	187 passengers

Stretching the DC-8

■ **DC-8 SERIES 10:** The first models of the DC-8 were all of the same size, variations being largely confined to powerplant, fuel capacity and range. Pan American were the first users of the type, flying 20 Series 10 aircraft on domestic routes.

■ **DC-8 SERIES 61 and SERIES 63:** Douglas offered a stretched version of the DC-8 in the mid-1960s, to compete with Boeing. The Series 61 and 63 models were 11.18 m (36 ft. 8 in.) longer than the original and could carry 259 passengers.

■ **DC-8 SERIES 62:** Stretched only by 2.03 m (6 ft. 8 in.), the Series 62 had extra fuel and aerodynamic refinements to give a very long range. The Series 63 incorporated the same improvements with the long fuselage of the Series 61.

DOUGLAS DC-8

CARGO CARRYING

● Cargo flyer ● Converted airliner ● Upgraded engines

▲ *The air cargo industry became a vital source of extra revenue for most airlines in the 1980s, because the profit margins on passenger flights were so low. This gave the DC-8 a new lease of life.*

One of the first long-range jet airliners, the Douglas DC-8, like its great rival the Boeing 707, still does a valuable job hauling cargo and equipment around the world. Introduced in 1958, the DC-8 was a pioneer of the jet age. Although most of the passengers have long gone to newer aircraft, the DC-8 has established itself as a winner in its second career as a freighter with new engines and refitted cargo bays.

DOUGLAS DC-8

▶ United Parcels
UPS was one of the most prolific users of the modified DC-8s. Specialist cargo carriers like UPS, Federal Express and Cargosur were very keen to acquire DC-8-62 airframes during the 1980s.

◀ Loading up
Typical of the air freight carried by the DC-8 are these small palletised loads. Although capable of lifting heavy weights, the DC-8 cannot carry large objects.

▲ KLM Admiral
This DC-8, named Admiral Richard E. Byrd, *served with KLM as a passenger liner. The DC-8 is now becoming rare in this role.*

▼ Into the sunset
Using freight conversions based on older airliners, operators of DC-8s must ensure that their aircraft satisfy present noise regulations.

▲ Big business
Growth in the express parcels business and computerised freight management saved the DC-8. Almost overnight, many aircraft went from scrap value to being in great demand.

FACTS AND FIGURES

➤ Of 556 DC-8s built, 262 were 'stretched' variants and about 150 have been used for cargo duty.

➤ The first cargo/passenger transport model flew in 1962.

➤ The long-fuselage DC-8-62AF was built with cargo doors and loading equipment.

➤ Fitting CFM56 turbofans has increased the DC-6-63's range by 25 per cent while carrying almost 40 per cent greater loads.

➤ In the DC-8-54AF most of the cabin windows were covered over.

➤ Freight variants of the DC-8 may still be in service as late as 2015.

PROFILE

Hauling freight in the DC-8

Success in the American market was vital, and United Airlines operated a large number of DC-8s.

The crew of a cargo DC-8's working life consists of crossing time zones, making brief stops in out-of-the-way places and spending a great deal of time in many of the world's less romantic airports.

The flight deck of this veteran, in its fourth decade of service, is not exactly 'user friendly', and the two pilots need all of their skill to make the most effective use of old-style, analogue instruments and dated navigation gear on a long flight.

Upkeep and maintenance of original specification aircraft is enough to keep pilots, engineers and mechanics fully occupied. But the old airliner still offers a respectable cargo capacity, especially in its stretched form, and many of the 250 surviving machines

have been upgraded with new technology CFM56 engines. These aircraft have greatly improved payload capacity and fuel efficiency, and lower levels of smoke and noise emission. Currently one of the mainstays of international mail and courier companies like America's giant United Parcels Service, the DC-8 looks set for many more years of effective service in the freight role.

Success in the American market was vital, and United Airlines operated a large number of DC-8s.

DC-8 Series 73

Type: long-range transport

Powerplant: four 97.87-kN (22,000-lb.-thrust) CFM International CFM56-2-1C turbofans

Maximum speed: 965 km/h (600 m.p.h.)

Range: 8945 km (5,558 miles) with maximum payload

Service ceiling: 11000 m (36,000 ft.)

Weights: empty 70800 kg (156,087 lb.); loaded 147400 kg (324,961 lb.)

Maximum payload: 30850 kg (68,012 lb.); DC-8s can carry an enormous variety of cargoes including farm equipment and live animals

Dimensions:
span 45.23 m (148 ft. 5 in.)
length 57.12 m (187 ft. 5 in.)
height 13.10 m (43 ft.)
wing area 267.91 m² (2,884 sq. ft.)

DC-8-55F JET TRADER

This DC-8 was operated by CargOman, and helped Rhodesia import aviation spares in defiance of the UN embargo. It was powered by JT-3 turbofan engines.

The latest DC-8 conversions have EFIS (Electronic Flight Instrumentation System) cockpit systems with glass displays. The nose cone covered a small Bendix or Collins weather radar.

Conversion to cargo-carrying often involves installation of larger cargo doors, a strengthened seven-track floor and a powered loading/unloading system.

Metal plugs are usually fitted in place of windows when passenger aircraft are converted to freight carriers.

Overwing emergency escape hatches were provided in the passenger version, but these are often deleted in cargo aircraft.

The DC-8 wing has two section ailerons which operate differently at varying speeds. At low airspeeds the outer ailerons deploy, but at high airspeeds the inner section only is used to reduce wing torsion.

The flight crew consists of a pilot, co-pilot, navigator and flight engineer. The loadmaster sits in a jump seat at the rear of the cockpit.

DC-8s were available with a variety of powerplants, including Rolls-Royce Conway turbofans in the DC-8-43, Pratt & Whitney JT-4s in most early versions and CFM56s in modernised aircraft. This version used the JT-3D-3B turbofan.

The inner section of the wing has double slotted flaps. A small section of the flaps hinges upwards to avoid the engine efflux.

The DC-8's fuselage was distinct in having a double-circular fuselage section, with the top half of greater diameter than the bottom.

Payload increase

TURBOPROP CARRIER: Turboprop airliners, like the CL-44, are efficient carriers, but except for the giant An-12 and An-22 they cannot match jets for sheer power and speed.

CL-44 28725 kg (63,327 lb.)

BOEING 707: The DC-8's great rival was also a useful cargo aircraft, and was more successful in gaining military transport and tanking roles. The Boeing could carry about 40 tonnes (44 tons).

MODEL 707 40324 kg (88,900 lb.)

DC-8 CARGO : With uprated engines and its capacious fuselage, the DC-8 was able to carry a much larger load than an equivalent Boeing 707.

DC-8 58410 kg (128,772 lb.)

ACTION DATA

MAXIMUM CRUISING SPEED

The introduction of jet airliners raised cruising speeds significantly, cutting time in transit by as much as two thirds. The DC-8 was even dived past Mach 1 in an experimental flight.

DC-8	890 km/h (553 m.p.h.)
CL-44	630 km/h (391 m.p.h.)
Model 707	980 km/h (609 m.p.h.)

RANGE

With a new generation of very efficient CFM56 engines, the already long-ranged DC-8-73CF could fly even further and with far better fuel efficiency than early Boeing 707s or previous generation DC-8s.

DC-8	8945 km (5,558 miles)
CL-44	5245 km (3,259 miles)
Model 707	5835 km (3,626 miles)

EMBRAER

EMB-110 BANDEIRANTE

● Twin-engined commuter ● Up to 21 seats ● Brazilian success

EMBRAER's twin-turboprop Bandeirante (Pioneer) was created for the Brazilian air force, but became a respected civil transport which played a key role in the foundation of Brazil's aerospace industry and development of the vast country's internal air network. The Bandeirante proved to be a fine short-haul airliner, providing good service to passengers and paving the way for the Brasilia airliner which is used worldwide.

▲ *An important market for the Bandeirante was the United States. It sold well there and around the world, with examples entering service as far apart as France and New Zealand.*

EMBRAER EMB-110 BANDEIRANTE

▼ Foundation for Brazilian industry
As well as helping to establish the country's internal air transport network, EMB-110 production was a cornerstone of Brazil's fledgling aviation industry.

▲ Brazilian air force C-95
The first customer for the Bandeirante was the Brazilian air force, which designated the aircraft C-95 and has become a major operator of the type.

Dolphin's dozen ▶
Dolphin Airways of Tampa, Florida, operated 12 Bandeirantes in the early 1980s, serving 22 cities in five US states. This is the EMB-110P1 version.

▼ Two variants
The EMB-110P1 and -110P2 were the two main commuter variants: the former had a 'quick-change' interior and cargo door, and the latter an 85-cm longer fuselage.

Conventional ▶ cockpit
The cockpit accommodated two pilots and its layout was fairly typical of similar aircraft in the 1970s.

FACTS AND FIGURES

➤ In all, 490 Bandeirantes were built by EMBRAER between August 1969 and September 1990.

➤ Currently being replaced by newer craft, EMB-110s still serve with several nations.

➤ The military prototype for this series of aircraft first flew on 26 October 1968.

➤ The first flight of a production EMB-110 Bandeirante was made successfully on 9 August 1972.

➤ French engineer Max Holste was mainly responsible for the Bandeirante's design.

➤ The EMB-110 was the basis for the short-fuselage EMB-121 Xingu business aircraft.

PROFILE

Brazilian pioneer twin

The hinterlands of Brazil, including vast stretches of Amazon jungle, have been opened up by the EMBRAER EMB-110 Bandeirante, a sensible and practical small airliner that is bringing civilisation to the wilderness. The 1968 decision to build this aircraft as the C-95 for the Brazilian air force led to the creation of EMBRAER the following year and to hundreds of Bandeirantes for small- and medium-sized air carriers.

The smooth-handling EMB-110 allows pilots to fly in and out of small airfields confident of having sufficient power to avoid take-off and landing mishaps. Both pilots and mechanics praise the simplicity and practicality of the Bandeirante, although its range and passenger-carrying capacity are limited.

The EMB-110 is used primarily as a feederliner and has seen service worldwide. There is also a seven-seat executive transport version, as well as a geophysical survey variant with additional wing tanks. Plans for a pressurised version were abandoned, but the experience gained was used in producing the subsequent EMB-120 Brasilia airliner. Production of the Bandeirante ceased in 1990 after 490 had been delivered.

YC-95 (EMB-100) serial number 2131 was the second Bandeirante prototype. The first production model, the EMB-110, had a longer fuselage and redesigned nose and cabin windows.

EMB-110P1 Bandeirante

This EMB-110P1 was operated by Florida commuter airline Dolphin Airways from 1981. Under the strict certification rules in the USA the EMB-110P1 was modified to allow a higher gross take-off weight.

The EMB-110's cabin was enlarged while the aircraft was in production. The initial commercial variant, the EMB-110C, held 15 passengers; the largest version was the EMB-110P2 which could accommodate 21.

A 450-W landing light was fitted to each wing so that the aircraft could both see and be seen.

Many American carriers operate large fleets of Bandeirantes and use it to bridge the gap between 8- and 10-seat light aircraft and the larger 30- and 40-seat turboprops.

Both the main and nose undercarriages retract forward, each leg being supported by a single wheel.

Two top-selling Pratt & Whitney Canada PT-6A turboprops supply the power to drive a three-blade Hartzell propeller.

The standard Bandeirante crew consists of a pilot and co-pilot. The stressed acrylic centre windscreen panels are 13 mm (½-in.) thick.

DOLPHIN

N61DA

The nose of the EMB-110 contains a Bendix- or RCA-built radar array.

The EMB-110P series introduces a forward passenger door, which was not fitted to the earlier, shorter models.

Internal wing fuel tanks have a total capacity of 1690 litres (440 gal.), giving a range of over 2000 km (1,250 mi.).

As the EMB-110P1 is able to be quickly converted to a cargo aircraft it is fitted with a large cargo door on the port side.

The EMB-110P2 version differs from the -110P1 not only in having a longer fuselage, but it also has provision for a toilet.

ACTION DATA

RANGE

In the vast Brazilian wilderness, where the Bandeirante is used, good range is important as airstrips tend to be some distance apart. The Metro on the other hand is intended for the relatively short distances between US airports.

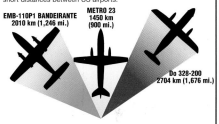

EMB-110P1 BANDEIRANTE 2010 km (1,246 mi.)

METRO 23 1450 km (900 mi.)

Do 328-200 2704 km (1,676 mi.)

PASSENGER LOAD

All three types are designed to carry around 18/19 passengers and larger versions have also been produced to transport bigger loads. Cargo doors can be specified so that the aircraft can be used for freight.

EMB-110P1 BANDEIRANTE 18 passengers

METRO 23 19 passengers

Do 328-200 19 passengers

MAXIMUM CRUISING SPEED

Fairchild's Metro is a relatively fast aircraft compared to others in the same class. The Do 328, although not as quick, has a good climb rate and cruising altitude.

EMB-110P1	411 km/h (255 m.p.h.)
METRO 23	534 km/h (331 m.p.h.)
Do 328-200	428 km/h (265 m.p.h.)

Small commuter propliners

BEECHCRAFT MODEL 99: The Model 99 Airliner was essentially an enlarged Queen Air executive twin with room for up to 15 passengers. Production ceased in 1986.

BRITTEN-NORMAN TRISLANDER: The Trislander of 1970 grew out of the successful twin-engined Islander. The last were built in 1984; plans to restart production have stalled.

DE HAVILLAND CANADA DHC-6: The Twin Otter STOL transport was built between 1965 and 1988 and considerable numbers remain in service worldwide, including floatplane variants.

FAIRCHILD METRO IIIA: Metros date from the 1960s and follow a Swearingen Aircraft design. Stretched and updated versions are still produced.

EMBRAER

EMB-120 Brasilia

● Brazilian design ● Pressurised twin turboprop ● Military versions

A number of projects aimed at producing a pressurised, higher capacity derivative of the successful EMBRAER Bandeirante 19-seater culminated in the 1979 launch of an entirely new design – the Brasilia. Seating up to 30 passengers and powered by two Pratt & Whitney Canada PW100 turbines, the EMB-120 has secured more than 300 orders from around the world and has been in service for more than a decade.

▲ Since the launch of the highly successful Bandeirante, EMBRAER of Brazil has developed into a respected aircraft manufacturer producing a range of commercial and military designs.

PHOTO FILE

EMBRAER **EMB-120 Brasilia**

▼ **Conventional cockpit**
Brasilia cockpits mainly have analogue instruments and feature a conventional array of avionics systems, including weather radar.

▲ **VIP transport**
The Brazilian air force's 6° Esquadrao de Transporte Aérea and Grupo de Transporte Especial operates 10 VC-97s.

▼ **Third prototype**
PT-ZBC was the third EMB-120 off the production line. Here it is seen in a factory finish with the EMBRAER logo on the fin.

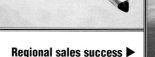

▲ **Launch customer**
Atlantic Southeast of Atlanta, Georgia, was the first customer and put the EMB-120 into service in October 1985. Early aircraft were powered by smaller 1119-kW (1,500-hp.) PW115 engines.

Regional sales success ▶
Comair is one of the largest US regional airlines and in 1997 operated a fleet of 40 Brasilias, providing feeder services for Delta Airlines.

FACTS AND FIGURES

➤ In June 1995, US airline SkyWest purchased 10 EMB-120ERs for $75 million; the cost included spare parts and training.

➤ Composite materials make up 10 per cent of the Brasilia's empty weight.

➤ The 300th Brasilia was delivered in September 1995.

➤ Brazil's air force has ordered five EMB-120SA early warning aircraft, equipped with fuselage-mounted radar.

➤ By January 1996, Brasilias had carried nearly 86 million passengers.

➤ EMBRAER's EMB-145 regional jet airliner uses EMB-120 parts, including the cockpit.

PROFILE

Improved successor to the Bandeirante

Although the Brasilia shared the Bandeirante's basic layout, it differed in some important respects. The fuselage was of circular section with a T-tail, but the low-mounted, unswept wings were retained.

After the prototype's first flight on 27 July 1983, the Paris Air Salon of 1985 was chosen to mark the first delivery to the launch customer – the US airline Atlantic Southeast.

From 1993 more powerful PW118 engines replaced the original PW115s (both members of the PW100 family), although a version with PW118A engines, had been produced in 1987. This model was designed for 'hot-and-high' operations in warmer climates.

In 1994 the EMB-120ER Brasilia Advanced became the standard production version. Improvements included a higher maximum take-off weight, to allow for greater fuel capacity and better range, and decreased cabin noise levels. Earlier aircraft can also be retrofitted to the -120ER standard. All-cargo and mixed configuration versions are also offered by EMBRAER, but have not yet been bought.

However, the EMB-120QC 'quick-change' variant (able to carry either 30 passengers or 3500 kg (7,700 lb.) of freight) entered service with Total Linheas Aereas of Brazil in 1993. A corporate version was ordered by United Technologies in 1986, while Brazil's air force has bought 10 VC-97 VIP transports.

Left: Air Midwest, at the time providing feeder services for American Eagle, was an early customer. It has since re-equipped with larger Beech 1900Ds.

Above: The United States is an important market and one in which the EMBRAER Brasilia has performed well. This aircraft belongs to United Express.

EMB-120ER Brasilia Advanced

Type: pressurised twin-turboprop transport

Powerplant: two 1342-kW (1,800-hp.) Pratt & Whitney PW118 or PW118A turboprops

Maximum level speed: 606 km/h (376 m.p.h.) at 6100 m (20,000 ft.)

Initial climb rate: 762 m/min (2,500 f.p.m.) at sea level

Range: 1575 km (975 mi.) at 9150 m (30,000 ft.) with maximum fuel, payload and reserves

Service ceiling: 9755 m (32,000 ft.)

Weights: empty equipped 7150 kg (15,730 lb.); maximum take-off 11,990 kg (23,353 lb.)

Accommodation: three crew and up to 30 passengers or 3500 kg (7,700 lb.) of cargo

Dimensions:
span	19.78 m	(64 ft. 11 in.)
length	20.07 m	(65 ft. 10 in.)
height	6.35 m	(20 ft. 10 in.)
wing area	39.43 m²	(424 sq. ft.)

EMB-120 BRASILIA

N180YV is one of a fleet of 20 EMB-120s operated by five airlines under the United Express banner, providing feeder services for United Airlines. Sixty cities are served from five main hubs.

Standard EMB-120 passenger configuration allows for 30 seats in one of two possible configurations, each with three seats abreast. Other features include an attendant's seat, galley and toilet. As well as pressurisation, air-conditioning is a standard feature.

Among the changes made to the EMB-120ER was the deletion of the de-icing 'boot' on the leading edge of the tailfin.

Baggage is stowed in a compartment behind the main cabin. 'Quick-change' freight variants use the cargo bay door to load the main cabin.

A crew of two flies the Brasilia from a modern cockpit. A small nose radome houses a weather radar scanner.

Passengers board via an airstair incorporated into the cabin door at the front of the port side of the aircraft. This allows the machine to operate from airfields with minimal ground facilities.

Pratt & Whitney's PW100 turbine family powers the Brasilia. The first examples used two PW115s, with later aircraft having more powerful PW118s or PW118As.

EMBRAER has marketed an all-freight version of the Brasilia with a 4000-kg capacity and the 'quick-change' EMB120QC variant with a maximum load of 3500 kg.

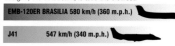

ACTION DATA

CRUISING SPEED

The Brasilia has a comparable cruising speed to other types in the 30-seater category, like the Jetstream J41 and Dornier 328, although the latter is marginally quicker. The oldest of these three designs, the Jetstream, is also the slowest.

EMB-120ER BRASILIA	580 km/h (360 m.p.h.)
J41	547 km/h (340 m.p.h.)
Do 328-110	620 km/h (384 m.p.h.)

PASSENGERS

All three designs are aimed at the 30-seat regional market. Both the J41 and Brasilia have sold well in the United States, although sales of the Dornier have been slow to materialise. Stretched versions of the Jetstream and Dornier have also been built or projected.

EMB-120ER BRASILIA ADVANCED
30 passengers

J41
29 passengers

Do 328-110
33 passengers

RANGE

Once again the most modern of these designs has the best performance. The Dornier, first flown in the 1990s, has a better range than the Brasilia, whereas the older J41's range is over 250 km (165 mi.) less than that of the Do 328. Long range is often a good selling point to airlines.

Do 328-110
1666 km (1,035 mi.)

EMB-120ER BRASILIA ADVANCED
1575 km (975 mi.)

J41
1403 km (870 mi.)

T-tailed pressurised turbine twins

■ **BEECHCRAFT MODEL 1900:** This 21-seat regional aircraft, derived from the Model 200, first flew in September 1982. The Model 1900D followed with a 35.6-cm (14-in.) deeper fuselage.

■ **DE HAVILLAND CANADA DHC-8 DASH 8:** Demand for 30- to 40-seat regional airliners in the late 1970s led DHC to design the Dash 8. This first flew in mid-1983 and worldwide sales followed.

■ **DORNIER Do 328:** Another 30-seater, the Do 328 has not been successful in what is a crowded market. First flown in 1991, the aircraft entered service in Switzerland in 1993.

■ **PIPER PA-42 CHEYENNE III:** Cheyenne III can trace its design origins back to the piston-engined PA-31 Navajo of the mid-1960s. The main cabin holds 11 passengers.

ENSTROM

SHARK

● Observation helicopter ● Passenger transport ● Trainer

First flown in its original form in 1962, the Enstrom 280 has been one of the most successful light piston helicopter designs ever. Whether teaching students to master the basics of helicopter flight, spraying crops, transporting businesspeople across cities or patrolling pipelines, the Shark has proved popular with pilots and customers alike. Remarkably, the successful design has not changed much as the Shark remains an excellent utility helicopter.

▲ Demonstrating the F-28's ability to remain stable in the hover, a brave employee is hauled into the air in front of the cameras as a marketing sales gimmick.

ENSTROM SHARK

▼ Blended body
The streamlined fuselage of the Shark – the result of a careful design study – is displayed for the camera.

▲ Light transport
Later versions of the helicopter were capable of carrying three passengers seated abreast. Although cramped, visibility from the cockpit was excellent.

Military service ▶
Operated by the Peruvian army, the helicopter is used for light observation and training duties, replacing the early Bell 47.

◀ High performance
Due to its lightweight design, the manoeuvrability of the Shark is exceptional, as demonstrated by this flying display at an air show.

Later Versions ▶
This late-model Enstrom development is test flown. A gradual upgrading of the design has taken place in an attempt to bring the helicopter wider service.

FACTS AND FIGURES

➤ First flight of the Enstrom Shark was on 26 May, 1962. it was the first of two three-seat pre-production models.

➤ The helicopter features a light alloy and glass-fibre cabin section.

➤ The US Army has shown an interest in the design, as a training helicopter.

➤ Military versions of the Shark serve with the Chilean and Peruvian armies as observation helicopters.

➤ A four-seat version was developed and flew in 1978; it was called the Hawk.

➤ The most recent development of the Shark is the five-seat Eagle.

PROFILE

Enstrom's Shark of the air

Enstrom was formed in 1959 specifically to build a light helicopter. The F-28, designed by Rudy J Enstrom, first flew in 1962. By the time the improved F-28A was built in 1968, Enstrom had been purchased by a bigger corporation. A turbocharged F-28B was built, along with a T-28 turbine-powered variant. By 1975, production of the F-28C had begun; this variant was phased out in 1981, when the current F-28F and 280 appeared.

These models became very popular and by 1993, over 900 of

these helicopters had been built. With a redesigned main gearbox, main rotor shaft, and an optional exhaust silencer, the F28 can be configured for crop-spraying with easily removeable hoppers, and is also available as a police variant (F28F Sentinel) with a searchlight. The 280FX is a substantially upgraded version, with new seats, tail fins, faired landing gear and a covered tail rotor shaft. More than 170 F-28F and 280FXs were in service in 1993.

The 280 achieved some success as a military trainer,

Above: Operating with the Chilean army, the Shark has proven to be an excellent utility helicopter.

with Chile, Colombia and Peru operating the type. The military-optimised TH-28, which lost out to the Bell TH-67 for the new US Army training helicopter requirement, is a similar aircraft.

Below: A US Army request for a new training helicopter saw a developed model of the Shark enter the competition. Though test flown by service pilots on occasion, the helicopter has not received an order and remains under development.

F28F Shark

- **Type:** Light trainer/transport helicopter
- **Powerplant:** one Textron Lycoming HIO-360F1 rated at 168 kW (225 hp.)
- **Maximum speed:** 180 km/h (112 m.p.h.)
- **Cruising speed:** 165 km/h (102 m.p.h.)
- **Range:** 423 km (262 mi.)
- **Endurance:** 3.5 hours
- **Climb rate:** 442 m/min (1,150 f.p.m.) from sea level
- **Hover ceiling:** 2345 m (7,700 ft.) out of ground effect
- **Dimensions:**
Rotor diameter:	9.75 m (32 ft.)
Length:	8.92 m (29 ft. 3 in.)
Height:	2.79 m (9 ft. 2 in.)
Rotor disc area:	74,66 m² (804 sq. ft.)

ACTION DATA

SPEED
Due to the small dimensions of the F-28F, its speed is limited by its engine size. The streamlined design allows respectable performance compared to larger types such as the twin-engine German-designed BO 105CB.

F28F SHARK	180 km/h (112 m.p.h.)	
R22 BETA	180 km/h (112 m.p.h.)	
BO 105 CB	242 km/h (150 m.p.h.)	

POWER
Although progressively updated during the course of development, the F-28F offers better performance in all flight areas than the Robinson R22. Although not as powerful as the Bo 105CB, the F-28F does not require as large of a load-carrying capacity.

F28F SHARK 168 kW (225 hp.)	R22 BETA 119 kW (160 hp.)	BO 105 CB 626 kW (420 hp.)

ROTOR DISC AREA
A large three-blade rotor disc offers excellent handling qualities for the F28F in the hover – a key selling point for the helicoper. Compared to the larger BO 105CB, the disc area seems too large for the small helicopter.

F28F SHARK 74,66 m² (804 sq. ft.)	BO 105 CB 75,40 m² (818 sq. ft.)
R22 BETA 46,21 m² (497 sq. ft.)	

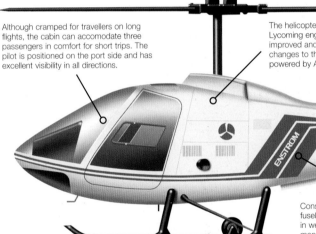

Although cramped for travellers on long flights, the cabin can accomodate three passengers in comfort for short trips. The pilot is positioned on the port side and has excellent visibility in all directions.

The helicopter is powered by an Avco Lycoming engine that has been progressively improved and updated to incorporate design changes to the airframe. Later versions are powered by Allison turboshafts.

A single rotor tail is positioned at the end of the boom. In later, larger variants it was moved to the port side to improve their handling qualities. The main rotor diameter has changed little during the course of development.

N2019H

Constructed from a light alloy and glass fibre, the fuselage offers exceptional strength at no penalty in weight. The tail boom is of an all-metal semi-monocoque construction. The resulting weight of the helicopter is surprisingly little.

280FX SHARK

Bringing helicopter travel to the masses has always been a driving principle for manufacturers. The Enstrom company has gone a long way to resolve this with its designs.

Light utility helicopters

■ **ROBINSON R22 MARINER:** Developed in the US, the R22 has been exported worldwide to serve as a utility and training helicopter. The design has proved very successful.

■ **EUROCOPTER ECUREUIL 2:** The AS 350 is larger than the Shark, but both are used in the same roles. The Enstrom achieves this at a lower operational cost thanks to a less fuel-thirsty engine.

■ **EUROPCOPTER GAZELLE:** The streamlined design looks very similar to the Enstrom Shark but the Gazelle has proved to be far more adaptable, serving widely in both civil and military roles.

EUROCOPTER
EC 120/135

● European design ● Latest technologies ● Quiet operations

▲ Both the EC 120 and EC 135 represent the cutting edge of helicopter technology for the next century. The Eurocopter company was formed in 1992 by the merger of the Aérospatiale and MBB helicopter divisions.

In order to match helicopter requirements in the next century, Eurocopter has produced its advanced EC 135 and EC 120 Colibri helicopters. Developed from the BO 108 technology demonstrator, the EC 135 is a high-tech successor to the MBB/Eurocopter BO 105, while the EC 120 is generally in the same class as Eurocopter's own Ecureuil and Gazelle. It meets the Bell JetRanger and MD 500 series head on, and is likely to sell well.

EUROCOPTER EC 120/135

Prototype ▶ formation
D-HECY, seen in the middle of this view of all three EC 135 prototypes, is the sole EC 135D-1 powered by the Pratt & Whitney PW206B engine.

First flight ▼
Eurocopter considers all EC 135 prototypes to be pre-production prototypes. D-HECX was the first example and is seen on its maiden flight.

▲ Before the EC 135
Messerschmitt-Bolkow-Blöhm (MBB) flew the first example of its Allison-powered BO 108 on 15 October 1988. The design subsequently evolved into the EC 135.

▼ French assembly
F-WWPA, the first EC 120 prototype, was assembled at Eurocopter's Marignane facility in France. The EC 135 was developed mostly in Germany.

Colibri programme ▶
By April 1997 two prototypes of the EC 120 were operational and had completed 250 hours of flight testing in preparation for certification.

FACTS AND FIGURES

➤ Having aimed to build 30 EC 135s in 1997, Eurocopter expects to increase production to 60 per annum thereafter.

➤ Eurocopter foresees a requirement for 700 EC 135s up to 2007.

➤ An Emergency Medical Service (EMS) layout is being developed for the EC 120.

➤ A number of EC 135s were flying with police forces in Germany and Spain by early 1997.

➤ The McDonnell Douglas MD 900 Explorer is a serious EC 135 competitor.

➤ Operating costs of the EC 135 are 25 per cent below those of the BO 105.

PROFILE

European helicopter challenge

With an upturn in the world economy causing a boom in the international helicopter market, Eurocopter was optimistic about the future of its EC 120 and EC 135 helicopters at the HeliExpo '97 trade show.

After certification during the summer of 1996, EC 135 deliveries totalled 10 by the year's end. Having first predicted orders for 20 EC 135s per year, Eurocopter has been forced to increase production to 30 in 1997 to meet demand.

Announced in February 1990,

the EC 120 Colibri is a joint venture between Eurocopter, CATIC/HAMC in China and Singapore Technologies Aerospace. The aircraft was officially launched at HeliExpo '97 and gained certification during the same year after, extensive flight testing. The Colibri is to be offered in a range of executive, police, training and utility layouts. A market of 1,600 to 2,000 examples is expected.

Both helicopters make extensive use of composites, the EC 120 being almost

entirely constructed from composite materials, and both employ a distinctive fenestron anti-torque system. This offers benefits in ease of maintenance and noise reduction, the latter being especially important in the policing and EMS roles.

Above: Eurocopter added an advanced fenestron anti-torque system to the MBB BO 108.

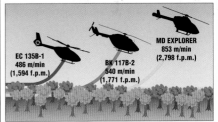

Above: Wearing its smart dark green colour scheme, D-HECZ introduced the EC 135 to America at HeliExpo '95 in Las Vegas. Strong competition for the type comes from the McDonnell Douglas MD 900 Explorer.

EC 135B-1

Type: five/seven-seat light helicopter

Powerplant: two 417-kW (560-hp.) (continuous rating) Turboméca Arrius 2B turboshafts

Maximum cruising speed: 261 km/h (162 m.p.h.) at sea level

Endurance: 4 hours at sea level

Maximum climb rate: 486 m/min (1,594 f.p.m.) at sea level

Range: 715 km (443 mi.) at sea level with standard fuel

Weights: empty 1370 kg (3,014 lb.), maximum take-off 2500 kg (5,500 lb.)

Accommodation: maximum of six passengers

Dimensions:
main rotor diameter	10.20 m (33 ft. 6 in.)
fuselage length	10.16 m (33 ft. 4 in.)
height	3.62 m (11 ft. 11 in.)
main rotor disc area	81.71 m² (879 sq. ft.)

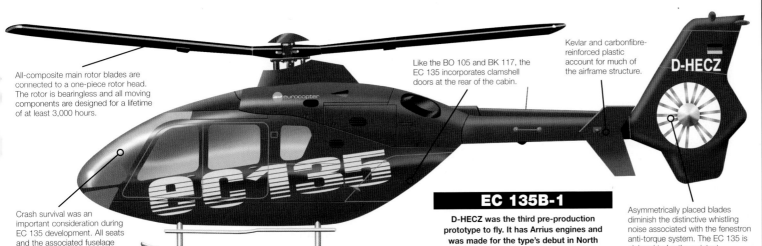

All-composite main rotor blades are connected to a one-piece rotor head. The rotor is bearingless and all moving components are designed for a lifetime of at least 3,000 hours.

Like the BO 105 and BK 117, the EC 135 incorporates clamshell doors at the rear of the cabin.

Kevlar and carbonfibre-reinforced plastic account for much of the airframe structure.

Crash survival was an important consideration during EC 135 development. All seats and the associated fuselage sections, are able to survive decelerations of 30 g.

EC 135B-1

D-HECZ was the third pre-production prototype to fly. It has Arrius engines and was made for the type's debut in North America – potentially a huge market.

Asymmetrically placed blades diminish the distinctive whistling noise associated with the fenestron anti-torque system. The EC 135 is claimed to be the quietest helicopter available.

ACTION DATA

NEVER EXCEED SPEED

Although aircraft rarely operate at their never exceed speed, the capability to achieve a high speed is useful. It might be especially important for an EMS or police helicopter responding to a call-out.

EC 135B-1	287 km/h (178 m.p.h.)
MD EXPLORER	296 km/h (183 m.p.h.)
BK 117B-2	278 km/h (172 m.p.h.)

MAXIMUM CLIMB RATE

McDonnell Douglas's MD Explorer offers superb climb performance, but cannot match the amazingly low noise signature of the EC 135B-1. The BK 117 is likely to lose sales to both types.

EC 135B-1 486 m/min (1,594 f.p.m.)
BK 117B-2 540 m/min (1,771 f.p.m.)
MD EXPLORER 853 m/min (2,798 f.p.m.)

COST

A comparison of 1995 prices shows that the EC 135 offers excellent value in its basic form. However, with optional equipment for alternative roles fitted, the price will increase.

EC 135B-1	BK 117B-2	MD EXPLORER
US$1.98 million	US$3.50 million	US$3.33 million

Eurocopter product line-up

AS 355 ECUREUIL 2: Still strong sellers, the AS 355 and single-engined AS 350 are especially popular with police forces, as well as private and corporate operators.

AS 332 SUPER PUMA: Also available as the military AS 532 Cougar, the Super Puma has been updated since Eurocopter inherited the design from Aérospatiale.

AS 365N2 DAUPHIN 2: Developed from Aérospatiale's initially unsuccessful single-engined SA 360, the Dauphin 2 offers customers high equipment and performance levels.

BK 117: Designed and built jointly with Kawasaki in Japan, the BK 117 was originally designed in co-operation with MBB. The aircraft is a competitor of the EC 135.

EUROCOPTER

AS 332 SUPER PUMA

● Oilrig support ● Search and rescue ● Tactical transport

Eurocopter's family of heavylift helicopters – Puma, Cougar and Super Puma – perform many duties around the world, but none more challenging as those in the petroleum industry. This is high adventure only a helicopter can provide – heading out over raging seas to bring supplies to oilrigs on the ocean. Fortunately, helicopters like the Super Puma handle extremely well when the going is rough.

▲ The Super Puma has been a great success in North Sea operations. It has proved very reliable, and can operate in marginal weather conditions that would severely inhibit less capable helicopters.

EUROCOPTER AS 332 SUPER PUMA

▲ Bristow Puma
The British operator Bristow Helicopters works its Pumas very hard. There is an average of 55 sorties a day leaving Dyce heliport near Aberdeen, heading out to the oilrigs and support vessels and back.

▲ Pre-flight checks
Puma pilots have to carry out an elaborate check procedure before flying. This begins with the pilot walking round and examining the airframe and rotor blades.

▲ Ready to go
With a close eye on the vicious and changeable weather and fuel states carefully calculated, the crew taxis out. The number of passengers is variable, depending on the fuel load needed.

◀ Long nights
Operating in the Shetlands means long summer days and early starts, but long winter nights allow few daylight flying hours.

▲ Night maintenance
Where possible work is carried out at night, as the Super Pumas have a very busy day schedule.

◀ Norwegian Puma
AS Lufttransport operates in the Norwegian sector, often flying in Arctic conditions.

FACTS AND FIGURES

➤ The prototype Puma first flew on 15 April 1965.

➤ The Super Puma took to the air for its maiden flight on 13 September 1978.

➤ About 420 Super Puma/Cougar helicopters have been built, about half of them used by civil operators.

➤ Petroleum Helicopters, the world's largest user of helicopters, uses Pumas and Super Pumas.

➤ The military Puma variant, the AS 532 Cougar, is used by 32 countries.

➤ The Super Puma Mk II introduced new main and tail rotors and transmission.

PROFILE

Flying for oil in the North Sea

Aérospatiale (now Eurocopter) has built a superb helicopter family with the AS 330 Puma, AS 332 Super Puma and AS 332L2 Super Puma II. With twin-engine reliability and an interior of 11.40 m³ (403 cu. ft.), the Super Puma offers brute hauling power. A survey of petroleum companies recognised the Super Puma as the most cost-effective helicopter in its class.

The Super Puma retains the original Puma's retractable undercarriage and adds glass-fibre rotor technology. The Super Puma is identified by its ventral fin and nose radome for weather radar.

For oilrig support, pilots praise its qualities, which also appeal to military users. Just as the rotors are deemed strong enough for 40 flying hours after hits by 12.7-mm (.50 cal.) small-arms fire, the fuselage and main rotors of the Super Puma can endure salt-water corrosion, high winds and the other challenges of petroleum industry flying.

The Super Puma supplements the older and larger Sikorsky S-61 Sea King (below) to service the oil industry. It has been a great success for the manufacturers, now called Eurocopter. The British operating company Bristow ordered 31 of a special variant known as the Tiger for offshore support work, and others are serving as far afield as the South Pacific and Abu Dhabi.

AS 332 Super Puma

Type: medium-size transport helicopter

Powerplant: two 1184-kW (1,590-hp.) Turboméca Makila 1A1 turboshafts

Maximum cruising speed: 266 km/h (165 m.p.h.)

Weights: empty 4460 kg (9,812 lb.); loaded 8600 kg (18,920 lb.)

Accommodation: crew of 2; 24 passengers in high-density configuration, or nine stretchers and three seated casualties, or 4500 kg (9,900 lb.) of cargo slung externally; some models have twin freight doors to accommodate bulky cargoes such as oil-drilling equipment

Dimensions:

main rotor diameter	15 m (49 ft. 2 in.)
length	18.15 m (59 ft. 6 in.)
height	5.14 m (16 ft. 10 in.)
rotor disc area	177.00 m² (1,905 sq. ft.)

A protective grille is fitted to the engine intakes to prevent ingestion of ice or debris. The engines drive at over 23,000 rpm, reduced by the gearbox to 265 rpm at the main rotor.

The more powerful Makila turboshaft replaces the original Turboméca Turmo of the original Puma.

The four-bladed main rotor is made of glass-reinforced plastic with a carbon fibre stiffening and moltoprene filler.

The Super Puma can be flown by a single pilot in visual flight conditions, but instrument flying in poor weather requires two pilots.

G-BFEU   BRISTOW

In 1994 lightning struck the tail rotor of a Bristow Super Puma, causing it to ditch into the North Sea, miraculously without injury to any passengers.

Offshore Pumas usually have a nose-mounted weather radar.

As in all helicopters, the passenger cabin of the Super Puma is quite noisy.

Flotation gear is essential when operating in bad weather over the dangerous North Sea.

The Puma airframe is of conventional aluminium with titanium skinning in critical areas.

AS 332 SUPER PUMA

The Super Puma serves in large numbers in the North Sea. Known as the Tiger to Bristow Helicopters, it serves with other operators including Helikopter Servis and Bond Helicopters.

ACTION DATA

CRUISING SPEED

The Super Puma is a thoroughly modern design, and is capable of maintaining a high-speed cruise through bad weather conditions. This is important, since in its unceasing search for new supplies the oil industry operates in some of the most hostile environments on Earth, from the violent winter storms of the North Atlantic to the Polar wastes of Siberia and Alaska.

MODEL 214	256 km/h (159 m.p.h.)
AS 332 SUPER PUMA	266 km/h (165 m.p.h.)
Mi-8	225 km/h (140 m.p.h.)

RANGE

North Sea helicopters need plenty of range, since the oil and gas production platforms they service are exploiting reserves in deeper and deeper water, at ever increasing distances from the nearest shore bases. The ability to fly these distances in severe weather conditions is also essential.

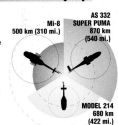

Mi-8 500 km (310 mi.)
AS 332 SUPER PUMA 870 km (540 mi.)
MODEL 214 680 km (422 mi.)

PASSENGER CAPACITY

Modern marine drilling platforms, especially those geared for deep-water operations in bad weather areas such as the North Sea, are massive structures housing hundreds of people. There is constant movement of men and equipment over wide areas, so large-capacity helicopters become essential to the smooth running of the oilfields.

AS 332 SUPER PUMA
24 passengers

Mi-8
28 passengers

MODEL 214
18 passengers

The Puma family

■ SA 330 PUMA: Developed initially as a military transport, the Puma could carry between 16 and 20 passengers. It was one of the first helicopters cleared for all-weather operation.

■ AS 332 SUPER PUMA: Based on the highly successful SA 330, the Super Puma has more powerful engines, better avionics, and a tougher airframe and landing gear.

■ SUPER PUMA II: The latest version of the Puma, first certified in 1992, is the Super Puma II. It is the longest in the series, with a stretched fuselage seating up to 29 passengers.

EUROCOPTER

AS 355/555 TWIN STAR

● Versatile lightweight ● Air taxi ● Police, ambulance, fire service

Known in the United States as the Eurocopter Twin Star, the bouncy little Aérospatiale Twin Squirrel is one of the world's most versatile flying machines. It is small, modest and relatively inexpensive, but it is an amazingly practical helicopter with dozens of everyday uses. From air taxi services to police and rescue work, the Twin Star gives solid performance at reasonable cost.

▲ *The Twin Squirrel is popular with everybody from air taxi services to TV stations, who appreciate the perfect view it gives when breaking stories.*

EUROCOPTER AS 355/555 TWIN STAR

▼ Police support
The Twin Squirrel is used by several police forces around the world, including Britain's Metropolitan police, who use it alongside the larger Bell 222.

▲ Safety tests
Modern helicopters undergo strict testing, such as stability analysis, before entering service.

Power-line surveillance ▶
Several UK electricity companies operate the AS 355. Its primary task is to locate damaged power cables allowing swift repair.

Neat interior ▶
The Twin Star has found its real niche as a comfortable air taxi. Its compact cabin can accommodate four passengers.

◀ Fennec
The military version of the Twin Star is known as the AS 555 Fennec. It is used for light utility work such as liaison and scouting, and can be armed with a Giat 20-mm cannon pod and pylon-mounted rockets.

▲ Light rescue
Equipped with a winch above the port door and a cargo hook, the Twin Squirrel can be used for search and rescue and light transport duties. The large mirrors under the starboard nose window allow the pilot to see the load carried by the aircraft's central cargo hook, essential for safety.

FACTS AND FIGURES

➤ A naval variant, the AS 555MN, is equipped with a chin-mounted radar, but is unarmed.

➤ The first Twin Squirrel made its maiden flight on 28 September 1979.

➤ The Twin Star has the best safety record of any helicopter in its class.

➤ Brazilian company Helibras builds Twin Squirrels with the designation CH-55 and VH-55 for the Brazilian air force.

➤ The Twin Squirrel's FADEC control system allows automatic engine starting.

➤ About 750 Ecureuils and Astars have been delivered to operators in 19 nations.

PROFILE

Eurocopter's versatile baby

The Eurocopter Twin Star is one of the world's best-selling light helicopters. Combining the twin-engined safety (essential for operating above dense urban areas) with the versatility and low costs of the AS 350 Squirrel, the AS 355 has been a great success. It has sold very well in North America, despite the dominance of the light helicopter market by the Bell 206 and Hughes 500.

The Twin Squirrel is derived from the single-engined AS 350 Ecureuil, driven by a single Turboméca Arriel turboshaft.

This aircraft featured a new rotor system and 'Starflex' rotor hub.

Like many helicopters in general use, the Twin Star can be equipped with a variety of flight instruments, avionics, radios and equipment options.

In use with civil operators, oil firms and police departments, the Twin Squirrel makes a superb air taxi. It is also ideal for primary training of fledgling rotary-wing pilots. The military AS 555 Fennec comes in naval and scout versions, and a missile-carrying version is under development,

The naval AS 355M2 has a chin-mounted 360° radar and can be armed with a pair of lightweight homing torpedoes. This version is in use with the Brazilian navy, which operates 11 UH-12Bs.

armed with anti-armour TOW rockets.

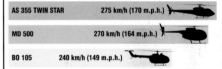

The AS 355 has a combined gearbox, with a shaft from each engine delivering power to the rotors.

The Starflex rotor system replaces the three conventional rotor hinges with a maintenance-free steel and rubber balljoint.

The main rotor blades are of glassfibre construction with a steel leading-edge sheath, combining strength, flexibility and light weight.

AS 355 Twin Star

Type: five-/six-seat general-purpose helicopter

Powerplant: two 340-kW (455-hp.) Turboméca Arrius turboshaft engines driving a three-bladed main rotor

Maximum speed: 275 km/h (170 m.p.h.)

Range: 720 km (446 mi.)

Service ceiling: 4000 m (13,120 ft.)

Weights: empty 1382 kg (3,040 lb.); loaded 2540 kg (5,580 lb.)

Accommodation: one or two pilots; six seats or up to 1134 kg (2,495 lb.) as an underslung load; various military loads can be carried including HOT or TOW anti-armour missiles, 20-mm Giat cannon pod or two homing torpedoes

Dimensions:
main rotor diameter	10.69 m (35 ft.)
length	13 m (43 ft.)
height	3.08 m (10 ft.)
rotor disc area	89.75 m² (966 sq. ft.)

COMBAT DATA

MAXIMUM SPEED

Helicopters are not the fastest of aircraft, but modern machines like the Twin Star can cruise quite comfortably at more than 200 km/h (125 m.p.h.). Coupled with their ability to operate from city centre heliports, they are often the fastest way of travelling from city to city.

AS 355 TWIN STAR	275 km/h (170 m.p.h.)
MD 500	270 km/h (164 m.p.h.)
BO 105	240 km/h (149 m.p.h.)

RANGE

Lightweight helicopters are the classic 'short-hop' transports. Although they do not have great unrefuelled ranges, they can stay in the air for several hours at a time. This is of great value in police surveillance or search-and-rescue work.

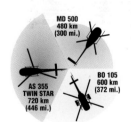

MD 500 480 km (300 mi.)
BO 105 600 km (372 mi.)
AS 355 TWIN STAR 720 km (446 mi.)

The Twin Squirrel has a simple two-bladed tail rotor, unlike the 'fenestron' or 'fan in fin' of its predecessor, the Aérospatiale Gazelle.

The latest AS 355 is powered by two Allison 250-C20F turboshafts. The original Ecureuil had a single Textron Lycoming or Arriel turboshaft. The twin-engined version first flew in 1979.

All AS 355s have a skid-type undercarriage for simplicity and low cost. This is slightly lengthened in military models.

Police Twin Squirrels often have a spot-light mounted under the belly, trained from the cockpit.

G-BOSK

POLICE

AS 355 TWIN SQUIRREL

The AS 355, known as the Twin Star for the American market, is known to most users as the Twin Squirrel. The Metropolitan Police was the first force in Britain to buy its own AS 355.

OGE HOVER CEILING

Helicopters generally have two hovering ceilings, depending on whether they are 'in ground effect' (IGE) or 'out of ground effect' (OGE). Using ground effect involves riding on the air generated by the rotor wash, which under certain conditions bounces back off the ground and acts as a cushion beneath the helicopter.

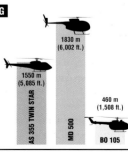

AS 355 TWIN STAR 1550 m (5,085 ft.)
MD 500 1830 m (6,002 ft.)
BO 105 460 m (1,508 ft.)

Aérospatiale's lightweights

ALOUETTE II: One of the most important helicopters in history, the Alouette II was the first turbine-powered rotary-winged craft to enter large-scale service.

ALOUETTE III: Taking the original Alouette concept a stage further, the Alouette III has a bigger cabin, a more efficient rotor system and more powerful engines.

LAMA: For operations in extreme conditions, Aérospatiale (now Eurocopter) introduced the high-altitude Lama, which is an Alouette II airframe with an Alouette III powerplant.

231

EUROCOPTER

HH-65A DOLPHIN COAST GUARD

● Search and rescue ● Coastal patrol ● Utility helicopter

S peeding to the rescue with the US Coast Guard, the HH-65 Dolphin has saved hundreds of lives since its was introduced in 1987. Serving in coastal locations across America, this short-range recovery version of the Eurocopter Dauphin multi-role helicopter has demonstrated impressive versatility. Fitted with advanced avionics and search equipment, the Dolphin is first to the rescue whatever the weather.

▲ A stretcher can be attached to the Dolphin's winch cable, which is particularly useful when picking up a casualty from a ship. The HH-65A is the US Coast Guard's most numerous asset, with nearly 100 examples currently in service.

EUROCOPTER HH-65A DOLPHIN COAST GUARD

▼ High-visibility paint scheme
The US Coast Guard has replaced its Dolphin's original white and red colour scheme (shown left) with an all-over high-visibility red, reflecting the helicopter's dedicated civil rescue role.

▲ Short-range rescue
The HH-65A is the short-range component of the modernised Coast Guard fleet, operating alongside the longer ranged HH-60J Jayhawk and fixed-wing HU-25 Guardian, a version of the French Dassault Falcon 20.

Advanced cockpit ▶
The Dolphin's modern cockpit is designed for minimum effort all-weather operations and includes comprehensive radio systems and datalink. The flight deck normally houses two, but it can be flown by a single pilot.

▼ Safety record
The HH-65A has a reputation as a very safe helicopter, thanks to its automatic flight control system, airspeed regulator, flotation bags, Rockwell-Collins navigation and Northrop SeeHawk FLIR.

◀ Rescue equipment
In addition to a winch and searchlight, the cabin contains first-aid gear, a removable stretcher and a sliding seat for the engineer.

FACTS AND FIGURES

➤ Israel purchased two HH-65s, and in trials operated them from the navy's fleet of fast patrol craft.

➤ Two HH-65s are used by the US Navy test centre at Patuxent River, Maryland.

➤ Flotation bags allow waterborne ditchings in bad weather – up to sea state five.

➤ The Dolphin was criticised for lacking power in hot and high conditions, but a re-engining programme was cancelled.

➤ The crew can be supplemented by a rescue diver for special missions.

➤ Dolphins were purchased to replace the elderly Sikorsky HH-52.

Coast Guard rescue helicopter

Around the coast of America, the United States Coast Guard waits patiently for calls for help. Teams of swimmers and boat crews are used for inshore rescues, and fixed-wing and larger rotary-wing aircraft, such as the Sikorsky HH-60J 'Jayhawk' and special versions of the C-130 Hercules transport, carry out the long-range work. The responsibility of the HH-65A Dolphin, a modernised

version of the Eurocopter SA 366 Dauphin purchased in 1987 to replace the elderly single-engined Sikorsky HH-52, is to undertake rescues at ranges up to 760 km (472 miles). Although built in France, the new HH-65A incorporates 70 per cent American components.

A total of 96 Dolphins serve around the United States from Astoria to San Diego. Fitted with advanced infra-red search systems, a winch, all-weather

avionics and a searchlight, the HH-65A is ideal for short-range rescue work.

Although the Dolphin has been a success, there was controversy over complaints voiced by the US Coast Guard that the aircraft lacked power, especially in the hot conditions around the coastlines of California and Florida in the summer. Re-engining the helicopter was considered, but rejected on the grounds of cost.

The HH-65A is seen here with its stablemate, the improved Eurocopter Panther 800. A more powerful and upgraded development, the Panther seems unlikely to serve with the USCG, which was not entirely satisfied with the Dolphin.

HH-65A DOLPHIN

The Eurocopter SA 366G Dolphin has been employed by the US Coast Guard since 1982, replacing the larger amphibious Sikorsky HH-52A in most units.

The HH-65's twin engines drive four-bladed rotors measuring 11.68 m (38 ft. 4 in.). Like the Gazelle and Panther, the tail rotor is the fenestron 'fan-in-fin' type.

Typically, the HH-65's crew will consist of a pilot, co-pilot and flight engineer/winch operator. The helicopter has a 1200-kg (2,640-lb.) stressed winch mounted above the starboard door.

The Coast Guard refit their French Dolphins with more powerful American-built Textron Lycoming LTS101 turboshafts, making the aircraft capable of a maximum speed of 324 km/h (200 m.p.h.).

4101

COAST GUARD

The Dolphin carries a sophisticated Planar array weather and search radar, plus equipment to allow joint missions with Coast Guard HU-25s, HH-60Hs, RG-8s and C-130s.

If the HH-65 is unfortunate enough to suffer a double engine failure over the sea, a successful ditching will be aided by the helicopter's pop-out inflatable floats.

The Dolphin's tailboom is sealed for enhanced buoyancy and contains an increased size all-composite Fenestron tail rotor. The aircraft's mainly composite structure leads to its nickname of 'plastic puppy'.

ACTION DATA

MAXIMUM SPEED

A generation ahead of the HH-3 or the Wessex and with considerably more streamlining, the HH-65A is capable of high speeds. SH-3s held speed records in the early-1960s.

HH-65A DOLPHIN	324 km/h (200 m.p.h.)
HH-3F	267 km/h (165 m.p.h.)
WESSEX HC.Mk 2	212 km/h (131 m.p.h.)

RANGE

With its much bigger fuselage, the HH-3 has greater fuel capacity and longer range. This allowed it to fulfil the long-range rotary search-and-rescue role in support of the inshore HH-65.

HH-65A DOLPHIN	760 km (470 mi.)
HH-3F	1005 km (625 mi.)
WESSEX HC.Mk 2	770 km (475 mi.)

HOVER CEILING

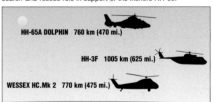

Hover ceiling is a theoretical figure measured during the first flights of the prototype. It can be affected very significantly by high temperature (this figure is calculated at a standard temperature of 15°C/59°F). The HH-65 often flies in hot weather at sea level.

HH-65A DOLPHIN	HH-3F	WESSEX HC.Mk 2
1627 m (1,000 ft.)	2500 m (1,550 ft.)	1220 m (760 ft.)

On patrol with the US Coast Guard

HC-130H: With a large APS-137 radar on the fuselage sides, the HC-130H can search large areas of ocean with great accuracy.

HH-52 SEAGUARD: The single-engined predecessor to the HH-65, the old HH-52 could land on the water, unlike the HH-65.

HU-25 GUARDIAN: Derived from the Dassault Falcon 20, the HU-25 can fly counter-smuggling or long-range rescue missions.

SCHWEIZER RV-8: For covert spying against smugglers, the low-light TV-equipped RV-8 wears a low-visibility paint scheme.

EUROCOPTER/KAWASAKI

BK 117

- European/Japanese co-operation ● Ambulance, rescue and utility

On 25 February 1977 Messerschmitt-Bölkow-Blohm and Kawasaki signed an agreement for the joint production of a new utility helicopter. Although the aircraft itself has been reasonably successful, it was the programme as a whole that demonstrated what can be achieved by a harmonious international project. BK 117s have found their most lucrative market in the rescue/emergency service role and continue to give life-saving service.

▲ With its large clamshell rear doors and twin-engined reliability, the BK 117 is a popular aircraft with civilian rescue and ambulance operators. It has also been licence produced by IPTN in Indonesia.

PHOTO FILE

EUROCOPTER/KAWASAKI BK 117

Armed and dangerous ▶
MBB displayed a multi-role military BK 117A-3M version at the 1985 Paris air show. The helicopter could carry the HOT anti-tank missile.

◀ Mountain rescue
Equipped with a cabin-mounted rescue winch and a searchlight, the BK 117 is a useful light search-and-rescue helicopter.

Off-shore support ▶
With its twin engines and 11-seat capacity, the BK 117 has considerable potential for maritime operations.

▼ Executive transport
Most BK 117s have been bought by civilian customers, and some are operated as corporate transports.

Fighting fires in Scotland ▶
Emergency services around the world appreciate the value of the helicopter for a variety of tasks. Many companies, such as McAlpine in the UK, lease aircraft to agencies such as the Strathclyde fire brigade.

FACTS AND FIGURES

- ➤ MBB abandoned its armed military BK 117A-3M, but 'civilian' machines have been sold to military customers.

- ➤ Kawasaki flew the first production BK 117 on 24 December 1981.

- ➤ Several features of the BO 105 were retained or modified in the BK 117.

- ➤ MBB abandoned its BO 107 design and Kawasaki its KH-7 project in favour of joint BK 117 production.

- ➤ The first aircraft from the MBB production line flew on 23 April 1982.

- ➤ Germany's ministry of defence used one BK 117 as a composites testing aircraft.

PROFILE

International multi-role project

Few international programmes have operated with as little controversy as that of the BK 117. Development costs were split equally between MBB (the German arm of Eurocopter) and Kawasaki and final assembly takes place in Donauwörth (Germany) and Gifu (Japan). Each company supplies the components it is responsible for, for example all fuselages are produced by Kawasaki and all rotor systems by MBB.

The majority of the BK 117's structure and production techniques was based on the BO 105, but, unlike its illustrious predecessor, the BK 117 failed to find any real military customers and this has limited the number of orders.

On the civilian market the BK 117 has proved ideal for emergency and rescue work, but this niche market has not allowed this helicopter to achieve the market success it truly deserves.

Above: MBB's BK 117A-3M demonstrator is armed with HOT missiles. Although more than 20 military customers exist, none uses the BK 117 offensively.

Right: Kobe City Fire Department's BK 117 is equipped with powerful spotlights for fire-spotting and other emergency duties.

BK 117B-2

Type: twin-turboshaft multi-purpose helicopter

Powerplant: two Textron Lycoming LTS 101-750B-1 turboshafts, each with 528-kW (708-hp.) take-off rating and 516-kW (692-hp.) continuous rating

Maximum speed: 278 km/h (172 m.p.h.)

Initial climb rate: 660 m/min (2,165 f.p.m.)

Range: 541 km (335 mi.) at sea level

Weights: empty 1727 kg (3,800 lb.) ; maximum take-off 3350 kg (7,370 lb.)

Accommodation: one pilot and a maximum of 10 passengers

Dimensions:
main rotor diameter	11 m (36 ft. 1 in.)
length	13 m (42 ft. 8 in.)
height	3.85 m (55 ft. 3 in.)
main rotor disc area	95.03 m² (1,023 sq. ft.)

BK 117

This BK 117 serves with the air proving wing of the Japanese Air Self-Defence Force.

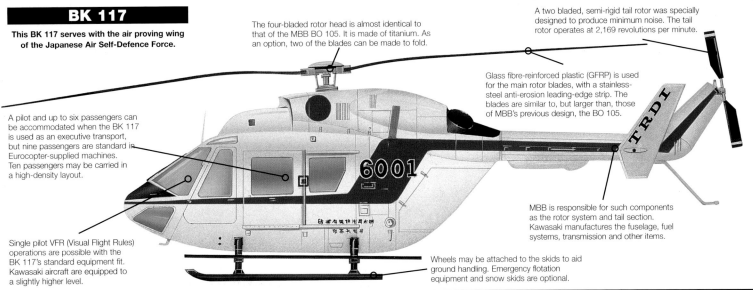

The four-bladed rotor head is almost identical to that of the MBB BO 105. It is made of titanium. As an option, two of the blades can be made to fold.

A two bladed, semi-rigid tail rotor was specially designed to produce minimum noise. The tail rotor operates at 2,169 revolutions per minute.

Glass fibre-reinforced plastic (GFRP) is used for the main rotor blades, with a stainless-steel anti-erosion leading-edge strip. The blades are similar to, but larger than, those of MBB's previous design, the BO 105.

A pilot and up to six passengers can be accommodated when the BK 117 is used as an executive transport, but nine passengers are standard in Eurocopter-supplied machines. Ten passengers may be carried in a high-density layout.

Single pilot VFR (Visual Flight Rules) operations are possible with the BK 117's standard equipment fit. Kawasaki aircraft are equipped to a slightly higher level.

MBB is responsible for such components as the rotor system and tail section. Kawasaki manufactures the fuselage, fuel systems, transmission and other items.

Wheels may be attached to the skids to aid ground handling. Emergency flotation equipment and snow skids are optional.

ACTION DATA

MAXIMUM SPEED

Although it can carry only two more passengers than the BK 117, the Dauphin 2 is far more powerful and hence faster. The comparatively low-powered Explorer does not use a tail rotor, which decreases drag.

BK 117B-2	278 km/h (172 m.p.h.)
AS 365N2 DAUPHIN 2	296 km/h (184 m.p.h.)
MD EXPLORER	296 km/h (184 m.p.h.)

MAXIMUM CLIMB RATE

Both of the lighter helicopters offer good climb performance. The much newer technology used in the Explorer is reflected in its superior performance.

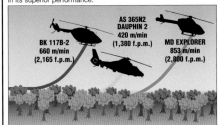

AS 365N2 DAUPHIN 2 420 m/min (1,380 f.p.m.)

BK 117B-2 660 m/min (2,165 f.p.m.)

MD EXPLORER 853 m/min (2,800 f.p.m.)

RANGE

Larger airframes have greater fuel capacity and therefore the Eurocopter AS 365N2 Dauphin 2 has the longest range. The BK 117, although incorporating older technology, offers a range almost as great as that of the Explorer. The BK 117 can be fitted with two internal and two external auxiliary tanks to increase its range.

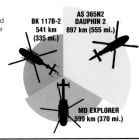

BK 117B-2 541 km (335 mi.)

AS 365N2 DAUPHIN 2 897 km (555 mi.)

MD EXPLORER 599 km (370 mi.)

Kawasaki aerospace projects

■ **KH-4:** Licensed manufacture of the Bell 47G-3B, as the KH-4, began in 1962. This aircraft was exported to the Thai police force.

■ **KV-107:** Kawasaki built the Boeing-Vertol Model 107 under licence, but production ceased in the early-1990s.

■ **OH-6:** Beginning in March 1969, Kawasaki manufactured the Hughes OH-6 under a licence agreement.

■ **369:** Civilian variants of the OH-6, designated the 369, have also been built in Japan, mostly for Japanese customers.

FAIRCHILD

MERLIN/METRO

● Executive airliner ● Turboprop engines ● Streamlined design

PHOTO FILE

FAIRCHILD MERLIN/METRO

▼ Magnificent Merlin
Fairchild undertook modifications to the Merlin series, allowing the aircraft to remain at the cutting edge of the highly competitive regional airliner market.

▲ Clean lines
The exceptionally streamlined design of the Merlin has enabled the aircraft to become one of the most eye-catching airliners around. This is highlighted by this example's attractive colour scheme.

European service ▶
Flying the demanding route over the Alps, Austrian airline Trans Adria utilises a Merlin IVA. The Merlin is proving to be a great success, able to provide a regular service in some of the most harsh weather conditions.

◀ Flying the flag
Operating within the United States as a commuter airliner, the Merlin is used to provide feeder connection flights to a host of major airlines. They operate from most of America's major city airports.

Multipurpose Merlin ▶
Often referred to as the 'sewer tube', because of its long circular fuselage design, the Merlin is equipped with a large rear-mounted cargo hatch and a forward passenger door.

O ne of the more distinctive turboprop commuter and business aircraft design families, the Merlin and Metro can trace their origins back to the 1960s. Swearingen Aircraft was founded in San Antonio, Texas, in 1959 by Edward J. Swearingen. His company began by offering turboprop conversions for existing aircraft, but in 1964 launched an all-new design – the Merlin. From this was developed a pressurised commuter aircraft – the Metro.

▲ With its long range and spacious internal design, the Fairchild Merlin and Metro series has found a ready market with both commercial and corporate users.

FACTS AND FIGURES

➤ Swearingen's financial difficulties in 1971 led to early merger talks with Piper, though these came to naught.

➤ PT6A engines were offered again on the Metro IIIA after requests from US airlines.

➤ One UC-26C was fitted with radar for use by the US ANG as a drug interdictor.

➤ The Metro II, introduced in 1974, offered an optional rocket unit for assisted take-offs from 'hot and high' airfields.

➤ An all-freight version of the Metro 23 is known as the Expediter.

➤ In 1997 Merlins and Metros share the same fuselage, but have different interiors.

PROFILE

Cutting edge commuter

Originally powered by two Pratt & Whitney PT6A turbines, the Merlin entered production in 1965. Pressure applied by AiResearch Aviation, who were marketing the aircraft for Swearingen, led to the Merlin being re-engined with Garrett AiResearch TPE331 turboprops, and the improved Metro series soon followed.

To comply with US regulations of the day regarding commuter aircraft, the Metro was initially restricted to a gross weight of 5670 kg (12,500 lb.). Its circular fuselage was derived from that of the Merlin and held 19 passengers.

By 1971, Swearingen had been taken over by Fairchild, with whom the Metro series had been jointly developed and, which had undertaken some sub-assembly work on early production aircraft.

Various improved Merlins and Metros followed, the Metro IIA of 1980 taking advantage of the relaxation in operational weight restrictions, and the Metro III

introducing 746-kW (1,000-hp.) TPE331s turboprops and an extension to its wingspan.

Having sold well, the Metro found customers in the US and abroad. A major boost to the programme came in the 1980s, when the US Air National Guard bought 50 Metro IIIs (C-26As and Bs). Incorporating features of these aircraft, Fairchild then introduced the civil Metro 23 with a 7484-kg (16,500-lb.) all-up weight.

Left: This example is operated by the Swiss airline Crossair. Regional flights are undertaken throughout Europe.

Right: Introduced in later models was the increased wing-span. This allowed the Metro to operate at greater weights as well as higher altitudes, so increasing range and reducing costs.

METRO III

Delivered in 1982, this aircraft operated with Houston Aircraft Leasing. After withdrawal from service, the Metro was passed to Chrysler Management Corporation as a company transport aircraft.

Metro III

Type: twin-engined regional airliner

Powerplant: two 746-kW (1,000-hp.) Garrett Air Research TPE331-11U-601G turboprops

Maximum speed: 555 km/h (344 m.p.h.)

Cruising speed: 513 km/h (318 m.p.h.)

Initial climb rate: 743 m/min (2,440 f.p.m.)

Range: 1149 km (712 mi.)

Weights: operational empty weight 3963 kg (8,719 lb.); maximum take off 6350 kg (13,970 lb.)

Accommodation: two flight crew and 19 passengers

Dimensions:
span	17.37 m	(57 ft.)
length	18.09 m	(59 ft. 4 in.)
height	5.08 m	(16 ft. 8 in.)
wing area	28.71 m²	(309 sq. ft.)

New features of the Metro III were uprated engines and a stronger wing, associated with the increase in gross weight. There was no increase in fuselage size or passenger accommodation. The aircraft was approved for up to 20 passengers, but in US operations this is limited to 19, since a cabin attendant is carried.

Streamlining the Metro design has played an important part in the aircraft refinement. To this end new Dowty-Rotol supercritical propellers were adopted and the nacelle lines were refined to reduce drag. Another drag-reduction modification allowed the landing gear doors to close after gear extension.

Positioned at the rear of the fuselage is a large cargo hatch. This allows the aircraft to be loaded with a limited amount of baggage. An interesting bonus of positioning the door at the rear is that during commercial flight operations, the aircraft cargo and passengers can be unloaded at the same time.

PIONEER AIRLINES

N30693

The forward-mounted passenger door is fitted with integral steps to ease the boarding for passengers. This door is also used by the flight deck crew.

Garrett turboprops are installed on the Metro III. These are equipped with an optional alcohol/water injection system to offer better performance in hot conditions.

The new wing of the Metro III is 3.05 m (10 ft.) longer than that of the original Merlin. To reduce drag, the wingtips are of a conical-chamber design.

With a general increase in the dimensions of the Metro series, the aircraft was fitted with a rear-mounted fillet. Earlier models were equipped with a small rocket pack, to reduce the take-off distance.

ACTION DATA

MAXIMUM CRUISING SPEED

Equipped with two turboprop engines like similar small regional airliners, the Metro 23 is able to offer an exceptionally high speed mainly because of its streamlined design. Slowest in this field is the Brazilian EMB-110.

METRO 23	534 km/h (336 m.p.h.)
EMB-110	411 km/h (255 m.p.h.)
JETSTREAM 31	489 km/h (303 m.p.h.)

RANGE

Continually upgraded, the Metro's range has allowed the aircraft to become one of the leading designs in the business commuter field. The increase in fuselage size and wingspan has allowed extra fuel tanks to be added.

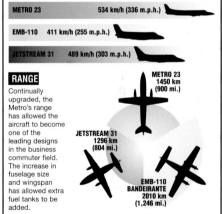

METRO 23 1450 km (900 mi.)

JETSTREAM 31 1296 km (804 mi.)

EMB-110 BANDEIRANTE 2010 km (1,246 mi.)

PASSENGER CAPACITY

Though not having a passenger load any higher than others within its class, the Metro's design allows a rapid turnaround in between flight operations. With the regular nature of commuter flights, the modest passenger capacity is therefore not a disadvantage.

METRO 23	19 PASSENGERS
EMB-110 BANDEIRANTE	18 PASSENGERS
JETSTREAM 31	19 PASSENGERS

First-class performer

■ **MILITARY:** Used as a squadron transport, this Merlin is flown by the Belgian Air Force. The aircraft also provides transport for high-ranking officers.

■ **COMMERCIAL:** Delivered in 1978, this Metro operated with Tavina in Colombia on internal flights. This example was once also operated by British Aerospace Inc.

■ **VIP TRANSPORT:** A substantial improvement was made to South Africa's military transport fleet with the purchase of a Merlin. The aircraft is employed as a long-range VIP transport.

FAIREY

ROTODYNE

● 'Compound' helicopter/fixed wing ● Heli-liner and cargo-lifter

▲ *Nothing before or since has been built like the Rotodyne. Basically an airliner with rotors and wings, it was a technical success which avoided many of the problems of today's 'tilt rotor' designs.*

I t has always been a dream – an airliner able to leap into the sky from the middle of the big city, traverse great distances and carry passengers direct to their destination. Fairey, Britain's Ministry of Supply and British European Airways became three-way partners in 1948 in pursuing this vision. The ambitious Rotodyne compound helicopter, or convertiplane, could have succeeded if boardroom politics by its manufacturer had not prevented it from entering production.

FAIREY ROTODYNE

▲ **Casualty evacuation**
A 1960 mock-up made for exercise 'White Swan' demonstrated that the Rotodyne could have made a highly effective flying ambulance.

▲ **Freight loader**
The Rotodyne could carry loads far beyond the capacity of most helicopters of the late 1950s.

Distinctive profile ▶
Like the huge Soviet Mil Mi-6, the Rotodyne featured wings and rotors, but no other aircraft featured twin turboprops as well.

▲ **Heavy lifter**
Thanks to its powered rotor, the Rotodyne could hover even with a girder slung underneath it.

Building a beast ▶
Because of the huge size of the Rotodyne, some very unusual construction techniques were required by Fairey. Only one example of this unique machine was ever completed despite its success.

FACTS AND FIGURES

➤ The Gyrodyne tested the concepts used on the Rotodyne and took a 200-km/h (124 m.p.h.) speed record in June 1948.

➤ In April 1958 the Rotodyne made its first transition to level flight.

➤ The production Rotodyne would have used Rolls-Royce Tyne engines.

➤ On 5 January 1959, the Rotodyne set a speed record in the convertiplane class by flying at 307.2 km/h (190 m.p.h.).

➤ Okanagan Helicopters and Japan Air Lines were interested in Rotodynes.

➤ British and American forces studied a possible military Rotodyne.

The ultimate helicopter

The Fairey Rotodyne was a bold attempt to build and sell a practical vertical take-off airliner. When it first flew on 6 November 1957, the Rotodyne was breathtaking – a new concept in aviation which could take off and land like a helicopter, but fly with almost the same performance as a conventional aircraft.

The Rotodyne's large, four-blade rotor for vertical flight was driven by tip jets which received compressed air from the two

Eland turbine engines. These also drove propellers for horizontal flight.

The Rotodyne had the potential to transform city-to-city travel. Kaman wanted to manufacture it in the US; New York Airways pledged to purchase five aircraft – then backed out. When Fairey merged with Westland in 1960 and numerous corporate changes took place quickly, the once-promising Rotodyne was suddenly deemed no longer

worth the investment it required.

Though the aircraft flew well and its technical problems could have been solved, the Rotodyne could not defeat Westland's cost accountants, and the project was cancelled in February 1962.

A huge chance was missed when the Rotodyne was cancelled. The potential for heavylift helicopters was shown by the subsequent success of the Boeing Chinook.

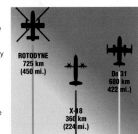

The prototype Rotodyne could carry two crew and 40 passengers, but production machines would have seated as many as 70 in a one-class configuration.

Because the main rotor was located above the centre of gravity, unlike a normal helicopter, the main cabin could be fully filled with cargo.

XE 521 was the only Fairey Rotodyne ever built. Flying between 1957 and 1960, it proved the potential of the convertiplane, but the aircraft was too costly to put into production.

The Napier Eland engines drove large four-metre Rotol propellers. Production Rotodynes were to have had the more powerful and reliable Rolls-Royce Tyne engine. A separate compressor generated high-pressure air which drove jets at the rotor tips.

The stubby wings provided lift in forward flight. They were equipped with trim tabs but no ailerons, roll control being effected through the rotor head.

The blade tip jets were known as Fairey High Pressure Combustion Chambers.

The cockpit was fitted with fairly limited equipment, but gave the pilots a superb view. The controls included a cyclic and collective pitch lever, as in a conventional helicopter.

FAIREY ROTODYNE

XE 521

FAIREY ROTODYNE

The Rotodyne's great weight required twin nosewheels to be fitted.

Fixed main gear was chosen in the prototype because of possible resonance problems.

The tail structure was similar to a conventional aeroplane, with fins, tabbed elevators, rudders and tailplane.

MAXIMUM SPEED

Although the Rotodyne was faster than any helicopter of the late 1950s, its rotary wing was less efficient than a conventional wing. The X-18's wing and engines tilted forward for normal flight, while the Dornier Do 31 was powered by two Rolls-Royce Pegasus turbojets, each delivering 7 tonnes of thrust.

ROTODYNE	307 km/h (190 m.p.h.)
X-18	400 km/h (250 m.p.h.)
Do 31	640 km/h (397 m.p.h.)

RANGE

The Rotodyne's range made it suitable for commuter airline operations, particularly with its ability to operate out of city centre heliports. The two experimental aircraft programmes had not addressed the problems of range before they were cancelled.

ROTODYNE 725 km (450 mi.)

Do 31 680 km (422 mi.)

X-18 360 km (224 mi.)

PAYLOAD

ROTODYNE	X-18	Do 31
40 passengers or 4800 kg (10,560-lb.)	capable of c. 2500 kg (5,500-lb.) lift	34 troops or 5000 kg (11,000-lb.)

The production Rotodyne would have had the passenger capacity of a medium-sized airliner, and its rear loading doors would have given it a significant cargo handling ability. The Dornier could have carried a similar payload far faster, but at much greater cost and, with its eight lift engines and two thrust engines, with many more parts to cause problems.

Vertical take-off load-lifters

■ **HELICOPTERS: (Mi-6)** The only practical vertical take-off lifters have been outsize conventional helicopters such as the giant Mil Mi-6 and Mi-26.

■ **COMPOUND HELICOPTERS:** (Fairey Gyrodyne) Combining a rotor with wings and engines for forward flight increases flying efficiency.

■ **CONVERTIPLANES: (Curtiss-Wright X-19)** These tilt the wing and engines through 90° for lift and forward flight.

■ **TILTING DUCTED FANS:** (Bell X-22A) This is a special variant of the convertiplane, with the propellers inside cowlings.

■ **LIFT AND THRUST: (Dornier Do 31)** Separate lift and thrust engines are the simplest solution, but they are bulky and add complexity.

FARMAN

F.60 GOLIATH

● Twin-engine biplane bomber ● Pioneer European airliner

esigned as a heavy bomber but completed too late to see service during World War I, the Farman F.60 became one of the world's first airliners. During the 1920s it was built in both military and commercial versions, equipping French air force and navy bomber units as well as helping pioneer airline services. Later military models with more powerful engines and the ability to carry bomb loads of up to 1500 kg (3,300 lb.) remained in service into the early 1930s.

▲ In August 1919
Frenchman Lucien Bossoutrot set a long-distance record, flying a Goliath with seven others aboard the 2044 km (1,270 mi.) from Paris to Casablanca in 18 hours 23 minutes.

FARMAN F.60 GOLIATH

▼ **Early airliner**
This aircraft started life with Belgian airline SNETA in April 1921, on services between Brussels and London. SNETA ceased operations in August after a crash and hangar fire. Its aircraft went to SABENA.

▲ **Farman Line to Brussels**
On 1 July 1920, Farman Line inaugurated a Paris to Brussels service, which was later extended to Amsterdam and Berlin.

At Le Bourget ▶
Two of Air Unions' Goliaths are seen here at Paris main airport in the 1920s. The other aircraft are an Air Union Blériot Spad 33 (rear) and a Fokker F.III belonging to Dutch airline KLM.

▼ **F.60 F-FHMU**
The Farman Line, operated by the company that built the Goliath, liked to incorporate the initials of its founders, Henri and Maurice Farman, in its aircraft's registrations.

▲ **On the tarmac at Croydon**
Air Union and Imperial Airways aircraft meet outside Croydon airport's terminal. Goliaths helped establish air services across the English Channel.

FACTS AND FIGURES

➤ A CGEA F.60 and a British DH.18 were involved in the first mid-air collision between two airliners on 7 April 1922.

➤ A Goliath was priced at the equivalent of $7055 in 1919.

➤ The fuselage, fin and rudder of an Air Union Goliath is preserved in France.

➤ A large number of F.60 airliners were re-engined with 300-hp. Salmson 9Az engines as the F.63bis.

➤ Bomber F.60s were built from 1922; the French army equipped six squadrons.

➤ After the 1930 crash of the first F.140, the French air force scrapped its last Goliaths.

Pioneer airliner from a French pioneer

Designed as a two-seat night bomber, the original Goliath proved readily adaptable to passenger transport. The original passenger conversion involved the creation of two cabins, one for four passengers in the nose and the other for eight behind and below the open cockpit.

On 8 February 1919, the aircraft carried 11 passengers plus a mechanic from Paris to London, returning the next day and flying to Brussels three days later. By the following year there were regular services linking the British, French and Belgian capitals.

Dozens of F.60s were used by fledgling French airlines during the 1920s. Others were operated in Belgium, Japan, Rumania and South America, and six aircraft were built in Czechoslovakia by Avia and Letov. Various engines were used, with the airplane's designation changing accordingly.

Farman also built 20 three-seat F.60M bombers for the French air force and 24 for the navy. Italy used the F.62 and Poland the F.68. In 1928 an improved F.160 series appeared of which there were nine separate variations. They included new floatplane torpedo bomber and transport variants.

Above: French airline Cie des Grands Express Aériens (CGEA) began a Paris to London service with F.60s on March 29, 1920. Flights were irregular at first.

Left: Another of Air Union's Goliaths, F-AEFC was named Provence. The last Goliaths in airline service were Farman Line aircraft in 1933.

F.60 GOLIATH

F-AECU Normandie was one of at least 15 aircraft operated by Air Union from 1923. Air Union flew aircraft inherited from CMA and Grands Express, airlines that flew the type on the London and Paris route.

F.60 Goliath
Type: Passenger transport.
Powerplant: Two 194-kW (260-hp.) Salmson CM.9 nine-cylinder air-cooled radial engines
Maximum speed: 140 km/h (87 m.p.h.)
Cruising speed: 119 km/h (74 m.p.h.)
Range: 402 km (250 mi.)
Service ceiling: 4008 m (13,150 ft.)
Weights: Empty equipped 2495 kg (5,500 lb.); max take-off 4760 kg (10,494 lb.)
Fuel load: 467 kg (1,030 lb.)
Accommodation: 2 crew plus up to 12 passengers (max useful load 1597 kg (3,520 lb.))
Dimensions: span 26.49 m (86 ft. 11 in.)
length 13.89 m (45 ft. 7 in.)
height 5.59 m (18 ft. 4 in.)
wing area 160.91 m² (1,732 sq. ft.)

Air Union named its Goliaths after regions in France, including Normandie. Other names included Languedoc, Alsace, Lorraine, Auvergne, Provence, Flandre and Gascogne.

In their 1.32-m (4-ft. 4-in.) wide fuselage, commercial Goliath variants had a nose cabin for four passengers and a rear cabin for up to eight. These were separated by the raised open cockpit for the two pilots.

Avia and Letov built a number of Goliaths in Czechoslovakia; five for the national airline CSA and one for VIP use by the air force. French-built aircraft served worldwide. Examples were sold in the USSR, Italy and Japan.

Early bomber variants were able to deliver 1043 kg (2,300 lb.) of bombs and carried a crew of three and three defensive 7.7-mm (.303 cal.) machine guns. The later F.140 Super Goliath could haul 1497 kg (3,300 lb.) of bombs.

The various commercial Goliaths were fitted with a variety of engines, the civil F.60 having two 172-kw (230-hp.) Salmson Z.9 radials. Other versions had powerplants by different makers, including Renault, Lorraine, Farman, Armstrong Siddeley and Gnome-Rhône.

The Goliath's sturdy undercarriage was fitted with trousered fairings and were supported by twin main wheels. Its structure was combined with that of the engine nacelle above the leg. The untapered wings with squared tips led to the rumor that they were built by the mile and cut to size.

Military Goliaths in action

TRAINING: After being declared obsolete as a bomber in Polish service, the Goliath found new roles as a parachute trainer and undertook crew familiarization flights.

1920s BOMBER: Despite obsolescence in the bomber role in Europe, France operated army F.60s and navy F.65s against Rif tribesmen in Morocco between 1925 and 1927.

FLOATPLANE TORPEDO BOMBER: The F.168 was a Jupiter-engined development which served with a number of units of the French Aéronautique Maritime from 1928 to 1936. The fuselage was modified to improve the pilot's view. About 60 entered service.

ACTION DATA

SPEED
Compared to airliner types that began to enter service in the late 1920s, the Goliath was short on top speed. It was soon outpaced by types such as the Handley Page W.8 and Vimy Commercial. The latter was another airliner developed from a bomber design.

F.60 GOLIATH	140 km/h (87 m.p.h.)
W.8	195 km/h (115 m.p.h.)
VIMY COMMERCIAL	158 km/h (98 m.p.h.)

RANGE
The Vimy had, albeit in modified form, demonstrated its ability to fly considerable distances in a series of long-distance route proving flights. Companies like Imperial Airways were able to pioneer services over longer routes than those flown by the F.60.

F.60 GOLIATH 402 km (250 mi.)
VIMY COMMERCIAL 724 km (450 mi.)
W.8 805 km (500 mi.)

WEIGHT
In the 1920s, manufacturers were more interested in providing their airliner designs with longer range than with increasing carrying. Thus, the W.8 and Vimy weighed in at less than one ton more than the Goliath. Most of the extra weight would have been fuel.

F.60 GOLIATH 4760 kg (10,494 lb.)
W.8 5598 kg (12,342 lb.)
VIMY COMMERCIAL 5658 kg (12,474 lb.)

FOKKER

F.VII

● Successful inter-war airliner ● Record flights ● Licence production

▲ By using all
of the experience he had gained
building World War I fighters, Anthony Fokker
was able to develop a world-beating series
of inter-war airliners.

In November 1918, with Germany in a state of collapse, Anthony Fokker fled to his native Netherlands, taking a large number of documents with him. Further intrigue followed. Fokker had been working on designs for a passenger aircraft. Prototypes were flown and it was the first F.II that Fokker's wartime test pilot, de Waal, secretly flew to Holland in 1920. The F.II established Fokker as a manufacturer of practical passenger airliners.

FOKKER F.VII

▼ American customers
Fokker supplied a number of airframes, usually without engines which were fitted locally, to America. This Standard Airlines F.VIIa had a Pratt & Whitney Hornet engine.

▲ Early Swiss airliner
HB-LBO was the first F.VIIa supplied to Switzerland, and was delivered to Balair in 1927. After service with Swissair it was retired in 1948 and later restored to be displayed in a museum.

▼ Tri-motor Bomber
F.VIIb-3ms were licence-built in several countries. Bomber versions were built in Czechoslovakia and Poland.

▲ Red Cross F.VIIa
Although it was originally H-NADP, by World War II this aircraft was in Finnish markings and serialed FE-2.

Famous Fokker ▶
On 9 May 1926 Floyd Bennett flew this F.VIIa-3m, the first F.VII tri-motor, over the North Pole. Purchased by Edsel Ford, it was later displayed in the Ford Museum.

FACTS AND FIGURES

➤ After testing an F.VIIa-3m the US Army bought a small number of US-built tri-motors; most were designated C-2s.

➤ F.VIIs were used by both sides in the Spanish Civil War.

➤ Licence-built F.VIIs included those built in Britain as the Avro Ten.

➤ Perhaps the most famous Fokker F.VII was Southern Cross, which crossed the Pacific non-stop in 88 hours in 1928.

➤ For a 1928 Antarctic expedition an F.VIIb-3m was fitted with floats.

➤ The very first F.VII first flew in 1924 powered by a Rolls-Royce Eagle engine.

PROFILE

From fighters to airliners

By 1923 work had begun on the prototype Fokker F.VII, which was very similar to the F.II and its successors. Powered by a 268.5-kW (360-hp.) Rolls-Royce Eagle engine, it flew in April 1924. This model could carry six passengers and only five were built.

The F.VIIa, which had a smaller wing and bigger engine to improve speed performance, plus an eight-passenger cabin, appeared in 1925. This model was used by airlines, including KLM, for both passenger and freight services.

When KLM issued a specification for a 10-seat airliner which was able to fly with a failed engine, the result was the F.VIIa-3m. The tri-motored Fokker was destined to become one of the most well-known commercial aircraft in the world. The first F.VIIa-3m made the first flight over the North Pole in 1926, while Charles Kingsford-Smith flew across the Pacific Ocean in 1928 in an improved F.VIIb-3m named Southern Cross. Between 1927 and 1933 the F.VIIb-3m was the world's premier airliner, and licence production was undertaken in seven countries.

Above: H-NACT was KLM's first F.VIIa. The Dutch company later requested a variant which had more engines to improve safety.

Below: This aircraft is one of four Armstrong Siddeley Lynx-powered F.VIIa-3ms registered in Britain. G-EBYI was owned by a Belgian financier.

F.VIIa

Type: single-engined 10-seat airliner

Powerplant: one 298-kW (400-hp.) Gnome Rhône-built Jupiter nine-cylinder radial engine

Maximum speed: 185 km/h (115 m.p.h.)

Cruising speed: 155 km/h (96 m.p.h.)

Endurance: 7 hours 35 min at cruising speed

Range: 1160 km (720 mi.)

Service ceiling: 2600 m (8,550 ft.)

Weights: empty 1950 kg (4,290 lb.); loaded 3650 kg (8,030 lb.)

Accommodation: two crew and eight passengers

Dimensions:
span	19.31 m (63 ft. 4 in.)	
length	14.35 m (47 ft.)	
height	3.90 m (12 ft. 9 in.)	
wing area	58.50 m² (629 sq. ft.)	

F.VIIB-3M

In Poland, E. Plage and T. Laskiewicz of Lubin built 19 F.VIIb-3ms for the Polish airline LOT. SP-ABK *Krysia* was one of 11 fitted with Wright Whirlwind J5A engines; the remainder were powered by Pratt & Whitney Wasp Juniors.

F.VIIb-3ms could be fitted with a wide variety of engine types with power outputs of between 149 kW (200 hp.) and 224 kW (300 hp.). In fact, at least 12 types are known to have been fitted.

The F.VIIb-3m had a larger wing than the F.VIIa to increase operating weights. Fuel tanks were located above the cockpit.

The welded steel tube fuselage structure and control surfaces were fabric covered. However, all-metal stressed-skin construction was fast gaining acceptance in the 1930s.

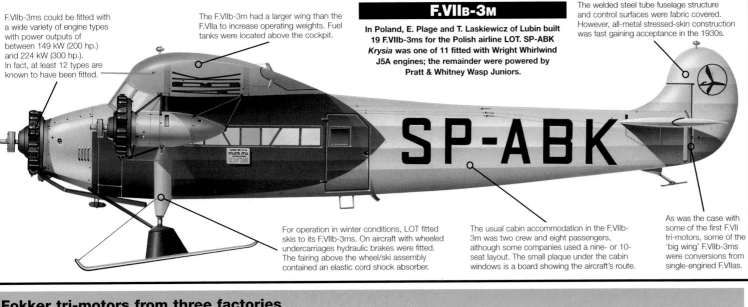

For operation in winter conditions, LOT fitted skis to its F.VIIb-3ms. On aircraft with wheeled undercarriages hydraulic brakes were fitted. The fairing above the wheel/ski assembly contained an elastic cord shock absorber.

The usual cabin accommodation in the F.VIIb-3m was two crew and eight passengers, although some companies used a nine- or 10-seat layout. The small plaque under the cabin windows is a board showing the aircraft's route.

As was the case with some of the first F.VII tri-motors, some of the 'big wing' F.VIIb-3ms were conversions from single-engined F.VIIas.

ACTION DATA

ENGINE POWER

The F.VIIb-3m was equipped with three engines and therefore had considerably more power than the contemporary Junkers W.33. The all-metal Ford Trimotor was even more powerful and was destined to replace the Fokker in the US.

F.VIIb-3m	W.33	5-AT-D TRIMOTOR
671 kW (900 hp.)	310 kW (416 hp.)	939 kW (1,260 hp.)

PASSENGERS

Even in single-engined form the F.VII could carry more passengers than the W.33. Three engines not only improved safety, but increased capacity. The Ford Trimotor was a considerable advance and also introduced greater levels of comfort.

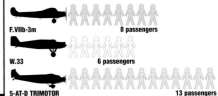

F.VIIb-3m — 8 passengers
W.33 — 6 passengers
5-AT-D TRIMOTOR — 13 passengers

RANGE

With a range of engine types available, the F.VII's performance tended to vary according to the powerplant. With three Wright Whirlwind J6 radials, 1200 km (750 mi.) was possible with a maximum fuel load aboard, more than 300 km (200 mi.) better than the Ford Trimotor.

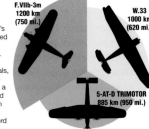

F.VIIb-3m 1200 km (750 mi.)
W.33 1000 km (620 mi.)
5-AT-D TRIMOTOR 885 km (950 mi.)

Fokker tri-motors from three factories

■ **FOKKER-BUILT:** KLM was a prominent user of both single- and three-engined F.VIIs. F.VIIb-3m PH-AFS was sold to Spain and served with the Nationalists during the civil war.

■ **ATLANTIC AIRCRAFT CORPORATION F-10/F-10A:** To overcome American manufacturers' opposition to a foreign design, Fokker set up a US factory. The F-10 was a modified F.VIIb-3m.

■ **POLISH F.VIIb-3m:** This Polish-built No. 211 Squadron aircraft was among a number built as bombers with an open mid-upper turret and bomb racks under the fuselage.

FOKKER

F27 FRIENDSHIP

● Turboprop powered ● Short-field performance ● Licence built

FOKKER F27 FRIENDSHIP

◀ **Successful sales**
One of the largest operators of the F27 was Air New Zealand. This Mk 500 was delivered in 1977 and served for 15 years.

▼ **Hot and high**
Good short-field performance made the F27 ideal for airlines such as Comair of South Africa.

▼ **Still going strong**
Despite Fokker introducing the more modern F50, the F27 is still in service around the world. This Mk 500 serves with Air UK.

▼ **First into service**
Aer Lingus was the first European airline to operate the F27, starting passenger services in November 1958.

▲ **North American pilgrim**
Pilgrim Airlines operated a pair of F27 Mk 100s on routes in north-eastern USA and into Canada. Praised for their reliability and performance, the aircraft have only recently been retired.

F okker's first turboprop airliner was a familiar sight on airline routes around the world for 30 years. This medium-range transport appeared on the scene in 1955 when Holland's best-known aircraft manufacturer began selling it to the airlines. Soon after, Fairchild built a version in the United States. The twin-engined, high-wing F27 was noisy and was said to shake like a cement mixer, but it provided affordable and efficient service.

▲ *As one of the first turboprop airliners, the F27 was initially regarded with suspicion. However, an excellent capacity plus economical performance made it a successful aircraft.*

FACTS AND FIGURES

➤ The Friendship was conceived initially as a possible replacement for the venerable Douglas DC-3.

➤ Friendships were purchased by 168 customers in 63 countries.

➤ The first of two F27 prototypes made its initial flight on 24 November 1955.

➤ During the Friendship's era, more F27s were manufactured than any other European airliner.

➤ The prototype for the enlarged Fairchild version took to the air in January 1966.

➤ Production of the F27 ended in June 1986 in favour of the Fokker 50.

PROFILE

Friendly ship of the world's skies

In the early 1950s, Fokker, backed by the Dutch government, began to develop this excellent twin-engined transport. The F27 was a response to a worldwide requirement for an aircraft able to carry 32 passengers over medium distances. Produced by Fokker in Holland and Fairchild in the US, the turboprop-powered F27 went into service in 1958.

Despite early reservations about the safety of a twin-turboprop airliner, the F27 has proved to be one of the safest aircraft in its class. While production was under way, both Fairchild and Fokker developed enlarged versions. The Friendship's passenger capacity was increased from 32 to 40 (as many as 52 in a high-density version), the fuel load was increased and a weather radar was added. In America, the enlarged version was 'stretched' and differed slightly in appearance from the Fokker-built version.

The F27 established a niche as one of the most economical airliners in its class. In some countries the F27 was also employed with great success as a freighter and VIP transport.

Above: One of the many African airlines to operate the F27 is Air Sinai of Egypt, which took delivery of three Mk 500s in the early 1980s. The aircraft pictured crashed in a sandstorm at Cairo airport in 1986.

Left: N334MV is an F27 Mk 500 delivered to Mississippi Valley Airlines in 1980. By 1990 it was based in France after having had several owners.

F27 Mk 300 Friendship

Type: passenger transport

Powerplant: two 1424-kW (1,910-hp.) Rolls-Royce Dart Mk 528-7E turboprop engines, each providing an additional 2.25 kN (506 lb.) of auxiliary thrust

Cruising speed: 428 km/h (266 m.p.h.) at 6100 m (20,000 ft.)

Range: 2010 km (1,249 mi.) with 3050-kg (6,724-lb.) payload and maximum fuel

Service ceiling: 9020 m (29,600 ft.)

Weights: empty 10,257 kg (22,612 lb.); maximum take-off 17,710 kg (39,044 lb.)

Accommodation: two pilots, flight attendant and 40 passengers (standard), or 52 in a high-density layout

Dimensions:
span	29.00 m	(95 ft. 2 in.)
length	23.50 m	(77 ft. 1 in.)
height	8.40 m	(27 ft. 7 in.)
wing area	70.00 m²	(754 sq. ft.)

FH-227B FRIENDSHIP

Originally delivered to Ozark Air Lines in July 1967, this FH-227 saw service with Delta Air Transport from 1977, and was leased to Air Lesotho for nine months between 1983 and 1984.

Two pilots are seated side by side, with a folding seat for a third crewmember if required. Weather radar, autopilot and instrument landing system aids are available to the flight crew.

F27s and FH-227s are powered by the Rolls-Royce Dart turboprop. The Dart engine went on to power a host of other aircraft and has proved to be highly reliable and economical.

The landing gear is of pneumatically-retractable tricycle type. The nosewheel is steerable and the mainwheels, which retract into the engine nacelles, can be used as airbrakes.

The all-metal fuselage is of a semi-monocoque fail-safe design. The only exception is the nose cap, which is made from glass fibre.

The tailplane is of all-metal structure, except for glass-fibre leading edges to the control surfaces. Goodrich de-icer boots are fitted to the leading edge of the fin and the tailplane.

7P-LAH

After establishing a production line for the F27 in the US, Fairchild-Hiller began to develop the aircraft. The FH-227 had a 1.83-m (6-ft.) longer fuselage. In all, 78 were built.

ACTION DATA

CRUISING SPEED

The F27 is one of the most economical aircraft in its class, and of comparable speed to its contemporaries. Top speeds of around 450 km/h were typical of turboprops of this size. The F27 outsold the YS-11 and Herald several times over.

F27 Mk 300	428 km/h (266 m.p.h.)
YS-11A	476 km/h (296 m.p.h.)
HERALD SERIES 200	428 km/h (266 m.p.h.)

PASSENGERS

Dutch-built Friendships were eventually produced with seating for 60 passengers, so that they could compete with larger aircraft like the YS-11. Manufacturers tend to match changes in competing airliners by developing new variants of equal or greater seating capacity, range and fuel economy, but with lower operating costs.

F27 Mk 300 FRIENDSHIP	52
YS-11A	60
HERALD SERIES 200	56

RANGE

The Mk 300 had an excellent range for a medium-size turboprop, allowing it to fly international flights within Europe. The YS-11A had an even better range performance. The Herald, originally powered by four piston engines, was eventually re-engined with Dart engines.

F27 Mk 300 FRIENDSHIP 2010 km (1,249 mi.)

YS-11A 2110 km (1,311 mi.)

HERALD SERIES 200 1786 km (1,110 mi.)

Friendship through the ages

■ **PROTOTYPE:** PH-NIV was the first Friendship to fly, in 1955. Its excellent performance led to the first orders from Aer Lingus.

■ **F27 TROOPSHIP:** Built for the Dutch air force, these were dedicated military transports. Some have been replaced by Fokker 60s.

■ **F27 Mk 500:** Production of the F27 continued into the 1980s with the improved Mk 500 version, which sold worldwide.

■ **F50:** The F27 was finally replaced on the Fokker production line by the F50, which owed many of its features to the Friendship.

FOKKER

F28 FELLOWSHIP

● Small airliner ● Domestic routes ● Twin engined

L ike the DC-9 and the BAC 1-11 of the same era, the Fellowship featured a moderately swept wing, twin turbofan engines mounted on the sides of the rear fuselage and a T-tail. It was smaller than both of these types, however, and slower than the DC-9, which also had a longer range. Consequently, it sold in relatively small numbers, and after only a few years in production Fokker switched to a bigger model.

▲ Its small size and reasonable operating costs meant that the F28 appealed to many Third World countries. The aircraft is still widely used from Bangladesh to South Korea.

FOKKER F28 FELLOWSHIP

◀ Peruvian landing
AeroPeru operated its F28s on domestic routes, often flying to remote high-altitude airfields.

▼ F28 in the Far East
Burma Airways made use of the Fokker F28's excellent hot-and-high performance.

▼ European service
Air France no longer uses the F28 on its short-haul routes, preferring more economical aircraft. Other major customers in Europe included TAT, KLM and Linjeflyg.

▲ Linjeflyg fleet
Sweden's domestic airline, Linjeflyg, operated an all-Fellowship fleet of 13 Series 4000s.

◀ Reliable engine
Like the turboprop F27, the F28 was powered by a Rolls-Royce engine, the Spey Mk 555. It was fitted with a special acoustic liner system to reduce noise.

FACTS AND FIGURES

➤ The Rolls-Royce Spey engine in the F28 also powered military jets like the RAF's Phantoms and Buccaneers.

➤ A freight-carrying version, the Mk 1000C, had an additional large door at the front.

➤ Many military operators, including Argentina's air force, use the F28.

➤ Several versions were built, including the Mk 6000 with a slatted wing and the high-density seating Mk 4000 for Linjeflyg.

➤ The Mk 3000R used water/methanol injection for hot-and-high operations.

➤ By the time the F28 was certified in February 1969, 22 had been ordered.

PROFILE

The great Dutch commuter jet

Developed in collaboration with Shorts of the UK, which supplied the wings, and Germany's HFB and VFW, which built the fuselage sub-assemblies, the Fellowship was powered by two Spey turbofans. It was designed to build upon the success of the turboprop F27 Friendship by offering the ability to carry more passengers at jet speeds over short and medium ranges.

The original Mk 1000 flew for the first time in May 1967

and could carry 65 passengers. The 79-seat Mk 2000 which followed had a slightly longer fuselage, and the Mk 3000 and 85-seat Mk 4000 had new wings and quieter engines. There was also a Mk 6000, which had leading-edge slats for improved take-off performance. This was certified in 1973, but Fokker was unable to find any buyers for this variant.

Germany's LTU was the first customer for the F28, and the last example manufactured was bought by Linjeflyg of

Sweden in 1987. By then Fokker had delivered 241 Fellowships to 59 customers in 39 countries, including a number of air forces.

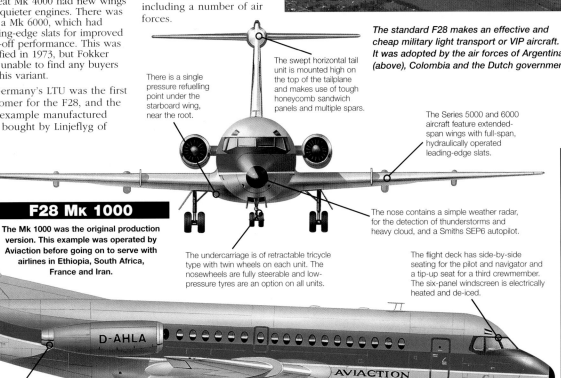

The standard F28 makes an effective and cheap military light transport or VIP aircraft. It was adopted by the air forces of Argentina (above), Colombia and the Dutch government.

The swept horizontal tail unit is mounted high on the top of the tailplane and makes use of tough honeycomb sandwich panels and multiple spars.

There is a single pressure refuelling point under the starboard wing, near the root.

The Series 5000 and 6000 aircraft feature extended-span wings with full-span, hydraulically operated leading-edge slats.

The nose contains a simple weather radar, for the detection of thunderstorms and heavy cloud, and a Smiths SEP6 autopilot.

F28 Mk 1000

The Mk 1000 was the original production version. This example was operated by Aviaction before going on to serve with airlines in Ethiopia, South Africa, France and Iran.

The undercarriage is of retractable tricycle type with twin wheels on each unit. The nosewheels are fully steerable and low-pressure tyres are an option on all units.

The flight deck has side-by-side seating for the pilot and navigator and a tip-up seat for a third crewmember. The six-panel windscreen is electrically heated and de-iced.

D-AHLA

AVIACTION

The tail unit is of cantilever alloy structure with a hydraulically actuated, variable-incidence T-tailplane. The elevators are hydraulically boosted and there is emergency tailplane actuation.

Two Rolls-Royce Spey turbofans are mounted in pods on either side of the rear fuselage. A six-chute silencing nozzle can be fitted, and the intakes are electrically de-iced.

F28 Mk 4000

Type: short- to medium-range twin-engined commercial transport

Powerplant: two 44-kN (9,900-lb.-thrust) Rolls-Royce Spey Mk 555-1P turbofans

Maximum speed: 842 km/h (552 m.p.h.)

Cruising speed: 787 km/h (489 m.p.h.)

Range: 3380 km (2,100 mi.) with maximum load and maximum fuel

Service ceiling: 10,675 m (35,000 ft.)

Weights: maximum take-off 31,523 kg (69,350 lb.)

Accommodation: two crew on flight deck plus a maximum of 85 passengers

Dimensions:
span	25.07 m (82 ft. 3 in.)
length	29.61 m (97 ft. 2 in.)
height	8.47 m (27 ft. 9 in.)
wing area	76.30 m² (821 sq. ft.)

ACTION DATA

MAXIMUM SPEED

The F28 has a respectable speed, well above that of its German rival the VFW 614, and nearly as quick as the larger, similar-engined BAC One-Eleven. Its service cruising speed is around 780 km/h, allowing improved fuel economy and increased range.

F28 Mk 3000	842 km/h (552 m.p.h.)
ONE-ELEVEN SERIES 200	882 km/h (547 m.p.h.)
VFW 614	735 km/h (456 m.p.h.)

PASSENGERS

For an aircraft of its size the F28 carries a relatively large number of passengers, thanks to its 'wide-body', five-abreast seating with an off-centre aisle. The F28's payload also makes it an attractive light- to medium transport aircraft for military operators.

F28 Mk 3000 — 65 passengers

ONE-ELEVEN SERIES 200 — 79 passengers

VFW 614 — 48 passengers

RANGE

British Rolls-Royce Spey turbofans give the F28 and BAC One-Eleven a useful range, greater than that of the fuel-thirsty VFW 614. Both the One-Eleven and the F28 were capable of flying across Europe, but the VFW 614 was limited to national and regional routes.

VFW 614
1126 km
(748 mi.)

F28 Mk 3000
3169 km
(1,965 mi.)

ONE-ELEVEN SERIES 200
2410 km (1,495 mi.)

Developments of the Fellowship

■ **FOKKER 70:** Powered by Rolls-Royce Tay turbofans, the 70 was developed to be a market partner for the similar 100. Seating was reduced to 79, and the aircraft first flew in April 1993.

■ **FOKKER 100:** Designed as the successor to the F28, and built on the same production line as its sister model the 70, the 107-seat 100 is flown by, among others, American Airlines.

■ **FOKKER 130:** This promising, larger development of the 100 series had not been built by 1996, when the Fokker company in the Netherlands was declared bankrupt.

FOKKER
F70/F100

● Advanced design ● Regional flights ● Partnership production

▲ In the competitive world of civilian airliners, the Fokker aviation company has produced a host of successful designs, all of which have achieved immense sales success.

A stretched version of the F28, the Fokker 100 flew for the first time in November 1986. It has a longer fuselage seating up to 107 passengers, redesigned wings, Tay engines instead of the F28's Speys, a new cockpit and modernised systems. The Fokker 70 is a shortened version. Using the same wings and engines, it can seat up to 79 passengers. Production of both types ended after Fokker was declared bankrupt early in 1996.

FOKKER F70/F100

▲ American bird
Seen wearing a patriotic colour scheme, this Fokker 100 is used for domestic flights within the United States.

▲ Hungry for success
Thanks to hard selling by Fokker, the F100 and F70 have been purchased by airlines in many European countries. This particular example serves with the Hungarian airline MALEV.

▲ Top deck
A vast range of colour schemes has been adopted by airlines using the aircraft. One of the most attractive is that of Korean Air.

▼ British operations
Operating with British Midland Airways for domestic flights, the Fokker 100 has proved itself to be an extremely cost-effective type.

▲ Partnership in practice
The soaring costs of developing a modern airliner made Fokker adopt the process by which sections of each aircraft are constructed in various European countries prior to final assembly.

FACTS AND FIGURES

➤ The initial purpose of the Fokker 70 was to replace the ageing F28 Fellowship with a more cost-effective aircraft.

➤ Fokker received their first order for F100s in 1984: 10 aircraft for Swissair.

➤ The first flight of the F100 was accomplished on 30 November 1986.

➤ Fokker gave the go-ahead to develop a short-fuselage variant of the F100 in 1992. This design became the F70.

➤ Launch orders for the F70 came from Pelita and Sempati Air in Indonesia.

➤ Fokker airliners are operated by more than 100 countries worldwide.

PROFILE

Fokker's last jetliner

As a result of a 1992 agreement under which Deutsche Aerospace took a major stake in Fokker, the company planned to develop a range of airliners based on the Fokker 100. This included an 80-seater and a 130-seat stretched version, but only the Fokker 70 materialised.

Quiet and efficient, the Fokker 100 enjoyed reasonable success. American Airlines became the type's biggest operator, with a fleet of 75, and a total of 290 had been ordered by the time of the

company's bankruptcy in 1996.

The Fokker 70 had been less successful, with total orders amounting to 71. However, it had appeared during a recession in the air transport market. It flew for the first time in April 1993 and entering revenue service with Indonesia's Sempati Air in March 1995. It might well have gone on to emulate the success of its larger predecessor had the manufacturer been able to stay in business.

As it is, the existing Fokker airliner fleet will be supported

by a new company, Fokker Aviation. There is a strong possibility that some aircraft will still be flying when the 100th anniversary of the founding of Fokker comes around in 2019.

Above: This Fokker 100 banks away from the camera. The type is widely praised by pilots for its performance.

Below: Only required to operate at medium altitudes for internal flights, the Fokker F100 is proving to be one of the most cost-effective airliners presently flying in Europe's skies.

F100

Type: twin-engined regional airliner

Powerplant: two 44-kN (9,900-lb.-thrust) Rolls-Royce Tay Mk 620-15 turbofans

Maximum speed: 861 km/h (534 m.p.h.) at operating altitude

Range: 1380 km (856 mi.) with maximum load

Service ceiling: 10,670 m (35,000 ft.)

Weights: empty 23,250 kg (51,150 lb.); maximum take-off 41,500 kg (91,300 lb.)

Accommodation: four crew (two flight deck and two cabin attendants) and 107 passengers

Dimensions:
span	28.08 m (92 ft. 1 in.)
length	35.31 m (115 ft. 10 in.)
height	8.50 m (27 ft. 10 in.)
wing area	93.50 m² (1,006 sq. ft.)

A high-set tail, which offers the best handling qualities, has become standard on almost all small regional airliners. A large rudder allows the Fokker 100 to operate from particularly small airfields where ground manoeuvring is restricted. All the controls on the tail are hydraulically boosted.

F100

Operating from its home country of Sweden, Transwede flies to a host of European countries as well as providing numerous internal flights. The aircraft wear a restrained colour scheme.

Only two flight crew are required to operate the F100. Pilots have found it easy to convert to the aircraft after gaining considerable experience on earlier Fokker airliners.

Under the terms of the partnership agreement, MBB of Germany undertook the construction of the mid-fuselage section and the rear tail. Positioned along either side of the fuselage are the usual airliner emergency exits.

A circular-section semi-monocoque light alloy design was used for the fuselage. It provided strength, with an overall saving in weight compared to conventional airliners. Seating for passengers can be adjusted according to the type of flight being undertaken by the airline operator.

TRANSWEDE

SE-DUB Fokker 100

Equipped with CRT displays, the flight deck is one of the most advanced of the current airliner fleet.

Construction of the wings was contracted-out to Short Brothers in Northern Ireland. Once completed, the sub-assemblies were delivered to Fokker for final assembly.

Positioned on the rear fuselage, the powerplants of the Fokker 100 are Rolls-Royce Tay turbofans. Each engine is equipped with a thrust reverser to reduce the landing run. This is a desirable feature for an aircraft that operates from city airports that may have restricted space. The engines have proved to be extremely reliable.

ACTION DATA

ACCOMMODATION

Operating in the competitive domestic routes market, the F100 is able to accommodate a large number of passengers, but still fewer than the other two aircraft featured. However, fuel efficient engines ensure the cost per passenger is low.

F100	107 passengers
A319	124 passengers
RJ100	128 passengers

CRUISING SPEED

The Fokker F100 is currently one of the fastest aircraft in its class; a high cruising speed is an attractive asset for business passengers. The fastest performer is the Airbus A319.

F100	861 km/h (534 m.p.h.)
A319	903 km/h (560 m.p.h.)
RJ100	801 km/h (497 m.p.h.)

MAXIMUM TAKE-OFF WEIGHT

The more weight that an airliner can lift off the ground, the more profitable it becomes, because the weight translates into freight and passenger revenue. Leader in this field, mainly because of its large size, is the European Airbus A319.

F100	A319	RJ100
41,500 kg (91,300 lb.)	64,000 kg (140,800 lb.)	44,425 kg (97,735 lb.)

Predecessors of the F100

■ **AÉROSPATIALE CARAVELLE:** Holding the distinction of being the first French turbojet-powered airliner, the Caravelle was used for short to medium-haul routes.

■ **BAC 1-11:** Once operated by a host of airlines across the world, this elderly British-designed aircraft is still in operation with a number of smaller airlines, for internal flights.

■ **FOKKER F28 FELLOWSHIP:** First flying in May 1967, the Fellowship had the capacity to carry a maximum of 79 passengers. Fokker was still receiving orders as late as 1980.

FORD

TRIMOTOR

● Bushplane ● Sightseeing platform ● Restored classic

O ne of the great workhorses of aviation, the Ford Trimotor started life as a regular airliner. Although it performed this role outstandingly for a good many years, it had another life as a bushplane, as a sightseeing platform around the Grand Canyon and as a movie star. Today just a handful are left, lovingly restored and cherished by their owners. Its working days are largely over, but for over 65 years the Trimotor has more than earned its keep.

▲ Ground crew
work to fix an engine on a Trimotor, using makeshift platforms. The Trimotor's systems were so simple that maintenance was routinely performed in the field.

▲ Air show performer
Trimotors have graced many air shows over the years, often performing amazing stunts. During the barnstorming era, they were used to transport crew for flying circuses around the US.

▲ Scenic survivor
One of the best-known surviving Trimotors is this superb Model 5-AT owned by Scenic Airlines, based at Las Vegas.

Canyon viewpoint ▶
Scenic operated two Trimotors, used by thousands to see the splendours of the Grand Canyon in style.

▼ Airliner progress
Used to illustrate the incredible advances made in aviation technology, in the 1970s this Trimotor donned American Airlines colours to pose alongside a 727.

▲ Crowd puller
The Trimotor is very evocative of the inter-war period, and draws a crowd wherever it goes. The few that still remain change hands for millions rather than thousands of dollars.

FACTS AND FIGURES

➤ One Trimotor was used by a typewriter company for a promotion campaign – dropping 210 typewriters from the air!

➤ In November 1929 a Trimotor was the first aircraft to fly over the South Pole.

➤ Trimotors were fitted with skis and floats to operate in remote areas of the world.

➤ Scenic's Trimotor is so valuable that it is insured for well over a million dollars.

➤ Ford were the first manufacturer to mass produce aircraft on a production line – just as they were with cars.

➤ The high drag factor of the Trimotor's corrugated skin slowed it down in flight.

PROFILE

Ford's 'Tin Goose'

When it first appeared in 1926, the Trimotor was the last word in airliner technology. With the reassuring Ford name behind it, the Trimotor was touted as the safest airliner around. In reality its performance with one engine gone was acceptable but with two out it could not retain altitude.

Some aircraft had rudimentary heating, but for most passengers the Trimotor was freezing cold (or sweltering hot, depending on the weather outside!) and impossibly noisy. Nevertheless,

it was a hit for the airlines until faster and more comfortable types appeared.

This may have spelled the end for lesser types, but the Trimotor was such a good aircraft that it could perform many other tasks. It could carry a good load in its cabin, and its huge wing allowed it to lift off from smaller airstrips. Above all, it was immensely tough, and could take any amount of punishment from rough fields, careless taxiing and the attentions of inexperienced pilots not fully familiar with its

strange flight peculiarities.

A long career in a wide variety of tasks followed, combining to give the Ford Trimotor a special place in the annals of aviation history.

Left: Lovingly referred to as the 'Tin Goose', the Ford Trimotor was built in two major models, the 4-AT and 5-AT. The 4-AT was much smaller and had a humped roof over the flight deck. The 5-AT (illustrated) had an angular roof.

Right: Trimotor's designer, Bill Stout, attempted to put a modernised version back into production during the late 1950s. The resulting Bushmaster 2000 eventually appeared in 1966.

Trimotor 4-AT

Type: passenger transport

Powerplant: three 313-kW (420-hp.) Pratt & Whitney Wasp C-series nine-cylinder radial piston engines

Maximum speed: 259 km/h (161 m.p.h.) at sea level

Cruising speed: 198 km/h (123 m.p.h.)

Range: 708 km (440 mi.)

Service ceiling: 7500 m (24,600 ft.)

Weights: typical empty 3447 kg (7,599 lb.); loaded 5738 kg (12,650 lb.)

Accommodation: flight crew of two side-by-side plus normal seating for up to 15 passengers or (later) 13 passengers plus steward or 1520 kg (3,351 lb.) of cargo

Dimensions:
span	23.72 m (77 ft. 10 in.)
length	15.30 m (50 ft. 2 in.)
height with tail down	3.66 m (12 ft.)
wing area	77.57 m² (835 sq. ft.)

The flight deck has side-by-side seating for two pilots. Although the Trimotor can be flown by a single pilot, the extra set of muscles is useful if an engine is lost, when control forces become almost impossibly high for one person.

Many Trimotors had the seats taken out and were used to haul cargo. In addition to the main cabin, the 5-AT had small holds in the thick inner-wing section, accessed via drop-down doors in the lower wing surfaces.

The whole surface of the Trimotor was skinned in corrugated aluminium. This had good strength, but did little for the aerodynamics. Cruising speed was typically under 200 km/h (124 m.p.h.).

The control cables that connect the stick to the moveable surfaces are external. Just below the flight deck is a rocker arm for the elevator control cables.

Over the years the strut-braced undercarriage of the Trimotor has proved to be immensely strong.

The cabin of the Trimotor typically has seating for around 12 passengers. Entering the Trimotor through the port-side door, the passengers had to contend with a steeply angled floor before they could reach their seats.

TRIMOTOR 5-AT

Perhaps the best-known of the remaining Trimotors is Scenic's aircraft. Unlike other survivors, this has worked all of its life. Until recently it was used to ferry sightseers over the Grand Canyon, but is now used only for promotional and film work, with occasional flights for rich pilots to get a check ride into their logbooks.

LEISURE TOURS

AUSTRALIA

Popular the world over as a pleasure flying aircraft, the BN-2 Islander has a high wing giving good downward vision. This BN-2 operates over Sydney Harbour.

ALASKA

Many of the world's most spectacular natural features can only be appreciated from the air. Tyee Airlines used Beaver floatplanes for sightseeing tours, operating from nearby fjords or lakes. This example is seen flying past the Misty Fjords National Monument near Ketchikan in Alaska. Other companies run tourist trips in the Alps, Himalayas and the Rockies, as well as to other famous landmarks such as Ayres Rock, Victoria Falls and Niagara Falls.

NEW YORK

The only way to fully take in the immensity of the skyscrapers in New York is on an aerial trip. In summer the sky is full of light aircraft and helicopters operating whistle-stop tours of the famous Manhattan skyline.

Flying across the Canyon

Pleasure flying in the Grand Canyon has been popular with tourists since the 1920s. Scenic Airways flew its first tours in 1926 and became famous operating the legendary Ford Trimotor. Now using a range of aircraft, including 20 specially modified Twin Otters, the airline caters for around 300,000 passengers per year. Its flagship Trimotor has a more leisurely life now, only flying occasional VIP trips.

LAS VEGAS

HOOVER DAM

HOOVER DAM: After taking off from Las Vegas the passengers are treated to the awe-inspiring view of Lake Mead and the famous Hoover Dam.

Mt TRUMBULL 2447 m (8,028 ft.)

COLORADO RIVER

THE GREAT SPECTACLE: The Trimotor then descends and flies along the rim of the canyon. The view is indescribable, with sheer walls dropping away from the plane and a myriad of towers rising from the canyon floor. Commentary is provided through headsets.

GRAND CANYON AIRPORT

BACK TO EARTH: At Grand Canyon airport the passengers disembark for a ground's eye view of the canyon before the straight run back to Las Vegas.

GAF

NOMAD

● Rugged and dependable ● Air ambulance ● Short take-off

▲ As well as being a superb flying ambulance, the Nomad seats up to 17 in the 'stretched' N24 variant. The key to the Nomad's performance is its remarkable short-field and rough terrain capability, making it well-suited to a range of operations throughout the Australasian continent.

I n the sprawling expanse of the Australian outback there is only one way a doctor can provide medical help to isolated communities – by air. Fortunately, Australia's Government Aircraft Factory (GAF) produced the twin-engined Nomad, an appealing plane that takes the doctors to the most remote regions. The Nomad short take-off and landing (STOL) aircraft also serves as an ambulance to evacuate patients requiring urgent intensive care.

GAF NOMAD

▲ Accommodation
The Nomad has a capacious cabin, with room for up to 13 passengers or 1685 kg (3,715 lb.) of freight.

▲ Short take-off
High-set wings, powerful turboprops and double-slotted flaps provide the GAF Nomad with its excellent short take-off and landing capability. This is essential for a flying doctor's work.

▲ Stretched version
The N24A's fuselage was lengthened by 1.14 m (3 ft. 9 in.) to accommodate 17 passengers and increase the maximum take-off weight to 4263 kg (9,398 lb.).

▲ Floatplane
In 1979 the N22B was certified to operate with floats for flights from lakes.

Flying doctor and air ambulance ▶
A major operator of the Nomad is the Royal Flying Doctor service in Australia.

FACTS AND FIGURES

➤ Australia's Northern Territory Aeromedical Service has flown more than 5,000 medical missions.

➤ The first GAF Nomad transport made its maiden flight on 23 July 1971.

➤ The Australian Customs Service operates radar-equipped Nomad Searchmasters.

➤ The flying doctors are on call 24 hours a day and can be airborne within 10 minutes of receiving an emergency call.

➤ The Nomad was designed specially for operations in Australia's outback.

➤ One N22B Nomad, equipped with floats, has operated as a seaplane and amphibian.

Life-saver of the outback

Developed in the mid-1960s as a light utility transport for civil and military work, the Australian-built Nomad has a rectangular-section fuselage, twin turboprops, a high-set tail, a high wing braced by struts, and pods which contain the retractable landing gear. Intended as an airliner, it has military and law-enforcement uses. And of its many duties, none better suits the Nomad than the difficult task of maintaining a medical lifeline in hard-to-reach locations.

With its short-field landing capability, the Nomad routinely lands at a sheep ranch or on a section of a highway. The speed and load-carrying ability of the Nomad enables it to carry plenty of diagnostic equipment and medicine in addition to a doctor. About 40 per cent of Australians live 500 km (310 mi.) or more away from the nearest full-service hospital, so the Nomad is truly an angel of mercy and a life-saver.

As well as serving numerous civil operators the Nomad has also found success with the military air arms of Australia, the Philippines, Thailand (as machine-gun-armed gunships), the Indonesian navy and Papua New Guinea.

The manufacturer GAF is now ASTA (Aerospace Technologies of Australia) and production of the Nomad has ended. The last completed airframe came off the production line in 1984, after 170 had been built. Nomads have been retired by the RAAF, but the flying doctor service continues to operate them.

The rough-field capability of the Nomad makes it ideally suited to civil utility, surveillance, agricultural and ambulance missions across Australia's vast and harsh rural expanses.

Nomad N22B

Type: STOL utility transport

Powerplant: two 298-kW (400-hp.) Allison 250-B17B (or 313-kW (420-hp.) 250-B17C) turboprop engines

Cruising speed: 269 km/h (167 m.p.h.)

Range: 1352 km (841 mi.)

Service ceiling: 6400 m (21,000 ft.)

Weights: empty 2150 kg (4,740 lb.); maximum take-off 3629 kg (8,000 lb.) (N22); 3855 kg (8,499 lb.) (N22B); 4263 kg (9,398 lb.) (N24A)

Accommodation: two pilots; 13 passengers (in the N22B) or 17 passengers (in the N24A); several configurations for stretcher-borne medical patients; or up to 1685 kg of medical equipment and personnel

Dimensions: span 16.52 m (54 ft. 2 in.); length 12.56 m (41 ft. 2 in.); height 5.52 m (18 ft. 1 in.); wing area 30.10 m² (324 sq. ft.)

NOMAD N22B

The Government Aircraft Factories Nomad served with the Army Aviation Corps for many years. This N22 was operated by No. 73 (GS) Squadron based at Oakey, Queensland.

The unusually tall tail unit contributes to the remarkable short take-off and landing performance. This can be as little as 200 m (660 ft.) for a N22B taking off fully loaded at 3855 kg (8,499 lb.).

Two American-built Allison 250-B17C turboprops rated at 313 kW (420 hp.) produce a cruising speed of 269 km/h (167 m.p.h.) over a reasonable range.

The spacious cabin can hold 13 troops or, more usually, up to 1685 kg (3,715 lb.) of freight or emergency supplies. Cargo must be tied down as take-offs and landings are very steep.

The flight deck features simple and reliable analogue controls and accommodation for a pilot and co-pilot. The large canopy provides superb visibility.

The sturdy tricycle undercarriage is housed in streamlined fairings, fitted to struts which brace the high wings.

Army Nomads were painted in this three-colour camouflage scheme when used in the rugged bush-covered areas of Australia in support of ground forces.

The Nomad's tough construction and simple layout made it an ideal military utility transport, which in times of conflict could carry 907 kg (2000 lb.) of weapons on underwing pylons.

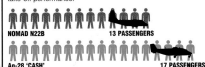

ACTION DATA

MAXIMUM PASSENGERS

The overall passenger figures reflect the aircraft's similar roles. The smaller Nomad sacrifices some of its payload for better short take-off performance.

NOMAD N22B — 13 PASSENGERS
An-28 'CASH' — 17 PASSENGERS
SKYVAN — 19 PASSENGERS

RANGE

The more modern Nomad and An-28 have a longer range than the veteran Skyvan. These two also have improved performance but lower payloads.

NOMAD N22B 1352 km (840 mi.)
An-28 'CASH' 1365 km (848 mi.)
SKYVAN 1115 km (693 mi.)

MAXIMUM SPEED

The Nomad's simple and rugged construction is not as conducive to speed as that of the streamlined An-28 and the powerfully engined Skyvan. Speed is not a high priority for this type of aircraft.

NOMAD N22B 311 km/h (193 m.p.h.)
An-28 'CASH' 350 km/h (217 m.p.h.)
SKYVAN 327 km/h (203 m.p.h.)

Flying doctor aircraft

BEECH KING AIR 90: A widely used business aircraft which is also operated by the US Army, the King Air 90 is a twin-turboprop 16-seat aircraft with pressurised fuselage.

CESSNA 425: Another popular business aircraft design, the Cessna 425 is powered by two PT6A turboprops. Standard accommodation is for six to eight passengers.

DE HAVILLAND DHA-3 DROVER: Six de Havilland Drovers were used by the flying doctor service. The eight-seat Drover was based on the Dove, but had three Gipsy Major engines.

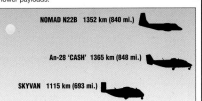

GRUMMAN

GOOSE/MALLARD

● Flying-boat ● Commercial flights ● Island hopping

T he Grumman Goose and Mallard were superb flying-boats built by a company better known for its carrier-based fighters. Development of the Goose began just before World War II, with that of the Mallard just after. Both were high-winged, twin-engined amphibians with two-step flying-boat hulls and retractable landing gear. These fine aircraft served as personal transport for many celebrities and as passenger liners for commuter airlines.

▲ Reflecting a bygone era, the Mallard is still operating as an airliner from the crystal blue waters off the Florida coastline. Here, a Turbo Mallard takes off at the start of another flight.

GRUMMAN GOOSE/MALLARD

▼ More power
In an effort to shorten the take-off run and also increase performance of the Grumman Goose, an extra pair of engines was installed on this example. The modification was not widely adopted.

▲ Land operations
With its engines at full power, a Grumman Goose prepares to lift off. The aircraft is fitted with a small undercarriage to allow amphibious operations.

◀ Executive model
After the end of World War II, Mallards were withdrawn from US Navy service and sold on the civil market. The interiors of the aircraft were completely refurbished to include a bar, sofas and sleeping quarters.

▼ Waterborne runway
Its passengers safely aboard, a Grumman Mallard eases its way into the water prior to a flight to Nassau.

▲ Former service
Having served with the US military forces during World War II the Goose aircraft were then sold to numerous small civilian operators.

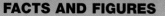

FACTS AND FIGURES

➤ The Mallard was the only non-military product built by Grumman in the post-World War II period.

➤ During World War II, Grumman Goose aircraft were used for reconnaissance.

➤ A retractable undercarriage allows amphibious operations to be undertaken.

➤ Grumman Goose flying-boats were used by the US Coast Guard, Canadian and British forces.

➤ One Grumman Goose was operated by the Bolivian air force.

➤ Chalk's International Airline have now become Pan Am Air Bridge.

PROFILE

Grumman's fantastic flying-boats

The Grumman G-21A Goose was developed for commercial use before World War II, making its debut in 1937. A versatile utility craft and short-distance cargo and passenger type, the Goose saw military service with the US Army, Navy and Coast Guard. It later became a familiar sight around the world in post-war years.

The replacement for the Goose, the G-73 Mallard, followed in 1946. It was larger and more powerful, with provision for between 10 and 15 passengers. Both aircraft were ideally suited to a variety of commercial activities, including VIP transport.

The Mallard had the advantage of placing the pilot well forward of the engines, offering improved visibility and (with its greater power) better performance. Unfortunately, the post-war market for commercial amphibians proved to be smaller than Grumman anticipated, and only a few companies purchased these fine aircraft straight off the production line. They have shown enormous durability, however, and Gooses and Mallards are still operating in several places around the world today on commercial routes.

Above: Although it is dated, no modern equivalent has yet been found for the Grumman Goose. This example has been modified with adjustable wingtip floats.

Left: Restored with its former wartime markings, this Grumman Goose is active on the American warbird circuit. The aircraft presents an unusual sight in the air.

G-73 Mallard

Type: light amphibian flying-boat; commercial transport aircraft

Powerplant: two 447-kW (600-hp.) Pratt & Whitney R-1340-SH31 Wasp radial piston engines

Maximum speed: 346 km/h (215 m.p.h.)

Cruising speed: 290 km/h (180 m.p.h.)

Range: 2221 km (1,377 mi.) with maximum fuel load

Service ceiling: 7010 m (23,000 ft.)

Weights: empty 4241 kg (9,330 lb.); maximum take-off 5783 kg (12,723 lb.)

Accommodation: two flight crew; up to 15 passengers

Dimensions:
span	20.32 m	(66 ft. 8 in.)
length	14.73 m	(48 ft. 4 in.)
height	5.72 m	(18 ft. 9 in.)
wing area	41.25 m²	(444 sq. ft.)

A separate flight deck was provided for the aircrew, and the main accommodation for 15 seated passengers was located in the rear fuselage, in two compartments. Very often, the interiors of the aircraft were air-conditioned, heated and soundproofed to provide maximum comfort.

The two Wasp radial engines were positioned high on the wing, away from the corrosive salt spray generated by operations at sea.

Grumman's Mallard was exceptionally well-designed. With a fuselage consisting of an all-metal stressed-skin design, and the addition of a two-step hull, the aircraft proved to be immensely strong.

A large cargo door was positioned on the port-side rear fuselage, the high setting of which allowed cargo to be unloaded while the aircraft was on the water.

To improve handling on the water a large rudder was fitted to the Mallard. Chalk's International Airline aircraft carry a small American flag on their tail, signifying their country of origin.

N2970

CHALK'S INTERNATIONAL

Retractable landing gear gave the Mallard an amphibious capability; when retracted, the main wheels were recessed into the fuselage.

Rigid balancer floats were mounted on either side of the wings to provide stability for the Mallard when operating from the water. They also served as extra fuel tanks.

G-73 MALLARD

Chalk's International Airline was founded in 1919 and by the early 1990s was the oldest airline still operating under its original title. It now operates as Pan Am Air Bridge.

ACTION DATA

MAXIMUM SPEED

Small and lightweight, the Grumman G-21 Goose offers exceptional performance when compared to the larger G-73 Mallard. Later models were fitted with uprated engines to improve the speed of the small flying-boat.

G-73 MALLARD	346 km/h (215 m.p.h.)
DHC-3 OTTER	212 km/h (131 m.p.h.)
G-21 GOOSE	391 km/h (242 m.p.h.)

RANGE

Despite its small size, the Grumman G-21 Goose had exceptional range compared to the larger utility aircraft. Although fitted with additional fuel tanks in its stabilising floats, the G-73 Mallard was unable to match the Goose's performance.

G-73 MALLARD 2221 km (1,377 mi.)

DHC-3 OTTER 1048 km (650 mi.)

G-21 GOOSE 2575 km (1,597 mi.)

SERVICE CEILING

Equipped with two powerful Wasp radial engines, the G-73 Mallard had a surprisingly high service ceiling for a large flying-boat. It was often utilised for long-range overseas flights. With only a single engine, the DHC-3 Otter's performance was particularly poor.

G-73 MALLARD	DHC-3 OTTER	G-21 GOOSE
7010 m (23,000 ft.)	5485 m (18,000 ft.)	6100 m (20,000 ft.)

Riding the waves of success

■ **CANADAIR CL-215:** Developed for the specialised role of fire-bombing, the CL-215 has been purchased by a host of European countries. Later variants feature turboprop engines.

■ **MARTIN MARS:** Having had an extremely brief military career, the Mars flying-boats now serve as fire-bombers and operate from lakes in British Columbia, Canada.

■ **SHINMAYWA US-1:** Japan has operated flying-boats for a number of years for coastal patrols and anti-submarine duties. The type re-entered production in 1992.

GULFSTREAM

I COMMUTER

● Executive transport ● Regional airliner ● Navigator trainer

I n the mid-1950s, Grumman – better known as a builder of naval warplanes – ventured into the light turboprop transport field. The Gulfstream was intended as an executive transport, although it was in the same class as small commuter airliners. Grumman manufactured Gulfstreams for more than 11 years for both civil and military use. Later this ship became retroactively known as the Gulfstream I.

▲ As an executive transport, the Gulfstream I is appreciated for its practical performance coupled with a roomy and well-furnished interior, although operating costs are high.

GULFSTREAM I COMMUTER

◄ **American Eagle**
Although more expensive to operate than its rivals, the Gulfstream I was found ideal for use as a feeder/regional transport. This stretched example operates within the United States.

High performance ►
Entering a market comprised mainly of converted World War II bombers, the Gulfstream offered better performance and economy.

Intruder trainer ►
Fitted with the nose of an A-6, this TC-4C was used to train future bombardier/navigators for the US Navy; six students and one instructor were carried.

▲ **European sales**
Most sales have been in North America, but a few examples have operated in Italy.

Sound design ►
Comparison of the American Gulfstream I in the background and the G-1C in front reveals a longer fuselage and the addition of two cabin windows.

FACTS AND FIGURES

➤ The Gulfstream had a fairly smooth flight test programme and was cleared for commercial operations on 21 May 1959.

➤ The prototype completed its first flight on 14 August 1958.

➤ Grumman manufactured 200 examples between 1959 and 1969.

➤ Although not a big success with airlines, the Gulfstream was ideal for use as an executive and government transport.

➤ Grumman used the first Gulfstream as a company transport for 40 years.

➤ Austria, Germany and Nigeria used the type as a government transport.

PROFILE

Grumman's executive liner

Left: Incorporating a fuselage extension of 3.25 m (10 ft. 8 in.) allowed a maximum of 37 passengers to be carried; otherwise, the aircraft was basically unaltered.

Grumman developed its G-159 Gulfstream to take advantage of the availability of the reliable Rolls-Royce Dart engine, which was already performing well on the Vickers Viscount airliner.

The Gulfstream became a superb executive transport, filling a gap that had opened when corporations sought to retire used transports of World War II vintage. Business leaders in need of efficient transport admired the Gulfstream for its practical performance coupled with roomy and well furnished, but not over-ostentatious, accommodation. Pilots enjoyed the Gulfstream for its snappy performance and excellent handling qualities.

The Gulfstream was fairly expensive for an aircraft in its class and was less successful when Grumman sought to sell it overseas. A number of these aircraft were adopted for government use in various countries, including an executive transport for the US Coast Guard and bombardier-navigator trainers for the US Navy.

The Gulfstream became the Gulfstream I when its name was taken over by a series of jet transports built by a new company formed by Grumman executives. Today, several dozen Gulfstreams are providing good service, four decades after the aircraft was created.Grumman's close association with the US Navy resulted in a bizarre modification to the Gulfstream's airframe. Grafted onto the nose was an A-6 Intruder nose, complete with avionics. Its purpose was to train future A-6 crews.

Above: British operations of the Gulfstream are restricted to executive flights for various companies. This example operates from Birmingham International Airport.

Gulfstream G-1

Type: twin-engined commuter or executive transport

Powerplant: two 1484-kW (1,990-hp.) Rolls-Royce Dart Mk 529-8X turboprop engines

Maximum cruising speed: 556 km/h (345 m.p.h.)

Certificated altitude: 9145 m (30,000 ft.)

Maximum ceiling: 11,245 m (36,900 ft.)

Range: 838 km (520 mi.) with payload

Weights: empty 10,747 kg (23,643 lb.); maximum take-off 16,329 kg (35,924 lb.)

Accommodation: 14 to 18 passengers in executive configuration or a maximum of 24 passengers as a commuter airliner

Dimensions:
span	23.88 m (78 ft. 4 in.)
length	22.96 m (75 ft. 4 in.)
height	7.01 m (23 ft.)
wing area	56.70 m² (610 sq. ft.)

GULFSTREAM G-1

A number of Gulfstream Is have been operated by commuter airlines in Europe. This example was operated for a number of years by Italian airline TAS.

Accommodation for the passengers could be adjusted to suit the requirements of the operator. In executive configuration 10 people were carried, but on regional feeder airline routes a high-density seating arrangement of 24 passengers could be installed.

For cargo operations, the fuselage could accommodate a maximum of 2753 kg (6,057 lb.). Loading was accomplished through a large door on the port side of the fuselage, positioned just aft of the wings.

The tall tail of the Gulfstream bestowed excellent stability, while its all-metal cantilever construction proved extremely reliable.

I-TASO

Seated side by side, the flight crew enjoyed excellent visibility from the flight deck. This was mainly because of the detailed research that Grumman undertook in its design.

Adopting an already proven engine design, two Rolls-Royce Dart turboprops were installed. Driving Rotol four-bladed constant-speed propellers, they were reliable and remained the powerplant for the entire production run.

The hydraulic-powered undercarriage included twin wheels on all three units. The main gear retracted forward into the engine cowlings, and the nose unit retracted forward below the flight deck.

Although intended only as a short-range feeder airliner, the Gulfstream I was fitted with a toilet compartment with hot and cold water. A hydraulically operated self-contained air-stair forward of the main cabin was also installed, providing easy boarding for passengers and crew and allowing a rapid turn-around.

ACTION DATA

MAXIMUM CRUISING SPEED

Despite being a 40-year-old design, the Gulfstream offers high speed. This is mainly due to a proven engine coupled with a fuselage that is exceptionally clean, when compared to the EMB-120ER.

G-1C	556 km/h (345 m.p.h.)
1900D	515 km/h (343 m.p.h.)
EMB-120ER	555 km/h (345 m.p.h.)

PASSENGERS

Feeder airliners are often described as spartan, but their main role is maximum capacity for relatively short flights. Set against more modern designs such as the 1900D, the G-1 is well equipped. Later Gulfstream models had increased capacity, accomplished by a fuselage extension.

G-1C 24 PEOPLE

1900D 19 PEOPLE

EMB-120ER 30 PEOPLE

RANGE

Range is considered to be the Gulfstream's main fault; the modern commuter market has been swamped with more advanced designs which are constantly being refined to operate more efficiently. New turboprop engines not only have lower fuel consumption but are also quieter.

G-1C 838 km (520 mi.)

EMB-120ER 1575 km (1,870 mi.)

1900D 2778 km (1,720 mi.)

Dart-powered derivatives

■ **CONVAIR 600:** Entering service in November 1965, this variant was the last of the series powered by Rolls-Royce Dart engines.

■ **DOUGLAS DC-3:** This classic airliner is seen here with experimental Dart engines fitted, although the conversion was not a success.

■ **FOKKER F27 FRIENDSHIP:** This German design utilising Dart engines has achieved sales in both military and civilian versions.

■ **HANDLEY PAGE HERALD:** Designed to fill similar requirements to the Gulfstream, this British aircraft also employed Dart turboprops.

GULFSTREAM

G IV

● Circumnavigation ● East and westbound flights ● Record times

▲ Early-production aircraft were used for both around-the-world flights. The long-range and high-speed potential of the aircraft was clearly and very publicly illustrated.

In January 1988 a Boeing 747SP set a new eastbound round-the-world record of 36 hours 54 minutes 15 seconds, knocking 8 hours 30 minutes off the previous record time, set five years earlier by a Gulfstream III. In June 1987 a Gulfstream IV, captained by the manufacturer's chairman, Allen Paulson, had added the westbound record to Gulfstream's collection of honours, and Paulson set about regaining the eastbound record in February 1988.

GULFSTREAM G IV

▼ Production prototypes
Four Gulfstream IV production prototypes, of which this is the first, were built. One was used for static tests.

▲ Proven powerplants
Gulfstream chose the well-proven and reliable Rolls-Royce Tay turbofan for the G IV.

September flight ▶
On 19 September 1985 the first Gulfstream IV made its initial flight. The aircraft was basically similar to production machines, apart from its nose boom.

▼ Long range by design
Winglets and other advanced aerodynamic features give the Gulfstream IV excellent range.

▲ Westbound around the world
Immaculately finished N440GA was the aircraft used to set a new westbound record in June 1987. The around-the-world flight was the primary goal, but the attempt actually set 22 world records in all.

FACTS AND FIGURES

➤ Having departed Le Bourget, Paris, westbound on 12 June 1987, N440GA returned 45 hours 25 minutes later. Westerly flights are slower because they are against the prevailing winds.

➤ N400GA's easterly flight covered 37093.1 km (23,048.5 miles), averaging 1026.29 km/h (637.7 m.p.h.).

➤ On a routine business trip between Tokyo and Albuquerque, N485GA, a Gulfstream IV-SP, set new world records.

➤ On this flight N485GA covered 9524 km (5917 miles) at 933.21 km/h (579.87 m.p.h.).

➤ N400GA's auxiliary fuel tank held an additional 3629 kg (8,000 lb.) of fuel.

PROFILE

Around the world with the Gulfstream IV

A brand new Gulfstream IV was chosen for the eastbound record attempt, with Paulson planning to fly from Houston, Texas. Previously he had crewed another Gulfstream IV from the Paris air show in 1987, to set the westbound record. An optional, temporary fuel tank was carried in the cabin, which had only a couple of seats and a divan rather than the normal luxurious cabin furnishings, in order to reduce the number of fuel stops.

To gain maximum advantage from the jetstream winds, the Gulfstream flew at an altitude of 10000-11000 m (32,800–36,000 ft.), well below its normal operating ceiling. To keep refuelling time to a minimum, Gulfstream ground crews were positioned at the planned stops.

The flight started from Houston on the morning of 26 February and the 37093-km (23,048-mile) trip routed the aircraft across the Atlantic to Ireland, then via the Middle East, India and China to Taiwan, and on to Hawaii. Each of the four fuel stops at Shannon, Dubai, Taipei and Maui took an average of just over 18 minutes

each, where the Boeing 747SP's two refuelling stops had consumed a total of 110 minutes. The difference was enough to see the Gulfstream home in 36 hours 8 minutes 34 seconds, over 45 minutes faster than the 747 which had set the record just 30 days before.

Below: N400GA was named Pursuit of Perfection for its flight. The Tay engines were only 22 hours old when the flight began.

Above: On its return to Paris, after having circumnavigated the globe in a westerly direction, N440GA had covered 36832.44 km.

Having been given a special colour scheme for its famous flight, N400GA became a Gulfstream Aerospace company demonstrator. Few manufacturers can match the long-range, record-breaking flights achieved by Gulfstream.

Gulfstream IV

Type: long-range business jet

Powerplant: two 61.6-kN (13,847-lb.-thrust) Rolls-Royce Tay Mk 611-8 turbofans

Maximum cruising speed: 936 km/h (582 m.p.h.) at 9450 m (31,000 ft.)

Range: 6728 km (4,180 miles) with maximum payload

Maximum operating altitude: 13715 m (45,000 ft.)

Weights: empty 16136 kg (35,573 lb.); maximum take-off 33203 kg (73, 200 lb.)

Accommodation: flight crew of two with one cabin attendant and up to 19 passengers

Dimensions:
span	23.72 m	(77 ft. 10 in.)
length	26.92 m	(88 ft. 4 in.)
height	7.45 m	(24 ft. 6 in.)
wing area	88.29 m²	(950 sq. ft.)

GULFSTREAM IV

N400GA's crew reported that its *Pursuit of Perfection* title was well earned, since the aircraft suffered no problems during its arduous flight.

Only four people were carried on the record-breaking flight, in order to save weight and reduce fuel consumption.

With a large auxiliary tank fitted in the cabin, there was little space for cabin furnishing. The standard Gulfstream IV is available with a range of luxurious cabin layouts, often finished to the particular requirements of individual customers, but can seat a maximum of 19 passengers.

Each of the Rolls-Royce Tay engines is fitted with a thrust reverser, the use of which allows the Gulfstream IV to land in only 1032 m (3,385 ft.) from a height of 15 m (49 ft.). The Tay engine also allows noise to be kept to a minimum, with take-off creating a mere 76.8 EPNdB (Equivalent Perceived Noise Decibels).

Light alloy is used for most of the Gulfstream IV's structure, but carbon composites are used for the ailerons, elevators, rudder, spoilers, tailplane components and parts of the cabin floor and flight deck. All flying controls are hydraulically operated.

"PURSUIT OF PERFECTION"

N400GA

Standard Gulfstream IV equipment includes a fully digital flight deck, with colour weather radar and comprehensive communications and navigation system. A satellite communications unit is optional.

The standard fuel load is carried in integral wing tanks and allows a range of 6728 km (4,180 miles) with maximum payload and reserves. A pressure refuelling point is located in the leading edge of the starboard wing.

Many modern designs employ upturned wingtips, known as winglets, which reduce drag and improve fuel efficiency.

ACTION DATA

FUEL CAPACITY

With 5342 litres (1,411 U.S. gal.) of fuel less than the Gulfstream IV-SP, the Challenger 604 proves its efficiency by achieving a range only slightly less than that of the American type. The capabilities of the Gulfstream IV-SP are illustrated by its record-breaking form in standard configuration.

GULFSTREAM IV-SP	GULFSTREAM V	CHALLENGER 604
16542 litres (4,370 U.S. gal.)	22960 litres (6,065 U.S. gal.)	11200 litres (2,958 U.S. gal.)

BASIC COST

Many customers purchase their aircraft in unfinished form, passing them on to specialist finishing companies, where cabin fittings and optional avionics are fitted.

GULFSTREAM IV-SP	GULFSTREAM V	CHALLENGER 604
US$24.625 million	US$30.5 million	US$17.95 million

MAXIMUM RANGE

In recent years, a new generation of ultra long-range business jets has become available. In the face of stiff competition from Canadair's Challenger, Gulfstream has produced the phenomenally long-ranged Gulfstream V, but with a considerable increase in purchase price.

GULFSTREAM V 12038 km (7,480 miles)

GULFSTREAM IV-SP 7815 km (4,856 miles)

CHALLENGER 604 7072 km (4,394 miles)

Global racing

GULFSTREAM VERSUS BOEING: The blue route is that taken by the eastbound Gulfstream IV, while that flown by United's 747SP is in yellow.

TAIPEI MEETING: Captain Lacy, pilot of the 747SP, was piloting a scheduled flight at the time of Paulson's record attempt and was obliged to delay landing at Taipei in favour of the record-breaking Gulfstream IV!

SEATTLE

SHANNON

ATHENS

MAUI

HOUSTON

FLYING WITH THE WIND: Strong tailwinds helped both aircraft to set their records, although, in retrospect, the 747SP pilot felt that he could have wrung more speed from his machine.

DUBAI

TAIPEI

HAMC

Y-11/Y-12

● Light transport ● Agricultural roles ● Short take-off and landing

The Harbin Aircraft Manufacturing Company (HAMC) started work on the Y-11 in the early 1970s after several years of building copies of the Soviet Mi-4 helicopter and Il-28 light bomber. Similar in configuration to the Pilatus Britten-Norman Islander, the aircraft flew for the first time in 1975. The Y-12 which followed had a longer fuselage to increase the payload, plus efficient 375-kW (500-hp.) PT6A-11 engines for improved performance.

▲ Built by the
Harbin Aircraft Manufacturing Company, the Y-11 and Y-12 are marketed abroad by CATIC. Harbin is also responsible for licence-built AS 365 Dauphin helicopters.

◀ Military applications
Y-12s have been delivered to the air forces of Cambodia, Eritrea, Mauritania, Peru, Sri Lanka, Tanzania and Zambia.

▼ Civil airliner
In China, the upgraded Y-12 is flown by five airlines, and by February 1996 101 had been built.

▼ Paradrop mission
Military configured Y-12s can seat up to 15 paratroops or carry an equivalent cargo load. Maximum payload of the improved Y-12 (IV) approaches 2000 kg (4,400 lb.).

▼ Agricultural application
After conversion to the agricultural role, this Y-12 will carry a 1200-litre (317-gal.) chemical hopper, four wing and two stub wing dispensers.

◀ Y-12 predecessor
Prior to the first flight of the Y-12 in 1982, HAMC produced the piston-engined Y-11.

FACTS AND FIGURES

➤ With 17,000 employees, Harbin currently constructs doors for the British Avro RJ series of airliners and freighters.

➤ The original Y-11 carried Chinese Zhuzhou HS6A radial powerplants.

➤ For very steep landings and rough-field operations, the Y-11 has a tail bumper.

➤ The first customer for the Teledyne Continental-powered Y-11B was Flying Dragon Aviation, based in China.

➤ For geophysical survey, the Y-12 (II) carries a long, kinked sensor tail boom.

➤ The Y-12 series has an American-made Bendix/King weather radar.

Harbin's utility transport

Able to carry one or two pilots and seven or eight passengers, the 40 Y-11s built were used mainly for agricultural and forestry work. They were powered by Chinese 213-kW (288-hp.) HS-16 engines, could take off and land in distances of as little as 140 m (460 ft.), and had a top speed of 220 km/h (136 m.p.h.).

Harbin flew the first of two Y-12 Is in July 1982, and the first flight of the Y-12 (II) followed in 1983. This variant features a new wing with integral tanks for 1600 litres (423 gal.) of fuel. Nearly half the all-metal structure is resin-bonded instead of rivetted. Hong Kong Aircraft

Engineering installed Western avionics and cabin furnishings in the sixth aircraft for greater appeal to foreign customers. The first Y-12 was exported to Sri Lanka in 1986, and nearly 100 more have followed to 18 other countries since then.

The main user of the type is the CAAC (Civil Aviation Authority of China), which may end up buying as many as 200. There is also a Y-12 (IV) version, powered by twin Pratt & Whitney Canada PT6A-27s, which incorporates winglets, a strengthened undercarriage and other improvements. Military variants are operated by Sri Lanka, Iran, Peru and Paraguay.

Below: More than 40 examples of the Y-11 were built before production switched to the Y-11B with US-built engines.

Above: HAMC currently produces the Y-12 (I) and the Y-12 (IV) with higher operating weights, modified wings, strengthened landing gear and seating for 19 passengers.

Y-12 (II)

Type: utility transport

Powerplant: two 507-kW (680-hp.) Pratt & Whitney Canada PT6A-27 turboprops

Maximum speed: 292 km/h (181 m.p.h.) at 3000 m (10,000 ft.)

Endurance: 5 hr 12 min

Range: 1340 km (830 mi.) at 250 km/h (155 m.p.h.)

Service ceiling: 7000 m (23,000 ft.)

Weights: maximum take-off 5300 kg (11,660 lb.)

Accommodation: crew of two, 17 passengers, 16 paratroops or 1700 kg (3,740 lb.) of cargo

Dimensions:
span	17.24 m (56 ft. 7 in.)
length	14.86 m (48 ft. 9 in.)
height	5.58 m (18 ft. 4 in.)
wing area	34.27 m² (369 sq. ft.)

Y-12 (II)

This profile represents a typical example of a civilian Y-12 (II). By 1996 there were 55 of this variant in service around the world, mainly employed as utility transports and small-capacity airliners.

Mounted at the very tip of the fin is a large anti-collision beacon, which provides a visual cue for other aircraft, particularly in poor weather.

Housed within the small cockpit are a pilot and co-pilot. Dual controls are standard and the instruments are thoroughly conventional and well laid out. Interesting features are the four-way adjustable crew seats, providing much needed comfort during longer flights.

All NAMC Y-12s are powered by proven Pratt & Whitney Canada PT-6 turboprops. These engines have established a solid reputation for being powerful and reliable and have been fitted to countless different aircraft types over the years. On the Y-12, they are rated at 507 kW (680 hp.) each.

Approximately 17 passengers can be accommodated in the main cabin with three-abreast seating. Alternatively, the entire cabin can be used for cargo, with a large double-hinged freight door similar to that seen on the de Havilland Canada Twin Otter, making access considerably easier.

Flying at relatively low altitudes does not require a pressurised cabin, so large square windows are a standard fitment on the Y-12.

The single mainwheels are fixed and are mounted on small sponsons projecting from the fuselage. For greater rigidity, large struts are attached between them and the wings.

External differences between the Y-11 and Y-12 include a large ventral fin fitted to the newer variant, plus slightly larger tail surfaces in general. The entire unit is of all-metal construction and the rudder features horizontal ribs for greater structural strength.

ACTION DATA

CRUISING SPEED

Although a decent aircraft in its own right, and blessed with exceptional STOL ability, the Y-11 is slower than designs such as the Do 228 and Let L-410.

Y-11	164 km/h (102 m.p.h.)
L-410UVP-E	380 km/h (236 m.p.h.)
Do 228-200	428 km/h (265 n.p.h.)

SERVICE CEILING

As a light utility transport, the Y-11 is ideal, being simple and sturdy. It cannot fly at as high an altitude as the Do 228; however, the German type is not really capable of short take-offs and landings. The poorer ceiling of the Y-11 is partly a consequence of the lower power of its piston engines.

Y-11	4030 m (13,200 ft.)
L-410UVP-E	6320 m (20,700 ft.)
Do 228-200	8535 m (28,000 ft.)

PASSENGERS

Both European types, the Czech L-410 and the German Do 228 were designed as feeder liners and are thus more advanced and quieter, with greater passenger capacity than the small Chinese twin. Despite its lack of capacity, the Y-11 excels in being a low-cost and reliable utility transport.

Y-11 — 8 passengers

L-410UVP-E — 19 passengers

Do 228-200 — 19 passengers

An ever-growing family

■ HARBIN (HAMC) SH-5: China still believes in long-range flying-boats. The impressive SH-5 fulfils a variety of roles, mainly anti-submarine warfare and search and rescue.

■ HARBIN Z-5: Essentially a copy of the Soviet Mil Mi-4 'Hound', this versatile helicopter was produced until 1979 and continues to serve in huge numbers in civil and military versions.

■ HARBIN Z-9 HAITUN: Derived from the French AS 365 Dauphin, the Z-9 has been in production since the mid-1980s. Current versions feature a substantial amount of local content.

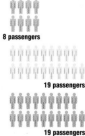

HAMILTON

H-45/H-47 METALPLANE

● Monoplane transport ● All-metal construction ● Twenty-nine built

Built by the Hamilton Metalplane Company of Milwaukee, Wisconsin, the Metalplane reflected the innovative spirit of aviation pioneers in the 1920s. When two H-45s joined Northwest Airways in September 1928, they introduced unimagined levels of comfort and modernity. Leather-covered wicker seats were nothing new, but cabin heaters and a 'comfort station' (toilet) were revolutionary. They were also the first all-metal airliners in US service.

▲ Most of the 29 Metalplanes built were sold to US operators, although a handful were exported to Canada and Panama. Single examples went to France and Italy.

HAMILTON H-45/H-47 METALPLANE

◄ Northwest service
Northwest's Metalplanes were first employed as mail carriers. Passenger services followed, including flights to Canada.

▲ Company demonstrator
NC538E (No. 24) was one of nine Metalplanes in the Northwest fleet, after having served as a sales flight demonstrator for Hamilton.

▲ Pioneering rail-air services
One of Northwest's early successes was the September 1928 establishment of co-ordinated rail-air services. Here, a Hamilton takes on cargo from a Chicago, Rock Island and Pacific train.

▼ Northwest H-45s
Aircraft 20 and 21 were H-45s powered by the Pratt & Whitney Wasp radial engine. They were in service long after the introduction of H-47s.

▲ In all weathers
Ski-equipped H-47s were the only aircraft able to operate from Chicago during the winter without having the runways cleared of snow.

FACTS AND FIGURES

➤ One Hamilton, used by a Panamanian airline, was taken on charge by the USAAC during World War II as a UC-89.

➤ The Metalplane could be fitted with a pair of Hamilton metal floats.

➤ The first Metalplane was the H-18, which had a rounded fuselage and open cockpit.

➤ A famous Arctic explorer, Carl Van Eissen, was killed in a Metalplane in the early 1950s.

➤ H-47s were nicknamed 'Silver Eagles'; those with floats were 'Silver Swans'.

➤ Most Metalplanes were built by the Hamilton Metalplane division of Boeing.

PROFILE

Forgotten pioneer metal airliner

Aviation pioneer Thomas F. Hamilton, assisted by others including James S. McDonnell (later of McDonnell Douglas fame), was responsible for the Hamilton Metalplane, a genuinely revolutionary aircraft which pointed the way to the future, changing the very face of air transport.

The first Hamilton Metalplane of 1925 was a one-off and carried only six people, but the bigger, more powerful H-45s and H-47s were the best airliners of their class. Northwest Airways and other carriers used

them on diverse routes in varying conditions, even in severe winter weather, when they were ski-equipped.

The Metalplanes were pleasant to fly and their cabins were, by the standards of the day, spacious and comfortable. Northwest dubbed them 'Silver Streak' and used them in the world's first co-ordinated rail-air service for passengers and express mail. Metalplanes were deemed economical by airline companies and continued to provide excellent service until World War II, by which time

Douglas DC-3s and other newer aircraft were on the scene.

At least one Metalplane has survived and been restored to airworthy condition.

The little-known Metalplane was an important type in the Northwest fleet. Nine were operated in all, between 1928 and 1941. By this time, the more advanced Douglas DC-3 had entered widespread service.

Northwest, the first and largest operator of the Metalplane, used the type to inaugurate the airline's first international service in 1935, over the border to Winnipeg, Manitoba in Canada.

The Metalplane's wings were wired to take a landing light on both the port and starboard wings.

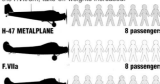

NC-7522

H-45 Metalplane

Type: all-metal monoplane airliner

Powerplant: one 298-kW (400-hp.) or 336-kW (450-hp.) Pratt & Whitney R-1340 Wasp nine-cylinder radial engine

Maximum speed: 222 km/h (138 m.p.h.)

Cruising speed: 185 km/h (115 m.p.h.)

Range: 1086 km (675 mi.)

Service ceiling: 3962 m (13,000 ft.)

Weights: empty 1315 kg (2,893 lb.); loaded 2449 kg (5,388 lb.) (empty 1650 kg (3,638 lb.); loaded 2608 kg (5,750 lb.) with 336-kW (450-hp.) engine)

Payload: 620 kg (1,364 lb.) (454 kg (1,000 lb.) with 336-kW (450-hp.) engine)

Dimensions:
span	15.57 m	(51 ft. 1 in.)
length	10.62 m	(34 ft. 10 in.)
height	2.62 m	(8 ft. 7 in.)
wing area	33.44 m²	(360 sq. ft.)

The H-45 was powered by a 298-kW (400-hp.) or 336-kW (450-hp.) Pratt & Whitney R-1340 Wasp nine-cylinder radial engine. Performance was greatly enhanced in the H-47, which was fitted with an R-1690 Hornet of 410 kW (550 hp.). At least one H-47 was fitted with a 391-kW (525-hp.) Wright Cyclone.

Two pilots crewed Northwest's Metalplanes seated in a cockpit behind the engine. The cabin boasted wicker seats (between six and eight), and was heated and featured a toilet; both were innovative features.

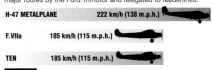

When first built, the H-45 was priced at $23,200, later raised to $24,500. The H-47 was as much as $26,000. Hamilton was purchased by Boeing in 1928.

The fixed undercarriage on the Metalplane was supported by two 'doughnut' low-pressure tyres. Wheelbrakes were a standard fitting (together with a metal propeller and an inertia-type engine starter).

Although not the first example built in the US, Hamilton's Metalplane was the first all-metal airliner to enter service in the US, beating Ford's Trimotor by several months. The use of an Alclad corrugated duralumin skin and a cantilever wing were major innovations.

H-47 METALPLANE

NC7522 was the last of two Wasp-engined and seven Hornet-engined Metalplanes delivered to Northwest Airways. Allocated the fleet number 28, it formed part of Northwest's 'Silver Streak' Hamilton fleet.

ACTION DATA

PASSENGERS

The Hamilton Metalplane was one of a number of monoplane airliner types of the inter-war period. Eight-seat passenger cabins were typical. Once more powerful trimotor designs appeared, like the F.VII/3m, take-off weights increased.

H-47 METALPLANE	8 passengers
F.VIIa	8 passengers
TEN	8 passengers

MAXIMUM SPEED

Compared to the two European designs, the H-47 had a healthy top speed of over 200 km/h. An aircraft's performance was a major area of competition between US manufacturers in the 1930s. For this reason, the Metalplane was soon outperformed on major routes by the Ford Trimotor and relegated to feederlines.

H-47 METALPLANE	222 km/h (138 m.p.h.)
F.VIIa	185 km/h (115 m.p.h.)
TEN	185 km/h (115 m.p.h.)

RANGE

The H-47's range was comparable to that of the F.VIIa at around 1100 km (700 mi.). The Avro Ten had a comparatively short range, some 500 km (290 mi.) less than that of the American and Dutch designs. Once trimotor aircraft like the Ford Trimotor and Fokker F.VII/3m entered service, longer routes were possible.

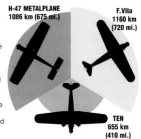

H-47 METALPLANE 1086 km (675 mi.)
F.VIIa 1160 km (720 mi.)
TEN 655 km (410 mi.)

Northwest's inter-war airliners

■ **STINSON DETROITER:** Northwest had four of these aircraft, the first enclosed cabin biplane airliners used by a commercial airline. In 1927, they inaugurated a Twin Cities-Chicago service.

■ **FORD 5-AT TRIMOTOR:** The first 'Tin Goose' was delivered to Northwest in 1927. It seated between 12 and 14 passengers and used three 313-kW (420-hp.) engines.

■ **SIKORSKY S-38:** In order to provide Duluth, Minnesota (on Lake Superior) with a service, Northwest used two S-38 amphibians, including NC303N, from 1930.

■ **LOCKHEED 10 ELECTRA:** Northwest was the first airline to put the Electra, the first truly modern airliner, in service, taking delivery of the prototype in 1934.

HANDLEY PAGE

HERALD

● Turboprop airliner ● Cargo carrier ● Military transport

▲ During 1959
the Herald underwent proving
flights throughout Asia, Australasia and South
America. It operated from rough strips in the
Himalayas, to the amazement of the locals.

Originally designed as a four-piston-
engined airliner, the Herald came
into its own when fitted with two of
the excellent Rolls-Royce Dart turboprops.
Built to compete with the Fokker F27 in
both the civil and military markets, the
Herald did not achieve the sales that its
safe and durable performance deserved.
However, over 40 years after entering
service it still undertakes regular cargo
flights around the UK.

HANDLEY PAGE **HERALD**

◀ **Dart power**
Designed with four
piston engines, the
Herald soon adopted
the more efficient Rolls-
Royce Dart turboprops.

◀ **Robust flight deck**
The two-pilot flight
deck was designed
with a 'military' feel
with substantial
controls and switches.

▲ **Foreign sales**
The Herald was aggressively marketed abroad,
especially in Commonwealth countries. This
example was bought by Air Manila in 1966.

▲ **Military service**
In 1963 the Royal Arab Air Force received
the first of its two Heralds. Despite Handley
Page's best attempts few Heralds were sold
to military customers.

◀ **Cross-Channel routes**
BAF operated the Herald on
routes between Southend
and the Continent.

▲ **Highlands and islands**
BEA found the Herald's
performance ideal for its
short-haul Scottish routes.

FACTS AND FIGURES

➤ The original version was fitted with
four Alvis Leonides Major piston engines
and was called the H.P.R.3.

➤ Early Dart-engined Heralds were priced
at £250,000 each.

➤ In 1959 the Herald completed a 55000-km
(34,000-mile) demonstration tour of South
America.

➤ In March 1960 a Herald undertook
emergency relief flights after severe
flooding in regions of North Africa.

➤ The H.P.R.8 was a high-capacity car ferry
version that was never built.

➤ At least 12 Heralds remain in use after
more than 35 years of service.

PROFILE

Forty years of the Herald

The Herald has led a varied life. Three impressive demonstration tours in 1959 took the new-look turboprop aircraft all around the world, proving its worth in places as far apart as the Caribbean and Australia.

With orders increasing the signs looked good until one of the prototypes crashed en route to the SBAC air show at Farnborough. This dented confidence in the aircraft and sales declined.

Despite the setback, Handley

Page developed the aircraft into the 'stretched' Series 200. With increased capacity this version entered service with airlines all around the world and proved that the faith the company had in the aircraft was not unfounded by building up an enviable reliability and safety record.

Channel Express still operate a fleet of cargo-configured Heralds in the UK and find these veteran aircraft to be ideally suited to the task.

Above: G-ARTC had its fuselage lengthened to Series 200 standard. In an attempt to capture military sales it is seen demonstrating a paratroop drop.

Right: Built to operate in any conditions, the Herald was very durable and strong with steady flying characteristics.

Each Dart engine drives a Rotol fully-feathering constant-speed auto-coarsening metal propeller. The four-bladed airscrew has a diameter of 3.66 m (12 ft.).

The Herald was one of the strongest aircraft of its era. It had a fail-safe reinforced wing which proved its worth when an early Herald lost an engine which separated from the wing. Only the strength of the wing saved the aircraft from destruction.

Similar to the F27, the Herald's main undercarriage retracted into the engine nacelles. The high wing caused the legs to have a particularly stalky appearance.

HERALD SERIES 200

Air UK operated a small fleet of Heralds in the 1980s, flying charter and scheduled flights in the UK and Europe.

The cockpit was designed for a two-man crew. The controls were robust, unlike the more delicate layout of its rivals the HS. 748 and the F27 Friendship.

The original Alvis Leonides piston engines were soon replaced by two Rolls-Royce Dart 527 turboprops, an engine which remains in use today.

Originally conceived as a 36-seater, its capacity was increased to accommodate 44 passengers when turboprop power was adopted. A further stretch allowed 56 seats in the Series 200.

G-APWE

Flying controls were entirely conventional. Control surfaces are of all-metal construction with associated trim tabs.

Herald Series 200

Type: medium-range passenger and cargo transporter

Powerplant: two 1570-kW (2,100-hp.) Rolls-Royce Dart 527 turboprops

Cruising speed: 428 km/h (265 m.p.h.)

Initial climb rate: 590 m/min (1,935 f.p.m.)

Range: 1786 km (1,100 mi.)

Service ceiling: 8505 m (28,000 ft.)

Weights: empty 11,703 kg (25,747 lb.); maximum take-off 19,504 kg (68,655 lb.)

Passengers: maximum of 56

Dimensions:
span	28.88 m (94 ft. 9 in.)
length	23.01 m (75 ft. 6 in.)
height	7.34 m (24 ft.)
wing area	82.31 m² (886 sq. ft.)

ACTION DATA

CRUISING SPEED

The more streamlined F27 had the highest speed of these three contemporary aircraft. Although the Herald was slower, its Dart engines were very efficient at normal cruising speed. Its wider fuselage created more drag but allowed a larger passenger load.

HERALD SERIES 200	428 km/h (265 m.p.h.)
F27 Mk 200	480 km/h (298 m.p.h.)
An-24 'COKE'	450 km/h (279 m.p.h.)

PASSENGERS

The improved Series 200 Herald could carry up to 56 passengers, which was at least six more than its rivals. The Herald and F27 competed directly for sales, with the Herald's larger capacity being a major selling point. However, the F27 generally outsold the Herald.

HERALD SERIES 200	56
F27 Mk 200	48
An-24 'COKE'	50

RANGE

One area where the Herald was inferior to the F27 was range. A fully laden Herald did not have the reach to connect cities in Europe to the degree the F27 could. The An-24 was also a good aircraft, which suffered from a lack of range. It was generally employed on short regional routes.

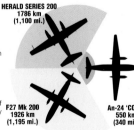

HERALD SERIES 200 1786 km (1,100 mi.)

F27 Mk 200 1926 km (1,195 mi.)

An-24 'COKE' 550 km (340 mi.)

Twin-turboprops of the 1960s

■ **ANTONOV An-24 'COKE':** First delivered to Aeroflot in 1962, the An-24 was designed as a rugged short-to-medium range transport for operations from a wide variety of airfields.

■ **FOKKER F27 FRIENDSHIP:** Of all the twin turboprops developed in the 1950s and 1960s the F27 is undoubtedly the most successful. It sold in significant numbers all around the world.

■ **NORD N 262 FRÉGATE:** Once regarded as a natural DC-3 replacement, the N 262 sold in relatively small numbers. A military version is still in service with the French navy.

HANDLEY PAGE

H.P.42

● Early luxury airliner ● Long-haul routes ● British Empire services

L ooking at it today, the Handley Page H.P.42 seems strange, with its exposed engines and its odd-sized, biplane wings. But in the 1930s, when Imperial Airways was harnessing the new science of aviation to carry passengers over great distances, the H.P.42 was a trailblazer. Although far from the state of the art, it was the first true intercontinental airliner operating with elegance and style.

▲ At a fuel stop in the desert, the crew of an H.P.42E supervise the replenishment of the aircraft's supplies. Such operations turned the journey into an adventure.

HANDLEY PAGE **H.P.42**

▼ Sumptuous comfort
This is the aft cabin of an H.P.42E, furnished in the traditions of a luxury Pullman train or Cunard liner of the time.

▲ 'Built-in headwind'
With its two wings and the maze of struts connecting them, the H.P.42 was hardly aerodynamic. In spite of the power of its four engines, the big biplane could barely manage 200 km/h (126 m.p.h.).

An exclusive passage ▼
The H.P.42 made long-range air travel a realistic proposition. But it was fearfully expensive: you had to be well off to fly.

▲ Western class
'Heracles' was one of the aircraft used only in the West, tailored for European routes with high-density seating.

◄ On-the-spot maintenance
Imperial Airways crew were trained to handle any emergency. The simple yet sturdy construction of the H.P.42 allowed them to undertake virtually all essential maintenance en route.

FACTS AND FIGURES

➤ The H.P.42 'Heracles' logged its one-millionth mile (about 1.6 million km) on 23 July 1937.

➤ The craft known as the H.P.42W was actually designated the H.P.45.

➤ The H.P.42 was one of the first airliners equipped with a kitchen, toilets and heaters for passenger comfort.

➤ The H.P.42 was so slow that Anthony Fokker joked that they were equipped with built-in headwinds.

➤ H.P.42s were retired on 1 September 1939 after almost a decade of service without a single fatal accident.

➤ The H.P.42 made its first flight on 14 November 1930.

PROFILE

Flying the Imperial routes

A famous name in Britain, the Handley Page team gave the world the H.P.42E (Eastern) and H.P.42W (Western) airliners at a time when air travel was a new and exciting adventure. These big aircraft of gleaming metal, their broad wings braced by enormous girders, became ocean liners of the sky, the four Eastern ships opening up new routes to India and South Africa while the four Westerners pioneered long trips in Europe.

'Up front' were two pilots and a wireless operator. The men at the controls of the H.P.42 faced challenges: the aircraft made plenty of noise, shook like a washing machine, and was difficult to land. But the pilots also held a commanding view, and enjoyed excellent control over the aircraft when aloft. It was a thrilling aeroplane to fly.

All eight H.P.42s had evocative names – Hannibal, Heracles, Horsa, Hanno, Hadrian, Horatius, Hengist and Helena. All true pioneers and great aircraft.

'Hannibal' was the class leader of the four Eastern aircraft, fitted out to perform the arduous journey linking Cairo to the Empire. One route flew south to Lake Victoria, another headed east for India.

H.P.42W

Billed as the world's largest airliner at the time of its service entry, the H.P.42 was something of an anachronism, for already more streamlined airliners were being built. Nevertheless, it had an elegance which transcended its meagre performance, and it was instrumental in establishing air travel.

H.P.42W/H.P.45

Type: civil transport aircraft

Powerplant: four 414-kW (555-hp.) Bristol Jupiter XFBM nine-cylinder piston engines

Maximum speed: 204 km/h (126 m.p.h.)

Range: 805 km (500 mi.)

Service ceiling: 6400 m (21,000 ft.) with moderate load

Weights: empty 8047 kg (17,700 lb.); loaded 12,701 kg (28,000 lb.)

Accommodation: maximum 18 passengers forward and 20 aft (total 38) with minimal baggage

Dimensions:
span	39.62 m	(129 ft. 8 in.)
length	28.09 m	(91 ft. 2 in.)
height	5.04 m	(16 ft. 6 in.)
wing area	277.6 m²	(2,990 sq. ft.)

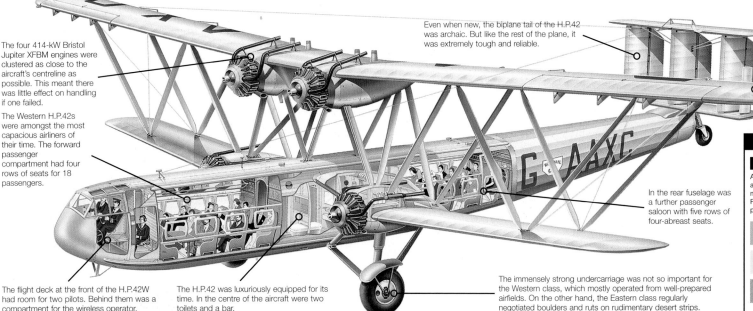

The four 414-kW Bristol Jupiter XFBM engines were clustered as close to the aircraft's centreline as possible. This meant there was little effect on handling if one failed.

The Western H.P.42s were amongst the most capacious airliners of their time. The forward passenger compartment had four rows of seats for 18 passengers.

The flight deck at the front of the H.P.42W had room for two pilots. Behind them was a compartment for the wireless operator.

The H.P.42 was luxuriously equipped for its time. In the centre of the aircraft were two toilets and a bar.

Even when new, the biplane tail of the H.P.42 was archaic. But like the rest of the plane, it was extremely tough and reliable.

The huge wing allowed the H.P.42 to take off in a very short distance, usually less than 200 m (600 ft.). Often it was airborne while still on the taxiway after leaving the terminal, and long before it had reached the recognised runway.

In the rear fuselage was a further passenger saloon with five rows of four-abreast seats.

The immensely strong undercarriage was not so important for the Western class, which mostly operated from well-prepared airfields. On the other hand, the Eastern class regularly negotiated boulders and ruts on rudimentary desert strips.

ACTION DATA

MAXIMUM SPEED

Airliners of the late 1920s and early 1930s were not the fastest of aircraft, and within a decade were to be completely outclassed by modern stressed-skin designs like the Douglas DC-3 and the Focke-Wulf Condor. But even though they were slow, they pioneered many of the world's long-range passenger routes.

F.VII
209 km/h (130 m.p.h.)

H.P.42
204 km/h (126 m.p.h.)

G.38
210 km/h (131 m.p.h.)

PAYLOAD

Although the massive Junkers G.38 was the biggest airliner in the world, it did not carry as many passengers as the long, slender fuselage of the H.P.42. The Fokker was much smaller, but competed directly with the Handley Page in opening the air routes out to the Far East.

H.P.42
38 passengers

F.VII
10 passengers

G.38
35 passengers

East to India

MEDITERRANEAN

CAIRO: This Egyptian airfield was the centre of Imperial's Empire land operations. From here H.P.42s flew south to the East African colonies, or east to the Indian sub-continent.

Cairo (Egypt)

DESERT REPLENISHMENT: The H.P.42 lacked range, and needed an interim stop in the Iraqi desert to pick up fuel.

ARABIA

Basra (Iraq)

Muharraq (Bahrain)

Sharjah (Trucial States)

Gwadar (Persia)

Karachi

INDIA: Taking the air route to India involved a considerable effort. Flying from Croydon in a D.H.86, passengers switched to a Short Rangoon flying-boat for the over-water trip from Brindisi in Italy to Egypt. From there, they transferred to the H.P.42 for the passage to India.

INDIA

HAWKER SIDDELEY

HS.748

● Sixty-seat airliner ● STOL capability ● Turboprop twin

Becoming a common sight on some of the world's more difficult short- to medium-haul routes, the HS.748 survived as a sound design through periods of great upheaval in the British aircraft industry. HS.748s were also built under licence in India, where the Series 2 standard aircraft was especially appreciated for its improved hot-and-high performance. Almost 40 years since its first flight, the HS.748 continues in limited airline service.

▲ *Many smaller airlines have bought the HS.748 and operate it from short or rough airstrips. Larger airlines have used them on feeder routes into major hubs, where their rugged durability is appreciated.*

PHOTO FILE

HAWKER SIDDELEY **HS.748**

Dart power ▶
Open nacelle inspection doors reveal the Rolls-Royce Dart RDa.7 Mk 531 turboprop fitted to an Andover CC.Mk 2 military HS.748 variant.

▲ Early customers
Aerolineas Argentinas was the second airline customer of the HS.748. Skyways Coach-Air in the UK also took Series 1 aircraft.

North American operations ▶
Buyers for the HS.748 were even found in the lucrative American market. Most carriers flew passengers into larger airports to meet major airline connections.

▼ Highlands and Islands
British Airways used its HS.748s on Scottish routes, where airports with short runways are common.

▲ Avro heritage
The HS.748 was originally, but only briefly, an Avro design. This very early aircraft carries Avro company titles and livery.

FACTS AND FIGURES

➤ Avro, which began design of the HS.748 in 1959, was absorbed by Hawker Siddeley in 1963 and became part of BAe in 1977.

➤ By the end of production in 1989, a total of 379 HS.748s had been built.

➤ Hindustan Aeronautics built the aircraft under licence in India.

➤ BAe used the HS.748 as the basis for its Advanced TurboProp, ATP, which was later marketed as the Jetstream 61.

➤ The HS.748 has been successfully converted for the fire-bombing role.

➤ The RAF Queen's Flight used six HS.748s as Andover CC.Mk 2s.

International STOL success

In 1957 a misguided British Government announced that the RAF would require no more new manned aircraft as guided missiles were the weapons of the future. Manufacturers of military types therefore sought new product lines and, to this end, Avro decided to develop a twin-turboprop machine as a cheap competitor to the Fokker F.27.

After producing 18 Series 1 machines, Avro switched production to the Series 2, which had more powerful developments of the Dart engine. After reorganisation it was Hawker Siddeley who put the new aircraft into production and developed the Series 2A, 2B and military versions.

Series 2A machines were further improved by the addition of even more powerful 1700-kW (2,280-hp.) Dart RDa.7 Mk 532-2L engines and the provision of a large freight door aft of the wing. Extended wingtips were introduced, plus other detail changes in 1979, to produce the Series 2B, now under the British Aerospace banner.

HS.748s will continue to fly with airlines who appreciate their low cost and dependability.

Series 2 HS.748s were favoured by airlines working out of hot-and-high airfields. Increased engine power from Dart RDa.7 Mk 531s gave better take-off performance.

HS.748 Series 2A

Type: twin-turboprop short-/medium-range airliner

Powerplant: two 1700-kW (2,280-hp.) Rolls-Royce Dart RDa.7 Mk 535-2 turboprops

Maximum cruising speed: 462 km/h (286 m.p.h.)

Initial climb rate: 393 m/min (1,290 f.p.m.)

Range: 1,891 km (1,176 mi.) with maximum fuel and provision for 370-km (230-mi.) diversion

Service ceiling: 7600 m (25,000 ft.)

Weights: maximum take-off 20,182 kg (44,400 lb.)

Accommodation: 40 to 58 passengers

Dimensions:
span	30.02 m (98 ft. 6 in.)
length	20.42 m (67 ft.)
height	7.57 m (24 ft. 10 in.)
wing area	75.35 m² (811 sq. ft.)

A circular section was chosen for the fuselage, since it produces a very strong structure.

Extended wingtips are fitted to Series 2B aircraft. These improve take-off and range performance.

HS.748 SERIES 2

The Series 2 was the most successful production version. Some Series 2 aircraft featured the 1425-kW Dart RDa.7 Mk 531; others were fitted with the Mk 533-2 of 1570 kW.

The 748s wings are set at seven-degrees dihedral and have an all-metal, two-spar fail-safe structure.

Three crew and 40 to 58 passengers are carried. The seats are arranged in pairs on either side of a central gangway.

Electrically operated flaps and powerful engines produce the HS.748's excellent short-field performance.

Black pneumatic de-icer boots cover all leading edges. These break off the ice by flexing.

Bahamasair

C6-BEE

BEE

Four-bladed Dowty Rotol propellers are standard on all HS.748s.

The maingear retracts forwards to lie in the lower section of the engine nacelles.

A rear door serves the passenger cabin and can be equipped with a power-operated entrance stair. The crew enter through the freight door ahead of the wings.

ACTION DATA

ACCOMMODATION

Considering its exceptional STOL performance, the large passenger load of the HS.748 is remarkable. Its Japanese competitor, the NAMC YS-11, never equalled the British aircraft's popularity and few remain in service.

HS.748 SERIES 2A — 58 passengers
YS-11A — 60 passengers
F.27 FRIENDSHIP — 52 passengers

TAKE-OFF DISTANCE

With its superb short-field and hot-and-high performance, the HS.748 was a versatile and rugged workhorse for smaller airlines. Some variants of the F.27 also had good hot-and-high performance, but their STOL capability was inferior.

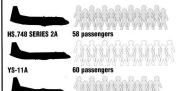

HS.748 SERIES 2A — 1006 m (3,300 ft.)
YS-11A — 1110 m (3,640 ft.)
F.27 FRIENDSHIP — 1250 m (4,100 ft.)

RANGE

Long range is important for airliners. While the YS-11 has largely disappeared from service, both the HS.748 and F.27 have been developed into more advanced versions. Interestingly, the Fokker 50 has proved far more attractive to airlines than the BAe ATP or Jetstream 61.

HS.748 SERIES 2A — 1,891 km (1,175 mi.)
YS-11A — 2110 km (1,300 mi.)
F.27 FRIENDSHIP — 1705 km (1,060 mi.)

HS.748 Avro ancestors

■ **ANSON:** Entering airline service in 1935, the Anson saw extensive wartime operations with the RAF. After the war it was again a favourite of the airlines.

■ **YORK:** Using the wings, tail unit, engines and undercarriage of the Lancaster bomber, 45 Yorks were built for airliner use. Skyways was also an early user of the HS.748.

■ **LANCASTRIAN:** Victory Aircraft in Canada modified a Lancaster B.Mk III for transport duties in 1942, and Avro adopted this as the basis of a long-range airliner.

■ **TUDOR:** The Tudor suffered a troubled career, plagued by crashes and changing requirements. It proved most successful during the Berlin Airlift.

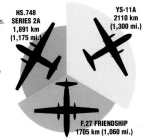

HAWKER SIDDELEY

TRIDENT

● Three-engined airliner ● 727 competitor ● de Havilland design

▲ The Trident first flew in January 1962, and on entering BEA service in April 1964 it became the airline's first jet transport. The Trident managed to fend off rival designs from both Bristol and Avro.

The Trident design was produced to meet a British European Airways (BEA) specification. In its original form it was to be powered by three Rolls-Royce Medway turbofans, be able to carry 111 passengers and have a range of more than 3300 km (2,050 mi.). But after ordering 24 in 1958, BEA changed its requirements. As a result, the aircraft had less-powerful Rolls-Royce Spey engines and could carry 97–103 passengers only 1500 km (930 mi.).

PHOTO FILE

HAWKER SIDDELEY TRIDENT

Tri-jet power ▶
The Hawker Siddeley Trident, shown here in its prototype form, was powered by three Rolls-Royce Spey 512 turbofans: one mounted on either side of the rear fuselage and the third buried in the tail.

▲ Trident in China
A total of 33 Trident 2E short-to-medium-range transports were purchased by CAAC, the national airline of the People's Republic of China. A number of these were later used by the Chinese air force.

▲ Iraqi orders
The Trident proved successful with airlines that could not afford or could not obtain Boeing's 727; Iraqi airlines for example bought the 1E model.

▲ British European Airways
The Trident had excellent low-speed handling, thanks to Krueger leading-edge flaps, spoilers and large double-slotted trailing-edge flaps.

Trident production ▶
Although not a great success, the Trident kept the Hawker Siddeley factory at Hatfield busy for 20 years.

FACTS AND FIGURES

➤ The Trident was originally called the de Havilland DH.121 and then the Hawker Siddeley HS.121.

➤ In all, 117 Tridents were built, the last main users being British Airways and CAAC.

➤ The first DH.121 Trident I (G-ARPA) made its maiden flight on 9 January 1962.

➤ The Trident 3 had a 'fourth engine' fitted; this was principally an auxiliary power unit (APU), but which added 23.3 kN of thrust.

➤ An innovation available on the Trident was a 'hands-off' autoland system.

➤ Tridents were to be built by Airco, a consortium including Fairey and Hunting.

PROFILE

Britain's tri-jet challenger

The Trident design was started by de Havilland, but by 1964, when the aircraft entered service with BEA, the company had been taken over by Hawker Siddeley. More significantly, though, Boeing had introduced the 727. This was also a tri-jet, but the 727's more powerful JT8D engines enabled it to carry up to 189 passengers over a distance of nearly 4000 km (2,480 mi.).

The result was inevitable. While Boeing went on to sell more than 1800 727s, Hawker Siddeley produced just 117 Tridents, most of them for BEA.

Succeeding Trident variants introduced more powerful engines, longer wings, enlarged fuel capacity and slight increases in passenger loads. Trident 1s and 2Es were delivered to BEA, and a handful of other airlines bought a total of 15 Trident 1Es. Cyprus Airways and the Civil Aviation Authority of China (CAAC) bought the Trident 2E.

A longer variant, the Trident 3B, could carry up to 180 passengers in a high-density seating arrangement on short-haul routes, and two still-heavier Super Trident 3Bs were built for the CAAC. The early decision to restrict range and payload, however, meant that the Trident never caught up with its rivals.

A surprising customer was America's Northeast airlines, which chose the Trident over the aircraft's US rivals.

Following the merger of BEA and BOAC (British Overseas Airways Corporation), the Trident 3 went on to serve in large numbers with British Airways.

The Trident 1E model introduced a superior increased-span wing with leading-edge slats.

Originally designed to incorporate the Rolls-Royce Medway engine, the Trident only ever flew under Rolls-Royce Spey 512 power.

Northeast was the Trident's sole American operator.

Like the Boeing 727 and the Soviet Tu-154 and Yak-40 of the same era, the Trident had three engines and a high-set, all-metal T-type tail unit.

The Trident 3E version was boosted during take-off by a Rolls-Royce RB.162-86 mini-turbojet. This was mounted in the rear fuselage below the rudder and above the third engine's exhaust.

TRIDENT 1E

As well as serving with Northeast airlines in the United States, the Trident 1E variant was operated by the national airlines of Kuwait, Iraq, Pakistan, and by Air Ceylon and Channel Airlines.

The long-span Trident 1E introduced accommodation for a high-density seating arrangement of up to 139 passengers.

An innovative feature of the Trident was its baggage hold, the forward portion of which could be pressurised for the carriage of animals.

The Trident's third engine was buried in the rear fuselage with an intake above the fuselage, and exhaust nozzle in the tail-tip.

The Trident's heavy-duty twinwheel nose landing gear was manufactured in the US by Lockheed.

Trident 2E

Type: three-engined short- to medium-range commercial transport

Powerplant: three 53.2-kN (11,970-lb.-thrust) Rolls-Royce Spey 512-5W turbofans

Maximum speed: 972 km/h (602 m.p.h.)

Economic cruising speed: 959 km/h (595 m.p.h.)

Range with typical payload: 3910 km (2,425 mi.)

Range with maximum fuel: 5726 km (3,550 mi.)

Weights: basic operating 33,250 kg (73,150 lb.); maximum take-off 65,090 kg (143,198 lb.)

Accommodation: up to 139 passengers

Dimensions: span 29.90 m (98 ft.)
length 34.98 m (114 ft. 9 in.)
height 8.23 m (27 ft.)
wing area 135.70 m² (1,460 sq. ft.)

ACTION DATA

CRUISING SPEED

The Trident 2E had a very similar top speed to its competitors. Speeds in the 950-975 km/h bracket were the norm for airliners of this size in the 1960s, when designing an airliner speed was less important than range.

TRIDENT 2E	959 km/h (595 m.p.h.)
727-200	964 km/h (598 m.p.h.)
Tu-154 'CARELESS'	975 km/h (605 m.p.h.)

PASSENGER SEATS

The Tu-154 was one of the largest tri-jet airliners produced and could carry more passengers than the Trident 2E. The Trident 3 addressed this problem and could carry 180 passengers. The Boeing 727-200 had slightly lower passenger loads.

TRIDENT 2E	115 passengers
727-200	145 passengers
Tu-154 'CARELESS'	154 passengers

RANGE

These three aircraft had very similar ranges. Range varies according to the ratio of fuel load weight to passenger load weight. Successive versions with higher gross weights tend to have shorter range unless they are modified to carry more fuel as well as a bigger payload.

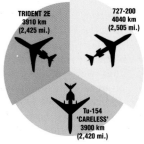

TRIDENT 2E 3910 km (2,425 mi.)

727-200 4040 km (2,505 mi.)

Tu-154 'CARELESS' 3900 km (2,420 mi.)

Disaster at Heathrow

Until the bombing of the Pan Am 747 over Lockerbie, the crash of a BEA Trident 1 on 16 June 1972 was Britain's worst air disaster.

1 TAKE-OFF: At 16.09 the BEA Trident codenamed 'Papa India' took off from runway Two-Eight Right at Heathrow, with Captain Stanley Key at the controls.

2 CLIMB: As the aircraft banked left to climb, turbulence in thick clouds buffeted the Trident's fuselage.

3 STALL: Flying at 162 knots (190 m.p.h.), the Trident's nose began to rise to an unacceptable angle. As speed decreased the nose was pushed up further still, and Captain Key suffered heart failure.

4 IMPACT: At 16.11 the Trident smashed into the ground, six and a half kilometres (four miles) from Heathrow. All 118 people on board were killed in the crash, which was eventually attributed to the poor health of the pilot.

HILLER
UH-12 RAVEN

● Lightweight 1950s design ● US Army's H-23 ● War veteran

F lagship for an exceedingly successful helicopter family which included the Model 360 and the military H-23 Raven, the UH-12 was created in 1948 by helicopter genius Stanley Hiller. As a test bed for his innovative 'Rotor-Matic' control system, it went on to be built in large numbers. At least 2,300 examples have provided excellent service to civil and military users, and many are still on duty, from Britain to New Zealand.

▲ Popular with civil and military operators alike, the Hiller was produced throughout the 1950s and until the late-1960s. After Hiller was taken over by Fairchild, production was restarted in 1973.

PHOTO FILE

HILLER UH-12 RAVEN

▼ Army H-23 Raven
The US Army operated the UH-12 as the H-23 Raven from 1950. This H-23B carries the wing of an L-20 Beaver.

▲ Powerful light helicopter
Hiller billed the UH-12E as the most powerful US-built light helicopter.

Piston-engined ▶
The earliest Hiller UH-12s were powered by Franklin engines, while later models used more powerful Lycoming flat-six powerplants. The final UH-12E-4s had an Allison 250 turboshaft as fitted to machines like the Bell 206 JetRanger.

▲ Over San Francisco Bay
Hiller marketed the civil Hiller 12C for land- or ship-based port work, such as personnel transport and the off-loading of light priority cargoes.

Large US Army orders ▶
US Army Ravens were delivered for 17 years from 1950. The most common variant was the OH-23G; 793 were built.

FACTS AND FIGURES

➤ An early UH-12 was the first commercial helicopter to log a transcontinental flight across the United States.

➤ Over 1,600 UH-12s went to the US Army and were used in Korea and Vietnam.

➤ As a flying ambulance, the UH-12 can carry two stretcher cases.

➤ UH-12s were exported to at least 18 countries, many via the Mutual Defense Aid Program.

➤ The Hiller UH-12 was the US Army's primary trainer until 1965.

➤ UH-12s were manufactured by Hiller in Palo Alto, near San Francisco, California.

PROFILE

Light helicopters from Palo Alto

In 1971 the US Army held a celebration to mark 100,000 accident-free miles flown by one of its veteran Hiller H-23 Ravens (the military designation for the UH-12). This kind of satisfaction by those who rely on the UH-12 is far from unusual. For decades the versatile Hiller UH-12 has enjoyed a reputation for safety and reliability in roles like police work and agricultural spraying, as well as military operations.

The UH-12 is of simple construction, incorporating two-blade main and tail rotors with a sturdy, upswept tailboom. Built in highly successful two-, three- and four-seat configurations, the type was fitted with a variety of Franklin and Lycoming piston engines. Aircraft built in the 1970s had almost twice the installed horsepower of the earliest models; there was even a turboshaft-powered version.

Production of what was at first known as the Model 360 began in the late-1940s and continued as the Fairchild-Hiller UH-12 and Model 12 until 1965. At least 300 Hillers were exported to overseas customers, both military and civil.

Stanley Hiller's son, Jeffrey, took over the business in 1994. The compnay continues to develop the UH-12 in piston- and turbine-engined versions and as a new five-seater – a testimony to the soundness of the 1940s design.

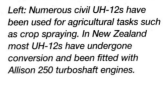

Left: Numerous civil UH-12s have been used for agricultural tasks such as crop spraying. In New Zealand most UH-12s have undergone conversion and been fitted with Allison 250 turboshaft engines.

Below: A number of UH-12s in the US are employed in a major insect control campaign in the Atlantic coast states. Over 1,000 UH-12s are still flying worldwide.

H-23D Raven

Type: three-seat light observation and training helicopter

Powerplant: one 186-kW (250-hp.) Lycoming VO-450-23B flat-six air-cooled piston engine

Max speed: 153 km/h (95 m.p.h.) at sea level

Cruising speed: 132 km/h (82 m.p.h.)

Initial climb rate: 320 m/min (1,246 f.p.m.)

Range: 317 km (200 mi.)

Weights: empty 824 kg (1,812 lb.); loaded 1225 kg (2,695 lb.)

Armament: normally none, although small-arms were often carried by crew in active service

Dimensions:
main rotor diameter	7.44 m (24 ft. 5 in.)
length	8.47 m (27 ft. 9 in.)
height	2.98 m (9 ft. 9 in.)
rotor disc area	91.51 m² (985 sq. ft.)

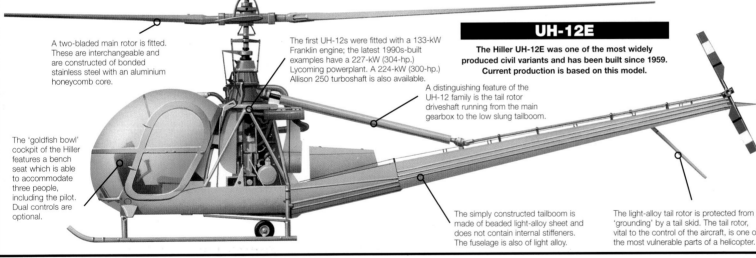

A two-bladed main rotor is fitted. These are interchangeable and are constructed of bonded stainless steel with an aluminium honeycomb core.

The first UH-12s were fitted with a 133-kW Franklin engine; the latest 1990s-built examples have a 227-kW (304-hp.) Lycoming powerplant. A 224-kW (300-hp.) Allison 250 turboshaft is also available.

A distinguishing feature of the UH-12 family is the tail rotor driveshaft running from the main gearbox to the low slung tailboom.

The 'goldfish bowl' cockpit of the Hiller features a bench seat which is able to accommodate three people, including the pilot. Dual controls are optional.

The simply constructed tailboom is made of beaded light-alloy sheet and does not contain internal stiffeners. The fuselage is also of light alloy.

The light-alloy tail rotor is protected from 'grounding' by a tail skid. The tail rotor, vital to the control of the aircraft, is one of the most vulnerable parts of a helicopter.

UH-12E

The Hiller UH-12E was one of the most widely produced civil variants and has been built since 1959. Current production is based on this model.

ACTION DATA

MAXIMUM SPEED

Speeds around 160 km/h (100 m.p.h.) were typical for the first mass-produced light helicopters. Bell's Sioux was widely used by US forces; the Mi-1 was an early product of the famous Mil factory.

H-23D RAVEN	153 km/h (95 m.p.h.)
H-13H SIOUX	161 km/h (100 m.p.h.)
Mi-1M 'HARE'	170 km/h (105 m.p.h.)

RANGE

The slightly larger Mi-1 had a considerably longer range than the two American types. This was largely due to the greater fuel capacity of the aircraft.

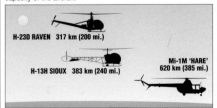

H-23D RAVEN 317 km (200 mi.)
H-13H SIOUX 383 km (240 mi.)
Mi-1M 'HARE' 620 km (385 mi.)

CLIMB RATE

The Raven, which entered service after the Sioux, demonstrated a marginally better climb rate. A more powerful engine in both the Raven and 'Hare' was the main reason for this difference.

Mi-1M 'HARE' 390 m/min (1,280 f.p.m.)
H-23D RAVEN 320 m/min (1,246 f.p.m.)
H-13H SIOUX 235 m/min (770 f.p.m.)

Hiller vertical risers

■ UH-5: Hiller's first helicopter with a main rotor/tail rotor configuration, the UH-5 also saw the first use of its 'Rotor-Matic' control system.

■ HJ-1 HORNET: Twelve of these two-seat ramjet-powered helicopters were built, plus a further 12 for the US Army as the YH-32.

■ FH-1100: Hiller's attempt to build a machine to rival the Bell JetRanger and Hughes 500 was derived from the unsuccessful military OH-5.

■ X-18: This unusual machine was flown in 1959 to test the practicality of tilt-wing aircraft. It was short-lived and the results were inconclusive.

HUGHES

H-4 'SPRUCE GOOSE'

● Largest aircraft ● Wooden construction ● Strategic transport

For more than three decades the Hughes HFB-1 (H-4) Hercules was the biggest flying machine ever built. It was a towering achievement of entrepreneurial spirit and aviation pioneering, all the more remarkable because the behemoth was built without essential wartime materials. Popularly called the 'Spruce Goose' because of its wooden construction, Hughes' flying-boat was an incredible sight, which flew just once.

▲ Variously known as the HFB-1, H-4 or HK-1, the monster flying-boat designed by Howard Hughes was a giant in every way. Even the flight deck had more space than the passenger cabins of many airliners of the period.

HUGHES H-4 'SPRUCE GOOSE'

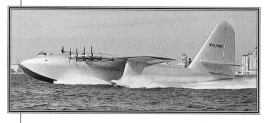

◄ The monster rises
At the end of the taxi trials, all of the guests left the aircraft. Hughes then took the 'Goose' out into the harbour for its one and only flight.

▼ Launch day
'Spruce Goose' was launched from its 88.4-m (290-ft.) dry dock into Long Beach Harbor on 1 November 1947.

◄ Eight-engine power
Propelled by eight huge Pratt & Whitney 28-cylinder radial engines, Hughes' flying-boat had more than twice the power of a Boeing B-29 Superfortress heavy bomber.

▼ Gathering dust
After its one flight, the mighty flying-boat was left in storage for 35 years, gathering dust and attracting fascinated tourists.

◄ Taxi trials
The HK-1 moved under its own power for the first time on 2 November. Hughes undertook a taxi trial with 18 crew, five officials and nine invited guests aboard before flying the H-4 himself.

FACTS AND FIGURES

➤ Hughes wrecked a Sikorsky S-43 while experimenting with centre-of-gravity and power settings for the HK-1.

➤ 'Spruce Goose' was flown just once, over Los Angeles harbour on 2 November 1947.

➤ The HK-1 was built in the world's largest wooden building at Culver Field.

➤ The huge flying-boat was taxi-tested with its eight engines controlled by four throttles harnessed in pairs.

➤ Hughes planned a larger flying-boat, the HFB-2, which was never built.

➤ 'Spruce Goose' was transported by barge to its present owners in Oregon.

PROFILE

The 'Spruce Goose' flies

In 1944, when Howard Hughes unveiled plans for the HFB-1 (Hughes Flying Boat First Design) or HK-1 (Hughes-Kaiser First Design) Hercules flying-boat, no one believed he was serious. He intended to build a seaborne giant that could carry up to 750 troops, without using steel or aluminium except in the engines. The airframe would be manufactured of non-strategic wood products. At that time, the Allies still thought that a large-scale invasion of Japan would be needed to bring the

Pacific War to an end, and the H-4 would have been much in demand as a flying troopship.

Everything about the HK-1 flying-boat was big. When it was built, it was the largest aircraft in the world. Today, the Ukrainian Antonov An-225 is larger, but the Hughes flying-boat still has a greater wing span.

Hughes and his experts saw the flying-boat as a great, globe-girdling craft which would change the way people and cargo were moved across vast distances.

Left: The huge wingspan of the 'Spruce Goose' was as long as a soccer pitch. Street lighting had to be dismantled at great expense to allow the road transportation of such a huge aircraft for final assembly in Los Angeles.

In a sense, this is what was accomplished decades later by the Boeing 747 jetliner.

Unfortunately, the very promising Hughes flying-boat was flown only once. Though it was a true pioneer, its potential was never fulfilled despite the genius of its design.

Above: The flight of the 'Spruce Goose' attracted great media interest, and Los Angeles harbour was packed with a flotilla of small boats. Little did they know that they would be the only people to see this great beast fly.

H-4 'SPRUCE GOOSE'

Type: very large long-range flying-boat transport

Powerplant: eight 2240-kW (3,000-hp.) Pratt & Whitney R-4360-4A 28-cylinder four-row radial engines

Maximum speed: 377 km/h (175 m.p.h.) at 1525 m (5,000 ft.)

Range: 4825 km (3,500 mi.)

Weights: empty estimated 90,000 kg (198,000 lb.); loaded 181,437 kg (400,000 lb.)

Accommodation: the Hughes flying-boat was built to carry up to 750 troops or more than 70,000 kg (154,000 lb.) of freight or cargo

Dimensions:
span	97.54 m	(320 ft.)
length	66.75 m	(219 ft.)
height	15.32 m	(79 ft.)
wing area	1029 m²	(11,072 sq. ft.)

H-4 'SPRUCE GOOSE'

The massive aircraft gained its popular name from the derogatory comment of a senator investigating what he saw as a waste of public money. "It's a Spruce Goose," he said, "it'll never fly."

'Spruce Goose' was powered by eight Pratt & Whitney Wasp Major R-4360 radial engines, each delivering some 2240 kW (3,000 hp.). These were the most powerful conventional piston-driven engines ever built.

The leading edge of the massive wings housed a catwalk which allowed inflight access to the engine nacelles.

The reason that such a large aircraft could be built from wood was that the Hughes Corporation had recently developed the Duramold process, which laminated plywood and epoxy resin into a lightweight but very strong building material.

Tailplanes and fin were of wood construction, though the rudder and elevators were fabric covered. The massive tailplane was longer than the wing of a Lancaster bomber.

NX37602

The 'Spruce Goose' was designed to be flown by two pilots. On its only flight the aircraft carried 18 working personnel, including flight engineers and flight test observers. There were also 15 airline-type seats on the upper deck for use by reporters and invited guests.

Although the nose of the aircraft was solid, its structure was designed to be easily fitted with clamshell doors to allow the loading of outsize cargo.

Up to 53,000 litres (14,000 gal.) of fuel were carried in 14 underfloor tanks.

The only flight of the Hercules

1 TAXI TO TAKE OFF: Hughes was supposed to keep the flying-boat on the surface, but to engineer Dave Grant's surprise the multi-millionaire ordered 15° of flap – which was the take-off setting.

2 LIFT OFF: Accelerating through 150 km/h (93 m.p.h.), the huge boat began skimming across the surface. Then, to the delight of thousands of people watching from the shore, it lifted slowly and gracefully into the air.

3 TOUCHDOWN: Hughes eased his huge machine back onto the water. The flight had lasted less than a minute, never more than 25 m (80 ft.) above the water and covering less than 1.6 km (one mile).

ACTION DATA

COMPARATIVE SIZE

When steel and shipping magnate Henry J. Kaiser proposed that Howard Hughes should build a giant transport flying-boat for use in the vast expanses of the Pacific, he could not have foreseen that the eccentric millionaire would produce the world's largest plane. Twice the size and more than four times the weight of a four-engined bomber or long-distance airliner, and as long as nine five-ton trucks, the H-4 flying-boat would have carried 750 troops or more than 60 tons of cargo. Its potential would not be matched for more than two decades, until the era of the 'Jumbo' jet.

H-4 'SPRUCE GOOSE' 66.75 m (219 ft.)

C-130 35 m (115 ft.)

HUGHES/SCHWEIZER

300/TH-55 OSAGE

● Lightweight helicopter ● Police operations ● Military trainer

I n 1948 the Hughes Aircraft Company began specialising in helicopters. Its second design, the Model 269/300, served as the basis for one of the most successful families of light helicopters. Having evaluated five examples as potential observation aircraft in 1958, the US Army adopted this simply constructed two-seater as its standard primary helicopter trainer in the 1960s. Hughes went on to build nearly 3,000 for both civil and military users.

▲ The success of the Model 269/300 family paved the way for the Model 369/500 design, which placed Hughes among the world's leading producers of light helicopters.

HUGHES/SCHWEIZER 300/TH-55 OSAGE

▼ Traffic watching
Robust and fuel-efficient, the 300 is an ideal machine for monitoring traffic conditions.

▲ Police service
More than 17 US city police departments have operated the Model 300 as a relatively economical surveillance platform. The 300 has also proved its military potential in the training role.

◀ Over California
A lieutenant from Whittier, California, keeps in touch with a police department 300.

▼ In the US Army
The Osage provided experience for the first generation of US Army chopper pilots.

▲ Schweizer production
By the time Schweizer began building Hughes 300s in July 1983, more than 2,800 had been built.

FACTS AND FIGURES

➤ Schweizer Aircraft bought the entire Model 300 programme in 1986; its 500th 300C was delivered in 1994.

➤ In 1996 a Model 300C training helicopter was priced at $187,500.

➤ Iraq acquired 30 Model 300Cs for crop-dusting, but used them for pilot training.

➤ In 1996 12 nations operated military Model 269s, including Indonesia, North Korea, Pakistan, Paraguay and Honduras.

➤ Kawasaki assembled 38 TH-55As as TH-55Js for the JGSDF.

➤ Schweizer builds a turbine development of the Model 300 – the Model 330.

PROFILE

Hughes' first successful chopper

Designated TH-55A Osage, the Hughes Model 269A-1 was delivered to the US Army after being selected in 1964. The Osage was a refinement of the civil Model 200 Utility, which was derived from the original Model 269 that had first flown in October 1966.

The next major variant was the three-seater Model 300 (269B), which, with an uprated Lycoming engine, became the Model 300C in 1969. This was the most widely produced version, with more than 1,000 being built by Hughes. Licence production was also undertaken by BredaNardi in Italy, as the NH-300C.

Popular with civil operators, the Model 300 has being used for roles as diverse as crop-spraying and policing duties. For the latter, the Hughes 300C Sky Knight, with a public address system and an infra-red sensor, was introduced.

In military service, several countries have adopted the type, principally for pilot training. TH-55As were supplied to Algeria, Haiti, Nigeria, Spain (designated HE.20s) and Sweden (as Hkp 5Bs). Other nations have acquired Model 300s, including Colombia and Japan.

Having acquired the programme from Hughes' new owners, McDonnell Douglas, in 1986, Schweizer introduced a new TH-300C trainer variant. Turkey was an early customer.

Above: This Hughes 300, based at Lakewood, Los Angeles, is fitted with a searchlight, a siren and warning light. Police versions often carry armour.

Below: For agricultural operations, the Hughes 300 often carries a crop-spraying or dry powder dispersal kit. Stetcher kits, cargo racks and slings may also be fitted.

Model 300C

Type: three-seat light utility/training helicopter

Powerplant: one 168-kW (225-hp.) Textron Lycoming HIO-360-D1A piston engine derated to 142 kW (190 hp.)

Max cruising speed: 153 km/h (95 m.p.h.)

Endurance: 3 hours 24 min at sea level

Initial climb rate: 229 m/min (751 f.p.m.) at sea level

Range: 360 km (225 mi.) at 124 km/h (77 m.p.h.) at 1220 m (4,000 ft.)

Weights: empty 474 kg (1,043 lb.); maximum take-off 930 kg (2,046 lb.), with external load of 975 kg (2,145 lb.)

Dimensions:
rotor diameter	8.18 m (26 ft. 10 in.)
fuselage length	9.4 m (22 ft. 2 in.)
height	2.66 m (8 ft. 9 in.)
rotor disc area	52.50 m² (565 sq. ft.)

The Hughes 300 series tail rotor is of the teetering type, with just two blades freely pivoted as one unit. Each comprises a steel tube spar with glass-fibre skin. A spring-mounted bumper protects the blades.

TH-55As can accommodate three crewmembers side-by-side, typically two students and an instructor, within the Plexiglass cabin. On either side of the cabin there is a forward-hinged removable door. Police versions of the 300 carry a siren, a searchlight, safety mesh seats, night lights, first aid kits and uprated electrical systems.

The fully-articulated, three-bladed main rotor of bonded metal construction has an aluminium core spar. A main rotor tie-down kit is standard on the Osage.

A simple pod and boom configuration on the 300 affords good handling characteristics. The light alloy tailboom has horizontal and vertical stabilising surfaces.

U.S.ARMY 18126

The AVCO-Lycoming flat-four piston engine is mounted directly behind the crew. A crash-resistant aluminium fuel tank can be supplemented by an auxiliary tank of 72 litres (19 gallons).

TH-55A OSAGE

Based at the Army Aviation Center at Fort Rucker, this TH-55A is one of 792 originally ordered by the US Army. Based on the 269C, the TH-55A is powered by a HIO-360-B1A engine. In 1996, 12 military users still operated the type; the US has retired its fleet.

ACTION DATA

NEVER-EXCEED SPEED

Never-exceed speed, or velocity (Vne), is greater than the true maximum safe speed of the aircraft. The older Series 300C is slower than its more recent, aerodynamically efficient and stronger counterparts, the Robinson R22 and Enstrom F-28F.

MODEL 300C	169 km/h (105 m.p.h.)
R22 BETA	190 km/h (118 m.p.h.)
F-28F FALCON	180 km/h (112 m.p.h.)

POWER

The Hughes 300 has more power than the smaller, but more recent, R22. Also flown by police forces, the Enstrom has the same powerplant as the Hughes, albeit turbocharged, and the 300C has its motor derated to 142 kW (190 hp.).

MODEL 300C 168 kW (225 hp.)	R22 BETA 119 kW (160 hp.)	F-28F FALCON 168 kW (225 hp.)

CLIMB RATE

The Hughes 300C lags behind in this category, but performed well against its 1960s contemporaries. For the military training role, as well as crop-dusting and observation, the practicality and economy of operation are more important factors.

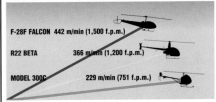

F-28F FALCON	442 m/min (1,500 f.p.m.)
R22 BETA	366 m/min (1,200 f.p.m.)
MODEL 300C	229 m/min (751 f.p.m.)

Piston-engined military training helicopters

BELL MODEL 47: Bell's Model 47 Sioux first flew in 1945, was used by at least 30 air arms. It stayed in production until 1974.

HILLER UH-12: A contemporary of the 300, more than 2,200 UH-12s were built. Military operators included the Royal Navy.

ROBINSON R22: Designed in the late 1970s, the R22 was bought by only one military customer, the Turkish army.

SAUNDERS-ROE SKEETER: Designed by Cierva, the two-seat Gipsy Major-powered Skeeter served with both Britain and Germany.

277

ILYUSHIN

IL-14 'CRATE'

● Eastern Bloc service ● Licence production ● Military transport

A ppearing in 1950, the Il-14 fulfilled the Soviet Union's requirement for a reliable transport for airline and military service. Developed from the problematic Il-12, the Il-14 was a much improved aircraft and was purchased by many Eastern Bloc countries. Licence production was successfully carried out in Czechoslovakia and East Germany, and a small number still remain in both military and civilian service.

▲ In 1943
Ilyushin began developing a transport aircraft to replace the Li-2. The resulting Il-12 and Il-14 equipped civilian and military organisations for the following two decades.

ILYUSHIN IL-14 'CRATE'

◄ Piston power
At a time when Western airlines were entering the turboprop era with aircraft like the F27, piston-powered Il-14s were still being produced for Eastern Bloc airlines.

Secret missions ►
A specialised Elint version, reportedly allocated the NATO codename 'Crate-C', was operated by some WarPac countries as well as by the USSR.

Pressurised comfort ►
Avia of Czechoslovakia built the Avia-14 Super version. This featured a pressurised cabin, circular windows and removable wingtip fuel tanks for extended range.

▲ Romanian 'Crates'
Romanian airline TAROM operated 18 Il-14s, the majority of which were built by VEB Flugzeugwerke in Dresden.

Photo survey ►
Fitted with a glass nose and an in-built darkroom for film processing, the Il-14FK was used for mapping and survey work.

FACTS AND FIGURES

➤ Total Il-14 production of all versions was about 3200; 2200 examples were built at the USSR's Khodinka factory.

➤ More than 100 examples of the Il-14 are estimated to be still flying.

➤ The first prototype, piloted by V.K. Kokkinaki, took to the air on 15 July 1950.

➤ Freighter versions of the Il-14 were loaded through a large 2.2-m (7-ft.) door on the side of the fuselage.

➤ The Il-14 was the first Soviet post-war aircraft to be widely exported.

➤ President Nasser of Egypt and the Shah of Iran were presented with luxury Il-14s.

Successful Soviet post-war propliner

Ilyushin's Il-14 was a successful attempt to solve the underlying deficiencies of the earlier Il-12. The 'Crate' had a number of improvements, including a new wing design and a strengthened fuselage.

In 1950 all transports were propeller-driven, and the Convair 340 and Martin 404 were demonstrating that a practical, twin-engined aircraft with tricycle landing gear was of great value. In fact, the Il-14's exhaust system, which had twin stacks that crossed over the wing and culminated in ejector nozzles at the trailing edge, was copied from the Convair. The American aircraft also influenced the design of the Il-14's anti-icing system.

During the 1950s and 1960s the Il-14 was the backbone of transport operations in the USSR and those of Soviet allies. In the USSR it was designed to do everything from transporting civil passengers to dropping paratroops and carrying out electronic intelligence-gathering missions for the Soviet air force.

Il-14s were licence-built by East Germany, which manufactured the aircraft at the Dresden State Aircraft Factory, and by Czechoslovakia, which produced the aircraft under the name Avia-14. More than 40 years after this enduring aircraft entered service, a number of Il-14s are still used on both passenger and cargo routes.

Left: Hungarian airline Malév operated a mixed fleet of VEB Il-14s and Ilyushin-built Il-14Ms, which were approximately one metre (3 ft.) longer and had additional capacity.

Above: Unlike its predecessor the Il-12, the 'Crate' handled well even if one engine failed.

Il-14M 'Crate'

Type: passenger and cargo transport

Powerplant: two 1417-kW (1,900-hp.) Shvetsov ASh-82T radial piston engines driving four-bladed AV-50 propellers

Maximum speed: 430 km/h (267 m.p.h.) at 2400 m (7,872 ft.)

Cruising speed: 300 km/h (186 m.p.h.)

Range: 1500 km (937 mi.) with maximum payload

Service ceiling: 7400 m (24,272 ft.)

Weights: empty 12,700 kg (28,000 lb.); maximum take-off 18,000 kg (40,000 lb.)

Accommodation: (typical) two pilots, radio operator, loadmaster and provision for 24, 28, 32 or 36 passengers in various models and configurations; maximum payload of cargo version 3300 kg (7,275 lb.)

Dimensions:
span	31.70 m (103 ft. 11 in.)
length	22.31 m (73 ft. 3 in.)
height	7.90 m (25 ft. 9 in.)
wing area	100 m² (997 sq. ft.)

Normal operating crew comprised two pilots and, aft of a semi-bulkhead, a navigator and radio operator. A flight engineer could be accommodated in a jump-seat. A cargo and baggage compartment was situated between the flightdeck and the passenger cabin.

The ASh-82T engine was developed from the wartime M-82 powerplant, which was itself a Soviet-built Pratt & Whitney R-1830 radial. This version had improved fuel efficiency and an exhaust system copied from the American Convair 240 airliner.

When the Il-14P entered service with Aeroflot it was fitted with 18 seats in pairs on the port side and singularly on the starboard side. This capacity was later increased to 24. The stretched Il-14M could carry up to 36 passengers in high-density configuration.

The newly designed square-topped fin and rudder gave a pronounced handling improvement over the Il-12 thanks to a 17 per cent increase in area.

The undercarriage was hydraulically operated, with the double-wheeled main units retracting forwards into the engine nacelles.

To help rectify the deficiencies of the Il-12, Ilyushin designed an entirely new wing. Built with three spars and a straight taper on the trailing edge, it was far more aerodynamically efficient.

POLSKIE LINIE LOTNICZE ·LOT·

SP-LNH

IL-14P 'CRATE'

Polish airline Polskie Linie Lotnicze followed up its purchase of five Il-12s by ordering 16 Il-14s in 1954. Nine were licence built in East Germany and one was a Czech-built Avia-14.

ACTION DATA

MAXIMUM SPEED

The Il-14 was more streamlined than the Il-12B and was fitted with a more powerful version of the ASh-82 engine, giving it greater performance. Western designs of the time, like the Convair 240, were far more advanced than their Soviet counterparts.

Il-14M 'CRATE'	430 km/h (267 m.p.h.)
Il-12B 'COACH'	407 km/h (252 m.p.h.)
CV 240	538 km/h (334 m.p.h.)

POWER

Fitted with an engine based on a wartime radial design, the Il-12 and Il-14 did not have the power of the Pratt & Whitney R-2800-powered 240. This series was the pinnacle of piston-engine design.

Il-14M 'CRATE'	Il-12B 'COACH'	CV 240
2834 kW (3,800 hp.)	2297 kW (3,550 hp.)	3579 kW (4,800 hp.)

PASSENGERS

Although originally designed to carry only 18 passengers, later versions of the Il-14 could hold up to 36 passengers in a high-density configuration. The more powerful 240 could carry the largest load.

Il-14M 'CRATE'	36
Il-12B 'COACH'	28
CV 240	40

The Il-14's Western rivals

■ CONVAIR 440 METROPOLITAN: The 440 was the last piston-powered Convair airliner, and more than 160 CV 440s were built.

■ CURTISS C-46: After the Japanese surrender in 1945 many ex-military C-46s were bought by civilian operators around the world.

■ DOUGLAS DC-3: A pre-war design, the DC-3 was built in huge numbers during World War II and continues to serve with civilian users.

■ MARTIN 4-0-4: Entering service at roughly the same time as the Il-12, the Martin series was overtaken by the onset of turboprop airliners.

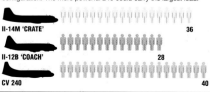

ILYUSHIN

IL-18 'COOT'

● 1950s airliner design ● Licence-built in China ● Pioneering turboprop

▲ If any aircraft could be said to have brought air travel to the masses in Eastern Europe, it was the Il-18. Operators found that the large turboprop, dismissed as obsolete in the jet age, was actually very profitable due to its much lower operating costs and fuel economy.

As the first (and largest) post-war aircraft construction project undertaken by the Ilyushin Design Bureau, the piston-engined Il-18 was an attempt to give Russia a much-needed long-range airliner with the minimum of delay. A second Il-18 was built in 1953 as a modern 75-seat passenger airliner. Powered by four turboprops, the Il-18 was later adapted to a military role as the Il-38 ASW aircraft, and also for signals intelligence work.

ILYUSHIN IL-18 'COOT'

▲ Traditional cockpit layout
The cockpit was well designed. The object in the centre is a weather radar scope.

▲ China service
Il-18s continued in service with China's CAAC airline until the early-1980s, flying throughout the country including Tibet. Serviceability was poor for the aircraft's last few years in China, resulting in a number of crashes. About 100 Il-18s were exported from the total of 800 built.

▲ Flying with the fleet
When Aeroflot was split up, the remaining Il-18s were inherited by new carriers. They are still operated by companies like Rossiya and SPAIR.

▲ Polish airlines
Most Warsaw Pact nations had Il-18s in their national fleet. LOT, the Polish national carrier, retired its last examples in the early-1980s.

Dnepropetrovsk ▶
Regional flights in the Soviet Union were the mainstay of the Il-18's work. This aircraft was the first to arrive at Dnepropetrovsk's new airport.

FACTS AND FIGURES

➤ The type had carried over 250 million passengers by 1981 and clocked up 14 million flight hours.

➤ The first 20 Il-18s used the Kuznetsov NK-4 turboprop engine.

➤ In the 1970s, the Il-18 was still Aeroflot's second most numerous airliner.

➤ The Il-18's flight deck crew numbered five – two pilots, a navigator, a radio operator and a flight engineer.

➤ From the early-1970s a number of Il-18s were converted to freighters.

➤ African operators such as Air Guinea, Air Mali and Air Mauritania also used Il-18s.

PROFILE

Turboprop liner for the USSR

Below: Due to the US trade embargo and cash shortages, Cubana, the Cuban national carrier, relied heavily on its Il-18s despite their age. This Il-18D, featuring uprated avionics, was still operating in 1986.

During the 1950s, Aeroflot decided, despite its still largely unmodernised infrastructure with many outlying airfields remaining in the 'dirt strip' category, to modernise its civil airliner fleet. The Il-18 was one of the results of this planning.

The specification that led to the Il-18 consequently called for a good rough field capability as well as cabin pressurisation and seating capacity for up to 75 passengers. Ilyushin opted for a conventional, single-fin/rudder

design powered by four turboprop engines and utilising a tricycle landing gear, the resulting aircraft bearing a superficial resemblance to the Bristol Britannia and DC-7. The prototype flew on 4 July 1957.

Five development aircraft proved little need for modification before production commenced and the Il-18 entered service with the Soviet state airline on 29 April 1959. Further models were produced including the Il-18V, which accommodated up to 100 passengers and which

Above: Despite the age of the design, Il-18 production only ceased in 1979 after 565 Il-18Ds had been built.

began flying with Aeroflot in 1961. Four years later the Il-18D appeared. This, the last Il-18 production model, featured a reconfigured fuselage interior to take up to 122 seats, greater fuel capacity and uprated engines. In total, at least 800 Il-18s were built for Soviet and foreign airline use, plus the military role.

Il-18D 'Coot'

Type: long-range turboprop airliner

Powerplant: four 2983-kW (4,000-hp.) Ivchenko AI-20M turboprops

Maximum speed: 685 km/h (388 m.p.h.)

Range: 3700 km (2,295 mi.) with maximum payload

Service ceiling: 9250 km (30,000 ft.)

Weights: empty 27,980 kg (62,678 lb.); maximum take-off 64,000 kg (93,500 lb.)

Accommodation: 110 in high-density seating

Dimensions: span 37.40 m (122 ft. 8 in.)
length 35.90 m (117 ft. 9 in.)
height 10.17 m (33 ft. 4 in.)
wing area 140 m² (1,506 sq. ft.)

IL-18 'COOT'

Still in limited service in Russia, the Il-18 was widely exported and many were sold to China before the Sino-Soviet split in 1960. They were operated by the national airline CAAC, which was split into smaller airlines in 1992.

In later years, Il-18s had a more complete avionics fit, including autoland (an automatic landing instrument). All versions contained the 'Emblema' weather radar in the nose and a Decca Flight Log navigation system.

Fuel was stored in 20 bag-type tanks in the wings, stretching from the wingroot to the ailerons.

Originally, Kuznetsov NK-4 engines were fitted, but these were replaced by Ivchenko AI-20s. The Il-18D (first introduced in 1964) was powered by AI-20Ms, which had about five per cent more power. The large 4.5-m (14-ft. 9-in.) propellers could be put into reverse pitch to give braking assistance on landing.

Electro-thermal engine de-icing was fitted as standard, and each engine had two SG-12 starter/generator systems. The main gear retracted forwards into the inboard engine nacelle.

All flight controls were manual, connected by cables. Hydraulic boosters were fitted to the ailerons and elevators, and there was a spring tab on the rudder.

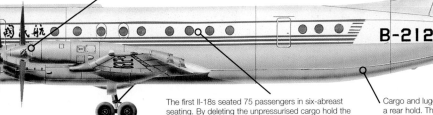

B-212

Five crewmembers were usually seated in the flight deck.

The first Il-18s seated 75 passengers in six-abreast seating. By deleting the unpressurised cargo hold the Il-18D increased this capacity to 110 to 120 passengers.

Cargo and luggage were stored in a rear hold. The only access to this was from outside the aircraft.

ACTION DATA

PASSENGERS

With the additional space produced by removing the rear cargo bay, the Il-18 could carry 110 passengers, albeit in Soviet-style seating which was noticeably spartan by Western standards. Early versions had 95 seats.

Il-18D 'COOT' — 110 passengers
BRITANNIA — 92 passengers
DC-7C — 105 passengers

RANGE

Turboprops are efficient engines, operating well at high altitude and giving a good compromise between the speed of jets and the economy of pistons. The following range figures are with maximum payload.

Il-18D 'COOT' 3700 km (2,295 mi.)
BRITANNIA 6869 km (4,259 mi.)
DC-7 5810 km (3,602 mi.)

PRODUCTION

The largest country in the world also had the largest airline, and the Il-18 was produced in quantity. The Britannia and DC-7 could not compete with the new jet-powered airlines.

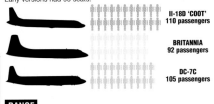

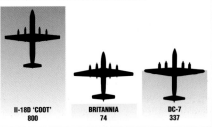

Il-18D 'COOT' 800
BRITANNIA 74
DC-7 337

Ilyushin airliners across the world

■ **Il-12 'COACH':** A Soviet equivalent to the C-47, the Il-12 was used by Aeroflot from 1947 and was also exported to Poland and China.

■ **Il-62 'CLASSIC':** The Il-62 was the only jet apart from the VC-10 to have four rear-mounted engines. It is still widely used.

■ **Il-86 'CAMBER':** The first four-engine wide-body Soviet jet, the Il-86 is still widely used on international routes by the airline ARIA.

■ **Il-96 'CAMBER':** Modifications to the Il-86 resulted in the Il-96, with a new wing and engines and advanced 'glass' cockpit displays.

ILYUSHIN

IL-62 'CLASSIC'

● Long-range airliner ● Rear-mounted four-jet layout

W hen the Ilyushin Il-62 was revealed to the world in 1962, this long-range airliner looked like a possible Soviet equivalent to the Boeing 707 and Vickers VC10. Until then, the USSR had never excelled at providing comfort and safety in a commercial transport, but the Il-62 met a high standard and served Moscow and its allies well. Although now obsolescent and costly to operate, many Il-62s still fly today.

▲ The Il-62M
served as a main component of the old Soviet airline Aeroflot and its successors. In the former Aeroflot, the aircraft set records for large payloads and speeds with an all-female flight crew.

ILYUSHIN IL-62 'CLASSIC'

▼ Four at the front
The Il-62 cockpit seats as many as four or five crew, including pilot, co-pilot, navigator, radio operator and flight engineer.

▲ Four at the back
Only the VC10 and the Il-62 share the four engines on the rear fuselage layout. This configuration allows the wing design to be clean and efficient, and reduces cabin noise to some extent.

Sheremetyevo ▶
The international airport at Moscow, Sheremetyevo, is still the main port of call for most Il-62s. Although newer replacements are now arriving, Il-62s remain in use with airlines such as Orbi and Aerovody.

◀ To Asia
The Il-62 serves many destinations in central Asia and the Far East. This example is seen at Subang airport in Malaysia; Aeroflot Il-62 services to this destination, via Delhi, began in 1970.

▲ Still going strong
Cubana is one of the last civil operators of the Il-62 outside the former USSR, with a few Il-62MK variants still in service.

FACTS AND FIGURES

➤ The first Il-62 flew in January 1963, powered by Lyul'ka AL-7 turbojets while awaiting delivery of NK-8-4 turbofans.

➤ The first scheduled Aeroflot service with an Il-62 took to the air on 10 March 1967.

➤ A total of 244 Il-62s had been delivered when production ended in 1990.

➤ When Germany was unified, the Luftwaffe flew former Interflug Il-62s until replacing them with Airbus A310s.

➤ The Il-62MK has a redesigned structure and undercarriage.

➤ The Il-62 closely resembles the proposed British 'Super VC10' of 1958.

PROFILE

Ilyushin's classic airliner

The Ilyushin Il-62 was developed as a long-haul jetliner for Aeroflot, primarily to replace the turboprop-powered Tupolev Tu-114. With its T-tail and pairs of side-by-side turbofans on the rear fuselage, the Il-62 resembles Britain's VC10.

Given the NATO reporting name of 'Classic', Il-62s have been continuously upgraded to keep pace with rapid improvements in technology elsewhere. Better thrust reversers, improved seats,

triplex inertial navigation and revised nacelles aimed at noise reduction are among the changes. Improved (Il-62M) and strengthened (Il-62MK) models, both with Soloviev engines replacing Kuznetsov NK-8-4 turbofans, carry passengers in Russia and allied nations.

Some surviving Il-62s serve as military transports and one aircraft transports the Russian president in his travels. But although the big Ilyushin was a genuine pioneer in its early

days, it has has become geriatric and increasingly difficult to maintain. As a result, many former Il-62 operators have taken advantage of the break-up of the USSR to acquire considerably more advanced aircraft like the Airbus A310 and Boeing 767 from the West.

The vast majority of Il-62s served with Aeroflot. Following the break-up of this airline they have been seen in many colours, including that of Aeroflot's main successor, ARIA (Aeroflot Russian International Airlines). Even so, many continued to fly in the old Aeroflot colour scheme for several years after the airline's demise.

Il-62M 'Classic'

Type: long-range airliner

Powerplant: four 107.8-kN (24,250-lb.-thrust) Soloviev D-30KU turbofans

Cruising speed: 900 km/h (558 m.p.h.)

Range: 8000 km (4,760 mi.) with maximum payload and reserves

Service ceiling: 11,440 m (37,500 ft.)

Weights: empty 69,400 kg (152,680 lb.); loaded 165,000 kg (363,000 lb.)

Accommodation: provision for flight crew of five; typically 186 passengers, with 72 in forward compartment and 114 in rear

Dimensions: span   43.20 m (141 ft. 8 in.)
length   53.12 m (174 ft. 3 in.)
height   12.35 m (40 ft. 6 in.)
wing area 282.2 m² (3,036 sq. ft.)

IL-62MK 'CLASSIC'

Linhas Aereas de Angola is one of the last African operators of the Il-62. They fly two of the Ilyushins on various routes including Luanda to Moscow and Havana.

The last Il-62s featured revised engine nacelles, giving reduced emissions and noise, although they could never meet the latest international noise abatement regulations.

The large bullet fairing improves airflow over the tail surfaces at high subsonic speeds.

A strengthened undercarriage on the IL-62MK is capable of supporting much greater all-up weights.

The Il-62M differs from earlier versions by the addition of an extra fuel tank in the fin, as well as completely revised avionics.

Il-62s have received several avionics upgrades. Many now have a triplex inertial navigation system, and the flight control system can be modified to permit operation in extremely bad visibility conditions.

The galley is located in the centre of the fuselage between the passenger compartments.

The Soviets were never as concerned with comfort as Western airlines, but later versions of the Il-62 have revised cabin layouts, giving increased passenger comfort.

During trials, the rear-engined high-tail layout caused the aircraft to have slender control margins at low speeds, so the wing was redesigned in production aircraft to give more lift.

LINHAS AEREAS DE ANGOLA

The Il-62M is fitted with the Soloviev D-30KU turbofan instead of the earlier Kuznetsov engine. Thrust reversers are fitted to the outer engines only.

The cabin seats up to 195 passengers in the Il-62MK version, in six-abreast layout with a central aisle. Up to 25 tons of cargo can be stored in containerised underfloor baggage holds.

Some Aeroflot Il-62s have an enlarged dorsal spine containing extra communications gear.

The long-range jet pioneers

■ **BOEING 707:** First of the modern four-jet airliners, the Boeing 707 entered service in the late 1950s. It revolutionised air transport, bringing the benefits of long-distance jet travel to more people than ever before.

■ **DOUGLAS DC-8:** The Boeing's great rival first entered service in 1959. Stretched many times over a long career, the DC-8 grew to seat 259 passengers in its final variants. It can still be seen around the world, primarily as a freighter.

■ **VICKERS VC10:** Designed to operate from 'hot and high' airfields, the sleek VC10 was a better performer than the 707 and DC-8. But operating costs were higher, and so it was not as great a commercial success as its American rivals.

ACTION DATA

PASSENGER LOAD

Seats in Russian aircraft are generally crowded more closely together than is the practice on Western scheduled flights; the reduced seat pitch allows for extra passengers to be carried, but in less comfort. The Tu-154 tri-jet carries almost as many passengers as the Il-62, but has a much smaller range.

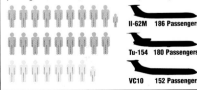

Il-62M   186 Passengers

Tu-154   180 Passengers

VC10   152 Passengers

ILYUSHIN

IL-86/96 'CAMBER'

● Modern airliner design ● Hi-tech redesign ● International services

▲ Il-86 prototype
Five years after development was announced, the first Il-86 was rolled out.

▲ Redesigning the 'Camber'
In an effort to solve the shortcomings of the Il-86, Ilyushin decided to redesign the aircraft. Although the resulting airliner, the Il-96, looks similar to the earlier 'Camber', it is, in fact, an almost completely new design.

▲ Aeroflot service
About 100 Il-86s were delivered to Aeroflot and fly high-density international routes.

▼ Increased capacity
The Il-96M, which has seating for a maximum of 375 passengers, has been test flown.

▲ Il-96 certification
As the Il-96 retained some of the Il-86's features, the new aircraft's test programme was reduced by 750 hours. Ilyushin had hoped that certification would be received in 1990, but it was not granted until 29 December 1992.

First flown in December 1976, the Il-86 started operating scheduled services with Aeroflot four years later. Range fell short of the intended 3600 km when carrying a 40000-kg payload or 4600 km with maximum fuel. As a result, fewer than 100 Il-86s had been delivered before the Il-96 appeared as a replacement in 1988. Although externally similar and having the same fuselage diameter, the -96 was a completely new design and incorporated several advanced features.

▲ With seating for 350 passengers in a 3+3+3 seating arrangement, Aeroflot and Ilyushin had expected the Il-86 to revolutionise Soviet air transport. Unfortunately, the aircraft's range was far less than expected.

FACTS AND FIGURES

➤ Genrikh V. Novozhilov announced the Il-86 at the 1970 Paris air show, after the retirement of Ilyushin himself.

➤ Originally, the Il-86 was to be an Il-62 with a wider fuselage and improved wing.

➤ Huge electrical pulses de-iced all of the Il-86's leading edges.

➤ Many Soviet airports had to be upgraded to make their passenger handling facilities compatible with the Il-96.

➤ A freighter version, the Il-96T, can carry 92,000 kg (202,400 lb.) of cargo.

➤ Ilyushin has proposed the Il-96MK variant, powered by NK-93 ducted propfans.

PROFILE

Success through adversity

In addition to being the first Soviet wide-body airliner and the first to have its engines in wing-mounted nacelles, the Il-86 also introduced a novel boarding system. To overcome the poor facilities at many Soviet airports, passengers could board the Il-86 through doors at ground level, stow their coats and hand baggage, and then climb internal stairs to the cabin.

The improved Il-96, which flew for the first time in September 1988, replaced the original NK-86 engines with PS-90s. It also introduced new structural components and used composite materials to reduce airframe weight. The wings are bigger and less sharply swept, and large winglets at the tips reduce drag.

Conventional doors located on the passenger deck level give access to the cabin. Up to 300 people can be accommodated in an all-tourist arrangement, or 235 in a three-class configuration.

Ilyushin intended to produce a range of Il-96 derivatives, including 200- and 375-

passenger models and a double-deck version with 550 seats. However, recent efforts have focused on installing Western avionics and engines to make the aircraft more attractive to airlines around the world.

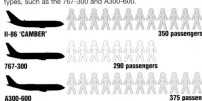

Below: Carrying a Russian registration number, this Il-86 serves with the Latvian airline Transaero. The airline operates two Il-86s.

Above: Aeroflot accepted its first Il-86 on 24 September 1979, but did not start operations until 1981, with a proving flight to East Germany.

Il-96-300 'Camber'

Type: wide-bodied airliner

Powerplant: four 156.9-kN (35,300-lb.-thrust) Aviadvigatel PS-90A turbofans

Cruising speed: 850–900 km/h (525–558 m.p.h.)

Take-off run: 2600 m (8,525 ft.)

Range: 9000 km (5,570 mi.) with 30,000-kg (66,000-lb.) payload

Service ceiling: 12,000 m (39,360 ft.)

Weights: empty 117,000 kg (257,400 lb.); maximum take-off 216,000 kg (475,200 lb.)

Accommodation: 235 passengers in three classes or a maximum of 300

Dimensions:
span	60.11 m	(197 ft. 2 in.)
length	55.35 m	(181 ft. 6 in.)
height	17.57 m	(57 ft. 7 in.)
wing area	391.6 m² (4,214 sq. ft.)	

IL-96-300

CCCP-96000 acted as the first Il-96 prototype, flying from Khodinka on 28 September 1988 and appearing at the Paris air show the following year. The -300 designation refers to the nominal seating capacity.

A six-screen glass cockpit replaces the conventional instruments of the Il-86. Unlike contemporary Western designs, Ilyushin has retained a flight engineer in the cockpit.

With its Aviadvigatel PS-90A turbofans, the Il-96 has a far better range than the Il-86. Fuel is contained in the wings and fuselage centre section, with a maximum capacity of 148,260 litres (39,170 gal.).

Abandoning the Il-86 wing entirely, Ilyushin designed a modern advanced wing of supercritical section for the Il-96. This included range-increasing winglets. The use of new technology has allowed Ilyushin to aim for a lifetime of 60,000 hours.

Neither the two-section rudder nor elevators have trim tabs. The Il-96M has a shorter tailfin, as the aircraft's lengthened fuselage provides increased directional stability.

A Triplex fly-by-wire system transfers pilot inputs to the control surfaces. The Il-96's tail surfaces have a higher aspect ratio and altered profiles, compared to those of the Il-96. They also have composite leading and trailing edges.

One of the few real similarities between the Il-96 and Il-86 is the four-unit undercarriage.

The Il-96 has a shorter fuselage than the earlier aircraft, with fewer seats and a greatly revised interior. The Il-86's unusual system of internal stairs for passengers has been discarded.

ACTION DATA

PASSENGERS

Even though the Il-86 has a respectable passenger load, its poor operating economies and unconventional passenger loading prevent it from competing effectively with comparable Western types, such as the 767-300 and A300-600.

Il-86 'CAMBER'	350 passengers
767-300	290 passengers
A300-600	375 passengers

TAKE-OFF RUN

For maximum operational flexibility, airlines require aircraft that have good field performance so that they can operate from smaller international airports. With its older technology engines the Il-86 trails behind.

- Il-86 'CAMBER' 2600 m (8,525 ft.)
- 767-300 2560 m (8,400 ft.)
- A300-600 2280 m (7,480 ft.)

RANGE

The Il-86 was intended to have a range of 4600 km (2,850 mi.), which was considerably less than the Boeing or Airbus models. In-service reports suggest that even this figure has not been achieved, with Interflug, the former East German airline, quoting a range of only 2500 km (1,550 mi.) in its sales publications. The Il-96 attempts to rectify this problem.

- Il-86 'CAMBER' 4600 km (2,850 mi.)
- 767-300 7408 km (4,600 mi.)
- A300-600 6759 km (4,190 mi.)

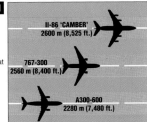

Airliners by Ilyushin

■ **Il-14 'CRATE':** A refined development of the Il-12 'Coach', the Il-14 was originally built as an 18- to 26-seat airliner. A stretched 24- to 28-seat variant was produced as the Il-14M. Several examples remain airworthy, most flying as freighters.

■ **Il-18 'COOT':** This four-engined turboprop first flew in 1957. It was Ilyushin's response to an Aeroflot requirement for a 75- to 100-seat medium-range transport. This aircraft flew VIP/staff transport duties with the Democratic and Popular Republic of Algeria.

■ **Il-62 'CLASSIC':** Very similar in appearance to the British Vickers VC-10, the Il-62 first flew in 1963 and was capable of accommodating a maximum of 186 passengers. A range of 6700 km was possible with maximum payload.

JUNKERS

W.33/W.34

● Single-engined civil transport ● F.13 development ● War service

One of the most advanced civil aircraft of the period, the Junkers W.34 set the standard in inter-war design. Intended for use as a cargo, mail and utility transport, this product of the forward-thinking Dr Hugo Junkers had a relatively brief, but bright, career. Developed in 1926 and bearing the distinctive lines associated with many Junkers aircraft, it was designed to replace the Junkers F.13 of 1919. It also served with the Luftwaffe until 1945.

▲ *In a demonstration of the type's reliability, Lufthansa W.33 D-1167 Bremen made the first East to West non-stop transatlantic flight by a single-engined aircraft on 12/13 April 1928.*

◀ **Record breaker**
W.33s and W.34s established a number of world records, including a duration record of 65 hours and 25 minutes set in July 1928. This reputation for reliability prompted Lufthansa (with 15 W.33s and at least eight W.34s) and a number of overseas airlines to purchase the aircraft.

Exported to Finland ▶
The K.43 was a three-seat reconnaissance bomber version built in unknown quantities in Sweden. Examples were exported to Colombia and Finland. This aircraft wears wartime markings.

▼ Canadian fire-bomber
Re-engined with a Pratt & Whitney Wasp, this W.34f was still in service in the early 1960s.

▲ **Luftwaffe service**
Both types saw German air force service and performed training and liaison duties until 1945.

Swedish-built K.43 ▶
Unmarked, having just left the factory, this K.43 can be identified by its dorsal machine-gun for self-protection and its extra cabin windows.

FACTS AND FIGURES

➤ The W.33 was first flown in 1926; in total 199 were produced, powered by Gnome-Rhone or Junkers engines.

➤ The W.33 and W.34 prototypes were converted from Junkers F.13s.

➤ A total of nearly 1800 W.34s was built in Sweden and Germany.

➤ A single Junkers W.33 is currently on display at the Henry Ford Museum in Dearborn, Michigan.

➤ Junkers W.34s were often used as VIP transports for very high-ranking officials.

➤ The prototype W.33, owned by Junkers, was named *Schildkrähe* (Hooded Crow).

German utility on land or water

An ordinary-looking aircraft, yet one that inspired transport aircraft design in the 1930s, the Junkers W.34 (and its alter-ego the W.33) was a superb monoplane that appeared on the scene at the right time. Earlier utility transports, dating back to the beginning of aviation, were hopelessly outmoded. This Junkers design, of sturdy construction, with a single wing and a clean shape (except for

bracing on the tail), represented the future. Although with their corrugated skinning they lacked aerodynamic elegance, these aircraft were immensely sturdy and capacious flying machines.

The designation W.33 was applied to the aircraft powered by an in-line engine, usually the Junkers L-5, but the designation was changed to the better-known W.34 with the installation of a radial powerplant. The aircraft was

available with wheel or float landing gear.

A total of 199 W.33s was built, and W.34s saw extensive service with the Luftwaffe from its formation until the end of World War II. In military service, in addition to their use as transports, these aircraft made fine navigation trainers. The freighter versions had a large compartment which was accessed via the side door.

Below: Like this example of a W.34, many W.33s and W.34s were built with open cockpits.

Above: NX7465 Queen of the Air *was a W.33 registered in the United States in the 1930s.*

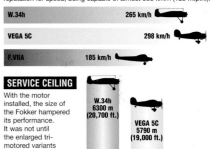

W.34F

Many W.33s and W.34s, like this Canadian-registered example, were exported. CF-AQB flew with Pacific Western Airlines. Float-equipped examples had an enlarged rudder and dorsal fin to maintain flight stability.

The principal difference between the W.33 and W.34 was the type of powerplant fitted. While the former had a liquid-cooled Junkers L-5 in-line engine, the W.34 was fitted with one of a number of different types of air-cooled radial motor.

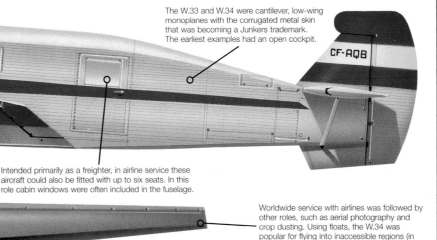

The W.33 and W.34 were cantilever, low-wing monoplanes with the corrugated metal skin that was becoming a Junkers trademark. The earliest examples had an open cockpit.

The first W.34 was powered by a 313-kW (420-hp.) Gnome Rhône Jupiter radial engine. Later examples used various motors, including Siemens, BMW and Bristol engines. In Canada, Pratt & Whitney Wasps were sometimes used.

Intended primarily as a freighter, in airline service these aircraft could also be fitted with up to six seats. In this role cabin windows were often included in the fuselage.

Worldwide service with airlines was followed by other roles, such as aerial photography and crop dusting. Using floats, the W.34 was popular for flying into inaccessible regions (in Colombia, for example). In Canada, aircraft like this one were used as fire-bombers.

ACTION DATA

MAXIMUM SPEED
Although the Fokker F.VIIa was powered by the same Jupiter engine as some versions of the W.34, its extra weight reduced its top speed considerably. Lockheed's Vega established an excellent reputation for speed, being capable of almost 300 km/h (185 m.p.h.).

W.34h	265 km/h
VEGA 5C	298 km/h
F.VIIA	185 km/h

SERVICE CEILING
With the motor installed, the size of the Fokker hampered its performance. It was not until the enlarged tri-motored variants appeared that this improved. The W.34 had the best ceiling capability of the three aircraft, although the Lockheed Vega was not far behind.

W.34h 6300 m (20,700 ft.)
VEGA 5C 5790 m (19,000 ft.)
F.VIIA 2600 m (8,500 ft.)

RANGE
Both the Vega and F.VIIa had a better range than the W.34h, despite the latter's record-breaking flights in the late 1920s. However, all three aircraft were still capable of flights of around 1000 km (600 mi.). The Fokker and Lockheed had 30 per cent more range, partly due to greater fuel capacity.

W.34h 900 km (560 mi.)
VEGA 5C 1165 km (720 mi.)
F.VIIA 1160 km (715 mi.)

Junkers inter-war civil transports

■ **G.31:** Flown in 1926, this tri-motored airliner was an enlarged development of the G.24, itself an extension of the F.13 design.

■ **G.38:** Only two of these remarkable four-engined airliners were built. They could accommodate 34 passengers.

■ **Ju 60:** A high-performance single-engined monoplane, the Ju 60 was intended to compete with the Lockheed Orion. Two were built.

■ **Ju 86:** The first twin-engined passenger and freight aircraft designed to employ diesel engines, the Ju 86 was used by airlines and the Luftwaffe.

JUNKERS
F 13

● Civil aviation pioneer ● All-metal airframe ● Lufthansa service

▲ *The F13 brought air travel to people all over the world, not just in Europe. These passengers flew on the first service by the Brazilian airline Varig in May 1927.*

When it first flew on 25 June 1919, the F 13 was the world's first all-metal commercial transport. It was the embodiment of everything scientific genius Hugo Junkers had learned in years of aviation pioneering, and Lufthansa instantly saw it as an aircraft worth having. For a single-engine machine, the F 13 was given a big job – and performed it with just the right mix of muscle and elegance.

JUNKERS F 13

Lufthansa on skis ▶
The adaptability and strength of the F 13 was a classic mark of all Junkers designs. Well able to operate in the harshest of conditions, more than 40 F 13s were converted to use either float or ski undercarriages.

◀ Modern lines
The profile of the F 13 was remarkably modern, especially when, like this Varig-owned example, it was fitted with the later square-topped tail. This shape of tail was to reappear on the classic Ju 52 transport and on late-World War II Junkers bombers and fighters.

Built like a tank ▶
The F 13's massive, chunky wing showed that all-metal construction was in its infancy in the 1920s, but the toughness this created contributed to the airliner's long life.

▼ Stopping for fuel
This F 13 and its partner, a Fokker F.III, would not have taken long to replenish. The entire fuel load of one of these aircraft would be less than a modern Lufthansa Airbus needs to simply get off the ground.

▲ Floatplane adventure
This F 13 was owned by a Norwegian, Miss Gidsken Jacobsen, and flown by Birger Johnsen. It was destroyed in a crash after its engine fell out while at about 1000 m (3,000 ft.) above Balestrand. Fortunately, no one was hurt.

FACTS AND FIGURES

➤ 322 F 13 aircraft (originally called J13) were manufactured in 11 years.

➤ In 1919, an F 13 broke the world altitude record by carrying eight people to a height of 6750 m (22,140 ft.).

➤ Lufthansa at one time operated no fewer than 55 F 13s.

➤ The last F 13 in service was finally retired by Varig Airlines in 1948.

➤ The Deruluft airline began F 13 flights to Russia, between Leningrad, Riga and Konigsberg, in 1928.

➤ F 13s served with operators in at least 28 countries around the world.

PROFILE

The world's first all-metal airliner

Hugo Junkers wanted to dispense with the cumbersome struts and wires that held the wings of an aircraft to the fuselage during the era of World War I. The monoplane F 13 resulted from his studies. Adopted quickly by Lufthansa, the F 13, with its characteristic corrugated sheet-metal skin, was virtually indestructible. It was eventually flown on all continents, with a conventional wheeled undercarriage, with floats as a seaplane, and even with runners for ice and snow.

Most remarkably, passengers in the F 13 travelled in comfort, in a closed, heated and ventilated cabin. Its seats were fitted with safety belts, and the F 13 was the first commercial aircraft to have more than one set of controls so that two pilots could relieve each other on long flights.

Junkers later built bigger and better airliners, but the F 13 was the ship which began a great revolution. Even when it was being retired, few other aircraft measured up to the F 13 in performance or efficiency.

Early all-metal aircraft designs like the F 13 were never pretty to look at. Nevertheless, the aircraft was a favourite with its crews, and F 13s frequently received female names.

F 13

Type: six-seat passenger transport

Powerplant: one 156-kW (210-hp.) Junkers L-5 piston engine (early versions: 138-kW (185-hp.) BMW IIIa piston or 119-kW Mercedes D.IIIa)

Maximum speed: 170 km/h (105 m.p.h.)

Range: 644 km (400 mi.)

Service ceiling: about 7000 m (23,000 ft.)

Weights: empty about 1500 kg (3,300 lb.); loaded 2495 kg (5,489 lb.)

Accommodation: two pilots, four to six passengers

Dimensions: span   17.70 m (58 ft. 3 in.)
length   20.50 m (31 ft. 6 in.)

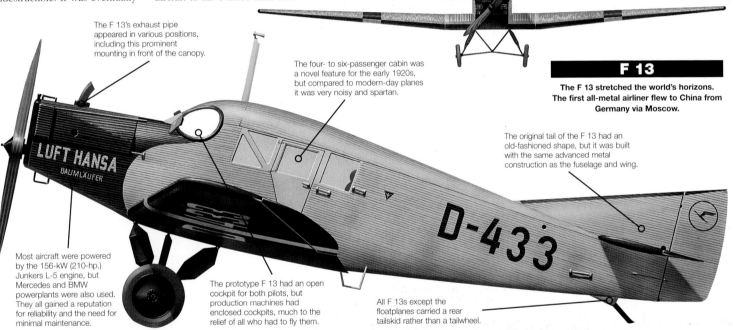

The first F 13s may have had an advanced structure, but most retained a traditional two-blade wooden airscrew.

The F 13's exhaust pipe appeared in various positions, including this prominent mounting in front of the canopy.

The four- to six-passenger cabin was a novel feature for the early 1920s, but compared to modern-day planes it was very noisy and spartan.

F 13

The F 13 stretched the world's horizons. The first all-metal airliner flew to China from Germany via Moscow.

The original tail of the F 13 had an old-fashioned shape, but it was built with the same advanced metal construction as the fuselage and wing.

Most aircraft were powered by the 156-kW (210-hp.) Junkers L-5 engine, but Mercedes and BMW powerplants were also used. They all gained a reputation for reliability and the need for minimal maintenance.

The prototype F 13 had an open cockpit for both pilots, but production machines had enclosed cockpits, much to the relief of all who had to fly them.

All F 13s except the floatplanes carried a rear tailskid rather than a tailwheel.

ACTION DATA

MAXIMUM SPEED

Airliners were a completely new concept in 1919 and 1920. Many were adaptations of military designs, like the DH.4, and as such had very good performance. But they offered far less passenger comfort than machines like the Junkers, which was designed as a passenger carrier from the start.

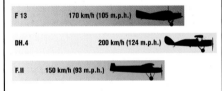

F 13	170 km/h (105 m.p.h.)
DH.4	200 km/h (124 m.p.h.)
F.II	150 km/h (93 m.p.h.)

PAYLOAD

| F 13 up to 6 passengers | DH.4 3 passengers | F.II 5 passengers |

The advantage of designing an aircraft as a passenger carrier was that payload space could be optimised. The DH.4 was larger and much more powerful than either the Junkers or the Fokker, yet it could carry fewer paying customers.

RANGE

The early airline routes were between the capital cities of western Europe, and the range of the Junkers was adequate for most journeys. It was not as good as the high-winged Fokker monoplane, however, which had been designed by Reinhold Platz to carry passengers non-stop between Berlin and Moscow.

| F 13 644 km (400 mi.) | DH.4 700 km (434 mi.) | F.II 1200 km (744 mi.) |

The first commercial travellers

■ **ENDURANCE TEST:** The first airline services used minimally converted open-cockpit World War I bombers. Exposed to the elements, passengers had to wrap up very well.

■ **WEATHER PROTECTION:** The amazing thing about the Junkers F 13 was that it offered passengers a fully enclosed environment, allowing them to travel in normal clothing.

■ **ENCLOSED COCKPIT:** Unlike many other aircraft of the period, Junkers pilots were protected, since the aircraft had a fully enclosed, if sparsely equipped, cockpit.

■ **TRAVEL IN STYLE:** It might not have matched a limousine of the period, but the cabin of the F 13 offered passengers plenty of comfort and a fine view through large side windows.

JUNKERS
G.38

- 34-passenger luxury airliner ● Largest landplane of its time

▲ *It was like nothing else in the skies, but despite its size and appearance the G.38 was a practical airliner. It was not fast, but its massive wing gave the huge machine good take-off and landing ability.*

Built in Dessau, the Junkers G.38 was a giant monoplane airliner with four engines, fixed undercarriage and a biplane tail – and windows in its wings. This amazing flying machine was the product of an easier, happier era of luxury air travel. Inside were upholstered lounge seats, a hat rack and two toilets. In Lufthansa colours, it gave top-quality catered service in the pre-war 1930s.

JUNKERS G.38

▲ Dwarfed
A light aircraft like the Junkers A.50 could almost land on the massive 44-metre wing of the G.38, which was the biggest in the world.

◀ Wing seats
The wing was so thick that the engines could be reached in flight. Two three-seat cabins were actually housed in the leading edge.

▲ Engine change
Changing an L8 engine was a complex affair, using cranes and pulleys and a lot of sweat.

▼ Flaps down
With its effective high-lift flaps, the G.38 had a short take-off run and a very low stalling speed.

◀◀ Lufthansa's pride ▶
The G.38 was the world's largest landplane and was a monument to the ingenuity of Junkers. It generated great interest in its services to Rome, London, Stockholm and many cities in Germany.

FACTS AND FIGURES

➤ The first flight of the Junkers G.38 took place on 6 November 1929.

➤ Lufthansa changed the second G.38's engines twice after receiving delivery.

➤ A single Junkers G.38 served with the Luftwaffe in 1939 for transport duties in Norway and the Balkans.

➤ The second G.38 was destroyed by RAF bombers at Athens on 17 May 1940.

➤ The first G.38 was modified to be the same standard as the second.

➤ Japan's copy of the G.38, the Ki-20, was destroyed by American bombing at the start of the war, along with a Ju 52.

PROFILE

Luxurious giant from Junkers

Even the landing gear of the G.38 was a unique piece of engineering. It carried two main wheels on tandem mountings, with a compressed air braking system powered by a diesel engine mounted in the wing.

N o feature of this behemoth of air commerce was more impressive than the large windows which made up the leading edge of the wings. Inside each wing, adjacent to the fuselage, was a compartment which housed three passengers in comfort. Remaining passengers in the Junkers G.38 occupied a fuselage, typically ribbed with corrugated metal, which gave them every

luxury – even a smoking lounge. When the 'Deutschland', the first of the two G.38s to be built, was shown to German airline officials, they knew it would be successful on long-distance routes. But the airline career of the magnificent G.38 was brief. The first example crashed in 1936 and was written off. After war was declared, the second, which had been named after President Hindenburg, was taken over by the Luftwaffe and

participated in the 1940 parachute assault on Norway. Six Mitsubishi Ki-20s, bomber versions of the Junkers G.38, were built in secret in Japan between 1931 and 1936. Designated Type 92 Super Heavy bomber, they had nine guns and a five ton bombload, and may have been intended for an attack on Singapore.

A small buffet and kitchen area was located at the top of the forward fuselage.

The nose area housed the navigator, radio operator and one or two engineers. Later, two or three passengers were allocated nose seats, which offered a superb view.

G.38

D-APIS was the second G.38, entering Lufthansa service in July 1932. It served in this role until 1939, when it was taken over by the Luftwaffe.

The 'President von Hindenburg' originally carried the serial D-2500, converting to the D-APIS registration shown here in 1934. In Luftwaffe colours it carried the serial GF-GG.

The wing contained a large number of separate fuel tanks. Baggage was stored in compartments behind the two leading-edge cabins.

The captain and first officer occupied the flight deck.

Hatches in the galley gave access to the wings and engines.

The tail unit of the second aircraft was extensively modified, having three fins and rudders.

The biggest change to the second aircraft was the installation of Junkers Jumo diesel engines, giving a significant increase in range.

The huge undercarriage spats were later removed, as they were found to make little difference to performance.

Passengers in the rear cabin sat in 13 rows of two. In the original configuration, the cabin just behind the cockpit could have beds fitted.

A second toilet was fitted at the rear of the cabin, behind the smoking compartment.

G.38

Type: long-range transport

Powerplant: four 559-kW (750-hp.) Junkers Jumo 204 12-cylinder horizontally opposed diesel engines

Maximum speed: 210 km/h (130 m.p.h.)

Range: about 2000 km (1,200 mi.)

Service ceiling: 5800 m (19,000 ft.)

Weights: empty 14,900 kg (32,780 lb.); loaded 25,488 kg (56,074 lb.)

Accommodation: seven/eight crew; 32 or 34 passengers (26 in main cabin, and three in each of two wingroot cabins); occasionally two passengers in the fuselage nose

Dimensions:
span	44.00 m	(144 ft. 4 in.)
length	23.20 m	(76 ft.)
height	7.00 m	(23 ft.)
wing area	294 m²	(3,163 sq. ft.)

ACTION DATA

MAXIMUM SPEED

The G.38 was not the fastest of aircraft even when new, being capable of only a stately 210 km/h (130 m.p.h.) at best. At that, it was marginally better than the contemporary British H.P.42, but both were to be left far behind within five years by new-generation airliners like the classic Douglas DC-3.

G.38	210 km/h (130 m.p.h.)
DC-3	370 km/h (229 m.p.h.)
H.P.42	204 km/h (126 m.p.h.)

RANGE

The diesel engines which powered the G.38 were fairly efficient for their time, and together with the massive fuel storage capacity of the huge wings gave the big Junkers airliner a very good range. The immense drag of the Handley Page's biplane wings meant that on long-distance flights it had to stop for fuel far more frequently.

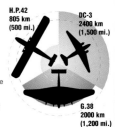

H.P.42 805 km (500 mi.)
DC-3 2400 km (1,500 mi.)
G.38 2000 km (1,200 mi.)

PAYLOAD

Although it was the world's biggest landplane, the G.38 could not carry as many passengers as the H.P.42 when the British airliner was used on European routes. When fitted with a luxury interior, however, the Handley Page only carried about 20 passengers. The DC-3 had a smaller load, but it could carry its passengers faster and over greater distances.

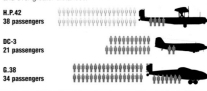

H.P.42 38 passengers
DC-3 21 passengers
G.38 34 passengers

The rise of Lufthansa

■ **AMALGAMATION:** Formed in 1926, Lufthansa combined the assets of early German private airlines like Deruluft, which pioneered the Berlin–Moscow route.

■ **ABOVE THE WEATHER:** The three-engined 10-seater Rohrbach Roland could fly at 5000 m (16,000 ft.), and in 1927 was used for trials across the Alps.

■ **ATLANTIC PIONEER:** Lufthansa led the way from Europe to South America. The South Atlantic sector was flown by long-range Dornier flying-boats.

■ **JUNKERS WORKHORSE:** From 1932, the reliable Junkers Ju 52 was used with great success on Lufthansa's European and Asian routes.

■ **CONDOR:** Entering service in 1938, the Focke-Wulf Fw 200 Condor was the most advanced airliner developed in Europe before World War II.

JUNKERS

Ju 52

● Three-engine transport ● 60 years of service ● Operated worldwide

▲ A Luftwaffe pilot refuels his Ju 52 during the Norway campaign in 1940. The dependable trimotor carried German forces throughout the war, proving reliable and sturdy in appalling conditions.

With it's corrugated metal skin and ugly exterior, the Ju 52 won no beauty contests, but this aircraft was loved: when a Ju 52 was restored by Lufthansa recently, the sight touched the hearts of airline pilots who had flown it long ago. Although designed as a pioneering airliner, the Ju 52 was also a military aircraft, serving the Luftwaffe as a bomber, transporter, trainer and minesweeper.

JUNKERS Ju 52

▲ French Junkers
The Ju 52 was built in France as the AAC.1 Toucan. In the early 1950s it was used as a bomber in Indochina.

▲ Makeshift bomber
Before World War II the Ju 52 was pressed into service as a bomber. A strange feature was the retractable 'dustbin' for the ventral gunner.

▼ Indestructible transport
Junkers had a reputation for making strong aircraft, and none came tougher than the Ju 52.

Post-war survivor ▲
Ju 52s are still flying today, a testament to their outstanding design. The Swiss air force flew three on transport tasks for years, although in their later life they were employed as film stars rather than serious military types.

Airliner success ▶
Before World War II the Ju 52 established itself as one of the world's top airliners, and sold around the world. Even British Airways operated the type.

FACTS AND FIGURES

➤ The Ju 52/3m (MS), or *Minensucher*, carried an enormous magnetised metal hoop to detonate mines at sea.

➤ Ju 52s were manufactured in France, Hungary and Spain after the war.

➤ The Junkers was fondly known to airmen as Tante Ju ('Auntie Ju').

➤ Although it looked similar, the Junkers Ju 52 was almost one-third larger and heavier than the Ford Trimotor.

➤ The Ju 52 was derived from a successful single-engine aircraft.

➤ Lufthansa has a Ju 52 that has been restored to its 1930s appearance.

PROFILE

'Auntie Ju': still proudly flying

The Junkers Ju 52 was one of the most important aircraft in European aviation history. In the world of aerial commerce the Ju 52 became the backbone of Lufthansa during the 1930s, operating from Norway to South America. For its time, the Ju 52 gave passengers a stylish experience and a level of comfort that had previously been impossible.

War changed the Ju 52. Intended as a servant, it became

a soldier. The Junkers trimotor was used as a bomber in early fighting, but became best-known as a military transport. Again and again, in the early days of fighting which were so successful for Germany, elite paratroopers leaped from the Ju 52 to make lightning assaults from Oslo to Crete. It also operated extensively in North Africa, and on the Eastern Front the Ju 52 was the Luftwaffe's most valuable transport asset.

The Ju 52 was equally at home on floats or skis as it was on wheels. This Swedish aircraft was used on airliner duties around the Scandinavian coastline.

Today, the few airworthy Ju 52s are priceless treasures of aviation. At air shows they give us the sounds, feel and smell of an earlier time when great aircraft performed pioneering feats.

To improve engine cooling without increasing drag, the Ju 52's outer engines were fitted with narrow-chord cowlings. In Ju-Air service they are painted royal blue.

Ju 52/3m

Type: airliner, medium bomber and troop transport

Powerplant: three 541-kW (750-hp.) BMW-built Pratt & Whitney Hornet (BMW 132A-3) radial piston engines

Cruising speed: 250 km/h (180 m.p.h.) at 900 m (3,000 ft.)

Range: 1290 km (800 mi.)

Service ceiling: 5900 m (19,600 ft.)

Weights: empty 5720 kg (12,620 lb.); loaded 9600 kg (21,200 lb.)

Payload: 17 passengers (plus three flight crew)

Armament: two 7.92-mm MG15 machine-guns plus up to 500 kg (1,100 lb.) of bombs

Dimensions:
span	29.20 m	(95 ft. 11 in.)
length	18.90 m	(62 ft.)
height	5.55 m	(18 ft. 2 in.)
wing area	110.5 m²	(1,200 sq. ft.)

Ju 52/3mg4e

HB-HOP was one of three Ju 52s delivered to the Swiss air force in 1939. When withdrawn from service in 1981 the aircraft was acquired by Ju-Air, which operates charter flights to help raise funds for the aviation museum at Dübendorf.

In civil trim, the Ju 52 can carry 17 passengers, though in military use 19 fully-equipped paratroopers or two tons of cargo was the standard payload.

In their military careers, Swiss Ju 52s performed a number of tasks. Paratroopers used the same door as the passengers to exit.

JU·AIR **HB-HOP** **A-703**

In its time, the Ju 52 has been powered by a variety of engines. The Ju-Air machine has the most common fit: three BMW 132 radial engines each delivering 392 kW (525 hp.).

The Ju 52 featured a conventional fixed undercarriage. Although the track was somewhat narrow, the large and fairly soft tyres meant that the aircraft could cope with rough fields.

Professor Hugo Junkers was one of the pioneers in the construction of all-metal aeroplanes. His aircraft were readily identified by their corrugated metal skin, which was used to stiffen the structure against torsion.

The Ju-Air trimotors retain the natural metal finish worn during their Swiss military service, along with Swiss national markings on the tail.

ACTION DATA

MAXIMUM SPEED

The Ju 52 first flew in single-engined form a month before the H.P.42. Although smaller, it was a generation ahead of the lumbering British biplane. But the Junkers was soon to be outclassed in turn by the classic DC-3.

Ju 52 290 km/h (180 m.p.h.)

H.P.42 160 km/h (126 m.p.h.)

DC-3 333 km/h (205 m.p.h.)

RANGE

The early 1930s saw the performance of commercial aircraft leap ahead tremendously. The Ju 52 had the range to fly between Europe's major cities non-stop, and proved immensely popular with airlines all over the Continent. The later DC-3 could eclipse all airliners of the time.

H.P.42 800 km (500 mi.)

DC-3 3400 km (2,100 mi.)

Ju 52 1290 km (800 mi.)

PAYLOAD

Air transport was expensive, and only a small number of people could afford to travel the skies. Nevertheless, demand soared in the 1930s, and aircraft carried two and three times as many passengers as their equivalents of only five years before.

H.P.42 4 crew and 38 passengers

Ju 52 3 crew and 17 passengers

DC-3 4 crew and 21-32 passengers

Versatile 'Tante Ju'

■ **AIRLINER:** The Ju 52 first rose to prominence as a 17-seat airliner. This aircraft flew the first Berlin-London service in 1932.

■ **SPANISH BOMBER:** During the Spanish Civil War the Ju 52 flew both transport and bomber missions. It could carry six 90-kg (200-lb.) bombs.

■ **NORWAY CAMPAIGN:** Nearly 600 Ju 52s took part in the invasion of Norway, where the type performed well on snow-covered airfields.

■ **MEDITERRANEAN TRANSPORT:** The Ju 52 is perhaps best-remembered for the attack on Crete, during which 174 of the type were lost.

■ **FLYING AMBULANCE:** One vital job assigned to the Ju 52 was the rapid evacuation of wounded soldiers away from the battle area.

KAMAN

K-MAX

● Twin-engined 'flying crane' ● Single-seater ● Intermeshed rotors

▲ 'WARNING: APPROACH FROM FRONT' reads the legend below the aircraft's rotor. While on the ground, the intermeshed rotors pass much lower than those on conventional helicopters.

Charles Kaman launched his helicopter company in 1945 when he was 26 years old. The K-MAX is the latest product from this now elderly trailblazer. The last living aviation pioneer of the 20th century, Kaman's principal contribution was the intermeshing rotor arrangement that dispenses with the need for a tail rotor. This arrangement is used on the K-MAX, known as the 'aerial truck', a machine capable of lifting almost 3 tonnes.

KAMAN K-MAX

Sales in Europe ▶
Helog of Switzerland became the first European K-MAX operator in May 1995, when this colourful example was delivered. Others have been delivered to France and Sweden.

◀ Versatility
Without a tail rotor, the K-MAX is able to manoeuvre into tight spots otherwise inaccessible to conventional helicopter designs.

▲ Slim profile
In this view of a Helog aircraft with an underslung load, the slim frontal profile of the design is seen. Angled cockpit windows give the pilot an excellent view.

▲ Connecticut factory
Pilots are trained using ex-military Kaman HH-43F Huskie helicopters. H-43s have a similar intermeshing rotor system.

◀ Prototype N3182T
In December 1991 the first K-MAX took to the air. This aircraft consisted of the basic airframe structure without a tailplane and fins.

FACTS AND FIGURES

➤ The K-MAX was originally known as MMIRA (pronounced 'Myra') for Multi-Mission Intermeshing Rotor Aircraft.

➤ The US Navy evaluated the type for use in resupplying warships at sea.

➤ In 1996 the price for one of these helicopters was $3.5 million.

➤ The K-MAX was the first helicopter structurally designed for repetitive external lift operations.

➤ Production rate at Kaman's Connecticut factory in 1996 was six per year.

➤ Kaman claims a 20-year life for K-MAX's airframe, at 1,000 hours per year.

Kaman's unique 'aerial truck'

When Charles Kaman revealed his company's K-MAX in March 1992, he signalled the introduction of a very special 'aerial truck' that has brought a revolution in the way helicopters handle cargo-hauling duties.

Kaman felt that the helicopter industry was focused on, and dominated by, 'people movers', the flying equivalent of the family car. Until the K-MAX, there were no helicopters

designed specifically for operators wanting logging, fire-fighting, construction, and cargo-hauling capabilities in a purpose-built machine.

The K-MAX, described by its Connecticut manufacturer as 'an efficient lifting workhorse', was designed as a twin-engined, single-seat heavy hauler to provide unsurpassed visibility for its pilot and to set new low levels of maintenance and operating expenses. Kaman's intermeshing

rotors mean that a conventional tail rotor is not required; this allows the aircraft to go into some otherwise dangerous or inaccessible locations.

First flown in late 1991, the K-MAX sold initially in the USA and Canada and has since found customers in Europe and Asia.

Above: This view of the inside of the Kaman factory shows the light alloy construction of a partly completed K-MAX.

Above: Kaman's helicopter designs have been intended to fill market niches. The company's vast experience with intermeshing rotors benefited the K-MAX design.

K-MAX

Type: single-seat external lift intermeshing-rotor helicopter

Powerplant: one 1118-kW (1,500-hp.) AlliedSignal T53-17A-1 turboshaft flat rated to 1007 kW (1,350 hp.)

Maximum speed: 185 km/h (115 m.p.h.) clean; 148 km/h (92 m.p.h.) with external load

Service ceiling: 7620 m (25,000 ft.) at 2722 kg (6,000 lb.) weight in standard atmospheric (ISA) conditions

Weights: operating empty 2132 kg (4,690 lb.); maximum take-off 2721 kg (6,000 lb.) without jettisonable load; 5216 kg (11,475 lb.) with external load

Dimensions:
rotor diameter (each)	14.73 m (48 ft. 4 in.)
length overall	15.85 m (52 ft.)
wheel track	3.56 m (11 ft. 8 in.)
wheelbase	4.11 m (13 ft. 6 in.)

AlliedSignal's (formerly Textron Lycoming's) T53-17A-1 turboshaft is a civil version of the military-specification T53 used in large numbers in aircraft like single-engined variants of the Bell UH-1 Iroquois.

Glass-fibre reinforced plastic (GFRP) and carbonfibre reinforced plastic (CFRP) are used in the construction of the rotor blades and tabs, for strength and lightness. Like the aircraft's engine (which is designed with a 10,000-hour life with a 1,500-hour time-between overhauls), these are designed to have a minimum maintenance requirement and therefore savings in operating costs.

A narrow fuselage and cockpit means that the K-MAX is a single-seat aircraft. The pilot sits in an impact-absorbing seat with a five-point harness. The K-MAX was also designed for unmanned radio-controlled operation in hazardous conditions.

K-MAX

First flown on 12 January 1994, N132KA was the first production K-MAX and the first of two leased to Oregon-based Erickson Air Crane on a $1,000 per hour, 1000 hours per year basis. Both aircraft were returned in 1995.

ERICKSON AIR-CRANE

N132KA

Constructed of light alloy, the K-MAX's airframe is both light and strong. The tail assembly weighs just 36.3 kg (80 lb.) and can be quickly removed by two people.

A wheeled tricycle undercarriage is a feature of the K-MAX and facilitates ground manoeuvring. Foot-operated brakes are standard. A 'bear paw' plate fits around each wheel for operations from soft ground.

ACTION DATA

MAXIMUM HOOK CAPACITY

The K-MAX is able to lift more than 2.7 tonnes on its single under-fuselage hook, thanks to its design which makes a higher proportion of the aircraft's engine power available for lifting. A minimal fuselage means that 'dead' weight is kept to a minimum.

K-MAX
2721 kg (6,000 lb.)

W-3A SOKOL
2100 kg (4,620 lb.)

TWIN TWO-TWELVE
2268 kg (5,000 lb.)

POWER

Compared with the PZL W-3A and Bell Twin Two-Twelve, the latter a civil version of the military UH-1N, the K-MAX has a modest power rating of just over 1100 kW. While the W-3A and Twin Two-Twelve have more powerful engines, they carry the extra weight of a heavy fuselage.

K-MAX
1118 kW
(1,500 hp.)

W-3A SOKOL
1342 kW
(1,800 hp.)

TWIN TWO-TWELVE
1193 kW
(1,600 hp.)

Logging by K-MAX

OPERATION ROANOKE: As part of Kaman's type testing, two pilots from logging helicopter operators took part in a five-day test in Virginia.

MARCH 1994 TEST: Selectively cut trees over an area of 162000 m² (531,360 sq. ft.) of inaccessible hillside were lifted out in 40 hours of operations in sub-zero temperatures.

SUCCESS: Only 90 minutes of unscheduled maintenance was required after the test. Kaman claims that, at a rate of 30 return logging sorties per hour, the K-MAX will have an airframe life of 20,000 flight hours.

KAMOV

KA-26 'HOODLUM'

● Co-axial rotor system ● Multi-role versatility ● Twin piston engines

F irst flown in 1965, the Ka-26 is widely used as an agricultural, ambulance, fire-fighting, survey and search and rescue helicopter. Its adaptability is largely a result of its unusual configuration. The piston engines are mounted on short wings and this allows a variety of payloads, including chemical spraying equipment, to be mounted aft of the enclosed cabin. It is a very compact design because the contra-rotating rotors mean that a tail rotor is not required.

▲ The layout of the Ka-26 'Hoodlum' has resulted in a practical helicopter which has sold well in at least 15 countries. It has a capacious fuselage and is easily adapted to different roles

KAMOV KA-26 'HOODLUM'

▼ Turboshaft conversion

After developing the Ka-126, Kamov passed responsibility for the production to IAR in Romania. Some customers have had their older Ka-26s modified to Ka-126 standard.

▲ Passenger pod

This Ka-26, fitted with spraying equipment, is shown alongside the alternative passenger/ambulance pod and the flat cargo platform. Conversion between roles is very rapid.

▼ Geological study

When configured for geophysical prospecting, the Ka-26 carries a large ring which produces electro-magnetic pulses.

German Kamovs ▶

Ka-26s were in use in both East and West Germany before reunification. This example was operated by the East German airline Interflug for short-range passenger or cargo flights.

▲ Compact people carrier

Even when configured for the carriage of seven passengers, the Ka-26 is a remarkably small helicopter. Few Russian aircraft have been exported so successfully.

FACTS AND FIGURES

➤ Kamov announced the Ka-26 in 1964 and the aircraft entered large-scale agricultural use in the USSR in 1970.

➤ Search-and-rescue variants have a winch for towing rescue boats.

➤ Full instrumentation is provided for flying by day or night, and in all weathers.

➤ In 1962 Ka-26s joined other helicopters transporting demolition teams whose task was to keep Soviet rivers free of ice.

➤ A towed 'bird' receives reflections from the emitter of the prospecting version.

➤ All payloads are carried at the Ka-26's centre of gravity.

PROFILE

Kamov's agricultural export

The compact dimensions of the Ka-26 allow it to fly from small ships as well as from land bases. It has even been fitted with floats and flown as a spotter aircraft from fishing boats. Military versions, designated 'Hoodlum' by NATO, were delivered to Bulgaria and Hungary for border patrol and liaison, and others may also be in service with Benin and Russia.

In 1981 Kamov started work on a turbine-powered version of the Ka-26. The original scheme involved replacing the piston engines by two small turbines, but this was abandoned in favour of a single 537-kW TV-O-100 above the cabin.

One Ka-26 was used as a testbed for Kamov's jet thrust anti-torque system, which was similar to the NOTAR (no tail rotor) concept developed by

McDonnell Douglas Helicopters. Kamov intended to use this system in the development of the Ka-118, which was planned as a five-seat business helicopter with just one main rotor.

By 1993 nearly 900 Ka-26s had been built and production was continuing at the Kumertaou Aviation Production Association. With its strength and versatility, the 'Hoodlum' is likely to remain in service for many years.

For crop-spraying the Ka-26 can carry 900 kg (200 lb.) of liquid, and when used as a duster capacity increases by 165 kg (360 lb.). Most Russian Ka-26s are used to treat orchards and vineyards.

Ka-26 'Hoodlum-A'

Type: general-purpose light helicopter

Powerplant: two 242.5-kW (325-hp.) Vedeneyev M-14V-26 nine-cylinder air-cooled radial piston engines

Maximum speed: 170 km/h (105 m.p.h.)

Range: 400 km (250 mi.) with seven passengers

Hover ceiling: 800 m (2,625 ft.) out of ground effect

Weights: empty in passenger configuration 2100 kg (4,620 lb.); maximum take-off 3250 kg (7,150 lb.)

Accommodation: pilot plus seven passengers, up to 1065 kg (2,340 lb.) of chemicals or cargo, or an 1100-kg (2,200-lb.) externally slung load

Dimensions:
rotor diameter	13 m (42 ft. 7 in.)
fuselage length	7.75 m (25 ft. 5. in.)
height	4.05 m (13 ft. 4 in.)
main rotor disc area	265.50 m² (871 sq. ft.)

The Ka-26 uses the co-axial contra-rotating rotor system which he had been used on the earlier Ka-25 'Hormone'.

Each of the air-cooled engines has a large fan fitted in the front of its nacelle. These ensure a sufficient supply of cooling air, even at slow airspeeds.

Kamov was one of the first helicopter manufacturers to use glass-reinforced plastic (GRP) rotor blades. They weigh only 25 kg (55 lb.) each and are de-iced by an alcohol-glycerine mixture.

Like the rotor blades, the tailbooms are manufactured largely from GRP. A tailplane is mounted at the rear of the booms and carries the twin endplate fins and rudders.

Operations are normally flown by a single pilot but a second pilot or passenger can be seated in the cabin, which is lightly pressurised. Agricultural models have an air filter system which prevents chemicals from entering the cockpit.

With its simple, but sturdy, four-leg undercarriage, the Ka-26 is able to carry a variety of payloads, attached directly to the fuselage between the rear legs. Only the rear wheels have brakes.

This detachable pod can accommodate six passengers. It has also been used to transport firemen and ice demolition teams.

Each of the fins is canted inwards at 15° and a large rudder is fitted to both. The external skin stiffening ribs on the tailplane are a characteristic feature of the Ka-26. They were previously used, but to a lesser extent, on the Ka-25.

KA-26 'HOODLUM-A'

Aeroflot has been a major user of the Ka-26. Very few military customers have emerged, but civilian operators appreciate the range of payload options available.

ACTION DATA

MAXIMUM PASSENGERS

Like the K-Max, the Ka-26 is used as a flying crane. The JetRanger III can also transport slung loads, but neither of the American helicopters can match the versatility of the Ka-26, which is able to carry seven passengers or fly as a crane.

Ka-26 'HOODLUM'	206B JETRANGER III	K-MAX
7 passengers	4 passengers	0 passengers

MAXIMUM SLUNG LOAD

As a specialised lifter, the K-Max can carry the greatest slung load. It has no facility for passengers, however, and is therefore aimed at a much narrower market than the versatile Ka-26. The Russian design has far greater load-carrying ability than the JetRanger.

Ka-26 'HOODLUM'	206B JETRANGER III	K-MAX
1100 kg (2,200 lb.)	680 kg (1,495 lb.)	2440 kg (5,370 lb.)

HOVER CEILING (OGE)

The Ka-26's flight performance is inferior to that of its Western rivals. With its piston engines, the Soviet helicopter does not have the altitude capabilities of the turbine-engined machines. This poor performance led to development of the Ka-126.

Ka-26 'HOODLUM' 800 m (2,625 ft.)	206B JETRANGER III 2680 m (8,790 ft.)	K-MAX 2440 m (8,000 ft.)

Piston-powered crop-sprayers

■ **BRANTLY-HYNES B-2:** Typical of the older generation of helicopters which have found use as sprayers, the B-2 is a lightweight two-seater.

■ **HILLER UH-12:** Used for agricultural spraying and power line inspection, the UH-12 is a common sight around the world.

■ **HUGHES 300:** In 1983 Schweizer acquired all rights for the 300. It has since developed a turbine-engined version, the 330.

■ **ROBINSON R22 BETA:** As one of the world's most popular basic training helicopters, the R22 is only occasionally used for spraying.

KAMOV

KA-27/29/32 'HELIX'

● Anti-submarine ● Assault/electronic warfare ● Civil transport

Using two rotors spinning in opposite directions the Soviet Kamov design bureau dispensed with the tail rotor normally used to give directional stability in helicopters. The design enabled shorter rotor blades to be used, which made it suitable for use aboard ships. The 'Helix' series of helicopters, which includes anti-submarine, assault transport and search-and-rescue versions, have served aboard a variety of Soviet warships.

▲ The Kamov Ka-27 'Helix' has progressively replaced the Ka-25 aboard ships of the Russian navy. The service now operates the Ka-27PL ASW helicopter, the Ka-27PS for SAR and utility duties, the Ka-29 naval assault variant and the Ka-31 for electronic warfare duties.

KAMOV KA-27/29/32 'HELIX'

▼ Export utility helicopter
The Ka-32T is a simplified utility helicopter for the transport of passengers/freight for civilian operators. The 32T lacks radar and other avionics of the 32S.

Inside the 'Helix' ▲
The naval Ka-27 family carry a crew of three: a pilot, tactical co-ordinator and ASW systems operator (PL model) or winch operator (PS model).

◀ Co-axial transport
Three major civil variants of the 'Helix' exist, and are used in Russia and abroad. Aeroflot operates approximately 150 Ka-32s including 32K cranes.

▼ Assault helicopter
The Ka-29 'Helix-B' is a heavily armed dedicated naval assault transport.

Search and rescue ▲
The Russian navy operates the Ka-27PS for air-sea rescue, utility and guard aboard aircraft-carriers.

FACTS AND FIGURES

➤ Russian navy Ka-27PLs carry Kh-35 anti-ship missiles, the heaviest to be carried by any naval helicopter.

➤ Ka-32s are operated by Swiss mountain rescue teams.

➤ Kamov is the world's only firm to have ever mass-produced co-axial helicopters.

➤ When flown by a single crewmember the Ka-32 can be left on autopilot while the pilot operates a winch from the cabin.

➤ The Ka-32K is a special version with a crane under the fuselage.

➤ In New Zealand Ka-32s are used for logging in remote hill areas.

PROFILE

Kamov's multi-mission wonder

First flown in 1974, the Ka-27PL 'Helix-A' anti-submarine helicopter carries dipping sonar and sonobuoys to locate submarines by their noise and has a radar under the nose.

The Ka-27PS 'Helix-D' is the search-and-rescue version. It is equipped with a rescue winch and floodlights instead of the sonar equipment.

An export version, designated Ka-28, is used by the Indian and Yugoslav navies. The Ka-29 'Helix-D' is an assault transport designed to ferry troops ashore during amphibious landings. It has a new fuselage and is armed with rocket launchers on the wings, plus a retractable nose gun. There is also a civil transport version, the Ka-32 'Helix-C'.

The Ka-32T is a basic load-carrier and is able to carry a payload of 4000 kg (8,800 lb.) internally or 5000 kg (11,000 lb.) externally. The Ka-32S is equipped with a radar and was designed to operate from ice-breakers and over barren terrain. It is used for such tasks as ice patrol, oilrig support and maritime's search and rescue in Russia's icy seas.

The flight deck of the Russian carrier Kuznetsov accommodates (left to right) a Yak-38 strike fighter, Ka-27PL ASW helicopter, Ka-29 assault transport and an electronic warfare Ka-31.

KA-29 'HELIX-B'

Shown here is one of the pre-production Ka-29s known as the Ka-27TB. The aircraft carries a non-standard flight instrumentation boom. Number 25 also lacks the fuselage mounted 30-mm gun.

The cabin door on the right of the Ka-29 does not slide as on other models, but hinges open rapidly for the 16 fully armed troops to disembark as quickly as possible. On the left side of the cabin there is now a sliding window where a light gun could be mounted.

The Ka-29 carries rocket pods, gun pods or guided missiles on its fuselage pylons.

The Ka-29 introduces a three-man side-by-side cockpit with a wider fuselage body as a result. The three flat front windscreen panels are bullet proof, and the cockpit is substantially armoured.

The two hydromechanically controlled Isotov turboshafts are uprated and heavily armoured to prevent any damage from enemy gunfire.

The nose contains retractable landing lamps, low-light television equipment, forward-looking infra-red and millimetric radar for use with anti-tank missiles.

Fixed armament on the Ka-29 consists of a four barrel 12.7-mm (.50-cal.) rotary machine-gun behind an articulated hatch inside the nose, and a starboard outrigger-mounted 30-mm single barrel cannon, with ammunition feed from the cabin.

Further protection is provided by flare and chaff cartridge launchers and the infra-red jammer above the fuselage. Production machines are likely to carry engine inlet filters and infra-red suppressors.

Ka-29 'Helix-B'

Type: maritime assault transport

Powerplant: two 1660-kW (2,225-hp.) Isotov TV3-117VK turboshaft engines

Maximum speed: 265 km/h (164 m.p.h.)

Maximum climb rate: 12.09 m/sec (40 f.p.s.) (inclined)

Combat radius: ferry range 800 km (500 mi.) with auxiliary fuel

Service ceiling: 4300 m (14,100 ft.)

Armament: one YakB-12 four-barrel 12.7-mm (.50-ca,.) machine-gun; one fuselage-mounted 30-mm 2A42 cannon; four pylons for gun pods, ASMs, rockets, fuel tanks or bombs

Dimensions:
rotor diameter	15.9 m (52 ft. 2 in.)
length	11.3 m (37 ft. 1 in.)
height	5.4 m (17 ft. 9 in.)
rotor disc area	198.60 m² (2,137 sq. ft.)

COMBAT DATA

MAXIMUM PASSENGERS

With its longer fuselage and improved engines, the Ka-27 can carry more passengers than the older Ka-25. The Lynx is a smaller machine and is also used for tactical support and naval missions.

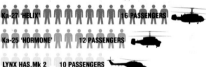

Ka-27 'HELIX' — 16 PASSENGERS
Ka-25 'HORMONE' — 12 PASSENGERS
LYNX HAS.Mk 2 — 10 PASSENGERS

MAXIMUM SPEED

The twin-rotor configuration and powerful engines make the Kamovs fast machines with a high rate of climb. A modernised Lynx still holds the helicopter speed record.

Ka-27 'HELIX' — 265 km/h (164 m.p.h.)
Ka-25 'HORMONE' — 193 km/h (120 m.p.h.)
LYNX HAS.Mk 2 — 230 km/h (143 m.p.h.)

RANGE

With additional fuel, the Ka-27 can fly further than a Ka-25 and almost as far as a Lynx. Twin-rotor helicopters are not as fuel-efficient as conventional types with a tail rotor.

Ka-27 'HELIX' — 800 km (500 mi.)
Ka-25 'HORMONE' — 650 km (400 mi.)
LYNX HAS.Mk 2 — 1000 km (620 mi.)

Versatile 'Helix'

DIPPING SONAR: The 'Helix' can search for submarines with a dipping sonar, as well as passive sonobuoys. The 'Helix' normally works in pairs in the anti-submarine role, but can operate autonomously if required.

LOGGING MISSION: A Ka-32 is used by a New Zealand timber company for hauling tree trunks from remote mountain sides. Operators are impressed with the aircraft's reliability.

AIR-SEA RESCUE: Ka-27 'Helixes' are used to rescue survivors of shipwrecks. The helicopter can drop a dinghy pack to survivors in the water as well as carry out a conventional rescue with a winch.

LEARJET INC.

LEARJET

● The first great 'biz-jet' ● Bill Lear's classic design

A sports coupé of the skies, the Learjet handles like a fighter (indeed, its sleek design is based on that of a Swiss fighter) and gives speed and luxury to business travellers. One of the most streamlined aircraft ever, the Learjet flies today in dozens of countries, not solely as an executive jet but also on military and scientific assignments. The Learjet is economical as well as speedy in getting small numbers of people quickly from one location to another.

▲ *Millionaire William P. Lear developed the Learjet from a single-seat fighter design for the Swiss air force. Since then the original Learjet has spawned an entire family of advanced business jets.*

▲ The Learjet family
Over the years the Learjet family has grown in number, and the aircraft in size. Note the increasing difference in length between the Learjet 24 (top), Lear 25 and Lear 35 in this picture.

▼ Special missions
The Japanese Air Self-Defence Force operates four converted Learjet 36As, called U-36As. They are packed with sophisticated radars and electronic jamming equipment.

▲ Eye in the sky
Its high cruising altitude and long endurance make the Learjet an ideal photo-survey aircraft. This Brazilian Learjet carries a special camera pack for the task.

◀ Mile-high style
While Learjets have always been a little on the small side, passengers can be carried in luxury and privacy exceeding that of any standard airliner.

Learjets around the world ▶
The early versions of the Learjet were fast, but short-legged. As Learjets grew in size, new engines and advanced wing designs gave the latest generation truly intercontinental range.

FACTS AND FIGURES

➤ The company making the Learjet has changed names seven times in 30 years.

➤ Eighty Learjets serve in the US Air Force as the C-21A.

➤ Golf celebrity Arnold Palmer flew a Learjet around the world on a goodwill journey in 1976.

➤ Sources say this executive jet has appeared in more movie and television films than any other aircraft.

➤ The original Learjet 23 of 1963 carried five passengers in its small interior; today's Learjet 60 can carry up to nine in a spacious 'stand-up' cabin.

PROFILE

The pocket rocket

The Learjet is one of the few aircraft named after a man, William Lear, who recruited designers to try features of a Swiss fighter on a revolutionary business jet. The goal was speed and luxury in business travel, and Lear achieved it. The aircraft provides the very best for hundreds of corporate jet owners.

A super ship to fly, the Learjet boasts pilot comfort, simple controls and easy handling. This familiar aircraft

Throughout its life the Learjet has been known the world over simply as the 'Lear'.

has a razor-like wing and twin engines out back; some models use winglets which poke up to improve the flow of air, affording better fuel consumption.

Although it is small enough to be very personal and can fly to and from the shortest of runways, the Learjet has global reach, able to cross oceans and

cruise at high altitude.

A few nations adapted this corporate jet for military work, giving the Lear patrol duties. But to most users Learjet means civilian journeys with speed, luxury and convenience.

All modern Learjets, such as the Learjet 31 and Learjet 60, are fitted with distinctive upturned winglets. These improve the aerodynamics and increase range.

Learjet 35/36

Type: long-range executive transport

Powerplant: two Garrett TFE-731-2-2B turbofan engines offering 15.57 kN (3,500 lb.) thrust each

Maximum speed: 850 km/h (528 m.p.h.) at 12,495 m (41,000 ft.)

Range: 5015 km (3,116 mi.) with four passengers and fuel

Service ceiling: 13,715 m (45,000 ft.) normal, but maximum operating altitude in excess of 15,000 m (49,200 ft.)

Weights: empty 4152 kg (9,154 lb.); loaded 8500 kg (18,739 lb.)

Payload: two pilots, eight passengers and 480 kg (1,058 lb.) of luggage

Dimensions:
span 12.04 m (39 ft. 6 in.)
length 14.83 m (48 ft. 8 in.)
height 3.73 m (12 ft. 3 in.)
wing area 23.53 m² (253 sq. ft.)

LEARJET 55 'LONGHORN'

The Model 55 Learjet was the first version to feature winglets. It was dubbed the Longhorn, as the winglets resembled the horns of longhorn cattle.

Despite all the changes that have occurred to the shape of the Learjet over the years, its long, slender nose has remained a constant trademark.

The Learjet 55 was powered by Garrett TFE-731 turbofans. This very versatile engine could also be found on many other 'biz-jets'.

Production of the Learjet 55 ended in 1992 after 147 had been delivered. It has been succeeded by the even larger Learjet 60.

Winglets – developed by a NASA engineer named Richard Whitcomb – are now found on many aircraft, but when they first appeared on the Learjet 'Longhorn' they were revolutionary.

The Learjet was the aircraft which popularised the term 'biz-jet' (short for business jet), and it opened up the global market for such aircraft.

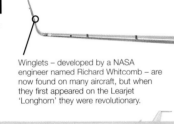

N90E

The Learjet 55 'Longhorn' was introduced in 1979. It was not the greatest-selling Learjet version, but paved the way for even more advanced designs.

'V'-shaped ventral fins were first seen on the Learjet 55C. They helped make the aircraft more stable in flight and have since been added to all subsequent Learjet designs.

ACTION DATA

PASSENGER LOAD

The original Learjet was very much the sports car of the executive jet world. Although small and compact, it was an immediate success. However, succeeding jets cater more to the corporate market, and can generally carry more passengers.

LEARJET 35 UP TO 8

CITATION II UP TO 10

MODEL 125-800 UP TO 14

MAXIMUM SPEED

Speed and luxury were Bill Lear's aims, and he achieved them with the Learjet, one of the fastest non-military aircraft flying today.

LEARJET 35	850 km/h (528 m.p.h.)
CITATION II	713 km/h (443 m.p.h.)
MODEL 125-800	840 km/h (522 m.p.h.)

SERVICE CEILING

The Learjet has superb altitude performance, being able to cruise higher than any other civil aircraft except Concorde. Flying at such heights it avoids all weather problems and can keep clear of congested air routes. However, care needs to be taken: the gap between maximum and minimum flying speeds at 15,000 m (49,200 ft.) can be as low as 90 km/h (56 m.p.h.), and it is possible to fall into a high-speed stall from which recovery can be difficult.

LEARJET 35 13,715 m (45,000 ft.)

CITATION II 7600 m (24,930 ft.)

MODEL 125-800 10,000 m (32,800 ft.)

A 30-year success story

LEARJET 23: When Bill Lear unveiled the first Learjet in 1963, the small yet speedy aircraft was soon dubbed the 'pocket rocket'. Note the large cabin windows.

LEARJET 35/36: The best-selling Learjets have been the Model 35 and 36. The latter is heavier, but both are identical from the outside. This is a military target-towing version.

LEARJET 55: The Lear 55 was a radical departure in Learjet design. Gone were the familiar wingtip fuel tanks; in their place came special drag-reducing winglets.

LEARJET 60: It resembles the Lear 55, but today's long-range Learjet 60 is a larger and far more advanced business jet. First flying in 1990, it is the ultimate Learjet.

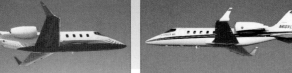

LET

L-410 TURBOLET/610

● Czech twin-turboprop ● Huge Aeroflot orders ● Rough-field capability

Flown initially in April 1969, the L-410 was one of the first aircraft designed solely by LET. The company had been established in 1950 on the site of the old Avia factory at Kunovice, and had graduated to transport aircraft after building military trainers, air taxis, gliders and agricultural aircraft. LET has built more than 1,000 L-410s, many of them for the Soviet Union, and, in December 1988, it flew the first prototype of the 40-seat L-610.

▲ LET found
that orders for the L-410 were slowing down by the early 1990s, after the loss of Aeroflot as its most important customer. The aircraft still serves in some numbers, however.

LET L-410 TURBOLET/610

▼ **Introducing the UVP**
In 1977, LET flew the first prototype of the L-410UVP. The aircraft had a slightly extended cabin and longer wingspan.

▲ **Multi-blade technology**
Five-bladed propellers by the famous Czech manufacturer, Avia, were introduced on the L-410UVP-E from 1984.

▼ **Soviet backbone**
L-410UVP-Es formed the backbone of Aeroflot's feederliner fleet and are still in service.

▲ **First of the 610s**
Similar in configuration to the L-410, the L-610 is, in fact, a completely new design. It has seats for 40 passengers.

◀ **Hungarian mystery**
This Hungarian L-410UVP carries a civilian registration and an unusual equipment fit. A bubble observation window is located at the rear of the flight deck, with unidentified blister fairings on the rear fuselage. The aircraft is most likely equipped for some form of geophysical survey or exploration.

FACTS AND FIGURES

➤ In 1991, LET began deliveries to satisfy an Aeroflot requirement for 600 L-610s, but financial problems intervened.

➤ Neither cabin pressurisation nor air conditioning is fitted to the L-410.

➤ At the end of 1992, LET had 50 unsold L-410s after Aeroflot cancelled orders.

➤ As an ambulance, the L-410 carries six stretchers, five seated patients and a medical attendant.

➤ An aerial photography L-410 for Hungary had a non-retractable nosewheel.

➤ The L-610 has been designed to replace the An-24 and Yak-40.

PROFILE

Czech-built feederliner

LET built only 31 of the initial L-410A model, with Pratt & Whitney PT6A engines, before switching to the L-410M. This used locally built Walter M-601 turboprops. Most of the 110 produced were delivered to Aeroflot, and the Czech army also used a small number.

The M-601B engine with water injection was used for the L-410UVP, which has longer wings, revised control surfaces and improved performance in hot-and-high conditions. More than 500 were built and, from 1986, the UVP-E introduced a bigger, 19-seat cabin and five-bladed propellers.

Aeroflot was the main customer for the L-410 and, in 1977, the Soviet airline asked for a bigger aircraft with more seats. The specified Motorlet M-602 engine would not be ready in time, so Aeroflot proposed a four-engined model with M-601s, only to change its mind again later.

The prototype L-610, with two M-602s, eventually flew in December 1988. LET then decided to build a version for the Western market with General Electric CT7 engines. It flew for the first time in December 1991, but the programme has subsequently been delayed.

Above: Although by far the largest operator of the L-410, Aeroflot was not alone in its use of the Czech workhorse.

Below: In the event of an engine failure, a bank-control surface pops up automatically ahead of the aileron on the side with the running engine, to reduce lift on that wing.

L-410UVP-E

Type: twin-turboprop regional airliner

Powerplant: two 559-kW (750-hp.) Motorlet Walter M-601E turboprops

Maximum cruising speed: 380 km/h (236 m.p.h.) at 4200 m (14,000 ft.)

Range: 1380 km (855 mi.) with maximum fuel at 4200 m (14,000 ft.)

Service ceiling: 6320 m (20,700 ft.)

Weights: empty 3985 kg (8,767 lb.); maximum take-off 6400 kg (14,080 lb.)

Accommodation: 19 passengers

Dimensions: span 19.98 m (65 ft. 6 in.); length 14.42 m (47 ft. 4 in.); height 5.83 m (62 ft. 9 in.); wing area 35.18 m² (379 sq. ft.)

L-410UVP-E TURBOLET

A maximum of 19 passengers are carried by the L-410UVP-E. The cabin is heated by engine bleed air and includes a wardrobe and toilet. Heating, and stowage for bulky winter clothing are especially important in Russia.

Although the earlier L-410 models had Pratt & Whitney engines, later variants such as the L-410UVP-E have indigenously-designed Motorlet Walter M-601E turboprops and Avia propellers.

Aeroflot employs its L-410UVP-E aircraft alongside An-28s for internal services. The harsh and variable Russian climate led the airline to specify an operational range of -50°C (-58°F) to +50°C (122°F).

An extra 200 litres (53 gal.) of fuel are carried in each wingtip tank. These tanks are optional fittings, but L-410s are never seen without them. Navigation lights are carried on the tanks and the starboard tank sometimes holds a powerful landing light.

The structure of the L-410 is almost entirely of metal. Unusually for a modern type, although the elevators and rudders have a metal structure, they are fabric-covered.

Alternative roles for the L-410UVP-E include aerial photography, ambulance duties, firefighting and parachute dropping. In the latter role, up to 18 parachutists and their jump master are carried. In the passenger role, the rear fuselage is occupied by a baggage compartment.

CCCP-67551
АЭРОФЛОТ

ACTION DATA

ECONOMIC CRUISING SPEED
Among these types, the L-410UVP-E offers the highest cruising speed; a useful feature in a feederliner which earns its keep by transporting passengers from smaller airports to important hubs.

L-410UVP-E 365 km/h (266 m.p.h.)
Do 228-212 333 km/h (206 m.p.h.)
An-28 'CASH' 335 km/h (208 m.p.h.)

TAKE-OFF RUN TO 10.7 M (35 FT.)
Although LET designed the L-410 for rough-field operations, it has only moderate STOL (Short Take-Off and Landing) performance, especially when compared to the PZL Mielec/Antonov An-28.

L-410UVP-E 685 m (2,250 ft.)
Do 228-212 793 m (2,600 ft.)
An-28 'CASH' 410 m (1,350 ft.)

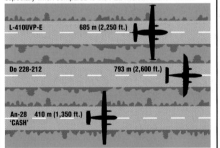

RANGE
Dornier's Do 228-212 offers excellent range and good operating economics. It is commonly used across Western Europe and in America, but has yet to break into the Eastern European market, which is still dominated by the L-410. The An-28 is now built only in Poland.

L-410UVP-E 1380 km (855 mi.)
Do 228-212 2148 km (1,330 mi.)
An-28 'CASH' 1365 km (850 mi.)

Post-war civil designs from LET

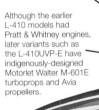

L-200A MORAVA: This twin-engined four-/five-seat light business and taxi monoplane first flew on 8 April 1957. More than 1000 were built in three versions; the L-200D entered production in 1962. Power came from two 156.5-kW (210-hp.) M-337 in-line piston engines.

Z-37 CMELAK: Flown in prototype form on 29 June 1963, this agricultural aircraft has also found applications as a mail and cargo transport during the winter months. An M-462RF radial of 234.7 kW (315 hp.) powered the aircraft, production of which ended in 1975. Around 600 were built.

Z-37T AGRO TURBO: A turboprop-powered Z-37, the Agro Turbo is built by Zlin as the Z-137T. Powered by a Motorlet Walter M-601Z rated at 365 kW (490 hp.), the aircraft has found sales in at least six countries. New features include a 1000-litre/900-kg (264-gal./1,980-lb.) hopper.

303

LOCKHEED

18 LODESTAR

● Based on the Electra ● Extensive military use ● Corporate aircraft

Lockheed's Model 14 Super Electra had a disappointing debut as Lockheed's then largest commercial design. Its high running costs resulted in slow sales. One early customer, Northwest Airlines, even withdrew its Model 14s from use after barely two years' service. Production was suspended and a redesign carried out, during which the new Model 18's fuselage was lengthened to accommodate two more rows of seats.

▲ Compared
to the Lockheed 14 Electra on which it was based, the Lodestar was slightly longer, allowing a few more seats and hence a lower operating cost.

LOCKHEED 18 LODESTAR

▼ Record-breaker
In the years immediately before World War II, mail delivery by air became well established in the United States. In 1940 a Lodestar flew the mail route between California, and Florida in just over nine hours.

▲ Flying the flag in war
BOAC acquired 38 Lodestars. During World War II, these aircraft were operated on services to Scandinavia, Malta, Africa and the Middle East.

Thoroughbred design ▶
Cruising at altitude, SE-BZE, in the livery of the Swedish Linjeflyg, displays the elegant lines of the Model 18 Lodestar. After the end of World War II, only a small number of Lodestars remained in regular use as airliners.

◀ Howard 350s and LearStars
Howard and Lear were among the companies which modified Lodestars into comfortable executive aircraft.

Post war service ▶
After wartime service as glider tugs and troop transports, surplus military Lodestars were snapped up by individuals and small enterprises and converted back into airliners. Some served on in this role into the 1960s and 1970s.

FACTS AND FIGURES

➤ During World War II, the British Overseas Airways Corporation (BOAC) operated 38 Lodestars on paramilitary duties.

➤ The first Lodestar was an ex-Northwest Airlines Model 14 rebuilt by Lockheed.

➤ The Lockheed Ventura wartime bomber was derived from the Lodestar.

➤ Kawasaki built 121 Ki-56s derived from a stretched version of the Model 14 and very similar to the Lodestar.

➤ In New Zealand, Lodestar airliners were converted into crop-dusters.

➤ Air forces to operate Model 18s included the SAAF, RCAF, RAF, RAAF and RNZAF.

Improving on the Electra

To disassociate the new Model 18 from the old Model 14, the new machine was named the Lodestar. Though the prototype had the wing, tail assembly and engines of the Model 14, production aircraft introduced a raised tailplane, a modified wing trailing edge and a choice of engines – Pratt & Whitney Hornets, Twin Wasps or Wright Cyclones. Lodestars entered service in March 1940 with Mid-Continent Airlines, the type seating either 15 or 18

passengers, depending upon whether or not a cabin attendant and galley were included.

The Model 18-07 offered operating costs close to those of the rival Douglas DC-3. Some aircraft with bench-type seating installed were able to carry as many as 26 people. However, despite these features, Lodestars sold in only small numbers in the US. Foreign orders, on the other hand, were more readily forthcoming, South African Airways becoming the largest civil operator with 29.

The US Navy ordered the first military Lodestars in 1940, as R5Os, but it was the USAAF that amassed the largest fleet during World War II, including impressed and new aircraft.

Post-war, Model 18s were outdated as passenger carriers and of limited use as freighters, though a significant number were converted for use as corporate transports.

Below: Handling problems, resulted in the trailing edge of the wing being extended, blunting the clean profile of the original Model 14 Electra.

Above: Even in the Southwest Pacific, Lodestars were to be seen in post-war civilian use. Trans-Australia Airlines operated the type on regional services shuttling passengers and mail between major cities.

Model 18-07 Lodestar

Type: medium-range airliner and civil transport

Powerplant: two Pratt & Whitney S1E2-G nine-cylinder radial engines

Maximum speed: 351 km/h (218 m.p.h.)

Initial climb rate: 296 m/min (970 f.p.m.)

Range: normal 2895 km (1,795 mi.); maximum 5150 km (3,193 mi.)

Service ceiling: 6220 m (20,400 ft.)

Weights: empty 5103 kg (11,227 lb.); normal loaded 7938 kg (17,464 lb.)

Accommodation: two pilots and up to 18 passengers

Dimensions:
span	19.96 m	(65 ft. 6 in.)
length	15.19 m	(49 ft. 10 in.)
height	3.6 m	(11 ft. 2 in.)
wing area	51.19 m²	(511 sq. ft.)

The Lodestar flight deck was virtually identical to that of the Electra. The two pilots sat side-by-side, though compared to the DC-3, the cockpit was narrow and cramped. Once the 'oscillating control' problem had been solved the aircraft proved well mannered in the air, with few vices.

Compared to the Model 14 Electra, from which it was derived, the Lodestar had a lengthened fuselage in order to accommodate extra seating and hence make the aircraft more appealing to airlines by increasing the revenue per mile. Maximum capacity was 18 passengers.

Early flight trials revealed elevator nibbling, so an attempt to cure the problem was made by splitting the elevators and adding servo trim tabs. The problem was eventually eliminated by raising the tail section a few centimetres, thus taking it out of the wing turbulence.

G-AGOD

Different powerplants were offered for the Lodestar, the most numerous in use being the Pratt & Whitney Twin Wasp series. Wright Cyclones were also optional, though they lacked the refinement of the Pratt & Whitney engines.

Extending the trailing edge of the wing also helped eliminate the control problem. Large slotted Fowler flaps mounted inboard of the engines gave the Lodestar exceptional short take-off and landing ability.

LODESTAR I

BOAC operated no fewer than 38 Lodestars for nearly seven years after their first delivery in March 1941. Despite their quasi-civilian role, a camouflage scheme was adopted for their dangerous wartime flights.

ACTION DATA

MAXIMUM SPEED

Pratt & Whitney engined Lodestars were slower than rival airliners in the late 1930s and the type never proved as popular in service as the Douglas DC-3. Boeing's Stratoliner was fastest of all, due in no small part to it being a four-engined design.

18-07 LODESTAR	351 km/h (218 m.p.h.)
DC-3A	370 km/h (229 m.p.h.)
SA-307B STRATOLINER	396 km/h (246 m.p.h.)

MAXIMUM TAKE-OFF WEIGHT

Having roughly the same seating capacity as the DC-3, the Lodestar was considerably lighter on take-off, though it was not able to carry as much cargo as the Douglas design.

18-07 LODESTAR	DC-3A	SA-307B STRATOLINER
8709 kg (17,464 lb.)	11,430 kg (25,146 lb.)	19,050 kg (41,910 lb.)

RANGE

In its day, the Model 18 Lodestar had an excellent range and this resulted in the type being employed on routes between the United States and the West Indies. It is ironic that the DC-3 had the shortest range of all, yet proved to be the most popular of the three in service.

18-07 LODESTAR 5150 km (3,193 mi.)

SA-307B STRATOLINER 3846 km (2,385 mi.)

DC-3A 2400 km (1,488 mi.)

Model 18s in the US armed services

■ **LOCKHEED LODESTAR:** Some 36 commercial Lodestars were acquired by the USAAF and pressed into service with the designation C-56. Many served until 1945.

■ **LOCKHEED R5O-1:** First order for military Model 18s came from the US Navy. The aircraft of the initial batch were used as staff transports and all were powered by Wright R-1820 engines.

■ **LOCKHEED R5O-4:** Four R5O-4 variants, destined for the USN, were diverted to the Coast Guard and entered service in 1942. They were used on administrative flights until 1946.

LOCKHEED

1, 2 & 5 VEGA

● High-speed monoplane ● Wooden monocoque ● Diverse roles

Although his first enterprise, the Loughead Aircraft Manufacturing Company, had failed, Allan Loughead did not give up. Convinced that wooden monocoque construction, as used in the Loughead S-1, had potential, he re-hired Jack Northrop and raised enough capital to found the Lockheed Aircraft Company in 1926. Its first aircraft, the Vega, was an immediate success as an airliner and set numerous records.

▲ *Corporate and private transport was one role tackled by the Lockheed Vega. Others were air ambulance, military transport and floatplane transport.*

LOCKHEED 1, 2 & 5 VEGA

LOCKHEED 1, 2 & 5 VEGA

▼ **Still flying in 1955**
Built in 1929 as a Vega 1, this float-equipped aircraft was modified to Vega 2D standard with a Wasp Junior engine.

▲ **Vega on skis**
Equipped for the colder climates of Norway, this Vega has skis fitted in place of wheels. Other ski-equipped Vegas were operated in Canada.

▼ **First trans-Arctic flight**
X3903 was only the fourth Vega 1 off the production line. On 15 April 1928 it took off on a historic flight from Alaska to Spitzbergen – the first ever crosing of the Arctic. In November it made an equally impressive trans-Antarctic flight.

▲ **Army Air Corps Vega**
The US armed forces' first Lockheed type was this Y1C-12 (DL-1), acquired for evaluation as a staff transport.

American airliner ▶
Transcontinental and Western Air Inc. (part of what later became TWA) operated this Vega 5C as a faster alternative to the larger, but slower, Ford Trimotor.

FACTS AND FIGURES

➤ Vegas were used to support American exploratory expeditions to both the Arctic and Antarctic regions.

➤ A Vega 5 made the first non-stop Los Angeles–New York flight in August 1928.

➤ In 1980, six Vegas remained extant; at least one was still airworthy.

➤ Jack Northrop chose the 'Vega' name, starting the tradition of naming Lockheed aircraft after stars and planets.

➤ The USAAC Y1C-12 (DL-1) flew a total of 999 hours before retirement in 1935.

➤ The last Lockheed-built Vega was used by the USAAC as a UC-101 until 1942.

PROFILE

Lockheed's first design

Below: This early production Vega has an uncowled Pratt & Whitney Wasp radial. Cowlings were often fitted later and increased top speed.

W ith its wooden fuselage, wooden internally-braced cantilever wing (as pioneered by Fokker) and a 149-kW (200-hp.) Wright Whirlwind nine-cylinder radial engine, the first Vega 1 had an unhappy fate.

Bought by newspaper owner George Hearst, it was entered in the 1927 Oakland to Hawaii air race. First flown on 4 July, the aircraft left Oakland, with seven other machines, on 16 August. It was never seen again. Despite the strange disappearance,

Lockheed went on to build 128 Vegas. A number were employed by US and Latin American airlines or as private transports. Others posted a number of speed, distance and altitude records between the late 1920s and mid-1930s.

The main production variant was the Vega 5 of 1928, which carried five or six passengers. In all, 35 were built, a few with floats. A Pratt & Whitney Wasp engine rated at between 306 and 336 kW replaced the Whirlwind. In July 1929, the

Above: In US airline service the Vega was used for passenger-carrying mail services. Although smaller than other airliners, it was considerably faster.

Detroit Aircraft Corporation bought Lockheed and developed a modernised Vega 5 as the DL-1. Two Vegas entered service with the USAAC and at least one flew with Republican forces in the Spanish Civil War as a transport and light bomber. A number are preserved.

VEGA 5

NC288W was flown by Varney Air Transport Inc. (later Continental Airlines) which was founded in the Rocky Mountains area in the early 1930s, with four Vegas, each equipped to carry nine passengers.

Exceptionally strong wing construction was a feature of the Vega. The wings were internally braced, removing the need for struts, and of cantilever design.

Lockheed's wooden monocoque construction methods were pioneered by company designer Jack Northrop (later a manufacturer in his own right).

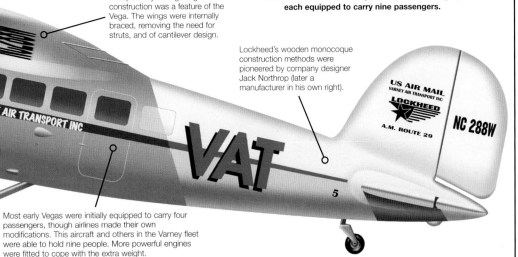

Vegas were fitted with a wide variety of engines. As the aircraft grew in size and capacity, more horsepower was required. Most engines were conventional radial designs, although at least one airframe was fitted with a diesel motor.

Most early Vegas were initially equipped to carry four passengers, though airlines made their own modifications. This aircraft and others in the Varney fleet were able to hold nine people. More powerful engines were fitted to cope with the extra weight.

US commercial types of the 1930s

■ **BOEING 247:** A revolutionary design at a time when American airliners were mainly heavy biplanes, the 247 was a mostly metal monoplane.

■ **CURTISS T-32 CONDOR:** This 15-seater from the early 1930s was built with seating and sleeping accommodation, and sold well.

■ **FORD TRI-MOTOR:** Built by Ford in 1926, after its acquisition of the Stout Metal Airplane Company. Large numbers were built until 1933.

■ **VULTEE V-1A:** An eight-seat airliner, the V-1A was powered by a Wright R-1820 Cyclone and served with American Airlines.

LOCKHEED

L-100 HERCULES

● Civil C-130 derivative ● Long service ● Still in production

Commercial Hercules have been in service almost as long as the C-130. Though initially dogged by poor sales through having to compete with cheaper freight conversions of older passenger types, the L-100 series remains in production after 30 years. By 1995, 115 had been delivered, mostly to civil operators around the world, though at least 21 have gone to air forces. Successive 'stretches' have culminated in the popular L-100-30.

▲ *Although built in limited numbers compared to the military Hercules, the L-100 has seen service in as many countries, especially on freight charters and humanitarian relief work.*

LOCKHEED L-100 HERCULES

◄ **Rough field expert**
Having cut its teeth on demanding military tasks, the Hercules design allowed civil users the same flexibility to operate from unprepared sites.

▼ **Early production for Delta**
Delta Air Lines was an early L-100 customer in 1966. Like a number of early production aircraft, N9268R was later converted to L-100-20 standard and in 1974 became an L-100-30.

▲ **Asian airlifter**
Merpati Nusantara of Indonesia flies this L-100-30 with cabin windows for passenger service.

▼ **L-100-30 in Africa**
Air Gabon flew this Dash-30, delivered in 1985, which has been leased to TAAG Angola Airlines.

◄ **Many owners**
Most early model L-100s soon changed ownership. This aircraft was with Southern Air Transport when it crashed in 1970.

FACTS AND FIGURES

➤ The latest proposed version is the L-100J – a civil variant of the updated and re-engined C-130J Hercules II.

➤ A twin-engined civil Hercules, the L-400, was suggested in the 1980s.

➤ First operator was Alaskan Airlines in March 1965, with a leased L-100.

➤ US operator Southern Air Transport has a number of L-100s configured for oil slick dispersal operations.

➤ A proposed L-100-50 with a further 6.1-m fuselage 'stretch' was abandoned.

➤ Three L-100-30s transported 50,000 Javan families during Indonesian transmigration.

PROFILE

'Herky Bird' for commercial operators

Having successfully introduced the C-130A into USAF service, Lockheed perceived a need for an aircraft for civil operators with large or heavy cargoes to carry over medium and long distances. On 21 April 1964 a prototype Model 382 (essentially a C-130E with its military equipment and underwing tanks removed) took to the air.

This and the Model 382B (the first version known as the L-100) sold in only limited numbers. Lockheed then 'stretched' the fuselage, since commercial operators needed more space as their cargoes tended to lack the density of typical military loads. The resulting L-100-20 was some 2.54 m (8 ft. 4 in.) longer and had uprated engines. It flew in 1968.

Freight airlines that had been unprepared for an aircraft with the Hercules' lifting capacity were now being offered a 150.26 m³ (5,306 cu. ft.) hold volume. Sales were encouragingly better; some Model 382B operators even converted their aircraft to Dash-20 standard.

The top-selling commercial Hercules has been the L-100-30 (Model 382G). It introduced another 'stretch', this time by 2.03 m (6 ft. 8 in.), providing 171.5 m³ (6,056 cu. ft.) of hold space. Between its first flight on 14 August 1970 and 1995, 78 were built; production continues.

Southern Air Transport is the largest L-100 operator, with one Dash-20 and 14 Dash-30s. SAT flew para-military duties with L-100s during the Vietnam War and today operates freight charters worldwide.

L-100-30 Hercules

Type: medium- to long-range transport

Powerplant: four 3362-kW (4,510-hp.) Allison 501-D22A turboprops

Cruising speed: 580 km/h (360 m.p.h.)

Initial climb rate: 579 m/min (1,900 f.p.m.)

Range: 2935 km (1,820 mi.) with a 23,014-kg (50,600-lb.) payload

Ferry range: 7435 km (4,600 mi.)

Service ceiling: 10,060 m (33,000 ft.)

Weights: empty 33,685 kg (74,107 lb.); loaded 70,307 kg (154,675 lb.)

Dimensions:
span	40.42 m (132 ft. 7 in.)
length	34.35 m (112 ft. 8 in.)
height	11.61 m (38 ft.)
wing area	162.16 m² (1,745 sq. ft.)

This colourful L-100-20 entered service with TAAG Angola Airlines in late 1979. In June 1986 it was damaged beyond repair in an accident in Dondo, Africa.

L-100-30 HERCULES

C-GHPW was delivered to Pacific Western Airlines in December 1978. In 1983 PWA leased the aircraft to Northwest Territorial Airways, with whom it carried the name *Capt. Harry Sorensen.*

Like the C-130, the L-100 family is powered by Allison's reliable and widely used T56 turboprop, driving a Hamilton Standard fully reversible four-bladed propeller. Known in civil guise as the Allison 501, this turbine design dates from the 1950s. Next-generation C-130Js (and L-100Js) will have entirely new and more efficient Allison AE 2100 engines driving six-bladed propellers.

Lockheed's factory in Marietta, Georgia undertook the first Hercules 'stretch', creating the L-100-20.

PACIFIC WESTERN

C-GHPW

As on military C-130s, the L-100 offers the ease of loading and unloading provided by the rear cargo ramp. The first Dash-30s were delivered to Saturn Airways in late 1970, specifically to fly powerplant sets (three Rolls-Royce RB.211 turbofan engines) for the Lockheed TriStar airliner from the UK to California.

Most commercial Hercules are configured for a freight role and are therefore fitted with a minimal number of cabin windows. However, the L-100-30 may be fitted with seating for up to 100 passengers, along with a galley and toilets.

Initial L-100 models omitted the standard military external fuel tank fit. The extra 5300 litres (1,400 gal.) of capacity that each of these tanks supplies was soon perceived as an asset by operators flying over longer routes, and the tanks were later offered as an option.

Such was the success of the stretched L-100-30 in commercial use that Lockheed offered the longer fuselage on the military Hercules. The C-130H-30 is 4.57 m (15 ft.) longer than the standard C-130H, with 40 per cent more internal capacity.

L-100 air freight around the globe

■ ALASKAN AIRLIFTER: Alaskan Airlines was the first customer for the L-100, the type later serving in the oil exploration support role with various airlines. Built to a military specification, 'Herks' can operate in all weathers.

■ ENGINES FOR THE TRISTAR: The first L-100-30s were delivered to Saturn Airways for a specific task – the delivery of Rolls-Royce engines from the UK to the US for fitment to new L-1011 TriStar wide-body airliners.

■ FAMINE RELIEF: Another well-known L-100 role has been famine relief flights (along with military C-130s), especially in Africa. Such life-saving flights often have to be made to rough unprepared airstrips in all weathers.

ACTION DATA

RANGE

Antonov's An-8 was designed for similar roles but appeared before the Hercules and was, at the time, a unique design. However, as a twin-engined aircraft it lacked the lifting capacity and range of the US type. The An-12 added two more engines and carried over twice the load, but with half the range capability.

L-100-20 HERCULES 2472 km (1,503 mi.)

An-8 'CAMP' 2280 km (1,410 mi.)

An-12BP 'CUB' 1450 km (900 mi.)

LOCKHEED

L-1011 TRISTAR

● Wide-body 'Whisperliner' ● Medium-/long-range tri-jet

I ntroduced as the 'Whisperliner' because of its quietness, the TriStar was the great rival of McDonnell Douglas' DC-10 tri-jet. With its Rolls-Royce RB.211 fan engines, it promised superb fuel economy and long range. Financial problems for Rolls-Royce and Lockheed almost caused the TriStar to fail before it flew, but it overcame these problems to become a superb airliner, well liked by passengers and pilots.

▲ The TriStar was designed at the end of the 1960s, when airlines wanted 'wide-body' fuselages with twin-aisle seating. Comfort was much better than in older narrow-bodies like the DC-8.

LOCKHEED L-1011 TRISTAR

▲ Delta launches the TriStar
Delta, one of the world's largest airlines, was a launch customer for the L-1011. It is a credit to the aircraft that Delta is still operating more than 50 examples of the tri-jet after over a quarter of a century in service.

▲ Wide body
Although the L-1011 looks similar to the DC-10, its third engine is buried in the rear fuselage rather than being mounted in the fin, as in the Douglas aircraft.

▼ Loading the hold ▶
Even though no dedicated TriStar freighter has been built, the basic airliner has a large cargo capacity.

▲ Tanker TriStar
In service with No. 216 squadron RAF, the TriStar has been a great success. Unlike its great rival, the DC-10, the TriStar has not been adopted by the US armed forces.

Needle nose ▶
The probe on the front of this test TriStar is a special 'gust boom' which measures air movement very accurately to check the aircraft's behaviour in turbulence.

FACTS AND FIGURES

➤ TriStars were originally priced at $14.3 million in the early 1970s, which is about the same price as an F-16 today.

➤ L-1011s are also operated by Saudia, Royal Jordanian and Cathay Pacific.

➤ The last TriStar was rolled out of Lockheed's Palmdale plant in 1983.

➤ Eastern Airlines and TWA received the first deliveries of L-1011s in April 1972.

➤ The RAF bought six TriStars from British Airways for £60 million in 1983.

➤ Lockheed built 250 TriStars; the first was rolled out in November 1970.

PROFILE

Lockheed's 'Whisperliner'

Designed as a medium-haul 250-seat airliner for American Airlines, with the emphasis on fuel economy and low maintenance, the TriStar almost fell victim to the financial problems of its manufacturer. Lockheed managed to pull itself together, and in 1966 the TriStar was born. It was marketed very aggressively by Lockheed, in ferocious competition with the longer range DC-10. By March 1968 the TriStar was selling well, with 118 delivered to Eastern Airlines, TWA and Delta. But just when sales looked good, disaster struck again as Rolls-Royce almost collapsed, stopping engine deliveries. After more financial dealings the supply of engines resumed and TriStars began selling again, but a large number of DC-10s had been sold in the meantime.

Range was improved in the L-1011-100 and -500, with more fuel tanks added, a wingtip extension and an active control

Like many major airlines, British Airways has now replaced its TriStars with newer aircraft.

system to reduce drag, but the aircraft never quite caught up with the DC-10. A small number were converted to tanker/transports for the Royal Air Force, and many still fly with airlines around the world.

Compared to a DC-10, the TriStar has a short fuselage and the wing is set further back, making it easily recognisable.

The undercarriage retracts into two large bays in the fuselage, just inside the wingroots.

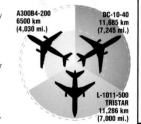

L-1011-500 TriStar

Type: long-range commercial transport

Powerplant: three 222.42-kN (49,900-lb.-thrust) Rolls-Royce RB.211-524B turbofans

Cruising speed: maximum 973 km/h (603 m.p.h.) at 9000 m (29,000 ft.); economy cruise 890 km/h (552 m.p.h.) at 10,500 m (34,000 ft.)

Range: 11,286 km (7,000 mi.) with maximum fuel; 9905 km (6,140 mi.) with maximum passenger and baggage load

Service ceiling: 13,200 m (43,300 ft.)

Weights: empty 111,311 kg (244,884 lb.); maximum 228,615 kg (502,942 lb.)

Accommodation: three flight crew; typically 24 first-class and 222 economy-class passengers

Dimensions:
span	50.09 m	(164 ft.)
length	50.05 m	(164 ft.)
height	16.87 m	(55 ft.)
wing area	329 m²	(3,540 sq. ft.)

L-1011-500 TriStar

The L-1011-500 was a long-range version of the TriStar, which was flown by British Airways on non-stop routes from London to New Orleans, Calgary and Edmonton. This aircraft was sold to the Royal Air Force in 1983, and now operates as a military tanker/transport.

The crew consists of a pilot, co-pilot and flight engineer. Cockpit noise levels are very low in the TriStar. An emergency escape hatch is fitted in the cockpit roof.

The wing has very large leading-edge slats, flaps, ailerons and outboard spoiler/speedbrakes. The wing of the 500 model contains very large fuel tanks, with a capacity of 34,000 litres (8,890 gal.).

The main cabin area typically seats up to 246 passengers in two classes, nine abreast in tourist class. Maximum load is 330, carried in a high-density 10-abreast economy layout.

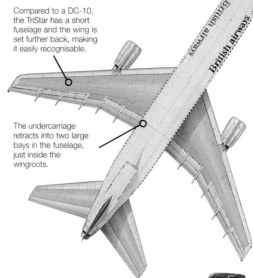

A forward galley is located just behind the cockpit.

The 500 series TriStar uses the RB.211-524 series turbofan engine. The RB.211 was consistently upgraded, mainly to compete with the Pratt & Whitney JT9-D in the Boeing 747, and it remains a highly efficient and quiet engine.

The Pratt & Whitney auxiliary power unit is located in a bay under the third engine feed duct.

Cowlings for the third engine are removable for maintenance access. A rear cabin door is fitted just ahead of the tailplane.

ACTION DATA

MAXIMUM SPEED

The TriStar was designed to take off from relatively short runways with a full payload. To achieve this it has an efficient aerodynamic shape, an effective wing and three excellent engines. These have the added benefit of making the big Lockheed design one of the fastest airliners around.

DC-10-40 **922 km/h (572 m.p.h.)**

L-1011-500 TRISTAR **973 km/h (603 m.p.h.)**

A300B4-200 **917 km/h (569 m.p.h.)**

RANGE

The TriStar was originally designed to fly the Chicago–Los Angeles route, but the 5000-km (3,100-mi.) range was insufficient for international users. Later models have greatly improved performance. The Model 500 has true intercontinental range, to match long-range variants of its great rival, the DC-10.

A300B4-200 **6500 km (4,030 mi.)**
DC-10-40 **11,685 km (7,245 mi.)**
L-1011-500 TRISTAR **11,286 km (7,000 mi.)**

PASSENGER LOAD

Long-range TriStars are four metres shorter than the standard variants, which reduces maximum passenger load from around 400 to 330. Passengers are seated 10 abreast in the high-density layout, although six abreast in first class and nine abreast in economy is a more normal configuration.

A300B4-200 **320 single-class high-density**
L-1011-500 TRISTAR **330 single-class high-density**
DC-10-40 **380 single-class high-density**

The wide-body generation

BOEING 747: First of the wide bodies, the epoch-making Boeing 747 'Jumbo Jet' is still the largest airliner in the world, over 30 years after its first flight. Most 747s are used on long-range high-density routes.

McDONNELL DOUGLAS DC-10: Smaller than the 747, the DC-10 was designed, like the TriStar, to fly somewhat shorter transcontinental routes than the 747. Longer range variants soon appeared which competed with the large Boeing jet.

AIRBUS A300: Europe's highly successful Airbus is the progenitor of a whole family of jets which compete with the Americans on all types of journey, from short-hop high-density flights to non-stop ultra-long-range routes.

LOCKHEED

10 ELECTRA

● All-metal design ● Twin-engined airliner ● Military versions

To many people, the Lockheed 10 Electra is known only as the aircraft in which Amelia Earhart disappeared. This unfortunate incident overshadows the career of a machine that was important in the development of passenger services with several US airlines during the 1930s. Most significantly, one of the greatest aviation engineers ever, Clarence 'Kelly' Johnson, the designer of the SR-71, was introduced to Lockheed via his work on the Electra.

▲ With the gradual passing of the airmail service, airline flights became accessible to more people, although they were still mostly for the rich. Lockheed's sleek, all-metal Electra was typical of the new breed of airliner in 1930s.

LOCKHEED 10 ELECTRA

On the flightdeck ▶
This 1930s photograph's caption claimed that the cockpit was equipped with 'every device known to science'.

▼ Museum piece
A US-registered Electra photographed at the Ontario Air Museum in 1966. Some Model 10s remain in airworthy condition.

▼ Wartime service
Several civilian Electras were impressed into Royal Air Force service. This machine joined No. 24 Squadron in April 1940.

▼ Northwest Electra
Very early aircraft were delivered with the prototype-style windscreen, but these were modified in service.

Flying on ▶
Many smaller airlines used Electras after the war. Provincetown-Boston Airlines were the last company to fly a scheduled Electra service in the early 1970s.

FACTS AND FIGURES

➤ Lockheed was part of the Detroit Aircraft Corporation until Robert Gross took the company over in 1932.

➤ A forwards-raked windscreen was fitted to early production aircraft.

➤ Lockheed used the name Electra again in 1957, this time for its Model 188 turboprop.

➤ The Electra was the first product of the 'new' Lockheed and the company's first twin-engined aircraft.

➤ Amelia Earhart's aircraft had more powerful engines and extra fuel capacity.

➤ Britain's Prime Minister used an Electra to fly to Germany in 1938.

PROFILE

Pioneering all-metal airliner

The head of the Lockheed Aircraft Corporation, Robert Gross, planned a 10-seat, all-metal, single-engined airliner. Before work began, however, market research indicated that a twin-engined machines would sell better and so the design of the Electra began.

In October 1934 the US Government banned single-engined aircraft from carrying passengers at night or over rough terrain, leaving Lockheed perfectly placed to pick up airline orders. The Model 10 helped the airlines through this difficult period, as most were quite new to passenger transport since airmail had previously been their main business.

Before the Electra was delivered to the airlines, it was wind-tunnel tested at the University of Michigan, where it was touched by the hand of genius. 'Kelly' Johnson was working as a professor's assistant and recommended a few changes to the airframe. Eventually, all of these modifications were adopted with great benefit to the design, and Johnson joined Lockheed.

In addition to the commercial version, a number of military models were built. Many found their way to South America and flew until the 1970s.

Above: A 1986 flight for a gleaming Electra. Johnson's twin-fin layout became a feature of subsequent Lockheed designs.

Above: South American Model 10 operators included the Brazilian state airline Varig. While some Electras were delivered pre-war, most South American aircraft were war-surplus or second-hand US civilian machines.

10-A Electra

Type: short-range light transport

Powerplant: two 336-kW (450-hp.) Pratt & Whitney Wasp Junior SB radial piston engines

Maximum speed: 325 km/h (202 m.p.h.) at 1525 m (5,000 ft.)

Cruising speed: 306 km/h (190 m.p.h.)

Initial climb rate: 347 m/min (1,140 f.p.m.)

Range: 1305 km (809 mi.)

Service ceiling: 5915 m (19,400 ft.)

Weights: empty 2927 kg (6,439 lb.); maximum take-off 4672 kg (10,278 lb.)

Accommodation: flight crew of two, plus 10 passengers

Dimensions: span 16.76 m (55 ft.)
length 11.76 m (38 ft. 7 in.)
height 3.07 m (10 ft. 1 in.)
wing area 42.59 m² (458 sq. ft.)

10-A ELECTRA

Northwest received the first production Electras. Operators and passengers were pleased with the aircraft's 306-km/h (190-m.p.h.) cruising speed, which was much faster than that of previous airliners.

Northwest was the first airline to place Electras in to service. The original forwards-raked windscreens were replaced by Northwest engineers. Aircraft were also given this Johnson-inspired modification on the production line.

A single aisle separated two rows of five seats. There were no overhead luggage bins and the cabin was very basic, although the windows did have curtains.

When the Electra was introduced into service it was the only US aircraft with complete metal skinning. The Electra was one of the first truly modern airliners.

All Electras, except for 18 Wright-engined 10-Bs for the US Coast Guard, were Pratt & Whitney powered, usually fitted with the Wasp Junior engine.

When retracted, the wheels of the main undercarriage were left partly exposed. The tailwheel was not retractable.

Lockheed felt that a slow, safe landing speed was important for commercial operations. To achieve this, split flaps were installed along the inboard wing trailing edge.

Northwest took a risk by introducing Electras into service early. On 7 August 1934 an Electra crashed, just four days before the award of an Approved Type Certificate.

During initial wind-tunnel experiments, small endplate fins were added to the conventional tail. Johnson recommended that twin fins and rudders would be more suitable and these were adopted.

ACTION DATA

MAXIMUM SPEED

Douglas and Boeing produced slightly larger airliners than the Electra, taking orders away from the Model 10. Although the DC-2 had 60 per cent more power, it was barely faster than the Electra.

10-A ELECTRA 325 km/h (202 m.p.h.)
DC-2 338 km/h (210 m.p.h.)
247D 322 km/h (200 m.p.h.)

PASSENGERS

While the capacity of the Electra was initially adequate, airlines soon required more seats. This meant that the Douglas design, especially as the DC-3, replaced the Electra in many companies.

10 ELECTRA 10 passengers
DC-2 14 passengers
247D 10 passengers

RANGE

Although it was designed to operate over shorter routes, the Electra could fly further than the larger Boeing 247D. It could not match the DC-2's range however, but this was a much larger aircraft, developed very closely with the airlines and therefore suited perfectly to their range and capacity requirements.

10 ELECTRA 1305 km (810 mi.)
DC-2 1609 km (998 mi.)
247D 1199 km (745 mi.)

Lockheed twin-tails

XC-35: This heavily modified Electra was used for testing cabin pressurisation techniques in 1937.

12 ELECTRA JUNIOR: The Electra was judged to be too large for feeder services and therefore this six-seat aircraft was built.

14 SUPER ELECTRA: Although designed to compete with the DC-2/3, the 14-seater Super Electra was still too small.

18 LODESTAR: A far more successful design than the Model 14, 625 of these 18-seat aircraft were built.

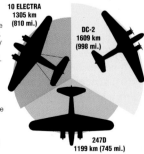

LOCKHEED

ER-2

● Research ● Ecological monitoring ● Sensor platform

NASA's ER-2 (ER for Earth Resources) is a peaceful version of the Cold War's U-2 spyplane. The nuclear stand-off between the West and the Soviet Union made it necessary to use high-flying reconnaissance aircraft, but the airframe became a less sinister tool when NASA began using it. ER-2s have been vital in recent years for monitoring the hole in the ozone layer, and for performing tasks that would otherwise be carried out by satellites.

▲ NASA operates just three ER-2 survey platforms, and all are based at NASA's experimental facility at Moffett Field. NASA-Ames has also operated civilian versions of the earlier U-2 aircraft.

LOCKHEED ER-2

▲ **Narrow body**
The TR-1 fuselage assembly is a narrow structure, a shape optimised for low drag in high-altitude flight.

▲ **NASA's special missions master**
The ER-2 is operated specifically by a unit of NASA known as the High Altitude Missions Branch.

▲ **Training variant**
Prospective NASA research pilots become accustomed to the unusual handling characteristics of the ER-2 in the USAF's tandem two-seat Lockheed U-2RTs of the the 9th Reconnaissance Wing.

▲ **Multi-mission cockpit**
Essentially similar to the military TR-1A, the ER-2's cockpit contains various sensor displays.

Foreign detachments ▶
As well as operating in the USA, NASA U-2s and ER-2s were often detached to Norway.

FACTS AND FIGURES

➤ One of NASA's three original U-2 pilots was a Briton, Ivor Webster, who trained for spy flight missions in the RAF.

➤ In 1980 an ER-2 studied volcanic eruptions from Mount St Helens.

➤ Two TR-1s were originally given to NASA and redesignated ER-2.

➤ Extra cameras used by NASA included Wild-Heerbrug RC-10 s with six- and 12-inch focal lengths.

➤ A third ER-2 (formerly a TR-1A of the 9th SRW) is now in service with NASA.

➤ The military TR-1 was used as a precision electronic reconnaissance aircraft.

NASA's civilian spyplanes

To most of the world the Lockheed U-2, manufactured at the top-secret 'Skunk Works', is remembered for being the spyplane shot down over Russia in 1960.

Originally, NASA (National Aeronautics and Space Administration) and its predecessor had only one connection with this Cold War spook, also called the 'Black Lady': NASA's civilian research was originally the 'cover story' for CIA spy flights in the U-2. But with the 1971 Earth Resources Satellite Technology programme (later called Landsat), NASA began operating

two U-2Cs (joined by the improved ER-2 model in 1983) for genuine, peaceful research using sensors and infra-red cameras. The U-2s complemented the satellite in providing a better understanding of the planet we live on, for example, measuring the chlorophyll content of vegetation. The ER-2 model carried most of its sensors in two 'superpods', one under each wing.

Although the U-2 is a difficult aircraft to fly, pilots appreciate this type of work because they are using a one-time clandestine weapon of war for a purpose that benefits mankind.

Above: ER-2s wear NASA's standard civilian-style paint scheme of upper surface gloss white with pale grey undersides and lateral blue stripe. The white paint scheme helps to prevent the systems overheating in strong sunlight.

Above: Lockheed ER-2s are useful to NASA because of their high ceiling. ER-2s regularly fly at heights of up to 24,000 m (78,740 ft.) and have a range of nearly 5000 km (3,100 mi.).

ER-2

Shown below is one of NASA's three ER-2 single-seat high-altitude earth resources aircraft, based at Moffett Field in the United States and detached to Bodø in Norway.

The ER-2's ultra-high-aspect ratio wings are similar to those of a glider, enabling the aircraft to act almost as a powered sailplane when at high altitude. They also make the aircraft probably the most difficult aircraft in the world to land, and several U-2 and TR-1 pilots have died in crashes after losing control just before touchdown.

The Lockheed U-2 series are the world's largest single-engined production aircraft, propelled by an enormous Pratt & Whitney J75 engine.

The long nose is hollow and can hold whatever equipment is suitable for the ER-2's particular mission profile. Further space is provided by the 'Q-bay' behind the pilot.

On take off the ER-2 jettisons its wing-mounted outrigger wheels, later coming in to land gently on one of its wingtip skids.

The cockpit is fully pressurised to withstand high-altitude missions and contains a single space-suited pilot.

Long, detachable 'superpods' are built under the wings and contain various different missions sensors.

A small composite tailwheel is housed in the rear fuselage, and outrigger wheels on the wings are used for extra balance.

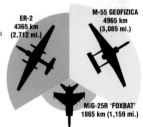

Environmental missions

OZONE RESEARCH: When detached to Norway, the ER-2's prime task is the continued monitoring of the upper atmosphere's ozone levels.

BIOLOGICAL RECONNAISSANCE: NASA has employed the sophisticated monitoring gear of its ER-2s to record a population boom in a species of moth which was destroying crops on the American coast.

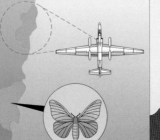

VOLCANIC MONITORING: The ER-2 was also successfully used to monitor the activity of Washington State's Mount St Helens during a period of eruptions in 1980.

LOCKHEED

CONSTELLATION

● Long-range airliner ● Last of the great piston transports

T he Lockheed Constellation had style. With its triple tail, porpoise-shaped fuselage and elliptical wing, the Constellation was queen of the skies in an era when airline passengers were pampered shamelessly. The Connie's accommodations were lavish. Stewardesses in elegant attire were under orders to spoil the customer. Even the strong, distinctive purr of four colossal R-3350 engines reinforced a passenger's sense of well-being.

▲ Aircraft of the Constellation's generation represented a huge advance in passenger comfort, being able to cruise high above most of the bad weather while retaining the sumptuous pre-war service.

LOCKHEED CONSTELLATION

▲ Ultimate 'Propliner'
The L-1649 Starliner represented the pinnacle of piston-engined airliner design. Sadly, these magnificent aircraft had their careers cut short by the arrival of the early jets, such as the Boeing 707.

▲ Baggage pannier
Many Constellations carried the Speed-Pak, an extra pannier attached to the aircraft's belly to hold extra baggage and cargo.

Sophisticated lady ▶
Lockheed workers swarm over a Constellation. The aircraft was a technological marvel, with extremely complex systems.

▼ Complicated cockpit
The Connie's flight deck was a mass of dials and switches, mostly concerned with the engines.

▲ Polished performer
Early Constellations carried a polished metal finish. Similar to the heavy bombers of the time, this finish gave the Constellation better range and speed performance as a coat of paint would add drag as well as weight to the aircraft.

FACTS AND FIGURES

➤ Eastern Air Lines Super Constellation services began in December 1951.

➤ Military Super Connies served as cargo and VIP transports, airborne radar stations and reconnaissance craft.

➤ The L-1049D was a cargo version with two large loading doors.

➤ Only 43 of the 'ultimate' L-1649A Starliners, which were late competing with the Douglas DC-7C, went into service.

➤ TWA's 1957 8850-km (5,500-mi.) non-stop Starliner polar service to London from San Francisco lasted 18 hours 32 minutes.

Constellation spanning the globe

Based on the triumphant Constellation which emerged from World War II, the longer and bigger Lockheed L-1049 Super Constellation became the top airliner of the propeller age.

The Super Constellation, which first flew on 13 October 1950, could seat 95 passengers compared with the 60-seat capacity of the original model. Wright, manufacturer of the engines, worked with Lockheed

to power the upsized 'Super' with a new R-3350 known as a turbo-compound. Once this truly beautiful craft began earning its keep with the airlines, it marked a high point in piston-engine transport. The Super Constellation flew millions of miles well into the 1980s.

The L-1049G, fondly called the 'Super G', was an advanced model. But the ultimate expression of the Constellation's class and quality was the

Lockheed L-1649A Starliner, a Super Connie with longer-span wings, stretched fuselage, and even more powerful turbo-compound engines. The Starliner was the last word in luxury travel in the late 1950s, but its days were to be numbered by the introduction of the first jet airliners.

Air France was among the many top airlines which operated the Constellation on its prestige routes, flying the big airliner on transatlantic and other long-range services.

The tall, stalky undercarriage, curved fuselage and distinctive triple tail made the Constellation one of the most recognisable aircraft of its time.

L-1049E Super Constellation

Type: long-range civil transport

Powerplant: four 2435-kW (3,165-hp.) Wright R-3350-972TC18DA-1 turbo-compound radial piston engines

Maximum speed: 590 km/h (370 m.p.h.) at 5670 m (18,000 ft.)

Range: 7950 km (5,000 mi.)

Service ceiling: 7225 m (23,700 ft.)

Weights: empty 34,665 kg (76,500 lb.); loaded 60,328 kg (133,000 lb.)

Accommodation: flight crew of three; two to four flight attendants; 95 to 109 passengers in various configurations

Dimensions:
span	37.49 m (123 ft.)
length	34.54 m (113 ft. 4 in.)
height	7.54 m (24 ft. 7 in.)
wing area	153.29 m² (1,650 sq. ft.)

L-1049G SUPER CONSTELLATION

Constellations were a familiar sight around the world in the late 1940s and 1950s. The L-1049G Super Constellations of TWA were among the first airliners to offer non-stop transatlantic crossings.

Constellations were designed for long-range operations, and the extra fuel carried in large wingtip tanks gave the Super Constellation true intercontinental capability.

The banana-shaped fuselage of the Constellation was a builder's nightmare. The passenger section in later Super Constellations was made cylindrical for ease of manufacture.

Originally carrying around 60 passengers, the Constellation's capacity grew with each new model. By the end of Lockheed's 13-year manufacturing run the Starliner was carrying more than 100 passengers across the Atlantic.

The Constellation flew long distance with a flight crew of five: pilot, co-pilot, flight engineer, radio operator and navigator.

The L-1049G was the first Constellation to employ weather radar, essential for these transatlantic airliners.

The L-1049G Super Constellation was powered by 18-cylinder Wright turbo-compound engines developing some 2423 kW (3,150 hp.).

The Constellation's wing was based upon the design of the P-38 Lightning fighter, but was enlarged and strengthened, as was appropriate for a large transport.

History of the Constellation

■ **MODEL 49 CONSTELLATION:** Flying eight years after the DC-3, the Model 49 was snapped up by the wartime US Army as a transport. Over 100 were ordered by airlines after the war.

■ **MODEL 749 CONSTELLATION:** More powerful engines and extra tanks gave this improved Constellation greater range. Many were acquired by the US Air Force and the US Navy.

■ **MODEL 1049 SUPER CONSTELLATION:** Stretched by nearly 6 m (20 ft.) and powered by turbo-compound engines, the Super Constellation was the biggest and fastest airliner of its time.

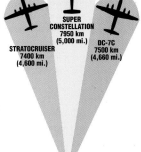

■ **MODEL 1649 STARLINER:** The ultimate Connie was a superb performer, but was too late to challenge the DC-7C. However, both were soon made obsolete by the new jets.

ACTION DATA

RANGE

It was the development of bombers during World War II which made intercontinental flight a possibility, and by the early 1950s airliners were carrying full passenger loads non-stop across the Atlantic, and with one stop across the Pacific. The Super Constellation was the ultimate long-range piston-engined airliner, and it inaugurated the non-stop polar route from San Francisco to London.

STRATOCRUISER 7400 km (4,600 mi.)

SUPER CONSTELLATION 7950 km (5,000 mi.)

DC-7C 7500 km (4,660 mi.)

MACCHI
M.5-M.67

● Fighting floatplanes ● Schneider Trophy winners ● Transports

One of the most famous names in aviation, the Macchi company built a series of seaplanes which gained fame not only during World War I, but also through legendary Schneider Trophy victories of the 1920s and 1930s. It was in 1915 that the Macchi company was asked to design a flying-boat to match those of the Austrian opposition. This was built in just over one month and paved the way for the record-breaking aircraft of the following decades.

▲ First appearing in 1918, the M.7 was the ultimate Macchi flying-boat of World War I. Post-war, the aircraft was developed into the successful M.7bis racer and M.7ter fighter.

MACCHI M.5-M.67

Venice victory ▶
Piloted by Giovanni di Briganti, an M.7bis won the 1921 Schneider Trophy. No less than five M.7s of various versions took part in the race.

◀ Trophy winner
Piloted by Mario de Bernardi, this M.39 won the 1926 Schneider Trophy at Norfolk, Virginia.

▼ Monoplane racer
Designed by Mario Castoldi, the M.33 was third in the 1925 Schneider Trophy at Baltimore, Maryland.

▼ Seaplane spotter
Macchi's first twin-boom design was the M.12 armed reconnaissance and bomber flying-boat.

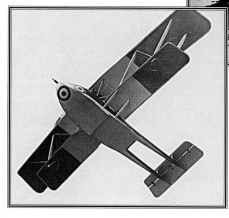

Famous fighter ▶
The highly agile, single-seat M.5 was the most successful Italian-designed fighter of World War I.

FACTS AND FIGURES

➤ Entering service in 1918, the M.7 served as the M.7ter in Italian training schools until as late as 1940.

➤ Three M.41s were delivered to Spain in 1936 and fought in the Civil War.

➤ The M.24 was used in torpedo-launching experiments during 1925.

➤ A number of M.3s were converted by Swiss company Ad Astra Aero for carrying passengers on pleasure flights.

➤ In 1929 one of the three Schneider Trophy M.67s crashed into Lake Garda.

➤ On 4 November 1927 the M.52 broke the 3-km (1.86-mile) world speed record at 479.29 km/h (297 m.p.h.).

PROFILE

Macchi's seaplane series

Macchi's first flying-boat design, the L.1 (L standing for Lohner), was basically a copy of an existing Austrian design. The company's first indigenous aircraft was the L.3 (later changed to M.3 in recognition of Macchi's design work). This aircraft, along with the M.5 and M.7 which were developments of this airframe, became highly successful fighters during World War I, matching any land-based opponent. They achieved export sales to the USA.

Post-war, the M.7 was developed into the M.7bis, which won the 1922 Schneider Trophy, and the M.7ter, of which more than 100 were built.

The success of the single hull, biplane wing, pusher-engine layout was to influence Macchi's designs over the next decade. Numerous designs were produced, each with more powerful engines and refined aerodynamics, culminating in the twin-engined M.24 commercial flying-boat capable of carrying eight passengers.

In 1925 Macchi began to specialise in floatplane racers. With financial backing from Mussolini, the company created the M.39 which won the 1926 Schneider Trophy and led, via the M.52 and M.67, to the world record-breaking M.C.72.

Below: Featuring a two-step hull, the M.24 was built as a reconnaissance bomber. The later M.24bis, as seen here, was designed for the civilian market.

Above: Developed for submarine-borne duties, the M.53 could be dismantled for storage aboard a submarine.

M.18

Type: three-seat bomber/reconnaissance flying-boat

Powerplant: one 186-kW (249-hp.) Isotta-Fraschini Asso in-line piston engine

Maximum speed: 187 km/h (116 m.p.h.)

Range: 1000 km (620 mi.)

Service ceiling: 5500 m (18,000 ft.)

Weights: empty equipped 1275 kg (2,805 lb.); maximum take-off 1785 kg (3,927 lb.)

Armament: one 7.7-mm (.303 cal.) Vickers machine-gun, plus four light bombs on underwing racks

Dimensions:
span	15.80 m	(51 ft. 10 in.)
length	9.75 m	(32 ft.)
height	3.25 m	(10 ft. 8 in.)
wing area	45 m²	(484 sq. ft.)

M.33

Designed for the 1925 Schneider Trophy air race, this example is one of two built. It later went on to serve with the Italian high-speed flight training school.

At a glance, the engine mounts appeared to be rather flimsy. Macchi realised that this area had potential for structural weakness and paid considerable attention to making the struts as strong as possible.

Power was provided by a single V12 in-line piston engine built by Curtiss in the United States. This powerful 19.7-litre (5.2-gal.) unit used fuel at a high rate which restricted range. However, since the aircraft was designed solely as a racing machine, range was not important.

The M.33 was of the high-wing configuration that was necessary to provide sufficient clearance for the outrigger floats. The wing was built in three major sections, with the outer units capable of mild flexing. Identifying features of the aircraft were the very long ailerons.

M33 48 6

A very streamlined fuselage was a characteristic of the M.33. Most of the hull, including the centre-section, was built entirely from metal. The two main sections were extremely robust in order to absorb the considerable forces exerted by air flow over the wing and engine supports.

ACTION DATA

MAXIMUM SPEED

The progression in flying-boat design is reflected in the relative speeds of these three aircraft. The M.3 of 1916 was a fast aircraft for its time, and the M.18, which appeared more than a decade later, was not significantly faster. The higher speed of the M.C.77 of the 1930s was a result of rapid increases in engine power.

M.3	145 km/h (90 m.p.h.)
M.C.77	279 km/h (173 m.p.h.)
M.18	187 km/h (116 m.p.h.)

RANGE

As a maritime reconnaissance flying-boat, the M.C.77 required long range, which was achieved by placing large fuel tanks in the fuselage and wing. The M.3 was designed as a fighter and its endurance of more than three hours was impressive for the period.

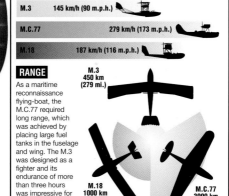

M.3 450 km (279 mi.)

M.18 1000 km (620 mi.)

M.C.77 3000 km (1,860 mi.)

TAKE-OFF WEIGHT

The M.3 could carry four bombs, which meant its take-off weight was higher than that of most of its contemporaries. The much larger M.18 could not carry significantly more because of a lack of power. The M.C.77, with significantly more power, could carry a much bigger load, but a large proportion of the weight was fuel.

M.3 1350 kg (2,970 lb.)

M.C.77 4835 kg (10,637 lb.)

M.18 1785 kg (3,927 lb.)

Land-based Macchis

M.14: In 1918 Macchi designed and built this single-seat scout. Only two were completed before development work was abandoned.

M.16: This ultra-light sport aircraft first flew in 1919. In 1920 the M.16 established a world altitude record for aircraft in its class.

M.20: Similar in appearance to the M.16, the M.20 could be used as a sport or training aircraft. It twice won the prestigious Coppa d'Italia.

M.70: First flying in 1929, the M.70 competed for Italian orders for a new training aircraft. It had a remarkable minimum speed of 55 km/h (34 m.p.h.).

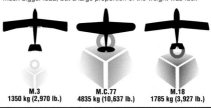

MacCready

GOSSAMER ALBATROSS

● Unorthodox design ● Repeated success ● Advanced technology

D r Paul MacCready ventured into the world of sailplanes in the 1970s when he began construction of the Condor, in response to a challenge laid down by industrialist Henry Kremer. In 1977, the Condor set a world record, flying in a figure of eight over a distance of 1.6 km (one mile). Two years later, another challenge was offered, to cross the English Channel by man-powered sailplane.

▲ *On 12 June 1979, a historic event took place. Bryan Allen, flying the MacCready Gossamer Albatross, became the first person to fly over the English Channel in a man-powered craft.*

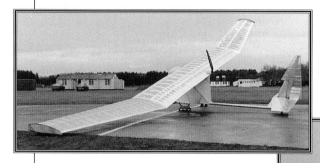

▼ Anatomy of the Albatros
Even today, the Albatross remains one of the most bizarre looking creations ever to take to the skies. It features a high-mounted wing and a pusher layout, with extremely large propellers for the greatest amount of thrust possible. It weighs only 97.5 kg (215 lb.) fully loaded.

▲ Rudimentary flying
This type of craft represents manned flight in one of its purest forms. Note the wing construction and the location of the spars on this Liverpuffin.

◀ Relying on solar energy
Similar in design to the Gossamer Albatross was the later Solar Challenger. As the name implied, this little contraption relied on energy from the sun, using no fewer than 16,218 photo-volatic cells to generate 2.2 kW (2.95 hp) of power.

▼ Scale aircraft technology
Looking like an experimental aircraft from the World War II period, this unidentified machine sports a slightly swept wing and pusher layout.

▲ Large span
This photograph of a Liverpuffin illustrates the extremely long-span wings common to sailplanes. Note the dihedral of the outer wings.

FACTS AND FIGURES

➤ Pilot Bryan Allen had broken a record in 1977 for flying in a figure-of-eight over a distance of 1.6 km (one mile).

➤ No batteries or energy storage devices were employed on the Solar Challenger.

➤ Allen won a total of £150,000 in prizes for his achievements.

➤ After the record-breaking Channel crossing, MacCready did it again in 1981, this time in the Solar Challenger.

➤ A British machine, Solar One, made the first solar/electric-powered flight in 1978.

➤ The first man to cross the English Channel by hang-glider was David Cook, in May 1978.

PROFILE

Across the Channel by pedal power

Unlike just about any other flying craft, the machines that emerged from MacCready's workshop near Los Angeles were built with one aim in mind: to break records.

The first of these, the Condor, had a wingspan of 29.26 m and was a pusher design, with a large two-bladed propeller mounted at the back and an auxiliary aerofoil placed well forward. The pilot sat in an enclosed cabin directly below the main wing. For the record-breaking flight which took place at Shafter, California, championship cyclist Bryan Allen was chosen as the pilot. On the hot August day in 1977, he flew the strange-looking Condor between the two pylons in 7 minutes 2.5 seconds.

Two years later, the industrialist Henry Kremer sponsored another challenge. This time it was more ambitious – to fly a pedal-powered sailplane across the English Channel. At MacCready, Vernon Oldershaw and his team built an improved version of the Condor, the Albatross. In many respects it was identical to the Condor and Bryan Allen once again piloted it on the journey. He landed at Cap Gris-Nez, near Boulogne, after pedalling 37 km (23 miles) over water.

Above: MacCready's man-powered sailplanes became household names during the late 1970s.

Left: This little craft is a Jupiter MPA. It was built by RAF apprentices at Halton.

Gossamer Albatross

Type: single-seat man-powered sailplane

Powerplant: one human via bicycle pedals

Maximum speed: 11 km/h (6.8 m.p.h.)

Endurance: 2 hours 49 minutes

Range: 37 km (23 mi.)

Weights: empty 31.8 kg (70 lb.); maximum take-off (including pilot) 97.5 kg (215 lb.)

Propeller RPM: 115

Dimensions: span 28.60 m (93 ft. 9 in.)
length (est) 18.00 m (59 ft.)
height (est) 7.00 m (23 ft.)
wing area (est) 73 m² (785 sq. ft.)

To make the Albatross as light as possible, materials used included balsa wood (for the propeller), Mylar (for the fuselage covering, aerofoil and wing sections), plus alloy and foam sheet for the leading edge of the wing.

Protruding rearward from the wing was another outrigger pole, which doubled as a ballast weight to help maintain stability while in flight.

Ahead of the main wing, mounted at the end of of a long cylindrical pole, was the auxiliary aerofoil section. It was designed to pivot universally on the outrigger pole.

Centrally located above the main outrigger spar was the air speed indicator. Although rudimentary, it was a vital piece of equipment, helping the pilot ensure that the speed of the Albatross was sufficient to keep the craft airborne.

To sustain level flight, the Albatross required at least 0.25 kW of power to the propeller. This factor alone ensured that the pilot had to be at peak fitness in order to complete the cross-Channel trip successfully, For turning, 20 per cent more power was required.

GOSSAMER ALBATROSS

Using technology from the preceding Condor, a single Gossamer Albatross was built. It was remarkably successful on its flight across the Channel, and inspired the solar-powered Penguin.

The pilot sat on a bicycle-type frame and power was by means of peddling. A chain drive and sprocket provided a direct link to the two-bladed balsa wood propeller. In flight, a maximum of 115 revolutions per minute was achieved.

For landing, twin bicycle tyres mounted in tandem could be fitted. They were non-retractable and protruded slightly from the floor of the Mylar-covered cabin. Contrary to popular belief, they were not pedal-powered, but purely freewheeling items.

FLIGHT OF THE ALBATROSS

1 MAKING HISTORY: Having established a world record in the USA for flying a man-powered sailplane in a figure of eight between two pylons spaced 1.6 km (1 mile) apart, pilot Bryan Allen realised another ambition: to be the first man to cross the English Channel in a man-powered sailplane. The journey would begin from Folkestone in Kent and finish at Cap Gris-Nez in France.

FOLKESTONE

ENGLISH CHANNEL

2 ENDURANCE TEST: On 12 June 1979, at 05.51, Allen set off, easing the odd-looking craft into the air. Flying across the Channel can present many problems, especially in a craft as flimsy as the Albatross. Luckily, no problems were encountered during the journey and Allen arrived safely at the Cap in just 2 hours and 49 minutes. He won a £100,000 prize for the trip, presented by British industrialist, Henry Kremer.

37 km (23 miles)

CAP GRIS-NEZ

Modern-day pioneers in aviation

■ **BEDE BD.5:** Jim Bede has made his reputation on marketing ultra-small and light homebuilt aircraft. The BD.5, a small pusher machine, made its first flight in 1972 and made speeds of up to 322 km/h (200 m.p.h.).

■ **ROBINSON R.22 BETA:** After working for Hughes, engineer Frank Robinson began developing a low-cost two-seat helicopter. Since its 1973 launch, the R.22 has become an extremely popular little machine.

■ **RUTAN DEFIANT:** Burt Rutan has been a pioneer in building small, low-cost aircraft, making extensive use of lightweight materials and advanced aerodynamics. The Defiant is one such machine.

MARTIN

2-0-2/4-0-4

● Twin-engined airliner ● Still in service ● Military use

MARTIN 2-0-2/4-0-4

▼ **Survivors**
A handful of 2-0-2s were passed on to small operators in the 1960s. This example was still flying in 1985 with Proair.

▲ **Problematic airliners**
Northwest was the only major airline to buy the 2-0-2 and in service they were not popular, being plagued by mechanical and structural problems.

◀ **First of the few**
Two prototypes were built and the second was distinguished by the greater dihedral (upward sweep) of its wings. Certification was given in mid-1947.

▼ **South American sales**
Among the few operators that actually purchased 2-0-2s was Linea Aeropostal Venezolana, which used it on its Latin American routes.

◀ **Thwarted production**
Production of the 2-0-2 variant was under way in earnest by 1947, though it was soon clear that many airlines wanted much larger, faster aircraft. Orders were cancelled and only 47 aircraft were built.

Determined to capture a slice of the lucrative post-war airline market, the Glenn L. Martin company built the twin-engined Model 2-0-2. The aircraft was the company's first attempt at producing a machine tailored for the civil market since the Clipper flying-boats, and ultimately proved unsuccessful. An improved variant, the 4-0-4 entered service in 1951 and most of these flew on into the mid-1960s.

▲ *A twin-engined airliner/transport, the 2-0-2/4-0-4 was externally very similar to the Convair 240, though it never achieved the same commercial success as its great rival.*

FACTS AND FIGURES

➤ After one aircraft crashed, killing all on board, Northwest Airlines promptly disposed of its remaining 2-0-2s.

➤ In March 1950, the larger and much improved 4-0-4 was announced.

➤ Eastern Airlines and TWA purchased a total of 103 of the improved variant.

➤ A pressurised version of the 2-0-2, known as the 3-0-3, was ordered by United Airlines, but later cancelled.

➤ One aircraft was converted into an executive transport for Frank Sinatra.

➤ Two aircraft, known as RM-1Gs, were delivered to the US Coast Guard.

PROFILE

Martin's postwar commercial

Nearly forgotten today, the Martin 2-0-2 and 4-0-4 might have been excellent aircraft, and in some ways deserved to succeed, but were plagued by numerous setbacks. The first 2-0-2 prototype flew in November 1946 and six customers immediately ordered the type. However, the market collapsed in 1947 and only Northwest Airlines actually purchased 2-0-2s. These aircraft proved troublesome in service. One was lost during a storm in 1947. Another was seriously damaged and cracks in the wings revealed a major flaw in the design. Martin addressed the problem but the airlines were unconvinced and only 24 of this variant were built.

The 4-0-4 of 1950 looked similar but featured a pressurised fuselage and was somewhat larger. These proved more popular, with two major airlines, Eastern and TWA, acquiring them. Some 4-0-4s serve into the late 1990s, flying charters in the Caribbean.

Above: Although similar in appearance, the 4-0-4 shared few components with its predecessor and featured a pressurised cabin. Compared to the 2-0-2 this variant was a success, with 103 built.

Right: Howard Hughes' TWA was an important customer for the Martin airliner, leasing a dozen 2-0-2s built from surplus parts before acquiring 4-0-4s. Several of these have been preserved.

4-0-4

Type: short/medium-range transport

Powerplant: two 1790-kW (2,400-hp.) Pratt & Whitney R-2800-CB16 radial engines

Maximum speed: 502 km/h (311 m.p.h.)

Cruising speed: 448 km/h (277 m.p.h.)

Initial climb rate: 580 m/min (1,900 f.p.m.)

Range: 1738 km (892 mi.) with maximum payload

Service ceiling: 8840 m (29,000 ft.)

Weights: empty 13,211 kg (29,064 lb.); maximum take-off 20,366 kg (44,805 lb.)

Accommodation: maximum of 40 passengers

Dimensions:
span	28.42 m	(93 ft. 3 in.)
length	22.73 m	(74 ft. 7 in.)
height	8.66 m	(28 ft. 5 in.)
wing area	80.27 m²	(864 sq. ft.)

4-0-4

Having reached the end of their careers with major airlines such as TWA, Martin 4-0-4s were passed on to smaller operators. Marco Island Airways flew this colourful example on its Caribbean routes.

On the 4-0-4 the standard crew for most flights was three, consisting of a pilot, co-pilot and navigator, though sometimes a fourth member was carried.

Despite a common external appearance, the 2-0-2 and 4-0-4 were structurally completely different aircraft. The 4-0-4 featured a larger, pressurised fuselage which proved more comfortable for both passengers and crew. Not surprisingly, the aircraft sold better than its unpopular predecessor.

The all-metal vertical tail followed contemporary fashion in having a very large dorsal spine which stretched nearly halfway down the fuselage. The tail unit was of all-metal stressed-skin construction and all control surfaces were powered. The aircraft was generally pleasant to fly and had few vices.

Marco Island Airways

N973M

The rather stalky tricycle undercarriage featured a single steerable nosewheel and double main units. All three units retracted forward for flight.

Among the improvements introduced on the 4-0-4 were uprated engines. The twin Pratt & Whitney R-2800 18-cylinder Twin Wasp radials featured turbo superchargers for better performance at high altitude.

Retractable steps were built in to the rear fuselage, dispensing with the need for a bulky, cumbersome staircase. This saved time and also enabled the aircraft to fly into airfields where ground support equipment was minimal.

ACTION DATA

CRUISING SPEED

Compared to their 1930s predecessors, the post-war generation of commercial twins could fly higher and faster, though the Soviet Il-14 Crate was slower and somewhat less efficient than Western rivals such as the Martin 4-0-4 and Convair 440.

4-0-4 — 448 km/h (277 m.p.h.)
IL-14 M — 300 km/h (186 m.p.h.)
CV-440 — 483 km/h (300 m.p.h.)

PASSENGERS

Although a capacity of 40 passengers may not seem impressive today, it was good back in the 1940s. Despite being excellent aircraft these designs were quickly superseded by larger types on major routes and ended up as regional airliners.

4-0-4 — 40 PASSENGERS
IL-14 M 'CRATE' — 36 PASSENGERS
CV-440 — 52 PASSENGERS

RANGE

A notable quality of the 4-0-4 was its superb range. This made it ideal for regional services across the United States and flights to the Caribbean islands. The similar Convair 440 proved more popular, despite its poor range with maximum payload. The Il-14 had a reasonable range by comparison, but was costly to operate.

4-0-4 — 1738 km (892 mi.)
IL-14 M 'CRATE' — 1034 km (640 mi.)
CV-440 — 739 km (285 mi.)

Rivals in the post-war market

■ BOEING 377 STRATOCRUISER: With its 'double bubble' fuselage the 'Strat' was the most prestigious airliner of the late 1940s.

■ CONVAIR 240: Also known as the 'Convairliner', this was the aircraft that beat the Martin 2-0-2 for airline orders.

■ DOUGLAS DC-3: In the austere, immediate post-war market, the DC-3 was an attractive buy for many commercial airlines.

■ DOUGLAS DC-7B: Ushering in a new era in air travel, were larger four-engined airliners such as the DC-7. Pan-American was a major user.

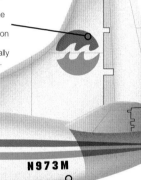

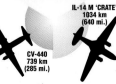

MARTIN

PB2M MARS

● Maritime patrol ● Water-bomber ● Four-engine flying-boat

MARTIN PB2M MARS

▲ Mightier Mars
The JRM-2 Mars, named 'Caroline Mars' by the Navy, was even heavier and more powerful than the first JRM-1s. It was fitted with Pratt & Whitney R-4360s, which were the most powerful engines in existence at the time.

▲ Mars formation
A rare sight even in the 1950s, this formation of four JRM-3s was headed by 'Philippine Mars' and 'Marianas Mars'. The JRM-1s were eventually upgraded to the same standard as the JRM-2, and were then known as JRM-3s.

▼ 'Hawaii Mars'
Flying cargo between the mainland and Honolulu, the Mars could operate in worse conditions than land-based aircraft and carried its larger load more economically.

▲ Pearl Harbor patrol
The first Mars was berthed at the Naval Air Station at Alameda, California. It made the round trip to Pearl Harbor in Hawaii in just five days, including all servicing and cargo loading. The massive wing contained large fuel tanks.

Few modern sights in aviation can equal that of a huge scarlet Martin Mars coming straight at you over a Canadian lake. These 50-year-old Navy veterans of World War II are among the biggest flying-boats ever built and hold the record as the largest aircraft used for fighting forest fires. Capable of dumping thousands of litres of water and foam to extinguish forest fires, the two remaining Mars 'boats' are survivors of six that were originally built.

▲ Like so many large flying-boat projects in the late 1940s, the Mars was an excellent aircraft that became irrelevant when the war ended. The fact that two are still flying shows just how useful the Mars is.

FACTS AND FIGURES

➤ Designer Glenn Martin saw the Mars as a flying battleship, carrying enough bombs and troops to storm an enemy island.

➤ All six Mars flying-boats were named after islands, the first being 'Hawaii'.

➤ Until the B-36 bomber, the Mars was the largest aircraft used by the US military.

➤ The Mars might have had a future after World War II if airlines had not opted to use landplanes rather than flying-boats.

➤ The US Navy retired its last Mars in August 1956 despite its success.

➤ Mars flew three sorties a week between San Francisco and Honolulu.

PROFILE

Patrol aircraft turned water-bomber

Designed to meet a US Navy requirement for a patrol bomber, the Mars started life as the Martin Model 170 or XPB2M-1. The flying-boat was so large that inside it was fitted out like a ship with separate mess rooms for troops, officers' quarters, staterooms and berths.

Flying for the first time on 5 November 1941, the twin-tailed Mars prototype did not become the forerunner of a huge wartime fleet of combat aircraft as designer Glenn Martin had hoped. Instead, the Navy

asked for a transport and the XPB2M was stripped of its turrets and bombing equipment. In this role the Mars was impressive and the Navy began regular runs across the Pacific, packing thousands of kilograms of freight into the huge interior.

After the war the Navy ordered 20 examples of an XPB2M derivative designated JRM-1 and fitted with a single fin and rudder, but in the event only five were completed. The original 'Hawaii Mars' and 'Marshall Mars' were destroyed in crashes, and the other four,

joined by a single example of the heavier JRM-2, served until 1956.

When no post-war boom in civil flying-boat operations materialised, the five aircraft were sold to Forest Industries Flying Tankers of Canada for use as water-bombers.

Post-war flying-boats were killed off by the introduction of larger jet-powered and turboprop-powered landplanes. Those that survived, however, were found extremely useful for everything from rescue to fire bombing.

JRM-1 Mars

Type: long-range flying-boat

Powerplant: four 1715-kW (2,300-hp.) Wright Duplex Cyclone R-3350 radial piston engines

Maximum speed: 360 km/h (225 m.p.h.)

Range: 7039 km (4,360 mi.)

Service ceiling: 4450 m (14,600 ft.)

Weights: empty 34,279 kg (75,414 lb.); loaded 74,844 kg (164,657 lb.)

Dimensions: span 60.96 m (200 ft.)
length 35.76 m (117 ft.)
height 11.73 m (38 ft.)
wing area 342.15 m² (3,681 sq. ft.)

JRM-3 MARS

Still flying after more than 50 years of continuous operation, the last two Martin Mars flying-boats are 'Hawaii Mars' and 'Philippine Mars'.

The Mars has a very spacious cockpit, entered via doors in the port and starboard side of the nose and stairs up to the flight deck.

JRM-1s were powered by Wright Cyclone engines, replaced by Pratt & Whitney R-4360s in JRM-2 'Caroline Mars'.

The original twin-tail was replaced by a taller, single-fin unit with a large rudder. This was essential for good handling on the water in windy conditions.

Dihedral tailplanes help give the Mars stable and slow handling in pitch and roll. The rudder has a large trim tab to assist in control movement.

High-wing designs were almost universal for flying-boats to ensure that the propellers and flying surfaces were as far above the water as possible. The long-span wing gives the Mars very long range.

A small access walkway was retained in the JRM-2 even though the rear fuselage had been extensively modified. Doorways to the rear fuselage are located ahead of the tailfin.

The Mars' planing hull is an excellent design, giving the aircraft very good handling on the water and making take-off and landing surprisingly easy for such a massive aircraft.

For the water-bomber role, the Mars contains enormous water tanks fitted in the fuselage. These can be filled in as little as 15 seconds as the aircraft taxies across the surface of a lake.

The main cargo-bay door is located in the fuselage side. It was the size of this door rather than payload weight limitations that dictated what a Mars could carry.

The bulk of a flying-boat fuselage could accommodate very large loads. In 1949, 'Marshall Mars' carried no less than 315 passengers as well as its crew of seven.

ACTION DATA

MAXIMUM SPEED

Flying-boats require range, capacious fuselages and a boat hull, all factors which mitigate against a fast design. With streamlining and powerful engines, the flying-boats of the 1940s were reaching almost 400 km/h (250 m.p.h.), an impressive achievement.

JRM-1 MARS	360 km/h (225 m.p.h.)
SHETLAND	424 km/h (263 m.p.h.)
BV 222 VIKING	382 km/h (237 m.p.h.)

RANGE

American aircraft were often built with impressive range, which was essential as long trans-oceanic flights were needed to reach other countries. The Shetland was designed with British Empire sea routes in mind and the availability of frequent fuel stops. The BV 222 was almost as long-ranged as the Mars.

JRM-1 MARS 7039 km (4,360 mi.) — SHETLAND 4000 km (2,480 mi.) — BV 222 VIKING 5988 km (3,713 mi.)

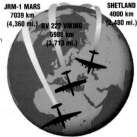

Flying firemen in North America

GRUMMAN TURBO FIRECAT: The Firecat is used extensively in North America as an effective fire-fighter even though it is a small land-based design. It has also been sold to France. The airframe is a turboprop variant of the naval S-2 Tracker anti-submarine warfare aircraft.

DOUGLAS DC-6: Fitted with a large canoe-shaped external fuel tank under the belly, this DC-6 named 'Spirit of '76' is another early post-war design which was pressed into service for fire bombing. Its tanks contain chemical fire-suppressant rather than water.

CANADAIR CL-215: Operated in Canada and across Europe, the CL-215 is one of the most common sights above a forest fire today. It was used by the French Securité Civile to fight the large fires near the Riviera region in 1985. It is also operated in Venezuela as a transport and in Thailand as a surveillance aircraft.

325

MBB (EUROCOPTER)

BO 105 AIR AMBULANCE

● Specialised emergency work ● Agile performance

▲ Health service helicopters
Despite being expensive to run, the air ambulance is so vital in many regions of the UK that funding has been made available for it.

▲ Quick load
The interior of the BO 105 can hold two stretcher cases along with two medical attendants.

▼ Dual role
Used for both medical and police work, this BO 105DBS/4 can be fitted with a powerful searchlight and infra-red imaging equipment.

▲ Mountain rescue
Swiss Air Rescue operate the BO 105CBS for mountain work. These aircraft are often used to rescue injured skiers or stranded hikers.

Far East connection ▶
Some Japanese operators fitted winches to their BO 105s giving them added rescue capabilities.

The MBB BO 105 light-utility helicopter is a masterpiece of simple but effective design that has won an excellent worldwide reputation. This fine helicopter is a veritable 'jack of all trades', suitable for a wide variety of civil and military duties. Well known in Europe as a military aircraft armed with a variety of weapons, the BO 105 is equally visible in America as a means of transporting casualties to hospital.

▲ Rearwards opening clamshell doors enable easy access for a casualty on a stretcher. The quick transfer from incident to hospital allowed by ambulance helicopters has saved hundreds of lives.

FACTS AND FIGURES

➤ Military BO 105s are valuable because they can fly nap-of-the-earth missions below treetop level.

➤ The prototype for the BO 105 series first flew on 16 February 1967.

➤ To date, 1,300 BO 105s have been delivered and 3,400,000 hours flown.

➤ Police/Medical Aviation Services Ltd currently operate five specially-equipped BO 105s in the emergency services role.

➤ Eurocopter claims that the BO 105 was the world's first light twin-engined helicopter.

➤ Sweden operates an unarmed SAR version known as the HR 9B.

PROFILE

Saving lives by air ambulance

The manufacturer's brochures for the MBB BO 105 helicopter call it a 'reliable, hard-working aircraft with multi-mission capabilities'. Several versions of this attractive and versatile helicopter are flown in many parts of the world. The BO 105 has been a popular choice in a variety of locations and is rugged enough to operate in almost any climate. The manufacturer boasts that it has "outstanding hot environment, high-altitude performance".

Such a versatile airframe has proved no less adaptable to the role of air ambulance. Clamshell

doors at the rear of the cabin make loading stretchers a simple task, while winches can be fitted to permit airborne rescues.

Design work on the BO 105 began in 1962. The German government was eager to support early testing of this design and to encourage its entry into service. Full production was well underway by 1971, with an improved version coming out of the factory by 1975. Civil BO 105s (as well as military versions) sold well, with air ambulance variants seeing service in the northern and southern hemispheres.

Above: The medical attendants, winchmen and pilots who operate ambulance helicopters have to undergo intensive training for their highly specialised duties.

Right: The helicopter is a vital tool for ambulance and rescue work. Not only can it reach areas inaccessible by road, it can also transport critical cases far more quickly, giving victims a better chance of survival.

BO 105CB

Type: five-seat light-utility helicopter

Powerplant: two 313-kW (420-hp.) Allison 250-C20B turboshaft engines

Max speed: 270 km/h (167 m.p.h.) at sea level

Range: 658 km (408 mi.) flying at 1525 m (5,000 ft.)

Operating ceiling: 5180 m (17,000 ft.)

Weights: empty 1256 kg (2,763 lb.); maximum take-off 2400 kg (5,280 lb.)

Armament: military versions carry up to eight Hughes TOW anti-armour missiles, or up to 38 air-to-ground rocket projectiles, or (typically) two 7.62-mm machine-guns; civil versions can carry 2800 kg (6,173 lb.) of cargo

Dimensions:
main rotor diameter	9.84 m (32 ft. 3 in.)
length	11.86 m (38 ft. 11 in.)
height	3 m (9 ft. 10 in.)
main rotor disc area	76.05 m² (818 sq. ft.)

The pilot and co-pilot or passenger have an excellent view in all directions. Extra equipment can include searchlights, doppler radar, infra-red imaging cameras or loudspeakers.

The BO 105's excellent agility is provided by the rigid titanium rotor head. Each of the four rotor blades is fitted with an anti-erosion strip and a vibration damper.

The twin-bladed, semi-rigid tail rotor unit is made from glassfibre reinforced plastic. Extra stability is provided by a horizontal stabiliser of light alloy construction with small endplate fins.

G-CDBS

BO 105DBS/4

G-CDBS is operated by Bond Helicopters on behalf of the Cornwall Ambulance Service in England. This vital service is entirely funded by donations from the people of Cornwall.

The landing gear is of skid type, designed with cross-tubes for energy absorption by plastic deformation in the event of a heavy landing. Inflatable emergency floats are fitted to this machine which can be removed. Entrance to the cabin is via side doors or the large rear-opening clamshell doors.

The fuselage is of the conventional pod and boom type and is constructed of light alloy metals. Two stretchers can be accommodated side-by-side in air ambulance configuration.

ACTION DATA

MAXIMUM POWER

All three of these types are currently used for mountain rescue in Europe. The added power of the A 109K2 is useful when lifting loads at altitude. The BO 105 has a good power-to-weight ratio, allowing it to winch casualties safely. All three types are fitted with twin-engines for safety and the added power they provide.

BO 105CB	626 kW (840 hp.)
AS 355 ECUREUIL 2	604 kW (810 hp.)
A 109K2	942 kW (1,263 hp.)

Air ambulances around the world

■ **SA 365N DAUPHIN 2:** Operated by the privately-funded company AirEvac, the Dauphin is used in major cities for medical evacuation.

■ **AS 350B ECUREUIL:** This AS 350 is seen operating for medevac company SAMU in France. The French police also use the Ecureuil.

■ **BK 117:** Operated by Life Flight on behalf of Stamford University Hospital, Connecticut, this BK 117 is specially equipped for medical duties.

■ **A 109K2:** Equipped with a rescue winch and skis, this A 109K2 is ideally suited to its mountain rescue duties in the Italian Alps.

McDONNELL DOUGLAS

DC-9

● Short- to medium-haul airliner ● Worldwide service ● New developments

McDONNELL DOUGLAS **DC-9**

◄ High-altitude cruise
Fitted with a long, clean swept wing, the DC-9 has economic, high-speed cruise capabilities. By mounting the wing low down the designers ensured the wing spars passed beneath the cabin floor.

Canadian colours ▶
Air Canada is typical of the airlines which have used the DC-9 to develop jet services on short- to medium-haul routes. The aircraft has proved efficient and reliable.

◄ Long Beach line-up
DC-9s await delivery from the McDonnell Douglas Long Beach plant. Several airlines bought the DC-9, but ultimately it lost out to the Boeing 737.

▼ DC-9 in Britain
As newer MD-80/90-series machines and other aircraft take its place, the DC-9 is becoming a less common sight around Europe.

▼ Soldiering on
Some older DC-9s require anti-noise and pollution modifications if they are to remain in service.

The Douglas DC-9 is among the most familiar aircraft in the world. More than 700 short- to medium-range DC-9s, together with later-generation derivatives which bear 'MD' (for McDonnell Douglas) designations, ply the world's airways. The DC-9 is often compared with the more numerous Boeing 727 and 737, but it began its career two years earlier than these aircraft. The pilots who fly the DC-9 regard it as the best aircraft in its class.

▲ Since its launch in April 1963 the DC-9 has continued the tradition of the DC-3, giving reliable and cost-effective service to operators around the world.

FACTS AND FIGURES

➤ Delta Airlines placed an order for DC-9s in April 1963, before the first aircraft had flown.

➤ The prototype for the DC-9 series made its initial flight on 25 February 1965.

➤ About 740 DC-9s remain in operation, most of them on US airline routes.

➤ Most DC-9s were offered in freight, convertible and passenger/freight configurations.

➤ Only about 100 DC-9s still fly routes within Europe.

➤ Although the DC-9 is narrow-bodied, Douglas gave it a wide-body look interior.

PROFILE

Setting new standards

With its low wing, a distinctive T-tail and twin engines astride the rear fuselage, the Douglas DC-9 established a winning design formula. The DC-9 was the first short- to medium-range jetliner to enter regular service, and over three decades of passenger flying it has amassed a fine record for both service and safety.

The original DC-9 design was manufactured in several versions with different dimensions, runway capabilities and passenger capacities. It is one of the most popular

airliners in the world and the basic design has paved the way for the more advanced MD-80/90 series, which is based on the original DC-9 configuration.

Since its first income-earning passenger flight with Delta Airlines on 8 December 1965, the DC-9 has remained popular with crews and passengers. The aircraft has responsive controls and is fairly inexpensive to maintain and operate. Many of the oldest DC-9s are still in service, and, with modifications to make them quieter, are likely to continue to fly for many years to come.

Right: When Pratt & Whitney developed the more powerful JT8D-15 and JT8D-17 turbofans, McDonnell Douglas produced the larger 139-seat DC-9 Series 50.

Below: A McDonnell Douglas DC-9 Series 40 development airframe flies over the Queen Mary. The first Series 40 aircraft was delivered in 1968.

DC-9 Series 30

Type: short- to medium-range airliner

Powerplant: two 62.3-kN (14,018 lb.-thrust) Pratt & Whitney JT8D-7 turbofan engines

Maximum speed: 926 km/h (575 m.p.h.)

Maximum cruising speed: 821 km/h (510 m.p.h.)

Range: 2775 km (1,724 mi.) at long-range cruising speed of 821 km/h (510 m.p.h.)

Service ceiling: 10,180 m (33,400 ft.)

Weights: empty 24,011 kg (52,935 lb.); maximum take-off 44,450 kg (97,995 lb.)

Accommodation: two pilots, flight engineer and 105 passengers; 115 passengers may be carried with limited facilities

Dimensions:
span	28.47 m	(93 ft. 5 in.)
length	36.37 m	(119 ft. 4 in.)
height	8.38 m	(27 ft. 6 in.)
wing area	92.97 m²	(1.000 sq. ft.)

DC-9 SERIES 30

In the 1970s Douglas developed versions of the Series 30 with more powerful JT8D engines, higher weights and auxiliary fuel tanks. These models were popular with European charter airlines.

Although only one main passenger entrance and exit door is available, two additional exits, above the left side wingroot, are available in an emergency. Each exit is equipped with an inflatable emergency escape chute.

Douglas produced the DC-9 to compete with the BAC One-Eleven, which was selling very well in the United States. The machines looked very similar, although the rear fuselage area was different. In the One-Eleven this area tapered, while in the DC-9 it was of near constant diameter, allowing five-abreast seating throughout the whole cabin length. This meant that the DC-9 could carry more passengers and offered greater flexibility than the One-Eleven.

To ease passenger loading at poorly equipped airports, a retractable airstair is fitted in the forward cabin doorway. This is the only passenger entrance.

A narrow, swept wing is efficient but produces high landing speeds. For good field performance the wing is equipped with leading-edge slats and large flaps.

Mounting the engines on the rear fuselage helps to keep cabin noise to a minimum and also allows a short undercarriage to be used. This was important as the DC-9 had to fly from less-developed airports with limited ground handling equipment.

The rear-mounted engines dictate the use of a high-set tail, or 'T-tail', which keeps the control surfaces clear of the jet blast. The tailplane of the DC-9 is all-moving for trim and has elevators for pitch control.

ACTION DATA

MAXIMUM CRUISING SPEED

Boeing's Model 737 was slightly faster than the DC-9, but it flew two years later and initially had an uphill struggle to win orders from the Douglas jet. Speed over short sectors is important to reduce journey times for passengers.

DC-9 SERIES 40	903 km/h (561 m.p.h.)
MODEL 737-200	927 km/h (576 m.p.h.)
ONE-ELEVEN SERIES 500	871 km/h (541 m.p.h.)

PASSENGER LOAD

Both the DC-9 and 737-200 were developed into variants which could accommodate more passengers than shown here. The BAC One-Eleven had reached its maximum capacity with the Series 500 and having inspired the DC-9, it lost out to it.

DC-9 SERIES 40	125
MODEL 737-200	130
ONE-ELEVEN SERIES 500	119

MAXIMUM RANGE

Learning from the experience of short- to medium-haul airliners already in service, Boeing was able to develop an aircraft more suited to the emerging needs of the market. Its 737-200 offered appreciably better range than the DC-9 Series 40, but was fitted with a similar number of seats.

DC-9 SERIES 40 2710 km (1,684 mi.)

MODEL 737-200 4075 km (2,532 mi.)

ONE-ELEVEN SERIES 500 3458 km (2,149 mi.)

DC-9s in many colours

■ **DC-9 SERIES 20:** This special 'hot-and-high' variant, used only by SAS, combined the short fuselage of the Series 10 with the long-span wings and more powerful engines of the Series 30.

■ **DC-9 SERIES 30:** With its 115-seat capacity, long-span wings giving efficient cruise and powerful engines in sound-treated nacelles, the Series 30 outsold all other DC-9 models.

■ **C-9 SKYTRAIN II/NIGHTINGALE:** USAF and US Navy aircraft have been used in the aeromedical, transport and VIP transport roles. Two passenger/cargo aircraft were supplied to Kuwait.

McDonnell Douglas

DC-10

● Wide-body transport ● Medium- and long-range tri-jet

BRITISH CALEDONIAN

O ne of the original three wide-body aircraft (the others being the Lockheed TriStar and the Boeing 747), the McDonnell Douglas DC-10 is a giant of air commerce. The aircraft has lived down an early tainted reputation to become a stalwart of the world's passenger routes and the inspiration for a family of jets which continues today with the state-of-the-art MD-11.

▲ Compared to the Boeing 747, the DC-10 has a roomy cockpit which is much appreciated by its crews. The majority of those with experience of all three first-generation wide-bodies prefer to fly the DC-10.

McDonnell Douglas DC-10

▼ **Air Force tanker**
Using the DC-10 airframe, McDonnell Douglas produced the KC-10 Extender for the US Air Force. This versatile aircraft can transport huge cargoes and refuel other aircraft in flight.

▲ **Prototype tri-jet**
The prototype of the DC-10 lifts off from Long Beach on its maiden voyage. Despite a series of early crashes, the DC-10 matured as a world-beating airliner.

▼ **Flying saloon**
The wide-body fuselage of the DC-10 allowed designers of aircraft interiors to provide spacious bars for first-class passengers.

▲ **Global travel**
In the long-range Series 320 version, the DC-10 could span the globe. Air New Zealand used it for a round-the-world service.

Best-seller ▶
The DC-10 proved very attractive to a wide range of airlines who wanted a prestige wide-body airliner without the huge capacity of the Boeing 747.

FACTS AND FIGURES

➤ The DC-10 was originally designed to enter a US Air Force competition for a military heavy-lifter, eventually losing out to the massive Lockheed C-5 Galaxy.

➤ The third engine mounted in the tail is supported by just four forgings known as 'banjo rings' – each weighs only 204 kg (250 lb.).

➤ DC-10 customers could choose between the GE CF6 engine or the PW JT9D.

➤ The Series 15 had more powerful engines for take off at 'hot-and-high' airports.

➤ Thanks to some well-publicised crashes, early DC-10s acquired an unearned reputation for unreliability.

PROFILE

Trans-oceanic tri-jet

In Germany both Lufthansa and Condor were staunch supporters of the DC-10's abilities.

When it first flew in 1970, the DC-10 was a brave step into the unknown. The three huge turbofans which powered it were themselves a new concept, and the tri-jet configuration, with one engine held high on the tail, was equally novel. Airlines flocked to the new design, and Douglas seemed to have scored a runaway success.

Success soon turned to tragedy when a spate of catastrophic accidents seriously damaged the aircraft's reputation. The name DC-10 became a household name for all the wrong reasons. However, the faults which had caused the crashes were fixed and the aircraft started to claw back its otherwise excellent reputation.

The airlines kept buying the DC-10 because it was so good, and since then it has shown exemplary performance, reliability and economy. Now in the twilight of its career, many still serve on passenger and cargo-hauling duties, while the tri-jet configuration and basic design goes on in production as the MD-11, a radically upgraded and modernised version.

Hugely powerful engines are needed to haul the DC-10 and its load into the air. Federal Express aircraft use the General Electric CF6 turbofan.

DC-10 Series 30

Type: long-range airliner and freighter

Powerplant: three 227.52-kN (48,100-lb.-thrust) General Electric CF6-50C high-bypass turbofans

Cruising speed: 920 km/h (570 m.p.h.)

Range: 7500 km (4,270 mi.) with max. payload

Service ceiling: 10,810 m (35,465 ft.)

Weights: operating empty 121,200 kg (2267,200 lb.); maximum loaded 263,000 kg (559,000 lb.)

Passengers: up to 405 passengers maximum; 323 passengers in typical two-class configuration; 293 passengers in three classes

Dimensions:
span	50.40 m (161 ft. 4 in.)
length	55.50 m (181 ft. 5 in.)
height	17.70 m (58 ft.)
wing area	367.70 m² (3,921 sq. ft.)

DC-10-10FC

The DC-10-10FC is a specialised freight version with a huge door in the side of the cabin. Rapid delivery specialists Federal Express bought a fleet to whisk parcels across America and around the world on a 24-hour delivery service.

The cabin of the DC-10 is 41.45 m (136 ft.) long, and together with the underfloor cargo areas allows the DC-10F to carry an astonishing 80,000 kg (176,370 lb.) of cargo on long-haul flights. The load is usually mounted on pallets, 30 of which can be carried in the main cabin alone.

Two pilots and a flight engineer fly the DC-10, although a freight version also carries loading specialists.

N303FE

The DC-10 differed from other tri-jets in having its third engine built into the tail rather than the rear fuselage.

Long-range versions of the DC-10 weigh considerably more than the short-range versions and consequently need an extra undercarriage leg to support the extra weight. This is located between the two mainwheels.

Federal Express has a huge fleet of parcel-carrying aircraft, ranging from small Cessna lightplanes to the monster DC-10 and MD-11.

ACTION DATA

CRUISING SPEED

Although the tri-jets are less powerful than the 747, having only three engines in place of four, they are only marginally slower than the big Boeing jet.

MODEL 747-200		980 km/h (610 m.p.h.)
L-1011 TRISTAR		925 km/h (575 m.p.h.)
DC-10		920 km/h (570 m.p.h.)

CAPACITY

By widening the fuselage to allow passengers to be seated eight, nine or even 10 abreast, the first generation of wide-body jets doubled the number of passengers that an aircraft could carry.

MODEL 747-200 — 365 passengers

L-1011 TRISTAR — 280 passengers

DC-10 — 300 passengers

RANGE

Although often used for medium- and even short-haul work, the DC-10 comfortably outranges the preceding generation of jets. Only the larger 747 with its bigger fuel load has better long-range performance.

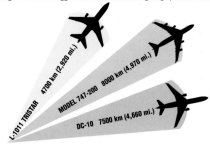

L-1011 TRISTAR 4700 km (2,920 mi.)

MODEL 747-200 8000 km (4,970 mi.)

DC-10 7500 km (4,660 mi.)

Douglas dynasty

■ **DOUGLAS DC-2/DC-3 (1930s):** These were the first stressed-skin airliners. Built in huge numbers, they were the foundation of modern air transport.

■ **DOUGLAS DC-4/DC-6/DC-7 (1950s):** A logical development of the DC-3, these four-engined airliners introduced long-range capability.

■ **DOUGLAS DC-8 (1959):** The highly successful DC-8 was, in stretched form, the world's largest airliner until the arrival of the Jumbo Jet.

■ **McDONNELL DOUGLAS DC-9 (1965):** The DC-9 and its advanced successors are some of the quietest and most economical short-haul airliners in service.

McDonnell Douglas
MD-11

● Successor to the DC-10 ● Electronic 'glass' cockpit ● Long range

As a modern development of the DC-10, McDonnell Douglas was certain the MD-11 would be highly successful. An all-digital flightdeck and new levels of passenger comfort made the aircraft attractive at a time when many airlines were looking to renew their fleets. Early deficiencies in range and the ailing fortunes of McDonnell Douglas, however, have robbed the MD-11 of the success it deserves.

▲ It is not known whether the MD-11 will survive as an airliner following the merger of McDonnell Douglas and Boeing. It is in direct competition with the Boeing 747, 767 and 777 wide-bodied airliners.

McDonnell Douglas MD-11

▲ **Six-screen cockpit**
Each member of the flightcrew has three screens, which display all flight information in multi-colour.

▼ **Shiny tri-jet**
Development MD-11s and those of American Airlines fly in a polished natural-metal finish.

▲ **On the way to Taipei**
Taipei-based China Airlines received the 100th MD-11 to come off the McDonnell Douglas Long Beach production line. At least 10 companies in America and Europe supply major components for the MD-11.

▼ **Delta MD-11 at Gatwick**
Although MD-11s belonging to American Airlines are familiar visitors to the UK, those operated by Delta Air Lines are rare. This Delta MD-11 was seen at Gatwick in 1997.

▲ **MD-11 in Hong Kong**
Hong Kong has become a centre of MD-11 operations with several Far Eastern airlines. The Pacific Rim is experiencing a huge growth in air transport, especially of cargo, and MD-11Fs are likely to play an important part.

FACTS AND FIGURES

➤ The first flight of the MD-11 was made on 10 January 1990 and five aircraft were used in the flight-test programme.

➤ The MD-11 is 5.66 m (18 ft. 7 in.) longer than the DC-10 and has about 50 more seats.

➤ In mid-1997 McDonnell Douglas was clearing a final backlog of orders.

➤ Specially converted, second-hand MD-11s are proving to be exceptionally useful in the pure-freighter role.

➤ In all-freight configuration the MD-11 has a maximum payload of 93304 kg.

➤ Federal Express is updating a number of DC-10s with MD-11 cockpit systems.

PROFILE

Douglas' last commercial aircraft?

During the mid-1980s McDonnell Douglas depended on sales of its wide-bodied MD-11 to keep the company alive as a supplier of large commercial aircraft. Unfortunately, early problems and the uncertain financial position of McDonnell Douglas meant that few orders were forthcoming.

Easy to distinguish from the DC-10, the MD-11, with its upturned winglets, introduced advanced engines and offered improved range, fuel efficiency and comfort. But when McDonnell Douglas was taken over by the Boeing empire, the future of its aircraft initially looked bleak. When details of the merger were finalised however, it became clear that Boeing were obliged to keep the basic MD-11 design alive.

Although the type is providing excellent airline service and new commercial customers would be easy to find, Boeing will probably develop the aircraft into a next-generation tanker-transport, possibly to replace the USAF's ageing fleet of KC-135 Stratotankers. In this way, competition with Boeing's established long-range airliners will be avoided.

By late-1997 Japan Airlines (JAL) was operating a fleet of 10 MD-11s. JAL gives its aircraft unusual names, with the MD-11s being known as the 'J Bird'. A total of 183 MD-11s were ordered worldwide and are likely to serve for many years.

MD-11

A number of airlines received the MD-11 and the majority are very pleased with its performance. From its inception, the aircraft faced stiff competition from Airbus Industrie and Boeing airliners.

The large fin gives the MD-11 excellent stability in the horizontal axis. A dual-section rudder provides directional control.

In common with most contemporary airliners, the MD-11 features range-extending winglets. Those of the MD-11 extend above and below the wingtip.

With a maximum internal width of 5.71 m (19 ft. 9 in.) the cabin allows nine-abreast seating. Plans for a twin-engined, small-fuselage derivative, the MD-20, have been abandoned.

Modern technology allows long-range operation of the MD-11 with only two flightcrew. Two observers may also be accommodated in the cockpit.

Customers may specify either Pratt & Whitney PW4460 or General Electric CF6-80C2D1F turbofans. Plans to develop a Rolls-Royce Trent 650-powered version were abandoned.

Composite materials form a significant part of the MD-11 airframe, including most of the control surfaces, engine inlets and other nacelle components, and wing/fuselage fillets.

One or two optional fuel tanks, each of 7472 litres (1,974 gal.), can be fitted in the forward, underfloor cargo hold. This extra fuel is carried at the expense of freight, but extends the MD-11's range considerably.

A centre fuselage undercarriage leg, as fitted to later DC-10s, spreads aircraft weight more evenly on runways and allows greater take-off weights.

The MD-11 has less sweepback on its tailplane and a more efficient aerodynamic design than the DC-10. In addition, 7571 litres (2,000 gal.) of fuel are carried in a trim tank.

MD-11

Type: long-range airliner

Powerplant: three 266.9-kN (60,042-lb.-thrust) Pratt & Whitney PW4460 or 273.57-kN (61,542-lb.-thrust) General Electric CF6-80C2D1F turbofans

Maximum speed: 945 km/h (586 m.p.h.) at 9450 m (31,000 ft.)

Range: 12,569 km (7,793 mi.) with 323 passengers

Weights: operating empty 131,035 kg (277,500 lb.); maximum take-off 273,289 kg (602,500 lb.)

Passengers: up to 410 passengers maximum; 323 in typical two-class configuration; 293 in three-class configuration

Dimensions:
span	51.77 m (169 ft. 6 in.)
length	61.24 m (200 ft. 10 in.)
height	17.60 m (57 ft. 7 in.)
wing area	338.90 m² (3,648 sq.ft.)

ACTION DATA

PASSENGERS

Although the MD-11 can seat 410 passengers in a single-class layout, 323 in a two-class layout is more realistic. The TriStar offers a similar capacity, but the Il-96 seats only 235 in a mixed layout.

MD-11	410 passengers
Il-96-300	300 passengers
L-1011 TRISTAR 100	400 passengers

MAXIMUM SPEED

Speed is important for an airliner as passengers want the shortest possible journey time. A programme of improvements has increased the efficiency of the MD-11 by reducing drag and increasing power, thereby giving an impressive speed performance.

MD-11	945 km/h (586 m.p.h.)
Il-96-300	900 km/h (558 m.p.h.)
L-1011 TRISTAR 100	925 km/h (574 m.p.h.)

THRUST

Modern, powerful and efficient turbofans give the MD-11 long range and good field performance. Early plans to offer a Rolls-Royce Trent 650-powered version were abandoned as the perceived demand did not warrant the financial investment necessary.

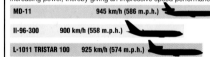

MD-11	Il-96-300	L-1011 TRISTAR 100
821 kN (180,123-lb.-thrust)	624 kN (140,375-lb.-thrust)	561 kN (126,203-lb.-thrust)

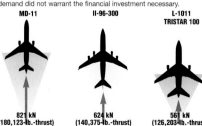

Tri-jet design

■ **HAWKER SIDDELEY TRIDENT:** In 1957 de Havilland began the design of the Trident to meet airline requirements for a 965-km/h (600-m.p.h.) short-haul airliner.

■ **LOCKHEED L-1011 TRISTAR:** Designed to match the requirements of American Airlines for a short- to medium-haul airliner, the Tristar was powered by Rolls-Royce engines.

■ **McDONNELL DOUGLAS DC-10:** Aimed at the same American Airlines specification as the Tristar, the DC-10 had a very similar configuration.

■ **TUPOLEV Tu-154 'CARELESS':** This medium- to long-range transport seats up to 167 passengers and remains in widespread service, especially in former Soviet countries.

McDonnell Douglas

MD-80

● Medium-range airliner ● DC-9 successor

McDonnell Douglas has
*persisted with its highly successful T-tail,
rear-engine airliners. The MD-80 series has
sold well around the world, despite fierce
competition from Boeing and Airbus.*

Beginning life as the DC-9, this
twin-engine airliner quickly became
popular on short- to medium-haul
routes. It sold well to carriers worldwide and
was developed into various different series
with configurations tailored to customer
requirements, this usually being achieved by
ever-longer fuselage 'stretches'. When the
Douglas Aircraft Company was restructured
in 1983, the DC-9 Series 80 became the
'new' MD-80.

▲ Sales success
*The MD-80 has sold well in the
U.S., where American Airlines
ordered more than 100 in the 1980s
as part of the largest order ever
placed for commercial aircraft.*

▲ Unducted fan
*In the 1980s, as oil prices rose,
fuel economy became a major
consideration for airlines.
McDonnell Douglas tested the
MD-UHB, featuring an unducted
fan engine which proved to be
efficient and quiet.*

▲ Ever-changing design
*The original DC-9 design was so sound that it
spawned the subsequent MD-80, MD-90 and MD-
95 series. Simple structural stretches and improved
engines have kept design costs low and yet still
produced world-beating airliners. The last 30 years
have shown that it is the ultimate 'rubber airplane'.*

▲ Economic performer
*Aéropostal of Venezuela flies the 165-seat MD-83,
which has a cost per seat-mile rate 12 percent
lower than its twin- and tri-jet competitors.*

Island-hopper ▶
*A highly-durable airframe is vital for high-intensity
routes. Multiple take-offs and landings test
durability, and the MD-81 passes with flying colors.*

FACTS AND FIGURES

➤ In April 1985, McDonnell Douglas signed
an agreement with China to have MD-
82s assembled in Shanghai.

➤ The larger MD-80 series can carry 26,276
litres (5780 gal.) of fuel.

➤ The MD series has sold particularly well
for domestic flights in the U.S.

➤ In 1989, the company tested an MD-80
with ultra-high-bypass (UHB) engines.

➤ When it entered service, the MD-83 was
the most fuel-efficient airliner in its class.

➤ The MD-90 Trunkliner is license-built in
China, with specially modified landing
gear for better rough-field performance.

PROFILE

The ever-changing "rubber" airliner

Left: The DC-9-80 was relaunched as the MD-80 in 1983. All subsequent aircraft in the series have adopted the 'MD' prefix.

Part of the "family" of McDonnell Douglas airliners, the twin-engine DC-9 (redesignated the MD-80 in 1983) was intended to serve short- to medium-haul routes and complement the long-range Douglas DC-8. Making its first flight on 25 February 1965, the DC-9 was in competition with the French Caravelle and British BAC One-Eleven. When it was 'relaunched' as the MD-80, the aircraft's main competitor was the Boeing 737, production of the earlier French and British rear-

engine airliners having stopped. Douglas had progressively stretched the DC-9's fuselage to allow space for more seats and extended the wingspan in the DC-9 Series 20, 30, 40 and 50.

Powered by re-fanned Pratt & Whitney JT8D-200 series turbofans, which offered more thrust yet were much quieter, the early MD-80s had a fuselage stretched by another 15 feet and a wing of greater span and chord than the Series 50.

The MD-80 began flight tests on 18 October 1979. The early

Right: The launch customer for the MD-80 was Swissair, which received its first aircraft in 1980. It was known then as the DC-9-81.

model was followed by the MD-81 and four more series models up to the MD-90, some of these later aircraft, reverting to a shorter fuselage and incorporating state-of-the-art systems, being intended to replace the old DC-9.

MD-87

Type: short- to medium-haul airliner

Powerplant: two 88.78 kN (19,950-lb.-thrust) Pratt & Whitney JT8D-217C turbofan engines

Maximum speed: 922 km/h (573 m.p.h.)

Service ceiling: 11,286 m (37,028 ft.)

Range: 4385 km (2,725 mi.)

Weights: empty 33,112 kg (73,000 lb.); loaded 63,370 kg (139,706 lb.)

Dimensions:

span	32.92 m	(108 ft.)
length	36.27 m	(119 ft.)
height	9.14 m	(30 ft.)
wing area	117.99 m²	(1,270 sq. ft.)

ACTION DATA

PASSENGER LOAD

The MD-83 and MD-90-30 both used the same stretched fuselage with a much increased passenger capacity than earlier models. The latest member of the family, the MD-95, will have a shorter fuselage comparable to that of the DC-9 Series 50.

DC-9-30 115

MD-83 172

MD-90-30 172

NOISE

As well as being more fuel-efficient, modern turbofans are much quieter in order to comply with strict noise regulations, especially for night operations. The DC-9 is noisy by today's standards, the MD-83 was one of the quietest airliners of the 1980s, and the even newer MD-90 with its IAE V2500 turbofans is quieter still.

DC-9-30 Maximum   **MD-83** Medium   **MD-90-30** Lowest

RANGE

The original DC-9 could hold less fuel than the "stretched" MD-83 and MD-90-30. More efficient engines and modifications to the wings have given the MD-83 and MD-90 much better fuel economy, allowing them to fly farther on the same amount of fuel.

MD-87

Finnair has long been a staunch McDonnell Douglas customer and was the first operator of the MD-87 in November 1987. The short-fuselage MD-87 can accommodate up to 130 passengers.

The MD-87 was the first of the MD-80 family to be fitted with an EFIS 'glass' cockpit and a head-up display, making the pilot's life much easier.

Following the success of the DC-9, the MD-80 series continues with rear-mounted engines, allowing a clean wing design. Its competitors, Boeing and Airbus, both use wing-mounted engines.

The most distinctive feature introduced in the MD-87 is the new re-sculptured aerodynamically-efficient tail and an extended low-drag tailcone.

A two-man crew is all that is needed to fly an MD-87; traditional flight engineer's tasks are automated.

To reduce development and testing costs, the same wing is used throughout the MD-80 series. The wing is an all-metal two-spar structure with riveted spanwise stringers. The wing trailing edge is fiberglass.

The main fuselage section has a galley at the end of each cabin, one toilet at the front and two at the rear. Three cargo doors to the underfloor holds are on the starboard side.

Power from the earliest DC-9 up to the MD-87 has been provided by continuously refined and upgraded versions of the excellent JT8 turbofan engine.

FINNAIR   *OH-LMA*   *md-87*

From DC-9 to MD-95

■ **DC-9 SERIES 50:** The Series 50 was the last version of the original DC-9 series and seated up to 139 passengers. Ninety-six Series 50s were built up to April 1981. Other features included new brakes and redesigned thrust reversers.

■ **MD-80:** Originally called the DC-9-80 'Super Stretch', the MD-80 family includes five different versions that are able to carry varying numbers of passengers over differing ranges. Structural and avionics improvements were also made.

■ **MD-90:** Intended as an advanced-technology follow-on to the MD-80, a major change was the adoption of the considerably more efficient and quieter IAE V2500 turbofan engines in place of the ageing Pratt & Whitney JT8Ds.

■ **MD-95:** This new version combines the short fuselage of the MD-87 (comparable to the DC-9-50) with the wing of the MD-80 and the avionics of the MD-90. New BMW Rolls-Royce BRT715 engines power the aircraft.

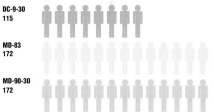

DC-9-30 3088 km (1,919 mi.)

MD-83 4839 km (3,007 mi.)

MD-90-30 4191 km (2,604 mi.)

McDonnell Douglas

MD-90

● Turbofan engines ● Medium-range airliner ● Advanced technology

The McDonnell Douglas MD-90 appeared in the 1990s as a high-technology airliner to replace ageing DC-9s and to compete with the successful Boeing 737. The MD-90 has enjoyed a respected commercial flying career, which is now being shortened by Boeing's 1997 purchase of the McDonnell Douglas company. The MD-90 is being discontinued to enable the firm to focus solely on the 737 in this class.

▲ Despite using some of the most advanced commercial aviation technology available, the MD-90 order-books have been revised downwards after initial interest in the design.

McDonnell Douglas MD-90

◀ **Sound design**
The MD-90 has the same fuselage length as the earlier designed MD-80. This greatly reduced the cost of the aircraft.

Graceful performer ▶
Banking away from the camera, an MD-90 displays its long elegant wingspan.

◀ **Delta direct**
An order for 50 examples from Delta Airlines and an option for a further 115 has now been significantly reduced by the operator. Responding to this, Boeing has decided to cancel the MD-90.

World market ▶
Although resembling many other twin-engined airliners, the MD-90 was most notable for its use of IAE V2500 turbofans.

◀ **Desert star**
Flying with Saudi Arabian Airlines these aircraft are occasionally used as VIP transports for Saudi royalty.

FACTS AND FIGURES

➤ The prototype for the MD-90 series completed its maiden flight on 22 February 1993

➤ Assembly of the first production MD-90 began at Long Beach, California.

➤ The MD-90-30T Trunkliner is fitted with a modified strengthened undercarriage.

➤ Shanghai Aircraft Manufacturing Factory (SAMF) was scheduled to build the MD-95. This deal has been cancelled.

➤ China is seeking at least 130 examples of the MD-90.

➤ Up to 20 MD-90s were to be assembled in China for its domestic market.

PROFILE

The MD-90, last of the DC-9 family

The low-wing, twin-engined MD-90 jetliner owes its elegant heritage to the successful Douglas DC-9/MD-80 series that are familiar on world airline routes. Thus, the MD-90's exterior has a familiar look, but on the inside this aircraft is different. The advanced-technology MD-90 uses new engines, power management system, cockpit instruments, and avionics.

The MD-90 (and the planned MD-95) were the most successful commercial aircraft conceived by McDonnell Douglas in California. Airline executives find them efficient and economical.

Passengers enjoy their quiet comfort. Pilots like the digital 'glass cockpit.' A robust career seemed in store when the manufacturer showed off the latest design at the Paris air show in 1991. Also promising were plans for co-production in China, where earlier MD-82/83 variants had already been manufactured for the Chinese airline market.

However, Boeing purchased McDonnell Douglas in 1997 and announced that, in order to allow it to concentrate on its 737 series, the much-admired MD-90 would be discontinued. However, the MD-95 is to remain in limited production.

Left: In an effort to increase sales, McDonnell Douglas undertook a world tour with the MD-90.

Above: The long fuselage of the MD-90 allows the aircraft to carry up to 172 passengers in relative comfort. Airline operators have praised the design and capabilities of the type.

MD-90-30

Type: twin-engine, medium-range airliner

Powerplant: two 111.21-kN (25,020-lb.-thrust) IAE V2525-D5 turbofan engines

Maximum speed: 844 km/h (523 m.p.h.) at 6960 m (23,000 ft.)

Maximum cruising speed: 809 km/h (502 m.p.h.) at 10,670 m (35,000 ft.)

Initial climb rate: 885 m/min (2,900 f.p.m.) at sea level

Range: 4200 km (2,604 mi.) with 153 passengers and fuel reserve

Service ceiling: 12,100 m (39,700 ft.)

Weights: empty 40,007 kg (88,015 lb.); maximum take-off 70,760 kg (155,672 lb.)

Accommodation: two pilots (flight deck); maximum of 172 passengers (standard 153), plus flight attendants

Dimensions: span 32.87 m (1017 ft. 10 in.)
length 46.51 m (152 ft. 7 in.)
height 9.33 m (30 ft. 7 in.)
wing area 112 m² (1,205 sq. ft.)

MD-90

Operated by Japan Air System, this is one of seven MD-90s that wear an elaborate and highly colourful paint scheme designed by the noted motion picture director Akira Kurosawa.

Pilots have found that, with the latest advanced flight controls, the performance of the aircraft is superb. The flight deck is fitted with electronic flight instruments and a complete full-flight management system. All this information is displayed to the pilots via two large cathode-ray tube displays.

The increased fuselage length allowed the total number of passengers to be increased to a maximum of 172. For general commercial flights however, this number is reduced to 153. Situated below the main fuselage deck is the larger lower-deck space for cargo and luggage.

With its tail adapted from the larger MD-87 the new MD-90 used a host of components from other airliners. This allowed the purchase cost of the aircraft to be greatly reduced.

As airline needs evolve, McDonnell Douglas intended to produce other MD-90s including variants with quieter engines and more fuel-efficient engines. Though interest in the MD-90 was promising further developments are now unlikely.

Retained on the MD-90 were the long slender wings from previous McDonnell Douglas airliners. Offering exceptional performance at high altitude, while allowing the aircraft to use relatively small airports, the design was a major breakthrough.

Internationally developed and manufactured, the V2500 turbofan engine represented one of the most advanced and fuel efficient jet powerplants for the time. The engine is a product of Pratt & Whitney in the USA and Rolls-Royce of Great Britain.

PROUD HERITAGE

Small wonder: Designed as a smaller companion to the DC-8, the McDonnell Douglas DC-9 (pictured below), entered service in the 1960s. The aircraft remains in use for short-haul routes and as a cargo carrier for courier operators.

'Stretched potential': Realising the requirement for a larger medium-range airliner, McDonnell Douglas developed the DC-9 with improved engines into the MD-80 (below). The aircraft operates around the world on domestic flights.

Customer demand: The go-ahead to develop the MD-95 (below) was given in July 1994. The aircraft is now the sole survivor of the company's airliner series remaining in production. The MD-95 will be fitted with Rolls-Royce engines.

Still going strong

AV-8B HARRIER II: With its unique abilities the Harrier II has seen extensive combat in recent conflicts, proving to be a capable attack platform.

C-17 GLOBEMASTER III: Fast becoming the standard transport aircraft within the USAF, the C-17 has served in Afghanistan and Iraq.

MD-11: Long-range coupled with a wide fuselage body are just two of the features that have allowed the MD-11 to become a success.

MD 520N: Representing a complete departure from normal helicopter design, the MD 520N has become an instant best seller.

McDONNELL DOUGLAS
MD 520

● **Advanced design** ● **No tail rotor** ● **Increased safety**

With its sleek shape and peppy performance, the McDonnell Douglas MD 520N is excellent for civil, commercial and police duties. The MD 520N combines a helicopter design from the 1960s (originally built for the military) with an evolving aerodynamic concept (the manufacturer's NOTAR, or 'no tail rotor' configuration) to produce the MD 520N, the helicopter everybody wants. As of 1996, McDonnell Douglas had sold 80 of the type.

▲ *Removing the tail rotor helps the NOTAR helicopter to operate from confined spaces. This has proved to be very convenient for commercial flight operations within large cities.*

McDONNELL DOUGLAS MD 520

Silent star ▶
The unique looks and performance of the MD 520 have meant that the helicopter has made numerous appearances in films and television programmes.

◀ Increased performance
Pilots have found adapting to the new helicopter's flying characteristics was easily accomplished without the need for extensive training.

▲ Staying afloat
Proving just as reliable as its earlier cousins, this MD 520N is equipped with two large floats.

▲ Police chase
Operating alongside a patrol boat, this MD 520N flies with a local sheriff's department in the USA.

◀ Proven design
Only minor modifications were required to install the NOTAR system on an existing helicopter's fuselage.

FACTS AND FIGURES

➤ In 1991 the Arizona Police Department, based in Phoenix, became the first operator of the MD 520N.

➤ This fine helicopter draws its basic design from the Vietnam-era Hughes OH-6.

➤ In September 1993, an MD 520N set a new Paris to London record of 1 hr 22 min.

➤ The NOTAR, or 'no tail rotor' concept is also used on the larger MD 630N and MD 900 Explorer helicopters.

➤ An MD 520N rescued four climbers from an 1800-m (5,600-ft.) mountain in Hawaii.

➤ Over 1,000 hours of testing was done before the MD 520N became operational.

PROFILE

Flying without a tail rotor

Pilots are delighted by the MD 520N, which springs aloft with a feisty enthusiasm. This is one helicopter that has plenty of power and carrying capacity, and it offers a quick response to the controls along with other excellent flying qualities.

Built in Mesa, Arizona, where McDonnell Douglas' helicopter division (originally the Hughes company) has decades of experience, the MD 520N is versatile and simply one of the world's best helicopters in the mid-sized class. It has proven popular with law enforcement officers, who value its agility and handling. The MD 520N can be equipped to carry a fascinating variety of police equipment, including searchlights and listening devices. Some police departments give the MD 520N a double-duty assignment, using it to stalk law-breakers but also to carry ambulance stretcher cases.

The MD 520N is a civilian spin-off of the military's OH-6 Cayuse (which differs in using a tail rotor, rather than the NOTAR blown-air system). A few military Cayuses have been converted to the NOTAR configuration, but only for America's special operations forces. It is rumoured that these helicopters have been utilised for recent covert operations around the world.

Left: High speed and the added safety of removing the tail rotor, suggest that the NOTAR type of helicopter will have a bright future ahead of it. Users of the MD 520 would agree.

Right: Heavily marketed as a potential replacement military helicopter, the MD 530N has undertaken various combat evaluations without success.

MD 520N

Type: five-seat civil helicopter

Powerplant: one 317-kW (425-hp.) Allison 250-C30 turboshaft engine

Max speed: 281 km/h (174 m.p.h.) at sea level

Cruising speed: 249 km/h (154 m.p.h.)

Initial climb rate: 564 m/min (1,850 f.p.m.)

Hover ceiling: 2753 m (9,030 ft.)

Range: 402 km (249 mi.) at sea level

Service ceiling: 4320 m (14,170 ft.)

Weights: empty 742 kg (1,632 lb.); maximum take-off 1519 kg (3,342 lb.)

Dimensions:
rotor diameter	8.3 m (27 ft. 3 in.)
length	9.8 m (23 ft. 2 in.)
height	3.01 m (9 ft. 10 in.)
rotor disc area	54.47 m² (586 sq. ft.)

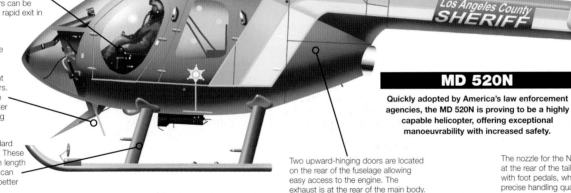

The heavily glazed cockpit offers the crew excellent visibility in all directions. For certain operations the doors can be removed allowing a rapid exit in an emergency.

A searchlight on the underside of the fuselage is now standard equipment on police helicopters. Protruding from the front is a cable cutter for protection during low level flying.

Skids are the standard landing equipment. These can be increased in length if required. Wheels can also be added for better ground handling.

MD 520N

Quickly adopted by America's law enforcement agencies, the MD 520N is proving to be a highly capable helicopter, offering exceptional manoeuvrability with increased safety.

Two upward-hinging doors are located on the rear of the fuselage allowing easy access to the engine. The exhaust is at the rear of the main body.

The nozzle for the NOTAR system is positioned at the rear of the tail boom. The pilot operates it with foot pedals, which give excellent and precise handling qualities.

ACTION DATA

MAXIMUM SPEED

The deletion of the tail rotor allows the MD 520N to have a high maximum speed compared to some other helicopters in its class. The lightweight Gazelle is as fast, but the MD 520N is a much more practical helicopter overall.

MD 520N	281 km/h (174 m.p.h.)
BO 105M	242 km/h (150 m.p.h.)
SA.342M GAZELLE	280 km/h (173 m.p.h.)

RANGE

Though a capable helicopter, the range of the MD 520N is poor when compared to the similar BO 105M. This has to be attributed to the new technology included in the design; later models will be better. The small Gazelle has exceptional range.

MD 520N 402 km (249 mi.)
SA.342M GAZELLE 670 km (415 mi.)
BO 105M 658 km (408 mi.)

SERVICE CEILING

Introducing the NOTAR concept to helicopter service has proved to be remarkably easy. Though it offers advantages in certain areas of flight, the ceiling of the MD 520N can only be described as average compared to some other designs.

MD 520N	**BO 105M**	**SA.342M GAZELLE**
4320 m (14,170 ft.)	5180 m (16,940 ft.)	4100 m (13,450 ft.)

The flying bugs

■ **HUGHES 500:** Originally developed by Hughes helicopters, this remarkable helicopter has seen numerous civil applications.

■ **OH-6 LOACH:** Having seen extensive use in Vietnam as a reconnaissance helicopter, the OH-6 continues in widespread service.

■ **MD 500E:** Developed for the executive helicopter market, this design has received numerous orders from across the world.

■ **500MD TOW DEFENDER:** A cheaper alternative to the AH-64 Apache, this helicopter is proving to be a highly capable attack platform.

McDONNELL DOUGLAS

EXPLORER

● NOTAR design ● Multi-role helicopter ● Police patrol

▲ The NOTAR concept removes one of the most troublesome parts of the helicopter, the tail rotor, which causes a great deal of noise, is very vulnerable to damage and needs extra maintenance.

The basic design of helicopters has changed remarkably little since the first practical machines flew in the 1940s. But McDonnell Douglas has taken a giant step in making rotary-winged flight both safer and quieter with its revolutionary NOTAR, or 'no tail rotor' concept. It was first used in the MD 520N and is now seen on the advanced composite construction Explorer. The NOTAR can even be reversed into trees or water and will still remain functioning.

McDONNELL DOUGLAS EXPLORER

▼ NOTAR family
McDonnell Douglas' NOTAR family has so far applied only to light helicopters, but this technology could also be relevant to much larger models.

▲ Tank killer
One possible role for the Explorer is anti-armour, which requires flying at tree-top height. Tail rotors can become entangled in trees, but the NOTAR system is much safer.

▼ Police squad
Law enforcement agencies operate the MD 520N with great success, with the low noise emitted by the NOTAR system being a great advantage.

▲ Rescue
NOTAR is useful for sea rescue missions, as it can operate even when immersed in water. Emergency floats can be fitted as optional extras for over-water operations.

▲ Safe and simple
It may seem strange for a helicopter not to have a tail rotor, but the NOTAR system uses almost no new materials or high technology, and is very simple.

FACTS AND FIGURES

➤ McDonnell Douglas estimates a worldwide demand for up to 1,000 NOTAR machines in the decade to 2005.

➤ The first NOTAR was declared ready after over 1,000 hours of test flying.

➤ By 1993 over 100 operators had taken out options on over 250 MD Explorers.

➤ In September 1993, an MD 520N flew the 215-km (130-mile) trip from Paris to London in a class record of 1 hour 22 minutes and 29 seconds.

➤ The first user of a NOTAR helicopter was the Phoenix Police Department, Arizona.

PROFILE

Goodbye to the tail rotor

Most of the noise and vibration generated by a conventional helicopter is produced by the tail rotor, which is designed to counteract the torque or twisting force caused by the main rotor.

The NOTAR, or NO TAil Rotor, system was developed in the early 1980s by McDonnell Douglas. It manages to dispense with the noise and complications by using an ingenious combination of aerodynamics and an air jet

produced by a fan buried in the root of the tailboom to provide directional stability and control. As well as being much quieter, NOTAR helicopters are safer: there is no risk of the tail rotor strikes that are the cause of many helicopter accidents.

The five-seat MD 520N, a derivative of the US Army's Vietnam-era Hughes OH-6 light observation helicopter, first flew in 1990 and most of the 70 examples delivered by

1995 have been sold to police departments and other law enforcement agencies.

McDonnell Douglas has also launched an advanced new NOTAR light-utility helicopter called the Explorer. Made largely from carbon fibre and composites, it first flew in 1992.

Military interest in the NOTAR system remains limited. However, the US Army conducted experiments with the concept for special operations, where its low noise was a useful asset.

MD 520N

The McDonnell Douglas Helicopters 520N is now in use with several private operators and police forces, and has proven the superiority of the NOTAR concept.

MD 520N

Type: eight-seat civil helicopter

Powerplant: two Pratt & Whitney Canada PW206B turboshafts delivering 469-kW (629-hp.) take-off power

Max cruising speed: 249 km/h (155 m.p.h.)

Initial climb rate: 853 m/min (2,800 f.p.m.)

Range: 600 km (373 mi.) at 1500 m (4,300 ft.)

Service ceiling: 5485 m (18,000 ft.)

Hovering ceiling: 3960 m (13,000 ft.) with ground effect

Weights: empty 1458 kg (3,214 lb.); maximum take-off 3035 kg (6,700 lb.)

Dimensions: rotor diameter 10.31 m (33 ft. 10 in.)
fuselage length 9.7 m (31 ft. 9 in.)
height 3.66 m (12 ft.)
width 2.79 m (9 ft 2 in.)
rotor disc area 83.52 m² (900 sq. ft.)

The main rotor system is a conventional five-bladed rotor with composite blades and an articulating hinged rotor head.

The fan is driven by a driveshaft via a secondary reduction gearbox, in a similar manner to a conventional tail-rotor driveshaft.

The port tail rotor fin moves to give directional control in autorotation, when power to the NOTAR fan is lost.

The engine exhausts through the rear fuselage, below the tailboom; this is to avoid interference of the hot engine gases with the NOTAR duct.

Yet another advantage of NOTAR is that the tailboom is slightly shorter than in a conventional helicopter. This makes it easier to manoeuvre the aircraft in confined spaces. The boom can even be reversed into foliage with care.

The flight controls of a NOTAR helicopter are identical to those of a conventional tail rotor craft. The one main difference is that the yaw control from the pilot's pedals is even more crisp and responsive than usual.

The MD 520 retains a conventional skid undercarriage similar to its distant ancestor, the Hughes 500. It is constructed of simple alloy tubing.

How NOTAR works

THE COANDA EFFECT: NOTAR works by utilising the Coanda effect. This is the tendency for air flowing over a curved area to follow the path of that surface. With the NOTAR concept, the tail rotor boom is the curved surface. NOTAR uses a fan to produce low-pressure air and a sleeve to control the airflow around the tailboom. This generates the anti-torque force. Instead of flowing evenly over the tailboom, it tends to flow towards the exiting air from the fan.

ROTATING SLEEVE: The air bleeds out through one side of a rotating sleeve. It then follows the profile of the tailboom, drawing more of the main rotor downwash over the slotted side than the unslotted side. This generates a force towards the slotted side, which opposes the rotor torque force.

TAIL CONE: Yaw control is generated by the rotating tail cone, which releases more air from the fan. This acts as a simple direct jet, and does not rely on the Coanda effect. In forward flight, most of the anti-torque is produced by the tail fins.

AIR INTAKE: Air is drawn in through a duct and blown by a simple fan.

ACTION DATA

MAXIMUM CRUISING SPEED

The efficient shape of the Explorer gives it a high cruise speed. The lack of a tail rotor also helps to reduce drag and wasted energy, as anti-torque force is produced by the fin in the cruise.

EXPLORER	275 km/h (170 m.p.h.)
EC-135	270 km/h (168 m.p.h.)
HAL-ALH	245 km/h (150 m.p.h.)

PASSENGERS

Both the Explorer and EC-135 are designed to be small multi-role machines, used for tasks such as city transport and police work, unlike the military ALH.

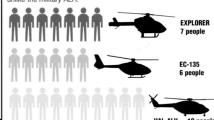

EXPLORER 7 people

EC-135 6 people

HAL-ALH 10 people

NOISE

The NOTAR system removes a major cause of noise, the conflicting airflow between a tail rotor and the main rotor. The EC-135 has a fan-in-fin, or fenestron, to help reduce this noise.

EXPLORER MIN

EC-135 MID

HAL-ALH MAX

McDonnell Douglas

MD500

● Single-engined turbine helicopter ● Top seller ● Civil OH-6

▲ The 500 family started out as the OH-6A Cayuse two-seat observation helicopter. The same US Army requirement also spawned the development of another very successful civil helicopter and one of the MD500's main competitors – Bell's Model 206 JetRanger.

The McDonnell Douglas MD500 is a 'great' of helicopter aviation – renowned for its economy, reliability and performance. The manufacturer tells cost-conscious operators that this aircraft offers the highest productivity per unit of any machine in its class. Whether supplying offshore oil platforms, helping the police in law enforcement or evacuating the sick by air, the MD500 is a bargain for its owners and a joy for pilots to fly.

PHOTO FILE

McDonnell Douglas MD500

Five-blade rotor ▶
The Hughes 500D introduced a five-blade rotor of smaller diameter to absorb the increased engine power.

▼ Small cabin
The original OH-6A was intended to carry just two crew; the rear cargo bay had two folding seats. Therefore, 500Ds had a fairly small cabin.

▼ Police patroller
This MD500E belongs to the Washington DC Metropolitan Police. It carries a powerful searchlight and additional antennas for a comprehensive radio fit.

▲ V-tail Hughes 500C
Initial civil versions of the OH-6 were the Model 500 and 500C. These can be distinguished from later variants by their V-tail and larger diameter, four-blade main rotor.

◀ MD500E
The main customers for this variant have been law enforcement agencies and utility operators in over 60 nations. This one carries a US registration.

FACTS AND FIGURES

➤ MD500s were built by RACA (Argentina), Breda Nardi (Italy), Korean Air and Kawasaki (Japan).

➤ Hughes was taken over in 1984: Hughes 500s became MD500s in August 1985.

➤ The 500 was the basis for NOTAR, the first helicopter sold without a tail rotor.

➤ First flown in September 1966, the MD500 carries 240 l (62 gal.) fuel compared to 231 l (60 gal.) in the military OH-6.

➤ An MD500 has been used by NASA to perform tests in engine and rotor noise.

➤ A military version of the 500D called the 500MD Defender has been sold widely.

PROFILE

The top-selling 500 family

D eveloped by Hughes Helicopters, which was purchased by McDonnell Douglas in 1984, the MD500 is a popular civil development of the US Army's OH-6 Cayuse observation helicopter.

Flown initially in February 1963, over 1,400 OH-6As were built for the US Army, serving with distinction in Vietnam. A few still remain in Air National Guard service.

Production of a commercial and export model, called the Hughes 500, began in 1968 and

was soon followed by the improved 500C. The 500D appeared in 1974 and had a more powerful engine, redesigned rotors and a T-shaped tail.

The last member of the family was the 500E, which had a reprofiled, pointed nose, replacing the familiar round cockpit allowing more cabin space. The 500th MD500E was delivered in April 1992.

Considered a very versatile helicopter, the MD500 has been popular with pilots as well as

cost-conscious operators. The military version, the Defender, could be armed with Stinger or TOW missiles and a Minigun pod. The related MD 520/530 family remains in production in Arizona.

Below: A major user of the 500 family have been police forces. This MD500E belongs to Oakland, California's Police Department and carries a spotlight under the cabin and wire cutters above and below the windscreen. Military MD500s are used in Colombia, Japan, Kenya, the Philippines and South Korea.

Above: Another popular use is that of executive transport, like the rival Bell 206. This smartly painted MD500E has extra clearance 'tall' skids.

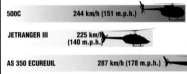

500C

Type: light utility helicopter

Powerplant: one 236-kW (316-hp.) Allison 250-C18A turboshaft engine

Max cruising speed: 244 km/h (151 m.p.h.) at 305 m (1,000 ft.)

Initial climb rate: 518 m/min (1,700 f.p.m.)

Range: 606 km (375 mi.)

Weights: empty 493 kg (1,085 lb.); maximum take-off 1361 kg (2,994 lb.)

Accommodation: two pilots and seven passengers or up to 800 kg (1,760 lb.) of freight

Dimensions:
main rotor diameter	8.03 m (26 ft. 4 in.)
length	9.24 m (30 ft. 4 in.)
height	2.48 m (8 ft. 2 in.)
main rotor disc area	50.60 m² (545 sq. ft.)

ACTION DATA

MAXIMUM SPEED

Speed has been one of the 500's major assets, giving it the edge over rivals like the Bell JetRanger. The AS 350 has a more powerful engine which allows an even better top speed.

500C — 244 km/h (151 m.p.h.)
JETRANGER III — 225 km/h (140 m.p.h.)
AS 350 ECUREUIL — 287 km/h (178 m.p.h.)

RANGE

Designed as a light observation helicopter for the US Army, the Hughes/MD 500, like the JetRanger and Ecureuil, had good range. This allowed longer times to be spent on patrol before the aircraft needed to return to a base to refuel. Later versions have greater fuel capacity.

500C 606 km (375 mi.)
JETRANGER III 730 km (298 mi.)
AS 350 ECUREUIL 730 km (413 mi.)

LOAD

The Hughes 500 has always had a reputation for good load-carrying capability due to its light weight which allows it to use its powerful engine to lift larger loads. The small diameter rotor of the 500D also improves manoeuvrability.

500C 800 kg (1,760 lb.)
JETRANGER III 680 kg (1,496 lb.)
AS 350 ECUREUIL 1030 kg (2,266 lb.)

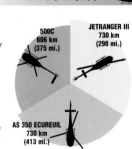

500D

This brightly decorated helicopter was a demonstrator for the British market. The MD 500 has gained a sound reputation for speed and lifting ability.

As it was originally intended as an army observation helicopter, the Hughes 500 had very good all-round visibility from the cockpit. Note that the windscreen extends up into the roof and that the side doors have especially large windows.

Most 500s are fitted with a set of either low or extended skids. Inflatable floats can also be fitted for operations over water. The front tip of each skid carries a navigation light.

Hughes 500Ds had a five-blade main rotor. The rotor hub has a curved fairing sometimes described as a 'coolie hat' fairing due to its shape.

The main rotor blades have an extruded aluminium spar hot-bonded to a wraparound aluminium skin. The flying controls are not hydraulically boosted.

The T-tail of the 500D and 500E was fitted to improve handling. It also improved the appearance of the helicopter.

G-BEJY

Allison's 250C engine, in various versions, powers all Hughes/MD 500 variants.

500Ds could be fitted with an optional four-blade tail rotor called the 'Quiet Knight' which, as the name suggests, was intended to reduce tail rotor noise.

The Hughes helicopter family

XH-17: The largest helicopter in the world in the early-1950s, the XH-17's rotors were powered by jet nozzles on each blade tip.

300C: Another design originally built for the US Army, the TH-55 Osage was a pilot trainer and later a very successful civil type.

AH-64 APACHE: The AH-64 is one of the most lethal attack helicopters in service, especially the latest Longbow radar-equipped variant.

MD520 NOTAR: The first helicopter to use the revolutionary NOTAR tail, the MD520 is already demonstrating much lower noise levels.

    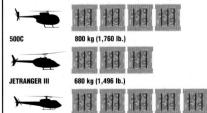

343

McDonnell Douglas

OH-6

● Equipped for night flying ● Light observation ● Police helicopter

▲ The OH-6 was used extensively by the US Army in Vietnam, armed with Miniguns and grenade-launchers. Many of the Border Patrol service's OH-6s are ex-Army machines in a new colour scheme.

Speeding along the border between Mexico and the United States at low level, the OH-6 Cayuse is exciting to fly. Hunting for illegal immigrants, the US Border Patrol service finds the OH-6 to be an ideal machine, fast and agile and providing a superb view of the terrain below from its bubble canopy. Patrolling the border in the agile and nippy OH-6 is a demanding task for these ex-Army pilots.

PHOTO FILE

McDonnell Douglas **OH-6**

▼ **Latest of the breed**
The sharp-nosed MD 500E is the latest of a long line that began with the OH-6. This MD 500E has a nose-mounted searchlight, and wears the badge of the Orange County Sheriff's Department.

▲ **Italian patrol**
The Italian air force also uses the OH-6. This one has a bubble-type observation window on the port side.

Baywatch ▶
Los Angeles County operates 10 MD 500s, which fly coastal patrols for smuggling ships and illegal immigration by sea.

▼ **Desert landing**
One of the less glamorous aspects of border patrolling is landing on empty stretches of desert to look for signs of life. Many OH-6s have the doors removed for cooling.

▲ **Highway patrol**
California's Police Highway Patrol department also uses the OH-6 (in its more modern MD 500 shape), to give warning of congestion on the freeways.

FACTS AND FIGURES

➤ The Hughes MD 500 Defender is an uprated version of the OH-6 airframe armed with TOW anti-tank missiles.

➤ The Model 500C could carry up to seven passengers or 776 kg (1,700 lb.) of cargo.

➤ The OH-6 was fitted with a new tail section and powerplant and became the MD 500.

➤ Hughes also developed a five-bladed OH-6 known as the 'quiet one' with a five-bladed main rotor.

➤ Hughes OH-6s and MD 500s were used by Argentina, Denmark, Mexico and Spain.

➤ Licence manufacture of the MD 500 was also undertaken by Kawasaki in Japan.

Patrolling with the Cayuse

First produced in response to a US Army request for a light observation helicopter (LOH), the Hughes OH-6 went to war in Vietnam soon after its introduction. It has also been sold to many civil users, but was overshadowed in the civil market by the Bell 206.

The OH-6 Cayuse really made its mark with the Border Patrol service in the United States. Flying in hot-and-high conditions along the desert border with Mexico, the Cayuse has the resilience to operate day after day in sand and heat. It offers an observer a superb view of the terrain below. The Border Patrol pilots are usually ex-Army, many of them having flown the OH-6 in Vietnam (where it was known as the 'loach', from the LOH designation).

A typical mission begins with a take-off from a small airfield only 15 km from the border, and check-in on the radio with a ground station. The pilot is alerted of unusual activity, and the OH-6 uses its spotlight to check out the border. There is no hiding from the 'flying eye', able to react at a moment's notice.

The Hughes OH-6 and MD 500 remain firm favourites with pilots for their superb handling. The classic egg-shaped fuselage remains in use on the new MDH NOTAR helicopters.

Government standard OH-6s are fitted with ARC-54 radios and the ASN-43 heading reference system.

The undercarriage is a simple, tubular steel skid, with integral shock absorbers.

The OH-6 has a side-by-side seating arrangement with full dual controls and two seats in the rear.

Clamshell rear doors provide access to the engine for maintenance.

The OH-6 uses a four-bladed main rotor and the main spar is hot-bonded to an aluminium skin. A trim tab is fitted to the end of each blade.

The fuselage of the OH-6 is of light alloy construction with the egg-shaped main cabin of semi-monocoque type. The shape gives good survivability in a crash as it tends to roll easily.

N67BP

The OH-6 is powered by an Allison T63-A-5A turboshaft engine.

Yaw control is effected through a simple two-bladed tail rotor. This OH-6 has a V-shaped tailfin, unlike the T-tail fitted to later models and MD 500s.

The OH-6 has a chin-mounted wire-cutter spike, potentially a life-saving piece of equipment for a helicopter that must fly at low level at night.

For night observation duty a powerful spotlight is fitted on the port fuselage.

OH-6A CAYUSE

The Border Patrol service operated four OH-6 helicopters, part of a mixed fleet of fixed- and rotary-wing aircraft responsible for assisting ground patrols in the border area with Mexico.

OH-6A Cayuse

Type: five-seat light multi-purpose helicopter

Powerplant: one Allison T63-A-5A turboshaft rated at 236 kW (315 hp.) peak power

Maximum speed: 241 km/h (149 m.p.h.)

Initial climb rate: 560 m/min (1,837 f.p.m.)

Combat radius: 611 km (379 mi.) at 1500 m (4,900 ft.)

Service ceiling: 2225 metres (7,300 ft.)

Weights: empty 520 kg (1,144 lb.); loaded 1090 kg (2,398 lb.)

Armament: provision for 7.62-mm Minigun or XM-75 grenade launcher on port fuselage

Dimensions:
rotor diameter	8.03 m (26 ft.)
length	9.24 m (30 ft.)
height	2.48 m (8 ft.)
rotor disc	50.6 m² (544 sq. ft.)

ACTION DATA

MAXIMUM SPEED

The OH-6 was one of the fastest light helicopters of its day, and could outrun the rival Bell 206. It was not as fast as the Aérospatiale Gazelle, which held several helicopter speed records for a short time in the early 1970s. All-out speed was not of primary importance to the designers of these helicopters.

OH-6A CAYUSE 241 km/h (149 m.p.h.)

GAZELLE 310 km/h (192 m.p.h.)

MODEL 206 225 km/h (139 m.p.h.)

RANGE

Range is an important consideration in light helicopters; all these machines were far superior to the older piston-powered aircraft. As all three were used by civil operators as well as the military, range meant potentially greater sales appeal. But despite its lack of range, the Bell 206 outsold its rivals in thousands.

GAZELLE 755 km (468 mi.)

OH-6A CAYUSE 611 km (379 mi.)

MODEL 206 549 km (340 mi.)

HOVER CEILING (IGE)

The hover ceiling is a product of the helicopter's weight and generated lift. Helicopters seldom ever fly at high level, and rarely ever reach their design ceiling after being test flown. Hover ceiling is measured both in and out of ground effect (the additional effect of sitting on a cushion of air that a helicopter experiences when near the ground).

MODEL 206 3900 m (12,800 ft.)

GAZELLE 3650 m (12,000 ft.)

OH-6A CAYUSE 3595 m (11,800 ft.)

Searching for illegal immigrants

CATCHING THE SWIMMERS: From its base at Brownsville Airport the OH-6 sets off at low level, flying across the town to the border, the Rio Grande river. The area offers many potential crossing points for illegal aliens. When a suspected sighting is made to the west of the town, the pilot circles slowly to give his observer the best view.

N

AREA OF SUSPECT ACTIVITY

BROWNSVILLE AIRPORT

RIO GRANDE RIVER

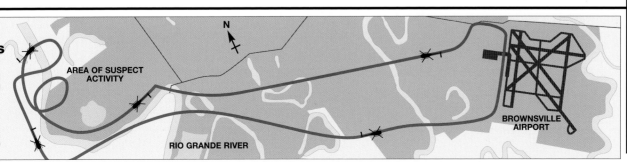

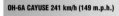

MIL

MI-6 'HOOK'

● Heavylift helicopter ● Speed record holder ● Heli-liner

S etting a trend for enormous gas turbine helicopters with massive load-carrying capability, the Soviet Union introduced the Mi-6 as a combined military/civil project in 1954. Intended primarily as a support vehicle for the air force's huge An-12 transport, the Mi-6 needed just two 'lifts' to equal the payload of the transport. Most Mi-6s were grounded in 1992, after a long service including wartime operations in Afghanistan and Africa.

▲ Mil's monster Mi-6 not only made every previous helicopter look minute, but it also proved a very viable and useful aircraft, unlike the later Mi-10 and Mi-12. Hence, it was exported widely and a handful are still flying.

MIL MI-6 'HOOK'

▲ Siberian giant
Transporting massive pieces of machinery for the oil industry was a common task for the Mi-6 in the 1960s.

▲ Long service
About 800 Mi-6s were built between 1957 and 1980. During the aircraft's busy life it ferried millions of passengers around the remotest regions of the USSR.

Troop truck ▶
With extra seating the Mi-6 could carry up to 90 troops, but it was rarely used in a tactical role as size made it vulnerable.

▼ Unique shape
The Mi-6 looked unique. It is an indication of the success of the design that the later Mi-26 has a similar configuration, but with no wings and an increased number of rotor blades.

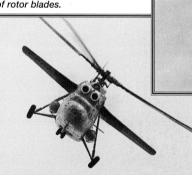

▲ Spacecraft recovery
Only the Mi-6 was big enough to carry the crew capsule from the Vostok space launchers. The wing was mounted at 15° to the fuselage and provided about 20 per cent of the lift when cruising. The wings could be removed for the 'flying crane' role.

FACTS AND FIGURES

➤ In 1961 the Mi-6 lifted 20117 kg to a height of 2738 metres and flew at 340.15 km/h over a 100-km circuit.

➤ The Mi-6P was a firefighting version with a water tank, but it did not have stub wings.

➤ By 1990 Aeroflot Mi-6s had carried 15 million tonnes and 12 million people.

➤ Mi-6 export customers included Algeria, Bulgaria, Egypt, Ethiopia, Iraq, Libya, Peru, Syria and Vietnam.

➤ The Mi-6R was a radio command post containing eight tonnes of equipment.

➤ The Mi-6's main rotor revolved clockwise at 120 rpm.

PROFILE

Mil's muscular 'Shestyorka'

During the 1950s the Soviets had industrial and military projects scattered across the country and the authorities faced huge problems in supplying them. It was for this reason that a fleet of large transport helicopters became necessary. The Mi-6 met the requirement from 1958.

Everything about the Mi-6 was large. Its engines were a giant leap in gas turbine technology as applied to heavylift 'flying crane' helicopters. It pioneered the use of supplementary wings for added lift and achieved an incredible performance for a machine in its weight class. Basically a freight carrier, military versions dominated the 800-plus production run which ended in 1981.

To cope with adverse weather conditions the Mi-6 had its own rotorblade de-icing system and an auxiliary power unit. The aircraft was known as 'Shestyorka' ('little six') by its crews. Variants included firefighters, military jammers, civil heli-liners and medevac aircraft. Military versions carried a machine-gun in the nose.

First flown in 1960, the Mi-10 was a developed 'flying crane'

Below: The Mi-6 carried loads such as oil drilling equipment, bulldozers, tractors and light artillery pieces.

Above: Although later Mils like the Mi-26 could lift more, they were not built in such large numbers as the versatile Mi-6.

version of the Mi-6, including the engines, gearboxes and stretched undercarriage. Not only was the Mi-6 the biggest helicopter in the world, it was also the fastest and had outstanding range.

Mi-6 'Hook'

Type: heavy-lift transport helicopter

Powerplant: two 4101-kW (5,495-hp.) Soloviev D-25V free-turboshaft engines

Maximum speed: 300 km/h (186 m.p.h.)

Range: 620 km (384 mi.)

Service ceiling: 4500 m (14,750 ft.)

Weights: empty 27,240 kg (59,928 lb.); loaded 42500 kg (93,700 lb.)

Armament: one (optional) 12.7-mm machine-gun in nose

Accommodation: flight crew of five and up to 90 troops or 41 stretcher cases

Dimensions:
main rotor span	35 m (115 ft.)
length	33.18 m (109 ft.)
height	9.86 m (32 ft.)
wing area	35 m² (377 sq. ft.)

MI-6 'HOOK'

Mi-6s were widely used in the Middle East, but almost all have now been retired. This helicopter was used by the Egyptian air force, which suffered from a lack of spares after the Soviets were expelled from the country.

For a helicopter the Mi-6 had an unprecedented equipment fit, including an autopilot. The flight deck had jettisonable doors on either side for the pilots and flight engineer. A navigator sat in the glazed nose and a radio operator was sometimes carried.

The massive gearbox weighed no less than 3200 kg (7,040 lb.). It also drove two 90-kVA alternators to feed the heavy load of electro-thermal de-icing systems and radios.

The five-bladed main rotor was based on an extruded steel main spar, with screwed-on aerofoil sections of duralumin. The blades were electro-thermally de-iced, and were connected to the head by conventional hinges and bearings.

Large clamshell doors made loading and unloading very easy. The main hold was 12 metres (39 ft.) long, had a volume of 80 m³ (61 cu. yds.) and included its own electric winch.

The tail rotor was a four-bladed AV-63B type with a steel spar and a Bakelite ply outer. Early versions had electro-thermal de-icing, which was replaced by alcohol in later models.

Big lifters in the West

AÉROSPATIALE SA 321F: The civil variant of the Super Frelon, the SA 321 is no longer in service. The military version is still used by France.

SIKORSKY CH-53: Still the biggest rotary machine built in the West, the CH-53 was a great success and is still in service in Germany.

SIKORSKY S-64: The West's answer to the Mi-10, the Skycrane was used extensively in Vietnam to recover shot-down UH-1s.

WESTLAND WESTMINSTER: Only two of these aircraft were ever built. It was cancelled in favour of the larger Fairey Rotodyne.

ACTION DATA

INTERNAL PAYLOAD

For sheer lifting capacity nothing could match an Mi-6. The Rotodyne also relied on wings, which limited its carrying capacity when taking off. The CH-47 had a smaller internal volume.

Mi-6 'HOOK' 12000 kg (26,400 lb.)

CH-47 CHINOOK 6300 kg (13,860 lb.)

ROTODYNE 4800 kg (10,560 lb.)

RANGE WITH PAYLOAD

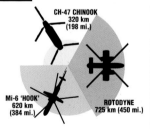

Another impressive feature of the Mi-6 was its range, a necessity in the vast expanses of the former Soviet Union. The Rotodyne was also very long ranged, but could not carry as much as the Mi-6. The Chinook was designed for shorter range operations.

CH-47 CHINOOK 320 km (198 mi.)

Mi-6 'HOOK' 620 km (384 mi.)

ROTODYNE 725 km (450 mi.)

MAXIMUM SPEED

These helicopters were all very fast, with the Rotodyne benefiting from extra engines and wings. The CH-47's twin rotors produced a large amount of thrust, whereas the Mi-6 relied on brute power.

Mi-6 'HOOK'	300 km/h (186 m.p.h.)
CH-47 CHINOOK	298 km/h (185 m.p.h.)
ROTODYNE	307 km/h (190 m.p.h.)

MIL
MI-8 'HIP'

● Assault transport ● Civil helicopter ● Gunship

A tough and resilient combat veteran, the Mil Mi-8 'Hip', and the closely related Mi-17, stands tall in its reputation as one of the most versatile helicopters in the world. The Mi-8 is the most widely used helicopter in service, and is cheap to run, easy to maintain and powerful. The 'Hip' is primarily a troop carrier and civil transport. Other roles include helicopter gunship, airborne command post, search and rescue and even communications jamming.

▲ One of the most enduring rotary designs ever, the Mi-8 has all the typical attributes of a Mil machine, combining strength and simplicity in a well-proven low-cost airframe.

MIL MI-8 'HIP'

▼ Shooting from the hip
The 'Hip-E' gunship version is one of the world's most heavily armed helicopters, and has been used extensively in Chechnya.

▲ Santa's sleigh
Even Santa Claus used the Mi-8 when travelling in distant areas of the Soviet Union. The Mi-8 was also vital to the Soviet oil industry, which explored in very remote areas.

Tourist flyer ▶
This Mi-8, belonging to Avialini Baltiski, flies tourists over St Petersburg on short pleasure flights in the summer.

▼ Assault transport
This Mi-8 of the Indian air force is landing troops close to the front. Soviet Mi-8s made thousands of air assaults in Afghanistan, and large numbers were shot down.

▲ KGB transport
Guarding the huge borders of the Soviet Union, the KGB needed a large number of Mi-8s to transport dog teams.

FACTS AND FIGURES

➤ More than 10,000 Mi-8s and Mi-17s have been built, with many hundreds being exported to more than 40 operators.

➤ The Mil Mi-17 is basically a Mi-8 with more power and a new tail rotor.

➤ The rare Mi-8PPA is a special communications jammer variant.

➤ The Mi-8 has fought in Afghanistan, Angola, Chechnya, Egypt, Mozambique and Nicaragua.

➤ The Czech Republic, Hungary and Russia use the 'Hip-G' command post version.

➤ The Mil Mi-14 'Haze' anti-submarine helicopter is derived from the Mi-8.

Helicopter workhorse to the world

Design of the Mi-8 'Hip' began in 1960. Unlike the earlier Mi-4 'Hound' which had its engine mounted in the nose, the Mi-8 has a more efficient shape with the turboshaft powerplant above the fuselage leaving maximum space for payload. Except on specialised models, large clamshell doors swing open at the rear fuselage.

Nearly a dozen versions of the Mi-8 and its upgraded Mi-17 derivative were used by Soviet forces and exported to Moscow's allies, and thousands of examples remain in service in

Russia and around the world. Despite the age of the basic design, the type remains in production and sales continue. From the Arctic tundra of Finland to the tropical jungles of Peru, the 'Hip' is always a formidable performer, whether dropping into a landing zone with a load of troops or flying scheduled airline or cargo services to remote settlements.

Military Mi-8s are often equipped to a high specification, including additional cockpit armour, infra-red jammers, chaff and flare dispensers

Mi-8s belonging to Interflug, former state airline of the DDR, have now all been retired.

and exhaust gas diffusers. The Mi-17 improved upon the original Mi-8 by introducing a titanium rotor head for greater strength, improved efficiency engines and a new gearbox.

MI-8T 'HIP-C'

The Mi-8 remains in service in very large numbers with Aeroflot's successor airlines in the former USSR, such as Baltiski, Baikal Avia, Orbi, Tajik Air and Tatarstan, as well as with many military air arms.

The Mi-8 was cheap enough to produce in thousands, giving the Red Army mass airlift capability.

The Mi-8 has a traditional rotor head with flapping hinges and bearings. The improved titanium rotor head of the Mi-17 needs less maintenance and is more bullet resistant.

Although slightly redesigned, the Mi-8's large five-bladed main rotor was also used by the later Mi-24 gunship. Like all Mil designs, it rotates clockwise when viewed from above. The rotors have an automatic ice detection and thermal de-icing system, essential for operations in Russian conditions.

In the Mi-8 the tail rotor is on the starboard side of the tail, but on the port side of the Mi-17.

The Isotov TV-2 engines of the Mi-8 are very similar to the TV-3 engines in the Mi-24 and Mi-17. The TV-3 proved more reliable and economical and dramatically improved performance in 'hot-and-high' conditions.

АЭРОФЛОТ 367H

CCCP-25852

The Mi-8 cockpit is surprisingly large. Israeli pilots flying captured examples in 1973 found that the machine had a totally different feel in flight to Western helicopters, and could easily outrun many of them.

Loading a Mi-8 is easy, thanks to the clamshell doors at the rear which can accommodate wide cargoes and allow infantry to exit very swiftly in an assault.

Mil's multi-role 'Hip'

Mi-8 'HIP-A': The first Mi-8 was the single-engined prototype that lacked power and only had a four-bladed main rotor.

Mi-8 'HIP-C': With two engines and five main rotor blades, the Mi-8 'Hip-C' became the main assault helicopter of the USSR.

Mi-8 'HIP-E': Probably the most heavily armed helicopter in service, the 'Hip-E' carried up to six pods of 32 rockets.

Mi-17 'HIP-H': The Mi-17 featured new engines, gearbox and rotor shaft and was a lot more powerful and economical than the Mi-8.

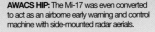

AWACS HIP: The Mi-17 was even converted to act as an airborne early warning and control machine with side-mounted radar aerials.

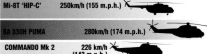

MIL

MI-26 'HALO'

● Largest production helicopter ● United Nations relief flights

◀ Subcontinent service
India has been the only export user and currently operates 10 examples, all with No. 26 Squadron.

▼ Commercial Mil
Mil has actively sought civilian customers; an Mi-26T variant is tailor-made for commercial use.

▼ Enormous capacity
The presence of these troops and a single jeep lend scale to the size of the Mi-26. The fuselage is as large as that of a C-130 Hercules and can accomodate up to 80 fully-equipped soldiers.

▼ Special requirement
A primary requirement prompting the design and development of this huge helicopter was for a machine able to carry substantial loads in vast, sparsely-populated areas, such as Siberia. The Mi-26 performs such tasks with ease.

◀ Continuing production
Although many Russian projects have fallen by the wayside due to a lack of funding, development of the 'Halo' continues, with new variants still emerging.

With the intention of surpassing the load-carrying capabilities of its mighty Mi-6 'Hook', Mil set about designing its Mi-26 'Halo' in the early 1970s. It was clear that the twin-rotor layout of the earlier V-12 had led to a developmental dead end, so Mil set out to produce a thoroughly conventional helicopter on a hugh scale, with a payload up to one and a half times greater than that of any previous rotary-winged type.

▲ Once again, Mil has entered the record books with the superb Mi-26 'Halo'. It is currently both the largest and the most powerful helicopter of its type in service anywhere.

FACTS AND FIGURES

➤ Flown for the first time in a hover on 14 December 1977, the Mi-26 was initially designated the V-26.

➤ Machined from titanium, the main-rotor hub is the largest in the world.

➤ External steps and handholds allow access to the tailboom and rotor.

➤ Variants include the Mi-26TZ tanker, which can carry 14040 litres (3,709 gallons) of fuel dispensed on the ground using 10 hoses.

➤ In the firefighting role, the Mi-26 can drop 7500 litres (2,000 gallons) of fire retardant.

➤ A special variant, designated Mi-26MS, is a fully-equipped airborne hospital.

PROFILE

Heavyweight 'Halo'

Using the world's only operational eight-bladed rotor system, and having a cabin cross-section similar to that of the Il-76T 'Candid' four-turbofan airlifter, the Mi-26 is truly a machine of superlatives.

With its eight rotor blades, the Mi-26 is able to handle its two 7,460-kW (10,003-hp.) turbines, with a rotor of smaller diameter than that of the Mi-6. Power is transferred to the rotor shaft by a gearbox of unique design. It is smaller than that of the 'Hook', but weighs 3,500 kg (7,720 lb.).

Its strength allows it to control the huge 90,000-kg (20,000-lb.) maximum torque of the engines.

A hook beneath the fuselage is stressed for slung loads of up to 30,000 kg (66,000 lb.). The principal motivation for the Mi-26 programme was support for exploration work in the remotest areas of Siberia, and a hook of such capacity is vital if heavy items of equipment are to be positioned in otherwise inaccessible areas. Such locations also require the highest levels of reliability, and 'Halos' often

Above: When the 'Halo' made its debut at Paris in 1981, the French had an apt nickname for it: 'Le monstre'.

operate under harsh conditions for up to a week without proper engineering support. As well as its many civilian roles, the Mi-26 is also employed by the Indian, Russian and possibly Ukrainian military.

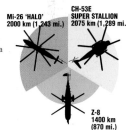

Above: Mi-26s have been actively used on United Nations humanitarian relief operations in recent years.

Mi-26 'Halo'

Type: heavylift civil/military transport helicopter

Powerplant: two 8,380-kW (11,237-hp.) ZMDB 'Progress' (Lotarev) D-136 turboshafts

Maximum speed: 295 km/h (183 m.p.h.)

Cruising speed: 255 km/h (158 m.p.h.)

Range: 2000 km (1,243 mi.) with auxiliary fuel; 800 km (497 mi.) with standard fuel

Service ceiling: 4600m (15,000 ft.)

Weight: empty 28200 kg (62,170 lb.); maximum take-off 56000 kg (12,350 lb.)

Payload: 20000 kg (44,100 lb.)

Dimensions:
main rotor diameter	32 m (105 ft.)
fuselage length	33.72 m (110 ft. 7 in.)
height	8.14 m (26 ft. 8 in.)
rotor disc area	804.25 m² (8,657 ft)

MI-26 'HALO'

This machine was one of the Soviet Frontal Aviation Mi-26s used during the clean-up of the Chernobyl nuclear power station in 1986. Later discovered to be radioactive, it was soon withdrawn from service.

At first glance, it would appear that the rotor design is very old fashioned and similar to that of its predecessor, the 1950s' vintage Mi-6 'Hook'. However, the head is extremely light and compact, and is the first in the world to carry eight rotor blades.

Unlike the main unit, the tail rotor unit was a completely new design and features five composite blades. The fin to which it is fitted incorporates a low-speed aerofoil section, which reduces load-bearing on the tail rotor, enabling better stability at cruising speed.

Rear access to the cavernous fuselage is provided by three clamshell doors: two hinge outwards, and the third incorporates a ramp, which can be lowered vertically.

At rest, the 'Halo' adopts a distinctive tail-heavy stance, similar to that of other Mil-designed helicopters. To protect the underside from damage when the helicopter is operating in 'hot-and-high' conditions, a heavy-duty tail skid is fitted.

ACTION DATA

POWER

No other helicopter can match the sheer power of the Mil Mi-26's twin turboshafts, which enable it to lift incredible loads. The nearest competitor is the 1960s' vintage Sikorsky Ch-53E Super Stallion, which is powered by three engines.

Mi-26 „HALO"	CH-53E SUPER STALLION	Z-8
16 560 kW	8268 kW	3468 kW
22 207 hp	11 087 hp	4650 hp

RANGE

Essentially a Chinese-built Super Frélon, the Z-8 has a surprisingly good range considering that it is an older design and is much smaller and less powerful than the other two giant machines.

Mi-26 'HALO' 2000 km (1,243 mi.)

CH-53E SUPER STALLION 2075 km (1,289 mi.)

Z-8 1400 km (870 mi.)

PAYLOAD

At present, the 'Halo' is able to carry the heaviest payload, though the giant Mi-12 holds the all-time record. The CH-53E is the West's largest heavy-lift helicopter.

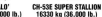

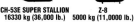

Mi-26 'HALO'	CH-53E SUPER STALLION	Z-8
24000 kg (53,000 lb.)	16330 kg (36,000 lb.)	5000 kg (11,0000 lb.)

Mil's milestone helicopters

MIL Mi-1: This little machine has the distinction of being the first series production Soviet helicopter of conventional configuration. Now a museum piece, it was a milestone in Russian design.

MIL Mi-8 'HIP': Numerically the most important European helicopter ever built, some 8000 examples have entered service over the years, with a number of operators around the world. Many remain in use.

MIL Mi-12 'HOMER': Only two examples of this, the largest helicopter ever, were constructed. The Mi-12 (or V-12) was powered by four engines; however, technical difficulties halted development.

MIL

MI-26 'HALO'

● Heavylift helicopter ● Largest rotor craft in the world

The Mil Mi-26 brings size and brute force to the bold adventure of taming the wildest terrain on our planet. To permit humans to tap the wealthy resources of inhospitable Siberia, Mil engineers produced the largest helicopter being used anywhere. They made it a flying powerhouse, able to get in and out of tight places in fearsome winter climates while carrying cargoes of record-breaking size and weight.

▲ It is the world's biggest helicopter, the size of the Lockheed Hercules. Flown by the Russian air force, it has been used to open up the trackless wastes of Siberia.

MIL MI-26 'HALO'

▼ Damage control
In the first panicked response to the disaster at Chernobyl, Mi-26s were used to dump tons of sand to smother the fires in the out-of-control nuclear reactor.

▲ Western visitor
The first sight of the giant Mi-26 was at Western air shows, but Russian operators are now pushing hard to market its unmatched heavylift capacity as a commercial proposition.

▶ Multi-role
With such a huge cargo hold, the 'Halo' can carry a wide variety of loads. Its maximum payload is 20 tons, and it can carry light armoured vehicles, oilfield equipment or more than 100 passengers.

▼ Wide body
With a fuselage the size of a C-130 Hercules, the Mi-26 is capable of carrying internally large loads which most, if not all, other helicopters would have to hoist as a slung load from external cargo hooks.

◀ Crewing the giant
Unlike Western helicopters, which have highly automated cockpits, the Mi-26 has a full four-man flight crew of two pilots, navigator and engineer.

FACTS AND FIGURES

➤ The fuselage of the 'Halo' is twice the size of a Douglas DC-3 transport.

➤ India was the only overseas customer for the 'Halo', purchasing 10 aircraft.

➤ The Mi-26 is larger inside than a C-130 Hercules, and is the biggest helicopter ever put into production.

➤ To ease freight handling, there are two 2500-kg (5,511-lb.) winches in the cargo hold.

➤ The circle created by the Mi-26's rotor has four times the area of the VS-300, an early helicopter.

➤ 'Halo' carries 30 times the payload of a light helicopter like the Bell JetRanger.

The world's biggest rotor craft

It represents one of the greatest advances in rotary-wing aviation. The Mil Mi-26 'Halo', first flown in 1977, boasts unbelievable strength and lifting power.

The Mil engineering team, experts at big helicopter design, took Russia by storm when their Mil Mi-26 began airline and military duties. Then the 'Halo' went to work, exploiting forestry, minerals and hydro-electric power in the frozen expanse of Siberia. The Mi-26 is so huge that it surprised no one when it picked up and moved a four-bedroom house.

The Mi-26 is big, but it is also a beauty. Two incredibly powerful engines drive its eight-bladed main rotor. Pilots love this friendly giant: it has a spacious flight deck at floor level with large windows bulged to permit a look at underslung loads, and TV cameras augment the pilots' all-round view. With the benefit of this amazing visibility, the crew have little difficulty in carrying out major chores with the Mi-26. One amazing feat of the 'Halo' was to fly over the burning Chernobyl reactor, dropping chemicals and concrete to try and staunch the radioactive flow.

Above: The Mil design bureau has long specialised in heavylift helicopters. One of the first to be seen in the West was the Mi-10 'Harke' flying crane.

Although the main rotor of the 'Halo' is smaller than that of the preceding 'Hook', its advanced design generates more lift.

MI-26 'HALO'

This heavylift helicopter is in service with the Russian air force, Aeroflot, the Ukraine, and the Indian air force.

Two 8380-kW (11,203-hp.) Lotarev turboshaft engines power the Mi-26. These deliver over 50 per cent more power than the three engines of the American Sikorsky CH-53E Super Stallion.

The Mil Mi-26 has been designed with the same internal cross-section as the Ilyushin Il-76 logistic freighter. At 3.2 metres square (34 sq. ft.), it can hold containers or medium-sized vehicles without any difficulty.

The eight-bladed rotor is of very advanced design and of lightweight but strong construction. It enables the Mi-26 to carry twice the load of its predecessors.

Currently utilising aluminium–lithium alloy in its rotors, the 'Halo' will be fitted with composite blades in the future.

CCCP-06141

АЭРОФЛОТ H-351

The 'Halo' is equipped with all the necessary systems to fly by day or by night, including a computerised flight/navigation system, automatic flight control and a weather radar in the hinged nosecone.

The 'Halo' can be quickly configured for passenger transport, freight, disaster relief or air ambulance duties. Access to the cabin is through a large pair of clamshell doors at the rear, with a lower door acting as a vehicle ramp.

COMBAT DATA

PAYLOAD

The 'Halo' has immense load-carrying ability thanks to its large size and very powerful engines.

Mi-26 'HALO'
Maximum payload 20 tons or 80 fully-equipped troops

CH-53E SUPER STALLION
Maximum payload 16 tons or 55 fully-equipped troops

CH-54 TARHE
Maximum payload 10 tons or 45 troops in cargo pod

Mil's monsters

■ **MIL Mi-6 'HOOK':** First flown in 1957, the massive Mi-6 was for two decades the world's largest operational helicopter. Using stub wings to provide extra lift in forward flight, it could carry 65 passengers or up to 12 tons of cargo internally.

■ **MIL Mi-10 'HARKE':** Although the cabin of the Mi-6 was big, it still could not handle outsize loads. The Mi-10, which first flew in 1960, was a flying crane variant capable of hoisting loads the size of a bus and up to 14 tons in weight.

■ **MIL V-12 'HOMER':** This experimental aircraft is the largest rotary-winged machine ever flown. Powered by two sets of Mi-10 engines and rotors, it carried a load of 40 tons to 2000 m (6,500 ft.), but control problems meant that it never entered production.

MIL

MI-34 'HERMIT'

● Military trainer ● Aerobatic ● Liaison aircraft

First flown in 1986, the Mi-34 was designed as a replacement for the Mi-1 and Mi-2 helicopter trainers. It was also offered for the observation, liaison and border patrol roles. The Mi-34 can carry a maximum payload of 165 kilogrammes (360 lb.) of fuel over a distance of 160 kilometres (100 miles) and it fuel consumption is a modest 45 litres (12 gallons) per hour. A twin-engine version, flown for the first time iin 1993, has two VAZ-430 twin-chamber rotary engines.

▲ *A pilot prepares to demonstrate the new Mi-34 'Hermit' for an airshow audience. His display will include such flight manoeuvres as barrel rolls and loops.*

MIL **MI-34 'HERMIT'**

▼ Slim design
Despite the compact layout of the Mi-34, the helicopter can accommodate two pilots and two passengers in the rear fuselage.

▲ Mixed materials
Although the Mi-34 relies heavily on conventional structures, the main rotor head and rear rotor blades are made of composite materials in an effort to save weight.

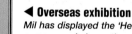

◄ Overseas exhibition
Mil has displayed the 'Hermit' at numerous airshows throughout the West as part of a sales drive.

▲ Pilot trainer
A military training variant has undergone flight testing with the Soviet armed forces as a possible replacement for the Mi-1/Mi-2.

◄ Flight performance
One of the latest helicopters developed in Russia, the 'Hermit' is sparsely equipped compared to its Western counterparts.

FACTS AND FIGURES

➤ The Mi-34 'Hermit' was designed as a replacement for the Mi-1/Mi-2 civil light helicopter and military trainer.

➤ 'Hermit' is the first Soviet helicopter capable of executing a loop.

➤ Composite materials are used for the main rotor and tail blades.

➤ Mil first flew the Mi-34 'Hermit' in 1986, using unboosted mechanical flight controls.

➤ A twin-engine version is built by the VAZ motor car works at Togliatigrad.

➤ The Mi-34VAZ features a totally new rotor head made from carbon fibre.

Russia's new lightweight

Using the same nine-cylinder piston engine as the Yak-52 trainer and Ka-26 helicopter, the Mi-34 has composite main and tail rotors attached to a straightforward light-alloy fuselage and non-retractable skids.

The 'Hermit' showed its competition-flying potential by becoming the first Soviet helicopter to perform loops and rolls. It can withstand loads of up to 2.5g for short periods at speeds of 50 to 150 km/h (30 to 93 m.p.h.), and can fly backwards at up to 130 km/h (81 m.p.h.).

As well as having a similar powerplant to other Soviet primary training aircraft – an important economical consideration – the Mi-34's reciprocating engine accelerates rapidly and is not disturbed by ingesting gases during acrobatic manoeuvres.

Although designed primarily for use as an aerobatic and training aircraft, the 'Hermit' offers scope for other duties, with space behind the dual-control flight deck for cargo or a bench seat for two passengers.

Left: After years of building military helicopters, the Mil design team is shifting its focus to the civilian helicopter market with the Mi-34

The twin engine Mi-34VAZ is built by the VAZ automobile factory. It has a new rotor head for enhanced control response, along with improved range, endurance and performance.

Above: The Mi-34 haas stunned airshow audiences with its flight demonstrations. An example is seen here about to enter a loop.

Mi-34 'Hermit'

Type: light military trainer/liaison helicopter

Powerplant: one 242.5-kW (325-hp.) VMKB M-14V-26 nine-cylinder air-cooled radial engine

Maximum speed: 210 km/h (130 m.p.h.)

Cruising speed: 180 km/h (112 m.p.h.)

Range: 450 km (280 mi.)

Hover ceiling: 1500 m (4,920 ft.)

Weight: Normal take-off 1080 kg (2,380 lb.)

Accommodation: two pilots and two passengers

Dimensions:
Span	10 m (39 ft. 7 in.)
Length	11.4 m (37 ft. 5 in.)
Height	2.8 m (9 ft. 2 in.)
Main rotor area	78,54 m² (845 sq. ft.)

Later versions of the 'hermit' have two engines and offer increased range and speed.

Exceptional visibility is provided by the bubble canopy. This approach has been copied from Aérospatiale's Gazelle, which the Mi-34 closely resembles.

Seating is provided for two pilots; the rear of the cockpit is devoted to cargo or an additional two passengers. Flight controls are unboosted mechanical controls requiring heavy inputs from the pilot during certain manoeuvres.

Composite structures are used throughout the helicopter, particularly in the main and tail rotor sections. This has reduced the overall weight and improved the safety of the design. Future Mil products will use more composite components.

МОСКВА 02

МИЛИЦИЯ

ОПАСНО

МИ-34

MI-34 'HERMIT'

The cancellation of a number of military contracts has caused many Russian aircraft manufacturers to turn their attention to the civil aviation field. Mil is now actively marketing the lightweight 'Hermit'.

All current production 'Hermits' have landing skids, although the design can be equipped with wheels if needed.

ACTION DATA

SPEED
The 'Hermit' has a lower speed than its Western equivalents mainly beccause of is relatively poor quality engine. For sheer speed Aérospatiale's Gazelle is the fastest helicopter in its class.

Mi-34 'HERMIT'	210 km/h (130 m.p.h.)
SA 342M GAZELLE	310 km/h (192 m.p.h.)
F28F SHARK	180 km/h (115 m.p.h.)

HOVER CEILING

In this field, the Mi-34 shows a drastic reduction in performance. Compared to the lightweight civil F-28F Falcon, the Russian design has a very low ceiling. Its inability to reach a high hover ceiling will greatly affect future sales of Mil's helicopter.

Mi-34 'HERMIT' 1500 m (4,920 ft.)	SA 342M GAZELLE 2850 m (9,350 ft.)	F28F SHARK 2345 m (7,700 ft.)

RANGE
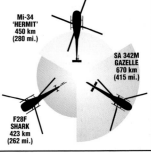
Mil gave the original 'Hermit' the ability to carry an additional fuel tank in the rear section of the fuselage to increase its poor range. Its range is reduced further when it is required to carry cargo. An improved 'Hermit' variant, with improved range, is now flying.

Mi-34 'HERMIT' 450 km (280 mi.)

SA 342M GAZELLE 670 km (415 mi.)

F28F SHARK 423 km (262 mi.)

Multiple Mils

■ **Mi-2 'HOPLITE':** Despite its small size, the Mi-2 is used for a variety of duties, including border patrols.

■ **Mi-6 'HOOK':** First of the heavyweight helicopters in service, the 'Hook' first flew in 1957 and remains in front-line service.

■ **Mi-17 'HIP':** Developed from the earlier Mi-8 in an effort to offer improved performance, the Mi-17 has seen widespread civilian service.

■ **Mi-35 'HIND-F':** Used as a battlefield attack helicopter, the 'Hind' has been constantly upgraded and has seen considerable combat.

MIL

V-12

● Twin rotor ● Heavylift helicopter ● Unbroken records

Everything about the V-12 was enormous. The twin-rotor giant shattered every record for helicopter payload, and made every previous rotary-wing machine seem like a toy. But the problems of operating such a machine were also enormous and, despite the ingenuity of the design, it was not really a viable machine for commercial use. After a memorable appearance at the Paris Air Show, the V-12 rarely flew again.

▲ Mikhail Mil, son of a mining engineer, was perhaps the best helicopter designer ever. The V-12 was his greatest creation, but only two machines were produced.

MIL V-12

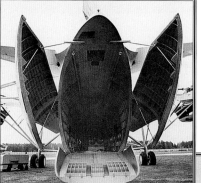

'Hook' power ▶
The engines, gearbox and rotors were all taken from the Mi-6 'Hook', albeit with some changes; rotor rpm was reduced to 112.

▼ Big wing
A large wing helped to offload the main rotors in forward flight. Its trailing-edge flaps were fixed after early trials.

▲ Loading ramp
Practical touches like the rear clamshell doors and loading ramp showed that the V-12 was not just a record breaker. The fuselage interior also had four cargo winches and a reinforced floor structure.

▼ Paris performance
The Paris Air Show was the V-12's greatest moment, attracting enormous attention. But there was little interest in the machine from foreign customers.

▲ Room at the top
The immense cockpit held a pilot, co-pilot, electronics operator and engineer, with the navigator and radio operator seated above.

FACTS AND FIGURES

➤ The enormous D-25 turboshaft engines were also used in other very large Mil helicopters like the Mi-6 and Mi-10.

➤ The one remaining V-12 can be seen at the Monino air force museum in Moscow.

➤ The V-12 had hydraulic flight controls, but it could also be flown manually.

➤ Fully loaded, the V-12 was as heavy as nine Mi-24 'Hind' gunships, or more than twice as heavy as an Mi-6.

➤ The main cabin of the V-12 was 28.15 m (93 ft.) long and 4.4 m (47 ft.) square.

➤ Optional ferry tanks could be carried inside the V-12 for maximum range.

PROFILE

Hundred-tonne helicopter

Produced by the man who had built the world's previous largest helicopter, Mikhail Leontyevich Mil, the V-12 was a giant. With a maximum take-off weight of over 100 tonnes, it was bigger than many transport aircraft.

Developed with the engines, transmission and rotors of the Mi-6, but in double pods outboard of a long reverse-taper wing, the V-12 had a huge fuselage space that contained one-tonne cargo hoists and seats could be fitted for more than 100 passengers. The V-12 even had a split-level flight deck, with pilots and flight engineer below and navigator and radio operator above.

The first V-12 was damaged in a crash in 1967, caused by resonance and control system problems. The second appeared at the Paris Air Show, and went on to break many helicopter payload records, most of which remain to this day. But despite its stunning performance and size, the V-12 was not really economical to use, and Mil

Below: The Soviet obsession with having the biggest and fastest of everything was manifest in the V-12. Mil turned his attentions to the more successful Mi-26 after the problems with the V-12 became apparent.

Above: Twin-rotor power was a new concept for the Mil company. Despite overcoming many of the technical difficulties, the V-12 was plagued by problems with resonance.

decided to develop the Mi-26 for heavy cargo work instead, leaving the V-12 in a museum.

V-12

Type: twin-rotor heavy transport helicopter

Powerplant: four 4847-kW (6,495-hp.) D-25V turboshafts driving in pairs with transverse shafting

Maximum speed: 260 km/h (161 m.p.h.)

Cruising speed: 240 km/h (149 m.p.h.)

Range: 500 km (310 mi.) with maximum payload

Weights: empty not disclosed; maximum payload 25 tonnes; vertical take-off 30 tonnes; maximum take-off 105 tonnes

Armament: none

Dimensions: span 19.55 m (64 ft.)
length 19.1 m (63 ft.)
height 4.88 m (16 ft.)
wing area 52.49 m² (565 sq. ft.)

ACTION DATA

PAYLOAD

The V-12 could carry a huge load, even more with a running take-off in which it benefited from transition effect (like all helicopters). The Mi-26 carries almost as much using a single rotor and has trouble-free handling.

V-12	CH-53E	Mi-26 'HALO'
25000 kg (55,000 lb.)	16330 kg (35,926 lb.)	20000 kg (44,000 lb.)

POWER

Using four engines from the Mil-6, the V-12 had awesome power. The modern Mi-26 has almost the same power from two more modern engines, which drive through a less wasteful transmission. The CH-53E is driven by three relatively small engines.

V-12	CH-53E	Mi-26 'HALO'
4 x 4847 kW = 19388 kW (4 X 6,495 hp. = 25,980 hp.)	3 x 3266 kW = 10798 kW (3 X 4,376 hp. = 13,129 hp.)	2 x 8380 kW = 16760 kW (2 X 11,229 hp. = 22,458 hp.)

MAXIMUM TAKE-OFF WEIGHT

The V-12 had a maximum take-off weight of 105 tonnes, or more than a loaded Vulcan bomber. The CH-53 is dwarfed by the much larger Mil helicopters, but is an impressive machine. The Mi-26 is almost as heavy as a fully loaded C-130 Hercules at maximum all-up weight.

V-12	CH-53E	Mi-26 'HALO'
105000 kg (231,000 lb.)	33400 kg (73,634 lb.)	56000 kg (123,458 lb.)

V-12

Number '21142' was the second Mil V-12 twin-rotor helicopter. In 1969, carrying a payload of 40204 kg (88,448 lb.), it was flown to 2255 m (11,224 ft.) by V. P. Koloshchyenko.

The podded engines had access panels on their undersides to allow easy maintenance. The whole engine assembly was mounted at a 4° nose down angle. Fuel was carried in the outer wing section.

The pilot flew the V-12 with the aid of an autostabilisation system. A ground-mapping radar was fitted under the nose.

The large central tailfin gave the V-12 some much needed stability in forward flight, supplemented by auxiliary tailfins outboard.

АЭРОФЛОТ
МИ
СССР-21142

Fuel was carried in two external tanks as well as the outer wing structure.

The engine and wing were suspended with complex bracing. Vibration of the rotors through this bracing to the undercarriage caused many of the V-12's problems.

Light vehicles could be loaded through its rear doors, and a side door allowed access for passengers.

Mil's family of helicopters

■ **Mi-4 'HOUND':** Still in service in some Third World countries, the Mi-4 can carry a 1300-kg (2,860-lb.) underslung load or an internal load of 1740 kg (3,820 lb.). Thousands of Mi-4s were built, including licence production in China.

■ **Mi-6 'HOOK':** Another Mil record breaker, the Mi-6 was the largest helicopter in the world for many years. It could carry 8 tonnes internally or 12 tonnes underslung. It used fixed wings to offload the rotors in forward flight.

■ **Mi-8 'HIP':** Using the same gearbox and rotors as the Mi-4, the Mi-8 has been produced in thousands and is the most widely used helicopter in the world. The Mi-8 could lift 4 tonnes internally or 4 tonnes externally.

■ **Mi-10 'HARKE':** Using the same engines as the Mi-6, the Mi-10 was developed as a flying crane with an extra long undercarriage for lifting bulky cargo. The Mi-10 could lift 15 tonnes internally or 8 tonnes underslung.

MYASISHCHEV

M-17/M-55 'MYSTIC'

- Balloon interception ● Reconnaissance ● Geophysical survey

In 1982 Western intelligence reported the sighting of an unidentified Russian high-altitude reconnaissance aircraft. Satellite photographs of the Zhukhovskii flight test centre showed an aircraft with twin tail fins and long, unswept wings, suggesting that it was a Soviet counterpart of the American U-2. It was known as 'Ram-M', and several years passed before the mysterious aircraft was finally identified as the Myasishchev M-17.

▲ *Russia's answer to the U-2 has not achieved the success or infamy of its American equivalent. The M-17s and M-55s have performed useful environmental research, however.*

PHOTO FILE

MYASISHCHEV **M-17/M-55 'MYSTIC'**

Record breaker ▶
During 1990 the single-engined M-17 Stratosphera set a total of 25 speed/climb/height records.

▼ **Environmental research**
The M-55 Geofizika was developed to help to study the problems of ozone depletion.

M-55 Geofizika ▶
The M-55 can carry equipment for Earth-resource missions, agricultural surveying, ground mapping and ice reconnaissance.

▲ **Air show star**
Geofizika has appeared in the West at the Paris and Farnborough air shows.

Mystic power ▶
Two 88.30-kN (19,865-lb.-thrust) Soloviev D-30-10V turbofans power the M-55.

FACTS AND FIGURES

➤ Subject 34 was cancelled when the CIA stopped using high-altitude balloons as reconnaissance platforms.

➤ Eduard Chyeltsov flew the first M-17 Stratosphera on 26 May 1982.

➤ In 1992 an M-17 'Mystic-A' investigated the Antarctic ozone hole.

➤ Chyeltsov also flew the M-55 Geofizika on its maiden flight on 16 August 1988; at least three more have flown since.

➤ A projected M-55UTS trainer was to have a periscope to aid back-seat vision.

➤ The M-55 'Mystic-B' can climb to 21 km (13 miles) in 35 minutes.

PROFILE

Master of the stratosphere

Originally planned in 1967 as an interceptor of high-altitude reconnaissance balloons under the designation Subject 34 and known as the Chaika (Gull), Myasishchev's new aircraft was first seen by NATO in the unarmed 'Mystic-A' form. Known as the Stratosphera in Russia, the M-17 retains some of its original mystery.

It resembles the U-2 in having a single engine with intakes on the sides of the forward fuselage, and was designed for a similar strategic reconnaissance role. But it has a greater wingspan and is slightly longer overall, with a shorter, deeper fuselage and a long tailplane carried on twin fins.

It was intended to replace the Yak-25RD, but one of the two M-17s that were built is now housed in a museum. The second aircraft has been used to investigate the ozone layer and pollution in the upper regions of the atmosphere.

Since 1994 a twin-engined version, the M-55 Geofizika ('Mystic-B'), has appeared at Western air shows. Designed specifically for environmental and geophysical research, it can carry a 1500-kg payload and has an endurance of seven hours.

From its operational altitude of 21500 metres, the M-55 can photograph an area 120 km (75 mi.) wide, and can also glide for a distance of 200 km (120 mi.).

Below: One of the two prototype M-17 Stratospheras (17103) survives in Aeroflot colours at the Monino aerospace museum near Moscow.

Above: According to Russian sources, development of the 'Mystic-B' as a strategic reconnaissance platform for military service is continuing.

M-17 STRATOSPHERA 'MYSTIC-A'

Although it achieved a number of world records, the prospect of the M-17 becoming a Soviet counterpart of the U-2 faded. The aircraft moved on to investigation of the Antarctic ozone problem.

The M-17's single pilot is seated on a K-36L ejection seat, under an upward-hinging canopy. Carried just behind the pilot are two oxygen canisters.

Compared to the unusual inverted gull wing of the Subject 34 interceptor, the M-17's wing is much more conventional in layout. The engine is started by a turbo-starter and fed with fuel from five separate wing tanks, which hold a total of 10,000 litres (2,650 gallons).

The M-17s were built at Kumertau, Bashkiri, primarily from lightweight metals. The entire aircraft is comprehensively ice-protected for high-altitude operations. In normal conditions the reconnaissance-configured M-17 would have carried 1000 kg (2,200 lb.) of advanced cameras and sensors.

This M-17, serial CCCP-17401, was the aircraft used during trials and preparation work for the M-55. It flew missions to monitor Antarctica's atmosphere. A number of environmental slogans were subsequently added.

CCCP-17401

'Mystic-A' carries a PRNK-17 navigation system radio compass and an RSBN Kobalt radar. These were also used in the M-55 'Mystic-B'.

A novel feature of the M-17 'Mystic-A' is its retractable landing lights, stowed under the front of the tail booms.

Designed for high altitudes, the RD-36-51V is based on the engine core from which the MiG-31's powerplants were derived.

Both the M-17 Stratosphera 'Mystic-A' and M-55 Geofizika 'Mystic-B' feature an unusual twin-boom tail, with vertical surfaces bridged by a long horizontal stabiliser.

Changing roles of the 'Mystic'

Since its conception in 1967, the 'Mystic' has seen its role change from balloon interceptor to research platform.

INTERCEPTOR: Armed with a turret-mounted GSh-23 cannon and two air-to-air missiles, the single-seat Subject 34 was intended to destroy spy balloons.

M-17 'MYSTIC-A': In its design role the M-17 would have flown high-altitude strategic reconnaissance missions over sensitive foreign installations.

CCCP 17401

M-55 'MYSTIC-B': An unusual role adopted by the M-55 is the conversion of hail into rain by the use of chemicals. Such weather alteration avoids excessive crop damage, helping the struggling Russian economy.

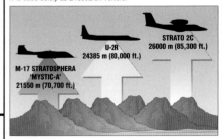

MYASISHCHEV

VM-T ATLANT

● Spacecraft carriage ● Converted bomber ● Heavylift specialist

▲ Dismissed as a failed bomber that was short of range, the Mya-4 'Bison' became a capable all-round aircraft used for inflight-refuelling, ocean reconnaissance and transporting outsize cargoes for the space industry.

While the USA and Europe have developed various 'Guppy'-type aircraft with outsize fuselages to carry large rocket assemblies, the Soviet Union uses several converted bombers as piggyback transports for complete aircraft wings and other large loads. The VM-T, or Atlant, is a version of the M-3M 'Bison-B' bomber which has been modified to carry bulky loads on top of its fuselage in support of the Soviet space programme.

MYASISHCHEV **VM-T ATLANT**

▲ **Fuel tank aboard**
Heaving aloft the massive Energiya fuel tank was no mean feat despite more powerful engines.

▲ **Shuttle transport**
The VM-T could also carry the Buryan re-usable space vehicle. The American Space Shuttle is carried on a Boeing 747.

▲ **Flying to Baikonur**
The VM-T was very busy, making over 150 flights to the Baikonur launch station from the factories.

▼ **New engines**
The VM-T was fitted with non-afterburning VD-7M engines (from the Tu-22 bomber) for extra thrust.

▲ **Standard 'Bison'**
Instantly recognisable, even from below, because of its single tailfin, the 'Bison' served until the late-1980s as a tanker and reconnaissance aircraft.

FACTS AND FIGURES

➤ The first flight of the VM-T Atlant carrying a payload was by A. Kuryurchenko and his crew in January 1982.

➤ Myasishchev died in 1978, shortly after beginning work on the VM-T conversion.

➤ Two VM-Ts (also known as 3M-T) were completed and first flew in 1980.

➤ Myasishchev also proposed a twin-deck military cargo variant of the 3M bomber, but this was never built.

➤ A proposed civil 380-seat airliner variant of the 'Bison' was also not produced.

➤ The 3M version of the 'Bison' bomber was a redesign with a new wing shape.

PROFILE

The Soviet big lifter

Never a great success as a bomber, only about 200 'Bisons' were built, and many of them were converted into tankers or maritime reconnaissance platforms.

More unusually, two examples of the M-3M 'Bison-B' version were adapted for transporting some of the structures produced as part of the Soviet space shuttle programme. To accommodate extremely long assemblies and to provide enough directional

stability to cope with the unusual sizes and shapes, the standard tail surfaces were removed. These were replaced by twin rectangular tailfins and rudders mounted on the ends of a new horizontal tailplane.

In this configuration the Atlant has been used to carry the Soviet Buryan space shuttle and sections of the Energiya launcher, including complete fuel tanks. They are secured on pylons mounted at various points on the front, centre and rear fuselage.

As the Atlant's payload is limited to 40 tonnes, the Buryan had to be stripped down before it could be carried, with the tail fin, orbital manoeuvring engines and other systems removed. The more recent An-225 Mryia can carry the complete shuttle orbiter on its back.

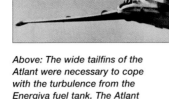

Above: The wide tailfins of the Atlant were necessary to cope with the turbulence from the Energiya fuel tank. The Atlant had quite good handling qualities.

Right: The Atlant used the airframe of the later 3MS 'Bison', recognisable by its longer nose profile. Only one of the aircraft had a flight-refuelling probe. The aircraft has the Cyrillic logo 'Aviaspetstrans' just above the Aeroflot badge.

VM-T ATLANT

RF-01502 was one of the two Atlant conversions of the Myasishchev 3M 'Bison' bomber used for carrying Energiya fuel tanks and Buryan shuttle bodies.

VM-T Atlant

Type: four-engine special transport aircraft converted from strategic bomber

Powerplant: four 93.2-kN (20,966-lb.-thrust) RBKM VD-7M single-shaft turbojets with afterburner removed for increased dry power rating

Maximum speed: 930 km/h (577 m.p.h.)

Take-off run: (3MS) 2950 m (9,676 ft.)

Range: 12,000 km (7,450 mi.) unloaded

Service ceiling: 14,900 m (48,875 ft.)

Payload: 40,000 kg (88,000 lb.)

Weights: (3MS-2) empty 75,740 kg (166,628 lb.); loaded maximum 192,000 kg (422,400lb.)

Dimensions:
span	53.14 m (174 ft.)
length	58.70 m (193 ft.)
height (approx.)	4.10 m (46 ft.)
wing area (est)	320 m² (1,050 sq. ft.)

The main modification to the Atlant was the fitting of a seven-metre fuselage extension, which was angled slightly upwards, and large fins on a dihedral tailplane. The majority of the design work was carried out after studies on three 3MN airframes.

The fuel tank was mounted on huge trusses at the front and rear of the fuselage.

The 3M bomber had RBP-4 radar located in the nose fairing. A flight-refuelling probe was fitted in the tip of the nose.

The Atlant nose was the same as the 3M bomber with the navigator located in a glazed nose compartment.

The Atlant and M3 used VD-7M engines unlike the Mikulin AM-3s and RD-3s in the early 'Bisons'.

Myasishchev designs

■ **DVB-102:** The first of the Myasishchev designs not to use the name of another design bureau, the DVB-102 was a fast light-bomber prototype. It flew in prototype form only, was delayed by the outbreak of war and was finally abandoned in 1944.

■ **M-17 'STRATOSPHERA':** Designed initially as a fighter to shoot down CIA high-altitude reconnaissance balloons, the M-17 was then converted to the high-altitude reconnaissance role itself. It was later used for ozone-layer research and geosurvey flights.

■ **M-50 'BOUNDER':** The M-50 had the biggest wing of any supersonic aircraft except for the American XB-70. The aircraft was designed as a strategic missile launcher, but engine development problems and limited range meant that it did not enter service.

ACTION DATA

PAYLOAD

With its uprated engines and redesigned fuselage, the Atlant could carry a much heavier payload than a standard 'Bison'. The Boeing 747 could carry even more, but is a much bigger and more powerful aircraft which was designed 10 years after the 'Bison'.

VM-T ATLANT	40,000 kg (80,000 lb.)
3MS 'BISON-B'	24,000 kg (52,800 lb.)
MODEL 747	70,000 kg (154,000 lb.)

NASA/AMES

AD-1

● One-off prototype ● Pivoting wing ● Advanced home-build

▲ NASA has inspired a number of highly unusual, one-off aircraft designs, but few have been as odd as the AD-1. The machine provided a great deal of valuable research information.

I n 1978, NASA turned to the Ames Industrial Corporation to manufacture one of the most exotic flying machines ever built. The Ames-Dryden AD-1 was a small, lightweight research aircraft intended to test the pivoting wing, also known as the oblique wing – a unique way of improving aircraft performance at varying speeds. The AD-1 was tested, but ambitious plans for an improved version did not proceed.

NASA/AMES AD-1

▼ Navy interest
An artist's impression illustrates the slender fuselage and twin podded engines of the AD-1. In addition to tests at NASA Dryden, flights were conducted by the Navy at Patuxent River.

▲ Truly unique
One of the strangest-looking machines ever to take to the air, the AD-1 nevertheless proved useful for research into oblique wing technology.

Supersonic benefits ▶
Due in part to its unique design, the AD-1 offered many potential advantages for future supersonic aircraft, including reduced engine power on take-off and reduced noise levels, an important environmental issue.

◀ Conventional position
While on the tarmac and during take-off and landing, the wing is kept in a conventional position for greater stability at low speed.

Maximum sweep ▶
Seen early in 1979, the then-incomplete AD-1 demonstrated the wing at its full oblique angle, which could be achieved only while flying at cruising speed.

FACTS AND FIGURES

➤ The AD-1 stemmed from research into a supersonic airliner/transport featuring a similar type of pivoting wing.

➤ Flight testing was conducted at NASA's Dryden facility between 1979 and 1982.

➤ A maximum oblique angle of 60° could be achieved while the aircraft was in flight.

➤ NASA provided the entire blueprints for the design; Ames was tasked purely with construction of the single AD-1.

➤ Gross weight of this bizarre machine is an incredibly low 816 kg (1,795 lb.).

➤ After years of inactivity, the AD-1 flew once again at Oshkosh in 1997.

PROFILE

Stranger than fiction

The principle behind the AD-1, designed by Burt Rutan, was similar to that of 'swing-wing' aircraft like the F-111, F-14 and Tornado. For operation at low speeds and during take-off and landing, the AD-1's wing was positioned in a 'normal' configuration. For flight at higher speeds, the wing pivoted to form an oblique angle of up to 60° – roughly the equivalent of shifting to greater sweep-back on a jet fighter – reducing drag and making possible greater speed and range with no noticeable increase in fuel consumption.

In tests, the AD-1 took to the air and flew with its wing at increasingly large angles, successfully demonstrating that the pivoting-wing principle worked as expected.

In 1986, NASA launched an effort to develop a short-span, 'joined wing' version of the AD-1. The new aircraft would have had removable wingtip panels, enabling it to be progressively modified for different wing sweep and angle configurations. This experiment did not proceed, but the AD-1 was a useful vehicle for research into such advanced concepts.

Left: High above the Californian desert, the AD-1 cruises with the wing pivoted. The large cockpit canopy gave outstanding visibility.

After increasing the angle of the wing during successive tests, NASA finally reached the full oblique of 60° during a flight on 24 April 1981.

Construction of the AD-1 comprised a semi-monocoque structure with a special foam core and glass-fibre epoxy for light weight.

For landing and take-off, the wing was kept at a conventional 90° to the fuselage. For the first few flights the wing remained in this position and it was only on the ninth flight that the angle was gradually increased.

For such a small and light machine, a suitable powerplant had to be devised. A pair of extremely compact Ames TRS 18-046 turbojet engines proved the ultimate solution.

AD-1

Only a single example of the NASA/Ames AD-1 was ever built. Construction at the Ames plant in Bohemia, New York, began in 1978, and this unusual creation took to the air for the first time in March 1979.

The cockpit was extremely long but very cramped, though excellent visibility was offered by the large canopy. The pilot sat very far back with his legs stretched out. Although nothing like it had ever flown before, the aircraft had surprisingly good handling qualities.

A conventional tricycle undercarriage was fitted, featuring single tyres on all three units. Ground clearance was minimal and landings were often quite bumpy.

In comparison to the unique main wing the tail unit was surprisingly conventional, with a standard vertical rudder and delta-style horizontal stabilisers featuring long elevators mounted on the trailing edges.

AD-1

Type: single-seat oblique-winged research aircraft

Powerplant: two rear-mounted 0.98-kN (153-lb.-thrust) Ames Industrial (Microturbo) TRS 18-046 turbojet engines

Maximum speed: 322 km/h (200 m.p.h.)

Service ceiling: 3600 m (11,800 ft.)

Weight: maximum take-off 907 kg (2,000 lb.)

Fuel capacity: 303 litres (80 gal.)

Accommodation: one pilot

Dimensions:
span	9.75 m (32 ft.)
span (oblique)	4.93 m (16 ft. 2 in.)
length	11.68 m (38 ft. 4 in.)
height	1.98 m (6 ft. 6 in.)
wing area	8.64 m² (93 sq. ft.)

NASA OBLIQUE WING PROPOSALS

LOCKHEED SUPERSONIC JET TRANSPORT: Dating from about 1975, this proposal from Lockheed Georgia and NASA was for an aircraft with a pivoting oblique wing. Studies undertaken by that time had shown that such a wing would provide benefits at supersonic speeds, notably reduced drag and fuel consumption. This ambitious project was later shelved, though the information gathered proved useful for the much smaller AD-1. NASA is currently still studying the concept of oblique-wing aircraft.

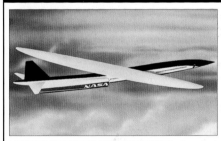

OBLIQUE-WING F-8 CRUSADER: With the AD-1 programme drawing to a close in 1982, NASA began to look for alternative testbeds on which to continue development. It was particularly interested in the slew-winged concept applied to a larger machine. One proposal involved modifying the Administration's fly-by-wire Vought F-8 Crusader with an oblique wing. Rockwell International's North American Aircraft division was awarded a contract for development of the project, but it was not built.

Studies into variable-geometry wings

■ **MESSERSCHMITT P.1101:** Captured by the Americans at the end of World War II, this unusual aircraft featured 'movable wings' which had to be altered manually on the ground.

■ **BELL X-5:** Taking the idea of the P.1101 a stage further, the X-5 featured true variable-geometry wings. In practice the design proved dangerous, one example being lost after entering a spin.

■ **GRUMMAN XF-10 JAGUAR:** Developed with operational service in mind, the Jaguar demonstrated the potential offered by swing wings, but it was years before the idea took off.

NH INDUSTRIES

NH 90

● European partners ● Advanced design ● Utility helicopter

T he NH 90 project began in 1985 as a co-operative project between European helicopter manufacturers for 'a NATO helicopter for the 1990s'. Today, more than 12 nations – including the original partners France, Italy, Germany and the Netherlands – operate a mix of helicopters as battlefield transports and shipboard ASW aircraft. Because of delays, delivery of the NH 90 to the initial partner nations began in 2006.

▲ To operate in the new century, the NH 90 uses some of the most advanced materials available for its construction. Though an excellent design, the helicopter faces an uncertain future.

NH INDUSTRIES NH 90

▼ Difficult start
Britain was one of the original partners, but decided to drop out of the project at an early stage, in 1987.

▲ Future perfect
To help promote the aircraft, various artists' impressions of the NH 90 were distributed to the aviation press.

◄ Military mock-up
Future military customers were shown full-scale models of the NH 90 to illustrate the potential of the design. This example was displayed at Farnborough.

◄ Shipboard warrior
Most European clients are interested in replacing their ageing Sea King fleet with a specialised variant of the NH 90. This version will be equipped with anti-ship missiles and torpedoes.

Future saviour ►
NH Industries has been quick to see the potential of the NH 90 as a rescue helicopter. Civilian operators have shown interest in the helicopter, although no orders have been forthcoming.

FACTS AND FIGURES

➤ Five European nations signed the memorandum in 1985 allowing the development of the NH 90.

➤ Two main versions (transport and naval) of the NH 90 are being developed.

➤ The naval version of the helicopter will be equipped with a search radar.

➤ The work is being shared by Eurocopter France (43%), Agusta (26%), Eurocopter Germany (24%) and Fokker (7%).

➤ Production of the NH 90 is expected to commence in 1999.

➤ The TTH version is expected to cost FF90 million; the NFH FF145 million.

PROFILE

A perfect partnership?

In September 1985, the defence ministers of five European nations agreed to co-operate on a new multi-role helicopter for the armies and navies of NATO. The British government withdrew from the project in 1987 during the design phase, leaving Germany, France, the Netherlands and Italy in the project.

A combined organisation named NH Industries was formed in 1992 to manage the project, and is based at Aix-en-Provence in France.

In service, the TTH (Tactical Transport Helicopter) version of the NH 90 will fulfil various roles, including tactical army support, command post, search and rescue, and medical evacuation duties. The NFH (NATO Frigate Helicopter) will perform ASW (anti-submarine warfare), ASVW (anti-surface vessel warfare), SAR and transport missions. Helicopters that will be replaced by the NH 90 include French, German and Dutch Lynxes, French Super Frelons and Super Pumas, and Italian Sea Kings and Agusta-Bell 212s. So far, 647 NH 90s have been ordered; the biggest customer is Italy, with 224 examples. The first production example of the NH 90 flew in May 2004.

Below: The flying prototype of the NH 90 has exceeded all the performance levels required for the design. Pilots have praised the helicopter's handling.

NH 90 (provisional)

Type: transport/ASW helicopter

Powerplant: two 1599.5-kW (2,145-hp.) Rolls-Royce/Turboméca/MTU RTM 322-01/9 turboshaft engines

Maximum speed: 295 km/h (183 m.p.h.)

Endurance: 5 hr 30 min

Combat radius: 1110 km (688 mi.)

Hovering ceiling: 3500 m (3,500 ft.)

Weights: empty 5700 kg (12,540 lb.); maximum take-off 9100 kg (20,020 lb.)

Accommodation: three crew and 20 fully-equipped troops

Dimensions:
main rotor diameter	16.30 m (53 ft. 5 in.)
length	16.81 m (55 ft. 2 in.)
height	5.42 m (17 ft. 9 in.)
main rotor disc	213.82 m² (2,300 sq. ft.)

The NFH version will normally carry a flight crew of three, comprising a pilot, a co-pilot and one system operator in the cabin.

The titanium main rotor hub supports the four composite blades, which have advanced aerofoils and curved tips to reduce drag. The NFH version will have automatic folding of the main blades.

The four-bladed tail rotor is of composite construction and rotates at 1235.4 rpm. The whole tail pylon can fold for storage on the NFH version.

Made by a European consortium of Turboméca, Rolls-Royce, MTU, Piaggio and Topps, the twin RTM 322-01/9 engines are expected to achieve new levels of reliability.

NH 90

F-ZWTI

NH90

The landing gear is retractable and consists of a twin-wheel nose unit and single-wheel main units. Emergency floatation gear will also be available.

The NH 90's fuselage is constructed in three countries. The front fuselage is built at Marignane, France; the centre at Ottobrunn Germany; the rear at Cascina Costa, Italy.

NH 90 PT2

PT2 is painted in naval-style light grey camouflage and is of basic configuration. As the second prototype to fly, on 19 March 1997, it also became the first example to operate with fly-by-wire controls.

MILITARY HELICOPTERS

MULTI-ROLE HELICOPTERS: European armies have long used the helicopter for combat operations. Whether flying troops low over a battlefield or searching for hostile submarines in the Atlantic, the capabilities of the helicopter are beyond doubt. Used as an aerial taxi for the French and British armies is the jointly developed Aérospatiale/Westland Puma (pictured below). The Puma will be replaced by the NH 90 in French army service.

For maritime operations the Sea King (below) has been a cornerstone of Western forces. A specialised variant of the NH 90 is in the process of being developed to replace the ageing Sea King in service. Italy, Germany and France have requested a variant equipped with a 360° search radar and hardpoints for anti-ship missiles and depth charges. The new helicopter was designed from the outset to be able to operate from small warships such as frigates and destroyers.

European rotorcraft projects

EH INDUSTRIES EH101: This Anglo-Italian multi-role helicopter has been ordered by Italy and the UK, and is being offered for export.

EUROCOPTER EC 135: This seven- or eight-seat, light, turbine-powered aircraft is projected to have achieved 700 sales by 2007.

EUROCOPTER TIGRE: Designed as an anti-tank and ground-support helicopter, the Tigre has orders for around 400 examples.

EUROFAR : Manufacturers from France, Germany and the UK are examining the possibility of building this twin-engined tilt-rotor aircraft.

NORTH AMERICAN

SABRELINER

● T-39 development ● Many still in service ● High performance

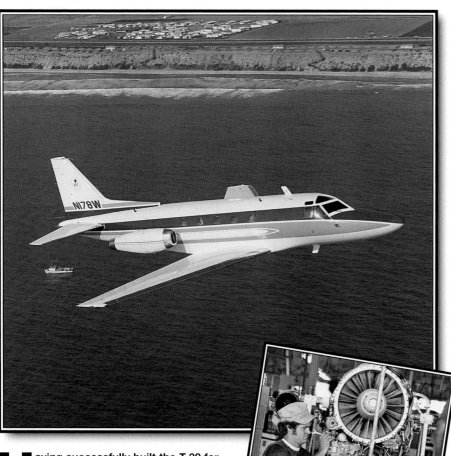

Having successfully built the T-39 for the US military, North American went on to produce the aircraft as the Sabreliner, or Sabre as it was often known, as one of the earliest biz-jets. From the initial Sabreliner 40, the company produced a series of improved variants which culminated in the Sabreliner Series 65, a turbofan-powered, 10-passenger executive transport equipped with a supercritical wing for transcontinental range.

▲ *Originally selling in considerable numbers, by the late 1960s the Sabre/Sabreliner was suffering a drop in sales because of the greater efficiency of turbofan-engined rivals.*

NORTH AMERICAN SABRELINER

▼ Final Sabre
The last of the Sabre series in production was the TFE731-3-powered, transcontinental Sabre 65.

▲ Taller, re-engined 75A
With greater cabin height and more efficient engines, the Model 75A was built until 1982.

Civil T-39A ▶
Initially, North American offered the Sabreliner Series 40. It was basically a civilian-certified version of the T-39A.

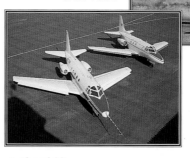

▲ 40 and 60
Two extra cabin windows distinguish the Series 60 from the Series 40.

Sabreliner into the 1980s ▶
This converted Series 60 was the prototype of the early 1980s Series 65.

FACTS AND FIGURES

➤ Production of the Sabreliner ceased at Rockwell's El Segundo plant on the day the facility's lease expired.

➤ A number of civilian-specification Sabreliners were used by the US Navy.

➤ The shortened Sabre designation was officially adopted in 1970.

➤ A simplified version of the Series 40, the Sabreliner Commander, was available for US $995,000 in 1971.

➤ Sabre production rights were passed to the Sabreliner Corporation in 1983.

➤ Sabreliner Corp's plans to produce an advanced Series 85 with Agusta failed.

PROFILE

North American executive dream

North American was quick to realise the potential of its military T-39 as an executive transport for the civilian market. The company had no civil marketing experience, however, and secured a tie-up with the Remmert-Werner group for finishing, distribution and marketing facilities.

North American became North American Rockwell in September 1967, trading under this title for a while before becoming Rockwell

International. The newly named company established a Sabreliner Division to continue Sabre production, which eventually ceased with the last Series 65 on 1 January 1982.

Evolution of the Sabreliner saw the aircraft develop into a 10-seater when the Series 40 was stretched by 0.96 m (3 ft. 2 in.) to become the Series 60, and sales remained high until more modern turbofan-powered aircraft appeared in the early 1970s. Rockwell responded with

the Series 75A, powered by General Electric CF 700 2D-2 turbofans, and later with the Garrett-powered Series 65, but the popular Sabreliner had reached the end of its development cycle.

A major boost for the Model 75A came from the Federal Aviation Administration (FAA), which ordered 15 for flight inspection duties. An expected Sabreliner order from the US Coast Guard failed to materialise.

A new wing of supercritical type allowed the Series 65 to cruise efficiently at high speeds.

All tail surfaces were of cantilever construction. The main structural material was light alloy, and the Sabreliner continues to maintain an excellent reputation for structural integrity.

SABRELINER 65

Seen in the markings of the Acopian Technical Company, this aircraft was the last of the 76 Sabre 65s built. The names Sabre and Sabreliner were both applied to the series.

Full blind-flying equipment was a standard feature of the Model 65's two-crew cockpit. A comprehensive range of avionics, including weather radar, was also available.

A maximum of ten passengers enjoyed the comfort of the Sabreliner's pressurised and air-conditioned cabin. All seating layouts included provision for a galley and toilet.

Unusual 'rounded triangular' windows were a feature of all Sabreliner models except for the Series 70/75 aircraft. The lengthened cabin of later aircraft incorporated five windows.

Rockwell gained certification for the Series 60 and 75A aircraft to fly from gravel runways after the nosewheel leg had been fitted with a special gravel deflector.

Garrett AiResearch TFE731-3-1D turbofans considerably improved the efficiency of the Sabreliner. Each engine was fitted with a hydraulically-actuated thrust reverser for improved landing performance.

N65L

Acopian

Sabreliner 60

Type: eight-ten seat, twin-engined business jet

Powerplant: two 14.68-kN (3,303 lb.-thrust) Pratt & Whitney JT12A-8 turbojets

Maximum speed: 906 km/h (563 m.p.h.) at 6550 m (21,490 ft.)

Range: 3239 km (2,013 mi.) with maximum fuel, with four passengers, baggage and 45 min reserves

Service ceiling: 13,715 m (45,000 ft.)

Weights: empty equipped 5103 kg (11,250 lb.); take-off 8877 kg (19,570 lb.) with four passengers

Accommodation: 10 passengers, or 1135 kg (2,304 lb.) of freight with the seats removed

Dimensions: span 13.61 m (44 ft. 8 in.)
length 14.30 m (46 ft. 11 in.)
height 4.88 m (16 ft.)
wing area 31.78 m² (342 sq. ft.)

ACTION DATA

ECONOMIC CRUISING SPEED

Several US manufacturers found a ready home market for executive jets in the 1960s and 1970s. When it initially entered the market, the Sabreliner was one of the highest performing types, but other manufacturers were quick to catch up.

SABRELINER 75A	772 km/h (480 m.p.h.)
MODEL 1329-25 JETSTAR II	811 km/h (504 m.p.h.)
GULFSTREAM II-B	777 km/h (483 m.p.h.)

PASSENGERS

In its lengthened Series 75A form, the Sabreliner could carry a maximum of ten passengers, although eight or nine was more realistic for maximum comfort. The Gulfstream II-B was a larger contemporary of the Sabreliner 75A.

SABRELINER 75A	10
MODEL 1329-25 JETSTAR II	10
GULFSTREAM II-B	19

RANGE

Even with the unusual CF 700 turbofan, featuring a turbojet core and rear-mounted fan, the Sabreliner 75A was unable to match the range of its US rivals. The other types were larger, heavier, more complex machines, and correspondingly were more costly to operate, however.

SABRELINER 75A 3174 km (1972 mi.)
GULFSTREAM II-B 6025 km (3,744 mi.)
MODEL 1329-25 JETSTAR II 4818 km (2,994 mi.)

Biz-jets of the 1960s

■ **ROCKWELL JET COMMANDER 1121:** Following first deliveries in 1965, the Jet Commander design was taken over by IAI.

■ **DE HAVILLAND DH 125:** Work began in 1961 on what was to become a huge sales success. This aircraft is still in production.

■ **LEARJET 23:** As the first model in a long line of highly successful biz-jets, the Model 23 had several features from a Swiss fighter project.

■ **MBB HFB 320 HANSA:** This unusual German design first flew in 1964, but was not as successful as its US and British contemporaries.

NORTHROP

GAMMA

● All-metal monoplane ● Airmail hauling ● Single pilot

T he beautiful Northrop Gammas of the early 1930s began as mail-carriers, but performed many duties. In an age when biplanes were made of wood and fabric, Jack Northrop's flying machines were silvery monoplanes constructed of metal. The Gammas were custom-built, and (except for a batch sent to China) each was different. Conceived in peacetime, later versions of the Gamma did see combat in China.

▲ *Ultra-modern for the period, the Northrop Gamma brought new standards to aircraft design. With its record-breaking flights, the Gamma was admired everywhere it was exhibited.*

NORTHROP **GAMMA**

▼ Great Gamma
Though not designed for air racing, the Gamma achieved a good reputation during the 1930s and set many inter-city records. This increased orders for the aircraft across the USA.

▲ Wheel covers
Huge fairings were placed over the wheels, leading to a more streamlined design.

▼ Wing design
The Northrop Gamma utilised one of the most efficient wings of its time. Northrop knew more about airfoils and strength than any manufacturer of the period.

▲ Ellsworth's Gamma
This example was equipped for a flight across the Antarctic, but was damaged before the attempt.

◄ Airline operations
Trans World Airlines flew the Gamma as an Experimental Overweather Laboratory aircraft, allowing information to be collected for future overseas routes. Mail was also carried within the fuselage.

FACTS AND FIGURES

➤ In 1933 Frank Hawks flew the *Sky Chief* from Los Angeles to New York in 13 hours 27 minutes, averaging 291 km/h (180 m.p.h.).

➤ Gammas influenced the design of later military planes, including the Dauntless.

➤ Howard Hughes flew a Gamma from California to New Jersey in nine hours.

➤ Forty-nine aircraft in the Gamma series were delivered to the Chinese government as light bombers.

➤ The Gamma lost out to North American's BC-1 as a military trainer.

➤ Variants of the Gamma were used as research aircraft in Great Britain.

PROFILE

Gamma's golden era

Jack Northrop (who broke away from Douglas to form his own company in 1933) spent a lifetime creating advanced aircraft, from his all-metal Gammas of the 1930s to the flying wings that evolved into today's B-2 bomber. The first two Gammas were built for celebrated pilot/adventurers Frank Hawks and Lincoln Ellsworth. Hawks used his ship, called the Texaco Sky Chief, to set distance records; Ellsworth, with Bernt Balchen, carried out dramatic explorations of the Antarctic.

Other Northrop Gamma aircraft were built to serve military missions and to carry mail. One Gamma became an Overweather Experimental Laboratory, contributing immensely to scientific knowledge of flight at high altitude. Yet another Gamma was flown to a distance record by Howard Hughes after having been raced by famous aviatrix Jacqueline Cochran.

The record-breaking flights by Gammas were all accomplished in the civilian world, but the majority of the Gammas built were military. Unfortunately, the Gamma bombers of the Chinese air force proved of little use when Japan invaded China.

Above: This Gamma was fitted with a Curtiss V-1570 Conqueror engine for the pioneering aviatrix Jacqueline Cochran. Unfortunately, this aircraft was destroyed in a crash in Texas.

Above: The Gamma's all-metal skin sparkles with the reflections from the sun. The type brought with it new advances in aircraft design.

Gamma 2A

Type: high-speed monoplane

Powerplant: typically (Gamma 2A) one 585-kW (785-hp.) Wright Whirlwind GR-1510 14-cylinder air-cooled radial driving a three-bladed propeller, or (Gamma 2B) one 373-kW (500-hp.) Pratt & Whitney Wasp SD nine-cylinder radial driving a two-bladed propeller

Maximum speed: 399 km/h (247 m.p.h.) at 2135 m (7,000 ft.)

Cruising speed: 354 km/h (219 m.p.h.) at 2135 m (7,000 ft.)

Range: 4025 km (2,495 mi.)

Service ceiling: 7130 m (23,400 ft.)

Weights: empty 1588 kg (3,494 lb.); loaded 3175 kg (6,985 lb.); max. take-off 3460 kg (7,612 lb.)

Dimensions:
span	14.63 m (48 ft.)
length	9.07 m (29 ft. 9 in.)
height	2.67 m (8 ft. 9 in.)
wing area	33.72 m² (363 sq. ft.)

GAMMA 2D

This Gamma was operated by Trans World Airlines. The type offered customers the means to carry a small number of passengers or mail at high speed across the United States.

The two cargo compartments were situated behind the engine. Hatches were positioned on top of the fuselage to provide access to the cargo. If passengers were carried seats were fitted to the fuselage sides in these sections. On most flights only mail was carried. The pilot's cockpit was situated under a simplified sliding canopy; visibility was adequate, although landing required a fair degree of experience.

To increase the performance of the aircraft the wheels were housed in large streamlined trousers, from which only about one third of each wheel protruded. Other variants of the Gamma were equipped with large floats.

The most revolutionary feature of the Gamma was its wing design, made of metal and incorporating a full multi-spar construction. The centre-section was built integrally within the fuselage, while the outer panels were bolted to the centre-section.

ACTION DATA

MAXIMUM SPEED

The Gamma had exceptional performance and many of the type established aviation records because of their high speed. Northrop's Delta used a similar layout to the Gamma but compared to other aircraft of the period, the Gamma was revolutionary.

GAMMA 2A	399 km/h (247 m.p.h.)
ORION 9	354 km/h (219 m.p.h.)
DELTA 1D-5	352 km/h (218 m.p.h.)

OPERATIONAL RANGE

In operation as a mailplane and small airliner, range was vital for the Gamma's future. Its ability to cover huge distances compared to its rivals gave Northrop aircraft sales success.

ORION 9 1205 km (747 mi.)
GAMMA 2A 4025 km (2,495 mi.)
DELTA 1D-5 2655 km (1,646 mi.)

SERVICE CEILING

By employing a sophisticated wing design, Northrop's Gamma was able to obtain a considerable altitude advantage over the Orion 9 and Delta 1D. Operating at a higher altitude meant the Gamma had reduced fuel consumption yet offered exceptional range.

GAMMA 2A 7130 m (23,400 ft.)
ORION 9 6705 m (22,000 ft.)
DELTA 1D-5 6095 m (20,000 ft.)

Numerous Northrops

■ **ALPHA:** Despite its ungainly appearance and fixed landing gear, the 1930 Alpha may be regarded as the first 'modern' airliner.

■ **BETA:** The Beta sporting monoplane was the first aircraft to exceed 322 km/h (200 m.p.h.) with its Wright Whirlwind radial engine.

■ **DELTA:** The United States Coast Guard operated a version of the Delta airliner as a transport for the Treasury Secretary.

■ **MODEL 8A:** The Northrop-designed but Douglas-produced A-17A was operated briefly by the USAAF before being sold to the RAF.

PIPER PA-25 PAWNEE

CROP DUSTING

● Agricultural use ● More than 4,000 built ● Pawnee Brave predecessor

▲
One of the first aircraft designed from the outset as an agricultural machine, the Piper Pawnee and its contemporary, the Snow S-2, set new standards in 'ag-plane' design.

Having had experience in adapting the ubiquitous PA-18 Cub for crop-dusting and spraying, Piper saw a market for a specialised agricultural design. The resulting PA-25 Pawnee was the first project tackled by the company's new development facility opened in 1957 at Vero Beach, Florida. More than 4,000 PA-25s were built over the ensuing 16-year period; the improved Pawnee Brave followed in 1972 and was produced until the late 1980s.

PHOTO FILE

PIPER PA-25 PAWNEE CROP DUSTING

◄ Four-bladed propeller
Agricultural operators often modify their aircraft to suit specific operating conditions. This Pawnee 260D has been fitted with a quieter four-bladed propeller.

Dusting at low level ►
Flying a few feet off the ground, this Pawnee makes a dramatic sight as it uses a spreader to distribute dry chemicals.

▼ Another load
With great care the driver of this hydraulic loader lines up a bucket of dry chemical over a PA-25.

▲ Ease of maintenance
Beginning in the late 1960s Piper redesigned the Pawnee, introducing numerous improvements which benefited the pilot and maintenance personnel alike. Among these was the introduction of removable fuselage panels to facilitate cleaning.

Chemical atomisers ►
This PA-25 Pawnee has four Micronair chemical spray atomisers fitted to its spray booms. They apply the chemical as a fine mist, thus giving better and more even coverage.

FACTS AND FIGURES

➤ Designs of both the Pawnee and Snow S-2 were based on work carried out at Texas Agriculture and Mining College.

➤ The Pawnee was designed by Fred Weick who also designed the Ercoupe.

➤ Total Piper PA-25 Pawnee production reached 4,438.

➤ Pawnee Brave production topped 1,000 before sales rights were sold to WTA Inc. who marketed a New Brave 375 and 400.

➤ Retired Pawnees have been converted for use as glider tugs.

➤ Like other agricultural types, the PA-25 may be used as a fire-bomber.

PROFILE

Piper's trend-setting crop duster

Named, like other Piper products, after a native American tribe, the first Pawnees were braced low-wing monoplanes powered by a modest 112-kW (150-hp) four-cylinder AVCO Lycoming engine and accordingly designated PA-25-150. Ahead of the cockpit was a 0.57-m³ capacity chemical hopper connected to a dust or spray distribution system, as perfected on the PA-18.

Given the dangerous nature of much agricultural flying, Piper was keen to incorporate features to reduce both the likelihood of an accident and enhance the pilot's chances of survival if a crash occurred. A high sitting position was built-in for an excellent all-round view, strengthened seat restraints were fitted and the cockpit structure was designed to remain undamaged in the event of a low-speed crash.

Sales figures around the world were encouraging, and Piper introduced more powerful engines of up to 194 kW (260 hp) and enlarged hoppers.

In 1972 the redesigned PA-36 Pawnee Brave introduced a new cantilever wing and even larger powerplants. More than 1,000 were built before the design was bought by WTA Inc. in 1981. Production of around 150 New Braves followed.

Above: Pawnees have seen service around the world. This example was one of a number sold in New Zealand.

Below: As well as being equipped to deliver dry chemicals from its hopper, the Pawnee is easily configured for spraying, using booms fixed to the trailing edge of the wing.

PA-25-235 Pawnee D

Type: single-seat low-wing agricultural aircraft

Powerplant: one 175-kW (235-hp) AVCO-Lycoming O-540-B flat-six, air-cooled piston engine

Maximum cruising speed: 161 km/h (100 m.p.h.) (duster); 169 km/h (105 m.p.h.) (sprayer)

Take-off run: 244 m (800 ft.)

Range: with maximum fuel 410 km (255 miles) (duster); 435 km (270 miles) (sprayer)

Weights: empty basic 725 kg (1,598 lb.); maximum take-off 1315 kg (2899 lb.)

Hopper capacity: 0.57 m³ (20.12 cu. ft.) allowing for 548 litres (144.7 U.S. gal.) of wet chemical or 363 kg (800 lb.) of dry chemical

Dimensions: span 10.97 m (36 ft.)
length 7.73 m (25 ft. 4 in.)
height 2.21 m (7 ft. 3 in.)
wing area 17.00 m² (183 sq. ft.)

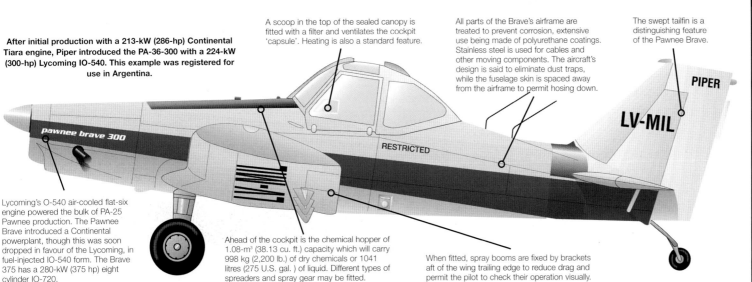

After initial production with a 213-kW (286-hp) Continental Tiara engine, Piper introduced the PA-36-300 with a 224-kW (300-hp) Lycoming IO-540. This example was registered for use in Argentina.

A scoop in the top of the sealed canopy is fitted with a filter and ventilates the cockpit 'capsule'. Heating is also a standard feature.

All parts of the Brave's airframe are treated to prevent corrosion, extensive use being made of polyurethane coatings. Stainless steel is used for cables and other moving components. The aircraft's design is said to eliminate dust traps, while the fuselage skin is spaced away from the airframe to permit hosing down.

The swept tailfin is a distinguishing feature of the Pawnee Brave.

Lycoming's O-540 air-cooled flat-six engine powered the bulk of PA-25 Pawnee production. The Pawnee Brave introduced a Continental powerplant, though this was soon dropped in favour of the Lycoming, in fuel-injected IO-540 form. The Brave 375 has a 280-kW (375 hp) eight cylinder IO-720.

Ahead of the cockpit is the chemical hopper of 1.08-m³ (38.13 cu. ft.) capacity which will carry 998 kg (2,200 lb.) of dry chemicals or 1041 litres (275 U.S. gal.) of liquid. Different types of spreaders and spray gear may be fitted.

When fitted, spray booms are fixed by brackets aft of the wing trailing edge to reduce drag and permit the pilot to check their operation visually.

ACTION DATA

POWER

Most agricultural designs have been progressively fitted with more powerful engines to boost flight performance and load-carrying capacity. The Pawnee D had a comparatively small engine.

PA-25-235 PAWNEE 175 kW (235 hp) | AT-401 B 447 kW (600 hp) | FU-24-950 298 kW (400 hp)

MINIMUM STALLING SPEED

Larger, heavier aircraft tend to have higher stalling speeds. The Pawnee D performs well in this respect, compared to the Air Tractor AT-401 and New Zealand Aerospace Industries FU-24. Slow-speed manoeuvres are commonplace in agricultural flying.

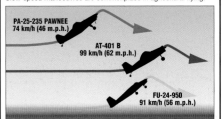

PA-25-235 PAWNEE 74 km/h (46 m.p.h.)
AT-401 B 99 km/h (62 m.p.h.)
FU-24-950 91 km/h (56 m.p.h.)

TAKE-OFF RUN

Pawnees and FU-24s share a take-off run of around 250 m (820 ft.), useful when operating from confined airstrips. The Air Tractor, on the other hand, needs around 400 m (1,312 ft.) in which to get airborne.

PA-25-235 244 m (800 ft.) | B 402 m (1,319 ft.) | FU-24-950 224 m (735 ft.)

US piston-engined 'ag-planes'

AIR TRACTOR AT-300/301: After handing production of the S-2 to Rockwell in the early 1970s, Leland Snow designed a new, larger aircraft, with a 336-kW or 447-kW radial engine.

CESSNA 188 AGWAGON: Another design to follow the lead set by Piper, the Agwagon first flew in 1965 and led to the AgPickup, AgTruck and AgHusky variants.

IMCO CALLAIR A-9: When IMCO acquired Callair in the early 1960s, their first new design was the A-9. Using the Pawnee's layout, the aircraft was also later produced by Rockwell.

SNOW S-2R: Leland Snow's well-known design has been in production since the late 1950s. Later built by Rockwell as the Thrush Commander, the S-2 is today built by Ayres.

PIPER PA-31

NAVAJO

- Business aircraft ● Commuter airliner ● Twin-engined safety

A s the first of a new series of large twin-engined executive aircraft, Piper's PA-31-300 Navajo was also aimed at the commuter airline and corporate markets. The Navajo family includes the Turbo Navajo, Navajo C/R, Pressurised Navajo and Navajo Chieftain. Each model in the series is available in standard, commuter or executive versions with differences in seating arrangements and interior cabin layouts.

▲ With its PA-31, Piper produced an aircraft which was universally popular. 'Customer friendly' features included the provision of baggage stowage space in the rear of the engine nacelles.

PIPER **PA-31 NAVAJO**

◀ Clean design
Each of the slim engine nacelles is positioned well forward of the low-set straight wings.

▼ Built-in stairs
For easy cabin access at poorly equipped airfields, the Navajo features a 'Dutch' door at the rear of the cabin; the top half hinges upwards and the lower half, with built-in steps, hinges downwards.

Freight version ▶
Removal of the Navajo's seats allows it to fly as a light freight transport. Here an assorted cargo is secured by webbing straps to strongpoints on the aircraft's floor.

▼ Instrumentation
Full blind flying instruments and night flying capability are common to all variants of the PA-31. This aircraft is finished in the standard Piper scheme.

▼ Pressurised Navajo
Changes from the initial Navajo design are evident in this picture of the pressurised version. There are fewer windows, a smaller windshield and an elongated nose.

FACTS AND FIGURES

➤ The pressurised version of the Navajo was designated the PA-31-425. A total of 258 was built.

➤ The prototype Navajo first flew on 30 September 1964.

➤ A total of 1824 Navajos was built and production ended in 1972.

➤ Introduced in 1973, the PA-31-350 Navajo Chieftain had a longer fuselage; 1942 examples were manufactured.

➤ The Navajo was the design basis for all of Piper's subsequent large twins.

➤ The Navajo has a main cabin cargo capacity of 6 m³ (211 cu. ft.).

Piper's big business twin

Piper introduced the Navajo in 1964 as an addition to its range of business twins which included the Apache, Aztec and Twin Comanche. With a pair of 224-kW (300-hp.) Lycoming IO-540 piston engines and greater capacity than previous models, the streamlined Navajo provided seating for up to eight passengers, although the standard layout held six.

Aimed primarily at the business market, the Navajo has been successfully employed as a third-level commuter airliner

and for air taxi operations. Various versions of the Navajo were produced, including the Turbo Navajo which had turbo-supercharged engines (whose propellers counter-rotated to cancel out engine torque).

A pressurised version, the PA-31P, was first flown in 1968, followed in the early 1970s by the Navajo Chieftain, later just called the Chieftain, which had a fuselage extension of 0.61 m and seating fitted for up to 10 passengers.

In 1969 the Navajo range was extended with the first

flight of the PA-31T Cheyenne, basically a turboprop version of the PA-31P. Certificated in 1972, it became Piper's first turbine-engined business aircraft and allowed Piper to compete with the Beech King Air. A number of Navajos also serve with air forces around the world.

Below: Argentina was one of several military customers, including a number elsewhere in South America, for variants of the PA-31.

Above: Basically similar to the standard Navajo, the PA-31 Navajo C/R introduced counter-rotating propellers and nacelle baggage accommodation.

PA-31 Navajo

Type: commuter airliner, executive and corporate aircraft

Powerplant: two 231-kW (310-hp.) Lycoming TIO-540-A2C flat-six piston engines

Maximum speed: 420 km/h (260 m.p.h.) at 6100 m (20,000 ft.)

Maximum climb rate: 372 m/min (1,220 f.p.m.) at sea level

Range: 1973 km (1,225 mi.) with maximum fuel

Maximum certified altitude: 7315 m (24,000 ft.)

Accommodation: pilot plus standard seating for six people, maximum seating for eight

Weights: empty 1816 kg (3,995 lb.); maximum take-off 2948 kg (6,486 lb.)

Dimensions:
span	12.40 m (40 ft. 8 in.)
length	9.94 m (32 ft. 7 in.)
height	3.96 m (13 ft.)
wing area	21.30 m² (229 sq. ft.)

Power comes from two 261-kW (350-hp.) six-cylinder horizontally-opposed air-cooled engines, fitted with Hartzell three-bladed, constant-speed, fully-feathering metal counter-rotating propellers. The engines are turbocharged.

The fuselage is a conventional all-metal, semi-monocoque structure. It has a long nose which can accommodate baggage as well as the undercarriage nosewheel.

In 'Standard Interior Group' configuration the cabin seats six passengers. In 'Commuter Interior Group' configuration, accommodation increases to a maximum of 10 and basic empty weight rises by 39.5 kg (87 lb.). Both configurations offer a choice of nine interior colour schemes.

All versions of the Navajo have the same swept-back cantilever all-metal vertical tail surfaces and variable-incidence tailplane. Trim tabs are installed on the rudder and starboard elevator.

PA-31-350 CHIEFTAIN

With its 0.61-m (2-ft.) fuselage extension, the Chieftain was a higher capacity version of the Navajo. It was the first aircraft in the series to incorporate the nacelle baggage holds.

FAR WEST AIRLINES

N27906

At the rear of the cabin a 91-kg (200-lb.) maximum capacity baggage compartment is provided. This is especially useful when the optional fuel tanks are installed, since they are accommodated in the baggage space at the rear of the nacelles.

ACTION DATA

BAGGAGE CAPACITY

In its original form, as described here, the PA-31 offered barely adequate baggage capacity for its six occupants. Both the Beech Model B55 Baron and Cessna Model 402C have considerably larger baggage holds capable of carrying heavy loads.

PA-31 NAVAJO 159 kg (350 lb.)	MODEL 402C 680 kg (1,500 lb.)	MODEL B55 BARON 317 kg (700 lb.)

ACCOMMODATION

All of these aircraft seat six passengers easily, although the PA-31 can seat eight with some detrimental effect on passenger comfort. Most operators are happy to fly with two crew members and four passengers.

PA-31 NAVAJO	8 PASSENGERS
MODEL 402C	6 PASSENGERS
MODEL B55 BARON	6 PASSENGERS

RANGE

Offering slightly greater range than either the Cessna or Beech models, the PA-31 was further improved in its Navajo C/R form. This introduced the option of additional fuel tanks in the rear of the engine nacelles. This feature was also available in the Cheyenne.

PA-31 NAVAJO 1973 km (1,225 mi.)

MODEL 402C 1822 km (1,129 mi.)

MODEL B55 BARON 1836 km (1,138 mi.)

Piper twins

■ **PA-23 AZTEC:** Piper developed the Aztec from its first twin, the PA-23 Apache. The Aztec introduced more powerful engines.

■ **PA-30 TWIN COMANCHE:** A twin-engined variant of the PA-23 Comanche, the PA-30 was powered by two 119-kW (160-hp.) engines.

■ **PA-31T CHEYENNE:** Adding turboprop engines to the Chieftain airframe produced the fast and comfortable Cheyenne.

■ **PA-34 SENECA:** Again, Piper developed a twin from a single-engined design. In this case, the PA-32 Saratoga led to the PA-34.

PIPER PA-34

SENECA

● Traffic monitoring over London ● Radio broadcasting from the air

Anyone who has experienced driving conditions in London, or any other large city around the world for that matter, will know of and appreciate the efforts of the 'flying eye' aircraft that circle overhead during the morning and evening peak traffic periods. These aircraft, sponsored by local radio stations, provide a bird's-eye view of the road network below, allowing advice to be given to drivers fighting their way through rush hour traffic.

▲ Providing a 'flying eye' service is an advertising and publicity opportunity for a radio station. It also gives a valuable service to the motoring public allowing better journey planning.

PIPER PA-34 SENECA

◀ Low-level flying
Much of a typical traffic-monitoring flight is undertaken at low level not only to allow observers a good view of the ground, but also to avoid airliner flight paths.

▼ Police operations
As well as those flights undertaken by radio stations, police forces often employ aircraft of various types (including helicopters) to keep watch on traffic flows.

▲ Twin engines for safety
Two engines give aircraft operating over urban areas an extra safety margin should they encounter mechanical problems. In London, flight regulations ban single-engined fixed-wing types.

▼ Monitoring motorways
As well as urban road networks, 'flying eyes' keep an eye on the motorways that feed them.

▲ Current 'flying eye'
The current Capital Radio aircraft, a Grumman Cougar, is appropriately registered G-FLII.

FACTS AND FIGURES

➤ The Seneca remained in production in 1997 as the PA-34-220T Seneca IV, with styling and other changes.

➤ Piper's Seneca has been built under licence in Poland and Brazil.

➤ In 1996, the standard equipped price for a Seneca IV was $459,900.

➤ The Seneca handles well on take-off as it has 'handed' propellers to counteract engine torque.

➤ The PA-34's avionics allow instrument flying; weather radar may be fitted.

➤ Senecas have a conventional light alloy semi-monocoque fuselage.

PROFILE

London's 'flying eyes'

As single-engined aircraft are prohibited from operating over London, twin-engined types are chosen for the 'flying eye' role. Popular types include the Piper PA-34 Seneca six/seven-seat cabin monoplane.

First announced in 1971, the design was essentially a twin-engined derivative of the well-known Cherokee Six. In 1975 a number of modifications were made, resulting in the Seneca II.

Major differences were the introduction of turbocharged engines and changes to the controls to improve low-speed handling, an important

consideration during traffic monitoring. The Seneca does not have a monopoly on such operations, however. Other twin-engined types are equally useful in the role, including the varied products of Cessna and other manufacturers.

A typical operation is that undertaken by Cabair Group on behalf of Capital Radio over

London. Based at Elstree Aerodrome, north of London, the 'flying eye' aircraft, a Grumman American GA.7 Cougar (which replaced a PA-34 Seneca), takes to the air during the morning and evening 'rush hours' to provide up-to-the-minute traffic reports to Capital Radio's in-car listeners stuck in London's traffic.

Above: Appropriately registered G-FLYI, this Seneca was employed as the Capital Radio Flying Eye traffic-monitoring aircraft, adorned with the London radio station's name and logo.

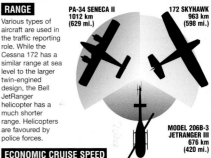
Above: Piper's Seneca has been a popular aircraft in the company's range. Based on the single-engined Cherokee Six, it was developed over a relatively short period and sold well.

PA-34-200T Seneca II

Type: six/seven-seat cabin monoplane

Powerplant: two 149-kW (200-hp.) Continental TSIO-360-E flat-four piston engines

Maximum speed: 362 km/h (225 m.p.h.) at 3660 m (12,000 ft.)

Maximum cruising speed: 352 km/h (219 m.p.h.) at 6100 m (20,000 ft.)

Economic cruising speed: 306 km/h (190 m.p.h.) at 7620 m (25,000 ft.)

Range: 1640 km (1,019 mi.) at 6100 m (20,000 ft.)

Service ceiling: 7620 m (25,000 ft.)

Weights: empty 1289 kg (2,842 lb.); maximum take-off 2073 kg (4,570 lb.)

Dimensions:
span 11.86 m (38 ft. 11 in.)
length 8.72 m (28 ft. 7 in.)
height 3.02 m (9 ft. 11 in.)
wing area 19.39 m² (209 sq. ft.)

PA-34-200 SENECA

Until recently, Capital Radio's Flying Eye was this aircraft, G-FLYI. More than 4500 PA-34s were built by Piper, including the turbocharged variants of the Seneca II and Seneca III, the latter with 164-kW engines.

As well as a flight crew of two and a broadcaster, most 'flying eye' traffic monitoring aircraft carry radio equipment to allow radio broadcasts from the air. The radio signal from the aircraft must be 'beamed' from the aircraft to the radio station and then out to the listeners below.

Gaudy colour schemes are often applied to aircraft engaged in this role as a means of advertising the sponsoring organisation. Corporate names are often applied in large letters on the undersurfaces of the wing.

Originally equipped with normally-aspirated Continental IO-360 air-cooled, flat-six engines, the Seneca was later re-equipped with turbocharged powerplants to improve performance.

The retractable tricycle landing gear fitted to the Seneca was based on that used on the single-engined Cherokee Lance.

As many twin-engined cabin monoplanes are six- or seven-seaters, radio stations using such aircraft for 'flying eye' work often offer seats to members of the public interested in seeing their home town from a different perspective.

'Personalised' out-of-sequence aircraft registrations are a common feature of corporate aircraft. They act as a low-cost means of advertisement for the aircraft's operators.

Piper twins in diverse roles

■ **AIRCREW TRAINER:** This PA-23 carries the colours of Greek airline Olympic. Twin-engined types are often used by airlines in a training role.

■ **BUSHPLANE:** Mounted on floats, this Aztec has been modified for use in the Pacific Northwest region of the United States.

■ **MINERAL SURVEYING:** Fitted with a magnetometer and other equipment, this Piper is equipped for mineral survey work.

■ **UTILITY TRANSPORT:** Designated UO and, later, U-11 by the US Navy, the PA-23 Aztec was ordered in small numbers as a transport.

ACTION DATA

RANGE

Various types of aircraft are used in the traffic reporting role. While the Cessna 172 has a similar range at sea level to the larger twin-engined design, the Bell JetRanger helicopter has a much shorter range. Helicopters are favoured by police forces.

PA-34 SENECA II 1012 km (629 mi.)
172 SKYHAWK 963 km (598 mi.)
MODEL 206B-3 JETRANGER III 676 km (420 mi.)

ECONOMIC CRUISE SPEED

A high economic cruising speed allows an aircraft to cover its patrol area quickly, though traffic monitoring is of necessity carried out at fairly low speeds to guarantee good visibility. High cruise speeds also allow aircraft to reach their monitoring areas quickly after take-off.

PA-34 SENECA II 306 km/h (190 m.p.h.)
172 SKYHAWK 160 km/h (99 m.p.h.)
MODEL 206B-3 JETRANGER III 214 km/h (133 m.p.h.)

MAXIMUM TAKE-OFF WEIGHT

The six/seven-seat Seneca has a maximum take-off weight of just over two tons, while the four-seater Cessna 172 is limited to just over one ton. While the Cessna 172 would be a cheaper aircraft to operate, it lacks the versatility and comfort of the Seneca.

PA-34 SENECA II 2073 kg (4,570 lb.)
172 SKYHAWK 1156 kg (2,549 lb.)
MODEL 206B-3 JETRANGER III 1451 kg (3,199 lb.)

PZL DROMADER

PEST CONTROL

● Polish agricultural aircraft ● Worldwide exports ● More than 600 built

SP-DAY

▲ Among radial-engined agricultural aircraft the Dromader has been one of the world's more successful types, selling especially well outside the Eastern Bloc.

Having designed and flown the conventional, piston-engined PZL-106 Kruk in 1972, and the somewhat bizarre, jet-powered M-15 Belphegor agricultural biplane the following year, PZL-Mielec returned to another conventional design for agricultural applications. The M-18 Dromader (Dromedary) was the result and remains in production after 18 years. More than 600 have been built, mostly for export.

PZL DROMADER

YV-505A

SP-PBZ

▼ Spray-boom equipped
This early-production Polish-registered M-18 is equipped with spray booms for the application of liquid chemicals.

▲ Venezuelan Dromedary
M-18s have found customers in Poland and 22 other countries, including Venezuela. The large size of the M-18 can be appreciated in this view.

Dual-control two-seater ▶
The M-18AS trainer was first flown in 1988 and built in only small numbers. The student sat in front of the pilot, a small hopper being retained for training flights.

▼ Long-range operator
This M-18, in the markings of Czechoslovak operator Slov Air, is carrying four long-range ferry fuel tanks. These allow operations away from base.

▲ Turbo Dromader
Known as the M-24T, this M-18 variant featured a Pratt & Whitney PT6A turboprop and an improved load and range. Only a prototype was built.

FACTS AND FIGURES

➤ In 1996 PZL was considering production of an amphibious water-bomber floatplane variant of the M-18.

➤ PZL proposed a scaled-down M-18 with a 682-litre (180 U.S. gal.) hopper.

➤ M-18s have been sold in countries as far apart as Australia, Chile and Turkey.

➤ PZL's US subsidiary Melex has developed a PT6A-engined T45 Turbine Dromader with a 3028-litre (800-U.S. gal.) hopper.

➤ Wingtip lights may be fitted to the Dromader for night-time operations.

➤ M-18s are built in batches of 30 to 50 aircraft; the 26th batch was built in 1996.

PROFILE

Hump-backed farming workhorse

Powered by the same 746-kW (1,000-hp) PZL-built Shvetsov ASz-621R radial engine as the Antonov An-2, the Dromader is similar in configuration to the PZL-106 Kruk, although it is a considerably larger machine.

With export sales in mind, PZL collaborated with Rockwell International and incorporated outer-wing panels from Rockwell's S-2R Thrush Commander to produce an aircraft to meet US FAA

standards. First flown in single-seat form on 27 August 1976, the basic M-18 and two-seat M-18A entered production in 1979 and 1984, respectively.

As at 1 January 1995 about 600 Dromaders had been built, with 90 per cent of these going abroad to operators in 22 countries. This total covers all versions, including the M-18AS dual-control training model and the M-18B, which has been the standard production model since 1994 and has better handling and a higher gross weight. In

1995 the first M-18C took to the air, fitted with an 895-kW (1200-hp) PZL Kalisz K-9 radial which improved flight performance.

Dromaders have proved popular in the highly competitive agricultural aviation market and are equally accomplished in both the crop-spraying and dusting roles. In Greece 30 M-18As are operated by the air force for fire-fighting duties, carrying water in the aircraft's 2500-litre (660-U.S. gal.) hopper.

PZL have marketed the M-18 in the water-bomber role.

From the outset the Dromader incorporated all-metal outer-wing panels which were identical to those of Rockwell International's S-2R Thrush Commander agricultural aircraft.

Dromaders are all-metal aircraft. All parts that come into contact with chemicals are coated in enamel or made from stainless steel to avoid corrosion.

Chemical dispersant systems fitted to M-18As include spray booms with nozzles or atomisers fitted to the wings, or a dry chemical spreader fitted directly below the hopper, as seen on this aircraft.

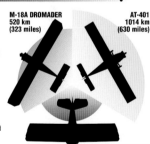

M-18A Dromader

Type: agricultural and fire-fighting aircraft

Powerplant: one 721-kW (967-hp) PZL Kalisz ASz-621R nine-cylinder supercharged radial piston engine

Maximum level speed: 256 km/h (159 m.p.h.)

Normal operating speed: 230 km/h (143 m.p.h.) at 4200-kg (9,259-lb.) take-off weight

Maximum climb rate: 414 m (1,358 ft.)/min at sea level

Range: 520 km (323 miles)

Service ceiling: 6500 m (21,325 ft.)

Weights: empty 2710 kg (5,975 lb.); maximum take-off 5300 kg (11,684 lb.)

Dimensions:
span	17.70 m	(58 ft. 1 in.)
length	9.47 m	(31 ft. 1 in.)
height	4.60 m	(15 ft. 1 in.)
wing area	40.00 m²	(430 sq. ft.)

M-18A Dromaders are fitted with a large glass-fibre epoxy hopper which can hold 2500 litres of liquid or 1350 kg of dry chemicals. Different dispersal systems are fitted beneath the hopper depending on the type of chemical being applied.

M-18 DROMADER

In the late 1980s Slov Air, a company based in Bratislava, Czechoslovakia, was engaged in agriculture-related flying, and operated a fleet of 40 helicopters and 250 crop-spraying aircraft.

Shvetsov's supercharged nine-cylinder ASz-621R radial engine, rated at 721 kW (967 hp) and built under licence by PZL, powers the M-18A.

PZL designed the Dromader with the emphasis on crew safety. The sealed and ventilated cockpit is stressed to withstand a 40g impact, giving the pilot some degree of protection in a crash. A second cabin, to accommodate a ground crewmember, is located behind the cockpit; on later aircraft this has a small window on each side.

ACTION DATA

MINIMUM OPERATING SPEED

Agricultural aircraft need to be manoeuvrable so that the pilot can apply chemicals exactly where required, minimising wastage and unnecessary flying. Low minimum operating speeds allow good manoeuvrability and increase the margin for safety in this potentially dangerous activity.

M-18A DROMADER	170 km/h (106 m.p.h.)
AT-401	193 km/h (120 m.p.h.)
AG-CAT SUPER-B/600	185 km/h (115 m.p.h.)

RANGE

The Dromader's range is between that of the Air Tractor AT-401 and Schweizer Ag-Cat. For ferry trips, the Dromader may be fitted with underwing fuel tanks, which can nearly double its range. These allow aircraft to be based at remote airstrips.

M-18A DROMADER 520 km (323 miles)
AT-401 1014 km (630 miles)
AG-CAT SUPER-B/600 318 km (198 miles)

POWER

The large ASz-621R supercharged radial engine makes the M-18 one of the most powerful piston-engined agricultural aircraft available. All three of these machines are also available in turboprop-powered versions.

M-18A DROMADER	AT-401	AG-CAT SUPER-B/600
721 kW (967 hp)	447 kW (599 hp)	335.5 kW (449 hp)

Radial-engined crop-dusters

GRUMMAN G-164 AG-CAT: Designed in the late 1950s, this manoeuvrable biplane was also produced by Schweizer Aircraft and is now built by the Ag-Cat Corporation.

LANCASHIRE PROSPECTOR: First flown in 1955 as the Edgar Percival EP.9, this design was acquired by Lancashire Aircraft in 1958 and re-engined with a Cheetah radial engine.

PZL-106 KRUK: PZL's first purpose-built, low-wing monoplane design, the Kruk was flown in 1973 with a flat-eight engine. It was produced with a radial engine until the early 1990s.

ROCKWELL THRUSH COMMANDER: Designed and built by Leland Snow from 1958 and later by Rockwell, this aircraft is now produced by Ayres in both piston- and turbine-engined models.

RAVEN

DOUBLE EAGLE II

- Gas balloon ● Atlantic crossing ● Seaworthy capsule

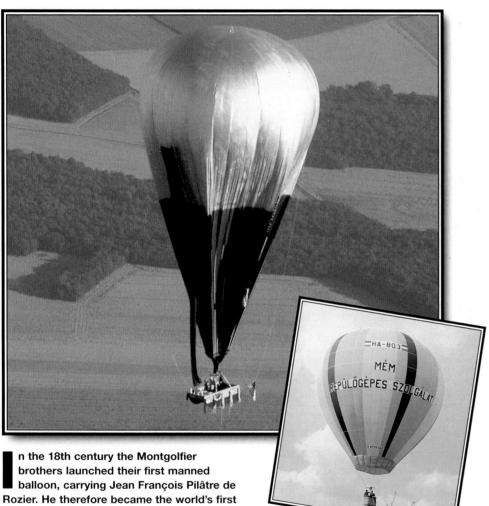

▲ Unlike today's more common hot-air balloons, Double Eagle II was filled with helium gas. Helium-filled balloons do not have to carry heavy fuel, which can give them longer endurance.

In the 18th century the Montgolfier brothers launched their first manned balloon, carrying Jean François Pilâtre de Rozier. He therefore became the world's first aeronaut. Almost 200 years later, the Double Eagle II gas balloon, piloted by L. Abruzzo, Maxie L. Anderson and Larry M. Newman, entered the record books by becoming the first balloon of any type to cross the Atlantic. This flight also set new world distance and endurance records.

◀ Final descent
After passing over the south coast of England, Double Eagle II began its final descent into northern France.

▼ Airborne advertising
Based in northern Germany, this Colt 90A hot-air balloon is sponsored by a computer company.

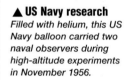

▲ US Navy research
Filled with helium, this US Navy balloon carried two naval observers during high-altitude experiments in November 1956.

▼ Height record
In 1957 another US balloon took a world record. This view of Minnesota was taken by Major D. Simons from 31090 m (101,975 ft.).

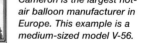

◀ British manufacturer
Cameron is the largest hot-air balloon manufacturer in Europe. This example is a medium-sized model V-56.

FACTS AND FIGURES

➤ Crew member Maxie Anderson was unsuccessful in a round-the-world record attempt in 1981.

➤ The Double Eagle II capsule is displayed at the Smithsonian Museum, Washington.

➤ The subsequent Double Eagle V became the first balloon to cross the Pacific.

➤ In honour of the crew, an airport at their home town of Albuquerque, New Mexico has been named Double Eagle II.

➤ Double Eagle V's crew included Abruzzo and Newman from the D.E. II team.

➤ The Double Eagle II crew enjoyed almost perfect weather for their flight.

PROFILE

Crossing the ocean

On 12 August 1978 the three-man crew of the Double Eagle II gas balloon lifted off from Presque Isle, Maine, on a journey which would end five days 17 hours and six minutes later in northern France. This journey not only established new world distance (5001.22 km/3,100 mi.) and endurance records, but set up the crew as the first people to cross the Atlantic by balloon.

The intention had been to touch down at Paris's Le Bourget airport, the same arrival point as Charles Lindbergh after his record-breaking transatlantic flight of 1927. A lack of food and exhaustion forced the crew down short of their intended destination, but the record had been taken.

The route had taken the craft across the North Atlantic and over southern England before crossing the coast of Dorset. Once the balloon had crossed the English Channel it was greeted by hundreds of members of the public. They followed the balloon in cars through northern France for over 30 minutes, causing a massive traffic jam. The craft eventually touched down in perfect conditions near Evreux, with the Stars and Stripes and the French tricolour draped from its gondola.

Above: It was not until 1987 that the first successful transatlantic crossing in a hot-air balloon was accomplished, by the Virgin team.

Below: The varying sizes of today's hot-air balloons are evident here. The single-seat Cameron V-20 is dwarfed by the Cameron A-530.

DOUBLE EAGLE II

The one-off Double Eagle II was produced in conjunction with the well-established Raven balloon manufacturing company in the USA. It underwent rigorous testing before the record flight.

Transatlantic journey

1 LIFT OFF: Departing from Presque Isle, Maine, the Double Eagle II used the prevailing west-to-east winds to carry it over Newfoundland. The winds enabled the craft to make good progress over the central area of the North Atlantic.

2 FRENCH FINALE: As the craft approached the British Isles, the wind eased and progress was slow. The balloon passed over southern England and the English Channel before finally touching down at Miserey.

Double Eagle II

Type: record-breaking gas balloon

Crew: three

Endurance: 137 hr 6 min (on record flight)

Range: 5001.22 km (3,100 mi.) (on record flight)

The top half of the balloon was covered in a reflective material to help prevent the sun's rays from overheating the helium gas contained within the envelope.

CROSSING THE ATLANTIC

John Alcock and Arthur Whitten Brown – On 14 June 1919 Capt. Alcock and Lt Brown departed St John's, Newfoundland on the first successful non-stop flight across the Atlantic. In their modified Vickers Vimy, they touched down at Clifden, Northern Ireland.

Charles Lindbergh – On 20-21 May 1927 Capt. Lindbergh made the first non-stop solo air crossing of the North Atlantic Ocean in the Ryan NYP (New York Paris) high-wing monoplane, *Spirit of St. Louis*, covering 5810 km (3,600 mi.) in 33 hours 30 min.

Amelia Earhart – Exactly five years to the day after Lindbergh made his epic flight, Amelia Earhart became the first woman to make a solo crossing of the North Atlantic. She flew a Lockheed Vega monoplane from Newfoundland to Northern Ireland.

Control ropes operated from the capsule were used to release some of the gas when necessary. This helped the crew control the balloon's altitude during the long flight.

Contained within the large air-tight envelope was helium gas. Helium is lighter than air and therefore causes the balloon to rise. Before World War II hydrogen was used for airships and gas balloons, but the flammable nature of this gas caused a number of disasters and its use was abandoned.

The three-man crew spent over five days in the cramped confines of their capsule. The capsule was designed to be seaworthy in case the balloon had to ditch in the ocean. The lack of space restricted food stocks, and it was for this reason that the crew was eventually forced to land.

ROBINSON

R22

● Two-seat light helicopter ● Cheap to own ● Private and business

▲ Short of buying and building a kit helicopter, about the cheapest way to own and operate a helicopter is to opt for the R22. This has been the key to its sales success in several countries.

For the beginner and the professional alike the Robinson R22 is the right helicopter. Since 1975, thousands of student pilots have earned their rotary-wing qualification flying the R22. Though it receives little publicity, the R22 is a popular, lightweight general aviation helicopter that is also economical. Few helicopters are tailored for people of modest means—but this aircraft is, making it the ideal training tool.

ROBINSON **R22**

▼ All tied up
Helicopter rotors can be surprisingly fragile. They must be carefully anchored to the fuselage to prevent windmilling on the ground.

▲ Simple controls
The R22 has a single cyclic stick connected by a cross bar with grips for each of the pilots.

▼ Crop duster
The R22 Agricultural is a version tailored for spraying pesticides and fertilizer. One person can install the spray equipment in five minutes without tools.

▲ Four-seat R44
The R44 is a four-seat version of the R22 incorporating many new features such as an automatic engine clutch and a rotor brake.

◄ R22 on floats
Another version of the R22 is the Mariner, which has inflatable floats and wheels for ground handling. The first examples delivered were used for fish spotting from tuna fishing boats off Mexico and Venezuela.

FACTS AND FIGURES

➤ It is estimated that over 13,000 student pilots have made their first helicopter solo in this aircraft.

➤ The first R22 prototype flew on August 28, 1975, and the second in 1977.

➤ Total production of the R22 had exceeded 2,500 aircraft by 1995.

➤ Despite the company's small size, Robinson achieved a production rate of about 30 R22s per month.

➤ The Turkish army is the only military user of the R22, as a basic flight trainer.

➤ Argentina's police forces are acquiring R22s fitted with both floats and wheels.

PROFILE

Popular light helicopter

It may sound like a lawn-mower flitting through the sky, but the Robinson R22 is actually a very efficient and pleasing lightweight helicopter.

This was also exactly what the world was waiting for. The manufacturer, which calls itself a small family in the California beach city of Torrance, recognized that there is a demand for a simple, easy-to-operate helicopter that can instruct students and perform basic missions.

Seeking to offer both simplicity and low cost, Robinson was so successful that in 1979, barely four years after starting flight tests, the company had already sold 524 of these fine aircraft.

With side-by-side seating and excellent vision through its rounded windshield, the Robinson R22 offers a superb ride for student and professional alike. Despite its small size, the R22 is basically but adequately equipped and carries

instruments and navigation gear for most kinds of routine flying. Pilots claim that the R22 is extremely stable and reliable, and that it will readily forgive mistakes.

Above: Brand new R22s awaiting their owners in the factory. The R22 continues to sell well.

Above: Helicopters have been operating over America's cities for many years. Only the safest and most reliable single-engine helicopters fly over the city.

R22 Beta

Type: Two-seat lightweight helicopter

Powerplant: One 119-kW (160-hp.) Lycoming O-320-B2C flat-four piston engine de-rated to 96-kW (130 hp.) for takeoff

Maximum speed: 180 km/h (112 m.p.h.)

Service ceiling: 4267 m (14,000 ft.)

Range: 595 km (370 mi.)

Hover ceiling: 2133 m (7,000 ft.)

Accommodation: 2 seats side by side in an enclosed cabin, dual controls optional.

Weights: Empty 346 kg (763 lb.); loaded 589 m (1,298 lb.)

Dimensions:
Rotor diameter	46.17 m² (25 ft. 2 in.)
Length	6.3 m (20 ft. 8 in.)
Height	2.6 m (8 ft. 9 in.)
Rotor disc area	46.2m² (497 sq. ft.)

R22 BETA

This U.S.-registered R22 is typical of the many serving worldwide. The aircraft is popular for training and as a low-cost personal transport.

View from the cabin is excellent and the doors may be removed if desired. Police and observation models can be supplied with bubble door windows.

A tall rotor pylon holds the main rotor well clear of the upper fuselage. This distinctive feature of the R22 has also been adopted on the four-seat R44. A special system is installed to prevent the rotor blades hitting the tailboom when starting in windy conditions.

A bright-red beacon flashes to warn other aircraft to the presence of the R22. Much basic helicopter training occurs over the airfield.

For anti-torque control the R22 uses a small two-blade tail rotor. The blades have a stainless steel spar and leading edge with light alloy skins and honeycomb filling.

The Lycoming engine is mounted on the rear part of the cabin and has a prominent cooling fan. Fuel is carried in a 72.5-litre (19-gallon) tank in the upper left part of the fuselage.

Mounted below the vertical tail surface on the right-hand side is a small tailskid. This keeps the tail rotor clear of the ground in the event of a tail-low landing.

With a track of 1.9 m (6 ft. 4 in.), the skid undercarriage provides a stable landing platform. Combined float and skid landing gear is available on the R22 Mariner, but this requires an extra tailplane to be fitted.

N2276X

ACTION DATA

SPEED

Turbine power for the Schweizer 330 results in it having a higher maximum speed. Speed, however, is not always of great importance in the initial stages of flying training and the more docile characteristics of the R22 may benefit the student pilot.

R22 BETA	180 km/h (112 m.p.h.)
330	199 km/h (124 m.p.h.)
EXEC 162F	153 km/h (95 m.p.h.)

COST

For flying schools and private buyers alike, the purchase price is of great importance. If initial costs to a school are low then it can pass on these benefits by providing cheaper lessons and so attracting more pupils. The low price of the Exec 162F results from it being supplied as a kit for home assembly, while the 330 is a more complex aircraft with a price to match.

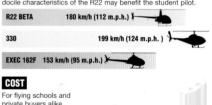

R22 BETA	EXEC 162F	330
$115,850	$56,000	$433,775

RANGE

All three of these small helicopters offer outstanding range due to their light weight and efficient engine design. The R22 is quite outstanding in this respect, providing novice pilots with the opportunity for long cross-country training flights.

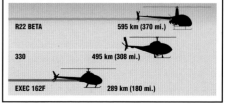

R22 BETA	595 km (370 mi.)
330	495 km (308 mi.)
EXEC 162F	289 km (180 mi.)

Helicopter lightweights

■ **ROTORWAY SCORPION TOO:** Designed by B. J. Schramm this aircraft is sold in kit form for assembly by amateur builders.

■ **BELL 47:** On 8 March, 1946, the American Bell 47 received the first ever Approved Type Certificate for a civilian helicopter.

■ **HUGHES 300:** Developed in the early 1960s, the Hughes 300 was also license-built in Italy and found favour with a range of operators.

■ **ENSTROM 280:** A more luxurious development of the F-28 of 1960, the 280 first flew in 1973 and remains a popular aircraft.

ROBINSON

R44

● Lightweight helicopter ● Proven design ● Brisk sales

Encouraged by the success of its two-seat light helicopter, the R22, the Robinson Helicopter Company of Torrance, California, created a slightly larger four-seater variant of the older machine for training and transport duties. Many proven features were retained in the interest of cost saving, simplicity and safety. The first R44 began flying in 1990, and by early 1994 around 300 R44s were in service around the world.

▲ *Robinson's R44 embodied many features of its predecessor. The simple controls kept the cost of the aircraft low, which is one of the reasons for the excellent sales figures.*

ROBINSON R44

▼ Value for money
At present, this little helicopter has a list price of just $265,000 in its home market, which makes it a very attractive buy.

▲ Trademark design
A distinctive feature of Robinson designs is the tall main rotor shaft. Many proprietary components are used on the rotor assembly.

Occupant protection ▶
Comfort and safety were prime aims for the R44, so an electronic throttle governor and safety restraints are standard.

▼ Popular in the US
Small helicopters have proved especially popular in the United States, and competition is fierce. The R44 has sold well.

Exceptional ▶ versatility
Base model R44s are known as Astros. They are also available for use as police helicopters, fire-bombers and for logging support.

FACTS AND FIGURES

➤ The first two R44s built accumulated more than 200 flying hours between 1990 and 1992.

➤ A total of $15,000 in deposits was taken on the first day of R44 sales.

➤ By January 1997, 308 R44s were operating in 38 different countries.

➤ The first R44 to reach 2,000 hours was the seventh production machine, which was returned for overhaul in mid-1996.

➤ The left-hand collective control lever and pedals can be removed if required.

➤ A float-equipped version, the Clipper, is available; it retails for $281,000.

PROFILE

Popular lightweight

Robinson's R44 has been an undisputed success story for the company. Since it was launched in the early 1990s, orders have continued to come in from customers in various parts of the world. A major reason for its popularity is the relatively low list price, which currently stands at around $265,000 in the USA.

Experience with the R22 resulted in the retention of the rotor design, which is unique in that it eliminates the need for the complicated hydraulic struts and shock absorbers found on most other rotary-winged craft. Other notable features include maintenance-free couplings in both the main and tail rotor drives, and spiral bevel gears.

Most R44s have been purchased for private use or as flying camera platforms by television news companies. Others have been bought by small police departments.

Above: N244H was the second R44 to fly and, like the first, was painted in this smart livery. It was later fitted with large floats in place of the skids and served as the demonstrator for the more upmarket R44 Clipper variant.

Below: R44s have enjoyed sales success outside the USA, too. This smart dark blue example is one of a number of machines currently registered in the United Kingdom.

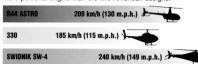

R44 Astro

Type: four-seat general-purpose light helicopter

Powerplant: one 194-kW (260-hp.) Textron Lycoming O-540 horizontally opposed six-cylinder engine

Maximum speed: 209 km/h (130 m.p.h.)

Initial climb rate: 305 m/min (1,000 f.p.m.)

Range: 643 km (400 mi.)

Service ceiling: 4270 m (14,000 ft.)

Weights: empty 635 kg (1,397 lb.); loaded 1088 kg (2,394 lb.)

Accommodation: one pilot and up to three passengers

Dimensions:
tail rotor diameter	1.47 m (4 ft. 10 in.)
length	9.07 m (29 ft. 9 in.)
height	3.28 m (10 ft. 9 in.)
main rotor diameter	10.06 m² (108 sq. ft.)

Proven equipment on the R22 was retained for its larger sibling. In the cockpit, this includes the Robinson central cyclic stick plus an automatic throttle governor and rotor brake which help to reduce pilot workload.

An innovative feature of Robinson helicopters is the main rotor unit. It is triple-hinged, eliminating the need for lag hinges, shock absorbers and hydraulic struts, increasing reliability and reducing maintenance time.

A two-bladed main rotor is standard on the R44 and both blades are metal-bonded for maximum strength and durability. The leading edges are fabricated from steel.

In both the main and tail rotor drives, maintenance-free flexible couplings are used as is a special elastic teeter hinge. This prevents the main rotor blades from making contact with the tail unit.

Light alloy is primarily used on the fuselage, with the cabin section comprising a steel cage covered with lightweight metal and plastic skinning. Extensive use of sound deadening material results in a low level of cabin noise.

R44 ASTRO

This colourful British-registered example is typical of the many R44s currently in service around the world. Orders have been strong and production looks set to continue for many years to come.

ACTION DATA

CRUISING SPEED

Faster than the rival Schweizer 330, the R44 has excellent performance for a lightweight helicopter, a factor which has been instrumental in its popularity. The Polish Sw-4 features a much more powerful engine than the two American designs.

R44 ASTRO	209 km/h (130 m.p.h.)
330	185 km/h (115 m.p.h.)
SWIDNIK SW-4	240 km/h (149 m.p.h.)

CLIMB RATE

It may be faster than the 330 in a straight line, but the R44 cannot climb as quickly as the Schweizer machine. PZL's redesigned Swidnik Sw-4 can climb 600 m in just one minute, which is more than twice as quick as the Robinson helicopter.

R44 ASTRO	330	SW-4
305 m/min (1,000 f.p.m.)	420 m/min (1,375 f.p.m.)	600 m/min (2,000 f.p.m.)

MAXIMUM RANGE

Depending on the role, range can have a varying degree of importance. The R44 has excellent endurance, a common characteristic of Robinson helicopters which makes it ideal for such tasks as crop-spraying. The Sw-4 is better still, capable of nearly 1000 km (560 miles) without being refuelled.

R44 ASTRO 643 km (400 mi.)

330 498 km (3009 mi.)

SWIDNIK SW-4 900 km (558 mi.)

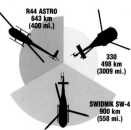

Robinson helicopters at work

■ **FISHING SUPPORT:** Fitted with floats, these helicopters support large fishing fleets.

■ **COW HERDING:** Many large farms in the USA use helicopters for rounding up cattle.

■ **POLICE WORK:** R22s (shown) and R44s are employed by various police departments.

■ **CROP-SPRAYING:** Robinson helicopters are often used in the crop-dusting role.

RUTAN

VOYAGER

● Ultra-long-range experimental craft ● Non-stop around the world

V oyager's glorious adventure enthralled millions in December 1986, when for the first time a crew of two pilots travelled around our entire planet without pausing or refuelling. With its bizarre shape, modern lightweight construction and enormous fuel capacity, this amazing aircraft was the right machine for a marathon endurance test. Its pilots were cramped but courageous throughout their incredible journey.

▲ Jeanna Yeager and
Dick Rutan were the two pilots of the Voyager for its incredible globe-circling flight. Dick's brother Burt was the designer of the amazing contraption.

RUTAN VOYAGER

◀ Voyager pilot
Dick Rutan not only co-piloted the Voyager on its round-the-world flight, but also made the type's first flight on 22 June 1984. To prepare for the global flight, Rutan and Yeager flew a 111-hour warm-up.

Flying fuel tank ▶
The layout of the Voyager was set by the need to carry more than 4500 litres (1,200 gal.) of fuel. Every available space in the wings, booms and fuselage was used for tanks.

▲ Flexible wing
The wingtip was so flexible that it moved up and down through 3 metres (10 ft.).

▼ Voyager meets the press
This was the public roll-out at Mojave airport. The amazing shape of the aircraft included winglets, but these were damaged on take-off on the record-breaking flight and were deliberately shaken off by some vigorous manoeuvring.

▲ Safe return
After nine days, three minutes and 44 seconds, Rutan and Yeager landed Voyager at Edwards AFB to a tumultuous reception.

FACTS AND FIGURES

➤ Ninety per cent of Voyager's construction is of light but strong graphite fibre.

➤ B-52 Stratofortress bombers, the only other non-stop around-the-world fliers, needed inflight-refuelling.

➤ One of Voyager's fuel tanks is 9.04 m (30 ft.) long, longer than some small aircraft.

➤ Voyager carried more than four tonnes of fuel when it set off around the world.

➤ Voyager's wings scraped the ground on take-off, but the pilots jettisoned the damaged winglets and pressed on.

➤ Voyager is now on display in the Smithsonian museum in Washington.

PROFILE

Non-stop Voyager

Voyager pilots Dick Rutan and Jeanna Yeager lived inside a cocoon of futuristic graphite for nine days in December 1986 when they guided this fantastic aircraft 40252 km (25,011 mi.) around the world. Like seafaring explorers of the past, they had to rely on skill and daring.

Their strange aircraft was a marvel of shrewd design and 21st century technology. For its purpose of going higher and further than any flying machine before it, the Voyager needed composite material for very light weight, a capacity for a giant-sized volume of fuel, and a graceful, sailplane-like shape which would allow it to be carried on its journey by the air and the wind.

The courageous pilots conquered dangerous weather, including Typhoon 'Marge' in the Pacific early in the flight. They used several methods of navigation to take their remarkable route around the Earth. After 216 hours in the air, they were greeted by an extraordinary welcome and by world acclaim.

When it lifted off for its around-the-world flight, Voyager used more than 4330 m (14,200 ft.) of the 4570-m (15,000-ft.) runway.

One of the small wingtip winglets was lost on take-off, so the other was shaken loose in flight without incident.

Voyager's wings were like those of a high-performance sailplane. The main spar was solid Magnamite graphite composite, covered with a Hexcel paper honeycomb and skinned with Magnamite sheets and a composite of aramid/epoxy/graphite.

Voyager

Type: special mission (around-the-world, non-stop) aircraft

Powerplant: one 82-kW (110-hp.) Teledyne Continental Motors Voyager 200 liquid-cooled engine at the rear of the fuselage and one standard 97-kW (130-hp.) Continental Model O-240 air-cooled engine at the front

Normal speed: 193 km/h (120 m.p.h.); with tailwind 238 km/h (148 m.p.h.)

Range: 41840 km (26,000 mi.)

Weights: empty 842 kg (1,850 lb.); world flight take-off weight 4472 kg (9,900 lb.)

Dimensions:
span	33.83 m (111 ft.)
length	7.86 m (25 ft. 6 in.)
height	3.18 m (10 ft. 4 in.)
wing area	30.10 m² (324 sq. ft.)

VOYAGER

Voyager was an aircraft built for a single task: to fly non-stop around the world. Designed by Burt Rutan and flown by his brother Dick and co-pilot Jeanna Yeager, it achieved its purpose in December 1986.

Voyager was powered by two Teledyne Continental piston engines, one of which was generally shut down for maximum economy during cruising flight.

The rear engine was slightly less powerful than the front, delivering 82 kW (110 hp.) against 97 kW (130 hp.). The propeller was fitted with a brake to stop it windmilling in the front engine's slipstream when in single-engine mode.

Voyager had two vertical fins, which were mounted on the end of the tailbooms.

The landing gear was fully retractable, but to save weight there was no power assistance: the wheels were pulled or wound up manually by the crew.

The cabin was just large enough for one pilot to sit to starboard while the off-duty crew member stretched out on a bunk alongside.

On the ground, the tips of Voyager's fuel-laden wings flexed nearly three metres downwards from their flight positions.

Voyager's fuselage and tailbooms were of Magnamite graphite/Hexcel honeycomb composite construction.

Only one of the two tailfins was fitted with a rudder.

N269VA

WINGS AROUND THE WORLD

DOUGLAS WORLD CRUISER

In the early days of flight, the US Army planned a spectacular trip around the world to publicise military aviation. Four Douglas DT-2s were modified as Douglas World Cruisers, with excess equipment removed and extra tanks fitted. On 6 April 1924, the flight took off from Seattle on a route which would take them via Alaska across the Pacific, through Japan, China, Southeast Asia, India, the Middle East, Europe, Iceland and Greenland. One aircraft crashed in Alaska and one was forced to ditch in the Atlantic, but the two survivors completed the route on 28 September. The flight had lasted 175 days, with a total of 371 hours 11 minutes actual flying time.

BOEING B-52 STRATOFORTRESS

The US Air Force made the first non-stop flight around the world. On 2 March 1949 a Boeing B-50 fitted with the newly developed aerial refuelling capability completed a 94-hour flight which had required the services of six tankers. Eight years later mid-air refuelling had become commonplace, and three eight-engined B-52B bombers completed the journey in 45 hours and 19 minutes. They had flown 39146 km (24,270 miles) at an average speed of 860 km/h (530 m.p.h.), refuelling several times en route.

Around the world in nine days

DAY 9 – rear engine stops and has to be restarted.

DAY 8

DAY 7 – violent storm puts Voyager into a 90° bank.

DAY 6 – climb high to avoid thunderstorms.

DAY 5

DAY 4

DAY 3 – route north around Typhoon Marge.

DAY 2

DAY 1

Edwards AFB

ACTUAL ROUTE

PLANNED ROUTE

WESTBOUND ROUTE: Voyager flew westbound to take advantage of the low-altitude trade winds in the Equatorial region. Most of the flight was at about 2450 metres (8,000 ft.), but over Africa altitude reached 6250 metres (20,500 ft.) to avoid thunderstorms.

PUSHED OFF COURSE: The plan was for Voyager to follow a great circle route taking it well into the southern hemisphere, but bad weather forced the aircraft north.

RUTAN

VARIEZE/LONG-EZ

● Advanced construction ● Fully aerobatic ● Cheaper than a car

▲ Burt Rutan's designs use advanced technology at astonishingly low cost and are highly original. The VariEze is fairly typical: a high-performance ship, appealing to the eye and offering simplicity with great strength.

Aircraft for everyone: that is the goal of California inventor Burt Rutan, maker of unorthodox glassfibre lightplanes which can be constructed by amateurs and flown by ordinary people. Since 1968 Rutan has given the world the VariViggen, VariEze, Long-EZ and Quickie. All are affordable, unconventional, and easy to construct and operate.

RUTAN VARIEZE/LONG-EZ

◀ **More space**
The Long-EZ is an improved and enlarged VariEze, and has an astonishing maximum range of more than 3200 km (2,000 mi.).

▲ **Foreplane control**
Foreplanes in place of tailplanes offer a pilot considerable low-speed handling advantages. Aircraft like the Quickie do not stall at slow speeds; they simply 'parachute' downwards without changing attitude, and a touch on the throttle has them flying again.

▲ **Viking Dragonfly**
The pioneering VariEze influenced a whole generation of designers. In 1980 the Viking company introduced the Dragonfly, a highly successful two-seater which could be built for less than $12,000.

▼ **Quickie**
Burt Rutan has helped several companies with designs. The Quickie, which first flew in 1977, is an easy-to-build kit which bears the unmistakable Rutan stamp.

▲ **VariViggen**
Named after the Swedish fighter, which was one of the first to use a canard configuration, the VariViggen is one of the most manoeuvrable aircraft ever to have flown, able to slow-roll at speeds where other aircraft would stall.

FACTS AND FIGURES

➤ Some Rutan homebuilds use a sidestick controller, like the F-16 jet fighter.

➤ The first VariEze, the Model 31, was built in a 10-week period in 1975 and performed perfectly on its first flight.

➤ Rutan's Defiant is a bigger, four-seat, twin-engine craft.

➤ The Popular Flying Association gives advice on flying and building VariEzes.

➤ The Long-EZ holds world distance records for homebuilds; in 1981 it flew 7725 km (4,800 mi.) non-stop.

➤ The prototype Defiant reached an altitude of 8535 metres (28,000 ft.) during trials.

PROFILE

Planes for the people

The Rutan VariEze, the best known in a series of fine lightplanes designed by Burt Rutan, first flew in 1975. From the start it enabled ordinary enthusiasts to build and fly an exciting small aircraft which incorporates glassfibre composites and other cutting-edge technology.

The maker of the VariEze provides homebuilders with all raw materials and most component parts of this recreational aircraft, including the Plexiglas canopy, moulded glassfibre nosewheel, two- or four-cylinder lightweight piston engine and glassfibre cowling.

With little more than written directions and a spirit of adventure, almost anyone can transform drawings into an actual VariEze aircraft that is able to fling itself around the skies at almost 300 km/h (185 mi.).

Not everybody is ready for the homebuilt revolution, however, and the radical shape of the Rutan VariEze still seems startling to many. But to those ready for a voyage of discovery, constructing a VariEze is a realistic undertaking which can cost less than the price of a mid-sized saloon car.

Because Rutan designs are sold in kit form, they have been built all over the world. This VariEze is from Switzerland.

A one-piece side-hinged canopy covers the single-seat cockpit. The Q2 has a wider cockpit, seating two side by side.

All flight surfaces are formed from glass-reinforced plastic (GRP) spars within a shaped core of low-density rigid foam. The outer skin is covered in a smooth layer of GRP.

VariEze Model 33

Type: two-seat sporting aircraft

Powerplant: one 74.5-kW (100-hp.) Continental O-200-B flat-four engine in the rear fuselage driving a two-blade pusher propeller

Max speed: cruising 313 km/h (195 m.p.h.); economy cruise 265 km/h (164 m.p.h.)

Stalling speed: 90 km/h (56 m.p.h.)

Take-off run: 275 m (900 ft.)

Range: 1126 km (700 mi.) at 75 per cent power; 1368 km (850 mi.) with max fuel at economy cruising speed

Service ceiling: 6705 m (22,000 ft.)

Weights: loaded 601 kg (1,320 lb.)

Dimensions:
span	7.96 m	(26 ft. 11 in.)
length	5.12 m	(16 ft. 9 in.)
height	2.40 m	(7 ft. 7 in.)
wing area	7.62 m²	(82 sq. ft.)

QUICKIE

The Quickie Aircraft Corporation of Mojave, California, asked Burt Rutan to use his VariEze experience in helping them to design an advanced composite aircraft for homebuilders.

The foreplane has marked anhedral – sloping downwards from the wingroots. The main wing, by contrast, has a small dihedral; it slopes upwards.

The Quickie's backward-sweeping tailplane is of similar construction to the wings, and is equipped with a single narrow-chord rudder.

The original Quickie was powered by a two-cylinder four-stroke engine delivering 13.5 kW (17 hp.) to a wooden two-blade fixed-pitch propeller.

Fixed undercarriage mainwheels are mounted in swept fairings at the tips of the downward-sloping foreplanes.

The Quickie's fuselage is of semi-monocoque construction. The banana-shaped body is formed from 25 mm (1 in.) of foam, surfaced by a thin layer of GRP for strength.

Built to a standard tailwheel layout, the Quickie has the rear wheel projecting to the rear and continuing the downward line of the fuselage.

G-BHUK

RUTAN SPECIALS

RUTAN MODEL 151 ARES

Burt Rutan was involved in design studies for the US Army to produce a low-cost battlefield aircraft, and used that experience in the design of the ARES. The name stands for Agile Response Effective Support and describes a lightweight jet armed with a 25-mm cannon, which has potential for anti-helicopter, close support, border patrol, drug enforcement and forward air control work.

BEECH STARSHIP

The Beech Starship takes all of Burt Rutan's characteristic design features and applies them to a business aircraft. The result is one of the most advanced and sophisticated private aircraft in the world: the Starship has jet-like performance and handling with the economy of a twin turboprop. The aft-mounted engines and pusher propellers give the eight passengers and two crew an extremely smooth ride.

A tradition of mould-breaking

■ **RUTAN DEFIANT:** In its first year, 150 sets of plans of the Defiant four-seater were sold to homebuilders.

■ **VIKING DRAGONFLY:** The Viking Aircraft Company's Dragonfly cruises at up to 275 km/h (170 m.p.h.).

■ **QUICKIE Q2:** The original Quickie was a single-seater. The Q2 is a side-by-side two-seater introduced in 1979.

■ **AT3:** Built by Scaled Composites, the AT3 is a 14-seat advanced-technology tactical transport.

■ **VARIVIGGEN:** Very easy to fly, the VariViggen can barrel-roll safely at speeds as low as 148 km/h (90 m.p.h.).

SAAB

90 SCANDIA

● Regional airliner ● DC-3 replacement ● Piston powered

▲ Production versions of the Scandia
could accommodate 24 passengers with
a three-abreast seating arrangement as
seen above. For high-density routes, 32
passengers could be accommodated in a
less comfortable four-abreast layout.

Saab's Scandia delighted pilots and
passengers. It was the ultimate
small, piston-powered airliner when
it made its debut after the end of World
War II. Sweden's innovative Saab company
had never built an airliner, but it hoped to
reap huge profits as the creator of a
replacement for the Douglas DC-3. Unfortunately, it was too late for piston power
and too early to consign the DC-3 to the
aircraft boneyard.

SAAB 90 SCANDIA

▲ **Piston power**
The original Pratt & Whitney R-2000
engine did not produce enough
power. Production aircraft were
powered by the bigger R-2180-E1.

▲ **Unveiling the prototype**
After a fairly secret development,
the first flight took place in
November 1946, with the pilot
Claes Smith declaring, 'In contrast
to the J 21 fighter, the Scandia
behaved exactly as predicted.'

▲ **Vikings of the air**
The only European operator of the Scandia was SAS
who named all their aircraft after famous Vikings.
This example was called Jarl Viking.

▲ **Export orders**
Some two Brazilian airlines
operated the Scandia. This
example flew for VASP.

Silver shine ▶
Like many of the classic propliners
of the postwar period the Scandia
flew in a polished bare-metal finish.

FACTS AND FIGURES

➤ Despite its great promise, only a total of
18 Scandias, including one prototype,
were manufactured.

➤ The prototype for Saab Scandia made its
initial flight on 16 November 1946.

➤ The first 12 airplanes were built by Saab,
and the last six by Fokker in Holland.

➤ Another Saab 90 was broken into
components and used as a ground
instruction trainer at Sao Paulo, Brazil.

➤ The final Scandia in service logged 15,683
hours and travelled 3,208,500 miles.

➤ One Scandia was preserved for display
at a museum in Brazil in 1975.

Saab's first airliner

A new age of air travel dawned at the end of the Second World War, and aircraft builders hastened to prosper from it. Saab, a new company whose experience was with combat aircraft, developed a conventional and perfectly acceptable short-range transport in the Saab 90 Scandia. The Scandia was offered to any airline that wanted to launch a modern fleet. Except for its tricycle landing gear, the Scandia resembled the DC-3 it was meant to replace.

The Scandia may have been available a little too soon for some countries rebuilding after the war. AB Aerotransport, the carrier that became the Scandinavian Airlines System, ordered a few of these transports, as did Aeroavias Brasil (later VASP).

Both airlines found the Saab 90 to be efficient and popular, and placed second orders. But the Scandia had drawbacks. It was not pressurized, though a pressurized version was planned. And by the time the world was ready for a DC-3 replacement, it was too late for

The prototype conducted extensive demonstration tours in Europe, Africa and later the United States and Latin America. It was also tested as a freight carrier, including an impressive nonstop flight between Albenga and Stockholm.

this piston-powered air plane to make major inroads into the civil transport market.

Each structurally conventional wing held two fuel tanks with a total volume of 29,700 litres (6,512 gal.).

The nosewheel leg was raised an extra 10 cm (4 in.) on production versions to give the propellers extra ground clearance.

The passenger cabin had 16 windows. There were also eight small windows in the cabin ceiling with built-in lamps to illuminate the cabin at night.

90 Scandia

Type: short-range civil transport

Powerplant: two 1,800-hp. Pratt & Whitney R-2180-E1 radial piston engines

Cruising speed: 389 km/h (242 m.p.h.) at 3048 m (10,000 ft.)

Range: 1480 km (920 mi.)

Service ceiling: 7498 m (24,600 ft.)

Accommodation: 4 or 5 flight crewmembers and 24 to 36 passengers.

Weights: empty 9939 kg (21,912 lb.); max takeoff 15,966 kg (35,200 lb.)

Dimensions: span   27.99 m (91 ft. 10 in.)
length   21.29 m (69 ft. 10 in.)
height   7.42 m (24 ft. 4 in.)
wing area 85.66 m² (922 sq. ft.)

90 SCANDIA

This Scandia was the second production aircraft and served with SAS until it was sold to Aeroavias of Brazil.

The Scandia would normally fly with a pilot and a co-pilot. Standard equipment included a Sperry A-12 autopilot.

The fuselage could accommodate 24 passengers in three-abreast seating or 36 passengers in a four-abreast arrangement.

This Scandia appears in the markings of Scandinavia Airline System (SAS) which was the only European operator.

SCANDINAVIAN AIRLINES SYSTEM   SAS   SE-BSB

Production Scandias were fitted with the 1342-kW (1,800-hp.) Pratt & Whitney R-2180-E1 engine.

The undercarriage retracted forwards into the engine nacelle to facilitate lowering in case of hydraulic failure.

Behind the passenger cabin was a cargo hold with a volume of 24.43 m³ (236 cu. ft.). The lavatory at the rear was fitted with a ceiling window.

The Scandia had a conventional tail layout with a rounded fin and tailplane. This feature resembled the aircraft it was designed to replace – the DC-3.

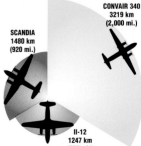

ACTION DATA

SPEED

The Scandia was much faster than the DC-3, which it was designed to replace. However, it could not match the speed of the more powerful Convair 340. The turboprop airliners that were being developed were faster still and made the Scandia look sluggish.

SCANDIA	389 km/h (242 m.p.h.)	
CONVAIR 340	447 km/h (278 m.p.h.)	
Il-12	349 km/h (217 m.p.h.)	

ACCOMMODATION

Although the Scandia could carry 36 passengers on high-density routes, this arrangement was very cramped. A more usual cabin arrangement would be for 24 passengers in comfortable reclining seats. The Soviet Il-12 carried a similar number of passengers.

SCANDIA   36 passengers

CONVAIR 340   44 passengers

Il-12   32 passengers

RANGE

Designed as a regional airliner, the Scandia had more than sufficient range for its tasks. The bigger Convair 340 had a much larger fuel capacity and could travel much longer distances. The Il-12 was generally used for domestic flights in the Soviet Union and had similar range to the Scandia.

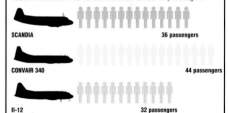

CONVAIR 340 3219 km (2,000 mi.)

SCANDIA 1480 km (920 mi.)

Il-12 1247 km (775 mi.)

Regional airliners that failed

■ DOUGLAS DC-5: The DC-5 first flew in 1939, but the outbreak of World War II reduced the demand for civil airliners. Douglas abandoned the project to concentrate on military production.

■ CESSNA 620: This pressurized 8- to 10-seat transport was powered by four Continental engines. It was abandoned when second-hand Convair 440s and Martin 4-0-4s became available.

■ LOCKHEED 75 SATURN: The Saturn was an excellent design. However, with many wartime transports becoming available it was not financially viable and the project was scrapped.

■ AVIATION TRADERS ACCOUNTANT: This 28-seat twin-turboprop airliner was marketed in the late 1950s. No sales were forthcoming and only one example was built.

SAAB

340

- Commercial airliner ● Corporate transport ● Military VIP aircraft

▲ *Since its first flight in 1983 the Saab 340 has been a success, with 280 aircraft delivered by early 1992. Production of the improved 340B continues at approximately 50 per year.*

Playing a major role in the growth of regional airline services, the Saab 340 extends passenger flights to markets that could not support a larger aircraft. Feeding major airline hubs, the 350-plus 340s in service make an average of six flights each per day. Around the world that means a Saab 340 either takes off or lands on average every 20 seconds. Each plane can carry a maximum of 37 passengers up to 1500 km (930 mi.).

SAAB 340

▼ Comair sale
Penetration of the American market was vital to the 340's success. The first customer was Comair, which took delivery of 19 aircraft.

▲ Propeller economy
Turboprop airliners are much favoured for their low noise and operating costs. Saab has achieved new levels of fuel economy with the 340 thanks to its low-drag airframe and highly efficient General Electric engines.

▼ Advanced wing
America's National Air & Space Administration designed an all-new, low-drag wing for the 340 when Fairchild were originally involved in the project. The tapered planform wing had a single-slotted, hydraulically operated honeycomb-alloy flap.

◀ More customers
By the late 1980s, with Saab running the project alone, the 340 had notched up customers in Asia, Europe, Australasia and America. The 340 prototype leads this formation.

▲ Metal frame
The new aircraft was largely built of alloys, with selective use of composites and Kevlar.

FACTS AND FIGURES

- ➤ Fairchild withdrew from the original 340 project after suffering financial difficulties in 1987.

- ➤ The largest customer for the 340 was American Eagle, which bought 100 aircraft.

- ➤ The 340 was temporarily grounded due to problems with the CT-7 engines.

- ➤ An airborne early warning version with a spine-mounted Ericsson radar has been developed for the Swedish air force.

- ➤ Asian customers include China Southern Airlines and Formosa Airlines.

- ➤ A Collins APS-85 autopilot and flight control system is fitted as standard.

PROFILE

Short haul in the quiet Saab

Launched in 1980 as a joint development by Saab of Sweden and Fairchild of the USA, the 340 project was later taken over completely by Saab. The first aircraft were delivered to Crossair of Switzerland in 1984. The initial American operator was Comair, and in 1985 the first corporate version was delivered.

In the years since then the 340 has proved a popular choice. It has enabled both established and start-up regional airlines to open up new routes while offering passengers high standards of speed and comfort.

In 1988 the improved 340B was introduced with more powerful engines. The resulting increase in operating weight allowed airlines to provide a better level of service, including, for example, hot meals to be served. Since 1989 this has been the standard model.

Ten years after the 340 entered service, Saab introduced a further upgrade. The 340

BPlus featured a new interior and active noise monitoring and control, using a system of microphones and loudspeakers. This reduced noise by about half. The first BPlus, and the 359th 340, was delivered to American Eagle in 1994.

Crossair of Switzerland have become an established operator of Saab aircraft, having been the launch customer for the Saab 340 and the larger 2000. The 340 has also been successful in the Far East.

The spacious cabin generally has three-abreast seating for up to 37 passengers in 12 rows. There is also provision for a galley, toilet and wardrobe or baggage module. Alternatively, a cargo or combined layout can be adopted.

The wings are constructed from aluminium spars with glass fibre and Kevlar panels and ailerons.

The horizontal stabiliser contains VOR/LOC antenna and the cockpit voice recorder.

340B

Type: regional commercial and corporate transport

Powerplant: two 1394-kW (1,870-hp.) General Electric CT-79B turboprops

Maximum speed: 522 km/h (324 m.p.h.)

Initial climb rate: 624 m/min. (2,048 f.p.m.)

Range: 2414 km (1,500 mi.) with 45-minute reserves and 30 passengers

Service ceiling: 7620 m (25,000 ft.)

Weights: maximum take-off 12,927 kg (28,439 lb.)

Accommodation: 33, 35 or 37 passengers seated three abreast

Dimensions: span 21.44 m (70 ft. 4 in.)
length 19.72 m (64 ft. 8 in.)
height 6.91 m (22 ft. 8 in.)
wing area 41.81 m² (450 sq. ft.)

340B

Continental operate the Saab 340 on short-range regional air routes in the United States. The aircraft is also ideal for business and VIP transport roles.

The modern flight deck has seating for two pilots and an observer. The flight attendant has a seat at the front of the cabin.

Two General Electric CT7-9B turboprops with Dowty four-blade reversible propellers provide a maximum of 1394 kW (1,870 hp.) of thrust and 1305 kW (1,750 hp.) for normal take-off. Refuelling points are over the wing and in the wing leading edge.

Located above the wing on either side of the fuselage is an emergency exit door for passengers. The crew's escape hatch is located in the flight deck roof.

Entry to the aircraft is via a single door at the front of the cabin on the port side, using an integral airstair which folds up into the forward fuselage for stowage during flight.

The main undercarriage is of twin-wheel type, retracting forward into the engine nacelle in flight.

Luggage is loaded into a rear fuselage bay via a large square section cargo door which slides upwards to open. All parts of the cabin are fully pressurised.

The tailcone contains discharge valve nozzles to jettison excess fuel prior to landing or in an emergency situation.

ACTION DATA

MAXIMUM CRUISING SPEED

Airlines do not operate turboprops for sheer speed, as regional jets are faster but more expensive to operate. Competition between manufacturers for performance means that all these aircraft are very closely matched in speed.

340B — 522 km/h (324 m.p.h.)
EMB-120 — 504 km/h (312 m.p.h.)
JETSTREAM 41 — 547 km/h (339 m.p.h.)

PASSENGER LOAD

Passenger capacity is all-important to regional airline operators, as a few empty seats can make all the difference between profit and loss. The Saab is slightly larger than most of its rivals.

340B 35 passengers
EMB-120 BRASILIA 30 passengers
JETSTREAM 41 29 passengers

RANGE

During the design stage Saab aimed the 340 at the US feederliner market as a result of the collaboration with Fairchild. The Jetstream and Brasilia were intended for the business sector and were designed with a shorter range.

340B 2414 km (1,500 mi.)
EMB-120 BRASILIA 1020 km (632 mi.)
JETSTREAM 41 1100 km (682 mi.)

Regional turboprop airliners

ATR-42: Built by a consortium of Aérospatiale of France and Alenia of Italy, the ATR-42 has been very successful and dominates sales of turboprops in the civil sector.

DHC DASH-8: The twin-engined counterpart of the Dash-7, the Dash-8 has the notable short take-off performance associated with DHC turboprops and is popular in North America.

LET 610: Produced in the Czech Republic by LET, the 610 uses General Electric CT-7 turboprops. It is aimed at existing customers of the LET 410 and was purchased by Aeroflot.

AIRTECH CN.235: Produced by a consortium in Indonesia and Spain, the CN.235 is operated by the military for maritime surveillance and transport and used by civilian customers as an airliner.

SAAB

2000

● 50/58-seat transport ● Swiss launch customer ● 340 derivative

On the back of considerable success with its 340 (more than 400 sales worldwide of its 35-seat feederliner), Saab secured an order from 340 operator Crossair of Switzerland in 1988 for 25 new Saab 2000s. As the name suggests, this was designed as an aircraft for the new millennium, but sales were sluggish as other operators chose regional jets over turboprops. Production of the 2000 came to an end in 1999.

▲ *Saab developed a new 50-seater for a fraction of the cost of a totally new design by basing the 2000 on the successful 340 35-seater. Common fuselage and wing cross-sections were used.*

PHOTO FILE

SAAB 2000

Swiss Phantom ▶
Crossair joined the growing list of airlines painting their aircraft in promotional colour schemes, with its 'The Phantom of the Opera' Saab 2000.

◀ Six-bladed propellers
Dowty Aerospace's efficient six-bladed propellers are of carbon-fibre sandwich construction. Their multi-blade design allows them to be rotated at reduced speeds, which minimises the 2000's noise footprint.

Saab's feederliners ▶
In this comparative view, some of the major differences between the 340 and 2000 are apparent.

◀ In German service
German associate of British Airways, Deutsche BA, was the second 2000 customer. Operators appreciate the jet-like speed of the type.

2000 prototype ▶
SE-001 was the first Saab 2000, which took to the air on 26 March 1992. Here it is seen on an early flight with its undercarriage extended. An instrumentation probe has been fitted to the aircraft's nosecone.

FACTS AND FIGURES

➤ Construction of large parts of the Saab 2000 was sub-contracted. The rear fuselage was built by Westland.

➤ The 2000's tail was built by Valmet in Finland; CASA built the wings in Spain.

➤ Crossair of Switzerland had the largest 2000 fleet with 25 in service.

➤ Sweden's government lent around US$180 million for Saab 2000 development, to be paid back by 2009.

➤ General Motors took delivery of the first corporate 2000 in October 1995.

➤ By August 1996, 33 Saab 2000s were in service, all but one in Europe.

PROFILE

Fast turboprop 2000

Saab's objective was to combine jet-like speeds with the economy of a turboprop aircraft. A cruising speed of 680 km/h (425 m.p.h.), a climb rate sufficient to take the aircraft to 6100 m (20,000 ft.) in 10 minutes, and cruising altitudes between 5485 m (18,000 ft.) and 9450 m (31,000 ft.) were the principal aims of the aircraft's designers.

Not simply a 'stretch' of the 340, the 2000 incorporates a number of new features. For example, power comes from two Allison AE 2100 turbines, the 2000 being one of the first types to use this new fuel-efficient engine. Each AE 2100 drives a six-bladed Dowty Aerospace propeller.

Features shared with the 340B are the fuselage cross-section and wing section, though the fuselage is naturally longer to accommodate up to 58 passengers. Wing span is increased by 15 per cent; the total wing area is 33 per cent greater. The engines are set further out from the fuselage to reduce cabin noise.

During the design phase, Saab made extensive use of computer-aided design and manufacture (CAD/CAM) to produce a prototype which took to the air for the first time on 23 March 1992, less than four years after programme launch.

The sixth aircraft off the production line was the first to be delivered, in August 1994, and entered service the following month.

Below: The Saab 2000 heralded a new era of fast, quiet turboprops which could compete effectively with jets over shorter sectors.

Above: SE-004 was the first production example and was later delivered to launch customer Crossair.

Most of the Saab 2000's primary structure is of aluminium alloy, like that of the 340B. The fin, propeller blades and cabin floor are of carbon-fibre, however, and limited use of composites is also made elsewhere.

2000

Type: twin-turboprop regional transport

Powerplant: two 3096-kW (4,150-hp.) (flat rating) Allison AE 2100A turboprops

Maximum speed: 682 km/h (423 m.p.h.)

Cruising speed: 594 km/h (369 m.p.h.) at 9450 m (31,000 ft.)

Initial climb rate: 685 m/min (2,250 f.p.m.) at sea level

Range: (at maximum cruising speed with 50 passengers and reserves at 1525-m (5,000-ft.) altitude) 2222 km (1,375 mi.)

Service ceiling: 9450 m (31,000 ft.)

Weights: operating empty 13,800 kg (30,360 lb.); maximum take-off 22,800 kg (50,160 lb.)

Accommodation: flight crew of three or four, plus 50 passengers ('European' configuration) or 58 (high-density configuration)

Dimensions: span 24.76 m (81 ft. 3 in.), length 27.28 m (89 ft. 6 in.), height 7.73 m (25 ft. 4 in.), wing area 55.74 m² (600 sq. ft.)

2000

Carrying its test registration SE-018, this aircraft was destined for Swiss operator Crossair. It was finished in a 'Phantom of the Opera' livery to mark the opening of the musical production in Switzerland.

An Ultra Electronics Active Noise Control (ANC) system uses 72 microphones and 36 speakers to monitor and neutralise cabin noise by means of an anti-phase sound field.

Some operators chose to move the cabin rear bulkhead further aft. This allows more space for the galley and wardrobe, which in turn frees cabin space for an additional eight seats, giving a 58-seat capacity.

A six-screen Collins Pro Line IV cockpit instrumentation system is standard. All aircraft also feature a solid-state WXR-840 weather radar and customers may specify turbulence-detecting weather radar.

A single control is used to adjust the Allison AE 2100A engines and their propellers, allowing for simplicity of operation. The engines have been moved outboard to minimise cabin noise.

A 10.2-m³ (361-cu. ft.) baggage hold is located in the rear fuselage, with access gained via a large door on the port side. If the rear bulkhead is moved aft, baggage space is diminished.

Certification of the 2000 was delayed by problems with the Powered Elevator Control System, which was replaced in late 1993. The first deliveries were delayed 18 months.

ACTION DATA

PASSENGERS

Usually flown in a 50-seat layout, the Saab 2000 may be configured with 58 seats. The new aircraft has a considerably greater capacity than Saab's 340B but holds fewer passengers than Jetstream's troubled ATP.

2000 — 58 passengers
340B — 37 passengers
ATP — 72 passengers

MAXIMUM SPEED

Passengers and airlines appreciate the benefits offered by an aircraft capable of near-jet speeds, with the economy of a turboprop. Jetstream's ATP (or 61) should have been a direct competitor to the 2000 but failed to offer adequate performance.

2000 — 682 km/h (423 m.p.h.)
340B — 522 km/h (324 m.p.h.)
ATP — 502 km/h (311 m.p.h.)

RANGE

Range is another strong point of the excellent Saab 2000. High-tech engines and other modern systems account for the aircraft's fine overall performance. The Saab 340B continues in limited production, while the ATP and its Jetstream 61 derivatives are no longer being made.

2000 — 2222 km (1,375 mi.)
ATP — 1739 km (1,080 mi.)
340B — 1732 km (1,075 mi.)

Civil Saab designs

 **90 SCANDIA:** Conceived during World War II and first flown in 1946, the Scandia entered service in Europe and with VASP in Brazil.

 **91 SAFIR:** This four-seat cabin monoplane dated from 1945. Around 320 were built for customers in 20 countries.

 **SAFARI TS:** The late 1960s Safari was originally powered by a 149-kW (200-hp.) Lycoming IO-360 air-cooled piston engine.

 **340:** Originally conceived in a joint venture with Fairchild (who withdrew in 1985), the 340 35-seater went on to sell in large numbers.

SAUNDERS-ROE

PRINCESS

- Last of the great passenger flying-boats ● Magnificent failure

A vision of a futuristic age of air travel that might have been, the Saunders-Roe SR.45 Princess was a magnificent flying-boat of the post-war era, and was to be the world's largest pressurised aircraft and turboprop. It was an enormous technical achievement, but the Princess suffered from nagging problems with its powerplant and it arrived on the scene after flying-boats no longer offered advantages over landplanes.

▲ The Princess, like the Brabazon, was another example of a technological wonder that had almost no relevance at all to the requirements of airlines in the 1950s and should never have been built.

SAUNDERS-ROE PRINCESS

◀ **Clean design**
The Princess was powered by engines located in pairs in the wing, driving the propellers via long shafts. This was an elegant aerodynamic solution, but it made the wing very complex and heavy.

▲ **Air show star**
The Princess flew at Farnborough to delight the crowds. At higher speeds the floats would have been retracted into the wingtips.

◀ **Saunders-Roe slipway**
The Princess shared its slipway at Cowes with the SRA-1 fighter. The Princess handled well on water, but the need for large flying-boats, like floatplane fighters, did not really exist.

▼ **Under construction**
The huge size of the Princess meant that it was built more like a ship than an aircraft. The twin pressurised hulls were constructed first, mounted one on top of the other, and the rest of the airframe was then assembled around them.

▲ **Waiting for engines**
The technical snag with the Princess was the disastrous Bristol Proteus turboprop. Even when the airframe was complete, the engines were delayed and were much weaker than expected.

FACTS AND FIGURES

➤ The first Princess made a delayed maiden flight on 22 August 1952.

➤ The 65920-litre (17,140-gal.) fuel capacity was housed entirely in wing tanks.

➤ By 1952 British Overseas Airways Corporation, the only potential customer, decided to operate landplanes only.

➤ A proposition to use six Tyne turboprops would have solved any power problems.

➤ The US Navy seriously considered using the three Princess prototypes to test an atomic powerplant.

➤ The only Princess to fly was towed to a salvage yard in 1967 and scrapped.

PROFILE

Britain's magnificent maritime failure

As the Princess thundered over Southampton Water on an early test flight, it looked down on the ocean liners it was designed to replace. This huge, majestic aircraft with its double-deck fuselage and 10 engines in six nacelles was intended as an ocean liner of the sky, to offer luxurious travel to the privileged and the discerning.

The dream died because no turboprop engine available in 1950 could offer the power the Princess needed – and because land-based aircraft then coming along, including the Boeing Stratocruiser, offered a similar standard of service at far lower cost to the operator.

The ambitious thinking behind the Princess led, in fact, to plans for a landplane version, as well as a 'Twin Princess' with two full-sized fuselages and 14 engines which would have been used as a cargo-hauler.

In the end, these grandiose plans came to nothing. At one stage the three Princess prototypes were to be converted into RAF troop transports. But this dream also died, and only the first prototype was ever flown.

The Princess belonged to the maritime world of Southampton. In many ways it had more in common with the ocean liners which it flew over than with the airliners with whom it would have shared the airways.

Princess prototype

Type: long-range passenger flying-boat

Powerplant: 10 2386-kW (3,200-hp.) Bristol Proteus 600 turboprops (eight in coupled units, plus two single units)

Maximum speed: 579 km/h (360 m.p.h.)

Range: estimated 9000 km (1,860 mi.)

Service ceiling: estimated 10000 m (33,000 ft.)

Weights: take-off 156492 kg (344,282 lb.)

Accommodation: flight crew of two pilots, two flight engineers, one navigator and one radio operator. As conceived for trans-ocean airline travel, the Princess would have handled 105 passengers in first class; as an RAF troop transport it would have carried 200 fully-equipped combat soldiers and all their equipment

Dimensions:		
span	66.90 m (219 ft.)	
length	45.11 m (148 ft.)	
height	17.00 m (56 ft.)	
wing area	487 m² (5,240 sq. ft.)	

The Princess was an incredible sight. But no matter how majestic its appearance, it was doomed to fail, beaten by the harsh demands of economics and market forces.

Powered control units in the rear of the hull operated the three-section electro-hydraulically operated rudder and twin-section elevators.

The flight deck housed two pilots, a navigator, two flight engineers and a radio operator.

Passenger accommodation was divided between two decks, with spiral staircases between them fore and aft. The rear cabin even had pull-down beds in the area where modern airliners have overhead baggage lockers.

SR.45 PRINCESS

The Princess prototype, G-ALUN, was the only one that flew out of the three built. The other two were put into storage on completion.

The wing leading edges were de-iced thermally, using air piped from the exhaust manifolds.

The tailplane was de-iced by kerosene-burning heaters with their own fuel supply, fed by an air intake in the base of the fin.

G-ALUN

The Princess used a capacious hold in the lower hull to carry cargo and baggage.

The hull bottom was an efficient hydrodynamic design. Take-offs and landings were notably smooth.

Giant cargo carrier

■ One of the more outlandish schemes to salvage the Princess programme was to develop a giant cargo carrier. Joining a pair of hulls with a common central wing would have created a transport able to carry 400 troops or 50 tonnes of cargo.

Princess landplane

■ A more practical proposition involved redesigning the hull with wheels and a rear loading ramp. Power would have been provided by six Tyne turboprops. Although the resulting airlifter would have been highly capable, the plans perished with the rest of the Princess programme.

ACTION DATA

TRANSATLANTIC TIME

To be fair to the aviation committees of the 1940s which first planned the Princess and the equally large but futile Brabazon, few people could have foreseen the revolution that the jet would bring to airliner performance. But by the early 1950s the Comet had sounded the death knell for such monsters, and the superb Boeing Model 707 was in the air less than two years after the first flight of the Princess.

PRINCESS 11 hours BRABAZON Mk I 14 hours BOEING 707 7 hours

RUTAN 151 ARES

● Lightweight ● Unique design ● Only one built

When Fairchild designed an aircraft around a single, big, multi-barrelled cannon, it materialised as the massive, tank-like A-10. Facing the same challenge, maverick designer Burt Rutan came up with something completely different. The Agile Response Effective Support (ARES) which his Scaled Composites company produced in the late 1980s matched a US Army requirement for a low-cost close air support aircraft. The emergent aircraft was unique.

▲ Rutan began studies on a light, low-cost battlefield support aircraft in 1981 and the result was the ARES. Customers were sought, but to no avail, and the project was shelved in 1995.

◄ Flying cannon
In some respects, the ARES represented a scaled-down A-10 Thunderbolt II, with a huge and tremendously powerful gun in the nose. Firing tests on this weapon began in 1991.

▼ Military transport, Rutan style
Another of Rutan's ambitious projects was the AT3 Advanced Tactical Transport. Like the ARES, it failed to win any orders.

▲ New standard in economy
Intended as a replacement for the Beechcraft Bonanza, the Catbird was an ultra-efficient five-seater light aircraft.

Demonstrator experience ►
In the past, Scale Composites had built many advanced prototypes.

◄ Too advanced?
An excellent aircraft in its own right, demonstrating superb performance and agility, the Rutan 151 ARES was perhaps too radical to succeed. It was nevertheless a very valuable research tool and demonstrator.

FACTS AND FIGURES

➤ Scaled Composites was bought from Burt Rutan by Beech Aircraft but later sold back to him in June 1985.

➤ Design on the ARES began in 1981, yet it did not fly until 1990.

➤ Initially, the project was private, with no additional funding from outside firms.

➤ The gun installation was designed so that the blast impinged on the forward fuselage and counteracted recoil.

➤ The single ARES prototype was finally grounded during 1996.

➤ A two-seat trainer variant was proposed but unfortunately never built.

PROFILE

Beyond frontiers and the battlefield

The reason for the location of the ARES turbofan engine on the left side of the aft fuselage was to keep the intake clear of the gases generated when the gun was fired. The gun itself was mounted at the aircraft's centre of gravity in a depression on the fuselage side, ensuring that the powerful recoil forces were balanced by the muzzle blast.

Aerodynamically, the aircraft used forward-swept canard foreplanes, a compound wing swept back 50° on the inboard sections and 15° outboard, and twin fins mounted on booms.

Low observability was another consideration. Although advanced stealth techniques were avoided to escape export restrictions, the position of the engine meant that its compressor blades were shielded from ground-based radars, while the twin fins masked the IR emissions of the exhaust.

The ARES flew for the first time in February 1990 and went on to complete live firing tests. However, the end of the Cold War meant the US Army no longer needed large numbers of low-cost ground attack aircraft, and the developing countries which were another target market generally opted for more versatile designs.

Distinctive canards are a feature of many Rutan designs, although, during flight testing, those on the Model 151 ARES were found to limit the angle of attack.

Extensive use was made of lightweight materials, notably carbon-fibre and poly vinyl chloride, resulting in a very light airframe.

Rutan Model 151 ARES

Type: experimental anti-helicopter and close air support aircraft

Powerplant: one 13.12-kN (2,949-lb.-thrust) Pratt & Whitney JT15D-5 turbofan

Maximum speed: 695 km/h (431 m.p.h.)

Range: better than 1850 km (1,149 mi.)

Internal fuel capacity: 771 kg (1,696 lb.)

Weights: empty (unarmed) 1308 kg (2,877 lb.); maximum take-off 2767 kg (6,087 lb.)

Armament: one General Electric GAU-12 25-mm cannon with 220 rounds of ammunition plus two Stinger or Sidewinder missiles

Dimensions:
span	10.67 m (35 ft.)
length	8.97 m (29 ft. 5 in.)
height	3.00 m (9 ft. 10 in.)
main wing area	17 m² (188 sq. ft.)
canard area	3.19 m² (34 sq. ft.)

RUTAN 151 ARES

Only one Model 151 was ever built. Allocated the serial N151SC (the last two letters indicating Scale Composites), it first flew in 1990 and began armament firing tests a year later. It is currently in storage.

From the outset, the entire aircraft was designed around the General Electric GAU-12 rotary-barrelled cannon. Despite its proximity to the cockpit, the pilot encountered few problems during gun firing, and a special shield protected him from the blast.

A clear one-piece bubble canopy offered superb all-round visibility, better than perhaps any combat aircraft, production or otherwise. For escape, the pilot sat on a UPC SIIS-3ER ejection seat.

Offsetting the single Pratt & Whitney JT15D-5 to port prevented gun gases being ingested by the air intake. Despite its location, the thrust line was central, being corrected by a curved jet pipe.

During flight testing, the Model 151 was cleared to carry a variety of ordnance. Two AIM-9 Sidewinder air-to-air missiles could be carried on the wing stations for air defence, or four of the smaller AIM-92 Stinger missiles.

One of the few conventional features of the ARES was the landing gear. Single wheels were fitted to each oleo and retracted backwards. The nose unit retracted into the fuselage and the main units retracted into the forward sections of the twin tail booms.

Mounting the fins and rudders on short tail booms resulted in the engine being shielded, making it less likely to be hit by ground fire.

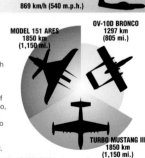

ACTION DATA

MAXIMUM SPEED

Powered by a turbofan, the Model 151 had decent performance. It was faster than the twin-engined turboprop-powered Rockwell OV-10 Bronco, but slower than the single-engined Cavalier Turbo-Mustang that was derived from the famous World War II P-51.

MODEL 151 ARES	695 km/h (431 m.p.h.)
OV-10D BRONCO	463 km/h (287 m.p.h.)
TURBO MUSTANG III	869 km/h (540 m.p.h.)

RANGE

Both the ARES and the Turbo Mustang had a range greater than 1850 km, which in a war scenario would give them considerable time over the battlefield if required. The Bronco, which was the only one of these three to enter service, ironically had the shortest range of all.

MODEL 151 ARES 1850 km (1,150 mi.)
OV-10D BRONCO 1297 km (805 mi.)
TURBO MUSTANG III 1850 km (1,150 mi.)

MAXIMUM TAKE-OFF WEIGHT

Extensive use of lightweight materials resulted in one of the lightest aircraft ever devised for the battlefield support role. Both the Bronco and the Turbo Mustang were real heavyweights by comparison and probably less suitable for the role.

MODEL 151 ARES 2767 kg (6,087 lb.)
OV-10D BRONCO 6552 kg (14,414 lb.)
TURBO MUSTANG III 6350 kg (13,970 lb.)

Failed battlefield support aircraft

CAVALIER MUSTANG II: Derived from the civilian Cavalier, the Mustang II proved unsuitable for the close-support role.

CONVAIR 44 CHARGER: One of two designs evaluated by the USAF in the 1970s, the Charger lost out to the OV-10 Bronco.

ILYUSHIN Il-102: An unusual design, the Il-102 was an attempt at a simple, very low-cost close-support aircraft.

SCHWEIZER

330

● American light helicopter ● Hughes ancestry ● Limited sales

Designed in the early 1980s to meet the US Army's requirement for a new flight training helicopter, the Schweizer 330 was produced with three sets of controls so that two students could be instructed simultaneously. It lost to the Bell TH-57 Creek in the military competition, but has been sold subsequently as a three- or four-seat light utility machine. It offers an attractive combination of low cost, high performance and mission flexibility.

▲ *Looking similar to the larger Hughes/McDonnell Douglas Model 500 series of light helicopters, the Schweizer 300 first flew in June 1988, and went on sale during 1993.*

PHOTO FILE

SCHWEIZER 330

▼**Common components**
In common with rival light helicopter designs, the 330 shares many components with another model, the Series 300. These include its basic fuselage structure and flying controls.

▲ **Army evaluation**
Schweizer's design was one of several tested for the US Army's New Training Helo requirement.

Sluggish sales ▶
Sales got off to a slow start, with only 12 Schweizer 330s being delivered by 1996.

▼ **First flight**
N330TT was the first 300 prototype and made its maiden flight on 14 June 1988.

Versatility ▶
The 330 was designed from the outset to fulfil a variety of roles, including fire fighting and law enforcement.

FACTS AND FIGURES

➤ Some design features of the 330 can be traced back to the Hughes 269, which first flew in 1956.

➤ The first Schweizer 330 in Europe was a demonstrator for Saab Helikopter.

➤ West Palm Beach Police Department in Florida operates a fleet of 330s.

➤ Main rivals in the US light helicopter market include the best-selling Robinson R44 and Enstrom 480 series.

➤ By January 1997 a total of 15 Schweizer 330 helicopters had been delivered.

➤ The Venezuelan army is one of the few military operators of the 330.

Lightweight performer

Schweizer's Model 330 is a turboshaft-powered development of the manufacturer's established Model 300. Originally a Hughes design, the Model 300 had been developed from the Model 269. Production was transferred to Schweizer in 1983.

The 330 was designed to combine safety and mission flexibility with outstanding performance. The unusual fuselage shape, combined with large stabilisers, make the 300 particularly stable, and the simple push-rod control system avoids the excessive weight and cost of hydraulic boost and stability augmentation devices. The fuselage also helps provide lift during forward flight and improves the flow of air to the main rotor.

Other safety features include a crash-resistant fuel bladder and a cabin floor and seat structure which has been specially designed to absorb sudden vertical impact during deceleration.

Left: An interesting and practical feature of the 330 is its ability to run on turbine fuel instead of Avgas if the operator wishes.

Right: This view of N330TT shows the similarity of the 330 to the elderly 300, especially the cockpit and doors.

330

Type: three-seat light utility helicopter

Powerplant: one 313.2-kW (420-hp.) Allison 250-C-20 turboshaft

Max cruising speed: 200 km/h (115 m.p.h.)

Range: 498 km (309 mi.)

Hover ceiling: 4300 m (14,100 ft.) in ground effect

Weights: empty 508 kg (1,117 lb.); loaded 1012 kg (2,226 lb.)

Fuel capacity: 227 litres (60 gal.)

Accommodation: one pilot and two passengers

Dimensions:
tailplane span	2.04 m (6 ft. 9 in.)
length	6.82 m (22 ft. 4 in.)
height	2.91 m (9 ft. 6 in.)
main rotor disc area	52.5 m² (565 sq. ft.)

Retaining many design features from the two-seat Series 300, the larger 330 offers an excellent view from the cockpit. The interior layout is flexible and three sets of full controls can be specified for student training.

Considerable attention was paid to ease of maintenance and this is reflected in the design of the rotor. Unlike the rival R44, the 330 features three blades and all are fully interchangeable. Elastometric dampers are incorporated.

On the original prototype, the tail boom was an open design, similar to that of the Series 300. The fuselage was later redesigned to produce an incredibly well streamlined integrated tail unit.

N330TT

A single Allison 250-C20 turboshaft powers the Schweizer 330. Flat-rated at just 175 kW (235 hp.), this engine has the ability to run on turbine fuel instead of Avgas and offers excellent hot-and-high performance.

330

Serialed N330TT, this particular machine was the first Schweizer 330 built and made its maiden flight on 14 June 1988. Originally painted white, it was subsequently modified with a more streamlined fuselage and repainted in this blue colour scheme.

CRUISING SPEED

Two of the Schweizer 330's main rivals in the light helicopter market are the Enstrom 480 and Robinson R44. Both these machines have better all-round performance than the 330, which may be a reason for the Schweizer's relative unpopularity.

330	185 km/h (115 m.p.h.)	
480	204 km/h (126 m.p.h.)	
R44 ASTRO	185 km/h (130 m.p.h.)	

RANGE

The Schweizer design also has much shorter range than its rivals. Enstrom's 480 is probably the better all-round helicopter and has seating for up to five, but retails for a similar price to that of the more advanced Schweizer 330.

330 498 km (309 mi.)

480 787 km (488 mi.)

R44 ASTRO 643 km (400 mi.)

POWER

Both the Schweizer and Enstrom helicopters are powered by single Allison 250 series turboshafts. Although the 330 therefore has a respectable 313 kW (420 hp.), it does not offer the same level of performance as the Enstrom. The R44 boasts far less power but also out-performs the 330.

330 313 kW (420 hp.)

480 313 kW (420 hp.)

R44 ASTRO 194 kW (260 hp.)

Proven utility helicopter designs

■ **AÉROSPATIALE ALOUETTE II:** Dating from the early 1950s, the Alouette was one of the first truly versatile light helicopters.

■ **AÉROSPATIALE GAZELLE:** Successor to the Alouette II, the Gazelle was also built under licence in the United Kingdom.

■ **BELL 206 JETRANGER:** One of the most successful helicopters in the world, the Jetranger is a familiar sight.

SHORT

330/360

● Twin-turbine feederliner ● Overseas sales ● Skyvan development

▲ Short
always envisaged the United
States as the primary market for the 330 and 360 and
took advantage of changes in the law which allowed
commuter airlines to operate larger aircraft.

With the success of the Skyvan and a perceived need for a larger aircraft in the 'DC-3 replacement' mould, Short embarked on the SD3-30. Originally conceived as a 26-seater, the aircraft was enlarged to take advantage of changed rules in the United States which allowed commuter airliners to carry 30 passengers. The 330, as it became, flew in 1974, and was followed by the 36-seat 360 in 1981.

SHORT 330/360

▼ **From the Isle of Man**
With an appropriate registration, the Manx airline's 360 G-ISLE rests on the tarmac before a flight across the Irish Sea to the British mainland.

▲ **In German service**
Few 330s or 360s have seen service in Europe. German company DLT operated a small fleet of the earlier aircraft in the 1970s.

▼ **330-200**
The Series 200 was introduced in 1985 and had an improved fuel capacity over the earlier 100 variant.

▲ **To the Western Isles**
Now trading under the British Airways name, Scottish airline Loganair has retired its 330s but continues to fly a number of 360s.

Multiple owners ▶
With feeder airlines preferring more modern pressurised types, 330s and 360s have been phased out by many early operators. This Casair 330 was sold after two years and is now owned by Short Aircraft Leasing Ltd.

FACTS AND FIGURES

➤ A number of former feederliner aircraft have had their seats removed and entered service as freighters.

➤ Owned by Bombardier of Canada since 1989, Short no longer builds aircraft.

➤ The 360 entered service with Suburban Airlines of Pennsylvania, USA, in 1982.

➤ Most of the USAF's C-23A Sherpas were transferred to the US Forest Service in 1990; the Air National Guard flies C-23Bs.

➤ Of the 104 Short 360s still in service in late 1996, 54 were based in the Americas.

➤ The Thai army operated two 330-UTT (utility tactical transport) variants.

Short Brothers' last airliner

Powered by the well-known Pratt & Whitney PT6A turbine engine, the SD3-30 was a development of the Skyvan design, and retained the earlier aircraft's square cross-section fuselage and twin tail. The wings and fuselage were longer, however, and the sponsored undercarriage was retractable, which was a major improvement.

The first SD3-30 flew in August 1974 and entered service, as the 330, in 1976 with Time Air of Canada. This was followed by the 330-200, which had increased fuel capacity. A quick-change version was also offered, along with a military 330-UTT transport (used by the US forces as the C-23).

When US aviation regulations were relaxed again, Short enlarged the 330 to carry 36 passengers. This version was called the 336, later 360. The first two 360s carried the descriptive registrations G-ROOM and G-WIDE and flew in 1981 and 1982, respectively. The last variant built was the 360-300 of 1987, which had up to 39 seats in an improved cabin and was fitted with an autopilot.

Production ended in 1992, after 139 330s and 164 360s had been built.

Deliveries of production 360s began in 1982. The following year Air UK received two aircraft, G-BLPV and G-BLPY.

360-300

Type: twin-engined feederliner

Powerplant: two 1062-kW (1,425-hp.) Pratt & Whitney Canada PT6A-65AR turboprops

Maximum cruising speed: 400 km/h (248 m.p.h.)

Initial climb rate: 290 m/min (950 f.p.m.) at sea level

Range: 745 km (460 mi.) with maximum payload and typical reserves at maximum cruising speed; 1178 km (732 mi.) with 31 passengers and at a cruising speed of 337 km/h (209 m.p.h.)

Weights: operating empty 7875 kg (17,325 lb.); maximum take-off 12,292 kg (27,042 lb.)

Accommodation: two flight crew and up to 36 passengers; in the freight role up to 3765 kg (8,283 lb.) of cargo

Dimensions: span 22.80 m (74 ft. 9 in.); length 21.58 m (70 ft. 9 in.); height 7.27 m (23 ft. 10 in.); wing area 42.18 m² (454 sq. ft.)

The 360's redesigned tail surfaces had several advantages over the twin-tail arrangement of the 330, including reducing drag which thereby increased fuel efficiency. The baggage capacity in the rear of the aircraft was also improved on the later type.

On the 330 the outer wing panels of the Skyvan were used, but the span was increased. The 360's wing panels and bracing struts were strengthened.

360-100

Delivered to Manx airlines in March 1984, the appropriately registered G-LEGS was named 'King Magnus Barefoot (1098-1103)' in 1989. It was later sold to Loganair and operates on commuter flights in Scotland.

As is standard on feederliner aircraft of this size, the Short 330/360 has a flightdeck crew of two pilots.

After problems with the engines originally chosen for the Skyvan, Short selected the proven Pratt & Whitney Canada PT6A turbine for the 330, along with a Hartzell five-bladed propeller.

In addition to the new tail, the 360 featured a stretched fuselage which was 0.91 m (three feet) longer than that of the 330. This was accomplished by inserting a section in the fuselage forward of the wing.

A luggage compartment was situated at the rear of the cabin. On the 330 a loading door was situated below the tail unit.

The 330's twin fin and rudder were similar to those fitted to the Skyvan, although they were larger. The 360 was a more streamlined design, and the twin fins were replaced by a conventional single swept fin. The 360 also boasted more powerful PT6A engines.

The 360, originally known as the 336, could carry 36 passengers.

The undercarriage was contained in small sponsons, but was retractable.

ACTION DATA

MAXIMUM CRUISING SPEED

The shape of the 330/360 was not as aerodynamic as contemporary feederliner designs, and would have contributed to its slow cruising speed. Other major factors which affect speed are wing design and engine power.

- 360-300 400 km/h (248 m.p.h.)
- 340B 522 km/h (324 m.p.h.)
- Do 328 620 km/h (384 m.p.h.)

PASSENGERS

All three types were designed in Europe but have sold extensively in the USA. A passenger load of 30 to 45 is the most economical configuration in this sector.

- 360-300 36 passengers
- 340B 37 passengers
- Do 328 33 passengers

RANGE

Range was the main weakness of the 330/360 once larger types came on to the market, especially in the USA where internal flights tend to be longer than elsewhere. The popular Saab 340 and the Dornier 328 could fly about twice as far as the Short aircraft.

- 360-300 745 km (470 mi.)
- 340B 1520 km (1,120 mi.)
- Do 328 1352 km (840 mi.)

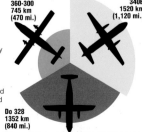

British twin-turbine airliners

BAe JETSTREAM: This family of feederliner and regional airliner was designed by Handley Page in the 1960s. The J41 has up to 29 seats.

BAe JETSTREAM 61: Originally known as the Advanced Turboprop, this 72-seat development of the HS.748 has new Pratt & Whitney engines.

HANDLEY PAGE HERALD: Flown in 1958, the Rolls-Royce Dart-engined Herald could seat 60 in its Series 700 variant. A total of 50 was built.

HAWKER SIDDELEY HS.748: The Dart-engined 748, designed by Avro, was first flown in 1960 and became Britain's best-selling turboprop.

SC.5 BELFAST

● Strategic airlifter ● Civilian freighter ● Tactical transport

A British long-range transport with much more potential development than it got, the Short Belfast production line ran to just 10 aircraft before 1970s defence cuts announced its end. The Belfast served with the RAF as a long-range strategic freighter until 1976. After retirement, the small fleet was purchased by the civil carrier HeavyLift, which from 1980 used it on charters to carry outsize loads around the world.

▲ Another example of wasted development that could have made a winner for British aviation, the Belfast is still seen all over the world in the colours of HeavyLift, the freight specialist.

SHORT SC.5 BELFAST

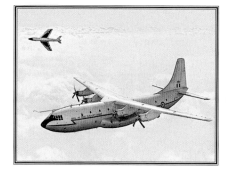

▲ Transport Command
Belfasts entered service with RAF Transport Command in 1966 and served for 10 years. No. 53 squadron was the only user. Some were sold to Pan African Freightliners in 1977 after the RAF retired them.

▲ Armour freight
Saladin armoured cars were no problem for the Belfast. The rear ramp door made fast loading of cargo simple.

◀ Built in Belfast
Named after the city where it was built, the Belfast did not keep the factories busy for long. Had the aircraft not been cancelled by the RAF, it may have attracted export orders.

▲ Worldwide lifter
With the capability to refuel in flight, the Belfast gave the RAF the ability to lift large cargoes anywhere in the world. The refueling probe has been removed from the HeavyLift Belfasts, since there is no need for it.

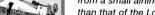

◀ Aircraft carrier
The Belfast could easily swallow up a fuselage from a small airliner. The fuselage was larger than that of the Lockheed Hercules, an interesting fact considering the arguments about the size of the proposed European FLA.

FACTS AND FIGURES

➤ The Belfast stemmed from a March 1957 design study into an aircraft called the Britannic.

➤ The Belfast was the first transport to have an automatic landing system.

➤ The Belfast prototype first flew on 5 January 1964; 10 were built for the RAF.

➤ Up to 10 Land Rovers and trailers or three Whirlwind helicopters could be carried by the Belfast.

➤ HeavyLift has carried Sepecat Jaguar fuselages to India in its Belfasts.

➤ Only two of HeavyLift's Belfasts remain in service today.

PROFILE

Heavy weight lifter from Belfast

HeavyLift Cargo Airlines, based at London's Stansted Airport, was set up in October 1978 specifically to operate Short Belfast freighters. These had recently come up for sale following their retirement from the RAF as an economy measure. Five were initially purchased by HeavyLift, three for mainstream operations and two held in reserve for use as spares.

The RAF's Belfast fleet was purchased to fulfill the shortage of high-capacity transport aircraft that existed in the late 1960s. The Belfast could carry the largest guided missiles, guns

and vehicles of the British army.

Each Belfast has a freight hold 90 feet long and 16 feet wide and the aircraft's high-strength airframe and four turboprop engines enable it to carry loads weighing up to 36,434 kg (80,323 lb.). Loading is accomplished from the rear of the hold via a ramp, often with the aid of an onboard powered winch. Now HeavyLift uses the Belfast's excellent cargo-carrying capacity to transport goods around the world. Despite being a wonderfully reliable aircraft, the 10 RAF aircraft were withdrawn in the late 1970s as

the United Kingdom's worldwide influence dwindled and the need for long-range heavy transport aircraft ended. It is ironic that the Belfast would subsequently have been a highly valuable asset in conflicts such as the Falklands and the Gulf.

Below: The Belfast showed remarkably benign handling for an aircraft that handled bulkier cargoes than a Boeing 747.

Above: The Belfast could also carry 150 troops in the hold, or up to 250 if a temporary upper deck was fitted.

SC.5 Belfast

Type: Long-range freighter.

Powerplant: Four 4124-kW (5,530-hp.) Rolls-Royce Tyne Mk 101 turboprop engines.

Maximum speed: 565 km/h (351 m.p.h.)

Service ceiling: 9144 m (30,000 ft.).

Range: 1609 km (1,000 mi.).

Weights: Empty 104,081 kg (229,460 lb.); loaded 139,008 kg (306,460 lb.).

Dimensions:
span	521.11 m	(158 ft. 10 in.)
length	41.66 m	(136 ft. 8 in.)
height	14.30 m	(46 ft. 11 in.)
wing area	245.73 m²	(2,465 sq. ft.)

BELFAST C.MK 1

Each of the RAF's Belfasts was given a personal name; XR367 was named *Hercules*. All military Belfasts served with No. 53 Squadron based at Brize Norton in Oxfordshire.

Flight crew in RAF Belfasts consisted of two pilots, a navigator, flight engineer and two loadmasters in the hold. Civil Belfasts have a similar crew configuration.

The excellent Rolls-Royce Tyne engines were so much in demand by the RAF when the Belfast was retired that Rolls-Royce bought five Belfasts and scrapped them just to recover the Tynes. This engine is also used in the Italian G.222 tactical transport.

The Belfast used basically the same wing as the Bristol Britannia. The ailerons were manually actuated through servo tabs, but the spoilers were hydraulically controlled and electrically activated.

The huge hold could also accommodate 10 Land Rovers with trailers, or two Wessex, or three Whirlwind helicopters.

The tail section, with its huge vertical fin, was also derived from the Bristol Britannia.

Unlike the rival An-12, the Belfast had an integral rear loading ramp and door for fast loading of vehicles.

ROYAL AIR FORCE

HERCULES

XR367

367

Belfast military loads

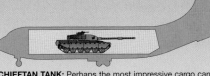

CHIEFTAN TANK: Perhaps the most impressive cargo carried by the Belfast was the Chieftan tank, a very heavy vehicle with a long gun barrel. The Chieftan could not be carried by similar aircraft like the C-130 Hercules.

SALADIN ARMORED CARS: Three Saladins fitted easily in the hold of the Belfast, with the rearmost vehicle facing forward. The weight of the Saladins was no problem, the limiting factor being the size of the cargo bay floor.

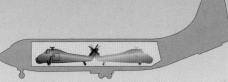

TWO WESSEX: With the helicopters' rotor blades removed and the airframes turned tail-to-tail, two Wessex could be fitted into the Belfast. This was an example of just how spacious the hold was given the shape of a Wessex.

ACTION DATA

RANGE

The Belfast was not as long-ranged as had been intended, mainly due to higher than expected drag. This was partly remedied in RAF service by the aircraft having air-to-air refueling provision, which the RAF C-130s did not have until 1982. Had the Belfast been designed from scratch rather than using Britannia parts, range could have been longer.

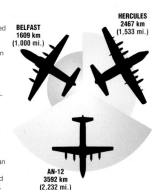

BELFAST 1609 km (1,000 mi.)

HERCULES 2467 km (1,533 mi.)

AN-12 3592 km (2,232 mi.)

SHORT

SC.7 SKYVAN

● Turboprop commuter ● Square-section fuselage ● Private venture

▲ Slotted in
among bigger aircraft, the
Skyvan became a well-known sight at numerous airports all around the world, providing feeder services for larger airlines.

I nspired by the Miles Aerovan, Short's Skyvan filled a niche in the civil market for an aircraft with an uncluttered box-section fuselage with provision for straight-in loading from the rear. Originally equipped with piston engines, the Skyvan was soon re-equipped with turbines. The aircraft sold well, starting a fashion that was followed by other manufacturers and followed up by the Short company itself with the enlarged Short 330 and 360.

SHORT SC.7 SKYVAN

▼ Olympic Airways
Greek airline Olympic was an early operator of the SC.7 and used it for short regional flights around Greece.

▲ Belfast's baby
Seen flying over Harland & Wolff's Belfast shipyard, this is the first of two Skyvans produced for Olympic Airways.

Flight testing ▶
Serving from 1979, with NASA's flight test facility at Wallops Island, Virginia, this sole example carried out mid-air retrievals of sounding-rocket payloads, which were used for atmospheric research. The aircraft was nicknamed the 'Ugly Hooker' and has now been retired.

▼ De-luxe travel
The Skyliner was an all-passenger variant which was introduced in 1970. It became the definitive commuter model of the Skyvan.

▲ Parachute training
Withdrawal of the balloon flight from RAF Hullavington left parachutist training to the operators of this example from Luxembourg.

FACTS AND FIGURES

➤ The Skyvan 1 prototype made its first flight from Sydenham, Northern Ireland, on 17 January 1963.

➤ Design of the Skyvan began as a private venture by Short in 1959.

➤ Civil Skyvans were used in Australia, the Middle East and the United States.

➤ When production ceased in 1985 154 Skyvans had been constructed; many are still in use.

➤ The Skyvan's roles included aerial survey, radio relay and fire spotting.

➤ Retractable skis can be fitted to the undercarriage of some variants.

PROFILE

Short's small wonder

Miles approached Short with a proposal that they build a version of the Aerovan, with high aspect ratio wings, called the HDM.106 Caravan. Although Short's purchased the design, they chose not to build it and instead designed a new aircraft along similar lines – the SC.7 Skyvan. This all-metal, beaver-tailed, rear-loading 'box van' aircraft had strut-braced rectangular wings and two Continental supercharged flat-six piston engines. Two

prototypes were built, and the first flew on 17 January 1963.

Early interest came from Alaska and Australia, where a reliable, economical aircraft was required. Within a matter of months, however, the prototype had been re-engined with Turboméca Astazou turboprops, which greatly improved its short field performance.

First sales came in 1965, when Aeralpi purchased Skyvans to operate between Milan and the Cortina d'Ampezzo ski resort.

Above: G-ASCN was the first Skyvan. Here it is seen fitted with a production tail unit and Astazou turbine engines.

Problems with the 'hot-and-high' capabilities of the Astazou engine led to the adoption of the Garrett TPE331 in 1967. When production ceased in 1985, 154 Skyvans had been built, including military examples.

Below: In flight the Skyvan looked ungainly, yet it proved to be an extremely practical design for light transport and passenger work.

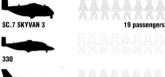

SC.7 Skyvan 3

Type: light utility transport

Powerplant: two 533-kW (715-hp.) Garrett AiResearch TPE331-201 turboprops

Maximum cruising speed: 327 km/h (202 m.p.h.)

Initial climb rate: 500 m/min (1,640 f.p.m.)

Range: maximum 1115 km (695 mi.); 300 km (185 mi.) with 1814 kg (4,000-lb.) payload

Service ceiling: 6860m (22,500 ft.)

Weights: empty 3331 kg (7,344 lb.); maximum take-off 5670 kg (12,500 lb.)

Accommodation: up to 19 passengers or 2086 kg (4,600 lb.) of cargo

Dimensions:
span	19.79 m (64 ft. 11 in.)
length	12.22 m (40 ft. 1 in.)
height	4.60 m (15 ft. 1 in.)
wing area	34.65 m² (373 sq. ft.)

With the Skyvan 2 Short introduced an optional weather radar installation contained in a more pointed nose radome (not fitted to this aircraft). The aircraft's controls are laid out for operation by a single pilot.

Garrett AiResearch's well-known TPE331 turboprop transformed the Skyvan's performance at altitude.

Inspired by the stillborn Miles HDM.106 Caravan, the SC.7 had a rectangular wing which produced STOL performance.

Between the prototype and production stages of the Skyvan's development various modifications were made, especially to the tail fins which were repositioned.

Skyvans in the feeder liner role were configured to carry 19 passengers. About a dozen 22-seat Skyliners were produced late in the production run.

At the time of its first flight the Skyvan was a unique design and gained orders worldwide. US operators generally viewed the type as a freighter.

SC.7 SKYVAN 3

Delaware Air Freight bought this Skyvan 3, which was first flown in July 1968, in 1973. The following year Delaware became Summit Airlines Inc. and flew the aircraft until it was sold in 1979.

ACTION DATA

PASSENGERS

Passenger versions of the Skyvan featured de-luxe comfort, but size was a limiting factor. Although other airliners were capable of carrying more passengers, this was in less comfortable conditions.

SC.7 SKYVAN 3	19 passengers
330	30 passengers
L-410UVP	15 passengers

ECONOMIC CRUISING SPEED

The square-section fuselage meant that performance was never outstanding compared to other airliners, like the Let L-410. The Skyvan more than compensated for its lack of speed, however, with its exceptional short take-off and landing capability.

SC.7 SKYVAN 3	278 km/h (172 m.p.h.)
330	296 km/h (184 m.p.h.)
L-410UVP	300 km/h (186 m.p.h.)

RANGE

Despite its ungainly design, the Skyvan had exceptional range, but at the cost of a reduced payload when compared to the later turboprop designs. The demands of expanding air travel forced larger passenger loads at the expense of range performance.

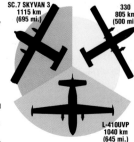

SC.7 SKYVAN 3 — 1115 km (695 mi.)
330 — 805 km (500 mi.)
L-410UVP — 1040 km (645 mi.)

Small turbine-powered transports

ANTONOV An-28 'CASH': A turboprop development of the An-14, the An-28 entered production in Poland in 1980.

CASA C.212 AVIOCAR: Intended to replace the DC-3, this Spanish design flew in 1971. More than 400 have been built for civil and military users.

HARBIN Y-12: An enlarged version of the Y-11, the Y-12 flew in 1982 powered by PT6A turboprops. Roles include geological survey.

IAI ARAVA: The first wholly IAI-designed aircraft, the Arava 20-seater, flew in 1969 and was produced in military and civil marks.

SHORT

MAYO COMPOSITE

● Long-range record holder ● Floatplane and mothership ● Mailplane

Short's Mayo Composite was an attempt to provide long-range air mail services by using two aircraft teamed together to carry out a single mission. This was a daring concept which looked bizarre. It was also a challenge to pilots, but it worked. During its brief moment of glory in the late-1930s, the Short Mayo combination established a long-distance duration record for seaplanes that will probably never be broken.

▲ An ingenious attempt at solving the problem of establishing a high-speed transatlantic mail route, the remarkable Short Mayo Composite performed brilliantly.

SHORT MAYO COMPOSITE

▼ **Pylon support**
A complicated pylon structure held the 'Mercury' securely on the S.21's back until separation.

▲ **Short S.20 'Mercury'**
'Mercury' was a completely new design and emerged as a sleek, four-engined floatplane with a long range.

Combining the aircraft ▶
Ground crew secure 'Mercury' on top of its 'Maia' mothership. Fully laden with fuel and 454 kg (1,000 lb.) of mail, the S.20 could not take off under its own power.

▼ **Separation**
'Mercury' was released at cruising altitude by the S.21. Although potentially dangerous, this operation never caused problems.

▲ **Eight-engined take-off**
A vital component of the Mayo Composite, the S.21 was based on the design of the successful 'Empire' flying-boat.

FACTS AND FIGURES

➤ With all eight engines running for take-off, the Short Mayo Composite had a total power output of 3760 kW (5,040 hp.).

➤ The normal cruising range of the loaded 'Mercury' was 6116 km (3,800 mi.).

➤ 'Mercury' was launched over Dundee, Scotland, for the record-breaking flight.

➤ On 6 February 1938 'Mercury' completed its first commercial, non-stop journey to Montreal in 20 hours 20 minutes.

➤ Changes in aerospace technology mean that the S.20's record may stand for ever.

➤ The second separation of the Mayo Composite was performed for the press.

PROFILE

Unique transatlantic mailplane

For its time it was one of the most incredible records in aviation history: 9652 km (5,984 mi.), from Dundee to the Orange River in South Africa.

In the 1930s, tests proved that an Imperial Airways 'Empire' flying-boat could achieve a transatlantic crossing if its entire payload only consisted of fuel, leaving no room for cargo or passengers. Since an aircraft can fly at a greater weight than at which it can take off, Robert Mayo proposed that a small, heavily loaded mailplane could be carried to operational altitude above a larger 'mother-plane' and then released to complete its long-range task.

Short designed and built a composite unit by modifying an 'Empire' flying-boat to carry the S.20 long-range twin floatplane. The system was a success, but World War II ended any further development.

'Maia' receives attention at its moorings. The S.21 flying-boat was destroyed by enemy action in May 1941, while the S.20 'Mercury' survived the war but was later broken up.

MAYO COMPOSITE

Short Brothers built only one each of the S.20 'Mercury' (G-ADHJ) and the S.21 'Maia' (G-ADHK). Both aircraft were finished in their natural metal colour with Imperial Airways titles.

Napier Rapier H engines, each of 254-kW (340 hp.), drove two-bladed propellers to power the S.20. On the flight to South Africa a cowling broke away adding extra drag to the problems posed by headwinds.

Three-bladed propellers fitted to Bristol Pegasus radial engines drove the S.21. The lower aircraft was only required to fly the short distance for launch before it returned to base.

An ingenious design, the pylon had to hold 'Mercury' securely but hinder the launch sequence as little as possible. This composite may have inspired the German Mistel projects.

'Mercury' was flown by a pilot and co-pilot, the latter also acting as the radio operator. For the record-breaking flight to South Africa the small S.20 weighed 12474 kg (27,443 lb.) on separation.

For the long-distance record attempt the floats were modified to hold extra fuel. Headwinds caused greater than expected fuel consumption, however.

To give the optimum water performance and to make lift-off as easy as possible, 'Maia' had a smooth two-step flying-boat hull.

MERCURY

MAIA

G-ADHJ

G-ADHK

The Mayo Composite concept

1 TAKE-OFF: Too heavily loaded to lift-off under its own power, the S.20 'Mercury' was hauled aloft by the S.21 'Maia'. Immediately after launch the 'mother-plane' returned to base.

2 SEPARATION: 'Mercury', still with a large fuel reserve, was released by 'Maia' at cruising altitude.

3 'MERCURY' LANDS ALONE: At the end of its long flight the S.20 landed on any suitable stretch of water. Return flights had to be made in stages since the 'mother-plane' was not available to carry 'Mercury' to altitude. This would have been a problem if the composite had entered regular service.

S.20 'Mercury'

Type: long-range floatplane mail carrier

Powerplant: four 254-kW (340-hp.) Napier Rapier H piston engines

Maximum speed: 339 km/h (210 m.p.h.); 314 km/h (194 m.p.h.) at maximum weight

Normal range: 6116 km (3,800 mi.)

Extended range: record flight 9652 km (5,984 mi.)

Weights: empty 4614 kg (10,150 lb.); maximum 7030 kg (15,466 lb.); normal Mayo Composite launch 9443 kg (20,775 lb.); record launch 12474 kg (26,752 lb.)

Payload: 454 kg (1,000 lb.)

Dimensions: span 22.20 m (73 ft.)
length 15.50 m (51 ft.)
wing area 56.80m² (611 sq. ft.)

SPECIFICATION
S.21 'Maia'

Type: flying-boat mother-plane for long-range upper component

Powerplant: four 686-kW (919-hp.) Bristol Pegasus XC radial piston engines

Maximum speed: 322 km/h (200 m.p.h.)

Range: 1360 km (843 mi.)

Service ceiling: 6100 m (20,000 ft.)

Weights: empty 11234 kg (24,715 lb.); max take-off 17252 kg (37,954 lb.); maximum for Mayo Composite launching 12580 kg (27,676 lb.)

Dimensions: span 34.70 m (114 ft.)
length 25.90 m (85 ft.)
wing area 162.50 m² (1,748 sq. ft.)

Record-breaking flight

DUNDEE

FLIGHT TO SOUTH AFRICA: Flying from Dundee, Scotland, to South Africa was a hazardous journey. Problems en route prevented 'Mercury' reaching its intended destination of Cape Town, and the crew were perhaps lucky to reach the Orange River unscathed.

ORANGE RIVER

SHORT

S.23 C-CLASS

● Flying-boat ● Trans-oceanic travel ● Mail service

The Short S.23 C-Class was a major technical advance in flying-boat design. It offered the latest features of the time – all metal structure, electrical flaps, variable-pitch propellers, a sleeping cabin, a promenade lounge and a steward's pantry. The S.23 entered service in 1937 and graced the skies for Imperial Airways and Qantas Empire Airways, among others. A trip in this aircraft was a memorable experience for any air traveller.

▲ 'Coriolanus' was beached for the last time in 1948, having flown over 4 million kilometres (2.5 million miles). Short's C-Classes were the last commercially successful flying-boats to fly in the British Empire.

SHORT S.23 C-CLASS

▲ Setting out
The C-Class flew as far afield as Cape Town, Egypt and Karachi, in addition to the European routes. Most of the cargo was mail, but passengers were also carried.

▲ Lifted ashore
Before the slipway was built at Queen's Island, 'Clio' had to be hoisted clear of the water by crane. When the slipway was completed, 'Clio' (renamed AX639 in RAF colours) was the first flying-boat to use it.

▲ Rest and refit
'Canopus' deserved its overhauls, having made many flights to Rome with British Imperial Airways.

▲ Wartime colours
Several C-Class aircraft were used as long-range transports in the war; some were lost in action.

Long service ▶
Travelling across the Empire built up huge numbers of flying hours, and 'Cameronian' flew 15,652 before it was scrapped.

FACTS AND FIGURES

➤ A Qantas S.23 flew the first commercial service between Australia and Southampton on 5 July 1938.

➤ First flight of an S.23 C-Class boat (Canopus) took place in July 1936.

➤ The Short S.23 was 26 km/h faster than the standard RAF fighter of its era.

➤ Among several S.23s impressed into RAF service, two became anti-submarine patrol aircraft.

➤ Together, the S.23, S.30 and S.33 were called Empire flying-boats.

➤ Thirteen of the Empire flying-boats were still airworthy at the end of World War II.

Flying ocean liners

When this magnificent flying-boat first appeared, it looked so promising that 28 were ordered before the first had even flown. The first boats in service operated from the new Imperial Airways flying-boat base at Hythe, Kent, where they provided air services to Australia, Bermuda, Egypt, Malaya, the United States and East and South Africa. The S.23 did not quite have the range for the transatlantic route, but its inadequacies led to early tests with flight refuelling. Short also developed the later S.30 and S.33 for longer flights. Thirty-one of Short's 42 Empire flying-boats were the S.23 C-Class (along with nine S.30s and two S.33s), which soon spread its wings far and wide. Australia at first resisted introducing flying-boats on its air routes, but by the late-1930s the S.23, then considered the most advanced aircraft of this type in the world, was performing well 'down under'. British Overseas Airways Corporation (BOAC) used the S.23 for heavy-duty wartime service, hauling people over long distances, and some were modified for patrol work.

Above: G-AFCZ, known as 'Clare', was lost in unknown circumstances after leaving Lagos, Nigeria, in 1942 while serving with BOAC.

Above: The first of the Empire boats, G-ADHL was later known as 'Canopus'. It was used for surveying the North Atlantic route and had extra long-range fuel tanks fitted.

S.23 C-Class

Type: mail/passenger flying-boat airliner

Powerplant: four 686-kW (920-hp.) Bristol Pegasus XC radial piston engines

Maximum speed: 322 km/h (200 m.p.h.)

Range: 1223 km (760 mi.)

Service ceiling: 6095 m (20,000 ft.)

Weights: empty 10,659 kg (23,500 lb.); normal loaded 17,655 kg (38,923 lb.); maximum take-off 19,732 kg (43,500 lb.)

Accommodation: two pilots, flight engineer, staff, and provision for up to 24 passengers or 3556 kg (7,840 lb.) of freight; later, the aircraft carried 17 passengers and 2000 kg (4,400 lb.) of mail

Dimensions:
span	34.75 m (114 ft.)
length	26.82 m (88 ft.)
height	9.70 m (31 ft. 10 in.)
wing area	139.35 m² (1,506 sq. ft.)

S.23 C-Class

G-AETY, known as 'Clio', flew mail from Southampton to Alexandria before being pressed into service as AX659 in 1940, after being modified for coastal reconnaissance with ASV radar by Short at Belfast.

An upper deck started just forward of the wing spar, with the flight deck ahead of it.

Four Bristol Pegasus engines powered the C-Class. The engines were installed in long chord NACA cowls with exit gills adjustable in flight to control cooling. Two large fuel tanks were located between the engine nacelles.

The distinctive tall tail of the C-Class was a feature that remained on later Shorts designs such as the wartime Sunderland.

The promenade cabin, with eight seats in two rows of four, had a wide 'promenade' along the port side with a railing below the windows.

The aft cabin had six seats. It was separated from the promenade cabin by a step up to the rear door. The seats were easily removable and were made to a luxurious standard.

The wingtip floats had waterproof compartments and bilge-pump connections and were wire-braced to withstand wave buffeting.

The main freight hold was at the rear of the aircraft, behind the passenger compartment. It was accessible via a door in the starboard side.

ACTION DATA

MAXIMUM SPEED

The requirement to land on water governed aerodynamics far more than the need for speed, which passengers did not expect in the 1930s. The powerful engines and streamlined fuselage gave the C-Class a respectable speed advantage over its rivals, and allowed it to compete with many land-based designs. On long routes to the Far East, travelling time was measured in days rather than hours, but the mail service was still far faster than in the days of shipping.

S.23 C-CLASS	322 km/h (200 m.p.h.)
Do R4 'WAL'	210 km/h (130 m.p.h.)
S-42	233 km/h (145 m.p.h.)

RANGE

C-Class flying-boats were relatively short ranged compared to their rivals, one reason being that the routes they flew to their destinations had a large number of refuelling stations in the British Empire. The Dornier flew to South America with fewer stops.

S.23 C-CLASS	1223 km (760 mi.)
Do R4 'WAL'	2000 km (1,243 mi.)
S-42	4000 km (2,485 mi.)

PASSENGER LOAD

Large flying-boats like the C-Class had impressive passenger facilities for their day. During the war years, the luxury passenger facilities of the inter-war period were dispensed with, giving the aircraft the ability to carry as many as 10 more passengers than the contemporary Dornier R4 'Wal'. The Sikorsky was a smaller aircraft carrying fewer passengers but had longer range.

S.23 C-CLASS	24 passengers
Do R4 'WAL'	19 passengers
S-42	12 passengers

Short's floating flyers

■ **1914 S.80:** Flown up the Nile as far as Khartoum in 1914, the S.80's first flight had taken place the previous year. It was able to carry up to four passengers thanks to its Gnome engine.

■ **1929 VALETTA:** Carrying 17 passengers in comfort, the twin-float Valetta was an advanced design, the largest floatplane of its day. It was later converted to a landplane.

■ **1931 KENT:** An enlarged version of the Short Calcutta, three Kents were built for Imperial Airways. Seating 15 passengers in comfort, the Kents also carried mail cargo.

■ **1934 SINGAPORE III:** These improved Singapores were used on civil routes to the Far East and also served with the RAF, replacing Short Southamptons.

SIKORSKY

S-62/HH-52 SEAGUARD

● Search and rescue helicopter ● Turbine-powered ● Overlooked

▲ *Looking like a scaled-down version of the S-61 Sea King, the S-62 was not a great commercial success and only a handful were built. It served with the US Coast Guard and in Japan.*

Conceived in the mid-1950s, the S-62 incorporated several new features. The US Coast Guard was sufficiently interested to purchase the type as the HH-52A Seaguard. A single T-58 turbine, a relatively spacious fuselage and amphibious capability made the S-62 an ideal search and rescue helicopter, particularly for coastal areas. It was capable of operating from almost any surface in just about any weather.

SIKORSKY S-62/HH-52 SEAGUARD

◀ **On land and water**
One of the prototypes performs a 'power-off' landing. As an amphibious helicopter, the HH-52 proved ideal in the coastal SAR role.

▼ **Northern search and rescue**
HH-52s operating from ice-breakers received a bright orange scheme with a white stripe for greater conspicuity over the frozen sea.

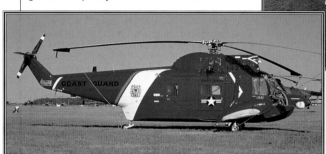

▲ **Rig support**
First order for the S-62 came from Petroleum Helicopters, which purchased a single example for serving large offshore oil rigs located in the Gulf of Mexico.

Sikorsky on the silver screen ▶
This strange-looking machine is actually a South African example, modified to represent an 'enemy' gunship, possibly an Mi-24, for film purposes.

◀ **Special equipment**
As first delivered to the US Coast Guard, HH-52s featured automatic stabilisation, towing equipment and other features tailored for the rescue mission.

FACTS AND FIGURES

➤ HH-52s based at Houston, Texas, frequently practised recovery of the NASA Apollo astronauts.

➤ First flight of the Sikorsky S-62 took place on 22 May 1958.

➤ A small number of Seaguards were put on display in museums after retirement.

➤ Nine examples were built under licence for service with Japanese Maritime Self-Defence Force (JMSDF).

➤ One US Coast Guard machine was used in the film *Airport '77*.

➤ A civilian S-62B model was built, but it was not popular on the civil market.

PROFILE

Unsung rescue helicopters

In commercial aviation, Sikorsky's S-62 was overshadowed by other helicopters. The US Coast Guard liked it enough to use the type from 1963 to 1989 for short- to medium-range rescue work. The ability to land on water, not found in any of today's Coast Guard helicopters, helped the HH-52A Seaguard in its rescue duties.

The HH-52A also joined the Coast Guard ice patrol operations aboard powerful ice-breakers. Typical was Operation Deep Freeze, the exploration of the

Antarctic in 1973. The aim of this project was to improve ice-breaking services, thus assisting the movement of maritime traffic through icy waterways.

Coast Guard pilots and crewmen were quite fond of the HH-52A – especially its ability to operate in all weathers. Although most flying was conducted from shore bases, Coast Guard crewmen also serviced the HH-52A onboard ship, which often proved to be a demanding task. By the time the last examples retired during 1989, HH-52s had

Below: This rare machine is one of a very small number of S-62s sold to non-US operators. It flew with the Canadian Department of Transport.

Above: Toward the end of their service lives, HH-52s were upgraded with Northrop forward-looking infra-red sensors, mounted in a small turret on the nose.

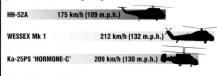

gained distinction for rescuing more people than any other helicopter. They were replaced by Aérospatiale HH-65 Dolphins.

HH-52A SEAGUARD

Some 99 examples of the Sikorsky S-62 were delivered to the US Coast Guard. They flew search and rescue (SAR) duties for nearly 30 years.

HH-52A Seaguard

Type: US Coast Guard all-weather amphibious rescue helicopter

Powerplant: one 932-kW (1,249-hp.) General Electric T58-GE-8 turboshaft engine

Maximum speed: 175 km/h (109 m.p.h.)

Cruising speed: 144 km/h (89 m.p.h.)

Range: 762 km (473 mi.)

Hover ceiling: 526 m (1726 ft.)

Weights: empty 2224 kg (4,900 lb.); loaded 3765 kg (8,300 lb.)

Accommodation: two pilots sitting side-by-side and one loadmaster, plus seating for up to 11 fully equipped troops if required

Dimensions: rotor diameter 16.15 m (53 ft.)
length 13.79 m (45 ft. 3 in.)
height 4.39 m (14 ft. 5 in.)

ACTION DATA

MAXIMUM SPEED
As one of the earliest turbine-powered helicopters, the HH-52 offered much better performance than several rival machines of the day. The 'Hormone' was twin-engined but was a relatively poor performer, unlike the single-engined Westland Wessex.

HH-52A 175 km/h (109 m.p.h.)
WESSEX Mk 1 212 km/h (132 m.p.h.)
Ka-25PS 'HORMONE-C' 209 km/h (130 m.p.h.)

SERVICE CEILING
Despite being single-engined, both the HH-52 Seaguard and the Wessex had impressive service ceilings, better than that of the twin-engined Ka-25 'Hormone'. The single-engined Wessex was essentially a licence-built, turbine-powered Sikorsky S-58.

HH-52A 3415 m (11,204 ft.)
WESSEX Mk 1 4298 m (14,101 ft.)
Ka-25PS 'HORMONE-C' 3350 m (10,990 ft.)

MAXIMUM TAKE-OFF WEIGHT
A light but strong all-metal fuselage, combined with the low weight of the turbine engine, permitted the HH-52 to carry a substantial payload if required. At maximum take-off weight the aircraft was much lighter than either the Wessex or 'Hormone'; the latter tipped the scales at almost 8000 kg fully laden.

HH-52A 3765 kg (8,300 lb.)
WESSEX Mk 1 5715 kg (12,600 lb.)
Ka-25PS 'HORMONE-C' 7500 kg (16,635 lb.)

In the late 1950s, the General Electric T-58 was one of the most advanced engines available for use in helicopters. It was light, powerful and efficient compared to piston engines of the period.

Although a considerable improvement over Sikorsky's S-55, the HH-52 did feature a sizeable number of components from the earlier machine, including the rotor blades, heads and gearbox.

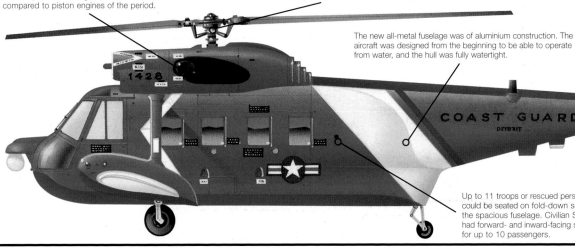

The new all-metal fuselage was of aluminium construction. The aircraft was designed from the beginning to be able to operate from water, and the hull was fully watertight.

Up to 11 troops or rescued personnel could be seated on fold-down seats in the spacious fuselage. Civilian S-62s had forward- and inward-facing seats for up to 10 passengers.

Like the main rotor, the tail rotor assembly was also from the S-55. Common components included the twin blades, the tail rotor head, auxiliary gearbox and shaft assembly. This permitted Sikorsky to save considerable time and reduce cost during manufacturing, and enabled the company to offer the S-62 at an attractive price.

Sikorsky's amphibious family

■ **S-61 SEA KING:** Similar in appearance to the smaller S-62, the Sea King was one of the most successful helicopters built by Sikorsky. It was widely exported.

■ **S-61N:** Clearly resembling the military Sea King, the S-61N was developed as a civil passenger helicopter. It retained amphibious capability and entered service in 1964.

■ **S-61R:** Yet another derivative of the basic S-61 design, this variant had a completely redesigned fuselage with a rear loading ramp and a retractable tricycle undercarriage.

SIKORSKY

S-76 SPIRIT

● Multi-role helicopter ● Army scout ● Passenger transport

▲ With the worldwide demand for oil rig support and business transport helicopters in the 1980s, Sikorsky pitched its S-76 against Bell's Model 222 and the excellent Agusta A 109. It did not gain much penetration in the military market despite its success in civil sales.

One of the family of highly successful Sikorsky rotorcraft of recent times, the S-76 is the first type since the S-62 designed by the company purely for the civil market. The main customer area was seen to be the offshore oil support industry, with the S-76 offering 12 passenger seats in standard form with IFR equipment and other navigational aids for all-weather operation. Among the 'optional extras' are long-range fuel tanks and air-conditioning.

SIKORSKY S-76 SPIRIT

◀ New York bird
This Heli Union S-76C is powered by Turboméca Arriel turboshafts. The S-76C first flew in 1990, and has also been sold to the Spanish air force.

▲ Screaming Eagle
Armed with rocket pods or guns, the S-76 was offered on the military market as the 'Eagle'. But it had to compete with the successful Agusta A 109.

▲ Passenger comfort
Compared to the A 109 and Bell Model 222, the S-76 was a much roomier machine, and the executive version could carry eight people in luxury.

▼ Spirit in action
Known as the 'Spirit' to civil operators, the S-76 soon demonstrated impressive performance compared to its smaller rivals.

▲ Sikorsky at sea
Operating from oil platforms was an important source of business for the S-76, with companies like Bond Helicopters in Scotland. Sikorsky had already cornered much of the market with the larger Sikorsky S-61 series helicopter.

FACTS AND FIGURES

➤ When configured for full day and night, all-weather offshore flying, the S-76 generally carries up to 12 passengers.

➤ Sikorsky sold 428 S-76s to customers in Canada, Mexico, the UK and the US.

➤ A harmonic control system tested on an S-76 reduced vibration by 90 per cent.

➤ The S-76 Shadow had a nose radar housing and fly-by-wire controls grafted onto the front section.

➤ The S-76B is operated in China, Germany, Japan, Korea and the Netherlands.

➤ The first S-76 prototypes flew in 1977 and deliveries began in 1979.

PROFILE

Sikorsky's middle weight

Having flown for the first time in 1978, the S-76 soon had a full order book and by the following spring over 200 had been ordered. The first production example, which in the meantime had been named 'Spirit', was delivered to Offshore Logistics of Louisiana in February 1979. Other early customers included Evergreen Helicopters Inc. based in Oregon, who ordered 20 Spirits in 1980.

The first British operator of the Spirit was Bristow Helicopters, which took delivery of the first two helicopters in November 1979. This and other sales reflected the boom in oil business at that time – one that did not last, and adversely affected requirements for new helicopters intended for offshore work.

Bristow soon demonstrated the speed which could be attained by a helicopter with fully retractable landing gear, by setting a new London to Paris record of one hour 15 minutes at a speed of 272.75 km/h. (171 m.p.h.). This bettered the previous record by some 26 minutes. On the return trip, the Spirit clipped another four minutes off its own record.

Sikorsky's development programme bore further fruit in 1985 when, on 24 June, it flew the first privately-funded S-76 Shadow. This acronym stood for Sikorsky Helicopter Advanced Demonstrator of Operator Workload.

Above: This 'fantail' variant was fitted with a fenestron-type tail rotor in trials for the Light Helicopter Experimental programme.

Left: With the space to accommodate a high standard of luxury features, the S-76 offered the ultimate in executive transport with its low-noise interior and high speed.

S-76 Spirit

Type: medium-capacity helicopter

Powerplant: two Allison 250-C30 turboshaft engines each rated at 484.7-kW (649-hp.)

Maximum speed: 289 km/h (180 m.p.h.)

Normal cruising speed: 269 km/h (167 m.p.h.)

Range: 1100 km (683 mi.)

Service ceiling: 1555 m (5,100 ft.)

Weights: empty 2241 kg (4,940 lb.); loaded 4400 kg (9,700 lb.); maximum take-off weight 5171 kg (11,400 lb.)

Dimensions:
rotor diameter	13.41 m	(44 ft.)
length	16 m	(52 ft. 6 in.)
height	4.41 m	(14 ft. 5 in.)

S-76 SPIRIT

First flown in 1979, the S-76 has sold widely in the North American market despite competition from the Bell Model 222 and Agusta A 109. The latest version is the S-76C with Arriel turboshaft engines.

To reduce vibration, the S-76 has bifilar vibration absorbers above the rotor head. The blades rotate on elastomeric bearings, with damping provided by hydraulic drag dampers.

The tail rotor is a conventional four-bladed type mounted on the port side.

Power is transferred from the engines to the tail rotor and main rotor through a gearbox, which also drives the twin hydraulic pumps and 200A DC generators. The engines have an automatic fire detection and suppression system.

S-76s are fitted with a high standard of cockpit controls, with full instrument flight rules equipment fitted and optional 'EFIS' and weather radar.

A baggage hold is located aft of the cabin with an external door on each side of the fuselage. The tail rotor was reconfigured in the S-76B to reduce weight.

The main undercarriage retracts under hydraulic power into the fuselage to reduce drag. The wheel brakes are also hydraulically powered.

The fuselage contains many composite and honeycomb structural components to reduce weight.

The main cabin can accommodate 12 or 13 passengers in an economy-type seating arrangement or can be configured in a four-seat flying office arrangement with additional soundproofing.

The many faces of the Spirit

■ **BATTLEFIELD EAGLE:** Fast and agile, the Eagle military transport could carry a squad-sized unit of 10 troops, as well as providing its own firepower with rocket and gun pods.

■ **FLYING AMBULANCE:** Equipped with full emergency medical service equipment, the S.76 air ambulance can provide full patient care en route to hospital.

■ **RESCUE MISSION:** The S-76 is used by the Government Air Service in Hong Kong as a search and rescue aircraft in the dangerous waters of the South China Sea.

■ **SHADOW:** A technology demonstrator for advanced cockpit instrumentation layouts, the Shadow paved the way for the advanced Boeing-Sikorsky LHX helicopter.

ACTION DATA

ACCOMMODATION

The S-76 was aimed at a gap in the market between helicopters like the Mi 8 and Bell 212, which were slower and bigger, and the Bell 222 and A 109, which were as fast as the S-76 but smaller.

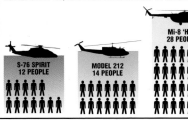

S-76 SPIRIT 12 PEOPLE

MODEL 212 14 PEOPLE

Mi-8 'HIP' 28 PEOPLE

SUPERMARINE

S.6B

● High-speed floatplane ● Record breaker ● Schneider race winner

S upermarine's S.6B was the fastest aircraft of its time. The company entered racing with its 1919 Sea Lion flying-boat and reached a pinnacle of performance with the S.6B of 1931. The combined talents of design genius R. J. Mitchell and fuel technician F. Rodwell Banks achieved Schneider Trophy glory, in the process laying the foundations of Britain's aerial defences during World War II.

▲ The experience
of competing in the Schneider races not only gave British aviation much prestige, but the lessons learned about the technology anticipated the shape of World War II fighters to come.

SUPERMARINE S.6B

▲ Taking to water
The S.5 makes a test flight at Calshot in preparation for the Schneider race of 1929. Its rival, the Macchi, is in the background.

Meeting the sponsor ▲
Lady Houston, who helped finance the prize-winning aircraft, meets members of the 1931 British team.

◀ Second winner
The original S.6 won the 1929 Schneider race. The engine was a 1417-kW (1,900-hp.) Rolls-Royce 'R', uprated in 1931 for the winning S.6B.

▼ Powerful engine
The S.6B needed the power of the 'R' series engine and special fuel, which was stored in the floats, to compete successfully.

▲ To be the best
The Supermarine company had a tradition of excellence, and built their aircraft to be the best. This attitude won them much acclaim, but meant that each aircraft required many man-hours on the production lines.

FACTS AND FIGURES

➤ In the 1927 Schneider race two S.5 monoplanes took first and second places.

➤ H. R. Wagborn flew the Supermarine S.6 to a record 528.87 km/h (329 m.p.h.) in 1929.

➤ A generous endowment by Lady Houston provided the finances for Britain's racing entry in 1931.

➤ On 29 September 1931 the S.6B became the first aircraft to fly over 643.7 km/h (400 m.p.h.).

➤ The S.6B was a top tourist attraction in London's Science Museum.

➤ One of the first plastic models sold in the United States was a Supermarine S.6B.

Schneider Trophy winner

The principal achievements of the Supermarine S.6B are in the record book for all to see: 547.3 km/h (340 m.p.h.) to win the Schneider Trophy outright for the United Kingdom at Calshot on 13 September 1931, and 654.9 km/h (380 m.p.h.) to establish an absolute world speed record at Ryde on the Isle of Wight on 29 September. The flights were made by pilots J. N. Boothman and G. H. Stainforth. These incredible records were all the more impressive because Britain's entry into the race had no government support and the S.6B was a modification of the earlier S.6 rather than, like many of the contestants, a new aircraft.

Before the S.6B made its mark in 1931, the S.5 and S.6 were among early monoplanes on the air racing scene and logged impressive flying records in their own right.

The great designer R. J. Mitchell had by now settled upon the general configuration of a sleek, graceful, high-speed aircraft, and was to use lessons learned to design yet another – the immortal Spitfire.

S.6B

Type: single-seat high-speed seaplane

Powerplant: one 1752.4-kW (2,350-hp.) Rolls-Royce 'R' piston engine

Maximum speed: 655.8 km/h (407 m.p.h.); 527.6 km/h (328 m.p.h.) in level flight

Landing speed: 152.9 km/h (95 m.p.h.)

Weights: empty 2082 kg (4,600 lb.); loaded 2760 kg (6,090 lb.)

Dimensions:
span	9.14 m	(30 ft.)
length	8.79 m	(29 ft.)
height	3.73 m	(12 ft.)
wing area	13.47 m²	(145 sq. ft.)

Taking off from water was safe enough, but pilots disliked using a periscope to see ahead. The aircraft were intentionally designed without a canopy to minimise drag and improve airflow.

S.6A

The original S.6 of 1929 was upgraded to S.6B standard for the 1931 race and was redesignated S.6A to distinguish it from the newer aircraft.

A small cockpit was another concession to high speed and low drag, but it was not a feature that pilots liked.

The thin wings were a good design for high-speed flight, but needed extra bracing to cope with the immense stress.

Success of the S.6 series owed much to the superb Rolls-Royce 'R' series engine, a direct ancestor of the wartime Merlin that powered the Spitfire and Hurricane, and which eventually went on to become the Griffon.

Engine cooling was a serious headache for aircraft designers in the 1930s. Use of ethylene glycol in flush-fitting radiators built into the underside of the wings helped solve the problem.

The sleek profile and long engine of the S.6 showed how designers tried to reconcile the need for maximum power with minimum frontal area to reduce drag and gain top speed.

The stressed-skin construction used to build the S.6 series was to prove extremely valuable to Supermarine in building the Spitfire seven years later.

The very minimum amount of fuel needed to complete the race course was carried in the large floats. One pilot discovered this when he miscounted the number of laps he had flown, and ran out of fuel!

ACTION DATA

ENGINE POWER

The development of engine power during the decade after World War I was the key to the vastly improved performance of the aircraft competing for the Schneider Trophy. Output increased dramatically from the victorious Curtiss of 1923 through the Macchi of 1926 to the triumphant S.6B of 1931.

CR-3 — 346.8 kW (464 hp.)

M.39 — 657 kW (880 hp.)

S.6B — 1752.4 kW (2,350 hp.)

MAXIMUM SPEED

Greater power and advances in aerodynamics saw the speeds achieved by Schneider Trophy competitors leap ahead. The lessons learned during the epic races were to stand the competitors in good stead as war clouds loomed in the 1930s.

1923 CR-3 — 285.6 km/h (177 m.p.h.)
1926 M.39 — 396.69 km/h (245 m.p.h.)
1931 S.6B — 547.3 km/h (380 m.p.h.)

Previous winners

■ **DEPERDUSSIN (1913):** The first Schneider Trophy race was won at Monaco meet at an average speed of 73.63 km/h (45.65 m.p.h.).

■ **SUPERMARINE SEA LION (1922):** After two post-war wins by Italy the Sea Lion won at Naples, at a speed of 234.48 km/h (145.38 m.p.h.).

■ **CURTISS CR-3 (1923):** The US Navy's Curtiss seaplanes were a revelation at Cowes, winning at 285.6 km/h (177.07 m.p.h.).

■ **MACCHI M.39 (1926):** Ordered by Mussolini to win the trophy, the Italians built the Macchi M.39, which achieved 396.69 km/h (245.95 m.p.h.).

■ **SUPERMARINE S.5 (1927):** First of the great Supermarine 'S' series, the S.5 won in Venice at an average speed of 453.29 km/h (281.04 m.p.h.).

415

TUPOLEV

Tu-104/Tu-124

● Based on Tu-16 bomber ● First Soviet jet airliner ● Medium range

▲ *When introduced in 1956, the Tu-104 dramatically reduced domestic and international journey times. As the second jet airliner in service in the world, it was the pride of Aeroflot's fleet.*

I n May 1954 Western observers first viewed the Tupolev Type 88 prototype and eight pre-production Tu-16 bombers. Analysts were rightly concerned that this bomber was a potential strategic threat. What they did not realise was that within two years a developed version, the Tu-104, would become the world's second jet airliner, upsetting the widely-held belief that Soviet aircraft were inferior to those in the West. The type served with Aeroflot for 25 years.

TUPOLEV Tu-104/Tu-124

Bomber origins ▶
Based on the Tu-16 bomber, the Tu-104 featured modified wing-mounted engine nacelles.

▼ Jet pioneer
The Tu-104 drew much attention when exhibited in the West, being the Soviet Union's first jet airliner.

Export 'Cookpots' ▶
This Tu-124K2 was exported as a VIP carrier for the Iraqi air force. Other users included the East German and Indian air forces.

▼ Visits abroad
In March 1956 the Tu-104 became only the second Soviet civil aircraft type to visit Britain. The Tu-104 was still operating to the UK in the 1970s. This example is seen at Gatwick Airport on an unscheduled service in August 1971.

▲ Sharply swept wing
An early production Tu-104A displays the wing trailing-edge fairings which held the four-wheeled main undercarriage.

FACTS AND FIGURES

➤ The prototype Tu-104, SSSR-L5400, was first flown by Y. I. Alasheyev from the Vnukovo factory on 17 June 1955.

➤ Two demilitarised Tu-16s used for crew training were designated Tu-104G.

➤ In service, the Tu-104 cut the Moscow-Irkutsk flight time by eight hours.

➤ Military use included the Tu-104Sh crew trainer as well as modified civil Tu-104Bs employed in cosmonaut training.

➤ In September 1957 a Tu-104A set three world records for an aircraft in its class.

➤ Two weather research Tu-104s were armed with cloud-seeding rockets.

PROFILE

From bomber to jet airliner

No other large jet transport aircraft has been placed into production in as little time and for as little money as Tupolev's record-breaking Tu-104. Designer S. M. Yeger was the man tasked with turning a strategic bomber into a passenger aircraft. The main modifications included a new fuselage with pressurisation and environmental control, and a new wing centre-section.

The prototype first flew in June 1955, and the excellence of the design was proved by successful, trouble-free flight trials. When the prototype visited Britain in 1956 it caused a great stir, as it was not only a rival to the Comet but, in several factors, showed technological superiority.After crews had been trained on a Tu-16, the Tu-104 entered service in September 1956. After only 11 aircraft, production was switched to the improved Tu-104A fitted out with a higher capacity, improved interior and more powerful engines. Despite

the aircraft's excellent record and low cost, the only export customer was CSA of Czechoslovakia which bought six Tu-104As. Further development led to the Tu-104B with a 1.21-m (4-ft.) stretch to the fuselage, increasing the capacity to 100 passengers.

Based very closely on the Tu-104, the Tu-124 short-haul airliner entered service in 1962 and compiled an impressive service history.

Right: Surprisingly, Czech national carrier CSA was the only export customer for the Tu-104, despite a low cost of £425,000 each.

The tail unit was basically the same as the unit fitted to the Tu-16, the major difference being a lower tailplane.

The control surfaces were all manually operated with hydraulic boost for the rudder. A trim-tab was fitted in the rudder and each elevator.

Tu-104A 'CAMEL'

Aeroflot was the main operator of the Tu-104 and flew all commercial versions of the type. From 1960 a few Aeroflot Tu-104As were converted to Tu-104D standard with luxurious forward cabins fitted with divans.

The Tu-104A was flown by a flight crew of five, consisting of two pilots, a navigator, an engineer and a radio operator.

The fuselage forward of the centre-section held a smaller cabin and on early versions was often fitted out for 16 first-class passengers. A toilet was situated at the front of the cabin.

The most radical difference between the Tu-16 and the Tu-104 was the fuselage, which was pressurised and had environmental control.

The wings were lowered from the mid to the low position to accommodate the passenger cabin. They were of anhedral swept design.

Like many early Soviet commercial aircraft, the navigator's position was in a glazed nose compartment.

А Э Р О Ф Л О Т

CCCP-Л5442

The wing centre-section reduced the height of the cabin. This area was used on early versions as the galley, with two windows fitted at a higher level.

The retractable tricycle undercarriage had four wheel main units which retracted backwards into trailing-edge wing fairings.

The rear cabin was separated from the front cabin by the galley. A wardrobe was situated opposite the rear door and a powder room, washroom and two toilets were situated at the rear.

Airliners based on bomber designs

AVRO 691 LANCASTRIAN: The Lancastrian was a high-speed long-range transport conversion of the Lancaster bomber. The Canadian-built versions could carry 10 passengers.

BOEING 377 STRATOCRUISER: In 1942 Boeing began developing a transport version of the B-29. The resulting Model 377 flew with both civil and military operators.

TUPOLEV Tu-114: As a civil counterpart to the Tu-95 'Bear' bomber, the Tu-114 was the largest and heaviest commercial airliner in the world when it appeared in 1957.

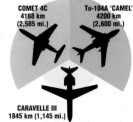

TUPOLEV

Tu-204

● New-generation airliner ● Western technology ● Growing orders

▲ Designed in the
early 1980s as a successor to the tri-
jet Tu-154, this medium-range airliner bears a
resemblance to the Boeing 757. Deliveries
began in 1992 and the first revenue-earning
flight took place in 1996.

Designed as a replacement for the
Tu-154, and flown for the first time in
January 1989, the basic Tu-204 was
just the first in a planned family of airliners.
The different models include versions with
Russian and Western engines, and offer
various combinations of payload and range.
Howver, development has been hampered
by lack of funding for flight testing and
certification. A version powered by Rolls-
Royce engines has achieved growing
interest from several airlines.

TUPOLEV **Tu-204**

▼ **Major improvement**
Compared to its
predecessor, the Tu-154, the
new airliner boasts greater
passenger capacity and
better fuel economy, making
the aircraft more attractive
to western airlines.

▲ **Joint venture**
After the collapse of the Soviet Union, Tupolev looked
for partners to secure funding for the Tu-204. This led
to the creation of BRAVIA (British Russian Aviation),
whose markings adorn this example.

▼ **State of the art**
Compared to previous Tupolev
airliners, the Tu-204 is an
engineering marvel. The wing has
a comparatively modest sweep
and features winglets which help
improve airflow.

▲ **Various powerplants**
As with many modern airliners, different engines
can be specified for the Tu-204. Series 100 aircraft
are powered by two Aviadvigatel PS-90 turbofans.

First flight ▶
Completed in 1988, the first
prototype made its maiden flight
in early 1989 from the Zhukhovskii
test centre near Moscow, with
Andrei Talalakin at the controls.

FACTS AND FIGURES

➤ Development of the Tu-204 was aided by
Armand Hammer, a US tycoon who had
many contacts inside the Soviet Union.

➤ Two-crew operation is possible, though
a third seat for a flight engineer is fitted.

➤ A Tu-204 fuelled by liquid natural gas has
been proposed, but so far not built.

➤ A smaller Tupolev design, yet to be
flown, the Tu-304 incorporates many
features of the larger Tu-204.

➤ BRAVIA has acquired a number of
aircraft which are intended for resale.

➤ A maritime version is being considered
by the Russian navy to replace the Il-38.

PROFILE

A new airliner for a new era

Finally awarded its Russian certificate of airworthiness in December 1994, the standard Tupolev Tu-204 is currently built at the Aviastar plant in Ulyanovsk alongside several other variants. They include the Tu-204-100, -120, and the 204C freighter variant with a large cargo door.

With each successive variant, maximum take-off weight has been increased and more powerful engines have been introduced to compensate.

Further variations include the Tu-224 and 324. These aircraft were designed for trunk route services and feature a shortened

fuselage with seating for up to 160 passengers and a range of 7200 km (4,465 mi.).

Russian airline Sirocco Aerospace placed an order for around 200 of the Rolls-Royce RB211-engined aircraft which are known as Tu-204-120s. A dedicated freighter variant is also available and features US avionics and Western cabin furnishings in addition to the British engines, resulting in a truly international aircraft. The first production version of the Rolls-Royce-powered Tu-204 rolled off the line in March 1997.

After a long and turbulent development process, the future

Above: Versatility has been demonstrated by the introduction of both combi and freighter versions of the Tupolev Tu-204.

of Tupolev's twin-engined medium-range airliner looks brighter than it did several years ago. Massive investment by Western organisations has aided the programme considerably.

Above: Proudly wearing the old Soviet-style Aeroflot colours, the first prototype SSSR-64001 sits quietly at Le Bourget. At that time the airline had intended to acquire 350 examples.

Tu-204-100

Type: medium-range airliner

Powerplant: two 157-kN (35,320-lb.-thrust) Aviadvigatel PS-90A turbofan engines

Maximum cruising speed: 850 km/h (527 m.p.h.)

Range: 4000 km (2,480 mi.)

Maximum fuel capacity: 40,730 litres (10,760 gal.)

Weights: empty 59,000 kg (129,800 lb.); loaded 103,000 kg (226,600 lb.)

Take-off run: 1450 m (4,760 ft.)

Accommodation: standard accommodation for two crew and 184 passengers, though a third crew member is often carried and passenger seating can be increased to 214

Dimensions:
span	42.00 m (137 ft. 9 in.)
length	46.22 m (151 ft. 7 in.)
height	13.88 m (45 ft. 6 in.)
wing area	182.40 m² (1,963 sq. ft.)

Tu-204

First flown in August 1992, this particular aircraft, RA-64006, was the first Tu-204 to be fitted with Rolls-Royce RB211s. It was fitted out by Hunting in the UK before being demonstrated at Farnborough '92.

The tail unit makes the most extensive use of composites, particularly on the moving surfaces. As in the much larger Boeing 747-400, the tail also holds an integral fuel tank.

Up front, the flight deck of the Tu-204 follows modern airliner practice in featuring a digital glass cockpit with TV type multi-function displays. Side-stick control columns, similar to those of the Airbus A340, were originally planned, but were discarded in favour of conventional yokes.

Depending on customer requirements, the cabin layout of the Tu-204 can vary considerably. A maximum of 214 passengers can be accommodated for charter flights, though for scheduled services a total of 184 passengers will normally be carried, comprising 30 in business and 154 in economy/tourist class.

Roughly 18 per cent of the airframe consists of composites. The fuselage also makes extensive use of titanium and aluminum-lithium for greatest possible strength and lowest possible weight.

RA-64006

This Tu-204 wears the markings of BRAVIA (British Russian Aviation), a consortium which was formed in the early 1990s. Through it, the aircraft received the Rolls-Royce engines and the door was opened for development of further variants of this promising Russian design.

Fitted to this variant are two RB211 Series 535 high-bypass-ratio turbofans. These engines are among the most popular on the civil market today and have gained a reputation for being ultra-reliable, fuel-efficient and powerful, not to mention quiet.

Under the cabin floor is the baggage compartment, which runs virtually the entire length of the fuselage, interrupted only by the fuel tanks. For greater payloads, a Tu-204 combi variant is available, in which a section of the normal cabin is reserved for freight.

ACTION DATA

MAXIMUM CRUISING SPEED

Not quite as efficient as the Boeing 757, the Tu-204 is nevertheless an economical aircraft and has a high cruising speed compared to other Russian airliners. The MD-90 is a modernised version of the 1960s' DC-9 and, not surprisingly, is somewhat slower.

Tu-204-100	850 km/h (527 m.p.h.)
757-200	935 km/h (580 m.p.h.)
MD-90-30	809 km/h (502 m.p.h.)

PASSENGERS

All three of these medium-range airliners are known as 'narrow bodies', in which passengers sit on either side of a single aisle. During the development stage, the Tu-204 was repeatedly stretched to accommodate more passengers; it still carries fewer passengers than the 757, though more than the lengthened MD-90.

Tu-204-100	214 PASSENGERS
757-200	239 PASSENGERS
MD-90-30	172 PASSENGERS

MAXIMUM RANGE

Today, medium-range airliners are capable of flying distances unheard of two decades ago. Though the basic design of the MD-90 is more than 30 years old, in updated form it still has a respectable range. The Boeing 757 is more capable, however.

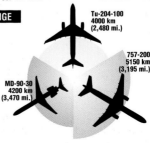

Tu-204-100 4000 km (2,480 mi.)
757-200 5150 km (3,195 mi.)
MD-90-30 4200 km (3,470 mi.)

Tupolev's previous jet airliners

■ **Tu-104:** This aircraft created a sensation in 1956 when it was the first Soviet jet airliner to appear in the West. It was, however, a crude machine, and performance was not spectacular.

■ **Tu-134:** An altogether better airliner, the Tu-134 was more refined and had a much lower level of cabin noise than the Tu-104, because of its rear-mounted engines.

■ **Tu-154:** Similar in concept to the Boeing 727 and Hawker-Siddeley Trident, the Tu-154 became a much-loved airliner in Aeroflot service. It is destined to be around for some time yet.

TUPOLEV

TU-114 'CLEAT'

● Long-range performance ● World's biggest turboprop airliner

With its unique combination of turboprop power and swept-back wings, the Tupolev Tu-114 'Cleat' was a flying giant of the 1950s. This famous transport was the largest, heaviest and longest-range civil aircraft of its era. Despite having propellers, it regularly cruised almost as fast as the newer swept-wing jets. In many respects, this was a 'jumbo jet', and was the world's heaviest aircraft before the advent of the Boeing 747.

▲ Despite its
ageing appearance compared to Western jet designs, the Tu-114 was a superb piece of engineering and remains the largest civil turboprop ever produced.

TUPOLEV TU-114 'CLEAT'

▲ Long legs
This Tu-114, at Heathrow Airport, shows off its extremely long nose undercarriage strut. The truck in the foreground gives an indication of just how massive the Tu-114 was.

▲ Passenger heaven
Another first for the Tu-114 was the introduction of four-by-four passenger seating for 220 passengers, although this configuration was not commonly used. Most aircraft seated 170 with a galley and divans.

Landing approach ▶
Landing was sedate in the Tu-114, the aircraft touching down at 205 km/h (127 m.p.h.) and stopping in about 1500 m (4,920 ft.). It needed about 1700 m (5,575 ft.) to take off.

▼ Low-wing design
To allow the passenger compartment to be as large as possible the Tu-114 was fitted with a low-mounted wing. This was the main structural difference between it and the military Tu-95, which features a mid-mounted wing.

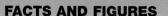

▲ Big spinner
The Tu-114's huge NK-12 turboprops featured contra-rotating propellers, which absorb more power from the engine.

FACTS AND FIGURES

➤ Cabin volume of the Tu-114 was 332 m³ (11,724 cu. ft.), making it by far the largest airliner of its era.

➤ The Tu-114 was also the world's fastest propeller-driven aircraft in 1960.

➤ The first of 31 Tu-114s, 'Rossiya' made its maiden flight on 15 November 1957.

➤ With an area of 64.90 m², the horizontal tail of the Tu-114 was larger than the wing of many aircraft.

➤ Tu-114Ds flew the 10,900-km (6,758-mi.) route from Moscow to Havana.

➤ The Tu-114 won the Grand Prix at the Brussels World Fair in 1958.

PROFILE

Mightiest of the turboprop airliners

Biggest, fastest and arguably the most impressive turboprop airliner, the Tu-114 'Cleat' gave the Soviet airline Aeroflot a colossal transport able to cover intercontinental distances with ease. Everything about this aircraft was big, new and different. Derived from the military Tu-95 'Bear', the Tu-114 was initially rather restricted in where it could operate in the Soviet Union, as few routes could use an aircraft that carried 200 passengers, and many airfields were too limited for its immense size, weight and long take-off run. Another problem

was that its doors were 5 metres above the ground. Plans for self-contained staircases never materialised, and finding steps that could reach the Tu-114 was a problem whenever it arrived at a new airport.

By the time the 'Cleat' began airline service from Moscow to Khabarovsk on 24 April 1961, becoming the first plane to routinely carry passengers a distance of 6500 km (4,000 mi.), this remarkable aircraft had established 32 records and had even flown Soviet Premier Khruschev on a non-stop Moscow to New York visit. The Tu-114 carried over six

Below: This Tu-114 duo appeared at Zurich airport in 1967, but more usual destinations were Delhi, Montreal, Tokyo and Conakry in West Africa. The aircraft's impressive range saved stop-over time.

Above: There was nothing like the sound of a Tu-114 landing, with its NK-12s whistling and propellers throbbing. Large flaps were fitted to reduce landing speed.

million passengers in its years of Aeroflot service before retiring in 1971. Some were converted to prototype Tu-126 airborne early-warning aircraft.

Tu-114 'Cleat'

Type: long-range airliner and transport

Powerplant: four 11,033-kW (14,784-hp.) Kuznetsov NK-12MV turboprop engines

Maximum speed: 880 km/h (545 m.p.h.) at 7100 m (23,000 ft.)

Cruising speed: 770 km/h (477 m.p.h.)

Range: 6200 km (3,853 mi.)

Service ceiling: 12,000 m (39,500 ft.)

Weights: empty 88,200 kg (194,000 lb.); loaded 179,000 kg (393,800 lb.)

Accommodation: flight crew of five (two pilots, engineer, navigator and radio/radar operator); typically eight or nine flight attendants; typically 170 passengers in three cabins holding 42, 48 and 54; maximum seating of up to 220 passengers

Dimensions:
span	51.10 m	(168 ft.)
length	54.10 m	(177 ft.)
height	13.31 m	(44 ft.)
wing area	311.10 m²	(3,347 sq. ft.)

Tu-116

As a parallel project to support the Tu-114, the Tu-116 was a direct civil variant of the Tu-95. This example was used for crew training for the Tu-114.

The powerplant was the same as used on the Tu-95 bomber. The four NK-12 engines were very powerful and drove the Tu-116 to an impressive top speed. The main undercarriage retracted to lie inverted in the rear of the inboard engine nacelles.

The fuselage skin was specially thickened adjacent to the propellers to give protection in case of engine failure. The NK-12 engine and its massive propeller system actually proved very reliable in service. The propellers were electrically de-iced.

The massive swept wing was identical to that of the Tu-95 and had the same main structure of three spars. A single spoiler ahead of the aileron assisted in roll control.

All control surfaces were hydraulically operated, a major innovation in this successor to the B-29-derived designs by Tupolev. The tailplane was of the variable incidence type.

Windscreen de-icing was by means of electric AC current, but the wing leading edges were de-iced by hot air bled from the engines and the tailfin by a flexible rubber boot.

An access tunnel linked the front and main cabins, passing through the skinned-over weapons bay.

The rear fuselage held up to 30 passengers in a two-by-two arrangement. A galley and two toilets were provided.

Inside the NK-12

TURBOSHAFT OPERATION:
A turboshaft engine is basically a jet engine with a turbine at the back that uses the gas produced to drive a propeller at the front through a central driveshaft. It is more efficient than a pure jet engine, and produces much more thrust than a piston engine of equivalent weight, as well as using cheaper fuel.

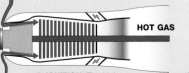

1 COLD AIR IN: The engine pushes air around the spinner and prop shaft, where it enters the 14-stage axial compressor and is pressurised.

HOT GAS

2 IGNITION: The high-pressure air from the compressor has kerosene injected into it after passing through stators and into the combustion chamber.

3 HOT GASES: The kerosene-filled air is ignited electronically in the combustion chamber. The gas produced has enormous energy, and as it burns it rushes through the rear five-stage turbine, spinning both it and the driveshaft. This, in turn, spins the propeller at the front of the engine, via reduction gearboxes.

DRIVESHAFT

HOT GAS

POWER TURBINE

EXHAUST GAS

Tu-114 MAIN WING SPAR

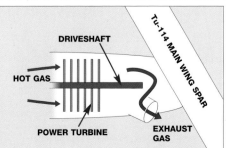

ACTION DATA

PASSENGERS

In its maximum density configuration, the Tu-114 carried more passengers than a Boeing 707, but a more usual load was around 170 in less cramped conditions. Soviet passengers on internal routes endured much lower standards of comfort than foreigners in jet airliners. However, air travel in the USSR was as cheap as taking a train.

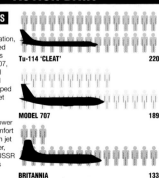

Tu-114 'CLEAT'	220
MODEL 707	189
BRITANNIA	133

TUPOLEV

TU-134 'CRUSTY'

● Medium/short haul ● Long serving ● DC-9 equivalent

As a contemporary of the British One-Eleven and American DC-9, the Soviet Union developed the Tu-134. Like those aircraft the Tu-134 has twin engines mounted on the rear fuselage and a T-tail, although its wings are more sharply swept. It entered service with Aeroflot in 1967, and nearly 800 were built. According to Tupolev, by the mid-1990s the Tu-134 and the Tu-154 were providing 65 per cent of all passenger transport in Russia.

▲ *Although a large number of Tu-134s remain in service after many years, the type is slowly disappearing as former Eastern Bloc airlines re-equip with more efficient Western aircraft.*

PHOTO FILE

TUPOLEV TU-134 'CRUSTY'

◄ Military transport
Many Tu-134s have been used for passenger transport and test duties with military agencies. The Bulgarian air force uses this Tu-134A as a transport.

'Crusty' cafe ►
As increasing numbers of Tu-134s are retired, the majority are being scrapped. Others, like this aircraft near Prague, gain a new lease of life serving in roles never envisaged by Tupolev's design team.

◄ African liner
This quasi-military Tu-134A belongs to the Angolan government. Many Tu-134s are finding their way to Third World operators.

Aeroflot original ►
Having been designed to satisfy Aeroflot requirements, the Tu-134 was used in huge numbers by the airline on its vast internal network.

◄ Middle Eastern service
Many of the countries flying Tu-134s were long-term allies of the Soviet regime. This Syrianair 'Crusty' was photographed in 1984. With the break-up of the Soviet Union, spare parts and other support services for older Russian aircraft are increasingly hard to find.

FACTS AND FIGURES

➤ Aeroflot began international service with the Tu-134 in September 1967, flying from Moscow to Stockholm.

➤ Only one Tu-134 prototype was built, flying for the first time in 1963.

➤ Tupolev designers claimed that the aircraft could fly from earth runways.

➤ The existence of the Tu-134 was not revealed until 1964, after 100 test flights had been completed.

➤ Early aircraft had no thrust reversers or auxiliary power unit.

➤ Tu-134s can land automatically and in fog when visibility is down to 50 m (150 ft.).

PROFILE

Soviet stalwart airliner

Known originally as the Tu-124A, the Tu-134 was developed from the earlier aircraft, whose layout was derived from that of the Tu-16 'Badger' bomber. As a result, with its engines carried in the wingroots, the Tu-124 was both inefficient and noisy, and as soon as it entered service work started on its replacement.

First flown in the early 1960s, the Tu-134 was a much improved aircraft. It started flying passenger services with Aeroflot in 1967, and in 1970

the Tu-134A introduced a lengthened fuselage with two extra rows of seats.

The type was also sold to several airlines outside Russia. In the mid-1990s it was still in service with Balkan Bulgarian, Czech, Malev Hungarian and LOT-Polish airlines, as well as Russia's Aeroflot, Samara and Tyumen.

The Tu-134 and early Tu-134As had a glazed nose for the navigator, but from 1971 a radar was installed in the nose. Various passenger layouts have

been used, with typical seating in later models for between 66 and 76. Variants include the Tu-134A3, which has lightweight seats for up to 96 passengers.

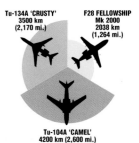

Appearing in an ever-changing series of liveries, the Tu-134 has become a reflection of the political turmoil of many Eastern Bloc nations. This aircraft belongs to the national airline of the Czech Republic.

TU-134 'CRUSTY'

Balkan Bulgarian airlines was one of the first Tu-134 customers. Six of the early model were delivered and the airline eventually flew a fleet of 16 aircraft. This is an early Tu-134 with a glazed nose.

On early machines the navigator sat in the glazed nose-cone with the RO3-1 weather and navigation radar housed in a radome to the rear of the navigator's compartment.

A 2.10-metre fuselage stretch allowed seating to be increased from the original 64 to 72 passengers, to between 72 and 80 in the Tu-134A. The Tu-134B-3 sub-variant could accommodate 96 passengers.

The incidence of the entire tailplane was altered for trimming, while the elevators were used for pitch control and had their own trim-tabs.

Sharp sweep and pronounced anhedral are distinctive features of the wing. Each wing contains three fuel tanks.

The two large wing fences on each wing help to reduce induced drag by preventing span-wise movement of air flowing over the wing. Reducing drag helps increase wing efficiency and thereby lowers fuel consumption and increases the aircraft's range.

As with all airliners having rear-mounted engines, the tailplane of the Tu-134 was high-set. The leading edge of the fin was de-iced electrically, while the fin was de-iced by hot air.

In common with many Soviet-designed aircraft, the retracted main undercarriage units of the Tu-134 were housed in large aerodynamic fairings behind the trailing edge of the wing.

The pilot and co-pilot sat side-by-side on the flightdeck. On aircraft with solid noses, the navigator was positioned behind the pilot, and the radar was moved into the nose radome.

Pilots relied solely on the wheelbrakes to stop these early aircraft, as no thrust-reversers were fitted.

From their experience with the Tu-104, the Tu-134's designers placed the engines at the rear to keep cabin noise to a minimum. The undercarriage was unusually tall for a rear-engined type to give the Tu-134 rough-field capabilities.

Tu-134A

Type: short- to medium-haul airliner

Powerplant: two 66.69-kN (15,000-lb.-thrust) Soloviev D-30-II turbofans

Maximum cruising speed: 900 km/h (558 m.p.h.)

Climb rate: 888 m/min (2,914 f.p.m.) at sea level

Range: 2000 km (1,240 mi.) with 8215-kg (18,075-lb.) payload or 3500 km (2,170 mi.) with 4000-kg (8,800-lb.) payload

Service ceiling: 12,000 m (39,400 ft.)

Weights: empty 29,000 kg (63,800 lb.); maximum take-off 47,000 kg (103,400 lb.)

Payload: 72 passengers or 80 passengers with reduced baggage space

Dimensions: span 29.00 m (95 ft. 2 in.)
length 37.10 m (121 ft. 8 in.)
height 9.02 m (29 ft. 7 in.)
wing area 127.30 m² (1,370 sq. ft.)

ACTION DATA

PASSENGERS

Several airlines were developed for the 70- to 80-seat short- to medium-haul market during the mid-1960s. Western designs faced very stiff international competition, but the Tu-134 had no rival for Aeroflot orders.

Tu-134A 'CRUSTY' 72 passengers

F28 FELLOWSHIP Mk 2000 79 passengers

Tu-104A 'CAMEL' 70 passengers

MAXIMUM CRUISING SPEED

Most passengers prefer to be airborne for as short a time as possible, so a fast, efficient cruising speed is highly desirable. The 'Camel' is the fastest of these three, but it offered little in the way of passenger comfort compared to the quieter Tu-134. The F28 has been developed into the advanced Fokker 100.

Tu-134A 'CRUSTY'	900 km/h (558 m.p.h.)
F28	843 km/h (523 m.p.h.)
Tu-104A 'CAMEL'	950 km/h (589 m.p.h.)

MAXIMUM RANGE

With its vast size, the Soviet Union demanded longer range from its short- to medium-haul airliners than was available from contemporary Western designs. With its bomber origins the Tu-104A offered outstanding range, but it was a crude airliner. The Tu-134 was a compromise between the Tu-104 and Western types.

Tu-134A 'CRUSTY' 3500 km (2,170 mi.)

F28 FELLOWSHIP Mk 2000 2038 km (1,264 mi.)

Tu-104A 'CAMEL' 4200 km (2,600 mi.)

Western 'Crusty' contemporaries

■ **BAC ONE-ELEVEN:** Some One-Elevens, usually with hush-kitted engines, still remain in service with smaller charter airlines in the UK and abroad. More than 200 aircraft were built, some under licence in Romania.

■ **BOEING MODEL 737:** With a maximum capacity of between 103 and 130 passengers, the 737 was unusual because Boeing opted to position its twin engines beneath the wings rather than at the tail. It has become the world's best-selling airliner.

■ **HAWKER SIDDELEY TRIDENT:** With its three Rolls-Royce Spey turbofans and seating for between 103 and 180 passengers, depending on the variant, the Trident was designed for short- to medium-range, high-capacity routes.

TUPOLEV

TU-144 'CHARGER'

● Supersonic transport ● Concorde competitor ● Technology testbed

irst flown on the last day of 1968, the Tu-144 was a product of the Cold War competition that saw the Soviet Union and the West repeatedly trying to outdo each other in various areas of aerospace technology. Alongside the space race, supersonic passenger transport was one of the most demanding areas of development, and one where the Soviets were determined to beat the Anglo-French team working on the aircraft that became Concorde.

▲ Before the fuel crises and strict noise regulations of the 1970s, Europe and the USSR were involved in a dramatic race to produce the first supersonic airliner, which the Tu-144 won.

TUPOLEV TU-144 'CHARGER'

Double-delta ▶
This view clearly shows the pronounced double-delta shape of the wing planform, which gave the Tu-144 a much more angular appearance than Concorde. The large air intakes are visible beneath the wing.

▲ Paris disaster
The second production Tu-144, 77102, suffered an inflight break-up during an unplanned violent pitch maneuver while participating in the 1973 Paris Show.

▲ Drooping moustache
For production versions, low-speed handling was improved by adding retractable canards just aft of the flight deck.

▲ Concorde copy
Many features of the Tu-144 were remarkably similar to Concorde, such as the distinctive drooping nose. It was later revealed that the KGB obtained blueprints of the Concorde design.

Afterburning engines ▶
The NK-144A engines fitted to production aircraft were designed by Kuznetsov. Uprated engines, which resulted in the Tu-144D, allowed cruise without afterburner, but never entered service.

FACTS AND FIGURES

➤ The original Tu-144 was smaller than the production version and did not have the high-lift canards fitted.

➤ The prototype first flew on 31 December 1968, beating Concorde by 61 days.

➤ The first Mach 2 flight by an airliner was made by the Tu-144 in May 1970.

➤ It has been alleged that the violent maneuver which led to the Paris crash was to avoid a French Mirage camera ship.

➤ Passenger service began in November 1977 between Moscow and Alma Ata.

➤ Only 102 revenue-making flights were flown before the Tu-144 was retired.

PROFILE

Catching up to the West, supersonically

In its efforts to overtake the West's lead in supersonic transport, the Soviet Union embarked on a concerted campaign of industrial espionage in the early 1960s. At the same time, a flight test program was started using a MiG-21 with a scaled-down version of the Tu-144's wing.

Thanks to the skill of their spies and an incredible amount of work by the design bureau, Tupolev won the race. The Tu-144 flew two months before Concorde, and started scheduled services in December 1975, nearly

five months ahead of its rival. No passengers were carried until November 1977, though, and after at least one had crashed the aircraft was withdrawn from service less than a year later.

Despite its commercial failure, the Tu-144 made a major contribution to the understanding of high-speed aerodynamics. Evidence of that came in the early 1990s, when the U.S. paid for one of the original Tu-144s to be refurbished as a technology testbed. The purpose was to help develop a second-generation supersonic transport.

Tupolev itself had been developing a successor to the 'Charger'. Designated Tu-244, it was intended to carry 300 passengers and have a range of 9173 km (5,700 mi.).

Above: The streamlined shape needed for attaining Mach 2 is evident in the design of the Tu-144. Its similarity to Concorde led to it being nicknamed 'Concordski' in the Western press.

Above: The prototype first flew in late 1968. It differed from production models by having less camber in the wings and no nose canards.

Tu-144 'CHARGER'

Aeroflot was the only operator of the Tu-144, making just 102 commercial flights before an accident in 1978 led to retirement.

Tu-144 'Charger'

Type: supersonic passenger transport

Powerplant: four 196.31 kN (44,115-lb.-thrust) Kuznetsov NK-144 afterburning turbofans

Maximum speed: 2494 km/h (1,550 m.p.h.)

Cruise height: 17,000 m (55,750 ft.)

Range: 6486 km (4,030 mi.) with 140 passengers at Mach 1.9.

Weights: 84,822 kg (187,000 lb.) empty; 167,376 kg (369,000 lb.) max take-off

Accommodation: 140 passengers typically

Dimensions:
span		94 ft. 6 in.)
length		215 ft. 6 in.)
height		42 ft. 2 in.)
wing area	437.85 m²	(4,713 sq. ft.)

During low-speed flight, takeoff and landing the nosecone droops by 12 degrees. A pair of canards also extend in this flight regime to improve the low-speed handling of the aircraft.

Production aircraft had redesigned engine nacelles with oblique rectangular inlets similar to Concorde. The intakes were electrically de-iced.

The virtually full-span powered control surfaces consist of four separate elevons on each wing. These act in unison as elevators, or in opposition as ailerons.

The double-delta wings have a leading-edge sweepback of about 76 degrees on the inboard sections and 57 degrees on the main panels. The wing also has a camber on both leading and trailing edges.

The Tu-144 is of largely light alloy construction. Titanium and stainless steel are used in the leading edges and control surfaces. Advanced flight controls and navigation systems are fitted.

Four afterburning Kuznetsov NK-144A turbofans powered the Tu-144. Afterburning was necessary to maintain supersonic cruise.

The Tu-144 had a normal flight crew of three with the two pilots seated side-by-side. The prototype was fitted with ejection seats for the crew, but these were removed in production aircraft.

The main landing gear was a 12-wheel bogie that retracted forward, rotating through 180 degrees to lie inverted in the wing. The long nose gear was based on the unit used in the Tu-114 and retracted forward into the fuselage.

The most common seating arrangement in the Tu-144 was for 11 first-class and 129 tourist-class passengers. The theoretical maximum was 167 passengers.

CCCP-77144

Aerodynamic features of the Tu-144

CRUISING POSITION: During supersonic cruise the nose is aligned with the fuselage, allowing for an extremely aerodynamic shape. The retractable visor is not transparent, giving the crew very poor forward vision.

LOW-SPEED POSITION: The nose droops by 12 degrees during low-speed flight, take-off and landing to give the pilots much better forward vision. The visor, which is armored to resist a supersonic birdstrike, retracts.

CANARDS RETRACTED: For high-speed flight the double-delta wing provides all the lift the aircraft needs and the rectangular canards, 6 m (20 ft.) long, retract back into the top of the fuselage to give a more aerodynamic shape.

CANARDS EXTENDED: To improve handling of the aircraft at low speeds the canards swing forward to zero-degree sweep, but sharp anhedral. Each canard is fitted with a double leading-edge slat and a trailing-edge flap.

ACTION DATA

SPEED

Of the two supersonic jet transports that have entered service, the Tu-144 was bigger and faster than the Concorde. Concorde, however, was commercially successful for more than 25 years. The DC-10 is a typical subsonic airliner of the time; it takes over twice as long as Concorde on Atlantic crossings.

Tu-144 'CHARGER'	2494 km/h (1,550 m.p.h.)
CONCORDE	2174 km/h (1,351 m.p.h.)
DC-10-30	954 km/h (593 m.p.h.)

VFW-FOKKER

614

- German airliner ● Overwing engines ● Rough-field STOL capability

VFW-FOKKER 614

▲ Overwing engines
Foreign objects were unlikely to enter the engines as they were protected by the wings.

▲ Flying in France
VFW-Fokker 614s had short airline careers, with Air Alsace using its jets only from 1976 to 1979.

Prototype number three ▶
After the first prototype crashed, the third aircraft was rushed into service to help with testing.

◀ Destined for Denmark
Cimber Air introduced the VFW-Fokker 614 into commercial service in 1975.

Icelandic runway ▶
According to a VFW-Fokker press release, the stones on this unprepared runway were 'fist-sized'. These tests were required for the aircraft to gain certification for rough-field operations. Tests were also undertaken in Saudi Arabia and north and west Africa.

Focke-Wulf, 'Weser' and Heinkel united as VFW in the mid-1960s to develop the VFW 614 airliner. In 1970 the VFW consortium joined forces with Fokker to produce the aircraft. It flew for the first time in July 1971, and by early 1975 ten operators had expressed their intention to buy a total of 26 aircraft. Two years later, though, only 16 had been ordered, and production ceased at the end of 1977 after just 19 had been built. Only four examples remain airworthy.

▲ A large number of orders were initially received for the 614, but few of these turned into deliveries. Airlines may have considered the aircraft too slow, or perhaps its unusual configuration and the early withdrawal of SNECMA from the project did not give potential buyers confidence in it.

FACTS AND FIGURES

- ➤ A merger of Focke-Wulf and 'Weser' Flugzeugbau produced VFW in 1963, with Heinkel joining in 1964.

- ➤ After 1969 Fokker became an equal partner in the company with VFW.

- ➤ Elevator tab flutter caused the crash of the first prototype in 1972.

- ➤ Early in 1973 VFW-Fokker had 23 orders for the 614, but only 19 were ever completed; 13 served with airlines.

- ➤ SABCA and Fairey in Belgium were also involved in production.

- ➤ MBB now uses its aircraft to test new technologies, including fly-by-light.

PROFILE

Radical airliner design

VFW designed the 614 as a modern version of the DC-3. Originally proposed as the E.614 by the Entwicklungsring division of Focke-Wulf, it could carry up to 44 passengers over ranges of around 600 km (372 mi.).

The most remarkable feature of the design was its overwing engines. Mounted on pylons, they enabled the aircraft to use very short undercarriage legs, which simplified passenger loading and helped to reduce the risk of engine debris ingestion.

Unfortunately, the idea did not prove popular and fewer than a dozen were sold before the manufacturers decided to stop production. The first 614 entered service with Cimber Air in Denmark, and Air Alsace operated three. Another three were delivered to the German air force, which still uses them as VIP transports.

In the mid-1980s one 614 was rebuilt as a research aircraft. It is used by the German aerospace research establishment, the DFW, to investigate new aerodynamics, systems and air traffic control technology. The projected 614-200 version, with a slightly longer fuselage and increased wingspan, would have carried 52 passengers.

Above: With a large flap area and strong undercarriage the VFW-Fokker 614 was destined to become a favourite with STOL operators, but it never happened.

Above: Three aircraft were delivered to the Luftwaffe and remain in service. Only one other VFW-Fokker 614 remains airworthy, operated by MBB.

614

Type: short-haul passenger transport

Powerplant: two 32.4-kN (7,290-lb.) Rolls-Royce SNECMA M45H Mk 501 turbofans

Maximum speed: 735 km/h (455 m.p.h.) at 6400 m (20,000 ft.); maximum cruising speed 722 km/h (448 m.p.h.) at 7620 m (25,000 ft.)

Climb rate: 1026 m/min (3,365 f.p.m.)

Landing run: 631 m (2,070 ft.) from 15 m (50-ft.)

Range: 2500 km (1,500 mi.) with maximum fuel; 667 km (414 mi.) with 40 passengers or 3680-kg (8,096-lb.) payload with fuel reserves for a 277-km (170-mi.) diversion

Service ceiling: 7620 m (25,000 ft.)

Weights: empty 12,200 kg (26,840 lb.); maximum take-off 18,600 kg (40,920 lb.)

Accommodation: 40 to 44 passengers

Dimensions:
span	21.50 m	(70 ft. 6 in.)
length	20.60 m	(67 ft. 7 in.)
height	7.84 m	(25 ft. 9 in.)
wing area	64 m²	(689 sq. ft.)

614

D-BABB was the second VFW-Fokker 614 prototype, flown on 14 January 1972, before the 1 February crash of the first aircraft, which claimed the life of its co-pilot. Its development was otherwise untroubled.

Pilot and co-pilot sat side-by-side with dual controls. An observer could be carried as an option. In addition to the flight crew, two cabin attendants were carried.

An engine pylon was mounted on each wing, just behind the rear spar at about two-thirds chord. This position left the wing leading edge well ahead of the engine and prevented debris entering it.

Rolls-Royce and SNECMA co-operated in the production of the M45H Mk 501 turbofan. It had been developed to power an Anglo-French strike fighter, but only found this one application.

The all-metal tailplane could be moved as a trimming method. A liquid de-icing system protected the leading edges.

Aircraft flying test duties, especially prototypes, are often fitted with large instrumentation booms. These collect a range of data about aircraft attitude and speed.

This forward door served as the main passenger entrance, with an in-built airstair. A cargo door for baggage was mounted opposite.

Massive flap guides were a result of the STOL capabilities of the design. The wing also had two spoilers for in-flight use and six for ground use.

A maximum of 44 passengers could be accommodated. Unfortunately engines mounted alongside the windows resulted in a noisy cabin.

ACTION DATA

MAXIMUM CRUISING SPEED

Some industry experts criticised the 614 for its low speed, although over the short routes for which it was designed this would not have been a problem.

614	722 km/h (448 m.p.h.)
ONE-ELEVEN SERIES 475	871 km/h (540 m.p.h.)
146-100	778 km/h (482 m.p.h.)

TAKE-OFF RUN

Even compared to the BAe 146, the take-off performance of the VFW 614 is remarkable. The 146 was to have been launched at the same time as the 614, but its manufacturers shelved the design after they judged that a market for the type did not exist at that time.

614	830 m (2,720 ft.)
ONE-ELEVEN SERIES 475	1676 m (5,500 ft.)
146-100	1116 m (3,660 ft.)

RANGE

Gaining a number of export orders, the One-Eleven was favoured for its long range, although it could not match the operational flexibility of the 614. Designed to the same philosophy as the 614, the 146 would have benefited from the incorporation of newer technology to produce an aircraft of greater overall capability.

614	2500 km (1,500 mi.)
ONE-ELEVEN SERIES 475	3677 km (2,275 mi.)
146-100	2872 km (1,780 mi.)

VFW aerospace projects

■ **VFW H3:** Typical of the innovative designs of VFW, this three-seat helicopter featured a compressed-air driven main rotor and shrouded propellers for forward flight.

■ **PANAVIA MRCA:** VFW was an early partner in the project that was to produce the Tornado, destined to become one of Europe's most important combat aircraft.

■ **VFW-FOKKER CH-53G:** A 1969 contract for 135 CH-53Gs to equip the German army resulted in VFW-Fokker building the type under licence from Sikorsky.

■ **FOKKER-VFW F.28 FRIENDSHIP:** VFW-Fokker was responsible for building fuselage sections and tail assemblies for the F.28 and contributed greatly to the type's success.

VICKERS
R.100

● Last British rigid airship ● Record-breaking flight ● Simple construction

▲ One of two competing airship designs, the privately funded R100 was a simple but sound craft. It is best remembered for its record-breaking endurance flight across the Atlantic.

Long range with a big payload and the ability to operate safely in conditions that would keep contemporary aeroplanes on the ground were the main attractions of the airship in the 1920s. One of the most successful rigid airship designs was the R.100, created by Barnes Wallis and built by a Vickers subsidiary called the Airship Guarantee Company. During its brief career the R.100 made the first transatlantic crossing by an airship.

VICKERS R.100

▲ First flight
Powered by conventional aero engines, the R.100 took to the air for the first time on 16 December 1929, piloted by G.H. Scott.

▲ Last British Airship
When it was built the R.100 was one of the largest rigid airships in the world. Built at the Airship Guarantee Company works in Howden, Yorkshire, it was the last made in Britain.

◀ Undignified end
No major problems were ever found with the design of the R.100, though the fate of its rival, the R.101 resulted in the airship concept falling from favour and to the R.100 being prematurely scrapped.

◀ Fit for Royalty
The accommodation on the R.100 was truly luxurious and even boasted a formal dining room capable of seating 56 passengers.

Simple construction ▶
The key factor in the strength of the R.100 was the geodetic design of its structure.

FACTS AND FIGURES

➤ Barnes Neville Wallis designed the R.100 and later became famous for creating the bouncing bomb during World War II.

➤ A disused RNAS air station was chosen as the site for building the R.100.

➤ When the airship was scrapped, Vickers had not covered all its costs.

➤ Geodetic construction used on the R.100 was later employed on the famous Vickers Wellington medium bomber.

➤ Neville Shute later wrote of the Atlantic crossing in his book *Slide Rule*.

➤ In 1924, the fixed price for the as yet unbuilt R.100 was set at £350,000.

PROFILE

Britain's best and last

It was the need for better communications with far-flung colonies that persuaded the British government to finance the development of two airships, the Vickers R.100 and the R.101, which was built by the Royal Airship Works.

Barnes Wallis used some novel construction techniques, including a system of wire mesh netting to keep the gas bags from being damaged by rubbing against the structural girders. There were three decks, with cabins for 100 passengers, a promenade area and a dining salon for 56.

After making its maiden flight in December 1929, the R.100 set out for Canada on 29 July, arriving on 1 August after 78 hours in the air. On the way it survived a violent thunderstorm over the St Lawrence River. The fabric covering on the stabilising fins was ripped, but the crew carried out repairs in flight before eventually arriving at Montreal. The return journey, to Cardington, took 58 hours.

Unfortunately, the rival R.101 crashed in France with many fatalities two months later, after setting out on a proving flight to India. As a result, the R.100 was taken out of service and scrapped, although it had already proved to be a safe and reliable craft.

Above: Seen in company with a German Zeppelin, the R.100 sits quietly, tied to its mooring mast. The German craft were filled with hydrogen instead of helium.

Above: In order to make the airship as streamlined as possible, Barnes Wallis and his team arranged the accommodation on three decks in the lower portion of the hull. A viewing promenade was also featured.

Barnes Wallis set out to build the R.100 in as straightforward and cost effective a manner as possible. The airframe was extremely strong and the Vickers craft proved to be much cheaper and easier to maintain than the entirely Government-funded R.101.

R.100

Type: rigid airship

Powerplant: six 500-kW (670-hp.) Rolls-Royce Condor piston aero engines

Maximum speed: 130 km/h (81 m.p.h.)

Endurance: 80 hr

Date of completion: 1929

Price: £350,000

Gross lift: 158.50 tonnes (174.7 tons)

Accommodation: on three decks, with sleeping berths for up to 100 passengers located on the upper decks and a gallery lounge on the bottom deck.

Dimensions: beam 41.15 m (135 ft.)
length 216.00 m (708 ft. 6 in.)
gas volume 147247.60 m³ (5,199,954 cu. ft.)

R.100

One of two designs submitted for a British long distance airship, the R.100 was completed in 1929. Built for use on the North American route, it completed only one, successful, flight before being withdrawn from service.

Although the R.100 was a relatively simple design, several construction techniques were pioneered on it. These included the use of wire mesh netting to contain the gas bags and prevent them from pressing on the main girders. The Vickers craft also had fewer main spars than other airship designs.

R-100

G-FAAV

At the very tip of the nose were anchor points for attaching the craft to a gigantic mooring mast. This also made entry and exit for the passengers and crew much simpler.

Propulsion was by means of six Rolls-Royce Condor IIIB aero engines. It had originally been intended to use experimental kerosene fuel engines, but the eventual choice proved to be a shrewd move.

In order to achieve the best aerodynamic efficiency, the R-100's stabilisers were smoothly blended in to the main structure.

The record-breaking journey

2 PROBLEMS STRIKE: While the R-100 was passing over the St Lawrence Seaway, a violent thunderstorm resulted in two damaged stabilisers and a hole being torn in the fabric. The crew made repairs in flight and the R.100 arrived safely.

3 JOURNEY HOME: The trip back took only 58 hours, though by this time the R.100 had made history by performing the longest-endurance flight ever by an airship.

MONTREAL

CARDINGTON

1 OUTWARD BOUND: Slipping clear from its moorings on 29 July 1930, the R.100 set off from Cardington on its record-breaking flight to Canada. No problems were encountered for most of the journey, although strong head winds resulted in the trip taking slightly longer than anticipated.

GOLIATHS IN THE SKY

SAGA OF THE R101: Rival to the R.100, though destined for the Far Eastern and African routes, was the ambitious R.101. Unlike the Vickers design, this giant airship was built by the Air Ministry at Cardington. It was a highly complex machine and no expense was spared during its construction. It suffered problems right from the beginning and proved to be underpowered and had poor handling. During its maiden voyage to India the R.101 crashed in France, bursting into flames and killing many of those aboard.

END OF AN ERA: After the R101 tragedy, Britain halted its development of long-range airships, though Germany persisted with the idea. The largest airship ever to emerge was the Graf Zeppelin Hindenburg. It was originally designed to use helium, but an international embargo resulted in highly flammable hydrogen being used instead. The Hindenburg completed 17 transatlantic crossings with success, though on a voyage in 1937, the huge airship burst into flames at Lakehurst in New Jersey, resulting in horrendous casualties. The era of the airship had finally ended.

VICKERS

VIKING

● Short-haul airliner ● Based on the Wellington ● RAF service

As World war II reached its climax in 1945, it became apparent that Britain urgently required an interim transport aircraft for short-haul work. Vickers designed the Viking, which was ideal for the task and could quickly be placed into production since it was based on the Wellington bomber. Vikings saw extensive service with British European Airways and served as transport and training aircraft, known respectively as the Valetta and the Varsity, with the RAF.

▲ Vikings replaced
DC-3s serving with a number of British airlines. The Vickers aircraft was one of the first airliners to feature personal steward call-buttons, adjustable headrests and air vents.

VICKERS VIKING

◀ Viking in production
Seen flying off the Isle of Wight, G-AGON was the first production Viking. It was used by BOAC's development flight, based at Hurn.

▼ Export Vikings
The first overseas customer was Indian National Airways, which named this aircraft Jumna.

▼ Jet power
On 6 April 1948 a specially converted Rolls-Royce Nene turbojet-powered Viking took to the air and became the world's first pure-jet transport aircraft.

▼ Metal wing
After the first 19 aircraft, stressed-skin metal wings were fitted, as these were easier to maintain.

◀ Linking Europe
Originally delivered to South African Airways, G-AMGG was one of 75 Vikings operated by BEA. The Viking was a vital component of BEA's fleet linking Britain to other European countries.

FACTS AND FIGURES

➤ Before the Viking name was chosen, the aircraft was also known as the Wellington Continental and the VC.1.

➤ The prototype first flew from Wisley airfield on 22 June 1945.

➤ British European Airways' Admiral-class Vikings could carry up to 36 passengers.

➤ Four Mk 1 Vikings were operated by the King's Flight on state visits to South Africa in 1947 and Nigeria in 1951.

➤ The RAF operated transport and training variants called Valetta and Varsity.

➤ A number of the 163 Vikings built were still operating charter flights in the late 1960s.

PROFILE

Britain's first post-war airliner

Post-war Britain had a demand for a civil transport aircraft, and before machines such as the Comet could enter service an interim aircraft was required. Vickers proposed the VC.1 (later the Viking), which combined the virtues of the tried-and-tested Wellington wing and Bristol Hercules engine with a new stressed-skin fuselage.

A year after design work began the VC.1 prototype took to the air. After a successful test programme, British European Airways (BEA) ordered 50 Vikings, with an improved stressed-skin wing, to replace its fleet of DC-3s. BEA operated the first Viking service on 1 September 1946.

In December 1946 icing problems were discovered, and operations were halted for four months. Solutions were found, however, and export sales were won after a successful 64,400-km (40,000-mi.) tour to New Zealand.

In April 1950 disaster nearly struck one of BEA's Vikings, Vigilant, when a saboteur's bomb exploded in the toilet over the English Channel. The strength of the design and the skill of Captain I.R. Harvey ensured the badly damaged aircraft made a safe landing. BEA's Vikings flew more than half a million hours and carried three million passengers before being replaced in 1954.

G-AHOS was one of the earliest Vikings and featured the geodetic wing.

The first 19 Vikings featured fabric-covered geodetic wings and tail. They were replaced by stressed-skin units.

Much of the wing design, including the main spar system, was based on the Wellington. Stressed-skin wings were introduced for ease of maintenance.

Viking Type 610

Type: twin-engined short-haul airliner

Powerplant: two 1260-kW (1,690-hp.) Bristol Hercules 634 piston engines

Maximum speed: 423 km/h (262 m.p.h.) at 3000 m (10,000 ft.)

Initial climb rate: 457 m/min (1,500 f.p.m.)

Range: 2736 km (1,700 mi.) at 338 km/h (210 m.p.h.)

Service ceiling: 7620 m (25,000 ft.)

Weights: empty 10,433 kg (22,936 lb.); maximum take-off 16,400 kg (36,080 lb.)

Accommodation: four crew and up to 27 passengers, or up to 36 passengers in Admiral-class layout

Dimensions:
span	27.20 m	(89 ft. 3 in.)
length	19.86 m	(65 ft. 2 in.)
height	5.97 m	(19 ft. 7 in.)
wing area	81.94 m²	(882 sq. ft.)

VIKING TYPE 610

G-AHPL, *Verdant*, was first delivered to BEA and was later renamed *Lord Anson*. It went on to serve with five other airlines, including Central African Airways.

Power was provided by two Bristol Hercules engines. They were chosen ahead of the Rolls-Royce Merlin because they had greater single-engine performance, and could meet new take-off regulations.

Unlike pre-war airliners, the Viking was designed with passenger comfort in mind. Sound-proofing was introduced to the cabin walls and ceiling, and a leather and moquette finish was applied to the interior.

Icing problems encountered on the tailplane were solved by increasing the flow rate of the de-icing solution.

The functional flightdeck had a central console with throttles, trim wheels, fuel-cock controls and the instrument panel. The wide-angle front and side windscreens were an innovative feature.

ACTION DATA

CRUISING SPEED

Capable of cruising at a higher speed than the ubiquitous DC-3, which it replaced, the Viking reduced travelling time for passengers. The later CV 240 and the the Il-12 'Coach' had more powerful engines, giving greater performance.

VIKING Mk 1B	338 km/h (210 m.p.h.)
CV 240 CONVAIRLINER	432 km/h (268 m.p.h.)
Il-12B 'COACH'	350 km/h (217 m.p.h.)

MAXIMUM PASSENGERS

In maximum passenger configuration the Viking could carry up to 36 passengers. A more typical load was 27, which gave greater passenger comfort. The CV 240 was a larger aircraft and offered more space for passengers and cargo.

VIKING Mk 1B 36 passengers

CV 240 CONVAIRLINER 40 passengers

Il-12B 'COACH' 32 passengers

RANGE

Built to operate British European Airways' services from London to major European cities, the Viking did not require, or possess, long range. The CV 240 and Il-12 were designed to cover the much larger areas of North America and the Soviet Union, and therefore required much greater range to meet the specific needs of customers.

CV 240 CONVAIRLINER 2880 km (1,800 mi.)

VIKING Mk 1B 837 km (520 mi.)

Il-12B 'COACH' 1250 km (775 mi.)

Vickers civil transport aircraft

■ **WARWICK:** Deliveries to British Overseas Airways Corporation (BOAC) started in 1943. Three Warwicks were used on North African routes.

■ **VISCOUNT:** Regarded as a milestone in air transport, the Viscount was the first turbine-powered aircraft to enter revenue service.

■ **VANGUARD:** Following on from the success of the Viscount, Vickers built the larger and faster Vanguard. It entered service on 1 March 1961.

■ **VC.10:** The four-engined VC.10 was built to a BOAC specification for a long-range airliner with good hot-and-high performance.

VICKERS

VC.10

● **First rear-engined four-jet** ● **Short take-off** ● **Long range**

▲ When it entered service with BOAC in April 1964, the VC.10 was the world's first long-range, intercontinental jet airliner with four rear-mounted turbofan engines. It was therefore the first of many airliners with a 'clean-wing' layout.

The Vickers VC.10 was a 'great' of the golden age of the 1960s, when jet-powered air commerce was new and airlines pampered travellers. It was chosen without hesitation by many carriers, including BOAC (British Overseas Airways Corporation), British United and Ghana Airways, with a military version joining the Royal Air Force. In addition, the popularity of the VC.10 led to the successful extended-body Super VC.10 model.

VICKERS VC.10

▼ Super VC.10
The stretched Super VC.10 had more powerful Rolls-Royce Conway engines, an additional fuel tank in the fin and extended wing leading edges. It carried more passengers over a longer range, but was not a great commercial success.

▲ Quick development
The design of the VC.10 began in March 1958, with the prototype becoming airborne for the first time four years later in June 1962. Within two years it was in regular service with BOAC.

◄ Tanker conversions
Retired airline VC.10s and Super VC.10s have been converted by British Aerospace as air-to-air refuelling tankers for the RAF. The first nine aircraft had holes cut in the tops of their fuselages to enable fuel tanks to be lowered into their cabins. The VC.10's five fuel tanks each hold 3182 litres.

▼ Spacious cockpit
The roomy cockpit provided accommodation for an airline flight crew of three.

▲ Tri-jet testbed
One of the RAF's 14 VC.10 transports had its two portside Conway engines replaced by a single RB.211 turbofan for flight testing. Large turbofans like the RB.211 gave next-generation airliners greater range.

FACTS AND FIGURES

➤ The Super VC.10 (Type 1151) was able to carry 163 to 180 economy-class passengers.

➤ BOAC introduced the first VC.10s on the London-Lagos route on 29 April 1964.

➤ First flight of the VC.10 prototype was made on 29 June 1962.

➤ When British Airways ended scheduled service in March 1981, VC.10s had carried over a million passengers.

➤ The lengthened Vickers Super VC.10 flew for the first time on 7 May 1964.

➤ The RAF ordered 14 of these Vickers transports for general support.

PROFILE

Britain's last big jet airliner

In the 1960s, when fewer than five per cent of all people in developed Western nations had even been inside an aircraft, the Vickers VC.10 offered a high standard of transportation for the lucky few who flew in it. The VC.10 was largely underwritten by BOAC, the airline since replaced by British Airways, but Vickers' fine servant of the skies appeared in many colours: Ghana Airways leased one to Middle East Airways which stationed the VC.10 in Beirut.

The success of the VC.10

jetliner paralleled faithful service by its military counterpart: RAF VC.10s are still used for long-range troop and VIP transport. A growth version, the Super VC.10, joined BOAC's North American routes in 1965. With greater capacity, the Super VC.10 had a lengthened fuselage, a fuel tank in the fin and more powerful turbojet engines.

All variants of the VC.10 sustained a fine record for reliability and safety; so much so that the RAF purchased a fleet of VC.10 airliners for conversion as air-to-air refuelling platforms.

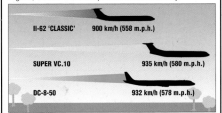

Below: The only new-build VC.10s to go directly to an overseas airline were two modified Model 1102s supplied to Ghana Airways in 1965.

Above: The first Super VC.10 entered service with BOAC in April 1965, and the 17 production aircraft were operated until 1981. Four new Super VC.10s, with large cargo doors and strengthened floors were built for East African Airways.

Super VC.10

Type: four-engined long-range passenger/cargo jet airliner

Powerplant: four 100.08-kN (23,030-lb.-thrust) Rolls-Royce Conway RCo.43 turbofans

Maximum speed: 935 km/h (580 m.p.h.)

Initial climb rate: 700 m/min (2,300 f.p.m.)

Cruise height: 11,600 m (38,000 ft.)

Range: 7560 km (4,698 mi.) with maximum payload

Weights: empty 66,660 kg (146,960 lb.); basic operating weight 70,479 kg (155,054 lb.)

Maximum payload: 27,043 kg (59,495 lb.)

Dimensions:
span	44.55 m (146 ft.)
length	52.32 m (172 ft.)
height	12.04 m (39 ft.)
wing area	272.4 m² (2,931 sq. ft.)

SUPER VC.10

As the fastest subsonic transatlantic airliner, the stretched fuselage of the Super VC.10 held up to 187 passengers. Its increased fuel capacity gave it a longer range.

The spoilers on the top of the wings were used as airbrakes.

The Super VC.10 was powered by four Rolls-Royce Conway RCo.43 turbofan engines, mounted in pairs on either side of the rear fuselage. Thrust reversers were fitted to the outer engines only.

The well-equipped flight deck had space for up to four crewmembers.

The Super VC.10 had a 4.27-m (14-ft.) longer fuselage, carried a bigger payload and had an additional toilet. The rear passenger door was moved aft of the wing.

The low wings, with 32° of sweep, made extensive use of fail-safe measures, with each aileron divided into two separate sections.

The flight deck was the first to become fully operational with the new Elliott automatic landing system, permitting hands-off landings in restricted visibility.

The inward-retracting main undercarriage units each used four-wheel bogies. It had twin wheels on the forward-retracting, steerable nose unit.

The Super VC.10 had an oval-shaped fuselage of light-alloy, semi-monocoque construction with conventional frames and stringers.

The cantilever, all-metal tail had the tailplane set at the top of the fin, ahead of a large bullet-shaped fairing at the junction. The fin also had an integral fuel tank.

Four-jet transports of the 1960s

■ **ILYUSHIN Il-62:** The first long-range, four-jet transport built in the USSR, the Il-62 remained in production for 30 years, with more than 250 delivered to airlines and military customers. It is longer and heavier than the VC.10, but with a lower top speed (901 km/h/580 m.p.h.) and shorter range (6700 km/4,587 mi.).

■ **McDONNELL DOUGLAS DC-8-50:** First flown in 1958, the DC-8, with its conventional underslung engines, was shorter overall than the VC.10 but could accommodate more passengers. It was not quite as fast as the Vickers' aircraft and did not have the range with maximum payload and reserves.

■ **VICKERS VC.10 C1:** With a standard VC.10 length fuselage, large forward loading door and strengthened cabin floor, the more powerful VC.10 supplied to the RAF in 1966 is still in service more than 30 years later. It is fast, with a maximum speed of 935 km/h (558 m.p.h.) and good range, up to 7560 km (4,154 mi.).

ACTION DATA

MAXIMUM SPEED

The Super VC.10 was the fastest subsonic transatlantic airliner when it entered service with BOAC in 1965. Possessing powerful engines, it is still one of the quickest airliners in the sky.

Il-62 'CLASSIC'	900 km/h (558 m.p.h.)
SUPER VC.10	935 km/h (580 m.p.h.)
DC-8-50	932 km/h (578 m.p.h.)

PASSENGERS

The rear fuselage-mounted engines reduce the interior cabin length available for passenger seating on both the Super VC.10 and Il-62. RAF VC.10 transports have rearward-facing seats for safety.

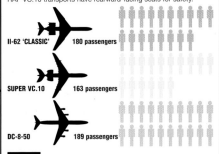

Il-62 'CLASSIC'	180 passengers
SUPER VC.10	163 passengers
DC-8-50	189 passengers

RANGE

The Super VC.10, with its additional fin fuel tank, has a markedly greater range than either of its 1960s competitors.

Il-62 'CLASSIC'	6700 km (4,154 mi.)
SUPER VC.10	7560 km (4,687 mi.)
DC-8-50	6440 km (3,993 mi.)

VICKERS

VISCOUNT

● Short-haul airliner ● World's first commercial turboprop ● Still in service

A revelation when it appeared soon after World War II, the much-loved Vickers Viscount was the world's first true turboprop airliner. With its four Dart turboprop engines, tricycle landing gear and a sumptuous interior which enabled the airlines to treat passengers in comfort, it was a great leap forwards for commercial aviation. Conceived as a short-haul transport for European routes, Viscounts are still flying today after more than 40 years.

▲ The Viscount
went through a phase of being unpopular when jets became fashionable, but it enjoyed a sudden revival in fortune when oil prices and operating costs rose.

VICKERS VISCOUNT

▲ Two engines only
Viscount pilots liked to perform at Farnborough. One display stunt was a low pass in front of the crowd, with the aircraft only using two engines.

▲ Star of the show
Despite its size, the Viscount put on an exciting performance at the 1955 Farnborough air show in 1955. This display was by a 700 series 59-seat aircraft.

▼ Third World workhorse
The Viscount gave some of its most valuable service to Third World countries in Africa and South America because of its reliability and low operating costs.

▲ Assembly line
The main assembly line at Weybridge normally had 12 aircraft in production at any one time.

▼ German Viscount
Nine Viscounts were operated by Lufthansa, the first arriving in October 1958 at Hamburg. The airline flew its Viscounts to European destinations until the end of March 1971.

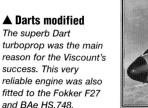

▲ Darts modified
The superb Dart turboprop was the main reason for the Viscount's success. This very reliable engine was also fitted to the Fokker F27 and BAe HS.748.

FACTS AND FIGURES

➤ The aircraft was originally named the Viceroy, but this was changed to Viscount when India gained independence in 1947.

➤ The first Viscount prototype made its initial flight on 16 July 1948.

➤ The RAF used Viscounts at its test pilot school and radar establishment.

➤ When the manufacturer delivered the last new-build Viscount in 1964, the production run had reached 444 aircraft.

➤ British World Airways operated the very successful Viscount Freightmasters.

➤ Viscounts survive in service in locations as varied as the Philippines and Zaire.

PROFILE

First turboprop airliner

The Viscount was one of the few successes of the Brabazon committee, established during World War II to oversee the future of British commercial aviation. Early Viscounts carried 47 passengers (32 in the prototype), and used turboprop power to set new standards of performance with British European Airways, Air France, Trans Canada and many others. Very attractive Viscounts were flown by Capital Airlines

of Washington DC, which was later absorbed by United Airlines.

The first improved Viscount offered underwing slipper tanks and more engine power. A 2.82-m (9-ft. 3-in.) cabin stretch and improved structural strength produced the Series 800, with increased power and carrying capacity. The definitive Model 810, produced in the early 1960s, seated 74 passengers.

The Viscount is out of date

today, but still turns heads when seen at airports. A few Viscounts were employed by air forces, including India and Turkey. The last Viscounts flying commercial services in Britain were eventually retired in Autumn 1996.

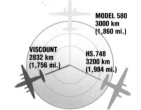

The Viscount came into its own when flying short inter-city flights, such as the London to Edinburgh route with British European Airways. The expense of flying jets on such routes meant that the Viscount remained a viable airliner even though its performance was much lower than jet 'feederliners'.

The Viscount tailplane had a very pronounced dihedral of 15°, and a distinctive rounded fin profile.

Irving-type ailerons and double slotted flaps were fitted to the wing. The structure was an all-metal frame covered with Alclad, and the wing was thermally de-iced.

VISCOUNT 708

Air France purchased 12 Vickers Viscount 708s, the first of which flew in 1953. This version, with improved Dart engines, could carry up to 48 passengers and was widely exported.

The flight crew consisted of only a pilot and co-pilot, with an optional crew station for a radio operator/navigator.

The original specification for the Viscount assumed that the Dart engine would produce about 600 kW (800 hp.), but final versions produced nearly 1600 kW (12,150 hp.).

The tail unit was of all-metal construction, with spring tabs on all control surfaces.

AIR FRANCE F-BGNK

Three large underfloor freight holds were accessible from a rear hatch.

The 700 series was different from earlier Viscounts in having a 1.5-m (5-ft.) longer wing and 2-m (6-ft. 6-in.) longer fuselage.

ACTION DATA

MAXIMUM CRUISING SPEED

The Viscount was so much faster than its piston-engined contemporaries that a number of manufacturers looked to re-fitting their aircraft with turboprops. Only the long-serving Convair twins proved at all successful, since by that time smaller, more economical purpose-designed turboprops like the HS.748 were coming into use.

VISCOUNT	563 km/h (349 m.p.h.)
MODEL 580	550 km/h (341 m.p.h.)
HS.748	450 km/h (279 m.p.h.)

RANGE

The Viscount's engines were more fuel-efficient than pistons, but four engines meant that consumption was higher than in smaller twin-engined rivals like the Convair 580 and HS.748, and the Viscount's range suffered slightly.

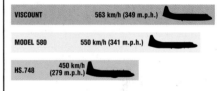

MODEL 580 3000 km (1,860 mi.)
VISCOUNT 2832 km (1,756 mi.)
HS.748 3200 km (1,984 mi.)

PASSENGER LOAD

Successive stretches to the Viscount airframe saw the passenger capacity rise from a planned 32 seats to as many as 74. When Viscounts began to be retired, they were often replaced by smaller aircraft like the HS.748, which were less capable but, being more modern, were cheaper to run.

VISCOUNT 74 passengers	MODEL 580 52 passengers	HS.748 36 passengers

The turboprop generation

■ **VICKERS VANGUARD:** The Viscount's big brother first flew in the late 1950s, but when it entered service the jet had become dominant and sales were disappointing.

■ **LOCKHEED ELECTRA:** Similar in concept to the Vanguard, sales of the Electra were also unspectacular. However, it was developed into the long-serving P-3 Orion ASW plane.

■ **BRISTOL BRITANNIA:** Best of the Western turboprops, the Britannia entered service on the transatlantic run. But it was soon outmoded by the arrival of the 707 and the DC-8.

■ **TUPOLEV Tu-114:** The greatest of the propliners, the Tu-114 used the wings and engines of the mighty 'Bear' bomber to fly further and faster than any other propeller-driven airliner.

■ **ILYUSHIN Il-18:** Jets were not as dominant behind the Iron Curtain, and the Il-18 was the most important Eastern Bloc airliner in the 1960s and 1970s, with more than 800 in service.

VICKERS

VANGUARD

● **Turboprop airliner** ● **Economical operation** ● **Freighter conversions**

V ickers developed the Vanguard in the late 1950s as a bigger counterpart to the successful Viscount. Its longer cabin could carry up to 139 passengers, nearly twice as many as the Viscount. Unfortunately, it had to compete with the new generation of turbojet-powered airliners designed to serve short- and medium-haul routes. Sales were disappointing and most Vanguards were converted to freighter configuration.

▲ *Although the Vanguard was not very successful, passengers appreciated its quiet cabin and airlines were pleased with its low operating costs. The last freighter version was retired in 1996.*

VICKERS **VANGUARD**

▼ Canadian Vanguard
Air Canada, as Trans-Canadian Airlines, was the only Vanguard export customer.

▲ Flagship of the fleet
G-APEA was the flagship of the British European Airways Vanguard fleet. This aircraft was actually named 'Vanguard'.

Wet start ▶
On 20 January 1959 the first Vanguard, known as the Type 950, lifted off from a very wet runway to make its first flight. The fin was neatly blended into the fuselage at this stage, but production machines had a large dorsal fin.

▼ Looking for customers
The second Vanguard undertook a demonstration tour of Europe, setting out for Hamburg on 6 March 1959. From Germany the aircraft visited Brussels and Rome, and is seen here in Italy on 4 June 1959. At the end of June it set off for a similar tour of Canada.

▲ Merchantman
The Air Bridge company was a major user of the Merchantman freighter conversion. Its overnight flights formed the bulk of the operations, with items such as letters, parcels and newspapers being the most common cargo. The company's last Merchantman was recently retired.

FACTS AND FIGURES

➤ Vickers studied 60 different proposals for their new airliner, including jet-powered and swept-wing designs.

➤ BEA decided that the new airliner would be named Vanguard.

➤ Vickers and BEA argued over whether the aircraft should be high- or low-winged.

➤ Vickers financed the development of the Vanguard and had no assistance from the Government.

➤ BEA's fleet of Vanguards was named after famous warships.

➤ A Vanguard flew from Canada to the UK in 8 hours and 15 minutes.

PROFILE

Airliner to freighter

First flown in January 1959, with much more powerful Tyne engines replacing the Darts that powered the Viscount, the Vanguard could fly further and faster than its smaller predecessor with nearly three times the payload. But, by then, the first medium-range jet airliners were starting to appear.

Turboprops were quieter and more fuel-efficient than turbojets, but at the time fuel was relatively cheap and airports were not subject to the same noise controls as they are in the 1990s. The jets were faster and had greater appeal to

British Airways Cargo operated six Merchantmen; G-APEK had previously flown with BEA as 'Dreadnought'. Airlines in Canada, France, Iceland, Indonesia and Sweden also flew freighter conversions.

passengers, so it was not surprising that the airlines preferred them.

As a result, Vickers sold only 43 Vanguards. Six Type 951s and 14 heavier Type 953s went to British European Airways (BEA), while Trans-Canadian Airlines (TCA) bought 23 of the Type 952. By the mid-1970s all had been retired from passenger service, but many were converted to Cargoliner freighters

in Canada or to Merchantmen in the UK. Journey time is less of a priority for short-haul cargo flights and the Vanguard's quiet engines helped to make it more acceptable on overnight freight services. For these reasons the Merchantman continued to serve into the late 1990s with a handful of specialist cargo airlines.

TYPE 951 VANGUARD

British European Airways named this Vanguard 'Euryalus'. The aircraft spent its entire career with the airline.

Part of the original BEA specification was for freight holds with a height of at least 1.22 m (4 ft.). The Vanguard's hold is 1.30 m (4 ft. 3 in.) high.

Large, four-bladed propellers drove the Vanguard. In recent years improved propeller design and multi-blade technology has seen an increase in the popularity of propeller aircraft.

All controls were manually operated and aerodynamically balanced. The Vanguard had a low approach speed.

The Vanguard had large oval windows, like those of the Viscount. These produce a very strong structure and allow the passengers an excellent view.

The distinctive dorsal fin was added to the tail unit to solve minor problems with the airflow around the rudder.

Route-proving trials prior to service entry revealed a number of engine problems which delayed BEA services until 1 March 1961.

Long, slender, high-aspect ratio wings gave the Vanguard good range and cruising speed characteristics.

A crew of three flew the Vanguard, with two cabin attendants.

The area within the wing box structure was sealed to form a fuel tank. The wing tanks held 23185 litres of fuel.

Like the Viscount, the Vanguard's tailplanes were angled upwards to improve directional stability and avoid jet wash from the engines.

Type 952 Vanguard

Type: four-engine medium-haul airliner

Powerplant: four 4135-kW (5,545-hp.) Rolls-Royce Tyne RTy.11 Mk 512 turboprops

Maximum cruising speed: 684 km/h (424 m.p.h.) at 6095 m (20,000 ft.)

Initial climb rate: 823 m/min (2,700 f.p.m.)

Range: 2945 km (1,825 mi.) with max. payload

Service ceiling: 9145 m (30,000 ft.)

Maximum payload: 10,886 kg (24,000 lb.)

Accommodation: 139 passengers

Weights: empty equipped 37,422 kg (82,328 lb.); maximum take-off 63,977 kg (140,749 lb.)

Dimensions: span 36.14 m (118 ft. 6 in.)
length 37.45 m (122 ft. 10 in.)
height 10.64 m (34 ft. 11 in.)
wing area 141.86 m² (1,526 sq. ft.)

Vickers' airliner designs

■ **TYPE 72 VANGUARD:** Only one of these 23-seat airliners was built. It entered service with Imperial Airways in 1928.

■ **TYPE 610 VIKING:** Offering seating for a maximum of 27 passengers, the Viking was a successful post-war airliner.

■ **TYPE 630 VISCOUNT:** This proved to be Vickers' most successful airliner and served for more than 40 years; 444 Viscounts were built.

■ **TYPE 1150 SUPER VC-10:** Most of East African Airline's VC-10s now fly with the RAF as tanker/transports.

ACTION DATA

MAXIMUM PASSENGER LOAD

With various seating arrangements, between 93 and 139 passengers could be accommodated in the Vanguard. BEA found that the high-density 139-passenger layout, with seats six abreast, was popular on many routes. The competing airliners shown were not able to offer this flexibility, although the Electra was also the subject of many freighter conversions.

TYPE 952 VANGUARD	139
ELECTRA	85
Il-18 'COOT'	120

WALLIS

AUTOGYROS

● 1950s design ● Many world records ● Film star

▲ Ken Wallis broke the world autogyro records for speed in a straight line (1986) and distance over a closed circuit (1988) flying this WA-116/F/S machine.

Wing Commander K.H. Wallis is the most famous name in post-war autogyro design. After his distinguished career in the RAF, his first machine took to the air in 1961. Since then his revolutionary designs have broken almost every autogyro world record. Trials were also carried out on a military reconnaissance version, but the aircraft which achieved the greatest fame was 'Little Nellie' in the 1967 James Bond film *You Only Live Twice*.

WALLIS AUTOGYROS

Record breaker ▶
Seen with its designer and pilot Ken Wallis, this WA-116/F broke an impressive nine world records.

▲ Army evaluation
The Beagle company helped produce early WA-116s, three of which were evaluated by the British Army.

First to fly ▶
After Wallis started design work in 1958, the first WA-116 was constructed by Beagle and flew in 1961. It had a 54-kW (72-hp.) McCulloch engine.

▼ Hand control
To keep the rotor blades steady when taxiing, the pilot can reach above his head to control them.

▲ 'Little Nellie'
For its starring role, 'Little Nellie' was armed with dummy air-to-air missiles, 44-mm rockets, rearward-firing 'flame-throwers' and two machine-guns.

FACTS AND FIGURES

➤ As well as the Bond movie, a Wallis design also appeared in and was used as a camera ship in *The Martian Chronicles*.

➤ A version built in conjunction with Vinten was designed for aerial photography.

➤ The WA-116 uses 27.5 metres (90 ft.) of runway during its take-off run.

➤ The Wallis WA-122 can be easily transported in a container thanks to its folding rotors and landing gear legs.

➤ The prototype WA-116 was flown by Wallis for the first time on 2 August 1961.

➤ The WA-119 Imp was powered by an engine from the Hillman Imp motor car.

PROFILE

Record-breaking autogyros

In 1908 Ken Wallis' father and uncle, H.S. and P.V. Wallis, designed and built the first aeroplane which employed steel tubing: the Wallbro monoplane. The family's position as revolutionary aviation designers continues 90 years on with the series of Wallis autogyros.

After constructing high-speed watercraft in the 1930s and a long career as a pilot in the RAF, including two operational bombing tours over Germany, Ken Wallis pursued a personal ambition of designing and building autogyros. The original design was the WA-116, which introduced many patented features, including a new rotor head design, a high-speed rotor shaft and a novel safe starting arrangement.

Three examples, built by Beagle, were evaluated by the British Army but never entered service. In 1967 G-ARZB 'Little Nellie' appeared alongside Sean Connery in *You Only Live Twice* and has since been displayed at air shows around the world.

Various versions of the basic WA-116 design have taken almost every autogyro world record, piloted by the original designer Ken Wallis.

Left: The WA-122 was a two-seat design with dual controls, making it suitable as a trainer. It is powered by a larger Rolls-Royce Continental 119-kW (160-hp.) flat-four engine.

Right: Since its film appearance G-ARZB has been displayed at shows as far away as Australia. The aircraft can be flown 'hands-off'.

WA-116/W

Type: single-seat general-purpose or reconnaissance autogyro

Powerplant: one 56-kW (75-hp.) Weslake 65/75 flat-twin engine driving a two-blade pusher propeller

Max cruising speed: 185 km/h (115 m.p.h.)

Loiter speed: 65 km/h (40 m.p.h.)

Endurance: 4 hours

Initial climb rate: 365 m/min (1,200 f.p.m.)

Range: 483 km (300 mi.)

Service ceiling: 4570 m (15,000 ft.)

Weights: empty 140.5 kg (309 lb.)

Dimensions:
rotor diameter	6.15 m (20 ft. 2 in.)
length	3.38 m (11 ft. 1 in.)
height	1.85 m (6 ft. 1 in.)

WA-116/Mc

This is the aircraft which appeared in the film *You Only Live Twice*. When it appears at air displays around the UK it is still fitted with the original dummy weapons.

This Wa-116 is powered by a 67-kW (90-hp.) McCulloch Model 4318A four-cylinder, air-cooled, two-stroke engine mounted aft of the rotor pylon. It drives a two-bladed propeller.

Constructed of wood, the two-bladed teetering autorotative rotor has metal reinforcements and internal mass balances. The initial rotor spin-up is achieved via a flexible shaft and engine clutch. A rotor brake is also fitted.

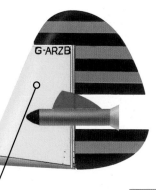

The dummy armament fitted to the modified WA-116 'Little Nellie' consisted of four jettisonable rearward-firing 'flame-throwers', fourteen 44-mm rockets, two air-to-air missiles, two nose-mounted machine-guns and 50 air mines deployed on parachutes.

A large fin and rudder, attached to the end of a short boom, help to control the aircraft in forward flight. They are constructed of hollow plywood and finished in Madapolam.

ACTION DATA

ENDURANCE

Powered by a very economical piston engine, the Wallis design has an excellent endurance for a craft of its size. This feature made it attractive to armed forces as a reconnaissance platform. The R22HP helicopter and Shadow microlight have lower endurance.

WA-116W	R22HP	SHADOW SERIES C
4 hours	2 hours 30 minutes	2 hours

THUNDERBALL: In the dramatic opening sequence of this film, James Bond fights and kills a SPECTRE secret agent at a chateau in France. Bond then makes his escape using a jet pack which enables him to fly over the castle's walls. A modified version of the jet pack was used during the opening ceremony of the 1984 Olympic Games.

Bond film aircraft stars

THUNDERBALL: Emile Largo was foiled by James Bond in his attempt to threaten the world with nuclear weapons obtained from RAF Vulcans that had ditched in the Caribbean Sea.

THE MAN WITH THE GOLDEN GUN: James Bond flew the Republic Seabee to Scaramanga's island in the South China Sea for a final showdown with the assassin.

GOLDFINGER: Pussy Galore's Flying Circus flew Piper Cherokees carrying nerve gas to disable US Army soldiers guarding the US Gold Reserves at Fort Knox, Kentucky.

WRIGHT

FLYER

● History's first powered heavier-than-air flight ● Home-built aircraft

WRIGHT FLYER

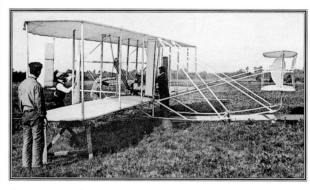

▲ Rail-launched
The Wright brothers' first experiments had been on dry sand which allowed take-offs on skids, but they had to find a way to reduce drag. One answer was a wooden railway, later replaced by wheels.

▲ Gliding record
In 1911, Orville returned to Kitty Hawk for the last time to set a world gliding record. He stayed aloft for 9 minutes and 45 seconds before landing safely.

▼ On camera
Keen to record their achievements, the brothers often filmed their flights. Here, Wilbur is seen photographing Orville during a test flight at Fort Myers in 1909.

▲ Wheeled undercarriage
The model 'R' was a sophisticated machine for its day, with twin propellers and wheels in place of the skids. The racing 'Baby Wright' was derived from this model.

◀ Passenger carrier ▶
The later Wright machines ('B' to 'R') could carry a passenger and had dual flying controls. The French aviation pioneer Paul Zens was Wilbur Wright's companion on this flight from Le Mans in 1908.

H istory was made when the Wright brothers flew their 'Flyer' a few metres over the sands of Kitty Hawk, North Carolina, in 1903. This short hop, in an aircraft that was less powerful and slower than a modern motor scooter, began the age of powered flight in heavier-than-air aircraft. The flight was less than the wing span of a modern airliner, but it opened up a whole new era of aviation.

▲ Flying the first aircraft
was nothing like flying modern aeroplanes. The builders and pilots devised their own control systems, built their own engines and airframes, and all too frequently caused their own deaths.

FACTS AND FIGURES

➤ The Smithsonian Institute refused to recognise the Wrights' achievement until the early 1950s.

➤ The Wright brothers opened their own flying school to train pilots.

➤ Wilbur Wright often kept his bowler hat on while flying his slow aircraft.

➤ Flyer III of 1905 had new propellers and a more powerful engine, and could be controlled easier than earlier 'Flyers'.

➤ Wilbur Wright had such a strong faith that he refused to fly on Sundays.

➤ The 'Flyer' Model D was a single-seater, two of which were sold to the US Army.

PROFILE

The first true powered aeroplane

Building experimental flying machines was a pursuit of cranks in the eyes of most people in 1903, but the Wright brothers were determined to achieve their goal of producing a practical, powered and controllable aircraft. Using the knowledge of previous aviation pioneers, they started building models and then small gliders, before rejecting many of the ideas as useless. With new plans of their own, such as controlling the aircraft with 'wing warping' and designing their own tiny engines, they produced the 'Flyer', a derivative of their 'Glider No. 1' of 1899.

Orville Wright took the controls of the 'Flyer' on 17 December 1903, a blustery day on the remote Kill Devil Hill. Mounted on a wooden railway track and watched only by a handful of local spectators, the 'Flyer' slowly climbed into the air and flew nearly 40 metres (120 ft.) before safely landing.

The brothers made four more flights that day, one lasting almost a minute.

Going on to demonstrate their flying machines to sceptical audiences all over Europe, they built bigger and better aircraft, cautiously correcting previous failures before going on to another flight. Thus, Wilbur Wright avoided being killed in an aeroplane crash like so many of his contemporary pioneers, instead succumbing to typhoid fever in his mid-40s.

Orville Wright (1871-1948) was the 'ideas man' of the duo. He holds a unique place in history after making the first controlled powered flight at Kitty Hawk in 1903 (below).

Wilbur Wright (1867-1912) was a quiet man, who once said that a parrot, the bird that talked the most, did not fly very high.

Wright Flyer 1903

Type: experimental heavier-than-air powered biplane glider

Powerplant: home-built four-cylinder in-line piston engine delivering 9 kW (12 hp.)

Maximum speed: c. 50 km/h (31 m.p.h.)

Height on initial flight: c. 3 m (10 ft.)

Distance on initial flight: 36.5 m (120 ft.)

Duration of initial flight: 12 sec

Take-off weight: c. 340 kg (750 lb.)

Dimensions:
span 12.29 m (40 ft.)
length 6.43 m (21 ft.)
height 2.81 m (9 ft.)
wing area c. 35.00 m² (510 sq. ft.)

WRIGHT FLYER

The Wright Flyer was based on earlier Wright glider designs. The 'Flyer' made history when Orville Wright flew it at Kill Devil Hill, Kitty Hawk, North Carolina, on 17 December 1903.

Wright-designed aircraft had no flaps or ailerons. Control was provided by warping the thin wood and fabric wings.

The structure was braced with wire for rigidity.

The wooden rudder was covered in fabric. In early Wright machines it was connected to the wing warping apparatus by cables, but was later controlled separately.

The Wrights built their own engines. The first 'Flyers' were powered by 9-kW (12-hp.) engines, with later ones having 16-kW (20-hp.) engines.

The Wrights had to carve their own chain-driven propeller, a fixed-pitch wooden unit.

The 'elevators first' layout was soon dispensed with. This layout has recently found favour with aircraft designers, and can be seen on many fighters.

Early Wright gliders were fitted with skids rather than wheels, with the 'Flyer' being built to the same pattern.

FIRST FLIGHTS

Man has probably dreamed of flight for as long as he has dreamed of anything. From the first caveman watching bats flitting out into the night, through the ancient Greeks and their myths of Daedalus and Icarus, to writers like Cyrano de Bergerac in the 17th century who fantasised about going to the moon in a carriage pulled by swans. But it was not until the 18th century, when the Montgolfier brothers harnessed the power of hot air in a balloon, that these dreams became an as-yet imperfectly achieved reality.

Dare-devils all over Europe followed the Montgolfier example, often with fatal results. Soon, people were experimenting with hydrogen to lift their balloons – much more controllable than hot air, but far more dangerous.

From there, the logical step was to fit some form of propulsion and steering mechanism. Experiments along these lines culminated in the last decade of the 19th century with steerable balloons, or dirigibles. Had anybody been taking bets in those days, most people would have put money on this being the future of flight. Few would have taken notice of the work being carried out by two mechanics in America, who were to achieve so much at Kitty Hawk in 1903.

The most important flight in history

LAUNCH RAMP: The Wright Flyer had no wheels. It took off by skidding along a polished wooden railway track.

HEAD WIND: The Wrights had chosen Kitty Hawk, on the North Carolina coast, for their flying experiments because it had a consistent steady wind blowing in off the Atlantic.

INTO THE AIR: There was a headwind of 43 km/h (21 m.p.h.) when, with Wilbur Wright at the controls, the 'Flyer' lifted into the air from the end of the launch rail.

ONE SMALL STEP: Although Wright was in the air for only 12 seconds, during which time the aeroplane covered 36.5 metres (120 ft.), the short hop was one of the greatest events in history. For the first time, man had flown under power in a heavier-than-air machine, and the way was paved for the 20th century's aviation revolution.

YAKOVLEV

YAK-40 'CODLING'/YAK-42 'CLOBBER'

● First Soviet feeder-liner ● Short take-off capability ● VIP transport

▲ The Yak-40
was a very useful aircraft for a
nation like the USSR, which has its population
spread over a massive area. The aircraft could
use airfields that Western jets could not.

The Yak-40 was designed as a short-range regional transport to replace older piston and turboprop aircraft. It featured a straight wing and accommodated up to 27 passengers, and could take off from small, 700-m (2,300-ft.) grass strips. The Yak-42 was a larger aircraft with a swept wing which significantly improved performance. Both aircraft remain in widespread use in Russia and former Soviet bloc countries.

YAKOVLEV YAK-40 'CODLING'/YAK-42 'CLOBBER'

▼ **Oil platform**
When Aeroflot split, many Yak-40s went to small regional carriers. This one is used to transport executives of the LUKoil firm.

▲ **Slovakian Yak**
The Slovak air force operates a small force of Yak-40s, based at Malacky with 32/1 Letka.

◄ **Fan test**
During a trials programme, this Yak-42E-LL tested the contra-prop D-236 engine. The front propeller had eight blades and the rear propeller six.

Prop nose ▶
This Yak-40 had a Czech M-602 turboprop engine mounted in the nose for test purposes.

◄ **Swept fin**
The Yak-40 had a curious mixture of traditional and new aerodynamics, with a straight wing for short take-offs and a sharply swept fin for fast cruising. The wing flaps were split, with three on each side.

FACTS AND FIGURES

➤ The prototype Yak-40 flew on 21 October 1966 and entered service in 1968; more than 1,000 had been built by June 1976.

➤ A Yak-42E-LL was used to test the D-236 experimental propfan.

➤ One Yak-40 was fitted with the nose section of a MiG-25R for trials.

➤ The Yak-42F, fitted with a cylinder containing electro-optical sensors, was an Aeroflot Earth survey aircraft.

➤ The Polish air force operates Yak-40s formerly used by the national airline LOT.

➤ The Yak-42 was the longest development project ever carried out by the Yak OKB.

First of the Aeroflot feeder-liners

Designed to replace the obsolete Li-2 and Il-14 propeller-driven aircraft in Aeroflot service, the Yak-40 was first ordered in 1964. Alexander Yakovlev himself was involved with the project, as was his son Sergei.

To fulfil the role of regional feeder-liner, which made up over half of Aeroflot's passenger requirement, the Yak-40 required a short take-off capability, plus the ability to cruise economically. Initially, it was planned to cruise on two

engines and use the third for maximum performance, but the two-engine requirement was soon dropped.

Although mainly seeing civil use as a 27-seat airliner, a few Yak-40s were used as military testbeds. Yak-40s were also sold to many air forces as VIP transports, including those of Ethiopia, Laos and Poland; many are still in service.

Work on the Yak-42 design began in 1972. It had the distinction of using the first high-bypass ratio turbofan in the

USSR. The first prototype flew in 1975. It was a much larger aircraft than the Yak-40, seating 120 passengers, but had a protracted development, and did not enter service until 1981.

The ultimate version, the Yak-142, entered service in 1993, and featured advanced avionics, flight-deployable spoilers and a new power unit.

Left: With flaps and undercarriage down, a Yak-40 lands at a Soviet airfield. The Yak carried on the tradition of the An-2 in operating from the small grass strips found all over the USSR.

Above: The Yak-42 featured a swept wing and relinquished much of the short-field capability of the Yak-40. High-lift devices meant that it could still use runways as short as 1800 m (5,900 ft.), however.

Yak-40

Type: three-engined short-haul feeder-liner

Powerplant: three Lotarev Ivchenko 14.71-kN (3,300-lb.-thrust) AI-25 turbofans

Maximum speed: 600 km/h (372 m.p.h.)

Economical cruising speed: 500 km/h (310 m.p.h.)

Take-off run: 340 m (1,115 ft.) at normal weight

Landing run: 340 m (1,115 ft.) at normal weight

Service ceiling: 8000 m (26,240 ft.)

Weights: empty 9000 kg (20,723 lb.); loaded 13,750 kg (30,250 lb.)

Payload: 2790 kg (6,130 lb.)

Accommodation: 2 crew and 27 passengers

Dimensions:
span	25.00 m (82 ft.)
length	20.36 m (66 ft. 10 in.)
height	6.40m (21 ft. 4 in.)
wing area	70 m² (754 sq. ft.)

YAK-40

The former Yugoslavian air force, one of many Eastern European air forces to use the type, operated Yak-40s in the VIP transport role. Yak-40s are still in use from Georgia to Sakhalin, and will continue to fly into the next century in the hands of civil operators.

The wing was first produced with 6° of dihedral, but this was later reduced. Each wing was produced in left and right halves, joined at the centreline. The wing skins were chemically milled and assembled by spot-welding, bonding and rivetting. Flaps are set to 15° for take-off and 35° for landing.

The intake mouth for the central (number two) engine is slightly raked back. The main cabin is 6.7 m (22 ft.) long and seats 24 people in a two plus one configuration. The fin leading edge is de-iced with engine bleed air.

A small auxiliary power unit is fitted above the air inlet duct for the central engine. This provides air for starting the main engine and for heating the cabin when on the ground. Early Yak-40s had a bullet fairing on the tailplane and fin junction, which was later deleted.

The Yak has a crew of two pilots, with an autopilot fitted for cruising. Grosa-40 weather radar and instrument landing systems are also fitted. The windscreen is electrically heated.

The front left cabin door is a service door, with the ventral hydraulic airstair being the main door. This Yugoslavian Yak has its designation written in Cyrillic script.

The Yak-40K had a large upward-lifting cargo door fitted in the port fuselage.

The fuel is contained in integral wing tanks forward of the main spar. The wing leading edge is de-iced by engine bleed air. The wing has manual ailerons, with a tab on the right wing only.

The Lotarev Ivchenko AI-25 turbofan has three low-pressure and eight high-pressure stages with cooled blades. The proposed Yak-40TL would have used two LF 507 engines and no thrust reverser, but it was never built.

71504

ACTION DATA

CRUISING SPEED

The bigger swept-wing Yak-42 had a slower cruising speed than the Western types but it had a similar maximum speed. The swept wing of the Yak-42 gave the aircraft much greater performance than that of the Yak-40. Being jet-powered the Yak-40 and Yak-42 both out-performed the piston-engined aircraft they replaced.

Yak-42	820 km/h (508 m.p.h.)
ONE-ELEVEN SERIES 475	871 km/h (540 m.p.h.)
F-28 FELLOWSHIP	843 km/h (523 m.p.h.)

PASSENGERS

The Yak-42 in standard fit could carry more passengers than the One-Eleven or the F-28. The proposed Yak-42M would have had 156 seats. The Yak entered service much later than the One-Eleven.

Yak-42 'CLOBBER'	121 PASSENGERS
ONE-ELEVEN SERIES 475	79 PASSENGERS
F-28 FELLOWSHIP	50 PASSENGERS

RANGE

The larger Yak-42 could carry 120 passengers more than 1900 km (1,100 mi.). This range was reduced to 1000 km (559 mi.) with maximum payload. Feeder-liners are used for flying passengers between cities in one country rather than between countries, but the size of the former USSR highlighted the Yak-42's lack of range.

Yak-42 'CLOBBER'	1000 km (559 mi.)
F28 FELLOWSHIP	2593 km (1,608 mi.)
ONE-ELEVEN SERIES 475	3001 km (1,860 mi.)

Three-engine airliners

BOEING 727: The world's favourite tri-jet, the Boeing 727 is still employed in large numbers, particularly on American domestic routes. Large numbers of 727 freighters were also sold.

HAWKER SIDDELEY TRIDENT: One of the few real success stories in British airliner history, the Trident was also produced in Romania under licence and was sold to the Chinese airline CAAC.

LOCKHEED L-1011 TRISTAR: Now a rare sight at the world's airports, the Tristar was popular with the major airlines in the 1970s because of its low noise and high fuel economy.

TUPOLEV Tu-154: Still in widespread service and produced in updated form, the Tu-154 was used by Aeroflot and Soviet-bloc nations on international medium-haul routes.

ZEPPELIN

LZ127 GRAF ZEPPELIN

● Commercial Zeppelin ● International flights ● Round-the-world trip

One of the most famous of the Zeppelin airships, **LZ127** *Graf Zeppelin* was made possible by the final relaxation in 1925 of restrictions on German airship construction put in place after World War I. This opened the way for a Zeppelin suitable for worldwide commercial use. With private and government funding, **LZ127** was built and flown in a little over 18 months and went on to make numerous notable flights, including a round-the-world trip in 1929.

▲ *The* Graf Zeppelin *and* Hindenburg *represented the pinnacle of hydrogen airship development that had begun before World War I and came to an end with the loss of the* Hindenburg.

ZEPPELIN **LZ127** GRAF ZEPPELIN

▼ Commercial prospects
LZ127's designer insisted that it was too slow for commercial transatlantic use, but it paved the way for more suitable designs like LZ129, the Hindenburg.

▲ Post-war restrictions
Germany's efforts to develop a commercial rigid airship were hampered by restrictions imposed by the Allies in 1918.

▲ Earlier commercial design
First flown in 1911, LZ10 carried up to 20 passengers. It was destroyed by fire in 1912.

▲ LZ130, the second Graf Zeppelin
Also named Graf Zeppelin, LZ130 of 1938 was effectively a helium-filled version of Hindenburg.

◄ Giant hangars
LZ127 was the largest Zeppelin able to be built in existing assembly halls at Friedrichshafen.

FACTS AND FIGURES

➤ Passengers on **LZ127's** round-the-world flight each paid US$9,900 for a berth on the well-appointed airship.

➤ **LZ127's** building costs reportedly totalled 6 million marks (£2.6 million).

➤ *Graf Zeppelin's* design was closely based on that of **LZ126** *Los Angeles*.

➤ During each of the seven years from 1928, **LZ127** flew an average of 1,900 hours – a creditable performance at the time.

➤ **LZ127's** first flight on 18 September 1928 was of 36 hours' duration.

➤ In all, **LZ127** accumulated 17,178 flying hours; its last flight was on 19 June 1937.

Most famous of the Zeppelins

First flown on 18 September 1928, LZ127 made its first transatlantic flight in October. This was followed by a number of special flights to various destinations (for which up to 20 passengers each paid a premium fare), intended to promote airship travel.

These flights included a number to South America, Spain and other parts of Europe, and an excursion to the Middle East. August 1929 saw the beginning of the round-the-world flight for which the Graf Zeppelin became famous. On 8 August the giant airship left Lakehurst, New Jersey, on the first leg of its circumnavigation.

Along with a crew of 36, a press contingent was joined at the end of the first leg in Germany by a few paying passengers who enjoyed the comforts of well-appointed cabins. From Germany, LZ127 crossed the Urals and northern Russia, before heading south to Japan. Bad weather delayed departure from Tokyo on the final leg across the Pacific Ocean and the United States, Lakehurst being reached once more on 29 August, just over 21 days after the airship had set off.

Other notable flights included the July 1931 Arctic exploratory flight, completed over seven days. The first flight to South America followed in 1930, paving the way for commercial flights during the 1930s.

Above: In parallel with airship development, Germany designed a number of large aircraft, like the Do X.

Right: After a series of trial flights, LZ127 was employed on a regular service between Germany and South America from 1932 to 1937. Between 27 April and 2 November 1933, 123 flights were made across the South Atlantic.

LZ127 Graf Zeppelin

Named on 8 July 1928, the 11th anniversary of Count Ferdinand von Zeppelin's death, by his daughter Hella, his only child, LZ127 saw almost 10 years of service before being broken up in 1940.

LZ127 Graf Zeppelin

Type: commercial rigid airship

Powerplant: five 395-kW (529-h.p.) Maybach VL2 reversible piston engines

Maximum speed: 128 km/h (78 m.p.h.)

Maximum range: 10000 km (6214 miles) at 117 km/h (73 m.p.h.)

Weights: empty 67100 kg (147,930 lb.); typical gross lift 87000 kg (191,800 lb.)

Accommodation: 36 crew and up to 20 passengers

Dimensions: max. diameter 30.50 m (100 ft.)
length 236.60 m (776 ft.)
gas capacity 75000 m³ (2,648,600 cu. ft.)

During LZ127's first Atlantic crossing in October 1928 bad weather caused the fabric covering of one of the airship's stabilisers to tear off, threatening to jam the rudder system. Crew were forced to climb on to the outside of the hull to make repairs as the storm raged.

LZ127's structure was, like its predecessors, of Duralumin. Sixteen gas cells held 75000 m³ (2,648,600 cu. ft.) of highly flammable hydrogen for buoyancy and 30000 m³ (1,059,440 cu. ft.) of Blaugas gaseous fuel for the five engines. *Graf Zeppelin* was the only rigid airship to operate on a gaseous fuel. As well as Blaugas, the engines could be run on petrol, 8000 kg (17,636 lb.) of which was carried.

After its final flight in 1937, LZ127 became a giant museum-piece in honour of Count von Zeppelin and his work. On 29 February 1940, Reichsmarschall Hermann Göring ordered the Zeppelin scrapped.

GRAF ZEPPELIN

D-LZ127

A large gondola under the forward section of the hull combined the control car with passenger accommodation. Cabins held up to 20 passengers, with a dining room and kitchens to give sustenance.

Five Maybach VL2 12-cylinder, vee-configuration piston engines powered LZ127, each being housed in its own power car. The engines were reversible and drove four-bladed wooden propellers.

Around the world in 21 days

FIRST AIRSHIP AROUND THE WORLD: On 8 August 1929 (after a 95-hour flight from Germany), LZ127 set off from Lakehurst, New Jersey, on the first leg of the flight, back to Friedrichshafen, which was reached in a record time of 55 hours.

OVER THE URALS: The second leg began on 15 August, when *Graf Zeppelin* headed across northern Europe and Russia, then south to cross the Sea of Japan, landing in Tokyo on 19 August. Total flight time was 102 hours, compared to four weeks by ship, or two weeks by train. By 29 August, the airship had reached Lakehurst, having covered 32790 km (20,374 miles) in 21 days, 5 hours and 31 minutes. The *Graf Zeppelin* returned to Germany in early September.

LOS ANGELES — LAKEHURST — FRIEDRICHSHAFEN — TOKYO

ACTION DATA

PASSENGERS

Graf Zeppelin was able to accommodate up to 20 passengers in its well appointed cabins. The British R100, which flew the year after LZ127, was intended to carry as many as 100 people, while the ill-fated *Hindenburg* had only half the R100's capacity.

LZ127 GRAF ZEPPELIN 20
LZ129 HINDENBURG 50
R100 100

Index